Social Studies for the Elementary and Middle Grades

Social Studies for the Elementary and Middle Grades

A Constructivist Approach

FOURTH EDITION

Cynthia Szymanski Sunal
University of Alabama

Mary Elizabeth Haas
West Virginia University

Boston   Columbus   Indianapolis   New York   San Francisco   Upper Saddle River
Amsterdam   Cape Town   Dubai   London   Madrid   Milan   Munich   Paris   Montreal   Toronto
Delhi   Mexico City   Sao Paulo   Sydney   Hong Kong   Seoul   Singapore   Taipei   Tokyo

Acquisitions Editor: *Kelly Villella Canton*
Editorial Assistant: *Annalea Manalili*
Vice President, Director of Marketing: *Quinn Perkson*
Marketing Manager: *Darcy Betts*
Production Editor: *Janet Domingo*
Editorial Production Service and Interior Design: *Elm Street Publishing Services*
Composition Buyer: *Linda Cox*
Manufacturing Buyer: *Megan Cochran*
Electronic Composition: *Integra Software Services Pvt. Ltd.*
Cover Designer: *Elena Sidorova*

For related titles and support materials, visit our online catalog at
www.pearsonhighered.com.

Between the time website information is gathered and then published, it is not unusual
for some sites to have closed. Also, the transcription of URLs can result in typographical
errors. The publisher would appreciate notification where these errors occur so that they
may be corrected in subsequent editions.

Cataloging-in-Publication data for this title is on file at the Library of Congress.

Printed in the United States of America

10   9   8   7   6   5   4   3   2   [EDW]   14   13   12   11   10

www.pearsonhighered.com

ISBN-10: 0-13-704885-8
ISBN-13: 978-0-13-704885-4

About the Authors

Cynthia Szymanski Sunal is Professor of Social Studies Education at The University of Alabama. She taught social studies at the early childhood, elementary, and middle school levels in several states and overseas. Her research focuses on constructivist teaching, teaching with technology, and on facilitating students' use of evidence as they carry out social studies investigations. She is Executive Editor of *Social Studies Research and Practice* and has authored numerous journal articles, chapters, and books on social studies education

Mary Elizabeth Haas is Professor of Social Studies at West Virginia University. She also serves as the chairperson of the West Virginia Commission on Holocaust Education. She taught social studies in grades 7, 8, and 9 in Indiana and social studies methods at universities in Arkansas and Mississippi. Her research concentrates on the teaching of social studies content, particularly geography, political science, and history. She has published extensively and collaborated with Dr. Sunal on four books in social studies education. She is currently serving as a senior editor for the elementary level of the NCSS journal *Social Education*.

Contents

Preface   xvii

1   What Is Powerful and Meaningful Social Studies?   *1*

EXPLORATORY INTRODUCTION   *1*
Chapter Overview   *2*
Chapter Objectives   *3*
DEVELOPMENT   *3*
Social Studies in the Elementary
   and Middle School   *3*
What Is Purposeful and Powerful Social
   Studies?   *6*
Social Studies Teaching and Learning Are
   Purposeful and Powerful   *8*
BUILDING ON DIVERSITY   Meaningful Social
   Studies   *9*
Defining Social Studies   *12*
Education for Active Citizenship   *12*

USING TECHNOLOGY   Deciding Whether
   and When   *13*
Social Studies Curriculum   *14*
Planning Powerful Social Studies
   Lessons   *17*
LEARNING CYCLE LESSON PLAN   From Tree to Paper   *18*
MAKING A LITERATURE CONNECTION   Using Trade Books
   in Social Studies   *23*
Social Studies Is Essential   *23*
EXPANSION   *24*
Twenty-First-Century Teaching
   and the Impact of Standards   *24*
Summary   *26*
Recommended Websites to Visit   *27*

2   How Do Students Engage in Powerful and Meaningful Social Studies?   *28*

EXPLORATORY INTRODUCTION   *28*
Chapter Overview   *29*
Chapter Objectives   *29*
How Is Social Studies Best Taught in Today's
   Classrooms?   *30*
DEVELOPMENT   *30*
Applying What We Know about Meaningful
   Learning to Social Studies
   Curriculum   *30*

*Using Constructivist Theory in Social
   Studies Instruction*   *30*
*Using Behavioral Learning Theory in Social
   Studies Instruction*   *31*
An Effective Strategy to Promote Conceptual
   Change   *32*
Phases of a Learning Cycle
   Lesson   *33*
LEARNING CYCLE LESSON PLAN   Scale   *34*

Exploratory Introduction   39
Development   40
Expansion   43
Lesson Summary   44
Choosing Activities for Each Phase of the Learning Cycle Lesson   45
Elementary Lesson Activity Choices   46
Middle Childhood Lesson Activity Choices   47
BUILDING ON DIVERSITY   Opportunities to Include Multiple Perspectives   48
Student Assessment in Each Phase of the Learning Cycle   49

Writing Your Own Learning Cycle Lesson   50
The Optimal Length of Time for a Learning Cycle   50
Working with the Learning Cycle   50
EXPANSION   53
Principles of Teaching and Learning that Support the Curriculum Standards for the Social Studies   53
Summary   54
Recommended Websites to Visit   55

3   How Are Social Studies Inquiry Skills Learned?   *56*

EXPLORATORY INTRODUCTION   *56*
Chapter Overview   57
Chapter Objectives   58
DEVELOPMENT   *58*
Using Inquiry Skills to Develop Students' Social Studies Ideas   58
BUILDING ON DIVERSITY   Early Inquiry Skills   59
Early Inquiry Skills   59
Social Studies Inquiry Skills   60
Data-Gathering Skills   64
Data-Organizing Skills   64
Data-Processing Skills   64
Communicating Skills   66
Reflecting Skills   66
USING TECHNOLOGY   Information and Communication Technology (ICT) Literacy   66
Observations, Inferences, and Hypotheses   68
Observations   68
Inferences   68
Hypotheses   68
Developing and Using Guiding Hypotheses   70

Teaching Lessons in Which Students Use Integrative Thinking Skills   72
Critical Thinking   73
Problem Solving and Decision Making   73
Investigating   73
Creative Thinking   75
USING TECHNOLOGY   Fostering Inquiry Skills   76
Creating Conditions that Promote Student Thinking in Social Studies   77
Lesson Characteristics   78
Planning Activities to Teach Inquiry Skills   79
EXPANSION   *80*
Applying a Learning Cycle to Teach an Inquiry Skill   80
LEARNING CYCLE LESSON PLAN   How Can We Classify Native American Food Plants?   *81*
Assessing the Use of Inquiry Skills   83
Hierarchy of Inquiry Skills   85
Summary   89
Recommended Websites to Visit   90

4 How Are Social Studies Concepts and Generalizations Developed? *91*

EXPLORATORY INTRODUCTION   *91*

Chapter Overview *92*

Chapter Objectives *92*

Concept Teaching Starts with Reflection and
  Practice *93*

DEVELOPMENT   *94*

Facts as Social Studies Content *94*

Forming Concepts *97*

  *Identifying All Important Attributes of a
    Concept 97*

Types of Concepts *98*

Interrelationships among Concepts *101*

Differences in Complexity and Abstractness
  of Concepts *103*

Powerful Concept Teaching *107*

  The Concept Learning Cycle 107

  *Teaching Concepts of Varying Complexity
    and Abstractness Differently 110*

BUILDING ON DIVERSITY   Cultural Factors and
  Concepts *110*

LEARNING CYCLE LESSON PLAN   Productive
  Resources *111*

Assessment of Concept Learning *113*

USING TECHNOLOGY   Examples of Resources for
  Helping Students Build Concepts *114*

Generalizations Show Relationships Between
  Concepts *115*

  Forming Generalizations 115

  Defining Generalizations 116

*Distinguishing Generalizations from Facts
  and Concepts 117*

*Using Generalizations to Make
  Predictions 118*

MAKING A LITERATURE CONNECTION   The Message Is a
  Generalization *120*

  Types of Generalizations 120

  Teaching Powerful Generalizations 121

The Exploratory Introduction Phase
  of a Generalization Learning
  Cycle *122*

The Lesson Development Phase of a
  Generalization Learning Cycle *124*

The Expansion Phase of a Generalization
  Learning Cycle *124*

LEARNING CYCLE LESSON PLAN   Using Technology
  to Investigate a Problem: Why Are
  Cities Built Where Rivers Come
  Together? *125*

Formative Evaluation and Assessment *128*

Inquiry Teaching and the National Standards in
  Social Studies *128*

EXPANSION   *129*

Applying Concepts and Generalizations to
  Create Powerful and Meaningful Social
  Studies *129*

Summary *130*

Recommended Websites to Visit *131*

5 How Do Students Develop Citizenship in Democratic and Global Societies? *133*

EXPLORATORY INTRODUCTION   *133*

Chapter Overview *134*

Chapter Objectives *135*

DEVELOPMENT   *135*

Defining Citizenship in a Democratic
  Society *135*

Developing Political Awareness   *137*

Citizenship and Standards   *139*

Key Concepts and Values   *140*

LEARNING CYCLE LESSON PLAN   Voting Is a Way to Make Decisions   *144*

Assessing Civic Education in U.S. Schools   *149*

Resources for Citizenship Education   *150*

Media Resources   *150*

MAKING A LITERATURE CONNECTION   Selecting a Trade Book That Stresses Social Studies   *151*

Law-Related Education   *155*

LEARNING CYCLE LESSON PLAN   Presidential Oath   *157*

Participating in Democracy   *160*
   School-Based Community Service Projects   162
   Participation in Student Government   164
   Political Participation   166

BUILDING ON DIVERSITY   The Challenges   *167*

USING TECHNOLOGY   Cybercitizenship   *168*

EXPANSION   *171*

Summary   *171*

Recommended Websites to Visit   *172*

6   What Is Social Studies' Contribution to Global Education?   *173*

EXPLORATORY INTRODUCTION   *173*

Chapter Overview   *173*

Chapter Objectives   *174*

DEVELOPMENT   *174*

Global Education: An Evolving Definition   *174*

Global Education Appropriate for Grades Kindergarten–8   *178*

Approaches to Global Education   *179*
   The Cultural Approach to Global Education   179
   The Problems Approach to Global Education   181

BUILDING ON DIVERSITY   Finding the Views of People in Other Nations   *181*

Interdisciplinary Connections   *182*

Teaching Global Education   *183*

LEARNING CYCLE UNIT PLAN Teaching about War to Help Create a More Humane World   *186*

Resources for Teaching Global Education   *194*
   Computers and the Internet   194
   Book Series   195
   Resources for Current Events   196

EXPANSION   *196*

Summary   *197*

Recommended Websites to Visit   *197*

7   How Do Teachers Use and Manage Social Studies Instructional Strategies Effectively?   *199*

EXPLORATORY INTRODUCTION   *199*

Chapter Overview   *199*

Chapter Objectives   *200*

DEVELOPMENT   *200*

Social Studies Pedagogical Content Knowledge (PCK)   *200*

Teaching Dimensions that Support Meaningful Learning   202
Best Practices: Teaching Strategies that Support Meaningful Learning   203

USING TECHNOLOGY Creating a Collaborative
Classroom *207*

A Continuum of Knowledge and
Instruction *207*

Matching Instructional Strategies
to Student Needs *209*
  *Expository, or Direct, Instructional Methods:
    Lower Student Control 209*
  *Guided Discovery Instructional
    Methods: Mixed Teacher and Student
    Control 210*
  *Inquiry and Problem-Solving / Decision-
    Making Instructional Methods: Greater
    Student Control 210*

Matching Types of Instructional
Activities to Each Phase of the
Lesson *211*
  *Useful Instructional Activities for the
    Exploratory Introduction Phase 213*
  *Useful Instructional Activities for the Lesson
    Development Phase 214*

MAKING A LITERATURE CONNECTION Reading
Literature *225*

BUILDING ON DIVERSITY Reading Activities *226*
  *Useful Instructional Activities for the
    Expansion Phase 231*

Classroom Management Strategies
for Powerful Social Studies *231*
  Advanced Planning 231
  Giving Directions 232
  Distributing Materials 232
  Organizing the Beginning 233
  Grouping Students 233
  Using Classroom Rules 233
  Crating Lesson Smoothness 234
  Being a Facilitator 234
  Assessment Considerations 234

EXPANSION *235*

Making Decisions about Which Instructional
Strategies to Use *235*

Summary *236*

Recommended Websites to Visit *237*

8 How Are Powerful and Meaningful Social Studies Units Constructed? *238*

EXPLORATORY INTRODUCTION *238*

Chapter Overview *238*

Chapter Objectives *239*

DEVELOPMENT *239*

Planning the Appropriate Focus for Social
Studies Units *239*
  Descriptive-Focused Units 240
  Thinking Skills–Focused Units 241
  *Conceptual and Thinking Skills–Focused
    Units 241*

Units that Integrate School Subjects *242*
  Theme Units 242
  Issue and Problem-Solving Units 245
  *How to Choose Appropriate Topics for
    Integrated Units 247*
  Planning Integrated Units 248

Developing Integrated Units *249*
  *Step 1: Generating Ideas
    for the Topic of a Unit 249*
  Step 2: Researching the Topic 250
  *Step 3: Developing Essential or Focus
    Questions 250*
  *Step 4: Identifying Special Needs among
    Students and Making
    Accommodations 251*
  *Step 5: Developing Intended Learning
    Outcomes 251*
  *Step 6: Categorizing Intended Learning
    Outcomes 252*
  Step 7: Creating an Idea Web 252
  *Step 8: Developing a Rationale and
    Goals 254*
  Step 9: Beginning the KWL Chart 255

*Step 10: Developing Learning
   Objectives 256*
Step 11: Developing an Assessment Plan 257
Step 12: Developing Lesson Plans 259
*Step 13: Developing Accommodations for
   Technology 259*

MAKING A LITERATURE CONNECTION   Incorporating
Social Studies Trade Books into Units 260
Step 14: Implementing the Unit 261

Step 15: Evaluating Student Learning 261
Step 16: Reflecting on the Unit 261

USING TECHNOLOGY   Databases and
Spreadsheets 262

EXPANSION   264

Conceptualizing an Integrated Unit 264
Summary 265
Recommended Websites to Visit 266

9   How Do Social Studies Teachers Facilitate Students' Development as Individuals and Community Members? *267*

EXPLORATORY INTRODUCTION   267
Chapter Overview 267
Chapter Objectives 268

DEVELOPMENT   269
Respect for Diverse Students and for Oneself
as a Teacher 269
The Classroom Environment 269
*The Curriculum Respects
   Diversity 269*

LEARNING CYCLE LESSON PLAN   Sharing and
Negotiation 270

Development of Self-Concept in Diverse
Students 275
Independence and Responsibility 275
Jealousy 277
Fears 278
*Aggressive Feelings, Bullying, and Conflict
   Resolution 279*
Friendship 282

USING TECHNOLOGY   Internet Safety and
Cyber-Bullying 283
*Empathy and Helpful Prosocial
   Behaviors 285*
Self-Esteem 285

Values and Moral Education in a Diverse
Society 286

BUILDING ON DIVERSITY   Learning from
the Voices of Our Family and
Community 286
Three Aspects of Morality 287
Moral Development Theories 288
*Teaching Approaches in Values
   Education 289*

Attitudes and Dispositions Promoting
Powerful Social Studies 296
Curiosity 296
Respect for Evidence 297
Reserving Judgment 297
Flexibility 297
*Responsibility to Others and to the
   Environment 298*
Values, Morals, and Aesthetics 298

MAKING A LITERATURE CONNECTION   Demonstrating
Powerful Attitudes and Dispositions 299

Assessing How Diverse Students Relate to
Individuals and Communities 300

EXPANSION   300

Confronting Challenges to Students' Active,
Responsible Development as
Citizens 300
Summary 301
Recommended Websites to Visit 302

10 How Can I Involve All Students in Meaningful Social Studies? *303*

EXPLORATORY INTRODUCTION *303*

Chapter Overview *303*

Chapter Objectives *304*

DEVELOPMENT *304*

Meaningful Social Studies for All Students *304*

"Best Practices": Giving All Students Greater Control of Their Social Studies Learning *305*

Social Studies Education for Students with Disabilities *305*

General Instructional Strategies for Inclusive Classrooms 306

USING TECHNOLOGY Adapting Instruction and Curriculum in the Inclusive Classroom *307*

Factors to Be Considered in Adapting Social Studies Curricula and Instruction 313

Social Studies Education in a Culturally Diverse Society *316*

BUILDING ON DIVERSITY Variations in Belief Systems *317*

Culturally Responsive Teaching 319

Sample Strategies for Multicultural Social Studies 319

Role Models and Relevancy 320

MAKING A LITERATURE CONNECTION Role Models *322*

Culture and Gender Differences in Student-Teacher Interactions *323*

Helping English Language Learners Participate in Social Studies *324*

Recognizing and Scaffolding Language Learning 324

Instructional Strategies for Helping ELL Students Understand Social Studies Content 325

Assessment of Social Studies Learning for All Students *326*

Maintaining an Equitable Approach 327

Assessing Using Technology 328

EXPANSION *328*

Applying Ideas for Helping All Students Learn Meaningful Social Studies *328*

Summary *330*

Recommended Websites to Visit *330*

11 How Do I Engage Students in Examining History? *331*

EXPLORATORY INTRODUCTION *331*

Chapter Overview *332*

Chapter Objectives *332*

DEVELOPMENT *333*

Definition of History *333*

History in Schools *335*

LEARNING CYCLE LESSON PLAN Learning from the Paintings and Drawings of Artists *336*

Standards for History *343*

Benefits of Studying History *346*

Students and the Learning of History *347*

Using Timelines to Develop Chronology *348*

Resources for Teaching History *350*

Locating and Using Historical Resources 350

People as Resources 351

Artifacts and Museums 351

The Community as a Resource 352

Documents as Resources   353
*Diaries, Letters, and Pictures as
    Resources   354*
Visual Literacy and History   *355*
Reenactments and Drama   *356*
Biographies and Historical
    Literature   *357*
BUILDING ON DIVERSIT   Pitfalls in
    Selecting Multicultural Books   *358*

MAKING A LITERATURE CONNECTION   Using Trade Books
    to Add Depth to History Units   *362*
USING TECHNOLOGY   Using Interactive Activities
    and Games in Learning History   *363*
Expanding Your Skills in History   *364*
EXPANSION   *364*
Lincoln Penny Worksheet   364
Summary   *369*
Recommended Websites to Visit   *370*

12   How Do I Engage Students in Interpreting the Earth and Its People Through Geography?   *371*

EXPLORATORY INTRODUCTION   *371*
Chapter Overview   *371*
Chapter Objectives   *372*
DEVELOPMENT   *372*
Defining Geography   *372*
The Five Themes of Geography   373
LEARNING CYCLE LESSON PLAN   People Change
    Their Environments   *374*
*Geography and the National Social Studies
    Standards   378*
*Geography Education Standards: The Six
    Elements of Geography Education   378*
Resources for Teaching Geography   *380*
USING TECHNOLOGY   An Important Contributor
    to Learning Geography   *381*
Developing Geographic Concepts,
    Generalizations, and Skills   *382*
*Research Findings on Geographic
    Education   388*
MAKING A LITERATURE CONNECTION   Books Provide
    Different Cultural Perspectives   *389*

*Research on Map and Globe
    Skills   390*
Helping Students Learn and Use
    Map and Globe Skills   *391*
Shapes and Patterns   393
Symbols   394
Direction   394
Distance   395
Grid Systems   396
*Remote Sensing and Digital
    Maps in the Teaching of
    Geography   397*
*Numbers: The Amount or Quality
    on Maps, in Atlases, and in
    Textbooks   399*
Reading and Maps   400
LEARNING CYCLE LESSON PLAN   Latitude and
    Longitude   *402*
EXPANSION   *408*
Summary   *409*
Recommended Websites to Visit   *409*

13 How Do I Assist Students in Making Economic Decisions? *411*

EXPLORATORY INTRODUCTION   *411*

Chapter Overview   *411*

Chapter Objectives   *412*

DEVELOPMENT   *412*

Economic Literacy   *412*

Defining Economics   *413*

National Social Studies Standards Related to
Economics   *414*

Voluntary National Standards in
Economics   *415*

National Standards in Personal Finance   *415*

Economic Concepts and Values   *419*

Microeconomic Concepts   421

Macroeconomic Concepts   421

MAKING A LITERATURE CONNECTION   Trade Books
Illustrating Economic Concepts   *422*

International Economic Concepts   423

LEARNING CYCLE LESSON PLAN   Economic
Interdependence   *424*

Measurement Concepts and Methods   427

Economic Decision-Making Skills   *428*

Economic Goals and Values   *431*

Children and the Learning of
Economics   *432*

Approaches to Teaching Economics   *434*

Resources for Teaching Economics   *435*

LEARNING CYCLE LESSON PLAN   Advertisements
and Making Good Choices   *436*

USING TECHNOLOGY   Investigating How to Use
a WebQuest with Your Students   *440*

EXPANSION   *441*

Summary   *442*

Recommended Websites to Visit   *442*

14 How Do I Teach Students to Learn through Multiple Assessments and Evaluation? *444*

EXPLORATORY INTRODUCTION   *444*

Chapter Overview   *447*

Chapter Objectives   *447*

DEVELOPMENT   *447*

Assessing and Evaluating Social Studies
Learning   *447*

*When Evaluation and Assessment Are
Needed   448*

*Guiding Principles for Assessment and
Evaluation   449*

National Testing of Social Studies   451

*Assessment and Evaluation Beyond
Testing   452*

BUILDING ON DIVERSITY   Promoting Individual
Needs   *464*

Modes of Assessment   *465*

*Identifying Assessments Within a Lesson
Plan   469*

Action Research and Reflection: Becoming
an Effective Social Studies Teacher   *469*

LEARNING CYCLE LESSON PLAN   Making Good
Rules   *470*

EXPANSION   *477*

Practicing Skills in Pre-Assessment   *477*

Summary   *478*

Recommended Websites to Visit   *479*

References   *480*

Index   *489*

Preface

Social Studies for the Elementary and Middle School Grades: A Constructivist Approach, Fourth Edition, views social studies as a powerful and purposeful part of the kindergarten through middle school program. Meaningful learning of social studies content, skills, and values promote democratic behavior in and among citizens.

This edition continues to focus strongly on *meaningful learning of powerful and purposeful social studies.* Such learning recognizes that students must construct knowledge in their own minds for it to be meaningful to them. To help teachers create powerful and purposeful social studies, we discuss: (1) strategies for teaching important social studies content, skills, and values; (2) the structure of the knowledge to be learned; and (3) the theory and research explaining meaningful learning in social studies. We base our discussion on over twenty-five years of public school teaching experience and an equal number of years in higher education teaching, supervising, and carrying out research.

The research literature in social studies and on constructivism contributes strongly to the approach we take in this book. We use the theories and strategies we discuss daily as we develop and teach social studies lessons, conduct research, and work with the research literature. We find that the learning cycle approach to structuring lessons and units is flexible and includes the best aspects of major theories describing how students learn. We apply the learning cycle in teaching social studies concepts, generalizations, skills, and values. Our chapters demonstrate the learning cycle as each begins with an exploratory activity challenging readers to remember and reflect on prior knowledge of the chapter's topic, moves into the more teacher-guided phase where readers find explanations and activities that develop their understanding and social studies pedagogical content knowledge (PCK), and end in an Expansion in which readers apply the chapter's main ideas in other contexts.

Social studies provides rich opportunities to involve students in active investigations of issues, problems, consequences, and successes encountered in our social world. Opportunities for application and reflection of the ideas in this book are found in the Time for Reflection: What Do You Think activities. These activities are intended to stimulate dialogue with the authors, instructors, and peers. They can serve as starters for class discussions building a community of teachers and learners who create powerful and purposeful social studies education.

There is a focus on twenty-first-century skills, civic action, and full involvement of diverse learners in social studies education. The National Council for the Social Studies Standards and the various content standards for history, economics, geography, and civics all are emphasized in the text and in the learning cycle examples presented. Assessment is integrated throughout and also discussed in depth in a separate chapter. The incorporation of the Internet and newer technologies is found within chapters and sample learning cycle. We guide users in planning and teaching powerful and purposeful social studies lessons and units incorporating all these components.

 # New to This Edition

The fourth edition has undergone reorganization to address important emerging needs and potentials of social studies education as we begin the second decade of the twenty-first-century. Recognizing the relationship between concepts and generalizations, the discussion of both has been combined into one chapter. The groundwork for building concepts and generalizations is supported by a strong focus on twenty-first-century skills necessary for inquiry learning. Democratic citizenship in the twenty-first-century at both the global and local levels is a major concept as well as goal in social studies and is represented in an enhanced discussion presented much earlier in this edition than in the third edition. Since social studies is best taught through units helping students to respond to important questions, the development of such units is considered earlier in this edition. This edition focuses on both individual development and students' development as a community member as represented in a specific chapter and also as included throughout. The fourth edition has enhanced and continues to present in-depth key ideas for teaching history, geography, economics, and other critical components of social studies.

A strong focus is included on the civic ideals and values needed for youth growing up in our twenty-first-century world in which technology impacts communications and classroom learning. A supporting emphasis on development of twenty-first-century skills extends the book's focus on citizenship in this century. The potential of reflection by students and teachers is emphasized by its inclusion as an important inquiry skill throughout the book. Additional emphasis is placed on second language learners, the use of appropriate literature, and addressing issues of diversity.

Each chapter has a new Exploratory Introduction and a new Expansion section to better demonstrate the learning cycle and to address new potentials and issues in social studies. Examples of learning cycles have been revised. Updated technology boxes and examples are woven through the chapters and supported by recommended interactive websites. The focus on incorporating appropriate literature has increased as has the focus on actively teaching our increasingly diverse student body.

We welcome your comments on the deep changes in this fourth edition and will continue to address those comments as we work daily with both students in social studies.

Features of This Fourth Edition

- *New!* **Learning Cycle Lesson Plans** illustrate ways of combining instructional strategies with important content from multiple social science disciplines to promote powerful and purposeful social studies learning.
- *New!* **Focus on Twenty-First-Century Skills** incorporated throughout the chapters show how these build the social studies learning needed by today's students.
- *New!* **"Using Technology"** boxes highlight incorporation of technology in social studies plus discussion and examples of technology use woven throughout chapters.
- *New!* **"Building on Diversity"** boxes plus discussion and examples woven throughout chapters illustrate actively involving diverse students in social studies.
- *New!* **"Making a Literature Connection"** boxes demonstrate how the use of literature in the classroom supports social studies instruction.
- *New!* **Activities** are included at the beginning of chapters, the "Exploratory Introduction," and at the end of chapters, the "Expansion," in every chapter.
- *New!* **Focus on the relationship between concepts and generalizations** shows how concepts can be related to construct generalizations.
- *New!* **Focus on both individual development and students' development as a community member** are represented in a specific chapter and also as included throughout.
- *New!* Inclusion of the potential of **reflection by students and teachers** is emphasized by as an important inquiry skill and throughout the book.
- Enhances and continues to present **in-depth key ideas for teaching history, geography, economics**, and other critical components of social studies.
- A strong focus is included on the **civic ideals and values** needed for youths growing up in our twenty-first-century world in which technology impacts communications and classroom learning.
- **"Time for Reflection: What Do You Think?"** activities, several times in each chapter, encourage students to reflect on their personal experiences and perspectives, and how they might relate to the chapter content.
- **"Classroom Scenarios"** are widely used throughout each chapter, emphasizing practical application of constructive theory.

 ## Instructor Supplements

The following ancillary has been created for instructors to use with the fourth edition. It is available for download from the password-protected Instructor Resource Center at www.pearsonhighered.com/irc. Please contact your local Pearson representative if you need assistance.

Instructor Manual/Test Bank

This manual, prepared by Mary Haas, has been fully updated for the new edition. It includes new class activities and handouts as well chapter objectives and a total of approximately thirty multiple choice, true/false, and essay questions per chapter.

 ## Acknowledgments

We would like to thank the reviewers of this edition for their helpful comments: David L. Buckner, Oklahoma State University; Rachel Finley-Bowman, Elizabethtown College; Barbara Hanes, Widener University; and Carol B. Tanksley, University of West Florida. We also thank our social studies colleagues who have examined and taught with the first edition and offered encouragement and suggestions. We are also grateful for the questions and suggestions from our students that have helped us to reflect on how they are constructing their ideas and skills for teaching meaningful social studies.

1

What Is Powerful and Meaningful Social Studies?

CLASSROOM SCENARIO

Ms. Park, a sixth-grade teacher, wants her students to think about the role of geographical characteristics in building a house at a particular site. She notes that there is some home building going on near the school on properties with very different characteristics. She begins by giving students information about two nearby 40-acre pieces of property for sale at similar prices. The information for each property contains an aerial photograph of the piece of land and some notes from a realtor about the characteristics of the property. One piece of property is high on a mountain ridge and is hilly with a thick forest. It has a stony stream that cuts a path back and forth through it. The other piece of property is located in a valley. It is mostly flat and swampy with very few trees.

Ms. Park presents a key question, writing it on the board: Which piece of property would be easier and cheaper on which to build a house and road? She divides the class into small groups, assigns roles, and says, "Discuss the question in groups for 5 to 10 minutes and be ready to explain to the class the reasoning for your answer."

All of the groups decide that the hilly property is a more difficult site on which to build a house and road. They do not consider that any problems might result from swampy ground. One group says, "When ground is flat, you can just put a house and road right down and don't have to worry about anything." Another group agrees saying, "You should pick the flat, swampy place because it will not cost you anything extra to build a road and house on it but you have to do some bulldozing to build in a hilly area." A third group notes, "This was easy because one place has a lot of problems and the other doesn't have anything to worry about."

Ms. Park thinks to herself, "We have been studying local geography for the last six weeks. They are not applying what they read about flooding in low-lying and swampy areas from all the rain we have had lately. They are not thinking through the information in the photos and the realtor's notes and identifying the problems found with each piece of property. Have our lessons really helped them get beyond their alternative perspective that 'flat land is always better and cheaper than hilly land to build on'?"

On the following day, Ms. Park had intended to provide the students with access to the Internet, a newspaper listing excavating companies and construction firms that they can call, and a map of the local area from the U.S. Geological Survey. In their groups, students would discuss the information they gather, make charts grouping the information, and decide whether this new information supports their earlier conclusions. Later, the students would be given more information on the properties, including a report indicating whether the soil is appropriate for a septic tank and how deep a well needs to be to get water.

Before continuing on with the activities she had planned for on the following day, Ms. Park decides she has to address the problems, "How can I help my students to really think about the information available?" and "How can I help my students make decisions based on the evidence they have, so that they don't rely on inaccurate ideas?"

To answer these problems, Ms. Park constructs the chart below:

Key Ideas I Wanted My Students to Consider in This Activity	Students' Ideas That I Need to Address	Ways I Can Help My Students More Accurately Use Available Information to Make a Decision

Summarize the ideas you listed in each column so you can share them with others. What did you find out? Examine the third column considering the question, "Are my suggestions focused more on involving students in active investigations and discussion of ideas or on telling the 'right' answer?" ∎

Chapter Overview

You have experience with social studies that you will use throughout this chapter to consider several questions: What is social studies? What are the sources of social studies content? What are the characteristics of social studies teaching? Over the years, social studies educators have offered many answers. As you work through this chapter and the book, you are presented with different perspectives on social studies. Reflect on these perspectives and discuss them with your peers. Do they view children and social studies learning in similar or different ways than you do?

Chapter Objectives

1. Describe the characteristics of powerful social studies.
2. Explain the model for meaningful social studies instruction.
3. Describe participatory citizenship in a democracy.
4. Define social studies as an integrated school subject with the goal of promoting civic competency.
5. Describe a structure for a social studies lesson and unit instruction that gives students greater control of their learning and thinking along the continuum from greater student control to greater teacher control.
6. Describe how the structure for social studies instruction demonstrates the use of best practices by teachers who have social studies pedagogical content knowledge.
7. Evaluate a social studies lesson plan by identifying the degree to which it applies social studies pedagogical content knowledge.

DEVELOPMENT

Social Studies in the Elementary and Middle School

Social studies is about our social world: It is about people, what they do, and how they interact with each other and with the world. Most of our lives and social worlds involve everyday experiences. Imagine children at a shopping mall. They observe, play, model people, and explore—all without being "taught." They might ask questions such as "Can you look at the mall map and find a short way to the toy store?" or "Where did Grandma and Grandpa go to buy their new shoes when they were little?" or "How does the baker know how many cookies to make for the cookie store in the food court?" or "How come all the teenagers hang out around the food court?"

These questions spring from a natural exploration of our social world that begins at birth and continues as the tools of language, reading, and mathematics are mastered and used to investigate the social world. Social studies happens every time a child figures out a shortcut to take home or asks a question about whether the classroom rules should be changed because "we keep fighting about whose turn it is." This book begins with a discussion of social studies in elementary and middle schools that examines the origin of children's knowledge and presents a glimpse of two classroom scenes that illustrate the teaching of social studies.

A FIRST-GRADE CLASSROOM SCENE

NCSS
Standard III

Ms. Blount, a first-grade teacher, identifies the question "What is a landform?" as the topic of a unit she will teach this school year, because it is part of the course of study in her state. She examines the national social studies standards and finds that this topic might best fit with the theme of People, Places, and Environments (National Council for the Social Studies [NCSS], 1994a). Yet, experience tells her that young students need a lot of help with their inquiry skills. In learning about landforms, observation and classification are important skills to emphasize. The students first must make observations of landforms and then classify them into categories, such as "island." She decides to begin the unit with a lesson on islands, while facilitating students' development of a higher level of skill in making observations. She recognizes that, because her students do not live in a region where they see islands, she will have to obtain multiple visual images of islands to use throughout the unit. After an Internet search, she finds several useful photos at a National Geographic site, Patterns in Nature: Island Aerials, that she bookmarks for her students to view (http://photography.nationalgeographic.com/photography/photos/patterns-island-aerials.html?source=pincl).

As the lesson begins, her students are in small groups. Each group has three different pictures of islands. Ms. Blount has the students look at the pictures and try to answer the key question written for them on a response sheet: "What differences do you see among these pictures?" Each group selects a recorder who lists the characteristics identified by group members. The group's recorder shares the list with the class while Ms. Blount creates a class list on chart paper. Ms. Blount quickly examines the class list to assess her students' prior knowledge about islands and their level of observational skill before moving on to the next part of the lesson.

Ms. Blount then has the students sit in a circle around three foam meat trays, each of which contains a clay model of an island: one is long, flat, and thin; a second has a hill with a gentle slope and a rounded top; and a third is rocklike, with a rough top and steep edges. She pours water into the trays. Ms. Blount calls on students sitting in different parts of the circle who have different views of the island to talk about the shape of the first island. Then, she calls on another group to talk about the shape of the second island and a third group to talk about the shape of the third island.

Next, Ms. Blount gives each student a paper cup and a worksheet titled "Cup Views." Recognizing that young students often are in the process of developing their spatial understandings, she involves the students in looking at the cups from different views. First, she has students place their cups upside down and then draw them, looking down from the top, because this "bird's-eye" view often is used in making maps. Then, they place the cups upside down on a table and squat down so they can draw them from eye level. Finally, students stand up and draw the cups from the view they now see.

After Ms. Blount asks them how the view changes in their drawings, the students are divided into three groups. Each group is given one of the island models to draw. Students turn over the worksheet to find "Island Views" on the back. Here, they draw the island from the top, from the side as they squat down, and from the side as they stand up. Students examine the pictures from the first lesson and compare them to the island models. Ms. Blount helps students complete a sentence on the board: "A place is an island if it . . ." (e.g., "is a piece of land that goes above the water"). Ms. Blount collects the students' cups and island-view drawings and assesses them in terms of how well they show the views the students saw.

Ms. Blount then has each student take a shoebox and some clay and a 3 × 5 card. She asks the students to construct an island that shows the features the class has identified as "a place that is land above water" and put it into the shoebox. This will become the students "landform box." Models of additional landforms will be added to the box as the unit progresses. Ms. Blount asks each student to write a sentence explaining why his or her model is an example of an island. She gathers the students together, and they briefly review the activities of the lesson and tell Ms. Blount what they think the lesson was about. Ms. Blount uses a rubric containing each of the key characteristics the class defined in the statement "A place is a island if it . . ." to evaluate each student's demonstration of the characteristics of an island.

A SIXTH-GRADE CLASSROOM SCENE

Mr. Valencia, a sixth-grade teacher, is planning a unit that considers the question, "What was the planned purpose of the Lewis and Clark Corps of Discovery Expedition?" The course of study for social studies in his school system identified an investigation into the purpose and accomplishments of the Lewis and Clark expedition as part of sixth-grade social studies. He has decided that the unit will address the national social studies standards theme of Time, Continuity, and Change (National Council for the Social Studies, 1994b).

NCSS

Standard II

The first lesson in the unit familiarized students with the personal backgrounds of Lewis and Clark and involved them in searching for sites that mapped out the trail taken by the Corps of Discovery.

The second lesson focuses on the purpose(s) of the expedition. In small groups, students are asked to describe and write out the purpose(s) such an expedition would have had early in the nineteenth century. After having each group share the purpose(s) it has developed, Mr. Valencia reminds the groups that the expedition occurred in the early 1800s and gives them a chance to talk about, and make, any revisions they might wish to make. Then, each group posts its final purpose(s) on a class discussion board. Mr. Valencia reviews each posting to assess how appropriate the purpose(s) are to the time period and the setting in which the expedition took place.

He has students read a *Letter from President Thomas Jefferson* (www.nwrel.org/teachlewisandclark/jefferson.html), in which President Jefferson states the purpose of the expedition, but Mr. Valencia encourages them to identify and use other sources as well. He gives them the following tasks: (1) identify the overall perspectives and attitudes expressed by Jefferson using evidence from the letter; (2) underline the subpurposes of the expedition as identified by Jefferson, circling evidence in the letter; (3) describe how the perspectives and attitudes expressed by Jefferson are similar to, or different from, those of U.S. citizens today; and (4) discuss how likely it is that they are able to understand the context of the times in which Jefferson identified the purpose of the expedition in terms of thinking as people of that time thought and knowing their values and aspirations. Mr. Valencia asks each group to post its responses for each of the four tasks on class discussion boards and to respond to the postings of two other groups. To bring closure on the purpose(s) of the expedition, Mr. Valencia asks the whole class to help him construct a table on the board to identify the major purposes of the expedition. When complete, students copy the table into their social studies notebooks. Then, he asks them to select one purpose from Jefferson's letter they would not expect to find in a letter from the current president about an expedition being sent to Mars and to list at least two reasons explaining why this might not be a purpose of the Mars expedition. He assesses the students' rationale to determine whether they are appropriately accounting for the different context of the times in which Jefferson's letter was written.

Mr. Valencia has students visit the website of the National Aeronautics and Space Administration (NASA) (http://spaceplace.nasa.gov/en/kids/mars_rocket4.shtml) to identify the purpose stated for the mission to Mars. Then, he has students individually construct comparison charts. First, students list the purposes of the Lewis and Clark expedition in column 1, then they list the purposes of the Mars mission in column 2, making sure to place a Mars purpose in the same row as a similar Lewis and Clark expedition purpose, if they find any similarities. Finally, as a means of summative evaluation, each student writes out conclusions made from the table regarding similarities and differences found between the purposes stated for the two expeditions. Mr. Valencia evaluates these conclusions to determine how accurately the student is drawing conclusions from the data available about these two expeditions. ∎

TIME FOR REFLECTION | What Do You Think?

1. What are some words you expect the students in Ms. Blount's class to use to describe social studies?
2. What do you think Ms. Blount's definition of social studies is?
3. What are some words you expect the students in Mr. Valencia's class to use to describe social studies?
4. What do you think Mr. Valencia's definition of social studies is?

The purpose of elementary social studies is to establish a learning environment and instruction that enable all students to understand, participate, and make informed decisions about their world. Social studies explains students' relationships with other people, to institutions, and to the environment. It equips them with the knowledge and understanding of the past necessary for coping with the present and planning for the future. Social studies provides students with the skills for productive problem solving and decision making, as well as for assessing issues and making thoughtful value judgments. Above all, it integrates these skills and understandings into a framework for responsible citizen participation, whether in the school, the local community, or the world (NCSS, 2008).

NCSS
Standard I

What Is Purposeful and Powerful Social Studies?

The view that students construct their own knowledge has great implications for social studies education. Students must have information to act on from their own experiences that can be related to the ideas and skills being taught. Students collect this evidence by making observations of, and interacting with, people, educational materials, and objects. Students think about information, relating it to their prior experiences and knowledge. They consider the information they acquire using familiar ways of thinking. They make predictions and encounter challenges. It is through such challenges to our present way of thinking that we come to understand new ideas (Brophy & Allemen, 2008).

Students need to classify and describe the materials, experiences, and information they observe. Performing such tasks comes naturally, but often students are uncertain about doing these tasks or are not particularly good at doing them. It is only after encountering activities that challenge them and make them think that students discover regular patterns in the world and make conclusions about them. A pattern is a regular activity that has occurred in the past and is expected to occur again in the future. The world is full of patterns, for example:

- People wear fewer and lighter clothes in summer.
- Groups have social relationships that tell members who should lead and who should follow.
- Past events influence current events.

Students' inferences and conclusions about their observations of the world are drawn from, and interpreted in terms of the values they, their families, and

This second grader's timeline showing her interest in the life of Abraham Lincoln is an example of active and purposeful social studies.
Photographer: Lynn A. Kelley

their communities have. These values are often challenged, reconsidered, and clarified during social studies activities. Throughout social studies instruction, students integrate information from a variety of sources that represent differing perspectives. They make decisions and solve problems about what they need and what is important to them. Social studies is a powerful construction process that goes on in students' minds.

The NCSS describes its vision of purposeful and powerful social studies teaching and learning in a 2008 position statement identifying five elements.

Social Studies Teaching and Learning Are Purposeful and Powerful

1. When They Are *Meaningful*. Effective teachers analyze students' knowledge, skills, and dispositions to make informed and purposeful decisions about what to teach and how to teach. By building on students' prior experiences, teachers design learning experiences challenging students to make meaningful connections and expand their experiences and viewpoints. Meaningful social studies occurs when teachers intentionally select what to teach, and students grasp the knowledge and skills taught. For meaningful learning, carefully planned, daily, sequenced learning experiences are needed.

2. When They Are *Integrative*. Elementary and middle school instruction should maintain social studies at its core so its features and goals are explicit. Social studies content, resources, activities, and assessment are integral to the students' world, and social studies is integrative by nature. Effective practice does not limit social studies to one specified period or time of day. Rather, teachers help students develop social studies knowledge throughout the day and across the curriculum. Students' everyday activities and routines are used to introduce and develop important civic ideas. The curriculum follows logical sequences, allows depth and focus, and helps students move forward in knowledge and skills. The curriculum should not become, in the name of integration, a grab bag of any social studies-related experiences that seem to relate to a theme or project. Rather, concepts must be developed in a coherent, planned manner.

3. When They Are *Value-Based*. Teachers make daily decisions about democratic concepts and principles that respect the dignity and rights of individuals and the common good. Thoughtful and deliberate classroom experiences related to controversial or ethical topics are used as opportunities to teach critical thinking skills and value-based decision making.

4. When They Are *Challenging*. Teachers have opportunities to be involved in the decisions that determine what is taught in social studies, how social studies is taught, and what resources will be used. Students are challenged by activities that can be accomplished, with some effort. A variety of approaches, strategies, and materials challenge students. Teachers think critically about when to take the lead during instruction and when to support the leadership of students in investigating ideas and issues.

5. When They Are *Active*. Teachers actively engage students in social studies. They monitor and adjust lessons and the curriculum, making decisions that consider whether students are experiencing meaningful, integrative, value-based, challenging, and active social studies.

Teachers incorporating these five elements into social studies understand that classroom instruction takes place along a continuum of instructional activities. They use activities incorporating greater student control to promote purposeful and powerful social studies learning.

Greater Student Control ◄──────────────────────────────► Greater Teacher Control

At one end of the continuum are instructional activities with greater teacher control that allow students little opportunity for input. An example is when the teacher presents a lecture or a video without offering students the opportunity to ask questions and to discuss the topic. At the other end of the continuum are instructional activities with greater student control that involve students as active participants who decide what issues they will study and how they will collect data on questions they have regarding those issues. An example is when students

Building on Diversity

Meaningful Social Studies

Every student brings to the classroom unique personal experiences, different perspectives on the world, and different ideas about how to act in social situations. Each student has inclinations toward certain ways of learning. Some students are excellent auditory learners, whereas others are excellent visual learners. Some students have traveled widely, whereas others have never left their community. Students come from two-parent families, single-parent families, extended families, blended families, or another type of family. The diversity found in every classroom is huge, even when that classroom is in a tiny rural community or takes in a close-knit ethnic community in a large city. Such diversity serves as a deep and broad resource for meaningful social studies experiences. When teachers build on the diversity found among their students, social studies is personal, relevant, and important. Students find there is much to be appreciated in diversity while recognizing that, despite our diversity, we all share

many experiences, wishes, and goals. Implementing the following practices as you begin the school year, shows you are welcoming the diversity your students represent.

- Treat each student as an individual, and respect each student for who he or she is.
- Convey the same level of respect and confidence in the abilities of all your students.
- Be evenhanded in how you acknowledge students' good work. Don't refrain from critiquing the performance of individual students in your class on account of their ethnicity or gender.
- Use assignments and exams that recognize students' diverse backgrounds and special interests.
- Become more informed about the history and culture of groups other than your own (accessed from http://teaching.berkeley.edu/bgd/diversity.html, 2008).

decide to investigate a problem such as heavy traffic outside the school and several instances when students were nearly hit by a car. The students decide to study traffic patterns and find that traffic is heaviest when school is starting and ending. Students conclude that a traffic signal is needed and go to the city council to advocate for placement of a traffic signal in front of the school. Additional examples appear in Figure 1.1. The more that we, as teachers of social studies, are able to use instructional activities that give students greater control of their learning activities, the more active their learning becomes.

As we strive to provide students with experiences in which they have control of lesson activities, we work to deepen our pedagogical content knowledge. As teachers, we need *content knowledge* specific to social studies and the *general pedagogical knowledge* used in teaching all subject areas, such as classroom management skills. Finally, we always need to be working to build our *pedagogical content knowledge (PCK)*, the knowledge of how to teach social studies (Shulman, 1986; Pajaras, 1992; Barton & Levstik, 2004). Figure 1.2 shows how these work together to accomplish social studies instruction. To teach social studies well, we

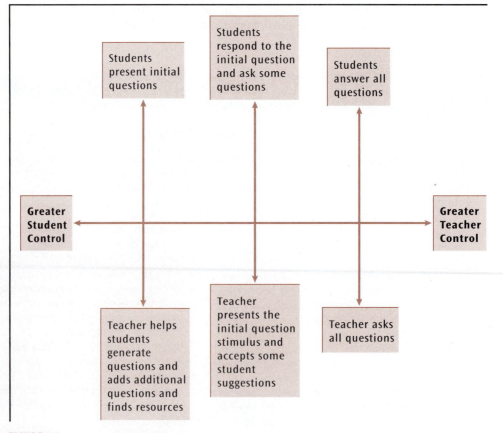

FIGURE 1.1

Continuum from Greater Student Control to Greater Teacher Control

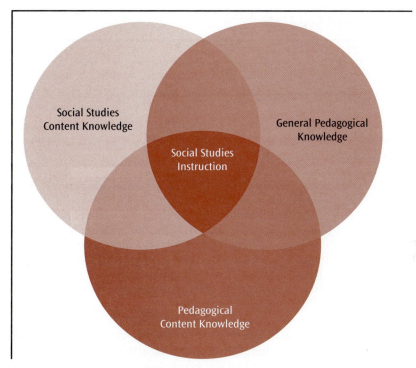

FIGURE 1.2
Teacher Knowledge Needed for Social Studies

must have PCK that helps us to select appropriate instructional strategies that will best help our students learn social studies content and inquiry skills. These often are called the *best practices* of teachers (Morine-Dersheimer, 1999). For example, how do we help students learn about historical events? What instructional strategies will help them understand that the Lewis and Clark expedition involved people who grew up in a world very different from ours? What strategies will help our students meaningfully understand the multiple perspectives of the members of the expedition, of the Native Americans from many different cultures who encountered the expedition, and of the French-speaking traders along the expedition's path? What strategies will help our students understand the limitations of the information we have about the people living at that time in North America? About which documents survived? About who had the skills to write letters and newspaper articles? All such decisions relate to our PCK in social studies. In later chapters in this book, we will talk about the PCK needed to use best practices in teaching the concepts and inquiry skills used in economics, geography, political science, history, and global studies, as well as other parts of social studies. Developing your PCK as an elementary or middle school teacher is a lifelong process. Through this process you become expert at helping students develop a powerful understanding of social studies that enables them to be active citizens making well-considered decisions for the common good.

Defining Social Studies

Powerful social studies is meaningful to students and is promoted by teaching that uses effective social studies PCK to actively involve students in learning. The National Council for the Social Studies has developed a formal definition of social studies and highlights it in *Expectations of Excellence: Curriculum Standards for Social Studies* (1994b). The NCSS describes how social studies integrates many disciplines to help fully develop our diverse students' ability to be active citizens in a democracy (1994b, p. viii).

> Social studies is the integrated study of the social sciences and humanities to promote civic competence. Within the school program, social studies provides coordinated, systematic study drawing upon such disciplines as anthropology, archaeology, economics, geography, history, law, philosophy, religion, and sociology, as well as appropriate content from the humanities, mathematics, and natural sciences. The primary purpose of social studies is to help young people develop the ability to make informed and reasoned decisions for the public good as citizens of a culturally diverse, democratic society in an interdependent world.

Civic issues, whether pertaining to health care, crime, or foreign policy, are complex and draw on several disciplines. Health-care issues, for example, require some understanding of law, biology, psychology, history, and sociology. The defining characteristic of social studies is that it is multidisciplinary in nature, encompassing and integrating knowledge and processes from many disciplines. The formal definition of social studies given above emphasizes the multidisciplinary aspect of social studies and the many perspectives it seeks to integrate. In a social studies unit about changes in the community, for example, history might take the lead while geography and economics support the unit. In a unit titled "New Jobs and Careers in the United States: What Is My Future?" the study of economics might lead with the support of geography, psychology, and history.

Education for Active Citizenship

A general goal for school curriculum should be facilitating students' development of an awareness, appreciation, and understanding of key social studies concepts and processes required for personal decision making, participation in civic and cultural affairs, and economic productivity (NCSS, 1994b; National Research Council, 1996). *Citizenship* means active participation in community and national decision making (Goodman & Adler, 1985; Sunal, 2008).

Being an active, participatory citizen means that students ask questions, decide on answers to questions based on related information, and act to bring about changes in their everyday social world. This process of awareness, appreciation, and understanding of the social world is learned fully only through social studies. As our technological society continues to change, it creates many concerns that require decision making from citizens. Making thoughtful decisions requires citizens to have content knowledge in many areas and to know how to use and evaluate the evidence their knowledge gives them. Yet, many students seem turned off by social studies when they enter middle school. This is a serious problem for a complex democratic society in which citizens are expected to make informed decisions. An important aspect of social studies is "promoting knowledge of and involvement in civic affairs" (NCSS, 1994b, p. vii).

The No Child Left Behind Act of 2001 identified three core subjects to be taught in K–12 that contribute to developing an understanding of citizenship in all students: civics and government, history, and geography. The National Assessment of Educational Progress (NAEP) tests students' knowledge of these three core subjects nationwide. States also test students' achievement in social studies and in these areas to track progress towards understanding citizenship knowledge and skills. The recent heavy emphasis on high stakes testing in elementary and middle schools sometimes pulls attention away from social studies. If students are tested in reading and in math, for example, teachers focus on those subjects and spend less time on other subjects (Boyle-Baise, Hsu, Johnson, Serriere, & Stewart, 2008). Sometimes,

Using Technology

Deciding Whether and When

Technology resources such as the Internet and CD-ROMs offer many opportunities for teachers to move away from using only textbooks as teaching resources. Teachers can use a website such as CNN Interactive at www.cnn.com to involve students in current issues or for relating historical events to today's issues. Or, teachers can use a CD-ROM such as Lewis and Clark Rediscovery developed by InfiMedia, Inc. (www.infimedia-inc.com) to enable students to use excerpts from the journals of members of the Lewis and Clark expedition to examine significant events in the journey and important decision points faced by the expedition.

Technology "is as old as the first crude tool invented by prehistoric people" (NCSS, 1994b, p. 28). Deciding when and how to use technology in social studies instruction is an example of real social studies problem solving. Technology has altered, and continues to alter, the course of education. It brings teachers surprises, and it challenges their beliefs and values.

Like all instructional resources, technology used to support the teaching of social studies must reflect social studies goals and learning outcomes. Both Mr. Valencia and Ms. Blount (see previous classroom scenes) used the Internet to find classroom resources for their lessons. Mr. Valencia integrated a letter from Thomas Jefferson and a NASA site as the major pieces with which his students worked. Teachers need to consider the following questions when deciding whether and when to use a technology:

1. How and when can technology facilitate the basic elements of instruction?
2. For which social studies activities are the costs in time and money of obtaining and using technology appropriate investments?
3. What learning experiences might be improved for my students if technology is used?

state testing includes social studies so teachers attend to it but might focus mostly only on those topics tested. Helping students be active citizens now and in the future is so important in today's world that, even though there are pressures from high-stakes testing, many teachers work hard to ensure their students develop the knowledge and skills they need to participate fully in a democratic society.

Social Studies Curriculum

During the 1990s, national standards were developed for social studies, along with other areas of education. These standards described

- What students from kindergarten through grade 12 should be taught
- How students should be taught
- How students' achievement should be evaluated (NCSS, 1994b, p. viii)

The 10 themes of the social studies standards are listed and defined in Table 1.1. Each theme incorporates one or more of the disciplines contributing to social studies content. Each theme also incorporates one to three major concepts associated with the disciplines. The first theme, Culture, incorporates ideas from anthropology, sociology, geography, and history. The second theme, Time, Continuity, and Change, emphasizes history along with other disciplines. The third theme, People, Places, and Environment, is strongly represented by geography and, to a lesser extent, economics, culture, and civic ideals. A major message is that social studies is multidisciplinary and not rooted in any single discipline. The themes of Science, Technology, and Society and Global Connections clearly demonstrate a multidisciplinary focus.

Expectations for Excellence: Curriculum Standards for Social Studies is a document created by a national task force of social studies teachers and teacher educators. It was designed for use by state governments and departments of education, school districts, schools, individual teachers, book publishers, parents, and community members. The complete document, published by NCSS as *Bulletin #89*, describes learning experiences in primary, intermediate, middle/junior high, and high school for each of the themes.

NCSS

Standards

Standards also have been developed for major disciplines contributing to social studies that describe what to teach in the discipline and how to teach it. Three standards books have been developed for history: *National Standards for United States History: Exploring the American Experience (Grades 5–12)*, *National Standards for World History: Exploring Paths to the Present (Grades 5–12)*, and *National Standards for History: Expanding Children's World in Time and Space (Grades K–4)* (National Center for History in the Schools, 1994). These describe what students should know about history and what thinking skills will help them investigate history. *Geography for Life: National*

TABLE 1.1

The 10 Themes of the Social Studies Standards

Theme	Description
Culture	Human beings create, learn, and adapt culture. Cultures are dynamic systems of beliefs, values, and traditions that exhibit both commonalities and differences. Understanding culture helps us understand ourselves and others.
Time, Continuity, and Change	Human beings seek to understand their historic roots and to locate themselves in time. Knowing what things were like in the past and how things change and develop helps us answer important questions about our current condition.
People, Places, and Environment	Today's students are aware of the world beyond their personal locations. As students study this content, they create their spatial views and geographic perspectives. Social, cultural, economic, and civic demands require such knowledge to make informed and critical decisions about relationships between people and their environment.
Individual Development and Identity	Personal identity is shaped by one's culture, by groups, and by institutional influences. Examination of various forms of human behavior enhances understanding of the relationship between social norms and emerging personal identities, the relationships between social processes that influence identity formation, and the ethical principles underlying individual action.
Individuals, Groups, and Institutions	Institutions exert enormous influence over us. Institutions are organizations that embody and promote the core social values of their members. It is important for students to know how institutions are formed, what controls and influences them, how they control and influence individuals and culture, and how institutions can be maintained or changed.
Power, Authority, and Governance	Understanding the development of structures of power, authority, and governance and their evolving functions is essential for the emergence of civic competence.
Production, Distribution, and Consumption	Decisions about exchange, trade, and economic policy and well-being are global in scope. The role of government in policy making varies over time and from place to place. Systematic study of an interdependent world economy and the role of technology in economic decision making is essential.
Science, Technology, and Society	Technology is as old as the first crude tool invented by prehistoric humans. Our modern life would be impossible without technology and the science that supports it. Today's technology forms the basis for many difficult social choices.

continued

TABLE 1.1 (Continued)

Theme	Description
Global Connections	The realities of global interdependence require understanding of the increasingly important and diverse global connections among societies. Persisting and emerging global issues require solutions.
Civic Ideals and Practices	All people have a stake in examining civic ideals and practices across time and in diverse societies, as well as in determining how to close the gap between present practices and the ideals on which our democratic republic is based. An understanding of civic ideals and the practice of citizenship is critical to full participation in society.

Source: Expectations of Excellence: Curriculum Standards for Social Studies, by the National Council for the Social Studies, 1994, Washington, DC: National Council for the Social Studies.

Geography Standards 1994 (National Council for Geographic Education, 1994) describes a set of 18 national standards identifying what students should know and what thinking skills will help them learn geographic content from kindergarten through grade 12. *Voluntary National Content Standards in Economics* (National Council on Economic Education, 1997) serves as a guide to helping K–12 students develop economic understanding. The Center for Civic Education (1994) produced the *National Standards for Civics and Government* to help teachers develop curricula to guide students' construction of key concepts of government essential for participation as a citizen of a democratic society. Each of the national standards documents focuses on three aspects of social studies that are essential in our lives: (1) supporting the community and the common good of its people, (2) identifying both common and multiple perspectives—unity and diversity in human society, and (3) applying social studies knowledge, skills, and democratic values to civic action.

The national social studies standards found in *Expectations for Excellence: Curriculum Standards for Social Studies* (NCSS, 1994b), as well as the discipline-specific standards in subjects such as geography, have been used in guiding the development of many state and local courses of study. Some states and school districts have added to or otherwise revised their courses of study so that they align with national standards. Other states and school districts have highly independent courses of study. So, whereas social studies represents a mixed picture in terms of its curriculum, guidelines are available from many sources to help teachers develop an appropriate and meaningful curriculum for their students. National, state, and local standards all indicate that the teacher's task is to support learning that really does increase a student's competence and confidence in using important social studies knowledge and skills to have a better life and to contribute more as a citizen.

TIME FOR REFLECTION | *What Do You Think?*

Return to the scenarios of the lessons taught by Ms. Blount and Mr. Valencia.

1. List the primary national social studies theme Ms. Blount identified for the lesson. Explain why you agree or disagree with her identification of that theme.

2. Identify one additional national social studies theme addressed by Ms. Blount's lesson and explain your interpretation of the theme's use.

3. Identify one performance expectation for the additional social studies theme you identified for Ms. Blount's lesson. Why do you think this lesson will help students move toward accomplishing this performance expectation?

4. Mr. Valencia identified Time, Continuity, and Change as his lesson's theme. Explain why you agree or disagree with his identification of that theme.

5. Identify one additional national social studies theme that also is addressed by Mr. Valencia's lesson and describe why it is addressed.

6. Identify one performance expectation for the additional social studies theme you identified for Mr. Valencia's lesson. Why do you think this lesson will help students move toward accomplishing this performance expectation?

 ## Planning Powerful Social Studies Lessons

Students have told us what instructional strategies they like to be used in social studies: less reading and more group projects, field trips, independent work, discussions, clear examples, student planning, challenging learning experiences, class activities, role-playing, and simulations (Schug, Todd, & Beery, 1984). Teachers of social studies have told us they use multiple resources in the classroom to address individual learning differences, cooperative learning, group learning, and individual choice in project selection (Haas & Laughlin, 1999a). If we consider both sets of information, then there appears to be positive connections between the instructional strategies students enjoy in social studies and the instructional best practices used by teachers with strong PCK in social studies. The PCK of effective teachers of social studies, however, goes further than using instructional strategies students prefer. Effective teachers also know how to carefully plan and assess lessons in which students have greater control of their learning so that powerful and meaningful social studies is experienced.

Powerful social studies helps students construct meaningful learning by helping them relate facts and concepts to explain the world. Content is challenging, integrative, and value based. Lessons involve students in active learning and processing of information described as "minds-on" learning. Teachers and students work together to keep a cooperative and supportive classroom climate that encourages students by providing opportunities to learn and grow rather than creating a

text continues on page 22

LEARNING CYCLE LESSON PLAN   *From Tree to Paper*

Grade Level: First or Second

NCSS Standards: Production, Distribution and Consumption; Science, Technology, and Society

NCSS
Standards
VII, VIII

Focus is on the inquiry skill of *sequencing* of events by time (the order in time during which they occurred).

Exploratory Introduction

Materials: Large plastic bag of paper discarded by students (have students throw used paper into a garbage bag for a few days before the lesson). Five sheets of rough newsprint with traces of wood; a set of paper items such as a shoe box, a piece of corrugated paper, a toilet paper roll, a paper towel, a piece of stationery, a discarded piece of paper from the printer, a newspaper page, a paper bag; tree artifacts (per group: one small log/wood piece, one small plastic bag of wood chips, one package of paper)

Objectives ⟶	Procedures ⟶	Assessment
1. Students sequence a set of artifacts according to their position in the papermaking process.	1. Have students sit in a circle. Bring out a large bag filled with discarded classroom paper. Dump it on the floor and have students tell you what these items are and whether they think they use a lot of paper in class. 2. Assign students to small groups and assign a materials manager, writer, observer, and reporter. If available, hold up a piece of rough newsprint in which some traces of wood are noticeable. Then give each group a sheet to examine while group materials managers go to a materials station and get a set of paper items, giving each group three to five items to put with the piece of newsprint. Ask, "Are all of your group's new items made from paper?" After providing students with time to make observations, ask each group to list on chart paper the items they think are paper and those that are not paper. If there are disagreements, ask groups to explain why or why not an item is paper and put a question mark by these items on the list. 3. Ask groups to discuss, "When was the last time you used something made of paper? What was it?" Record a list of paper products on chart paper. Note that many objects are made of paper and that we use many kinds of paper (soft, firm, shiny, rough, etc.).	1. Use a checklist to record whether each group was able to sequence the items in the correct order: first, tree; second, wood chips; third, paper.

continued

4. Ask groups to discuss the key question: "What is all of this paper made from?" Share ideas, creating a list on chart paper.

5. Have groups go to tables and instruct the materials manager to get one set of tree artifacts. Tell groups that paper is made from trees. Ask groups the key questions "What should we look for to put these items in order with the paper last to show how paper is made?" and "Which item would be first, second, last?" Ask students to give their reasons for the sequence they used. Ask students why they think the wood chips are in this artifact set.

Lesson Development

Materials: A. Mitgutsch (1986). *From Wood to Paper* (New York: Carolrhoda Press). Artifacts from the exploratory introduction; eight pictures of the papermaking process: (1) tree, (2) cut into logs, (3) bark is stripped, (4) ground into wood chips, (5) mixed with pulp (water in a slurry), (6) poured on to a screen, (7) ironed, and (8) packaged. Papermaking Process website at www.wipapercouncil.org/process.htm; URLs for current and past papermaking techniques and for making recycled paper (ww.paperonweb.com/pmake.htm)

Objectives ⟶	*Procedures* ⟶	*Assessment*
1. Students sequence artifacts in order by where they occur in the papermaking process.	1. Read *From Wood to Paper*, calling students' attention to the sequence described and to the papermaking production process. 2. Have groups check their three artifacts and rearrange the sequence as needed based on the information in the book. Write "first," "second," and "last" on the board and have students tell you which artifact picture should be laid on the chalk tray underneath "first," which goes under "second," and which goes under "last." 3. Ask, "What do we look for to put things in order when we talk about tree to paper?" 4. Return to the book and give each group a set of pictures showing steps in the papermaking process. Reread the book, stopping at appropriate places so students can put their pictures into the sequence described in the book.	1. Write a brief note describing whether students are able to indicate accurately which artifact is first, second, and last in each part of the sequence.

continued

2. Students order eight events in the tree-to-paper process by time sequence.

5. Have each group describe the picture sequence it developed, referring to the book as needed. During this discussion, construct a sequence of pictures on the chalk tray with labels on the board from first to last. Emphasize the need to be certain that the events are ordered by time, so that, for example, the event just before that shown in picture 3 is placed as second and the event after picture 3 is placed as fourth.

6. **Closure.** Create a consensus statement that describes how we can place things into a sequence that shows which occur first, second, and so on, until we get to the final step. Write the statement on chart paper and post it where it can be seen.

2. Use a checklist to record which groups accurately ordered the eight pictures by time sequence.

3. Have each student write or draw the first and last event and then the fourth and fifth event. Examine their work, indicating on a checklist which students accurately identified the fourth and fifth events.

Expansion

Materials: Drawing paper and markers for each student

Objectives ⟶	Procedures ⟶	Assessment
1. Students add the "store" for purchasing paper as an event following the papermaking process.	1. Ask, "Where do we buy the paper we use?" Write down students' ideas. Have students make a quick drawing of where their paper is purchased. Remind students that they have been sequencing events in the papermaking process. Now they are going to add where the paper goes after it is made. Add a student's drawing to the sequence on the chalk tray.	1. Using a checklist, record which students identified the store as the location where paper is purchased.
	2. Ask, "Do we need to change or add to the labels, as we now have nine events?" Erase "last," change to "eighth," and label the store as "last."	
2. Students indicate that an additional	3. Have groups identify another event to add to the end of the chain (e.g., taking the paper home, but	2. Write a brief statement indicating how

continued

label must be added to the sequence of events.

students may identify other appropriate events), make a drawing of it, and add it to the chalk tray. Review the events added. Decide whether they all qualify for the last event or if some come before others. Number the events groups have added.

4. **Lesson summary.** Have students help you briefly describe the sequence of activities in this lesson. Then, have them tell you "what we do when we put things that happen in a sequence."

difficult students find adding an additional event to the sequence.

Summative Evaluation Ask each student to draw three events, in sequence, that occur in getting paper from home to the student's desk at school and to label the events as "first," "second," and "last." Use the Summative Evaluation Rubric to score the assignment.

Summative Evaluation Rubric

Criteria	Score			
	3	2	1	0
Three appropriate events are identified.				
The three events identified are in correct order.				
Each event is labeled.				
Each event is labeled appropriately.				

restrictive atmosphere based on a fear of failure. The Learning Cycle lessons shown on pp. 3–6 present lesson plans that employ powerful social studies ideas in a way that facilitates meaningful learning and construction of knowledge by students.

The Learning Cycle Lesson Plan on pp. 18–21, From Tree to Paper, is designed for grade 1 or 2. Its focus is on helping students develop a higher level of ability to *sequence* their observations of events. To develop a higher ability of this skill, the students work with content relating to theme VII: Production, Distribution, and Consumption from the national social studies standards. A second theme in the content is VIII: Science, Technology, and Society. Although the lesson content addresses how paper is made from trees, the teacher focuses on helping students develop their skill at ordering the observations they are making.

This lesson is set within a unit that addresses the social studies content theme of "How do people make items we use every day?" Some other parts of the unit address: "How do people make plant fibers into clothes?" "How do people make grain into bread?" "How do people make paper into paper money?" and "How do people make milk into ice cream?" Because each lesson involves these young students in learning about how people process various natural resources into finished products that we use every day, the skill of sequencing is important to meaningfully understand the social studies content of the unit. Each lesson works to help students apply their skills of observation and sequencing and recognize that they can use those skills in different kinds of activities focused on answering the question "How do people make items we use every day?"

TIME FOR REFLECTION | What Do You Think?

Read the Learning Cycle Lesson Plan, From Tree to Paper, on pp. 18–21. Reflect further on it using the following questions. Write down your responses and, if possible, discuss them with a peer.

1. What are two different assumptions the teacher made about the prior knowledge and experiences of the young students for whom this lesson was planned?

2. How do the key questions asked in the exploratory introduction tie into the phases of the lesson?

3. What lesson development activities help to explain how events are sequenced by the learner?

4. What is the purpose of the closure at the end of the lesson development phase of the lesson?

5. During the expansion phase of this lesson, how does the teacher help students expand on their more developed abilities, sequencing events beyond what was done earlier in the lesson?

6. How does the teacher "wrap-up" the lesson?

7. To what extent will the summative evaluation activity let the teacher know how well each student has developed his or her ability to sequence events to a higher level than existed before the lesson?

Making a Literature Connection

Using Trade Books in Social Studies

Trade books can be used to develop and expand on the main idea of many social studies lessons. Lessons following From Tree to Paper could use Gallimard's (1995) *Trees and Forests* (New York: Scholastic Inc./Gallimard Jeunesse). This interactive book with eye-catching art and impressive graphics examines a range of topics, from the first plants to grow on land to modern cultivated tree farms. This range can be confusing to young children, so although this book offers opportunities to expand on the skills and ideas in From Tree to Paper, the teacher must decide how to use it and which parts would be appropriate.

Another possible trade-book selection is Oppenheim's (1995) *Have You Seen Trees?* (New York: Scholastic). In this book, poetry and watercolor illustrations encourage readers to use their senses while exploring trees, leaves, and fruits. It also includes a tree identification key. This book is best used *after* students have had an opportunity to first use their five senses to explore real trees, leaves, and fruits so they have some concrete experiences with which they can better understand the representations in the book.

A book on Johnny Appleseed, such as that by Lynda Durrant (2005), *The Sun, the Rain, and the Apple Seed* (New York: Clarion) can be the basis for an expansion activity. This novel tells the story of Johnny Appleseed's life. Johnny Appleseed traveled through the American West in the 1790s planting apple seeds to feed the hungry and to produce seeds for planting and trading. This story could

be used to sequence seed to tree to new seeds to trading those seeds, focusing on ordering these events and the concepts of production, distribution, and consumption.

Another possible expansion is to involve students in recycling paper. A book by Nancy Elizabeth Wallace (2005), *Recycle Every Day*, may also be helpful. This story follows a rabbit family for a week and chronicles their recycling activities. Children could consider how many materials, including paper, can be recycled.

Other books that deal with various aspects of trees could serve to expand on the lesson's major skill and ideas. S. H. Shetterly's (1999) *Shelterwood* takes the reader on a summer journey through the woods to learn how environmentally conscious foresters protect the inhabitants by selectively cutting trees, leaving shelter for animals and protecting young trees. W. Pfeffer's (1997) *A Log's Life* uses stunning cut-paper collages and descriptive text to introduce the life cycle of a tree. Children learn about the many animals that depend upon the tree for food and shelter and the role of the log in the decay process.

Each of these books is best used in lessons that follow From Tree to Paper. The beginning of a lesson engages students in an active experience that brings out their prior social studies knowledge and motivates them to investigate and learn the inquiry skill or idea on which the lesson is focusing. Each of the books described here is best used to support the development or expansion of a lesson's main ideas and skills.

Social Studies Is Essential

Social studies plays a critical role in our lives. When social studies consists of memorizing facts, reading textbooks, watching videos, answering questions, and doing Internet searches to find as many facts as you can, its impact on students is minimal. These activities provide little help for students when they try to understand how and why people act as they do and whether particular behaviors are good or worthy of adopting. But when social studies is perceived as an integral part of the intellectual development of students, and as a set of relevant experiences, it becomes an essential part of the curriculum.

When social studies focuses students' attention by confronting interesting problems related to their social world, students will naturally want to observe, ask questions, research information, express observations and ideas in drawings, argue for their viewpoints, and act to change things. When students "do" social studies, they draw on thinking skills and knowledge from the entire school curriculum as they construct an understanding of their social world and seek to solve the problems it presents.

If students are, and will continue to be, effective participants in a democratic society, then social studies must be an essential part of the curriculum in the elementary and middle school years. In a world that demands independent and cooperative problem solving to address complex social, economic, ethical, and personal concerns, the social studies are as basic to survival as reading, writing, and computing. Knowledge, skills, and attitudes necessary for informed and thoughtful participation in society require a systematically developed program focused on concepts from history and the social sciences (NCSS, 2008).

EXPANSION

 ## Twenty-First-Century Teaching and the Impact of Standards

The social studies content and skills needed by citizens for twenty-first century learning require higher-order thinking, real-world experiences and skills, and the ability to solve authentic problems. Students' development of such content knowledge and skills is a gradual process requiring practice at every grade level. Ted McCain (2005) identified six actions teachers must take to accomplish these goals.

1. Resist the temptation to "tell."
2. Stop teaching content out of context, as just a set of facts to learn.
3. Stop giving students the final product of your thinking as a teacher. Involve them in the process that gets to the final product or conclusion.
4. Give the problem first. Teach the topic of which the problem is a part after students have been challenged by the problem.
5. Progressively withdraw from helping students so they become independent learners.
6. Continuously assess students' performance of skills and their learning of content knowledge not just their final content knowledge products.

In the last years of the twentieth century, professional organizations developed standards such as those in social studies. States also frequently developed standards, which may or may not have aligned with national standards. As teachers focus on how to best help students be active, responsible citizens in the twenty-first century, they recognize they must teach in ways promoting needed skills and knowledge, as McCain suggested in the six actions he identified. National standards are being revisited to address twenty-first-century teaching and twenty-first-century learning.

TIME FOR REFLECTION | *What Do You Think?*

Teachers are required to address existing state social studies standards when these exist. Recently, many states have rewritten their social studies standards and matched them carefully with their state's tests. Other states are in the process of doing such alignment. Standards often are controversial. Some common concerns about state social studies standards include the following (Peterson & Hess, 2008).

- The standards are too broad in nature making them too difficult for teachers to understand and present in age appropriate ways.

- The standards stress low-level thinking and memorizing of trivia or facts that are not meaningful to children, youth, or adult life and fail to promote in-depth examination or learning.

- There are too many standards to complete in a year's time.

- The standards are static and/or archaic and do not allow for local needs, current events, or unique occasions to be examined.

- The standards are too dictatorial and undermine opportunities for students' and teachers' decisions to be incorporated into the curriculum.

- The standards are too open and encourage teachers to make too many of their own decisions, so there is no continuity in the social studies curriculum from year to year.

Your state's specific state social studies standards can be found at teachinghistory.org/teaching-materials/state-standards. Select a specific grade level and read through the list of standards for this grade.

1. Write a response in regard to the six concerns listed above, giving examples from your state's standards indicating whether the concern is or is not justified.

2. Conclude your comments by describing a social studies idea, value, or skill that you might teach at this grade level to address one or more of your state's standards in a positive and meaningful way with students.

Many states include twenty-first-century technology standards and reading /literacy standards as a part of the standards for each of the school subjects.

3. Do you find evidence in the state's standards at this grade level that indicates a teacher is to relate technology or literacy specifically to the content and the special skills used in the teaching of social studies? If so, give examples of such evidence.

4. Do you conclude that the emphasis on learning skills in your state's standards is or is not focused on mastering social studies with its essential and unique skills and values? Give examples from your state's social studies standards to support your conclusion.

Quickly look at the social studies standards for a grade either three levels above or below the grade you selected.

5. What, if any, are noticeable connections in the social studies standards at this new grade level with the standards you first examined?

6. Why do you think states try to make such connections across grade levels in their standards?

7. What happens to students' meaningful learning if a teacher at the lower grade level does not teach purposeful and powerful social studies?

Summary

Participatory citizenship is an important goal in the development of every student. A participatory citizen has an awareness, appreciation, and basic understanding of key social studies concepts and processes required for personal decision making, participation in civic and cultural affairs, and economic productivity. Powerful social studies facilitates the construction of knowledge about the social world and our role as a participating citizen in it. Planning and teaching effective social studies lessons in elementary and middle school classrooms is an exciting and complex task. Powerful social studies teaching involves students in activities, confronting them with situations they cannot adequately understand using only their prior knowledge.

Instructional activities range along a continuum from greater student control to greater teacher control. As teachers develop their pedagogical content knowledge (PCK) in social studies, they seek to become experts at using best practices that encourage greater student control of learning. Best practices include encouraging students to make observations, to gather and communicate evidence, and to form conclusions through a variety of activities. This text describes ways of creating and using powerful social studies to develop lessons that support students as they construct their social studies inquiry skills and understanding of content to become active participants in a democracy.

Recommended Websites to Visit

National Council for the Social Studies
www.ncss.org
No Child Left Behind Act of 2001, Pub. L. No. 107-110
www.loc.gov
National Center for History in the Schools: National Standards in History
www.sscnet.ucla.edu/nchs/standards
National Geography Standards
www.nationalgeographic.com/education/xpeditions/standards/matrix.html
Voluntary National Content Standards in Economics
http://store.ncee.net/volnatconsta.html
National Standards for Civics and Government
www.civiced.org/stds_toc_preface.html

2

How Do Students Engage in Powerful and Meaningful Social Studies?

EXPLORATORY INTRODUCTION

Read the following sample passage, which is similar to those found in some fifth-grade social studies textbooks.

> Several important explorers were sent by different countries in Europe to find a route to the Far East that was shorter than sailing from Europe around Africa. They came to the New World, even though they were trying to find the Far East. Some of these explorers were Christopher Columbus, John Cabot, Ferdinand Magellan, and Jacques Cartier.
>
> In 1492, Christopher Columbus was the first of these explorers to try to find a route to the Far East by sailing west across the Atlantic Ocean from Europe. Instead of finding the Far East, he explored the Caribbean and the coasts of Central and South America. Five years after Columbus's first voyage to the New World, John Cabot sailed west across the Atlantic Ocean, but farther north than Columbus. He explored parts of eastern Canada, thinking he was in Asia. He tried again on another voyage and ended up in Greenland. Later, in 1519, Ferdinand Magellan sailed across the Atlantic Ocean, heading west and south with five ships, and was able to sail all the way around South America to the Pacific Ocean. He crossed the Pacific and landed in the Philippines, where he died. But one of his ships got back to its home port in Spain, managing to go all around the world. In the mid-1500s Jacques Cartier left France to find China by traveling northwest across the Atlantic Ocean. He explored the St. Lawrence River, but did not get to the Far East.

Respond to the following questions.

1. What is the main idea of this passage?
2. Does this passage provide conditions that encourage student thinking in social studies? Why or why not?
3. What additions can you suggest that might motivate students to use higher-order thinking skills and understand the concept more meaningfully?

Your response to questions 2 and 3 should include a consideration of further concerns. The goal of a social studies lesson on the efforts of Europeans to find a shorter route to the Far East involves several ideas. One is that resources that were much desired and expensive in Europe, such as spices, were to be found in abundance in the Far East. Another is that through lots of experimentation and testing, Europeans had developed sailing ships that could manage a long and difficult journey.

As we consider this passage and any other topic we plan to teach, it is important to consider some questions: How can teachers help students learn important social studies content so that it is meaningful to them? What social studies teaching procedures are based on an understanding of how students learn? How would you begin the lesson? What would you do next? How would you end the lesson? The planning, design, and implementation of your social studies lessons should demonstrate answers to these basic concerns and questions.

Chapter Overview

Teachers strive to increase meaningful learning in social studies and to help students revise their alternative conceptions about the social world. This chapter focuses on how teachers plan lessons facilitating students' meaningful learning of social studies, developing an awareness, appreciation for, and ability to make decisions and participate successfully in everyday life (NCSS, 1994b).

Teaching social studies effectively requires teachers to help students know, for themselves, how to obtain information and use it to make decisions supporting a democratic society. How do students begin to learn about their social world in a meaningful way? How can teachers create conditions that help students learn powerful social studies content so that it will be meaningful to them? How can teachers structure social studies lessons to apply what is known about how students learn? These questions form the focus of this chapter.

As you read and respond to this chapter, you will be provided with a flexible structure for developing lessons. The same lesson structure can be applied to learning all levels and types of social studies information and inquiry skills and to developing attitudes, values, and morals.

Chapter Objectives

1. Explain the importance of understanding students' prior knowledge about the social studies content and skills to be taught.
2. Describe the effect of prior knowledge on learning new social studies knowledge.
3. Explain how rote memory learning of social studies differs from meaningful social studies learning.
4. Describe how students begin to understand social studies content, skills, attitudes, and dispositions.

5. Describe a planning strategy that can be used to facilitate meaningful social studies learning.
6. Select activities for the various phases of a powerful social studies lesson.
7. Describe the essential parts of each phase of the learning cycle.
8. Explain why each phase of the learning cycle lesson must be included for successful student learning.
9. Construct appropriate activities for each phase of the learning cycle lesson.

 ## How Is Social Studies Best Taught in Today's Classrooms?

Social studies educators have long advocated that students must form meaning in their own minds by their own active efforts (Fraenkel, 1977; Saunders, 1992; Taba, 1967). Meaning cannot be pushed or poured into the mind by someone else. The meaning of cooperation with others, the process of identifying types of governments, the understanding of why citizens should vote, are examples of the range of social studies knowledge for which students must develop their own conception. To do so, students must work with social studies ideas until these ideas mean something to them. Teachers facilitate meaningful learning by planning and using social studies experiences that engage students in working through social studies ideas in their own minds.

DEVELOPMENT

 ## Applying What We Know about Meaningful Learning to Social Studies Curriculum

When confronted with a new idea in social studies, a student generally responds first by recalling prior knowledge of a seemingly related idea or skill. Then, the student makes observations of the context in which the problem is set. Next, the student attempts to solve the problem. Most of these early actions result in confusion and even failure at understanding the new idea. If the teacher has set up *conditions* that enable the student to work toward understanding, however, the *sequence* of activities in the lesson will help the student solve the problem and experience the satisfaction that comes with solving a problem.

Using Constructivist Theory in Social Studies Instruction

Meaningful social studies learning is an active construction process. It creates a network of experiences, ideas, and relationships that educators call *knowledge*. Starting with the earliest experiences in life, we begin building ever more complex networks of social studies knowledge. Meaningful social studies learning is a process of integrating and building various social studies ideas by adding, modifying, and connecting relationships between ideas. Making relationships also includes the abilities to explain, predict, and apply social studies information to many events (NCSS, 1994a). Learning social studies depends on the *prior knowledge* the learner brings to a situation, whether the learner's *attention is focused* on the ideas being presented, and the *mental and physical actions* of learners as they interact with events, people, and objects during instruction.

Using Behavioral Learning Theory in Social Studies Instruction

Teaching for active learning differs from traditional and behavioral orientations to social studies teaching. Traditional teaching views knowledge as transmitted by the teacher or textbook. When the teacher asks questions or gives an assignment, it is primarily to find out whether students have received the message. Such traditional social studies teaching is viewed as transmission and begins with the teacher or textbook presenting summarized information the student is expected to "recite" at a later time. Sometimes, this telling is followed by a highly teacher-guided activity designed to show the "truth" of the information. Telling students that cities are often located on rivers or asking them to repeat the definition of a city are examples of the traditional transmission view of instruction.

The transmission view of the social studies curriculum is focused on a list of items to be transmitted, a catalog of facts. Traditional teaching uses strategies that enhance memorization and recall. Students often enjoy memorizing facts they view as useful. The issue is whether the goal of the social studies curriculum is committing to memory a list of facts *or* whether it is meaningful learning that enables individuals to personally explain relationships and decide how to be involved with social events in ways that are consistent with their values and culture. A traditional program centered on memorizing facts does not encourage students to find meaning in what they are learning, nor does it help them make and test their decisions.

Memorization is useful for recalling facts such as that 50 states make up the United States or that the name of one type of government is *monarchy*. But if students do not understand the meaning of those facts, they cannot connect them to form a bigger idea. Teaching social studies in this way fails to make connections with what a student already knows about the world. Direct teaching narrows learning objectives and limits social studies learning to the particular solution explained. When direct instruction dominates lessons, teachers often find it necessary to devote much attention to motivating and disciplining students because students can become bored and distracted rather than engaged in social studies learning.

Teaching for meaningful learning does not replace all traditional strategies. Traditional social studies methods and behavioral teaching methods are appropriate for encouraging the recall and comprehension of information and the initial teaching of skills, such as spelling social studies words, identifying names of presidents, citing an example of a propaganda technique in a commercial, learning to measure distance on a map, or recording data from a survey on a chart or graph. Traditional teaching is sometimes appropriate, but it deserves a small portion of students' and teachers' time and efforts.

Some school systems have responded to the "No Child Left Behind" legislation (U. S. Department of Education, 2001) by moving toward more traditional fact-based social studies learning. As schools struggle with reaching Adequate Yearly Progress goals, large amounts of time are allocated to reading. Teachers then feel pressure from some administrators to reduce time for other subjects such as social studies. Students are quickly taught sets of facts to memorize and have little time to discuss and think about important social studies ideas. Despite the pressures, however, many teachers continue to keep in mind the need to help their students learn social studies in ways that are meaningful to them.

 ## An Effective Strategy to Promote Conceptual Change

Social studies knowledge begins when the learner actively works with events in everyday life, both in and out of a classroom. It is saved in the learner's mind as a *new construction* made from sensory information obtained in the world and *reconstructions* of prior knowledge. For meaningful learning to occur in school, classroom experiences must first be perceived by students. Then, students mentally reconstruct the perception in their minds. This representation is transformed by each student to fit his or her own prior knowledge. Figure 2.1 illustrates the mental processes involved in meaningful learning.

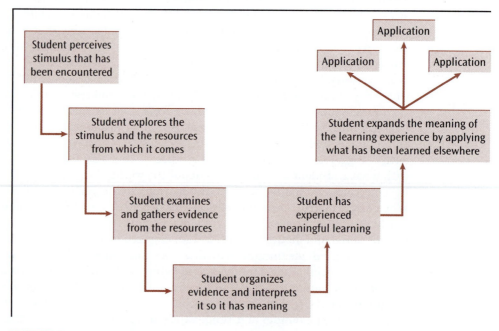

FIGURE 2.1
The Process of Meaningful Learning during a Social Studies Lesson

Conceptual change occurs when students change their concepts. This is not easy to do. Students form their existing ideas from the experiences they have had. These ideas make sense to them. They do not give up their ideas without being convinced that the new idea is better and more useful in their lives. So teachers involve students in meaningful social studies activities that foster conceptual change. They plan lessons that

- Motivate students to recall related prior knowledge
- Connect the new social studies idea to students' prior knowledge
- Allow students to compare and confront their prior knowledge with the new social studies idea
- Encourage students to use metacognition, to think about their own thinking (Costa, 2002; diSessa, Elby, & Hamner, 2002).

 ## Phases of a Learning Cycle Lesson

The learning sequence represented in the following lesson on scale uses a research-based teaching strategy called the *learning cycle* that is effective in planning social studies lessons that promote conceptual change and increase students' powerful and meaningful learning (Sunal, McCormick, Sunal, & Shweny, 2005; Sunal & Sunal, 1999). The learning-cycle approach is designed to sequence the key elements, or conditions, implied by constructivist learning theory so that *all students*:

- *Become aware* of their prior knowledge
- *Confront* their prior knowledge as they encounter a new social studies idea
- *Resolve* their confrontation *by constructing* their "new" social studies idea
- *Connect* the new social studies idea to what they already know
- *Apply and transfer* the new social studies idea in novel situations (Appleton & Asoko, 1996, Atherton, 2005)

Because the learning cycle incorporates these constructivist elements, it is better able to foster meaningful learning in social studies than are traditional teaching approaches (see Figure 2.2 on page 37). The carefully selected active experiences of the *exploratory introduction* phase of the learning cycle enable students to become more aware of their own reasoning. As this occurs, they recognize shortcomings in their prior knowledge. During the *lesson development* phase of the learning cycle, students are engaged in experiences that enable them to search more effectively for new patterns in their experiences (see Figure 2.2). They reconstruct their prior knowledge into these new patterns, which represent concepts, generalizations, inquiry skills, attitudes, values, or dispositions. As this reconstruction occurs, students practice with the new pattern to better understand its characteristics and use. This practice stabilizes this new thought pattern in their mind so that it can be accessed from long-term memory when needed. During the *expansion* phase of the learning cycle, students apply the new

text continues on page 38

LEARNING CYCLE LESSON PLAN   *Scale*

Grade Level: Fourth or Fifth

NCSS

Standard III

NCSS Standards: People, Places, and Environment

This learning cycle on scale is an example of a lesson plan promoting meaningful learning by students by incorporating strategies for conceptual change. Geographers use a scale to show how one place is located in relationship to another on maps and globes of varying sizes.

Exploratory Introduction

Materials: For each group, provide two objects that are the same except for size (e.g., two blocks of wood with one larger than a half sheet of paper and one smaller) and three half-sheets of drawing paper per student.

Objectives	Procedures	Assessment
1. Students identify reducing the scale of two objects as a means by which both can be drawn on paper that is too small to draw both at full scale.	1. Place students in small groups. Have a group materials manager get drawing paper and two objects that are the same except for size. Give students the task of drawing the smaller object on the half sheet of paper. Then, ask students to draw the bigger object. 2. Discuss the problems that arose. Ask, "Is there any way you can think of to draw both of these on just one half sheet of paper?" Discuss student suggestions. 3. Ask students to try out their ideas on another sheet of paper. Discuss results of their efforts. Ask, "Which of the drawings has solved the problem? How was this done?"	1. Review final drawings to determine whether they (a) reduced both objects to a smaller size in their drawings and (b) used the same scale for both objects, using a checklist to identify successful students in each task.

Lesson Development

Materials: Provide pairs with 5 to 7 sheets of graph paper, plain paper, wood block or other square object (6 × 6 inches), scissors, and glue

Objectives	Procedures	Assessment
1. Students define *scale* as a ratio where one square represents more squares (e.g., 1 to 5).	1. Use common classroom materials, such as pencils and books, noting that many ordinary objects are found in different sizes. 2. Refer back to the exploratory introduction problem, reviewing solutions tried. Ask, "How did we try to solve the problem of getting everything on one small piece of paper? Were we successful?" 3. Assign pairs. Give each pair a sheet of graph paper and a wood block. Have pairs position the block so	1. On a checklist, record whether students produced a scaled drawing of an object that is larger than their sheet of graph paper and identified the scale used.

its sides are on lines. Have students draw a line around the block, lift up the block and count the squares inside the block they have drawn, then write down the number of squares. Have them cut out the square outlined and glue it to a piece of paper.

4. Repeat the procedures in number 3 above with a 3 × 3 square and a 1.5 × 1.5 square. Have students glue these squares using the same piece of paper on which the block was drawn. Ask: "How are the three shapes on the paper alike?" "Does this activity give you ideas about how you can draw something that is large on a small piece of paper?"

5. On a sheet of graph paper, ask each pair to draw a scaled down drawing of a desktop or of a book that is larger than the graph paper. Work with students to establish a scale, such as 1 square = 5 inches, of the item. Encourage pairs to use different scales as long as they are successful at the task. Show students how to write the scale 1 square = 5 inches. Have pairs identify their scale and write it on the drawing.

2. Students draw the same object in two different scales.

6. Give each student a sticky note. Have each draw it on graph paper to size, then reduce the scale in another drawing, and label the scale for each drawing.

7. **Closure.** Based on what we have done in these activities, "How can we define a *scale*?" Use students' ideas and write the definition on the board. (Note: It should be similar to "a scale is a ratio where a square represents or stands for several squares (e.g., 1 to 5)."

2. On a checklist, record whether students used two different scales to draw an object and labeled the scale for each drawing.

Expansion

Materials: 1 × 1 inch strip of paper; globe; several maps containing a map scale; yardstick for each pair and two sheets of graph paper; for each student provide graph paper and pencils, blueprint of school or scaled diagram of school or scaled diagram of a local mall (optional)

Objectives ⟶	Procedures ⟶	Assessment
1. Students define *scale* in geographic terms. 2. Students draw a room at home to scale and	1. Ask, "What are some very large things you have seen drawn or shown on a piece of paper?" Take suggestions. Point out that a very big thing to try to draw is the world. Tell students that because the	1. Students change their earlier definition of scale so that miles or kilometers are used.

continued

accurately identify the scale used.

world is so large, geographers use scales when they make maps.

2. Show a globe. Place a 1 × 1 inch strip of paper on the globe. Ask: "Do you think that one inch on this globe is equal to five inches on the earth?" "What is your guess about what the scale might be?" Locate the scale on the globe and read the answer. Have sets of two pairs look at one or more map and find the scales.

3. Ask the class to revisit the definition of scale. Have students revise the definition so it is like one that a geographer might use.

4. Tell students to watch carefully so they will know what to do at home. Have one pair measure the classroom's length and another pair measure its width using a yardstick. Write the measurements on the board. Have student pairs draw the classroom to scale on graph paper and indicate the scale they used. Note the different choices students made for their drawings.

5. Homework assignment. Have each student measure a room at home and draw it to scale, writing the scale used on the drawing. Note: Students can ask a family member to help. Tell students to bring drawings back to class.

6. Display drawings of rooms and note the scales used. Identify several of the most popular scales used. If possible, share with students the architect's blueprint of the school. Look for the scale on the blueprint. Option: Use a scaled diagram of the school or a local mall.

7. Note that geographers are not the only people who use scale drawings or models. Ask, "Has anyone seen anything else that is made to scale?" (e.g., model cars and trains, doll houses)

8. **Lesson summary.** Ask students to briefly describe their activities in this lesson and what they think was the main idea of the learning cycle.

2. Use a checklist to record whether students accurately indicated the scale used on a drawing made of a room at home.

Summative Evaluation Have each student draw a scaled plan of another room in the school (e.g., library, cafeteria) using length and width measurements for the room and a door into the room, which you provide. Ask them to indicate the location of the door to the room and identify the scale used. Consider whether (1) the scale used was appropriate, (2) the scale was used consistently in the drawing, (3) the door was in the correct location, and (4) the door was drawn to scale.

TIME FOR REFLECTION   What Do You Think?

Consider the learning cycle lesson plan on scale. Respond to the following questions. If possible, discuss your responses with a peer.

1. How does the task in the exploratory introduction present students with a challenge?

2. How does the key question used by the teacher in the exploratory introduction engage students' prior knowledge? Around which concept is this lesson focused?

3. How does the teacher help students develop the concept of scale as a ratio through the lesson development activities? How do these activities help students recognize scale as a ratio?

4. On what two components of the concept of scale does the teacher bring closure, after students have had time to further develop their concept of scale in the middle portion of this lesson?

5. How does the teacher work with expanding students' use of scale during the expansion? What procedures in the plan indicate that the teacher first involves all the students in a carefully guided practice activity with the concept? What procedures describe an individual activity with the concept? What benefit might there be to the students when they are first involved in a carefully guided practice activity then in an individual practice activity?

Exploratory introduction: **Social studies learning experiences are designed to encourage students to**

- Recall and relate prior knowledge to the new idea by focusing attention, making observations, and collecting data
- Respond to a "key" open question, involving students in trying out the new social studies idea
- Make public their prior knowledge related to the new social studies idea
- Confront their prior knowledge with the new social studies idea

Lesson development: **Social studies learning experiences are designed to encourage students to**

- Discuss the results of the exploratory introduction activity, providing connections to the new social studies idea that is the focus of the lesson
- Explain the new idea, how to use it, when to use it, the purpose for which it is used, and/or how to know when it is used appropriately
- Practice clear examples or model the new idea
- Practice activities using the new idea in interesting examples, not repetitive practice
- Provide closure for the new idea, describing the steps necessary to use it appropriately

Expansion: **Social studies learning experiences are designed to encourage students to**

- Apply the new idea in several new and relevant contexts
- Transfer the new social studies idea to real-world events
- Provide a summary of the development of the new social studies idea in the completed lesson

FIGURE 2.2
Learning Cycle Format

thought pattern to solving related problems (see Figure 2.2). Students are asked to transfer the new thought pattern to contexts different from that in which it was originally learned. The order of phases used in the learning cycle organizes the conditions needed to help students modify or discard prior knowledge, promoting conceptual change.

Teaching is a process of continuous decision making that involves planning, implementation, and evaluation. If teachers base their decisions on an understanding of how students learn social studies effectively, they can increase their ability to develop social studies lessons that work. Figure 2.2 outlines the components of each of the three phases of the learning cycle lesson. The criteria for making planning decisions vary with each phase of the learning cycle. When planning each phase of the learning cycle, teachers should ask themselves questions derived from constructivist learning theory to ensure they are addressing each element important to that phase (see Figure 2.3). These questions demonstrate that the learning cycle process is not a blueprint or cookbook that teachers follow, but rather a set of decision points using important criteria that help teachers address important conditions for students' meaningful learning of powerful social studies.

The following questions are designed to help adapt social studies instruction to assist student learning in a social studies lesson.

Exploratory Introduction

- What activities will enable my students to *become aware* of and make public their prior knowledge and reasoning about the new social studies idea in a safe environment?
- What activities will provide my students with the opportunity to *try out* their prior knowledge in the new setting?
- What activities will enable my students to *compare* their prior knowledge to the new social studies idea and recognize shortcomings in their prior knowledge?

Lesson Development

- What activities will provide my students with a clear *explanation* and sufficient practice examples or model to allow them to *connect* the new social studies idea to what they already knew?
- What activities will enable my students to *construct* their own "new" social studies knowledge based on the new idea and to search more effectively for the new patterns in their environment?

Expansion

- What activities will enable my students to *apply* the new social studies knowledge in relevant contexts?
- What activities will help my students develop successful procedures for making decisions and solving problems while *transferring* the new social studies idea to other and novel settings, especially in settings more relevant to students' personal needs?

FIGURE 2.3
Brief Outline of Questions for Learning Cycle Planning Decisions

The learning cycle sequences its three phases beginning with the *exploratory introduction*, working through *development*, and ending with *expansion*. Each phase has a different purpose, and, therefore, requires different student and teacher actions and interactions. All three phases need to be completed in a lesson before a single idea can be meaningfully learned. If one phase of the learning cycle social studies lesson is inadequate or missing, or if the sequence of phases is changed, significant loss in achievement of the new social studies idea is expected.

Exploratory Introduction

Teachers make a number of decisions when planning a lesson, such as what social studies content to include, what new social studies skill the lesson will teach, and what previously learned skill and information will be reviewed. Teachers consult national standards and state guidelines for suggestions for appropriate topics and skills. These are weighed against students' experiences. Objectives are developed that incorporate the guidelines and students' past experiences. The entire lesson usually has a primary objective and a number of secondary objectives. A teacher also may want to use a particular activity or set of resources. These can assist in lesson planning, because it is often possible to write a lesson objective that combines the content and skills required for use of the desired activity or material.

After identifying the lesson's objectives, the teacher begins planning the lesson, starting with the first phase, the exploratory introduction. The teacher's role during the exploratory introduction involves confronting students' thinking, raising questions, and facilitating students' exploration. The students' role involves controlling much of their own learning behavior through exploring, observing, recording, and testing prior knowledge (see Table 2.1 on page 40).

During the exploratory introduction, students get involved with a social studies idea that is new to them. They do this by engaging in an open-ended activity that makes their prior knowledge public and enables the teacher to diagnose their existing ideas. Finally, the activity begins to relate their prior knowledge to the new social studies idea. The three questions in Figure 2.3 guide the teacher's decisions in *selecting instructional activities* for this exploratory phase of the lesson. By answering the questions, the teacher identifies several open-ended activities that promote a safe environment in which students control the direction of their responses and specific responses are not expected. The activities are focused with a carefully planned open-ended key question or two. The key question (see the scale learning cycle) enables students to understand the topic or direction of the lesson. During the exploratory introduction activities, the teacher uses cooperative learning groups and pairs to encourage social interaction as students work with materials and share ideas. Students interact as they collect and organize data, select resources, discuss their tasks and observations, and argue the evidence they have at hand. To accomplish all this, the teacher must allow sufficient time. If enough time is not provided, students will not be able to relate their prior knowledge to the new knowledge.

Many types of activities work well during the exploratory introduction phase, including student observation and exploratory introduction of an event, problem

TABLE 2.1

Consistent and Inconsistent Exploratory Introduction Activities

	Actions Consistent with the Learning Cycle Strategy	Actions Inconsistent with the Learning Cycle Strategy
Teacher's Actions	Creates interest in topic Generates curiosity Raises questions Elicits responses that uncover what the students know or think about the concept/topic Encourages students to work together without direct instruction Observes and listens to students as they interact Asks probing questions to redirect students' investigations, when necessary Provides time for students to solve problems Acts as a consultant to students	Explains concepts Provides definitions and answers States conclusions Lectures Provides answers Tells or explains how to work through the problem Provides closure Tells the students that they are incorrect Gives information or facts that solve the problem Leads students step-by-step to a solution
Students' Actions	Respond with interest to the stimulus question, task, or artifact Ask questions, such as "Why did this happen" or "What do I already know about this?" Show interest in the topic Think freely, but about the topic Test new predictions and hypotheses Form new predictions and hypotheses Try alternatives and discuss them with others Record observations and ideas Suspend judgment	Ask for the "right" answer Offer the "right" answer Insist on answers or explanations Seek one solution Let others do the thinking and exploring Work quietly with little or no interaction with others (only appropriate when exploring ideas or feelings) "Play around" indiscriminately with no goal in mind Stop with one solution

solving, a discovery field trip, an inductive demonstration, a task for which decisions are to be made, drawings and discussions of students' understanding of a concept, and question-and-answer discussions about evidence observed in small groups. Chapter 7 describes several of these types of activities in depth.

Development

During the lesson development phase of the learning cycle, the teacher provides more guidance than was provided in the exploratory introduction phase (see Table 2.2). During the lesson development phase, the teacher's role is to provide an explanation

TABLE 2.2

The Learning Cycle: Consistent and Inconsistent Actions during the Lesson Development Phase

	Actions Consistent with the Learning Cycle Strategy	Actions Inconsistent with the Learning Cycle Strategy
Teacher's Actions	Encourages students to explain ideas in their own words	Accepts explanations that have no justification
	Asks for justification, evidence, and clarification for statements	Neglects to solicit students' explanations
	Provides definitions, explanations, and new labels	Introduces unrelated concepts or skills
	Helps students link previous experiences to social studies learning	
Students' Actions	Explain possible solutions or answers to others	Propose explanations from "thin air" with no relationship to previous experiences
	Listen critically to others' explanations	
	Question others' explanations	Bring up irrelevant experiences and examples
	Listen to and try to comprehend explanations offered by the teacher	Accept explanations without justification
	Refer to previous activities	
	Examine maps, charts, pictures, and narrative data resources	Do not attend to other plausible explanations
	Support explanations with data	

for the key idea or skill, to interact with students, to promote student practice of the idea, and to provide closure on the key idea or skill. The students' role is to construct, question, and practice the alternative explanations.

In the development phase, the teacher explains and provides examples and nonexamples of the key social studies idea or skill. The teacher guides students in reconstructing their prior knowledge. Although the teacher is a stronger guide in this phase of the lesson, a variety of instructional strategies can be used. The teacher may have students use a WebQuest, listen to a short lecture, watch and discuss a video, read a textbook, or participate in a simulation. When students give evidence of having reconstructed their prior knowledge, the teacher brings this phase of the lesson to a close by clearly defining and describing the idea or skill, often involving the students in arriving at a consensus statement that defines the new idea. The two questions in Figure 2.3 for the development phase guide the teacher's decisions in *selecting instructional activities* for this phase of the lesson.

The teacher recognizes that the development phase continues the development of the new social studies idea or skill through directed reflection and discussion, following up on the activities in the exploratory introduction phase. If the exploratory phase's activities challenged students' prior knowledge by confronting it or by puzzling the students, the development phase's activities communicate information about the new idea to help students resolve the confrontation or puzzle.

To resolve the confrontation, the students work through a variety of activities, investigating all of the important aspects, ranges, contexts, and uses of the new social studies idea or skill. Such activities are sequenced into a structure that organizes data related to the new social studies idea or skill so that the students see how the various components fit together. Students need to see clear examples of what the new social studies ideas or skills represent. At first, students' practice of an idea or skill is guided or modeled by the teacher. This enables them to receive feedback. Without such guidance, the students may practice errors creating alternative conceptions that require a great amount of effort to unlearn. One or more examples demonstrating the idea or skill are presented at this point in the lesson. Sometimes this consists of demonstrating a social studies idea or skill through guided practice, analogies, or working models. It also can involve taking the students through a step-by-step process. The more ways in which an idea or skill is modeled for students, the more meaningful it will be to them.

The development activities are varied. The focus is on providing more than one form of explanation, giving clear examples, using modeling, and checking for understanding. Using several activities enables students to question, try out, and practice the new social studies idea. Because most students have limited short-term memories, the teacher provides important information as concretely as possible. When more concrete materials or visuals, such as hands-on materials, pictures, graphs, demonstrations, and modeling, accompany verbal explanations, more information can be stored efficiently. The use of concrete materials facilitates meaningful learning and long-term memory storage. After students have worked with an activity aimed at providing an explanation of the new social studies idea or skill, they need to practice using it in concrete activities similar to the situations just experienced in the explanation activity. Throughout this phase of the learning cycle, the teacher is a guide who helps students accommodate their thinking to new social studies ideas or skills, restoring the equilibrium lost during the Exploratory Introduction when their prior knowledge was confronted.

Key terms should be provided and defined during the discussion, following up on activities carried out during the development phase. When terms are defined at the beginning of the phase, before students have worked with examples and explanations, they will have little meaning.

Some students will discover the new social studies idea during the exploratory introduction phase and some will develop it during the development phase's activities. Still others may not be clear about the new social studies idea even after working with development activities. It is important to make certain that all students have closure, a clear description of the idea or skill with which they have been working that they will apply in the last part of the lesson, the expansion. Closure can occur by providing a brief clear description, demonstration, or modeling of the main social studies idea or skill orally, and in writing, at the end of the development phase. The closure states or shows clearly and concisely the main objective of the lesson. Alternatively, students state the main idea of the lesson orally, write the idea on the board, or demonstrate the skill.

Expansion

Following the development, or explanation, phase of the lesson, the teacher helps students apply and transfer the new social studies idea or skill to different situations. This is the purpose of the expansion phase of the learning cycle. During the expansion phase of the learning cycle, the teacher provides less guidance than during the development phase (see Table 2.3). The teacher's role in the expansion

TABLE 2.3
The Learning Cycle: Consistent and Inconsistent Actions during the Expansion Phase

	Actions Consistent with the Learning Cycle Strategy	Actions Inconsistent with the Learning Cycle Strategy
Teacher's Actions	Expects students to use previously learned formal labels, definitions, and explanations Encourages students to apply or extend concepts and skills in new situations Reminds students of alternative explanations Refers students to existing data and evidence and asks: "What do you already know?" and "Why do you think…?" (strategies from the previous stage also apply here) Looks for evidence that students have changed their prior knowledge Asks open-ended questions, such as "Why do you think…?" "What evidence do you have?" "What do you think about…?" and "How would you explain…?"	Provides definitive answers Tells students that they are incorrect Lectures Leads students step-by-step to a solution Explains how to work through the problem
Students' Actions	Apply newly learned labels, definitions, explanations, and skills in similar situations Use previously learned information to ask questions, propose solutions, or make decisions Draw reasonable conclusions from evidence Record observations and explanations when performing activities Check for understanding among peers Demonstrate an understanding or knowledge of the concept or skill Ask related questions that encourage future investigations	"Play around" with no goal in mind Ignore previous information or evidence Draw conclusions from "thin air" Use those labels provided by the teacher in discussions only

is to provide for, and encourage, students' application and transfer of the social studies concept or skill. The students' role is to attempt to apply and transfer their newly reconstructed idea or skill in new situations and contexts where it has not been previously used and to make connections to real-world experiences.

Practice and application during the expansion phase helps students retrieve the social studies idea from memory. Providing additional experiences that help students transfer the new idea to other settings and contexts is necessary, because transfer does not automatically occur. Two questions (see Figure 2.3) guide the teacher's decisions in *selecting instructional activities* for this final phase of the lesson.

During the expansion phase, the teacher helps students broaden the range of application of a new idea or skill. The teacher asks the students to differentiate the new idea from other related ideas. The teacher asks the students to describe not only the solution, but also the process used to find a solution and to relate prior knowledge to the new idea or skill learned.

Have you ever thought you understood an idea, but later found that you didn't really understand it, or were no longer able to remember it when needed? It is likely that either you did not construct a meaningful understanding of the idea or that you did construct it, but then had little or no practice in applying it. As a result, the idea was poorly, if at all, connected to your prior knowledge and to the knowledge structure in your mind. Application and transfer experiences with a new idea and skill enable us to connect it to a relevant knowledge structure and to access it from our long-term memory. Expansion experiences are spaced out over time so the idea or skill is used in situations similar to, but different from, those experienced in the exploratory introduction and development phases of the learning cycle. Students begin using and applying the new social studies skill or idea in settings similar to those experienced in the lesson. Then, they are ready to transfer it to different situations. This step often is omitted because students have given some evidence of learning the new idea or skill earlier in the lesson. Although students seem to have reconstructed their prior knowledge, they need experience in using the social studies idea in a new context over a period of time before the new thought can be stabilized in the long-term memory (Perkins, D., 2009; Baker & Piburn, 1997).

Many types of experiences enable students to apply and transfer a new social studies idea or skill. These include reflecting on hands-on activities, taking field trips, problem solving, decision making, interviewing or surveying other students, drawing events, playing a part in a simulation, playing a game where the idea is needed to arrive at a successful conclusion, creating an analogy or model of the new idea and describing how it works, using the Internet to find applications of the new idea, completing paper-and-pencil exercises, and engaging in question-and-answer discussions in small groups (see Chapter 7 for a discussion of instructional strategies).

Lesson Summary

When sufficient practice and application experiences have occurred, it is important to involve students in generating a brief chronological summary of the learning cycle. A summary is aimed at consolidating the lesson's experiences into a

---

TIME FOR REFLECTION | ## What Do You Think?

Use the following questions to reflect on the expansion phase of the learning cycle on scale earlier in this chapter. Respond to each question. Then, discuss your ideas with a peer, if possible.

1. What activities are expansion experiences that involve students in applying their understanding of the social studies idea?

2. What activities are expansion experiences that involve students in analyzing a problem with the new social studies idea?

3. How can the expansion experiences involve students in considering tentative solutions to a problem based on their previous experiences with the new idea?

4. How can the expansion experiences involve students in trying out the tentative solutions to a problem that use the new social studies idea?

5. How can the expansion experiences involve students in evaluating the effectiveness of the tentative solutions to the problem by using the new social studies idea?

6. What activities serve as expansion experiences to involve students in using the new solutions to the problem in different and increasingly real-world contexts?

---

related event. Such consolidation is particularly important when the learning cycle takes place over more than one day. Students should be asked to give the summary, including the important ideas and events in each phase of the learning cycle just completed. When students are involved in constructing the summary, the teacher is able to check on their understanding of the events of the lesson, how they were related, and their purpose.

 ## Choosing Activities for Each Phase of the Learning Cycle Lesson

Elementary and middle school students' social and cognitive development enables them to benefit from a variety of instructional strategies. As students gain experiences and become able to work in ever more complex situations, teachers use more activities that rely on cooperative and collaborative research, discussion, problem solving, and decision making. Teachers of younger students employ small-group instruction with more careful guidance, and often use learning centers where students explore events and work out simple solutions to problems. Many learning activities are used across the grade levels but become more complex and more abstract in both their goals and procedures as students progress through the years. An example is interviewing, an activity that requires students to develop relevant questions, understand a question asked of them, and respond to an effective question with more than a yes/no answer. Research among kindergarteners and second graders by Lynn Kelley (2006, 2009) found that even young children could learn these important skills and develop and conduct interviews. The teacher, however, had to help these young children learn to ask and answer questions with a "yes" or "no" response, and then to ask and answer questions with an open-ended relevant answer. By middle school, students who have had effective instruction can develop, conduct an interview, and respond to interviews by others with increasing depth using several well-chosen questions targeted at the problem or event that is the focus of the interview.

Now, try recognizing which actions belong to which phase in a lesson designed to teach the map skill of using the grid system and gaining information through observation. Two sets of activities describing ways to teach using grid systems are presented. The first set is for elementary students, and the second set is for middle childhood students. From each set, select one activity to use for the exploratory introduction phase, one to use during the development phase, and a third to use in the expansion phase. Record the numeral of each choice on the line provided at the end of the list of activities. When you have made your choices for each lesson, reflect on your reasons for the selections or discuss your selections with a classmate.

Elementary Lesson Activity Choices

1. The teacher says: "Think about where you are sitting. For example, I am sitting in front of Ellen and next to the sink. I will ask some students to tell the class where they are sitting in the room." Have each student pick another student's name from a jar and describe where that student is sitting. The teacher asks: "Did anyone have any problems in trying to describe the locations or in deciding who the person was whose location was being described?" Discuss student responses.

2. Create a grid on all or much of the classroom floor. Move students' desks so that each is in a square of the grid. Tape cards to the floor that identify rows with numbers and columns with letters. Ask students to identify their "address" by using a number and a letter. Have them put their address on any drawings or other papers they turn in. At the end of each day, select one or two students to act as mail carriers for the day, using the addresses to deliver finished papers and drawings for students to take home.

3. Using masking tape, make two columns on the floor. Divide them both by another tape strip to create four squares. Identify each row with a picture of a bird (e.g., robin and cardinal) and each column with a picture of a piece of clothing (e.g., pants and sweatshirt). Ask one student to stand in a square. Ask the other students to tell you which square the student is standing in. Repeat with students standing in different squares. Students should soon discover that each square has two names (it can be robin–pants, robin–sweatshirt, cardinal–pants, or cardinal–sweatshirt). Encourage them to use both names. Repeat on another day with six squares, and later with eight squares. Eventually, introduce letters and numerals so the squares can be identified as A1, A2, B1, and so on.

4. Introduce students to the game bingo. Use cards that have letters and numerals identifying rows and columns. Play the game several times over a few weeks.

Write the number of the activity you choose from those above on the line beside the phase in which you would use that activity.

Exploratory Introduction   _____
Development   _____
Expansion   _____

Discussion.   The first activity in the list is the approach that best represents an exploratory introduction activity. The development phase of a lesson formally introduces the new idea or skill, guiding students to construct new knowledge from their experiences. A combination of discussion and a floor grid, found in elementary lesson activity 3, forms an effective development activity for defining a grid system, a concept essential to eventually understanding latitude and longitude. The expansion phase is the final part of any effective lesson designed for meaningful learning. Students apply the new idea in additional situations. Activity 2, in which students act as mail carriers, is an effective expansion activity with which to conclude the lesson. A follow-up to activity 2 for the expansion phase could be activity 4. Because it is more abstract than is activity 2, it is not preferred as a first expansion activity.

Middle Childhood Lesson Activity Choices

1. Provide students with travel magazines and other magazines with pictures of interesting places to visit. Have them select one they would most like to visit, but keep it a secret. Help them find it on a world map. Ask them to plan a 1-or 2-minute presentation for the class describing the place they would most like to visit, their "mystery place," without naming it. Next, tell them to give the other students clues by describing where it is located using two neighboring places. Have the other students try to guess what the mystery place is. Discuss problems that arose as they tried to guess each mystery place.

2. Ask groups of three students to plan a treasure hunt through five cities. Each city can be identified only by its location using latitude and longitude. Students should do some library research to identify an item that is made in each city. They should draw the item or find a picture of it, then place it in an envelope identified with the name of the city.

Each team goes on a treasure hunt designed by another team. Using a world map, they find each city by using its latitude and longitude coordinates. When all five cities have been located, each team makes a list of the names of the cities found at particular pairs of coordinates. Then they claim the envelopes printed with the names of these cities. They glue the items found in the envelopes onto a map, identify the city that belongs with each item, and display the map on a Treasure Hunt bulletin board.

Building on Diversity

Opportunities to Include Multiple Perspectives

The learning cycle format offers many opportunities to build on the cultural diversity represented by students. Because the Exploratory Introduction phase is open ended, it is expected that students' prior knowledge is diverse. As each student's prior knowledge is brought out, other students often discover varying perspectives among their classmates, setting up a confrontation to what the student currently thinks. During the Development phase, the focus is on reconstructing prior knowledge into a new idea or skill level or attitude. So, all students have equal opportunities to reconstruct their prior knowledge. The different perspectives and skill levels among the students are used to both broaden and deepen the reconstruction. During Expansion, students use their newly reconstructed idea, skill level, or attitude in a new application that is different from the context in which they learned it. The more diverse the students, the wider is the possible set of applications.

3. Tape yarn onto a world map, forming a grid with 10 rows and 10 columns. Ask students to suggest a way of labeling the grid. (They might suggest, for example, letters and numerals.) Label the ends of each row and column with the system suggested. Then, have pairs of students pull a card out of a box and try to find the city named on the card. After finding it, ask the students to identify its location as closely as possible using the grid. Talk about problems they encounter, such as not being able to pinpoint a location well if it is in the center of a square or not directly on a grid line.

Ask whether anyone can tell the class what the equator is and where it is on the grid. Identify the equator for the students, if necessary, and label it. Ask them to identify whether their city is above (north) or below (south) of the equator on this map. Repeat this procedure with the prime meridian. Discuss whether these designations help students identify the location of their city or make it more confusing. Ask whether anybody can share something about latitude and longitude. Discuss comments. Then describe how the grid system currently on the map relates to latitude and longitude. Introduce finding locations with latitude and longitude. Introduce a globe and find latitude and longitude lines on it. Are these lines easier to understand with the globe? Practice finding their cities on the globe.

4. Ask students to find a city of their choice on the globe and then write down only its latitude and longitude on a strip of paper and place that in a jar. Ask each student to select a strip out of the jar, use the coordinates given to find a city, and write the name of the city on the strip of paper. Offer to assist any student who is having difficulty. Then have the class generate a list of cities they have heard of in the news. Ask students to choose five cities, find their coordinates, and write them on a sheet of paper. Check papers for accuracy.

Discussion.   The first activity in the list is the approach that best represents an exploratory introduction activity. For the development phase of the lesson, activity 3 is a good choice. It starts with a map and a simple grid system and uses these as beginning points for helping students invent for themselves an appropriate understanding of latitude and longitude. For the expansion phase, asking students to construct their own situation, as in the treasure hunt in activity 2, is an effective expansion activity with which to conclude the lesson. Activity 4 also would serve as a useful expansion activity because it engages students in demonstrating and practicing their own construction of the idea just explained in the development phase of the lesson.

 ## Student Assessment in Each Phase of the Learning Cycle

Formative assessment occurs throughout a learning cycle. Assessment in the exploratory introduction phase primarily involves diagnosing prior knowledge. In the development phase, assessment focuses on monitoring students' actions and statements that indicate they are developing a meaningful understanding of the key social studies idea or skill. During the expansion phase, assessment checks for students' understanding of the new social studies idea or skill and their ability to apply and transfer it, leading to the *summative evaluation* of each student. Chapter 14 discusses assessment and evaluation of students' meaningful learning in depth.

Teachers monitor individual students and student groups during the exploratory introduction and development phases of the lesson. Small and whole groups can be monitored by having students respond to teacher questions with a yes or no card that they hold up. The teacher can ask a question of the class, have student groups discuss the question, and then get responses from group representatives. Students can quiz each other on the main idea during the development's closure. Checklists and lists of performance levels can serve as guides for recording assessment information.

During the expansion phase of the social studies lesson, the teacher continues observing students in group discussions, working with activities, and as they share answers. After the student groups apply the social studies idea in a new situation, the teacher gives students a similar problem to which individuals must develop a response. The lesson summary then gives the teacher information on how the new idea or skill has been constructed by the students. After offering opportunities to apply and transfer the new idea or skill during the expansion phase, the teacher carries out summative evaluation, checking for understanding in assignments or quizzes involving application-type assessment questions and performance activities. Many teachers plan more expansion phase activities than are needed and use the extra activities for summative assignments or quizzes following the lesson. Assessment that probes students' meaningful understanding rather than rote memory enables a teacher to decide whether to move on, to stop and clarify, or to recycle students through another set of activities.

Writing Your Own Learning Cycle Lesson

You have practiced identifying the characteristics of the phases of the learning cycle. Now, try to write a learning cycle lesson of your own choosing either the early grades or the middle grades.

For the early grades, plan a brief lesson on family groups. Assume that the students in your class come from homes with two parents, homes with a single parent, and homes with an extended family, and present information on only these three forms of families. For the middle grades, plan a brief lesson on how a person's family and friends influence his or her development of a personal identity.

1. Design an exploratory introduction activity suitable for introducing the topic you chose at a specific elementary or middle school grade level that will explore students' prior knowledge of it during a social studies lesson.
2. Design a development activity to follow the exploration that helps students meaningfully understand the topic.
3. Describe an expansion activity to follow the development activity that helps students apply their new understanding of the topic in a new time or place.

The Optimal Length of Time for a Learning Cycle

The optimal length of a learning cycle is a single class period. Some social studies ideas, especially very abstract concepts and generalizations, will take longer. Typically, if a more complex concept is to be taught, the lesson begins on day 1 with the exploratory introduction and development phases and ends on day 2 with the expansion phase. Other variations are found in Figure 2.4 and include one phase each day, with a learning cycle scheduled over three or four days. When a learning cycle lesson is completed, a new connecting concept is selected, leading to a new learning cycle. For example, a learning cycle on the concept of scale as a ratio can lead to consideration of small-scale microclimates occurring near a lake shore or in a mountain valley versus macroclimates occurring over a region of the country such as the Southwest, or students could work with directions on a map and then with the compass rose. Each learning cycle builds on the previous one (see Figure 2.4). However your teaching is structured, recognize that you will need to begin using the learning cycle slowly at first, through trial lessons. This will provide the time needed for you and your students to become familiar with the activities found in learning cycle lessons.

Working with the Learning Cycle

The format for planning a complete lesson using the learning cycle is shown in Figure 2.5 on page 52. This basic format identifies the concerns and issues to be considered when planning for meaningful and powerful social studies learning. The learning cycle

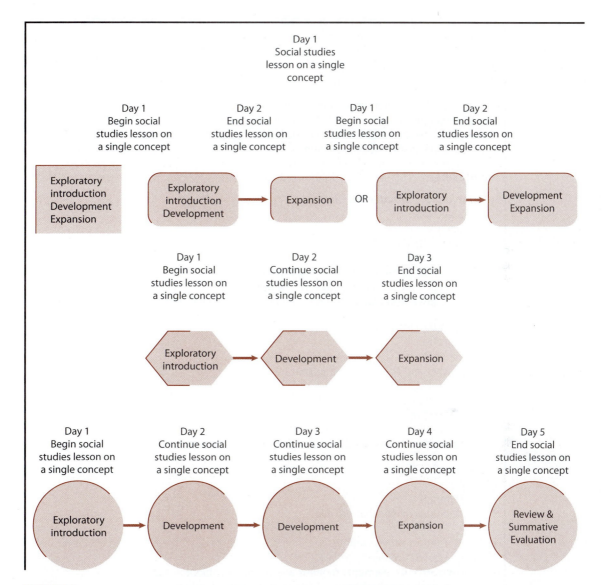

FIGURE 2.4

Learning Cycle Planning Patterns on Consecutive Class Days

approach is used best as part of a social studies program that stresses the importance of social studies for all students; effectively uses cooperative learning groups; and assesses and rewards development of thinking skills such as critical thinking, creativity, and the development of self-worth, self-reliance, and respect for the opinions of others. For conceptual restructuring to occur and for meaningful learning to result from a learning cycle strategy, several prerequisites need to be considered:

The learning cycle lesson plan requires the identification of:

- Classroom information
- Key Idea
  - Lesson goal
  - Expected student prior knowledge
  - Prerequisite skills and concepts needed
  - Social studies standards to be addressed (national, state, and local)
  - Special needs accommodation

Procedure:

1. *Exploratory Introduction Phase*
   Objectives
   Materials
   Introduction to lesson
   Student activities that
   - Try out and confront prior knowledge
   - Relate previous knowledge to new idea
   Formative Assessment: monitor and diagnose student needs

2. *Lesson Development Phase*
   Objectives
   Materials
   Teacher and student activities that provide
   - Explanations
   - Examples
   - Practice
   - Closure
   Formative Assessment: monitor and diagnose student needs

3. *Expansion Phase*
   Objectives
   Materials
   Student activities that provide
   - Application
   - Transfer to new settings
   - Lesson summary
   Formative Assessment: monitor and diagnose student needs
   Summative Evaluation: evaluate student understanding

FIGURE 2.5
Learning Cycle Lesson Plan Format

1. Change in the social studies idea or skill should not be too great; it should be challenging, but not overwhelming, to students.
2. Lesson content must be related to the background experiences and daily lives of the students as much as possible. Such a relationship helps to create a knowledge structure to which the new idea or skill can be connected. This

knowledge structure is important if the new social studies idea or skill is to be easily retrievable from long-term memory.

3. Many hands-on/minds-on examples are used in real situations during a learning cycle. Using technology can be very helpful.

4. Students should have many opportunities to work through practice situations using real or simulated actions while conceptual learning is occurring. Learning usually takes place in cooperative learning groups.

5. Students should have time to reflect, make mistakes, and form the new ideas or skills in a safe environment.

6. Less coverage of content occurs but there is increased understanding of basic concepts.

7. Only those critical concepts are selected that are basic to understanding the idea under investigation and are suggested as key ideas in the social studies standards. As time permits, other less important concepts are taught using the learning cycle or in a more direct instructional style.

8. All phases of the learning cycle are addressed in the order supported by the research literature. Deleting a phase will create significantly less meaningful learning.

Other prerequisites may exist in various situations, but these eight are essential. Although most students benefit from use of the learning cycle, gifted students may require less dependence on use of the learning cycle and more open general inquiry activities for conceptual reconstruction to take place. The learning cycle may be planned to teach different types of objectives. Teaching a thinking skill, concept, generalization, attitude, disposition, or value all follow the learning cycle model but use a number of different instructional strategies because the learning objectives focus on different goals.

EXPANSION

Principles of Teaching and Learning that Support the Curriculum Standards for Social Studies

In the *Curriculum Standards for the Social Studies*, the National Council for the Social Studies (1994b) outlined its principles for teaching and learning. Five main principles tell us that social studies teaching and learning are powerful when they are meaningful, integrative, value based, challenging, and active. This chapter has applied these principles. It has introduced an overview of social studies teaching and learning supported by the five main principles.

Do the following Time for Reflection Activity to expand your abilities at planning a learning cycle lesson in social studies. As you think through possible activities for your lesson, keep in mind the five principles that should apply to social

TIME FOR REFLECTION: *What Do You Think?*

Design activities, by yourself or with a small group, to use in a learning cycle addressing one of these concepts: (a) assembly line, (b) population density, or (c) needs and wants. (Note: These are two concepts usually taught together.) Describe the following.

1. Concept chosen and grade level addressed:

2. Key characteristics or attributes students must include in order to demonstrate a meaningful understanding of the concept. Possible examples for the concepts are:

   (a) assembly line: division of labor and _____

   (b) population density: number of people and _____

   (c) needs and wants: what is required if a person is to live and _____

3. Describe your exploratory introduction activity:

4. Describe your lesson development activity (make sure it logically follows your exploratory introduction activity):

5. Describe your expansion activity for the concept:

6. Reflect on whether the five principles are found in the activities. Describe which principles you are able to identify within the activities.

studies activities. Consider whether your activities are meaningful, integrative, value based, challenging, and active.

Summary

Social studies teaching must be appropriate to students' own prior knowledge if it is to be effective in helping them construct meaningful social studies learning. Before any formal social studies lesson, students are likely to have their own ideas about the concept, skill, or attitude that, until now, enabled them to explain and predict events to their satisfaction. Instead of teaching students entirely new content in social studies, teachers find it necessary to spend much of the instructional time helping students restructure their social studies knowledge, fostering conceptual change.

When students are presented with ideas in their social studies lessons, they have to modify and reconstruct their prior knowledge to understand the new ideas. This requires a willingness and an effort on the part of the learner to construct her knowledge schema through additional interactive experiences with the social world. It involves reorganizing prior knowledge along with newly acquired knowledge. A student's learning is not passive. Students control their own learning by their willingness to mentally engage in lessons. Teachers help each student construct ideas by using the ideas students bring with them to the classroom.

The purpose of this chapter is to introduce the teaching of social studies for meaningful learning. The following points summarize teaching as it is used to facilitate students' meaningful learning of social studies. The most worthwhile objectives of social studies units are learning major concepts, generalizations, inquiry skills, values, attitudes, and dispositions. This requires a strategy of instruction different from traditional teaching used to recall facts. For these important social studies ideas and skills, teachers plan activities that encourage meaningful understanding.

Teachers identify important key social studies ideas and skills in advance, using a strategy that promotes conceptual change and meaningful learning. Lessons consist of a three-phase sequence of purposeful, interactive activities: exploratory introduction, development, and expansion. These phases help students explore their prior knowledge, integrate new ideas into their thought patterns, and apply new ideas and skills in diverse settings. Teachers continually assess progress toward attaining lesson objectives and may return to an earlier phase if further explanation or application of an idea, skill, or attitude is needed.

Recommended Websites to Visit

Econ Ed Link Learning Cycles
http://www.econedlink.org/cyberteach/cycles.php
Learning Cycle Workshop: Modifying lessons to the learning cycle
http://www.sahra.arizona.edu/education/pbl_workshop/TheLearningCycle.htm
The Awesome Library (of social studies lessons)
www.awesomelibrary.org/Classroom/Social_Studies/Social_Studies.html
Library of Congress/National Digital Library
www.loc.gov/
Marco Polo: Internet Content for Your Classroom
www.marcopolo-education.org
PBS Teacher Source
www.pbs.org/teachersource/

3

How Are Social Studies Inquiry Skills Learned?

Read the following passage from the beginning of an interview. Respond to the questions that follow.

> My name is Elly Van Aspert. My family's name was Neeter, and my Christian name is Esther. I was born in Utrecht, in central Holland, on February 12, 1924. I am the oldest of four girls in my family. My sisters are Miep, Jos, and Emi. We were an ordinary Dutch family who were Jewish.
>
> My parents owned what today we would call an electronics store in Amersfoort, 20 Kilometers from Utrecht, but this was before modern electronics, so the store sold electrical items like radios and vacuum cleaners. Mother was always in the shop.... She always welcomed people to the shop and would give them a cup of coffee whether or not they bought anything.
>
> After the Germans came into Holland in 1940, we had to wear the yellow star on our clothes so everyone would know we were Jewish. Dutch Jewish children could not go to high school after age fourteen and a half, so I could no longer go to my high school. So, I went to a school for Jewish children in Utrecht.... After a while, all Jews were told that we had to turn in our bikes because we were no longer allowed to have bikes. So, I could not get to school in Utrecht any more.
>
> Of course, the Nazis wanted more than just our bikes! They wanted our gold and other valuable things. My parents gave our bikes but not our gold, even though we were always afraid of the Nazis. My parents knew we probably would need the gold sometime and maybe need it to survive. But, we gave in our bikes because we never wanted to confront the Nazis. When we would walk down the street, we would try to walk with other children, not alone, because it was safer. Many Jewish people never came out at all. (Personal interview by Cynthia Szymanski Sunal on July 21, 2005)

1. Why do you think Ms. Van Aspert is being interviewed?
2. What do you think happened in her life through the period ending in April 1945?
3. What evidence do you find in this early part of the interview to support your responses in questions 1 and 2?
4. Because only part of the interview is available to you, what conclusions can you make about how your responses are limited by having partial data?
5. What social studies inquiry skills have you been using in reading this passage and in responding to questions 1 through 4?

Chapter Overview

NCSS

Standards

Inquiry in social studies involves the diverse ways in which we study our social world and propose explanations based on evidence for various events. Inquiry also refers to the activities students engage in as they investigate the social world and develop their knowledge of ideas in social studies. Students ask, find, and determine answers to questions growing out of everyday experiences. Learning involves developing thinking, or inquiry, skills (NCSS, 1994b). Table 3.1 lists the general abilities students need to carry out social studies inquiries. Most elementary and middle school students are ready for experiences that give them concrete foundations for understanding abstract social studies ideas (Anderson, 1997; NCSS, 1994b; Educational Broadcasting Corporation, 2004). These foundations constitute

TABLE 3.1

Abilities Needed to Do Inquiry

Grades K–4	Grades 5–8
Ask a question about phenomena/events in the social world	Identify questions that can be investigated
Plan and perform simple investigations	Plan and conduct investigations
Use simple equipment, technology, and tools to gather data	Use tools and technology to gather, analyze, and interpret data
Use data to develop descriptions and explanations	Use a range of inquiry skills to develop generalizations and models using data
Communicate descriptions of investigations and explanations	Communicate procedures for investigations and explanations
Make plans for how and when to do a task and recognize when you have completed the task	Reflect on your own learning process, asking questions on your concentration and motivation

the *inquiry skills*: (1) early inquiry skills, (2) social studies inquiry skills, (3) inquiry attitudes and dispositions, and (4) integrative thinking skills.

Inquiry skills help us develop an "explanation" for what we observe or investigate. The explanation students develop is the social studies "idea" or "knowledge" to be learned in the lesson. Students at various age levels and with various types of experiences develop different explanations from their personal experiences depending on the inquiry skills used or available to them. The challenge for the teacher is to make common experiences meaningful to students through the use of inquiry skills. Skill development requires classroom instruction during which students interact with each other. Assessment of inquiry skills is essential. Such assessment is communicated to students to help them understand that a high value is placed on learning inquiry skills.

Chapter Objectives

1. Explain the importance of planning for the development of social studies inquiry skills.
2. Describe types of skills needed by students to develop meaningful social studies learning.
3. Describe the difference in emphasis when planning social studies inquiry skills for the early childhood and middle childhood levels.
4. Describe the process of teaching social studies inquiry skills.
5. Identify conditions necessary for effectively teaching social studies inquiry skills.
6. Describe methods for assessing social studies inquiry skills during a lesson or unit.

DEVELOPMENT

 ## Using Inquiry Skills to Develop Students' Social Studies Ideas

NCSS

Standards
III, VI

Knowledge develops through our experiences with the world and other individuals. Students use their prior knowledge and information from their experiences to construct new social studies knowledge. The success of this learning process depends on the level and kind of inquiry skills available to students. Throughout the year, inquiry skills are developed, practiced, and used in every social studies unit (Chu, Chaw, Tse, & Kulthau, 2008). The transfer of an inquiry skill from one context or topic area to another is an important goal. Transfer does not occur automatically when a skill is first learned (Kuhn, Black, Keselman, & Kaplan, 2000). Transfer of an inquiry skill is likely to occur automatically only after a student has had many opportunities to practice the skill. For example, in a unit on landforms, students identify and classify landforms to learn to distinguish hills from mountains. A few weeks later, the class begins working with a unit on economics in the community. The classification skill students developed in the earlier unit on landforms does not automatically transfer when they try to classify types of community businesses, such as manufacturing and service companies. The following discussion describes and examines inquiry skills in an effective K–8 social studies program.

Building on Diversity

Early Inquiry Skills

Kindergarteners begin school with numerous early inquiry skills developed through interactions with those around them and with their physical environments. Very young students are usually skilled at filling and emptying containers, smelling objects and people, spreading sand and mud, throwing objects, running, whining, whispering, and so forth. Such early inquiry skills enable young children to investigate social situations, often testing others' reactions—for example, how significant adults around them react to a thrown object, to whining, or to a whispered confidence.

Every student has a different set of early experiences. The culture of the home and its occupants dramatically affects the student. The neighborhood also exerts an influence, as do the media and the larger regional and national cultures. These influences are diverse, so children start school with different levels of skill development. Some students have advanced classification skills, while others' skills are limited. Some students have had lots of opportunities to talk with adults, while others have had few opportunities. Children use their inquiry skills to examine their social worlds. Teachers expect wide ranges of skills among their students and engage them in physical activities that foster early inquiry skills among those who lag in development and build on existing inquiry skills among others, creating a foundation for social studies inquiry skills.

 ## Early Inquiry Skills

People use their five senses to investigate the environment: sight, hearing, taste, touch, and smell. Preschool children apply their senses to develop numerous early inquiry skills as they play: pushing, pulling, sliding, and rolling. Children run their fingers through people's hair, touch clothes of different textures, feel the warmth generated by sitting in a comfortable adult lap, taste everything they can get into their mouths, and listen to the cadences of a caretaker's speech. These skills facilitate the investigation of the very young child's world. Later, other inquiry skills such as observation develop through continued experiences.

These early skills are learned before children experience any social studies content. Very young children, for example, feel the textures of a variety of clothing items before they understand how money is exchanged for clothing or how the seasons determine which clothing items are worn at various times. These early skills are basic prerequisites for understanding social studies concepts such as wants and needs, money, and production and distribution of goods. They also are prerequisites for later social studies inquiry skills. Early social studies experiences are important and focus on building these early inquiry skills.

Social Studies Inquiry Skills

The early inquiry skills developed by very young children are incorporated into social studies activities to develop social studies inquiry skills. These skills include both basic and higher-level integrative thought processes. They are important in social studies because they are necessary for exploration and investigation of the social world. Most children, and many adults, however, are not very good at using them (Kuhn, Black, Keselman, & Kaplan, 2000; Nugent, Kunz, Levy, Harwood, & Carlson, 2008). Examples of social studies inquiry skills include observing, classifying, estimating, using maps, inferring, predicting, isolating and using variables, and interpreting data. The basic social studies inquiry skills are prerequisites for more complex inquiry skills. Table 3.2 provides examples of student behaviors related to each skill.

Each inquiry skill is built on a number of subskills, which need to be addressed. Table 3.2 describes behaviors that are necessary to use each inquiry skill effectively. For instance, as younger students learn the skill of observing, teachers address the need for them to make many observations using all their senses. Teachers also encourage students to examine both qualitative and quantitative characteristics. If an event involves change, students are encouraged to make observations of the event during the change process as well as before and after it. In middle school, teachers help students use the observing behaviors they have built to distinguish between statements that are based on observations and those based on inferences. Younger students, for example, visit a bank and observe money being counted, being given to clients, and being received from clients. Middle school students use those prior observations to make observations of an Internet banking site in which they identify the location on the site where a specific amount of money can be deposited, where information on the amount of money deposited is reported to a client, and where a copy of the transaction can be printed. Because they have been to a bank and observed money being exchanged, they try to make observations on the Internet site that include the components found in a bank. They are making an inference that actual money is being transferred on the Internet site and are able to distinguish this inference from observations of the different parts of the site.

Social studies inquiry skills can be grouped into five areas by their functions: data gathering, data organizing, data processing, communicating, and

TABLE 3.2
Social Studies Inquiry Skills K–8

Basic Skills	
	Associated Behaviors
Observing	1. *Identify* and *name* characteristics of an object or event by using at least four senses. (Use of the sense of taste is restricted to specific teacher-designed situations.) 2. *Be aware of the need* to make numerous observations of objects and events. 3. *Pose questions* focusing on observations of objects, people, and events. 4. *Construct* descriptive and quantitative statements of observations. 5. *Construct* statements of observations describing observable changes in characteristics of an object or during an event. 6. *Distinguish* among statements based on observations and those based on inferences.
Communicating	1. *Describe* the characteristics of an object or event in sufficient detail so that another person can identify it. 2. *Describe* changes in the characteristics of an object or during an event. 3. *Use* pictures, maps, tables, and graphs to communicate results obtained from observations. 4. *Describe* relationships and trends orally, in writing, in drawings, and using graphics.
Classifying	1. *Identify* and *name* observable characteristics of objects or events that could be used to group them. 2. *Order* a group of objects or events based on a single characteristic. 3. *Construct* a one-, two-, or multistage classification of a set of objects or events and name the observable characteristics on which the classification is based. 4. *Construct* two or more different classification schemes for the same set of objects or events with each scheme serving a different purpose. 5. *Construct* an operational definition of a single object or event based on a classification scheme.
Inferring	1. *Construct* one or more statements or explanations from a set of observations. 2. *Identify* observations supporting a given inference. 3. *Describe* alternative inferences for the same set of observations. 4. *Identify* inferences that should be accepted, modified, or rejected on the basis of additional observations.
Predicting	1. *Construct* a forecast of future events based on observed events. 2. *Order* a set of forecasts or predictions in terms of your confidence in them. 3. *Identify* predictions as (a) interpolations between observed events or (b) extrapolations beyond the range of observed events.

continued

TABLE 3.2 *(Continued)*

Basic Skills	
Measuring and Estimating	1. *Demonstrate* the use of simple tools to describe length, distance, and time. 2. *Describe* objects and events using measurements consistently during investigations. 3. *Construct* estimates of simple measurements of quantities such as length and area. 4. *Apply* rules for calculating derived quantities from two or more measurements. 5. *Distinguish* between accuracy and precision.

Integrative Skills	
	Associated Behaviors
Organizing, Interpreting, and Drawing Conclusions from Data	1. *Describe* the overall appearance of a graph or map and the relationships between individuals and groups of data. 2. *Construct* maps, tables, and graphs using information from observations. 3. *Construct* one or more statements of inferences or hypotheses from the information given in a table of data, graph, map, or picture. 4. *Use and construct* maps and graphs of various types to interpret data. 5. *Describe* data using the mean, median, and range where applicable. 6. *Use* technology hardware and software to gather, analyze, and interpret data. 7. *Distinguish* between linear and nonlinear relationships in data.
Isolating and Using Variables	1. *Identify* factors that may influence the behavior or characteristics of an event or set of events. 2. *Distinguish* among variables that are manipulated, responding, or held constant in an investigation or description of an investigation. 3. *Construct* a test to determine the effects of one variable (manipulated variable) on a second variable (the responding variable). 4. *Distinguish* among conditions that hold a given variable constant and conditions that do not hold a variable constant.
Formulating Hypotheses	1. *Distinguish* among statements of inference and hypothesis. 2. *Construct* a hypothesis relating potentially interacting variables. 3. *Construct* a test of a hypothesis. 4. *Distinguish* between observations that support a hypothesis and those that do not. 5. *Reconstruct* a hypothesis to increase its power to explain.
Solving Problems, Making Decisions, Investigating, Thinking Critically, Thinking Creatively, and Reflecting	1. *Acquire* background information. 2. *Establish* initial conditions for the investigation. 3. *Write* focus questions to guide inquiry. 4. *Collect and analyze* data while attempting to develop explanations. 5. *Reexamine and rewrite* explanations/plans if necessary. 6. *Reflect* on steps used, questions asked, and conclusions reached.

What Do You Think?

Look closely at the photograph in Figure 3.1. Then answer the following questions without looking back at it:

- What is your first impression of where this picture was taken?
- What do you think the people in this picture are doing?

   Look at Figure 3.1 again and respond to the following questions:

- What details do you notice on a second look that you did not notice when you first looked?
- Do these details support your first impression of where this picture was taken? If not, where do you now think it was taken?
- Do the details you noticed on a second look support your first impression of what these people are doing? If not, what do you now think they are doing?
- What can you remember seeing, experiencing, or reading that supports your idea of what these people are doing?

This activity asked you to look at a picture without telling you anything about it. Then you were asked to make some inferences regarding where it was taken and what is happening in it. After having a second opportunity to make observations about the picture, you were asked to recall anything you might have seen that would support your ideas. These

FIGURE 3.1
What Are These People Doing?

questions incorporated the three characteristics that should exist in an exploration activity beginning a skills lesson: (1) diagnosing what students now know, (2) focusing students' attention, and (3) relating students' prior knowledge to the new learning.

By asking what your first impression was and what you could remember that might be related to the picture, the activity was diagnosing your prior knowledge and relating prior knowledge to new learning. The activity focused your attention by asking you to look at the picture and make some inferences about it. By reflecting on your responses to the questions above, you should be able to evaluate how appropriate your inferences were about the picture. We will return to this photograph later in the chapter.

---

reflecting (see Table 3.3). This sequence is used when planning an inquiry lesson or unit. Early in the lesson, several data-gathering skills are used. Later, data-organizing and data-processing social studies skills are used. Student activities involving communication occur throughout the lesson. A stronger focus on communication occurs near the end of the lesson when final conclusions are made, shared, and evaluated. As the lesson ends, students reflect on what they did and how well they did it. A well-planned social studies lesson or unit involves skills from each area.

Data-Gathering Skills

Data gathering is where learning begins. A number of skills are used to gather data in social studies: observing; measuring and estimating; researching and referencing; questioning; interviewing and surveying; interpreting books, charts, graphs, and maps; hypothesizing; and using technology to gather data.

Data-Organizing Skills

Data gathering is the beginning point. The information gathered has little meaning to students unless they are helped to organize it so that it is usable. Skills that are important in organizing data are classifying, ordering or sequencing, isolating and using variables, and using technology to organize data. These skills enable us to take individual pieces of information and make some sense of them. We do this by putting together pieces that show similar characteristics.

Data-Processing Skills

Once data is organized, it can be processed into concepts and generalizations using one or more of these skills: constructing tables, maps, charts, and graphs; finding patterns; predicting; interpreting observations; finding relationships; inferring; making conclusions; evaluating hypotheses; and using technology to process data.

TABLE 3.3
Functions of Social Studies Inquiry Skills

Data Gathering	Data Organizing	Data Processing	Communicating	Reflecting
Observing	Classifying	Constructing tables, maps, charts, and graphs	Reporting	Monitoring our planning, progress, and recognizing when tasks are done
Measuring and estimating skills	Ordering or sequencing	Finding patterns	Writing	
Researching and referencing skills	Isolating and using variables	Predicting	Using graphing, mapmaking, and drawing	Self-evaluating our planning, progress, communicating, selection of possible alternatives, and use of information
Questioning	Using information and communication technology (ICT) to organize data	Interpreting observations	Formal discussing	
Interviewing and surveying		Finding relationships	Informal discussing	
		Discussing to clarify ideas		
Interpreting books, charts, graphs, and maps		Inferring	Discussing to persuade	
		Making conclusions		
Hypothesizing		Evaluating hypotheses	Using information and communication technology (ICT) to communicate data	
Using information and communication technology (ICT) to gather data		Using information and communication technology (ICT) to process data		

Communicating Skills

Communicating is part of what defines us as social beings. It is essential to the thinking process enabling us to share the questions we raise, the hypotheses we develop, and the answers we find. Language in written, spoken, or signed form involves us in communication. Communication is a large part of our lives and takes place both formally and informally. Communication skills include reporting; writing; graphing, map-making, and drawing; formal discussing; informal discussing; and using technology to communicate data and conclusions.

Reflecting Skills

Reflecting occurs in all parts of inquiry learning. We monitor our progress to determine whether we are planning and carrying out a task as well as we can, whether it is data gathering, communicating, or any other part of our inquiry. We evaluate ourselves as we work through our inquiry and after it is completed, considering how we carried out our tasks, whether we carried them out when we should have done them, and whether there were alternatives that may have helped us to have a stronger inquiry. Reflecting builds our inquiry abilities so that our next inquiry is more thoroughly planned and carried out.

Using Technology

Information and Communication Technology (ICT) Literacy

Information and communication technology (ICT) literacy involves critical thinking skills related to finding, accessing, evaluating, and using information, the media, and technology (Partnership for 21st Century Skills, 2008). Many of these are skills that have been associated with the traditional use of the libraries and archives. In the twenty-first century, digital media is so present in our lives and arrives so quickly that it is essential to master these skills to be able to rapidly seek the accuracy of the data and claims. Two sets of ICT skills are used in social studies.

1. *Information literacy skills*: accessing information via technology efficiently and effectively, evaluating information critically, using information accurately and creatively to address the problem, and having a fundamental understanding of the ethical and legal issues surrounding the access and use of information.

2. *Media literacy skills*: understanding how media messages are constructed, for what purposes, and using which tools, characteristics, and conventions; examining how individuals interpret messages differently, how values and viewpoints are included or excluded, and how media can influence beliefs and behaviors.

As students develop these two sets of skills they become better able to function in our society and economy using digital technology, communication tools, and/or networks. When digital tools are used effectively to access, manage, integrate, evaluate, and create information, citizens can better reflect on their world.

Source: Partnership for 21st Century Skills, Information, Media, and Technology Skills. Accessed December 15, 2008. http://www.21stcenturyskills.org/index.php?option=com_content&task=view&id=61&Itemid=120

TIME FOR REFLECTION | What Do You Think?

This activity asks you to use your present knowledge to determine the skill used to form each of the statements below. Identify each statement as observation, inference, or hypothesis.

Classroom Event

A game was placed in a learning center. Students were told they could play the game throughout the school week in groups of two to four when they had finished their work and had some free time. The students found that the board game had colored squares on it in a pattern that covered the board. They also found nine small objects in a box on top of the board. They did not find the rules to the game, nor would their teacher tell them how to play it. Students were asked to write about the game and their experiences with it in their social studies journals whenever they wanted to do so. Listed below are some of the statements students made during the week. Read their statements and identify which statements are observation, inference, or hypothesis, O, I, or H, respectively.

1. "The game has squares on it." (Day 1)

2. "The pieces go with the game." (Day 1)

3. "All games have rules." (Day 1)

4. "The game has a box on top of it with nine pieces in it." (Day 3)

5. "We counted the squares in the game and there were 14 red ones, 6 blue ones, 12 yellow ones, and 9 purple ones." (Day 3)

6. "The game is like Monopoly." (Day 4)

7. The following statement was made by a small group of students who brought in several board games to compare to the one in the learning center: "All board games have the same kinds of parts." (Day 5)

8. "Rules are what make a game work." (Day 5)

9. "We tried to play the game nineteen times." (Day 5)

10. "When there are no rules for a game, people will start arguing because they can't agree on what to do." (Day 4)

11. "Someone must have lost the rules." (Day 1)

12. The following statement was given by a small group of students as a starting point for a project: "The more parts to a game—like the more squares of different colors it has and the more pieces—the harder it is to play."

How did you do? Check your responses with the following answers:

Statements 1, 4, 5, and 9 are observations.
Statements 2, 3, 6, 7, 8, and 11 are inferences.
Statements 7, 10, and 12 are hypotheses.

Observations, Inferences, and Hypotheses

Everyone has been involved with social studies inquiry skills in school. Yet, many people have difficulty distinguishing among them or describing them. This is especially true of observing, inferring, and hypothesizing skills.

Observations

Observations state characteristics of objects or events observed through the use of the senses. You should be able to identify the sense that is used to make an observation. Consider the following observation: The arrowhead felt smooth except for three sharp points along each side and a sharp point on top. This observation clearly involves the sense of touch. The arrowhead *feels* smooth. Sharp points can be *felt* on the top and sides, and the number of points can be *counted* on each side. Indirect observations are those made by another person: "Miranda told me that the beef jerky Tomas brought to class tasted salty." Observations represent a single case or event. They may be valid but cannot be used to make predictions. Observations lead to statements of fact.

Inferences

Inferences use observations, but extend beyond what has been observed with the senses. Inferences are best-guess statements such as "It looks like it's raining outside." They are only partially supported, or even unsupported, descriptions or explanations of what has been observed. Inferences summarize and go beyond a set of observations that have common characteristics.

Any activity focused on developing a skill uses some content. To teach a skill well, the lesson should be integrated with content, but priority is given to the skill (Eggen, Kauchak, & Harder, 1979; Sunal & Haas, 1993).

Hypotheses

A *hypothesis* describes the relationship of two or more variables constructed for investigation and testing. Simple hypotheses usually contain only two variables: the cause and the result. For example, consider the following hypothesis: The most popular lunch served in the school cafeteria is one that you can pick up in your hands and eat. Two controls might be added to this hypothesis for a class investigation: (1) All the lunches have been served on different days of the week. (2) All the lunches have a dessert. Another hypothesis may claim that whenever the same variables are combined, the same event results. For example, any lunch that has a main part you can pick up and eat, such as pizza or hot dogs, is popular with students at this school.

Hypotheses typically condense large amounts of data and are general statements that cover all cases, not only those that are actually observed. Once a hypothesis has been stated, it is investigated and tested. A special word of caution is needed at this point: Hypotheses can be *proved* only if all possible cases are investigated and tested. Testing all cases is impossible, so hypotheses can only be *well supported* so one feels quite confident about the relationship. The first set of data found that contradicts the hypothesis results in the hypothesis no longer being supported. An unsupported hypothesis must be either dropped or revised to account for the new information.

People of all backgrounds carry out investigations, devising and using tests. Trying out different kinds of hand lotion on severely chapped hands and deciding which brand of garbage bag best holds one's garbage without breaking when carried out to the garbage can are examples of investigations that involve a test. Rarely do these investigations accurately test hypotheses, however, because the variables being tested are restricted by conditions, and testers may have little control over the conditions affecting the situation. For example, the person testing two types of hand lotion on chapped hands might not take into account how frequently the lotions are applied, how much is applied, and whether the furnace is on, drying the air and making it easier for the hands to remain chapped when one of the lotions is tested.

Effective problem solvers design tests that require more observations of the proposed related variables covered by the hypothesis than do the ones just described. For example, an individual may investigate the effectiveness of different types of hand lotion on severely chapped hands by requiring a variety of hand-wetting tasks when testing different brands of lotion. The individual wants to make sure extra tasks, such as washing the floor, are not performed while a brand of lotion is being tested. Such extra tasks may wet the hands more and cause the test of lotions to be unfair.

In summary, a statement that attempts to describe the relationship between variables and is general in the sense that it covers all cases, both observed and unobserved, is called a *hypothesis*. A hypothesis is a statement that can be investigated. A useful hypothesis statement clearly relates two variables in a general way. A hypothesis may be disproved when one set of observations does not agree with what the hypothesis predicts. An acceptable hypothesis is one with a lot of support. Students must practice rewriting a hypothesis that needs to be modified or that was rejected when it was investigated. It is not an easy task.

Helping Students Develop Hypotheses.   Younger students can ask questions and carry out investigations when they are working with familiar items or situations. The hypothesis is developed as a response to a specific inquiry (Sunal & Sunal, 1999; Baral, 2003). This process occurs in the lesson development phase of the learning cycle. Students are asked questions to get them thinking about what is needed to decide whether their original inquiry can be addressed:

What do you need to know to answer your question?
What do you now know about this?
What do you need to try out?

NCSS

Standards
VII, VIII

How could this material or activity help us come up with answers to
   our question?
What should be changed?
What will happen as a result of the change?

Cooperative learning groups offer an opportunity for the give and take of ideas and are effective when trying to develop hypotheses.

Evaluating Hypotheses.   After data is gathered and presented, students decide whether their hypotheses are supported. Four results are possible:

1. If the data is inadequate for making a decision, students decide they need additional data.
2. If the hypothesis is supported, students invent a generalization.
3. If the hypothesis is not supported by the data, students reconstruct their hypothesis.
4. If the hypothesis is not supported by the data, students reject the hypothesis and construct a new tentative hypothesis based on the additional information.

Developing and Using Guiding Hypotheses

In social studies, students often develop *guiding hypotheses*, which have characteristics different in some ways from the hypotheses just described. Guiding hypotheses are tools that help an investigator raise questions and search for patterns. These hypotheses are not as precise as those just discussed. The investigator starts with an inquiry and then develops some guiding hypotheses to investigate it further. As interesting patterns are found in the search, a guiding hypothesis may be discarded and another one developed.

Teachers help students develop guiding hypotheses for different kinds of investigations. Students might do an *exploratory* investigation, a process that investigates something they do not understand very well. In this case, it is not possible to develop a hypothesis that clearly links variables and describes a test that can be carried out. Instead, students are trying to discover or identify the important variables. Examples of questions that can be used in an exploratory investigation follow:

NCSS

Standards III,
IV, VI, X

What is happening in this event? (For example, "Are all of the class rules
   being enforced?")
What are the important patterns we are seeing? (For example, everyone
   seems to ignore the rule about not borrowing pencils and other supplies
   from one another.)
How are these patterns linked to one another? (For example, students don't
   enforce the rule about borrowing materials because everyone gets short of
   materials once in a while and knows he or she will have to borrow from
   someone else.)

TIME FOR REFLECTION What Do You Think?

Elementary and middle school students constructed the following hypotheses to test during a week of school. Read the pairs of hypotheses below. Identify the statement that identifies the better hypothesis in each pair.

1.a. The later the hour in the day, the more likely it will rain.

1.b. It rains more often on September 20 than on October 20.

2.a. A candidate who has the most debates with opponents will win an election.

2.b. The more debates there are, the more people notice a candidate.

3.a. The greater the perceived threat from another as determined by the number of attacks on communities by an opponent's soldiers, the more frequently protective walls are built around both large and small communities.

3.b. People build big structures such as castles or the Great Wall of China to protect themselves.

4.a. The longer a country has had a flag, the more likely it is to be a representative democracy.

4.b. Placing the flags of countries on a timeline will give us an answer.

5.a. Students who are taller than 5 feet are older than students who are 5 feet or less in height.

5.b. The taller the student, the older in months he or she will be.

6.a. Lots of towns are located along rivers.

6.b. The longer a river is, the greater the number of towns located along it is.

7.a. As inflation increases, the amount of money required to buy a house will increase, keeping up with the rate of inflation.

7.b. The more unstable the economy is, the greater the rate of inflation is.

8.a. People keep others farther away from them in the afternoon than in the morning.

8.b. The later in the day it is, the farther away people like to be from those standing near them.

9.a. The more hours of sunlight there are, the more tasks people report accomplishing.

9.b. The more sunlight there is, the more we do.

Answers and rationale follow.

In statements 1a, 2b, and 8b, the hypotheses are generalized statements.
In statements 3a and 9a, the hypotheses show clear relationships of two or more variables and are more readily disproved.
In statement 4a, the hypothesis attempts to describe a relationship between variables.
In statements 5b and 7a, the hypotheses are testable.
In statement 6b, the hypothesis is a generalized statement that shows a relationship between two or more variables.

Students also might develop guiding hypotheses as part of an *explanatory* investigation. In this case, they try to explain the factors that are causing an event or action. They also may want to identify plausible networks of causes that shape the event. Questions they may ask follow:

What events, beliefs, attitudes, and policies are shaping this event? (For example, a new bridge across a nearby river has been proposed, and students note that three different locations are being considered, each having its vocal supporters or detractors.)

How do these factors interact to result in the event? (For example, the location for a new bridge across a nearby river has been chosen even though it means that a toxic dump at the foot of the bridge location will have to be cleaned up at great expense and a rare species of wildlife is endangered at the site of the other end of the bridge. What factors caused this bridge location to be chosen over the other two proposed locations?)

Another type of investigation using guiding hypotheses is the *descriptive* study. Here students try to document the event of interest to them. To do so, they ask a question, such as "What are the important behaviors, events, beliefs, attitudes, and processes occurring in this event?" (For example, our school seems very crowded, and people are beginning to talk about adding on to the building. What is happening to make people think it is crowded?).

A last type of investigation using guiding hypotheses is the *predictive* study. Students try to predict the outcomes of an event. They also might try to forecast other events or people's behaviors as a result of this event. They may ask the following questions:

What will happen as a result of this event? (For example, what will happen to class sizes if an addition is built on to the school?)

Who will be affected by this event? (For example, will any of the students now in the school still be here when the addition is finished? Will new teachers have to be hired for the additional classrooms?)

In what ways will students be affected? (For example, will students be feeling less stressed because they have more personal space? Will students argue less over where to put stuff in the classrooms?)

This type of investigation often is closest to the studies carried out to test hypotheses that were discussed previously (Marshall & Rossman, 1995).

Teaching Lessons in Which Students Use Integrative Thinking Skills

In everyday life, people make decisions, evaluate, and form judgments about their world. In responding to life's problems and issues, people need to be able to make careful and appropriate choices. To make such choices, people engage in critical thinking, problem solving and decision making, investigating, and creative thinking (see Figure 3.2). These skills involve students in using many cognitive and affective skills as they reach a conclusion to a problem or issue they are studying in a social studies lesson.

Critical Thinking

Standards

Critical thinking involves having good reasons for what you believe. *Critical thinking* includes careful, precise, persistent, and objective analysis of any knowledge claim or belief to judge its validity and worth (Ennis, 1991). Both before and after arriving at a conclusion, students need to be aware of, and willing to consider, the thought process they followed to reach the conclusion. Were their methods logical? Were they making unwarranted assumptions? Was a necessary step skipped? Did the evidence support the conclusion? Throughout the process is there an evaluation of the methods used? What limitations exist? What are the problem areas? How could things be done differently? Should the process be done differently? We engage in critical thinking when we think about and assess our plans, procedures, and conclusions, purposely seeking conditions that lead us to refute our conclusion. Critical thinking is demanding, but also creative, because we come to recognize that it enables us to identify problems and construct alternatives. Figure 3.2 describes the elements that are part of critical thinking.

Critical thinking involves a complex set of dispositions and abilities (see Figure 3.2), including seeking reasons, trying to be well informed, taking into account the total situation, and looking for alternatives (NCSS, 1994b). In addition, critical thinking involves abilities such as focusing on a question, judging the credibility of a source, making and evaluating value judgments, defining terms, and deciding on an action (NCSS, 1994b; Willingham, 2007).

Problem Solving and Decision Making

Problem solving is an activity with which we are involved every day at many levels. Students need our help in learning how to solve problems well, how to use a variety of problem-solving strategies, and how to proceed efficiently. Problem solving involves a complex sequence of thought processes (see Figure 3.2). Teachers help students become reflective problem-solvers by (1) listening to students' ideas; (2) modeling thinking; (3) acting as a guide for students; (4) designing social studies activities that involve learning as problem solving and investigation; (5) planning, monitoring, and evaluating student progress; and (6) empowering students toward self-direction (Anderson & Krathwohl, 2001).

Investigating

Daily life involves continual *investigating*; examining your actions, at times, in order to see what follows (Evans, Newmann, & Saxe, 1996; Partnership for 21st Century Skills, 2008). Although students have some skill in investigating, they

Critical Thinking—Understanding New Knowledge

Being open minded
Asking questions
Focusing on a question
Distinguishing relevant and irrelevant knowledge statements, value statements,
and reasoning
Willing to analyze arguments and knowledge statements in terms of how well they explain
Desiring to use credible sources
Judging credibility of an argument or source
Tolerating ambiguity
Respecting evidence
Waiting for considerable evidence before judging
Being willing to search for more evidence
Being willing to revise in light of new evidence

Problem Solving—Resolving a Difficulty

Sensing a problem
Identifying important components of the problem
Putting elements of the problem into one's own words
Constructing or identifying a problem statement
Identifying alternative solution plans
Selecting a plan appropriate to the type of problem identified
Anticipating and planning for obstacles
Trying out the planned solution
Monitoring the process of working toward the solution
Adapting procedures as obstacles are encountered
Describing the solution resulting from the procedure
Validating the findings in terms of procedure and goal
Determining the efficiency and effectiveness of the overall process

Investigating—Testing an Idea or Explanation

Writing operational definitions as needed
Constructing a question to be answered
Writing a hypothesis that answers the question
Collecting and interpreting data related to the hypothesis
Writing a report of the investigation, including a statement about whether the
data supports the hypothesis

Creative Thinking—Creating Novel Ideas or Products

Demonstrating an interest in exploring the novel and the unexpected
Willing to try to create innovative or original thoughts, patterns, products, and solutions
Willing to take risks in creating and exploring new ideas and different viewpoints
Being aware of the potential of generating alternatives
Being aware of the potential of applying ideas, analogies, and models in new contexts
Being ready to change ideas or approaches as the situation evolves
Being willing to work at the edge of one's competence and to accept confusion and uncertainty
Learning to view failure as normal, interesting, and challenging
Being willing to set products or ideas aside and come back later to evaluate them
from a distance
Feeling comfortable with and being motivated by intrinsic rather than extrinsic rewards

FIGURE 3.2
Sample Student Behaviors Involved When Using Integrative Skills

need help in becoming more organized and efficient, in becoming better planners, and in identifying alternatives and limitations, among other components. Teachers should pose "what if" questions and encourage students to pose them and follow-up by designing and carrying out investigations that examine responses to their questions.

Three problems often arise when a person is not very good at investigation.

1. Collecting too few pieces of data can lead to an erroneous conclusion.
2. Collecting more data provides more information, but that data must be organized; otherwise, relationships among the pieces of data may not be obvious.
3. Even when organizing the information, too small or too large a sequence may result in data that isn't very helpful.

Teachers help students refine their investigating skills by encouraging them to share their information with the class. Data collected by one group of students may lend or reduce support for one or more of several competing hypotheses. Sharing information is likely to broaden students' understanding of a problem because they come into contact with a wider range of data organized in varying formats by different groups.

During a learning cycle lesson involving investigating, students are encouraged to take different paths in their investigations depending on whether the data they collected are inadequate, support the hypothesis, or do not support it.

If the data collected are inadequate and no decision can be made regarding whether a hypothesis is supported, students need to decide whether to try to collect more data and/or more appropriate data. If this can be done, they plan how to do it and then collect the additional data. Students sometimes find that it is not possible to obtain adequate data. For example, students interested in the lives of a local group of Native Americans living in Nebraska during the late 1700s, before this region became a part of the United States, may find little or no information available. They might decide to pursue a different but related problem for which more information is available. If their hypothesis is not supported, the students repeat the processes of gathering, organizing, and presenting data and deciding whether the hypothesis is supported by this new set of data. If it is, they have developed a generalization as a result of their second attempt to solve the problem. If their data does not support the reconstructed hypothesis, they need to modify or construct a completely new hypothesis and repeat the process.

NCSS

Standards I, II

Creative Thinking

Creative thinking uses the basic thought processes to develop constructive, novel, or aesthetic ideas or products. Emphasis is on the use of prior knowledge to generate other possibilities in the same context or similar possibilities in other contexts, or to extend ideas in new directions. Creative ability builds on and extends awareness, interest, and willingness to explore, create change, and generate novel thoughts, products, and solutions (see Figure 3.2).

Lesson activities allow students to generate, or select among, different purposes for exploring and understanding basic concepts. Students explore the range of meaning ideas have. Lessons on local government, for example, might include helping students construct an idea of the role local government has in necessary but ordinary aspects of our lives, such as trash collection, the removal of snow on school bus routes, thus reducing the number of "snow days" for which schools are closed, and paving dirt roads in the 1950s as more people began to own cars. Students select and revise a problem related to a key idea, choose the methods to study the problem, and defend ideas derived from their study. Such assignments challenge students to use what they already know, applying it to what they see as new and challenging problems. They use their skills in the more difficult tasks of combining information, generating ideas, and communicating their ideas.

TIME FOR REFLECTION | *What Do You Think?*

Return to the passage from the interview with Elly Van Aspert at the beginning of this chapter. Examine the last paragraph. What example(s) of problem solving and decision making do you find in this paragraph? If possible, share and discuss these with your peers.

Using Technology

Fostering Inquiry Skills

Technology can be used to expand students' control over their own learning by increasing the quality and extent of their experiences with information. Students' inquiries are facilitated by many public agencies. The federal government, for example, is making much of its current information and many of its archives and library resources available to the public. The Library of Congress, www.loc.gov/, is just one public agency with an ambitious program for placing its documents and pictures online. This website's pictures, sound recordings, maps, and documents interest students and prompt them to think about and ask questions.

Many newspapers have websites, and many allow free access to their articles. Examples are the *Washington Post* and *New York Times*. News organizations such as CNN, British Broadcasting (BBC), and C-Span have tapped their video archives, developing special programs and picture essays often sold with teacher guides. C-Span is a joint venture of many local and national news agencies providing free downloads of programs and lesson plans targeted at middle schoolers. The rights to use such materials vary among the programs.

Teachers use technology as a tool to facilitate social studies inquiry in six ways.

1. By providing authentic learning activities such as those found at the website of the Library of Congress.
2. By having collaborative groups of students use several resources found via the Internet to explore an issue, for example, "What were the actual purposes of the Lewis and Clark Corps of Discovery Expedition?" (see middle school learning cycle in Sunal, Sunal, & Staubs, 2007).

3. By providing information-rich instruction possible through sites such as that of the Smithsonian Institution.
4. By involving students in considering current and historical issues through making and watching podcasts and digital movies. These widely available digital presentations overcome barriers and provide all with a reinvention of traditional guest speakers, field trips, and primary sources (McAninch, Swan, & Hofer, 2007). *Learn Out Loud* at www.learnoutloud.com, for example, allows students to listen to Martin Luther King's "I Have a Dream" speech when studying the civil rights movement. *Colonial Williamsburg* at www.history.org/media/podcasts allows students to see saddles and tools being made using seventeenth-century methods.
5. By involving students in discussing questions and posing problems to specialists. Eric Langhorst reports such student involvement when they had questions about the Jamestown colony. His students sent an e-mail to the official Jamestown site at http://historyisfun.org/videos-and-podcasts.htm, and located an on-site archaeologist who responded to their questions (Keeler & Langhorst, 2008).
6. By involving students from a range of schools and classes in jointly investigating issues through blogs such as the bookblog used by Eric Langhorst (Keeler & Langhorst, 2008), with *The Year of the Hangman* by Gary Blackwood (2002). Langhorst reviewed student's comments before posting them and had the students use only first names or pen names to ensure student responsibility and safety. A later bookblog involved Pat Hughes, author of *Guerilla Season* (2003), who participated in the blog as students commented on her book and also in an audio conference in which she talked about the process and excitement of engaging in historical research and writing historical fiction.

Creating Conditions that Promote Student Thinking in Social Studies

Teaching for thinking requires deliberate planning and classroom conditions facilitating student interaction. Three strategies help create a proactive approach to teaching thinking in social studies: questioning, structuring, and modeling (Allen, 1996; Costa, 1991).

Questioning students' prior knowledge of an idea is the beginning point. Several questions may follow up students' initial responses:

What can you tell me about your past experience with this?
What is your evidence for that statement?
What can you do now to become more sure about, or comfortable with, your answer?

Effective social studies teaching involves helping students ask more questions and providing them with fewer answers. To accomplish more effective questioning, teachers must be aware of, and plan for, higher-level thought questions, that ask for evidence to support responses, and require students to become aware of their own thinking.

Lessons should provide opportunities for students to engage in asking questions. Planning for questioning requires the use of wait time, waiting 3 to 5 seconds before asking a student to respond to your question and before responding to a student's answer. It is a research-supported technique that has been correlated with increased student thinking about ideas, with longer responses from students, and with more effective use of evidence in constructing responses (Rowe, 1987).

Structuring involves planning interactions between students and the learning environment. It is important that teachers maintain and extend student thinking about social studies ideas for greater periods of time than is now common in many classrooms. The classroom and outside school environment can be arranged so students interact with real people, real objects, and real social experiences. Students need regular and frequent opportunities to talk about their thinking and to be involved in at least some risk taking in the learning process. A safe learning environment with a positive and creative atmosphere encourages students to listen to others' ideas and to work with each other. Such an environment helps students look at problems from many perspectives.

Modeling involves posing a problem and thinking out loud while demonstrating a solution. Using materials to provide observable cues is effective. For example, a teacher demonstrates how to use a map scale properly to measure distance on a map by acting out a complete procedure, explaining each step. Putting into action questioning, structuring, and modeling encourages students to integrate higher-order thought processes with social studies content.

Lesson Characteristics

An inquiry skill lesson has four major characteristics.

- A primary focus on a skill used in inquiry
- Concrete and/or manipulative experiences
- Use of content in an organized fashion
- Extensive practice of the skill (see these in the lesson plan on pages 81–82)

NCSS

Standard II

Concrete experiences use materials students can experience with their own senses. Such experiences might involve students in activities that feature a guest speaker dressed in Vietnam War military clothing, a 1910 glass bottle, a copy of the Declaration of Independence, or a video of a recent debate among presidential candidates. Students might try on a Vietnam War helmet, pick up a 1910 glass bottle and note its weight, handle the copy of the Declaration of Independence and try to trace an original signature with their finger, or count the number of times a presidential candidate looked over at an opponent during a 2-minute period allotted for initial comments. Students need time to explore the materials or information available to make observations for use in later parts of the lesson.

Processing unfamiliar information is a difficult task that is made easier when concrete materials are available. Evidence shows that children have limited space in their sensory memories (Glatthorn & Baron, 1991). They can address only a few items coming in through their senses at a time. When all the sensory memory space is being used, items simply are not addressed; no attention is paid to them. Having concrete examples in front of them allows students to work with greater amounts of new information. They do not have to hold it all in their sensory memory at once. A student can refer to the item and work with a greater variety of information at the same time. When concrete materials are not available, the teacher should decide whether to defer the topic until students can more adequately deal with it in the absence of examples or whether photographs, video, computer software, Internet sites, or other less concrete materials can be used.

In the lesson, many different activities encourage and emphasize the development of inquiry skills. As opportunities to teach content occur during the activity, the teacher takes advantage of them.

Planning Activities to Teach Inquiry Skills

Planning includes everything a teacher considers and prepares for classroom activities. Planning for skills activities includes

- Identifying the key skill that students will develop to a higher level
- Writing objectives
- Deciding which activities to use and sequencing them
- Developing assessments that address the key skill
- Obtaining the materials that will be used during the activity
- Setting up the grouping arrangement for the activity (Sunal & Haas, 1993)

Goals and Objectives. A skills lesson has two goals for students: developing skills and gathering an unspecified body of information (Sunal & Haas, 1993). Objectives for a skills lesson are developed from its goals. They identify the specific skill(s) students are to be constructing.

Teaching Materials. To develop skills, students need information to process. The teacher provides students with materials that give them access to the information needed. If possible, each student or pair of students should be provided with a set of materials with which to work. When it is not possible to provide enough materials, the following alternatives can be considered:

- Ask the students to bring in materials.
- Set up a learning station if just a few materials are available.
- When just one object is available, organize opportunities for each student to explore the object with the teacher and/or person providing the object.
- When no materials are available, use media or electronic technology.

Grouping. Skills activities should use grouping arrangements that give students maximum opportunity to work with materials. Large groups, small groups, learning stations, or one-on-one interaction can be used equally well with careful planning.

EXPANSION

 ## Applying a Learning Cycle to Teach an Inquiry Skill

Developing and using a learning cycle lesson focused on helping students further develop their knowledge of an inquiry skill, of when to use it, and of how to best use it requires expertise. Inquiry learning and teaching place responsibility for the outcomes of the learning cycle lesson on both students and teachers. Both will be developing expertise over the long term as it takes time for the community of learners needed for inquiry teaching and learning to form.

At the beginning of a lesson, the teacher involves students in a task in which they try to use the lesson's key skill. The task is somewhat challenging. As the students try to work through the task, the teacher diagnoses their prior knowledge of the skill, how it is used, and what it is used to do. If the skill is that of making inferences about a photograph, for example, the students may find they can make inferences but are not too sure about how appropriate their inferences are. The teacher notes students' tentativeness and is able to diagnose their current level of ability at making inferences. During the activity, the teacher does not focus on students' learning of content knowledge, but on their ability to make inferences from the content with which they are working.

In the second phase of the inquiry skill learning cycle lesson, the teacher guides students to a higher level of development of the lesson's key skill. He asks leading questions, gives explanations, and provides examples of using the skill. The teacher might, for example, demonstrate how he makes inferences from the photographs the students used in the exploratory introduction's task. He might show students how he first makes sure he has really looked at the entire photograph by looking at the middle, then at what is shown in each of the four corners of the photo. Then, he might demonstrate questions he asks himself about the photograph, "When was this photograph taken?" "What kind of clothes are the people in it wearing?" "What kinds of buildings or land are in the photograph?" When the students seem to be demonstrating a high level of ability at making inferences, the teacher gets them together and helps them bring their new ideas on when and how to use the skill together into a closure. The closure involves students in deciding, together, and writing down, a statement describing how and when to make inferences.

Now that the students have a higher ability at making appropriate and accurate inferences, they need to practice it and expand its use to other types of situations. At first, the teacher guides their practice, asking for the observations that support an inference they have made so it is more than just a quick guess. As students take responsibility for explaining their inferences, they become better able to independently use their higher level of making inferences. When the teacher recognizes that the students are using the skill at a higher level with little guidance, he calls the class together to finish the learning cycle with a lesson summary. The students are asked to briefly describe the activities with which they have been working and the usefulness of the important skill they have learned.

text continues on page 83

LEARNING CYCLE LESSON PLAN **How Can We Classify Native American Food Plants?**

NCSS
Standards I, IX

Grade Level: Kindergarten–First Grade

NCSS Standards: Culture

Inquiry Skill: Classification

Exploratory Introduction

Materials: Sweet potatoes, peanuts, tomatoes, squash, pumpkin, field corn, yellow corn, sunflower seeds (at least four items per group)

Objectives ⟶	Procedures ⟶	Assessment
Students will make observations of a sample of Native American plants and sort them into two groups: eaten and not eaten.	1. Arrange students in a circle around a set of plants such as sweet potatoes and field corn. 2. Have students examine items. Ask, "What does each of these look like? How does each one feel? Smell?" 3. Ask, "Which of these do people eat?" Assign groups of 3 or 4. Have groups show what they think by sorting items into two groups: eaten and not eaten. 4. Tell students these foods are all from plants that Native Americans had but people in Europe did not have. All can be eaten, but the field corn is so tough, usually only animals eat it.	Students place plants into two groups.

Lesson Development

Materials: Foods from Exploratory Introduction, knife, bowls, paper plate for each student

Objectives ⟶	Procedures ⟶	Assessment
Students will demonstrate that items can be classified using various criteria by reclassifying the plant items.	1. Have students discuss observations and classification of the items. Are they familiar with each item? 2. Examine the items sorted as eaten and not eaten, asking each group, "Why did you put each in its group?" 3. Cut larger items such as sweet potatoes and pumpkin into pieces and put in bowls. Ask groups to resort the items any way they want into new groups. Talk about how they are sorting by asking questions like "Why	Students will appropriately identify the characteristic they used to classify three items on their plate.

did you put these together?" and "What is the same about those in this pile?"

4. Have each student choose three items that go together and put them on a paper plate. Ask some to share why they chose these three. Ask each to write/draw why the items on their plate go together.

5. Closure: Ask, "What do people do when they put things into groups?" or "How do you decide that some things go in one pile and other things belong together in another pile?"

Expansion

Materials: Small raw and cooked samples of the food plants, toothpicks, plastic spoons, paper plates, newspaper supermarket ads, scissors, glue sticks, paper cut into the shape of a dinner plate

Objectives ⟶	Procedures ⟶	Assessment
Students will use the sense of taste to classify plant items.	1. Have students taste small raw and cooked samples of the foods. 2. Have them sort foods into groups using sense of taste and identify their favorite. Ask students to think of another food that tastes something like their favorite. 3. Have students use newspaper supermarket ads to find pictures of foods they like that are the same in some way, cut them out, paste them on a piece of paper shaped like a dinner plate, and write/draw a description of how these foods are similar. 4. Lesson summary: Briefly, talk about what we did in this lesson and have students tell how they put things into groups and why it is possible to change and make new groups.	Students will appropriately describe the characteristic(s) shared by a set of foods each has selected from a newspaper advertisement.

Summative Evaluation: Give students a worksheet to take home on which they will draw three items at home that share a taste, share a color, or feel the same and on which they identify the characteristic shared. Assess the accuracy of the characteristic identied for the classification, talking with students to clarify as needed.

What Do You Think?

Examine the learning cycle, *How Can We Classify Native American Food Plants?*

1. The learning cycle's title identifies classification as the key skill of the lesson. After considering this lesson, how well do you think it helps students develop a higher level of skill at classification? What evidence from the lesson supports your conclusion?

2. If this were part of a unit on Native Americans, what other materials might the teacher have used to teach the skill of classification? What are three characteristics students might use to classify those materials?

3. If this lesson were part of a unit on Native Americans, what lesson might follow next to involve students in applying their newly developed higher level of skill at classifying?

 ## Assessing the Use of Inquiry Skills

Regular daily recordkeeping makes the assessment of skills doable within the demands of a busy teaching day. Assessment of student thinking skills uses different types of records for different purposes. The type of recordkeeping depends on whether the record is intended for the parent, teacher, student, or for another purpose, such as assessment by special education personnel.

A *task completion* record indicates a student has finished a task. It can indicate how well or to what level a task has been finished. A *task performance* record uses events occurring within a social studies unit. For example, a student task record in an early grades unit investigating geographic features of the neighborhood involves the completion of specific tasks as shown in Table 3.4.

The type of information recorded for assessment ranges from a simple checkmark to a numerical rating scale, rubric, or a narrative comment. See Chapter 14 for more discussion of assessment. A checkmark indicates the student demonstrated or completed the task. Checkmarks are useful as a way to identify that progress has occurred, but they usually are not sufficient for evaluating student progress. The use of numerical, rubric, and narrative assessments helps diagnose students' strengths and weaknesses. Rubrics use criteria to assess and evaluate learning performance. See Table 3.5 on page 84 for a sample rubric assessment. Rubric and narrative assessment ratings are useful in deciding on future social

TABLE 3.4

Task Performance Record of Student Social Studies Activities

Topic	Student			
	Tanya	Travis	Natalie	Umberto
Drawing two geographic features using a variety of materials	X	X	X	X
Listing observable characteristics of geographic features	X	X	X	X
Constructing a model of one geographic feature	X	X		X

studies instruction. Table 3.6 identifies levels for curiosity, an important disposition in learning. Records may be kept on individual or classroom charts. Comparing student progress to the overall development of the skill or to other students allows a teacher to provide a more supportive and powerful social studies program.

TABLE 3.5
Record of Student Skill Development

Topic	Student			
	Tanya	Travis	Natalie	Umberto
Observing				
Use of more than one sense while investigating the observable characteristics of a geographic feature	X	X	X	X
Classifying				
Classification of a variety of geographic features by their shape		X	X	X
Identifying Variables				
Identification of the height of the land as a variable related to the observable characteristics of some of the neighborhood's geographic features			X	X

TABLE 3.6
Sample Development Assessment for Curiosity

Curiosity Assessment				
Lesson or Activity _____				

Rating Level	Student			
	Tanya	Travis	Natalie	Umberto
Level 1				
Unaware of new things and shows little sign of interest even when these things are pointed out				
Level 2				
Often seems unaware of new things and shows little sign of interest even when these things are pointed out				
Level 3				
Is attracted by new things but looks at them only superficially or for a short time. Asks questions mostly about what things are and where they come from, rather than about how or why they work or relate to other things				

Level 4

Usually shows interest in new or unusual things and notices details

Level 5

Shows interest in new or unusual things and notices details;
seeks, by questioning or action, to find out about and to explain
causes and relationships

 # Hierarchy of Inquiry Skills

The categories of inquiry skills provide a way to scaffold the introduction of these skills in social studies lessons. During the early elementary grades, social studies lessons focus on basic skills such as observation, classification, communication, and measurement. At the middle school level, social studies lessons focus on students' independent use of basic skills and facilitate their learning of integrative inquiry skills. Table 3.7 illustrates the ever-increasing complexity of the skills addressed during the K–8 years. The learning cycle lesson teaches inquiry skills (see Table 3.8 on page 86).

TABLE 3.7

Developmental Use of Thinking Skills in Social Studies Lessons

Thinking Skill	Components of Skills Used at Particular Grade Levels		
	Kindergarten	**Elementary School**	**Middle School**
Observation	Descriptive; uses all senses; needs to use real experiences	Quantitative; observes change; uses familiar situations	Relates theory and observations; can use imagined situations
Classification	Uses one attribute to classify	Can use multiple attributes to classify; can use a hierarchical system	Can create a hierarchical system
Communication	Can describe information coming directly from the senses, can begin recording data	Can make inferences from experiences; can begin graphical representation	Can describe using maps, charts, graphs qualitatively
Measuring and Estimating	Can make comparisons	Measures with some accuracy; begins estimating	Can use abstract measures and relations
Inferring	Uses inference but unaware of using it	Distinguishes among observations	Uses inference in developing theory

continued

TABLE 3.7 (Continued)

Thinking Skill	Components of Skills Used at Particular Grade Levels		
	Kindergarten	**Elementary School**	**Middle School**
Predicting	Uses prediction but unaware of using it	Makes descriptive, concrete predictions	Makes quantitative, thorough predictions; uses qualitative description; uses abstract variables
Using Variables	Uses a single variable	Identifies, selects, uses multiple variables	Controls multiple variables
Hypothesizing	Begins using fair tests	Makes simple, concrete hypotheses; identifies hypotheses; judges; uses inductive thinking	Identifies and constructs tests; judges; uses inductive and deductive thinking
Investigating	Begins developing concept of fairness	Uses hypothesis testing	Uses and generates hypotheses
Reflecting	Can describe what he or she has done in a task	Describes procedures used, choices made, problems encountered, other procedures/choices that could be made	Identifies and implements procedures to produce a more appropriate/useful process, acts on problems encountered, seeks choices that benefit the common good

TABLE 3.8
Teaching Inquiry Skills Using the Learning Cycle

Exploratory Introduction

Help students try out and confront their prior knowledge of the inquiry skill.
Provide an opportunity for students to display the skill focused on in the lesson. Start students thinking with a "key" question involving them in an activity using the skill.
Relate previous experience to the lesson skill.

Lesson Development

Discuss the results of the exploratory activity, providing connections to the focus skill.
Provide an explanation of the new skill, describing how to use it, when it is used, for what purpose it is used, and how to know when to use it appropriately.
Provide clear examples or model the new skill.
Provide closure for the new skill, describing the steps necessary to use it.

Expansion

Provide practice activities for the new skill. Use interesting examples, not repetitive practice.
Provide activities where the skill is applied in new, relevant contexts.
Provide activities helping students transfer the new social studies inquiry skill to more and more real-world events.
Provide a summary of the skill, when it is used, and how to use it correctly.

CLASSROOM SCENARIO: The Mystery in the Backyard

One day Ms. Laughlin told her class about a woman she knows who has always enjoyed watching the birds, and has a bird feeding station in her backyard. One morning she saw something had happened overnight. The teacher showed the class two pictures.

She asked, "How could this mess have happened?" "Where are the seeds that were in the three feeders?" She noted, "Something even ate everything that was in the plastic square of suet and seeds for woodpeckers." Ms. Laughlin asked, "How did the heavy pole get broken? My friend didn't think the wind could have done this." The class agreed that the wind was not the culprit, noting there were no tree limbs on the ground and the feeders all seemed to be near the pole. They asked their teacher for the answer to this mystery but she said that she was not certain and that she thought the class might help her find a good explanation.

Ms. Laughlin asked "Do you think it was a hawk or an eagle?" When the student said, "No, a bird can't knock over a pole," she asked, "What about a raccoon or a opossum?" After some thought, Alex suggested that deer eat seeds, and said he had heard that deer frequently go into backyards, even in cities. Sylvia said she had heard that too, but thought "it would need to be something bigger than a deer or any other of the animals we have been talking about to break the pole." "What about an elephant? I saw them pushing over trees on a TV program. An elephant

could knock down and break off a metal pole," said Ahmed. Then Ahmed asked, "Does your friend live in Kenya where elephants might be migrating through?" The teacher replied that her friend lives in the United States and asked, "Would it help you to know state in which my friend lives?" "How would you use that information?" The students replied that they would look up information about the state in reference books or on the Internet. Ms. Laughlin agreed that was a good plan to follow.

   She told the students that her friend lived in West Virginia and pointed out the area on the map of the United States. The class decided to spend some time on the classroom computers looking for information on animals in West Virginia. After some time searching the Internet, the teacher asked the class if anyone had found information that might help solve the mystery in her friend's backyard. Betty said, "Besides eagles and hawks West Virginia has lots of wild turkeys, but I don't think they would be strong enough to break the pole." Alex said, "I found there is a deer hunting season and seasons for hunting bear in West Virginia." Carl said, "The state animal is the Black Bear." The class decided that bears were strong enough, eat seeds, and move around during the day and also in the night when the bird feeder was damaged. The students told Ms. Laughlin to ask her friend if there were bears or bear sightings in her area of West Virginia. They also suggested she should tell her friend that if there have been bear sightings, she should look carefully before going out into her backyard because they thought a bear probably was the cause of the broken pole and emptied feeders. ■

TIME FOR REFLECTION | What Do You Think?

1. In this classroom scenario Ms. Laughlin used the pictures and asked questions to begin the investigation. What about these questions encouraged the students to contribute ideas and evaluate what they heard?

2. It would have been quicker and easier to tell the students the answer. Why do you think it is important for the teacher to devote scarce class and computer time to this short inquiry study?

3. How might these pictures, and additional pictures, be used to help nonreaders or beginning readers to inquire into what happened in the backyard and to reach the conclusion that a bear probably was responsible for breaking the pole and eating the seeds and suet?

4. How might this presentation be aided through the use of technology if the students were nonreaders?

5. What key elements in the lesson do you identify as necessary to assure the lesson is a success?

Summary

Ideas are made up of information and the related inquiry skills necessary for using and interpreting information meaningfully. Students perceive and interpret information from their experiences and use their prior knowledge to construct new knowledge. Construction of new knowledge is dependent on the level and kind of inquiry skills available. Beginning social studies lessons focus on helping students derive meaning from their everyday experiences by encouraging the development of their inquiry skills. After students have specific social studies experiences in an area and have developed basic inquiry skills, the focus of social studies teaching moves from a skills emphasis to a skills-and-content emphasis. Assessment and evaluation of a wide range of inquiry skills places a higher value on them and focuses instruction on meaningful learning in students.

Recommended Websites to Visit

Decision Making, a lesson plan for grades 4, 5, and 6
http://askeric.org/cgi-bin/printlessons.cgi/Virtual/Lessons/Social_Studies/Psychology/PSY0004.html
Critical Thinking Strategies, a lesson plan for all grade levels
http://askeric.org/cgi-bin/printlessons.cgi/Virtual/Lessons/Interdisciplinary/INT0013.html
The Process of Sequencing: A Picture Card Game
http://askeric.org/cgi-bin/printlessons.cgi/Virtual/Lessons/Interdisciplinary/INT0059.html
Data Gathering: Vietnam, a middle school lesson
http://askeric.org/cgi-bin/printlessons.cgi/Virtual/Lessons/Social_Studies/World_History/Vietnam/VET0200.html
Environmental Explorer: A lesson using observation skills to analyze changes that people have made to the natural environment
www.nationalgeographic.com/resources/ngo/education/ideas58/58environ.html
iTECH Inc: School Acceptable Use Policy Links
www.aupaction.com/aupsonweb.html
Partnership for 21st Century Skills, Information, media, and technology skills. Accessed December 15, 2008
http://www.21stcenturyskills.org/index.php?option=com_content&task=view&id=61&Itemid=120
"How Can You Decide Among Competing Responsibilities?" A lesson building the skill of decision making.
http://www.civiced.org/index.php?page=fod_ms_resp07_sb

4

How Are Social Studies Concepts and Generalizations Developed?

EXPLORATORY INTRODUCTION

Consider the following objective: "After examining a situation involving two children and one gift, students will define *jealousy*."

1. What is the major concept used in this objective?
2. If this objective is to be accomplished, students must be able to use which inquiry skill?

The concept of "jealousy" is emphasized in this objective. In order to accomplish this objective, students must have skill in making predictions.

3. Rephrase the objective so that it focuses on an inquiry skill rather than on the concept of jealousy.

There are a number of ways in which this objective could have been restated. One example is, "Students will predict whether an individual would be jealous when involved in a situation where there are two children and one gift."

4. In order to plan the lesson development phase of a learning cycle lesson, a teacher first needs to answer the question, "What do you think are the most important characteristic(s) of the definition of *jealousy*?" Write down the definition of *jealousy* as a second grader might explain it. Then, write down the definition of *jealousy* as a fifth grader might explain it. What activity would help students identify these important characteristic(s) of jealousy?
5. As part of the Expansion in this learning cycle lesson, students might be involved in developing and performing a scenario where jealousy is displayed. Why would the teacher be involving students in the scenario?

When teaching a concept, teachers must clearly identify those characteristics of the concept their students can meaningfully understand. Then, the lesson is developed to help students actively work with those important characteristics. Reading a text or memorizing a definition from a glossary or dictionary is not enough to meaningfully understand a concept.

Reading a text passage or memorizing the statements in the passage is not enough if students are to develop a meaningful understanding of the concept it contains. Students need to understand the characteristics of each concept so that they can differentiate related concepts.

Chapter Overview

Standards

Social studies involves mastery of key concepts and processes required for personal decision making, active participation in civic and cultural affairs, and economic productivity (NCSS, 1994b).

Factual information, or *facts*, is based on observations and inferences about objects and events. Examples of two facts are (1) the Bill of Rights is part of the Constitution of the United States of America and (2) this author's family has two children, one girl and one boy. Concepts summarize a set of facts that have a common characteristic and distinguish any and all examples of the concept from nonexamples. The first fact, about the Bill of Rights, may be part of a set of facts used to construct the concept of governing documents. The second fact, about this author's family, may be part of a set of facts used to construct the concept of family.

The most useful and powerful ideas in social studies are generalizations. A generalization describes two or more concepts and the relationships among them. Generalizations enable us to explain processes and events we experience. They often are explanations of cause and effect that allow us to predict future events. Generalizations develop from inferences we make about many observations. They also arise from results gained from testing hypotheses. A generalization provides more information than does a concept. Teachers help students construct meaningful generalizations through asking and investigating significant questions. This chapter involves the reader in activities that focus on enhancing students' understanding of key concepts and generalizations in social studies.

Chapter Objectives

1. Identify and classify different types of concepts.
2. Identify and classify different levels of abstraction between concepts.
3. Describe the rationale for assessing and planning for working with students' alternative social studies conceptions.
4. Describe important elements of a teaching strategy that encourages and facilitates conceptual change and reconstruction.
5. Explain why generalizations are an important part of social studies content.
6. Suggest appropriate questions and activities for an inquiry lesson that helps students construct a generalization.
7. Describe the teacher's role in an inquiry lesson developing a generalization.

8. Describe how the process of developing and revising generalizations is continuous.
9. Describe thought processes used to construct generalizations to solve everyday personal and civic problems.

 ## Concept Teaching Starts with Reflection and Practice

In lessons that focus on helping students construct a new concept or reconstruct an existing one, the teacher's role involves two tasks: (1) providing students with information to work with and (2) asking questions to focus their attention on important aspects of the information. Although the teacher serves as a guide during lesson development, activities are centered on interactions between students and their social environment. Activities enable students to work with examples of the concept. Eventually, students reconstruct their ideas or invent a definition of the concept using the information they have worked with during the lesson development.

A FOURTH-GRADE CLASSROOM SCENE

As an exploratory activity for her students, Ms. Carlson asked them the following questions. How do you think her fourth-grade students responded?

"Think about who sits next to you in your art class."
"If someone sits on your left, is it a boy or girl? What is this person's name?"
"If someone sits directly in front of you, is it a boy or girl? What is this person's name?"

Then, Ms. Carlson instructed her students to draw a simple map showing themselves and the students sitting near them. Later, Ms. Carlson asked, "Do you know the people who sit near you better than those who sit farther away from you?" Finally, she asked the students to think about what characteristic, or attribute, they used to select the people to include on their map. She asked her students, "What attribute did they all have in common?"

The attribute that was the focus of this exploratory activity was *location*. Students were asked to think about who was sitting in a classroom location near to them. They were not asked about others located farther away. To build on the exploratory activity, the following lesson development occurred. ■

Ms. Carlson asked the students to imagine the following scenario.

Imagine that the classroom walls have moved farther out so that the classroom is twice its size. When this happened, your chairs ended up being farther away from each other. Now the distance between your chairs is twice what it was before. The person who was on your left is still on your left. The person who was directly in front of you is still in front of you. The only thing that has changed is how far apart your chairs are. Even though the people around you are farther away from you, they are still on your left, or in front of you.

Ms. Carlson: What might we call someone who sits next to us in class or who lives next door to us at home? [The students quickly decide that such a person is called a *neighbor*.]

Ms. Carlson: Using the location, how would you define *neighbor*?

Brian: A neighbor is "someone who is in a place close to you."

Ms. Carlson: Do you think Brian's definition of *neighbor* is a useful one for you? [The students tell her they think it is a useful definition. Ms. Carlson writes it on the board as their working definition.]

Ms. Carlson: Using Brian's definition of *neighbor*, if the person sitting on your left switched seats with someone on the other side of the room, would that person still be your neighbor? [After some discussion, students agree that the student who switched seats would no longer be a neighbor. They decide that an important attribute of neighbor is location and, specifically, closeness in location.]. ∎

DEVELOPMENT

 ## Facts as Social Studies Content

Facts are statements of observations about objects, people, and events that provide evidence we use to develop meaning for concepts, generalizations, attitudes, and values. Without an adequate background of facts based on concrete experiences, a student's understanding of concepts such as *consumer, peace, society, place*, or *authority* remains vague. *Factual information,* or fact statements, is based on the observations we make about objects, people, and events. The following are examples of facts: "There are 20 houses under construction in this neighborhood," "The new road will be open on November 20," and "In 1874, the Women's Christian Temperance Union came together to fight alcohol use." However, facts in any social studies curriculum must be related to specific concepts that are part of the key ideas of the social studies standards. Factual information by itself is useless to students.

Concepts differ from facts in two major ways. First, facts are isolated bits of information acquired through the senses: seeing, hearing, tasting, feeling, or smelling. A concept involves more than a simple observation. Second, concepts summarize and group together observations into categories on the basis of shared characteristics, or *attributes*. In other words, concepts refer to a set or class rather than a single object, person, or event. Concepts are formed by finding similarities between many facts and temporarily emphasizing those similarities. For example, *lake* is a concept formed by focusing on the shape, contents, and sources of various bodies of water. In forming the concept of lake, we ignore small differences between lakes, such as their size and where they are found. Concepts are defined by humans and reflect our cultures: people living in rainforest cultures who encounter high humidity in their daily environment will construct the concept of *shelter* differently than those living in low-humidity desert cultures. Concepts are the fundamental building blocks of the social studies curriculum. We use concepts and their relationships to form social studies generalizations.

The *summarizing* capability of a concept is very important. For example, people ride in many kinds of vehicles: big and small, with room for two or six, with or without air conditioning. To remember each of these with a name would take up a lot of mental capacity, so we form concepts that group together similar vehicles by shared attributes: such as pick-up truck, sport utility vehicle, or hybrid.

Understanding concepts involves identifying attributes that must be present. These are *essential attributes* for an object, person, or event to be a member of a grouping. Learning concepts also involves identifying those essential attributes that can vary over a range but are still part of the same concept. Variations can relate to a range in color, size, shape, place, and other essential attributes that still include the members of the set that represents the concept. So, whether you are short or tall, brown or blue eyed, right or left handed with any of these variations, you still belong to the concept category of "human being."

Examples are any and all individual members of a category that have the essential attributes of a given concept. *Nonexamples* are any and all individuals that may have some but not all of the attributes that make them examples of a given concept.

To summarize, concepts

- Represent a group of objects, people, events, or symbols of two or more members
- Include members sharing common attributes
- Include members identified by a name or label

CLASSROOM SCENARIO: Constructing a Concept of Aggression

Three teachers are involving their students in a unit on the concept of aggression. Mr. Hernandez decides to use examples of accidental aggression. He chooses three examples: tagging a friend too hard in a game of hide and seek, telling a joke that unexpectedly hurts someone's feelings, and crushing a butterfly in your hand in an effort to keep it from flying away. Ms. Wenta focuses on a set of examples of a child enjoying an aggressive action that inadvertently hurts someone: Roger feels satisfaction in a well-placed karate chop that knocks down Sammy's block building, and Elizabeth laughingly bites Tulana because it feels good. Ms. Michaels focuses on hostile aggression. Claudia pushes Jenny away from the water fountain because Jenny was first in line last time. Claudia sees this as "getting even," so it is premeditated and deliberate. Marisol grabs Bernardo's pencil box and stamps her foot on it, cracking it because Bernardo's pencil box was decorated with stickers that she envied.

Each of these teachers is working with examples of planned or inadvertent aggression. Each example is a specific fact. When they are put together, their similarities convey a type of aggression. Each of these types of aggression is a concept: accidental aggression, aggression that inadvertently hurts someone, and hostile aggression. Each concept includes the facts or specific events used as examples by the teacher. But, each fact is not powerful by itself. It becomes powerful when it is grouped with similar facts into a social studies concept. Each of these concepts can, of course, be grouped into a deeper concept of aggression that is even more powerful. This deeper concept includes each of these three types of aggression, helping students to recognize that aggression is not just a "fact." ■

Facts are single occurrences, taking place in the past or present. They result from observations. Facts do not allow us to predict an event or action (Eggen & Kauchak, 2001). Using a fact about the number of houses built in a new development, we cannot predict the number of houses that will be built in the next development begun in the city. Effective strategies for learning factual information differ greatly from those used in learning other social studies content.

Meaningful social studies content is not acquired by using or recalling facts when constructing or interpreting concepts. When recall is needed, a rote memory learning strategy can facilitate the learning of social studies facts. Rote memory learning requires repetition, immediate feedback, breaking down the content into small pieces, associating new material to be memorized to information previously learned, mnemonics, and attention to the motivational needs of the student (Joyce & Weil, 1992). Games, rewards, mnemonics, and quick pacing of instructional events are all effective techniques to facilitate the memorization of facts. Such rote instructional techniques should make up only a small part of social studies, probably no more than 10 percent of instructional time. Terminology, symbols, and spelling are factual information that might be included in a social studies curriculum. Useful facts a teacher might have students learn are the names of continents; the major steps for making a law; procedures for constructing a timeline; and names of coins used as money in our society.

Teachers plan in advance for the memorization of facts and relate these facts to important social studies objectives. In a fourth-grade unit on landforms, for example, the names of specific mountains and volcanoes such as Mt. McKinley, Mt. Everest, and Mt. Kilimanjaro are facts that might be learned as a minor objective and activity in the unit. In the absence of direct personal experience on the part of the students, a teacher may focus on teaching some facts so that students are better able to develop and understand more important concepts and generalizations. When the teacher shows students a video on mountains and volcanoes, such as one on Mt. McKinley, the video is the only source of common experiences the teacher knows the students can share. Direct experiences and the use of references for information provide important classroom sources of facts to be used in developing concepts.

NCSS

Standard III

In the past, traditional social studies lessons focused on fact-learning strategies. These often resulted in elementary and middle school students having weak understandings of more interesting and advanced concepts needed to form conclusions and make value decisions (NCSS, 1994a). Today's teachers realize that only rarely should facts be the focus of what is taught.

A heavy use of fact-learning teaching strategies neglects important social studies concepts. For example, emphasis on facts reduces learning the structure of

U.S. government to memorizing the names of the branches of government and a statement explaining their powers. Yet the powerful social studies objective is developing a comprehensive, personal understanding of the judiciary, legislative, and executive branches of U.S. government. Each branch of government is a concept and should be taught using concept learning strategies.

Without an adequate background of facts, a student's understanding of concepts, such as *individual, group,* or *consumer*, remains vague. Facts are a necessary part of instruction, but should not be the final outcome of lessons and units. Facts can only provide examples or partial meaning for important social studies concepts.

 ## Forming Concepts

Concepts are formed by finding similarities between several facts that we have acquired from our experiences. For example, we construct the concept of *parent* from the parents with whom we have had contact. We ignore gender, age, cultural background, and other attributes. We use similarities, particularly caring for children and providing for the basic physical, emotional, and health needs of one's children, to construct the concept.

Identifying All Important Attributes of a Concept

For effective instruction, it is important to identify all attributes *essential* to a social studies concept. When concepts are complex, a child begins with a simple definition. As the child's experiences increase his or her abilities to understand an idea, the concept is refined and new attributes are added to its definition. Many social studies concepts such as democracy and justice have meanings that evolve over time as individuals mature and cultures change.

For example, in learning the concept of *friendship*, young children may consider a friend's similarity to themselves an essential characteristic (Buysse, Goldman, & Skinner, 2003). With help, students experience and consider several characteristics of friendship: (1) perceived similarity in age, race, sex, interest, degree of sociability, and values; (2) existence of mutual acceptance, admiration, and loyalty; (3) willingness to help each other and to be satisfied by the help received; (4) caring about what happens to a friend; and (5) mutual understanding and closeness with an expectation that friends be useful to each other (Kostelnik, Stein, Whiren, & Soderman, 1998). The fourth and fifth characteristics usually are understood by students in middle school, but not by younger students. However, all elementary and middle school students can learn that some attributes, such as the size or hair color of a friend, are not essential. It is important to help students distinguish nonessential characteristics from those that are essential.

Identify which of the following are facts.

1. The sand is white.

2. The line that forms a border around an area delimiting that area is its boundary.

3. People's lives are changed by revolutions in technology as new jobs are created and existing jobs disappear.

4. Juan Ponce de Leone explored Florida in 1513.

5. The quickest way for women to gain the right to vote was to amend the U.S. Constitution instead of having a law giving them the vote passed in each state.

Of the five items above, items 1 and 4 are facts. Item 1 describes a specific observation. Item 4 identifies a specific event. Item 2 is a concept statement defining a *boundary*. Item 3 is a generalization because it describes a pattern relating three concepts: people's lives, their jobs, and technology. Both items 2 and 3 describe and summarize a set of similarities found between the facts from which they were formed. Item 5 is an inference, a statement that goes beyond the observations made.

For older students, a learning cycle could involve asking students, during the exploratory introduction phase, to make and discuss predictions and carry out tests using written scenarios in learning stations for several essential attributes. During the lesson development phase, students could discuss the results of the tests of their predictions. As the discussion progresses, they are provided with clear explanations of examples and nonexamples. The examples are carefully selected to make obvious the essential and nonessential characteristics of the concept. The expansion phase involves asking students to make further applications and transfer the concept to situations outside the classroom context. This could involve an everyday situation, such as how to help a friend who has left his backpack at home and doesn't have any paper or pens, or a not-so-common situation, such as how to help a friend get elected as class representative to the school legislature even though you were thinking about trying to get elected yourself.

 ## Types of Concepts

Concepts can be communicated in three ways:

1. *Formal definition:* A carefully worded sentence often using abstract terms, for example, that given in a dictionary
2. *Concept name:* A name indicated by a label or term
3. *Operational description:* A definition that describes the concept in practical, everyday language often accompanied by an example

Understanding a *formal definition* is a difficult task for students. Read the following example of a formal concept definition for *bar scale*: "A bar scale is a series of marks made along a line at regular intervals to measure distance on a map." This type of definition is commonly found in elementary and middle school textbooks. Understanding this definition of *bar scale* requires knowledge of what is meant by a "series of marks," an "interval," a "regular interval," "measurement," "distance," and "map." Only when the student understands each of these concepts can they be put together to form a relationship that has meaning and can be applied to the bar scale found on a map.

Concept names are the labels or terms used to communicate the concept, for example, "bar scale." *Map* is a concept name used to describe a class of objects. *Suffrage* is a concept name given to a class of actions and events. Some of the many concept names that are important in social studies are *culture, time, environment, individual, production, global connections, civic ideals*, and *governor*. Concept names communicate different meanings to individuals. Young students may be able to focus only on one aspect of *governor*: "can get things for me that I need." Older students may visualize a person who manages the work of many others and is responsible for putting into practice laws others make. Giving an event or object a concept name is a common textbook approach to social studies instruction. But, just labeling something does not give it meaning. It is important to provide students with experiences, discussion, and time to reflect so they can give meaning to the concept name.

Operational definitions describe a concept by providing a test for deciding whether an object, action, or event is an example of the concept. The test is described in terms and experiences that are familiar to the student. The definition excludes all reasonable statements that do not represent the concept for students. If the object or event does not meet the test, it does not represent an example of the concept. An example of an operational definition is "Acting on impulse means that a person acts without thinking ahead: an idea or desire pops into their heads, and they are in motion; they see something they want and grab for it; they think something and blurt it out" (Calkins, 1994, p. 59). Frequently, operational definitions have two parts. The first part describes the conditions. The conditions include what is done in an event or to an object being defined, such as, "an idea or desire pops into their heads, and they are in motion." The second part describes the effect of what is observed or what happens as a result of what is done, for example, "they see something they want and grab it." Powerful social studies instruction focuses on the use of operational definitions to communicate the meaning of concepts.

Some operational definitions are difficult to use or construct. For example, for a definition of *hyperactivity*, one might say that it is "inappropriate activity at a high energy level." However, one may find that all children are involved in inappropriate activity at times. Also, children usually show a high energy level at certain times during the day. So this operational definition may be more appropriate in some situations than in others. Additional description may be added to the definition. The operational definition of hyperactivity may be made more useful to a teacher by expanding it as follows: "a persistent pattern of inattention and/or impulsivity that is more frequent and severe than is typically observed in individuals at a comparable level of development, often leading to inappropriate activity at a high energy level."

TIME FOR REFLECTION | *What Do You Think?*

Below is a sample elementary social studies textbook passage describing a portion of U.S. history. As you read the passage, pay close attention to how the key concepts are defined with specific attributes.

> Women's **suffrage**, or the right to vote, was important to many people. But, for a long time, women could not vote. After the Civil War, the Fifteenth Amendment gave African American men the right to vote. But women did not get the right to vote.
>
> Between 1890 and 1919 the women's right to vote movement grew. Women gained the right to vote in many states, such as Montana. In 1916 Jeanette Rankin was elected to Congress by the people of Montana. She was the first woman to serve in the House of Representatives. Jeanette Rankin, Harriet Stanton Blatch, and Carrie Chapman Catt were some of the women who worked for suffrage for everyone.
>
> Women were given the vote by one state, then another. But this was slow. The quickest way for all women to get the right to vote was by amending the Constitution.
>
> Some men believed women should not take part in government. They also thought that women could not do certain kinds of work or understand certain ideas. The work that women did during World War I helped change people's ideas. They saw that women could contribute much in government and work.
>
> In 1919, Congress passed an amendment to the Constitution. It said women could not be kept from voting. The amendment went to the states for **ratification**, or approval. Enough states gave their approval by August 26, 1920.

1. Identify and name the two important social studies concept(s) being defined in the sample passage.

2. Describe the attributes provided for the concepts in the passage.

3. For each concept listed, determine whether examples and nonexamples are provided in the passage. If provided, describe them; if not, indicate they are not present.

The major concept introduced in the sample textbook passage is the women's suffrage movement. Ratification is another social studies concept essential to the process of women gaining suffrage in the United States. Attributes of the women's suffrage movement provided in the passage are (1) the right to vote for all women; (2) some states gave women the right to vote; (3) some men were against women's suffrage; and (4) an amendment would be the quickest way for all women to obtain voting rights. Among the examples provided is that Montana and some other states granted women suffrage. A nonexample is the Fifteenth Amendment giving African American men the right to vote.

Other examples and nonexamples of women gaining the right to vote are possible. Ratification appears once in the passage and is defined as "approval." The word *approval*, but not *ratification*, appears in the concluding sentence. The passage fails to mention any time limit or the number of states required for ratification. It does not mention that the amendment had to be approved by state legislatures at special state conventions called for the purpose of approving the amendment. No examples of states that ratified the amendment or of states that voted against it or failed to consider it are given. The names of three women who worked for suffrage are given. But no specific information about how they approached and accomplished their task is provided. The passage indicates that the approval of the amendment ended the women's suffrage movement on August 20, 1920.

Attention to the complete meaning of the concepts and the use of multiple examples and nonexamples would strengthen this textbook passage presentation of the concepts of the women's suffrage movement and ratification of amendments to the U.S. Constitution. Doing so would make the passage more realistic. It would help students understand that the rights of democracy must be claimed and used by its citizens if democracy is to continue to exist.

 # Interrelationships among Concepts

Concepts are interrelated. Two concepts often share some of the same facts, and most concepts include other concepts as subconcepts. A garage, for example, can house a car, but it can also be a workshop or a storage area. People are flexible in the concepts they form, allowing them to account for the diversity in the social world.

A key concept in elementary and middle school social studies is *government*. Government includes the subconcept of *branches of government*. Branches of government, in turn, involves the subconcepts of *judiciary, legislature*, and *executive*, as well as other subconcepts. Executive, in turn, includes *president, governor*, and *mayor*, in addition to other subconcepts. These related concepts form a hierarchy. In a hierarchy, a key concept can incorporate many subconcepts. In turn, a concept can be a subconcept to another more inclusive concept. So *judge* can be a subconcept to *judiciary*, and *judiciary* can be a subconcept to *branches of government*. Providing concept maps and having students make their own concept maps can be an important tool to help students assess their own learning. Concept maps also help teachers diagnose learning problems.

Concept maps and *concept webs* are terms that often are used interchangeably. A concept map helps students develop interrelated knowledge and understandings. The concept map has been defined as a process that identifies concepts in a set of materials being studied, and that organizes those concepts into a hierarchical arrangement from the most general, most inclusive concept, to the least general, most specific concept (Farris & Cooper, 1994).

Consider a very simple concept map:

People—*eat*—apples.

Such a concept map shows how two concepts are related but does not describe a hierarchy. As an instructional or assessment device, a teacher might draw a concept map for students and leave some blank spaces in it. In the example, the teacher might leave a blank space where *apples* is found. Students might use the map in one or more of a number of ways: to discuss and decide what concepts should be written in the blanks or to carry out investigations and other activities to decide how to fill in the blanks.

Teachers may use a concept map throughout a unit, beginning with students' prior knowledge and adding to it and revising it as the unit progresses. A concept web is very similar to the concept map. In a concept web, the most general and

TIME FOR REFLECTION | *What Do You Think?*

The following activity works with identifying and developing the skill of defining a concept by using operational definitions. For students, this skill is closely related to the skill of communicating. Making clear statements to others about the world is important. Also important is the idea that more than one satisfactory statement can be used to define a concept. Operational definitions define concepts so that they can be used in everyday situations.

Part I

Identify the type of concept description each of the following statements represents.

1. A branch is a stream or river that flows into a larger stream or river.
2. Children are self-disciplined when they can judge for themselves what is right and wrong and then behave appropriately even when nobody else is available to tell them how to behave or to make sure that they do it.
3. Culture.
4. A schedule is an organized pattern of blocks of time that is arranged in a certain order allowing individuals following it to predict future activities.
5. A continent is one of the Earth's main areas of land.

Items 1 and 5 are examples of formal definitions. These definitions involve language and terms that require additional definition. Items 2 and 4 represent operational definitions. These definitions adequately describe a procedure, concept, event, object, or property of an object in the situation in which it is used. Item 3 is a concept name.

Part II

Two definitions are provided for each of the following concepts. Choose the more appropriate operational definition for a sixth-grade student.

1.a. *Humor* is something that is perceived as funny because it is not compatible with the normal or expected pattern of events.

1.b. *Humor* is when something silly happens.

2.a. A *game* involves other players, has rules, and is highly social.

2.b. A *game* is not work.

3.a. A child taking on a *character role* is involved in pretend play.

3.b. A child taking on a *character role* engages in many behaviors appropriate for the part and demonstrates that the role is temporary and is defined by the actor in the present situation.

Humor and *game* in items 1 and 2, respectively, are more appropriately defined operationally using the first definitions (1a and 2a). The second choice (3b) is the more appropriate operational definition for *character role*. More appropriate definitions allow the student to follow a procedure or carry out an activity whose result defines the concept. The less operational statements refer to abstract procedures or terms or may involve experiences that students are not likely to have had.

Standard VII

inclusive idea is placed in the center. Subconcepts are arranged around it and connected to it with a line. Then another layer of sub-subconcepts of each subconcept is arranged around the outside of each subconcept and connected to it with a line. Software is available to make concept webs easy to draw. One example of such software is Inspiration (Inspiration Software).

Teachers perform a *concept analysis* to assist them in considering how concepts are related to each other. The analysis requires the teacher to make decisions about each part of the analysis. Each teacher may make different decisions based on the age and experiences of the students. The following is a concept analysis of the concept of *parent* (Eggen & Kauchak, 2001):

1. Concept: parent
2. Definition: A parent is a person who has responsibility for raising a child because of genetics or adoption.
3. Attributes: A parent assumes financial responsibility for a child, takes care of a child's basic needs, provides emotional support for a child, and oversees a child's education.
4. Examples: mother, father, stepmother, stepfather, foster mother, foster father
5. Superordinate concept: family
6. Subconcepts: mother, father, stepmother, stepfather, foster mother, foster father, relatives, guardian
7. Coordinate concept: caregiver

A *superordinate concept* is a "bigger" or more inclusive concept into which a concept fits. *Family* is a superordinate concept for *parent*. A *coordinate concept* is one that is equivalent in some way to the concept under consideration. The two concepts may be related in terms of just one characteristic. *Stream* and *brook* are coordinate concepts. *Mother* and *stepmother* are coordinate concepts. *Capitalism* and *communism* are coordinate concepts for *socialism*. Coordinate concepts are related to each other but are not subconcepts nor superordinate concepts for each other.

Concepts are a major portion of the social studies content that students need to construct. Individuals must learn each concept and process the information it represents on their own. As a result, each of us and every student within a class has a somewhat different understanding of a concept. The strength of well-defined concepts is such that even though we each form our own mental construction of a concept, its essential attributes are recognized by all of us.

Differences in Complexity and Abstractness of Concepts

Concepts differ widely in their *complexity* and level of *abstractness* (Setti & Caramelli, 2005). Because of this difference, the level of abstractness of concepts must match students' developmental level of thinking. Consider the following concepts: *wants, puddle, map, money, decade, highway, election, individual*, and *interdependence*. Of the concepts listed, *wants* and *puddle* can be understood by very young children. Both are closely tied to everyday experiences in a child's world.

TIME FOR REFLECTION | *What Do You Think?*

1. Identify a concept that includes *supply* and *demand* as subconcepts.

2. Identify one or more subconcepts of *supply*.

3. Identify a concept that includes *socialism* as a subconcept.

4. Identify one or more subconcepts of *socialism*.

A concept that includes *supply* and *demand* as subconcepts is *price*. Possible subconcepts of *supply* include *manufactured goods* and *producer*. Possible concepts that include *socialism* as a subconcept are *political system* and *economic theory*. Each of these includes *socialism* as one system or theory along with others. Possible subconcepts of *socialism* include *governmental ownership* and *state control of production*.

A label and an operational definition can easily be associated with *wants*. A *puddle* is a concrete object a child can play in. Whereas both *wants* and *puddle* can be complex concepts, each is also tied to a number of concrete experiences the child can have. As a result, children having these experiences typically form an appropriate partial concept before or during the early grades. Experiences later in life contribute to a more complete understanding of each concept.

The concepts of *map, money, decade, highway, election*, and *individual* are appropriately introduced to, and understood at least partially by, elementary students. First- and second-grade students can experience properties of *map* subconcepts through

- Playing in a sandbox where they try to reproduce the schoolyard
- Playing with trucks and cars on the floor
- Drawing an object, such as a drinking cup, from different perspectives—from above, below, the side
- Sitting in different parts of playground equipment, examining the same view from different locations
- Arranging models of furniture in a doll house or on a tabletop

Fourth- and fifth-grade students should investigate map subconcepts such as *scale, symbols*, and *grid systems*. Investigating grid systems begins with arranging items in straight rows and columns, and playing bingo. These and later experiences build an increasingly deeper understanding of the key concept of grid systems. These understandings, in turn, become part of the more inclusive concept of *map*.

Among the most complex and abstract of the concepts listed is *interdependence*, which refers to a relationship in which two or more people, objects, or events depend in some ways on each other. It is a relationship that can be personally experienced in complex as well as simple ways. You can be interdependent with your dog, for example. You feed the dog and it gives you affection in exchange. Both of you benefit from the relationship. Our states and nation are interdependent with many other states and nations because each trades its natural resources and manufactured products for those others produce. Interdependence has some concrete, or directly observable, characteristics that can be appropriately experienced by elementary and middle school students. But, often it is not directly observable or is on such a large scale, as in the case of interdependence among nations, that it is difficult for students to have relevant experiences.

The ease with which a concept can be learned depends on several factors:

- The number of critical attributes it has
- How concrete these attributes are
- The reasoning skill level required to provide meaningful learning of all aspects of the concept (Tennyson & Cocchiarella, 1986)

A teaching technique that focuses on beginning with the simplest concepts or versions of a concept and moving gradually to more complex concepts was described by Robert Gagne (1965). He stressed the need to examine the entire learning sequence, then work in small steps from the simple to the complex.

Three types of concepts were described by Bruner, Goodnow, and Austin (1962): conjunctive, disjunctive, and relational. A *conjunctive* concept has a single, fixed set of characteristics that define the concept. An example of a conjunctive concept in social studies is a globe. It is a spherical object with a map of the earth drawn on it. This is the least complex type of concept to learn.

A *disjunctive* concept has two or more sets of alternative critical attributes that define it. A parent, for example, can be the father or mother of a child, by genetics or by adoption.

A *relational* concept is the most complex type of concept. It lacks clearly defined attributes. Instead, its attributes are defined by comparisons and relationships with other objects or events. An example of this concept is *rich* or *wealthy*. A million dollars may make you rich in a town where the average household income is $40,000 per year. But if you live in a town where several people have incomes of millions of dollars every year, you are not considered rich. Other social studies concepts that are relational are *far away, justice, fairness, busy, democratic*, and *hardworking*.

Much social studies content requires the use of diverse and higher-order reasoning. Yet most students' ability to do abstract thinking is limited. It is important to plan the learning of social studies concepts according to the reasoning patterns needed to understand the content communicated in the lesson. Although not limited to these specific stages, concepts *may* be called *sensory* or *preoperational, concrete*, or *formal*, depending on the type of thought processes required to begin constructing meaning about the concept. These labels indicate differences in the thinking required to understand a concept even at a basic level. Effective teachers begin with sensory or concrete concepts and gradually progress to higher-level concepts.

Sensory concepts develop from students' use of early inquiry skills (see Chapter 3). In learning the concept *boundary*, for example, very young children use all their senses with each boundary encountered. They see, touch, smell, and perhaps bite each item, forming a physical boundary. They lie down on it, kick it, try to throw it, put it under things, and so on. These investigations are repeated with each boundary they encounter until they are able to group all of these attributes into the concept of *boundary*. Then, when a boundary is encountered, not only do young students name it as a *boundary*, but they understand it as a meaningful concept.

Concrete concepts develop as students begin to use a full range of inquiry skills (see Chapter 3) to investigate real people, objects, and experiences. Some concrete concepts, such as *prejudice* and *map*, are examples of concrete concepts for which higher-level inquiry skills are needed. Drawings, maps, globes, and models establish many concepts as concrete. However, learners need direct experience with a concept to develop a meaningful understanding of it. If the materials represent an abstract model with which students have had no experience, then the concept is not concrete for the learner. For example, if a learner has never seen or worked with a globe, a drawing of a globe is not enough to make this a concrete concept.

Formal concepts are not based on information we get through our senses. We must use our imagination or we have to develop logical relationships among the subconcepts and attributes that are part of the formal concept. Examples of formal concepts are *ethnic group, third-world nation*, and *revolution*. If a student uses only concrete reasoning patterns, then this student will find it difficult to use information from a lecture or a textbook to meaningfully understand formal concepts such as *freedom* or *political system*. Instead, instruction must begin with exploration experiences and with helping students meaningfully understand concrete concepts that contribute to the understanding of the formal concept. Beginning with a concrete concept makes a more secure connection to students' prior knowledge.

School is a concrete concept. What attributes of this photograph of a Paraguayan school fit with the attributes you use to identify a school? Photographer: Dennis W. Sunal

Powerful Concept Teaching

Meaningful teaching of social studies concepts involves the following elements:

1. Identifying all essential attributes of the concept
2. Identifying examples and nonexamples of the concept
3. Identifying students' everyday thinking about the concept
4. Using a learning cycle to teach the concept
5. Teaching concepts differently from teaching facts
6. Using operational definitions in teaching concepts
7. Teaching concepts of varying complexity and abstractness differently
8. Teaching interrelationships among concepts.

These elements are taught effectively using the learning cycle.

The Concept Learning Cycle

Student descriptions of social studies concepts often differ from those descriptions accepted in the professional literature. These *alternative conceptions* have been called *critical* barriers to learning, and *misconceptions*. Students have developed their alternative ideas through their experiences, family members' ideas, and sound bites from the media. The students generalize this everyday knowledge into their alternative conceptions. For example, a child may have noted that everyone waiting in line to vote at a polling place was talking about how angry he was with a recent raise state legislators had voted for themselves. The child may decide that you cannot vote unless you are angry about an issue. Although the concept is inaccurate, it represents an effort by the child to abstract similarities.

Teachers must assess prior knowledge and then work to help students reconstruct alternative conceptions so that they better represent the concept (Sanger & Greenbowe, 1997). If teachers do not do so, students consider the concept "school knowledge" that has to be memorized, especially if it is tested, but do not use it in their everyday lives. Teachers have an important role. They provide opportunities for students to have experiences that will add to their inventory of facts that form the concept. Teachers also must provide opportunities for students to discuss the facts they have acquired and to relate them to the concepts formed. Teachers must be aware that students have alternative conceptions about each concept area in social studies.

How can teachers influence students' understanding of social studies concepts? In order to learn a new concept, students must be mentally involved in conceptual change, a process of reshaping and restructuring their prior knowledge. This type of teaching has been labeled *conceptual change teaching*. Their prior knowledge is common everyday knowledge. This knowledge has proven successful for the student in the past. However, it is different from the intended knowledge to be gained as an outcome of the social studies lesson.

During the early part of every social studies concept lesson, the exploration, each student identifies his or her own existing concept. A social studies experience that involves students in working with a problem related to the concept followed by discussion encourages students to think about their views. If they hold an alternative conception, thinking about their views leads to a confrontation between the alternative conception and the conception intended by the social studies lesson. Dissatisfaction with existing conceptions is *critical* to the process of conceptual change. Only when they are dissatisfied do students realize they must reorganize or replace their prior knowledge because their existing concepts are inadequate to understand the new experiences. To be useful, retained, and transferred to a new setting, the new conception must be clear, understandable, plausible, and successful for the student (Thagard, 2008). This process of *awareness, reconstruction*, and *application* makes up the sequence of events in the learning cycle.

For meaningful learning, activities are planned to help students identify the essential attributes of a social studies concept. Table 4.1 summarizes the planning for each phase of a learning cycle focused on teaching a social studies concept.

- *Exploratory Introduction.* Help students become aware of the ideas they bring to the lesson (their prior knowledge). This part of the lesson focuses attention on encouraging students to describe, write, draw, and act out their understanding or meaning of the data related to the concept the lesson is teaching. Questions are asked to find out what students think about the object or event. What words do they use to describe or explain it? What evidence are they using to describe or explain it? Helpful activities include sorting activities, student-only group discussion, small- and large-group discussions with the teacher, and one-to-one informal discussions with the teacher during class activities, with students' ideas often presented on paper or electronically. Annotated drawings and diagrams, sequenced drawings, structured writing, and personal logs are encouraged. For example, ask students in small groups to draw and discuss their prior ideas on aggression and make observations of scenes of various kinds of aggression drawn on cards in order to identify essential attributes of aggression.

- *Lesson Development.* Involve students in discussing the results of the observations. As the discussion progresses, provide them with clear explanations of all essential attributes, showing a range in attributes and practicing identification of examples and nonexamples. The examples should make obvious the essential and nonessential attributes of the concept, as well as variable ranges in the essential attributes.

  Communication is important, particularly during the development phase of a learning cycle when students are guided to construct a new concept or reconstruct an existing one. Students present their ideas to others and learn to appreciate the ideas of other students and the teacher. Often, small-group discussion challenges students to find evidence for their ideas. Large-group discussions bring a number of ideas together for consideration. Don't present ready-made concepts and expect students to understand them without providing time for them to construct their own meaning for the concepts.

TABLE 4.1

Teaching a Concept Using the Learning Cycle

Phase	Planning Required
Exploratory Introduction	Help students try out and confront their prior knowledge of the social studies concept.
	Ask probing questions to diagnose students' prior knowledge of the social studies concept.
	Focus students' attention on social studies experiences.
	Encourage students to work cooperatively in groups to relate prior knowledge to the concept.
	Make public students' prior knowledge of the concept.
Lesson Development	Provide concise, brief closure for the new social studies concept.
	Ask students to reflect on and explain exploratory experiences, concepts, and terminology in their own words to provide connections to the concept focused on in the lesson.
	Provide definitions, terminology, clear explanations, all characteristics, and elements of the new social studies concept as concretely as possible.
	Involve students in clear examples and nonexamples of the new social studies concept.
	Ask students to clarify the new idea and justify statements with evidence.
	Provide for student practice using the new social studies concept.
Expansion	Provide additional practice to help students use terms, definitions, and explanations of the concept experienced in the lesson.
	Provide application activities for the social studies concept in new, relevant contexts while at the same time helping students recall their original alternative explanations.
	Provide activities to help students transfer the new social studies concept to increasingly real world events.
	Provide a summary of the important events in the social studies lesson leading to the new social studies concept.

- *Expansion.* Involve students in making further applications and in transferring the concept to situations outside the classroom context. Students need to use the new concept to make sense of a variety of new experiences. Through reflection, the consideration of observations, and communication, students realize the usefulness of the new concept in interpreting the world around them. For example, ask them to describe and then to observe settings concerning everyday exposure to aggression in school hallways, the cafeteria, at the mall, and in local sports events. Ask students, "Where is aggression most likely to be found more frequently or more severely?" "What conditions are needed for aggression to thrive?" "What are the conditions where aggression is not commonly found?" "Where are these conditions found in school? Elsewhere?"

Teaching Concepts of Varying Complexity and Abstractness Differently

Teachers determine how concrete or abstract a concept is and its level of complexity. Then, activities are designed to give students sensory and concrete experiences with which to build meaning for the concept. With a complex and abstract concept such as *government*, teachers plan a unit with several learning cycles. Learning cycles might address a different essential attribute of the concept of *government* earlier in the unit. One or two learning cycles later in the unit help students put the individual essential attributes together into the major concept of *government*.

Building on Diversity

Cultural Factors and Concepts

Lynch (1998, p. 24) described culture as a "second skin" that becomes visible only when we brush up against one that's different. Sometimes well-prepared lessons fail to help students operationally define a concept. When this happens, a teacher might well remember Lynch's simile. Students' culture might be involved. Because our culture is a framework for our lives, it includes our food, clothing, furniture, art, games, and habits, as well as our deep beliefs and values. The way we look at the world, the way we relate to one another, and the way we bring up our children are culturally defined (Ayers, 1993). It is important for teachers also to recognize that there are many variations within each culture, including educational level, socioeconomic status, occupation, temperament, and personal experience, all of which are factors that influence our values and beliefs. Finally, children might not reconstruct the concepts we are trying to help them build because of other factors in their lives stemming from the culture they bring to school, including race, language, ethnicity, religion, gender, family, age, lifestyle, and political orientation. In such a case, students do not all achieve the lesson's objectives. What does the teacher do? Reteaching the lesson using different strategies might help. Some students, for example those from Middle Eastern cultures, consider their role in a group to be important. These students might benefit from a cooperative group approach to activities through which the concept is constructed. To teach concepts well, teachers need to know some basic information about the cultures and languages of their students. Resources describing learning styles of students from various cultures and appropriate teaching styles are *Understanding Your International Students: A Cultural, Educational, and Linguistic Guide*, edited by J. Flaitz (2003); *Passport to Learning: Teaching Social Studies to ESL Students*, Bulletin 101, by B. Cruz, J. Nutta, J. O'Brien, C. Feyten, and J. Govoni (2003), *Reflective Teaching in Second Language Classrooms* by J. Richards and C. Lockhart (2000); *Educating Hispanic Students: Effective Instructional Practices*, Center for Research on Education, Diversity & Excellence, Practitioner Brief #5, by Y. Padrón, H. Waxman, and H. Rivera (August 2002); and *Bilingual and ESL Classroom: Teaching in Multicultural Contexts*, 4th ed. by C. Ovando, C. Combs, and V. Collier (2006).

LEARNING CYCLE LESSON PLAN *Productive Resources*

NCSS

Standard VII

Grade Level: Primary and Intermediate

NCSS Standards: Production, Distribution, and Consumption

Exploratory Introduction

Objectives ⟶	Procedures ⟶	Assessments
1. Students review previous knowledge by identifying examples of natural, human, and capital resources.	1. Ask: "Do you like brownies?" The teacher says: "Let's make some. What do we need to make brownies?" List items on the board. Affirm all items are necessary to make brownies.	1. Record, on a checklist, students who offer appropriate suggestions.

Lesson Development

Materials: A set of three pictures of natural, human, and capital resources each, for each group

Objectives ⟶	Procedures ⟶	Assessments
1. Students define productive resources as the natural, human, and capital resources used to make a product or perform a service.	1. The teacher divides students into groups. Each group is given a set of pictures of natural resources. The teacher asks students to discuss the set in their groups. 2. Write *Productive Resources* on the board and identify some of the pictures in the set as natural resources. Then, write *natural resources* on the board under the heading Productive Resources. Ask students to identify other pictures in the set as natural resources and explain which characteristics in the picture they used to make the identification. 3. Repeat the process with the other two sets of pictures. Have students consider the following questions: What (natural) resources do you see in this picture? Are these people examples of human resources? Why? Why not? 4. Return to the list for brownies. Have students classify each item on the list. Ask: "What can we say a productive resource is?" 5. *Closure:* Write the class definition of a productive resource on the board. Have students decide whether it needs revision. Have students write the final definition they develop in notebooks.	1. Correct classification of items on the list is recorded on a checklist. 2. Class states an appropriate definition.

continued

Expansion

Materials: A set of five pictures of livestock production for each group

Objectives	Procedures	Assessment
1. Given a set of pictures of livestock production, student groups identify which of the items pictured are or are not productive resources in this business.	1. In groups, have students develop a list of items from the pictures that are productive resources used in livestock production and a second list of items that are not used. Then, have students identify at least two examples of human, natural, and capital resources on their lists. The group recorder writes on the board. The class and the teacher compare checklists. 2. *Assign Homework:* Talk with a parent or neighbor about his or her job, and identify the productive resources required in it. Then put an *N* by those that are natural resources and a *C* by those that are capital resources. Be prepared to share this information the next day. 3. Have students share findings from homework interviews and create a list of productive resources used by the people they interviewed. Ask: "Why did some of the people you interviewed only use capital resources? How can we describe the jobs that used both natural resources and capital resources?"	1. Check group lists for at least 80 percent accuracy.

Lesson Summary: Students briefly identify their lesson activities and conclude that those who produce goods are more likely to encounter natural resources as they work than are those people who perform services. Students conclude that natural resources were used to make the capital goods all workers use.

Summative Evaluation: Ask each student to complete the following tasks: (1) Identify a job someone else described in class. (2) Identify productive resources used in the job. (3) Identify each productive resource with an *N* for natural resource or a *C* for capital resource. Determine accuracy and appropriateness of parts 2 and 3 using the following rubrics.

continued

Productive resources rubric

All resources appropriate to the job were identified.	Most resources appropriate to the job were identified	Some resources appropriate to the job were identified	One or no resources appropriate to the job were identified
5 points	4 points	2 points	1–0 points

Natural and capital resources rubric

All resources for the job were identified and categorized appropriately	Most resources for the job were identified and categorized appropriately	Some resources for the job were identified and categorized appropriately	One or no resources for the job were identified and categorized appropriately
5 points	4 points	2 points	1–0 points

TIME FOR REFLECTION | ## What Do You Think?

Read the concept lesson on Productive Resources and answer the following questions.

1. What concept and subconcepts are the primary focus of this lesson?

2. What makes the presentation of the concept and its subconcepts appropriate for elementary students?

3. What examples and nonexamples are provided in the lesson?

4. List at least two critical attributes, presented for the concept and each of its subconcepts in the lesson.

5. How is the concept applied in the expansion phase, and how is its use expanded to contexts beyond that in which it was learned during the development phase?

6. What purpose does the homework assignment serve in this lesson?

 ## Assessment of Concept Learning

Concept learning can be assessed using a variety of the forms of assessment (see Chapter 14). Planning for assessment begins when the teacher constructs a concept web, map, or analysis. The teacher must decide how to operationally define the concept and determine the essential attributes that will be taught. These decisions are made by considering the developmental level of the students, the kinds of experiences they bring to class, the prerequisite concepts they have, and how the concept fits into the local, state, and national social studies standards. Constructing a concept web, map, or analysis involves the teacher in making these decisions.

Concepts have little use if they cannot be applied when needed. Therefore, assessment must involve the student in applying the concept. True/false, matching, and fill-in-the-blank items typically do not involve students in such application. A better paper-and-pencil assessment would be to have students complete a concept web. Or, a web might be constructed by a student at the beginning of the lesson and then revised after the lesson so the teacher can examine the changes made. Students can be given a task that is a version of a task they did during the lesson's expansion phase, as in the learning cycle on productive resources.

Using Technology

Examples of Resources for Helping Students Build Concepts

Technology offers a wide range of resources that can be used to expand students' experiences as they construct new concepts and reconstruct existing concepts. Recordings represent an older but still very useful technology that engages students' sense of hearing, while a picture engages their sense of sight. When the two are combined, an opportunity to process many more observations is created. For example, students may understand a historical scene very differently when hearing it described by a bystander during an audiotaped interview than they might when looking at photographs of the same event. The teacher must preview each resource before using it with students. Some videos, audiotapes, and similar resources are outdated, are biased, have little useful information, or are of poor quality. Before using a technological resource, teachers decide on its purpose:

Will it stimulate students' exploration of a concept?
Will it help students construct the concept?
Will it expand a concept into new contexts?

Teachers introduce students to the focus of the resource before it is used. Students know whether they will be presented with information that cannot be personally experienced except by audiovisual means. Next, teachers outline key observations students should try to make and discuss how these observations are recorded. After examining the resource, students share and discuss their observations. Teachers then ask prepared questions to help students extend their observations. Subsequent activities build on these experiences.

Video has the advantage of being easily made. Video can be of a field trip, a guest speaker's visit, student presentations, local sites of interest to the social studies program, or of any number of other events and activities. Video can be edited and used on websites or in PowerPoint presentations. A script is prepared for a video by the students, teacher, or students and teacher working together. The script may lay out the exact words to be spoken, as in the case of a class play on a concept such as *human resources* or *voting*. More often, a script indicates a sequence of activities and who is involved in each. Plans for activities and scripts are often general with specific details ad-libbed. Scripted videos allow for retakes if a major blunder occurs during videotaping. Digitizing video allows it to be watched when needed. The video title, credits, and other components can be added by using programs on the computer.

The criteria used in assessing the students must include whether they recognize the essential attributes of the concept that have been explained and the examples of these attributes with which they have worked and whether they can display their understanding of an operational definition of it. So, an assessment that asks students to give a definition of a concept can examine whether students memorized a dictionary or other definition. If students have to draw their understanding of the concept, describe it in a scenario, determine which of several statements show a person is using it, or apply it in some other way, it is possible to assess their meaningful understanding of the concept.

 ## Generalizations Show Relationships Between Concepts

As students construct concepts, they quickly try to build relationships between concepts that are called generalizations. Three generalizations follow. Middle school students developed these generalizations while investigating the question, "How are newer technologies, such as the cell phone, affecting communication between people?" Consider the evidence that does or does not support the generalization, and which concepts it is relating.

1. Newer technologies, such as the cell phone, have rapidly transformed communication between individuals and groups and have increased our stress as we are made aware of events as they are happening but cannot judge the quality of the information being communicated.
2. Cell phone technology has changed social life because we communicate very frequently with others but are less likely to reflect on what we say before we say it.
3. Text messaging encourages a sense of communication but also encourages isolation, because we do not need other people to be physically present while we communicate with them.

Forming Generalizations

Before formal schooling starts, students construct alternative or inaccurate generalizations from their limited experiences (Graue, 2006). For example, one generalization taught in social studies is that we depend on workers with specialized jobs and the ways in which they contribute to the production and exchange of goods and services. This generalization leads to statements such as "We use money to pay specialized workers and to exchange goods and services" and "An economic system determines what is produced by whom, how products are distributed, and who consumes them." Students might form an alternative generalization from a single experience, for example, that people can do other people's jobs easily. This generalization can result when a child notes that a parent is able to take care of a garden, make and fire a clay pot, and put new windshield wipers on a car. Social studies experiences provide students with a great number of opportunities to help them investigate relationships in the social world, construct generalizations through experiencing the interaction among concepts, and develop the knowledge and skills needed in reconstructing existing generalizations they brought into the classroom.

In a lesson constructing a generalization, a problem or question is posed. Questions are raised in the learner's mind by having students interact with information related to the topic during the exploratory introduction phase. Teachers help students identify questions using different strategies. Teachers can put students in a situation in which the information they acquire conflicts with what they expect or raises a question. They often find their prior knowledge isn't sufficient to resolve the conflict or to answer their questions.

Defining Generalizations

Generalizations are typically reconstructed as students gain more experience with the concepts included in the generalization. Instruction designed to help students construct meaning and learn generalizations is called *inquiry learning*. Distinguishing generalization statements from other statements is critical in deciding which instructional strategy to use. Social studies experiences with generalizations often begin with early childhood students and focus on personal decisions. As students grow cognitively, the curriculum content becomes more abstract and focuses on the civic or community impact of problems. Generalizations make up more of the content of social studies for older elementary and middle school students.

It is important to select and teach appropriate ideas that help students construct meaningful generalizations (Bianchini, 1998; Social Studies Center for Educator Development [SSCED], 2008). Generalizations are "big ideas." Reading about a generalization, or having a teacher tell you what it is, might not be rich enough in meaning for students to recognize the generalization as something relevant in life and worthwhile to learn.

Consider the following sample fifth-grade textbook generalization statement linking the economic concepts of *specialization, productivity*, and *profit*:

> The more specialized a worker is, the more profit can be made from the
> work, because each does the specialized work faster and with more accuracy.

On the basis of students' own experiences, the statement can only be accepted on authority and learned through memorization. This statement is not useful in students' everyday lives and only partly relevant to their prior experiences, so they may have difficulty understanding concepts such as specialization. Students do not encounter mass production as it is carried out in business and industry. They most likely see people individually completing an entire product, whether it involves building a model airplane or sewing a pair of drapes for the living room. Their own experiences with hobbies and class work are most often individually completed.

Even if students become highly specialized in particular tasks, such as assembling model airplanes or accessing information from the Internet, they are not likely to profit financially. Nor are they likely to understand the role of increased profits in the growth and success of business. Making or writing statements that try to simplify an idea so that a fifth grader can understand it is largely futile. The student does not have the necessary prior experiences with which to understand the relationships in the statement, so memorization results rather than meaningful understanding. Memorized information has little chance of being applied in new settings because it is not linked to real experiences.

Generalizations differ from facts and concepts because they:

- Identify relationships between two or more concepts
- Construct explanations of cause and effect
- Enable predictions of a future occurrence of the relationship stated in the generalization (Eggen & Kauchak, 2001)
- Are expressed as follows—an idea is expressed in a complete sentence while a concept is expressed in a single word or short phrase
- Are stated objectively and impersonally and require evidence to be gathered to support them

Linking words and concepts together to form sentences is part of natural communication. In the following discussion, a third-grade student named Spencer uses both concepts and a generalization to describe an experience:

> The president makes speeches. The president meets important people. He signs laws. The president gives big dinners. He talks to television reporters and answers their questions. *You have to be good at doing a lot of different things to be president.*

Among the concepts Spencer uses are *president, speeches, laws, dinners*, and *reporters*. These concepts summarize Spencer's experiences with each of these events and items. Spencer also makes a generalization that goes further than the concepts alone. He relates being president to having many abilities.

An example of a well-supported generalization that can be constructed by middle school students is, "Revolutions change people's ways of living because different opportunities for them to earn money become possible." In this generalization, the concepts of "revolution," "people's ways of living," and "earning money" are being related. Students can examine the American Revolution to see if there is support for this generalization. Then, they could consider revolutions in Russia, in France, and elsewhere. If they find there is support in each of these cases, then the generalization becomes well supported and highly accepted. If students find the generalization is not supported in each case, then they revise it to match what they have found.

Distinguishing Generalizations from Facts and Concepts

Because objectives for social studies lessons can be learning facts, concepts, or generalizations, teachers need to distinguish among them. The choice of an instructional strategy in a social studies lesson is matched to the type of statement selected for the learning objectives. Sometimes people mistake generalizations for facts. Consider the following statement: Riding in a limousine means you have a lot of money. This statement is a generalization, not a fact, for several reasons:

- The statement was not formed from one observation alone. We may have seen limousines and the passengers riding in them. We may have noted the quality of the clothes the passengers were wearing. But we have not seen their bank records or credit card bills. We are summarizing our experiences, not reporting a single event.
- The statement involves two concepts: *limousine* and *money*. The statement also describes a relationship between those two concepts when it connects "riding in a limousine" to "you have a lot of money." This statement can be used to make the prediction that anyone who we see riding in a limousine has a lot of money. We can check our prediction to see if it applies to the person we see riding in the limousine. Because we can use it to make a prediction and to check that prediction, it is a powerful statement, much more powerful than a statement of a concept. Of course, we are likely to find that this generalization statement is not supported when we investigate it. We might find that the person riding in the limousine hired it to celebrate a one-time personal event, such as prom night or an anniversary. Generalizations range in the amount of support they have. Yet, whenever a relationship is described between two or more concepts, we have a generalization. If the data we collect when we investigate the generalization indicates that it is not supported, then we can change our original generalization. Our generalization can be thought of as a hypothesis we are making and then investigating to decide whether it has enough support to continue using it.

Using Generalizations to Make Predictions

Generalizations are used to organize facts and concepts by summarizing them and describing the relationships among them. Once a generalization is formed, it can be used to make predictions of actions and events. Using the generalization that riding in a limousine means you have money, we can predict that a person who rides only in limousines would be considered wealthy by others in the community. If you have formed the generalization, "Text messaging encourages a sense of communication but also encourages isolation, because we do not need other people to be physically present while we communicate with them," we would predict that teenagers, who usually text message more than sixty-year-olds, might have less desire to gather together with friends than would the older people. Generalizations can be a starting point leading to the creation of a hypothesis and a test. If we use the hypothesis about text messaging and isolation, we could ask teenagers and adults of different ages to keep notes of how much time they are spending texting during a day and of how much time they are communicating in person with someone else. We can compare the information to decide whether there is any evidence that texting substitutes for in-person communication. The results of our data collection are limited, of course, but might lead us to change our original hypothesis and create a new generalization.

What generalization might this young child construct in the future
using his experience with such a big machine?
Photographer: Lynn A. Kelley

The predictive ability of generalizations is important because being able to predict events and actions gives us some control over our lives. Social studies helps students learn to predict, understand, and control events in their lives and as citizens of their society. Teachers help students form generalizations about their everyday life and use them to make predictions that affect their daily lives. They also help students discover inaccuracies in the generalizations they have formed and reconstruct the generalizations so that they have better predictive value.

Making a Literature Connection

The Message Is a Generalization

Some literature for children and youth involves messages that are generalizations. One example is from *Not One Damsel in Distress: World Folktales for Strong Girls*, a book of stories compiled and retold by Jane Yolen. The message is "Anyone can be a hero if he or she has to be—even girls—especially girls." This generalization connects the concept of hero with that of girls and with that of a cause "if he or she has to be." It establishes a positive relationship between girls and heroism. Another book, *Cuban Kids* by George Ancona, uses many photographs to foster the generalization that "Cuban children come in all shapes and sizes." *On the Same Day in March: A Tour of the World's Weather* by Marilyn Singer, emphasizes another generalization, the relationship between geography and various weather patterns: "Weather patterns are affected by the geography of a region." *How I Became an American* by Karin Gundisch, explores the generalization: "For immigrants to the United States, the hardships of language, finding work, and keeping a family united are balanced by the opportunities available." *Oh, Rats! The Story of Rats and People* by Albert Marrin discusses the generalization "people, rats, and the environment influence one another." *50 American Heroes Every Kid Should Meet* by Dennis Dennenberg and Lorraine Roscoe fosters the generalization that "everyday individuals have the potential to be heroes." *Dancing with Katya* by Dori Chaconas constructs the generalization that "disease can not only disable your body, but your spirit as well." *Ladies First: Forty Daring Women Who Were Second to None* by Elizabeth Cody Kimmel provides life stories that support the generalization, "People can go beyond traditional barriers to achieve their goals and make a difference in the world."

Types of Generalizations

Generalizations come in many forms. Some generalizations describe a simple relationship among a few concepts with which we have had many experiences, so we find the generalization easy to understand. For example, we find it easy to understand the generalization "All people must eat to survive." A simple generalization often is limited in its ability to explain and/or predict.

Other generalizations are complex yet we have had many experiences with them so we do not find them difficult. "Newer technologies, such as the cell phone, have rapidly transformed communication between individuals and groups and have heightened tensions as we are made aware of events as they are happening but cannot judge the quality of the information being communicated" is a complex generalization, but we have had experiences that enable us to understand it. More complex generalizations often have better power to explain and/or predict. Some generalizations are highly complex and relate many concepts, show complex relationships, and/or make predictions with a higher degree of certainty or accuracy and a greater degree of confidence. These are laws, principles, and theories. These highly complex generalizations require many experiences with the concepts they include and the relationship described in order to understand them.

Our experiences can be reviewed to decide whether we find instances where the generalization is not supported. If we do find such instances, we *must* revise the generalization or discard it. "Historical knowledge and the concept of time are socially influenced constructions that lead historians to be selective in the questions they seek to answer and the evidence they use" is a complex generalization. Our experiences may be limited if we have not had many opportunities to examine sets of primary historical documents that discuss an event from different perspectives. For example, we might read documents describing a march in 1878 in favor of giving U.S. women the right to vote from the different perspectives of those in the march, bystanders who did not want women to have the right to vote, bystanders in favor of giving women the right to vote, and women who wanted the right to vote but were afraid of what their neighbors would say if they marched. Until we have more of such opportunities and are involved in experiences in which we reflect on those opportunities, we will not be able to understand the generalization well nor to decide how well it is supported.

Teaching Powerful Generalizations

Generalizations are the most powerful form of social studies content for understanding and having some control over our lives. Generalizations also are the most difficult form of social studies content to learn. To understand a generalization, a student must first develop an understanding of the concepts used in the generalization, and then repeatedly experience the relationship among these concepts.

Reflect on the following generalization: "The features of the earth's surface vary as a result of geologic events, weather, and human decisions." The effects of a heavy rain on the playground dirt need to be observed several times to ascertain

---

TIME FOR REFLECTION | What Do You Think?

1. Below is a list of social studies concepts. Write three or four statements linking together some of the concepts to form generalizations.

consumer	producer	election	law
advertisement	candidate	political party	leadership
voter	family	workers	investor

2. Illustrate, by writing or drawing, your understanding of one of the generalizations you wrote.

3. Suggest several topics or problems that upper elementary or middle school students might study to learn aspects of this generalization.

4. What inquiry skills might students need to study these topics or problems?

If students are to apply a generalization at appropriate times, teachers must help them understand the concepts and relationships found in the generalization. Memorization of a generalization with little understanding of the concepts it includes results in students being unable to use it or even judge when to apply it.

the validity of this generalization. Students need to note that a heavy rain causes channels to form in the dirt and creates a delta where the dirt being carried off in the channel hits the sidewalk. They need to notice that lighter rain produces smaller erosion and deposits less dirt. They can measure approximately how long a rainstorm lasts and how much rainwater is collected in a rain gauge. They can predict the effects of storms of varying length and strength on the erosion of playground dirt, then go out to sketch and measure the depth and length of channels in the dirt after a storm.

At other times, students can build small dams out of heavy cardboard to see how they affect runoff and erosion on the playground during rainstorms. This is a time for checking predictions developed from prior knowledge against reality and modifying the generalization as needed. Eventually, students have enough experiences that they are able to apply them to the earth as a whole. They can begin meaningfully to understand the generalization that the earth's surface features vary as a function of geologic events, weather, and human culture.

A lesson focusing on a generalization has the following phases:

1. *Exploratory Introduction:* Identification of a problem or question
2. *Lesson Development:* Formation of a working hypothesis responding to the question; gathering of data (information) related to the hypothesis; evaluation of the data to decide whether it supports the hypothesis
3. *Expansion:* Application of the generalization constructed if the hypothesis is supported, or reconstruction and testing of the generalization if the hypothesis is not supported

The complete cycle used in teaching a generalization is described in Table 4.2.

The Exploratory Introduction Phase of a Generalization Learning Cycle

The question developed in the exploratory introduction phase is the starting point of a lesson helping students construct a generalization. A question can be posed by the teacher or, more meaningfully, by the student or a student group. Good questions are stimulating, making students take a closer look at something in their social and physical worlds (Schug & Beery, 1987). The question focuses the student on a cause and its result, or on an explanation. Good questions often start out as general "what" questions followed by more specific ones. Examples of general questions are: What happens? What do I see, hear, or feel? What does it do? What do you think? What happens if...? How many? What group...? Can you make...?

Poor first questions ask students about their knowledge of words or what the text or teacher previously said. They limit social studies to the recall of information

TABLE 4.2

Teaching Generalizations

Phase	Planning Required
Exploratory Introduction	Help students try out and confront their prior knowledge of the social studies generalization.
	Provide an opportunity for students to identify a question on which the lesson is focused. Start students thinking with a *key question* that involves them in an activity.
	Encourage students to work in cooperative groups and relate prior knowledge to the question.
	Bring out and make public students' prior knowledge of the question.
Lesson Development	Ask students to investigate a social studies generalization as a response to the question in the exploratory introduction activities.
	Allow students to gather data to provide evidence for a solution to their question while investigating the generalization.
	Ask students to analyze the data and formulate a conclusion to their question, comparing it to the generalization previously introduced.
	Provide closure on important aspects of the new generalization.
Expansion	Provide application activities for the social studies generalization in new, relevant contexts while at the same time helping students recall their original alternative explanations.
	Provide activities to help students transfer the new social studies generalization to more and more real-world events.
	Guide students in summarizing the important events in the social studies lesson that lead to the new social studies generalization.

by encouraging students to answer with what the teacher thinks is the "correct" reply instead of with what the students understand. If students ask poor questions, teachers need to help them rethink them (Kelley, 2009). Good first questions ask students to focus their observation of an event, pose problems, initiate data collection, and make comparisons.

Students probably will not understand the generalization if they cannot (1) clearly identify the concepts, (2) identify the relationships in the generalization, and (3) actively engage in experiences and use data involving the relationships.

In planning the lesson, teachers think about students' understanding of the concepts involved in the question, possible generalizations that could resolve the question, and what kind of information students need to collect to determine whether their generalizations are supported by evidence.

The Lesson Development Phase of a Generalization Learning Cycle

The inquiry lesson continues as students gather information about their question. Teachers provide guidance by asking questions such as the following:

What are some possible sources of information to be gathered?

What methods would help us gather the most useful information: direct observation, carrying out investigations, library and Internet research, surveys, or a combination of a few methods?

What materials and equipment do we need to carry out our investigation?

Can this method provide us with enough information to investigate our problem or do we need to combine it with another method to gather some different kinds of information?

How can we record and store the information obtained?

How can we communicate the information obtained to others?

How can we analyze the information we gathered?

Once students decide how they want to gather information, they are given enough time to do this. Some data gathering may be done out of school. Some in-school time is necessary, however, because students often need to discuss a next step in data gathering with their cooperative learning groups or they need advice on how to find and use an information source not previously considered.

As students gather data, they decide how to organize, classify, and categorize it. Data should be presented in a way that allows it to be easily and clearly shared with others. Students might use tables, charts, graphs, bulletin boards, drawings, oral reports, written reports, dramatic skits, panel discussions, models, or demonstrations. Well-organized data enables students to use it more successfully to decide the level of confidence they have in a generalization. Poorly organized data collection or presentation is of little use. It may not display identifiable patterns, encouraging false conclusions about the generalization.

The Expansion Phase of a Generalization Learning Cycle

Teachers help students construct a usable generalization. They also help students understand that, once they have a usable generalization, they need to apply it and transfer it to a variety of settings. When students begin to apply a generalization, it is always necessary to encourage them to think about its limitations. This can be accomplished by asking students questions such as the following pair: When is this generalization useful? Does the generalization always make good predictions? Students decide how widely the generalization can be applied. For example, do all

text continues on page 128

**LEARNING CYCLE
LESSON PLAN**

Using Technology to Investigate a Problem: Why Are Cities Built Where Rivers Come Together?

NCSS

Standards
II, III

Grade Level: 5 or 6

NCSS Standards: People, Places, and Environments and Time, Continuity, and Change

Exploratory Introduction

Materials: A set of drawings of Fort Duquesne (now Pittsburgh) for each small group (available at www.u-s-history.com/pages/h1195.html and/or http://members.aol.com/tabletopstd/Page4.html

Objective ⟶	Procedures ⟶	Assessment
1. Students identify a question related to Fort Duquesne that can lead to a generalization they can investigate.	1. Assign students to small groups. Have groups study drawings of Fort Duquesne. If needed, guide them to recognize that later the site would be Pittsburgh. 2. In discussion of the pictures, facilitate development of the question, "Why was the fort built in this location?"	1. A question is posed by students about Fort Duquesne that can lead to a generalization that can be investigated.

Lesson Development

Materials: Maps of the location of Fort Duquesne resources (a useful map with a close-up view of the three rivers found there can be found at www.expedia.com), chart paper and markers for each group; access to the following websites:

- An overview of the site of Fort Duquesne (www.socialstudiesforkids.com/wwww/us/fortduquesnedef.htm)
- A map and description of the role Fort Duquesne played in the French and Indian War (www.u-s-history.com/pages/h1195.html)
- Pictures and historical models of Fort Duquesne (http://www.spdconline.org/history/Facts/FortDuquesne.html)
- An overview of means of travel in the colonies (www.usgennet.org/usa/topic/colonial/book/chap10_4.html);
- Information on the use of the Hudson River for transportation (www.nypl.org/research/hudson/history/his1.html)
- Map showing a wagon road (http://www.ncmuseumofhistory.org/collateral/articles/Great.Wagon.Road.pdf)
- Access to www.google.com to locate sites dealing with cities on rivers in the United States and in other countries

continued

Objectives $\longrightarrow$	Procedures $\longrightarrow$	Assessment
1. Students' analysis of the data gathered supports the following generalization: "People used the river systems to transport themselves and their goods because roads were few and poor."	1. Provide maps of the region so student groups can discuss them and develop a response to the question. 2. Have each group write its hypothesis answering the question on chart paper and put it on a bulletin board. 3. Encourage students to search for information beyond maps to decide whether the data supports their hypothesis. Talk with them about what kind of data-gathering sources will be used. Suggest Internet sources (see materials). 4. Decide together how data will be presented. Help students recognize that groups must use a similar format in order to compare data gathered and to determine whether the data support a hypothesis. Note: charts may be useful. 5. Have student groups collect, organize, and present their data. 6. Have students compare data and decide whether any hypotheses are rejected because they do not have support. 7. Work with students to decide which hypothesis has the most support. The data will support the hypothesis "Fort Duquesne was built at its location because the Monongahela and Allegheny come together to form the Ohio at that point and *people used the river systems to transport themselves and their goods because roads were few and poor*. If groups have not developed a hypothesis similar to this one, and cannot support their hypothesis, have them reconstruct their hypotheses and collect and analyze additional data. 8. *Closure:* Write the supported hypothesis on chart paper and post it on the bulletin board, underlining the generalization that has resulted.	1. Student groups agree that the data support the generalization: "People used the river systems to transport themselves and their goods because roads were few and poor."

continued

Expansion

Materials: Internet resources

Objectives $\longrightarrow$	Procedures $\longrightarrow$	Assessment
1. Students' analysis of data supports the generalization: "Cities often are built where two or more rivers join because the goods and people going up and down the rivers all come together there."	1. Talk with students about whether they think the following expansion of the generalization has support: "Cities often are built where two or more rivers join because the goods and people going up and down the rivers all come together there." 2. Have student groups investigate this generalization using Internet sources to locate cities in such locations, explore their history, and determine whether there is evidence to support this generalization. 3. Have groups present their data using the agreed upon format used with the initial generalization. 4. Have the class decide whether the expanded generalization is supported or needs to be revised with additional data. 5. *Lesson summary:* Have students briefly describe the activities with which they have been involved and the initial and expanded generalizations for which they found supporting evidence.	1. Student groups agree that the data support the generalization: "Cities often are built where two or more rivers join because the goods and people going up and down the rivers all come together there."

Summative Evaluation Have each student locate a city in another country that fits the generalization: "Cities often are built where two or more rivers join because the goods and people going up and down the rivers all come together there." Then, have each student prepare an outline citing three pieces of historical evidence and three pieces of modern evidence supporting the generalization. Consider whether the city is an appropriate choice and whether each piece of evidence is appropriate and accurate.

places where rivers join have a city? As questions are raised, students are encouraged to investigate them through further surveys, interviews, or the use of a website that sends queries to students at schools all over the world. Generalizations can be reconstructed when students find they no longer address the data they obtained.

Formative Evaluation and Assessment

Students are assisted in reviewing their investigative activities to determine which activities are productive and which could be done differently. For example, some data sources may be very helpful, whereas others are limited. Some ways of organizing data may be more effective than others. Evaluating their activities enables students to make better decisions, better direct their own learning, become more aware of their own thinking and planning, and become more dependent on internal rather than external reinforcement. This is important to teaching meaningful and powerful social studies that develops citizens who are independent judges and decision makers.

Assessment is incorporated into the inquiry procedures that are used in a learning cycle focused on constructing a generalization. The teacher's role is that of a facilitator. In order to facilitate, the teacher works closely with groups to determine how well they are planning and collecting, organizing, and analyzing the data. Because such inquiry-oriented activities typically are done by small groups, the teacher uses checklists, anecdotal notes, and other means of recording how well each student is accomplishing his or her role in the group's work. At the end of the learning cycle, the teacher involves each student in a task that indicates whether each individual has a meaningful understanding of the generalization constructed in the lesson and is able to apply it.

Inquiry Teaching and the National Standards in Social Studies

NCSS

Standards

The "Principles of Teaching and Learning" in the *Curriculum Standards for Social Studies* describes five major components of a powerful social studies program (NCSS 1994b, pp. 11–12). These components enable students to carry out inquiry-based social studies: meaningful, integrative, value based, challenging, and active. These principles note that in social studies, students learn *connected networks* of knowledge, skills, beliefs, and attitudes that they find useful both in and outside school. Furthermore, the principles indicate that meaningful learning activities and assessment strategies focus students' attention on the most important ideas embedded in what they are learning. Teachers model seriousness of purpose and a thoughtful approach to inquiry. Teachers also show interest in and respect for students' thinking but demand well-reasoned arguments rather than opinions voiced without adequate thought or commitment. These principles, adopted by this national organization devoted to teaching social studies, support teacher and student involvement in inquiry-based and investigative learning aimed at helping students construct generalizations.

EXPANSION

Applying Concepts and Generalizations to Create Powerful and Meaningful Social Studies

The national social studies standards identify ten themes around which curriculum should be built at all grade levels. These themes represent major concepts in social studies such as "culture," "global connections," "power," "civic ideals," and "civic practice." Concepts such as these are called key concepts, major concepts, essential concepts, big ideas, superordinate concepts, etc. Although different labels are used for such concepts, it is clear that they are so important that it is not possible to meaningfully understand social studies without addressing them. It is also clear that students of different ages and with differing experiences will have different levels of understanding of such concepts. Teachers will work throughout the grade levels to help students continue to develop their understandings of these concepts, and likely this development will continue lifelong.

As students construct meaningful concepts, they also construct linkages, or relationships, between those concepts in order to explain events. As two or more concepts are related, they become generalizations that are applied in our experiences. To have a sense of control over our lives, each of us tries to explain why and how an event has occurred and to predict what might happen in future similar

TIME FOR REFLECTION | *What Do You Think?*

Using the national social studies standards, identify a major concept appropriate for study by a group of students whom you are observing or with whom you are working.

1. Construct a concept analysis for the identified concept.

2. Then, prepare a set of three to five interview questions to investigate how these students are constructing their idea of the concept.

3. Reflect on, and identify, important attributes that are and are not included in the concept by the students.

4. Identify experiences that could be implemented to help the students understand those attributes important to the concept.

events. It took people millennia to relate hygienic practices such as hand washing and keeping rodents out of homes to a reduction in disease. As people related the concepts of hygiene and disease, a great deal of evidence was found over time to support the generalization that, "Appropriate hygiene reduces our chance of getting a disease such as a cold." Today, this generalization allows people to have greater control over their health than did many of their ancestors. Generalizations are a very powerful part of social studies content.

TIME FOR REFLECTION | **What Do You Think?**

Generalizations are powerful, yet any generalization we form may be more or less inaccurate. We refine generalizations we use over time so they more accurately represent the experiences we have and the events we are trying to relate.

1. Develop three generalizations about one of the following topics that would be appropriate for learning cycle lessons for upper elementary or middle grades students: maps and map reading, elections and the electoral process, jobs and careers, advertisements and advertising, and the media and new technologies.

2. Explain why upper elementary and middle grades students should have opportunities to carry out investigations leading to the construction of a generalization even if the resulting generalization may be somewhat inaccurate.

3. Outline a learning cycle lesson that would involve upper elementary or middle school students in constructing one of the generalizations you developed in #1 above.

4. Assume your elementary or middle school students have applied the generalization they developed as a result of the lesson you outlined in #3 above in a new setting that is different from the one in which they constructed it. They found their generalization did not explain events in that setting. Describe how you might encourage them to consider the inaccurate generalization further and facilitate their reconstruction of it.

Summary

The development of generalizations is a primary goal in elementary and middle school social studies teaching. It is the most powerful type of social studies content students learn. Knowledge of generalizations provides meaningful predictions to help control events in our daily lives and our civic associations. To create meaningful learning, students must be able to interact in relevant ways with the concepts and relationships involved in a generalization. Generalizations are meaningfully understood only through active involvement. For children and youth, such involvement is both physical and mental. It enables students to work with data used to construct the generalization and to predict the outcome of a generalization. Therefore, the generalization is verified each time it is used.

In teaching generalizations, the three phases of the learning cycle help students identify a problem/question related to the generalization (*exploratory introduction*), collect data with which to verify the validity of the generalization and to predict the results of the generalization (*development*), and apply or transfer the use of the generalization to different contexts (*expansion*). One significant step in planning a generalization learning cycle is checking the application of the generalization in a new situation during the expansion phase. Students need to use their generalizations in a variety of situations if they are to become usable pieces of knowledge. They also need to discover that the generalizations they construct (1) may not satisfactorily explain a different situation or their investigation, (2) may not use appropriate procedures or resources, or (3) may need additional or more diverse information. Because the modern world involves students in complex and changing situations, it is important that they use generalizations in a variety of situations to learn when they are appropriate and when they need to be reconstructed. If students are not able to do this, they will be less able to participate fully as citizens.

Concepts are a basic component of powerful social studies content. Although factual information is necessary for forming concepts, social studies content is not acquired by memorizing facts. Teachers planning lessons identify and distinguish among the concepts they teach. Most concepts have more than one level of meaning and may be sensory, concrete, or formal, depending on the instructional methods used. All concepts are abstract because they are abstracted from many specific instances and examples.

The learning cycle helps teachers prepare lessons that provide the four conditions needed for conceptual change. The learning cycle fosters cooperative learning and a safe, positive learning environment; compares new alternatives to prior knowledge; connects new ideas to what students already know; and helps students construct their own "new" knowledge and apply it in ways that differ from the situation in which it was learned. When a teacher uses learning cycles in a classroom with a positive environment in which it is safe to take risks when learn-

ing and sharing ideas, students are more likely to have success in constructing powerful social studies concepts.

Recommended Websites to Visit

ESL Lounge: This excellent teachers' site is loaded with lesson plans, worksheets, teaching tips, printable board games, and reviews of notable ESL books.
www.esl-lounge.com

Pathways to School Improvement: An easy-to-navigate point of entry to gain access to some of the best resources on the Internet for teaching at-risk students.
www.ncrel.org/sdrs/areas/at0cont.htm

"Fighting Cholera With Maps." A lesson plan teaching the generalization: Mapping techniques can be used to understand social issues and to solve problems.

www.nationalgeographic.com/resources/ngo/education/ideas58/58cholera.html
"What's My Interest?" A lesson in economics education on the concept of interest
for grades 3–5
www.econedlink.org/lessons/index.cfm?lesson=EM377
"All in Business." A lesson on the concepts of costs and benefits for grades 6–8
www.econedlink.org/lessons/index.cfm?lesson=EM376
"Look You're Wearing Geography." Teaching the concept of interdependence.
www.nationalgeographic.com/resources/ngo/education/ideas58/58wearing.html
"Regions: A Hands-On Approach." Teaching the concept of region.
www.nationalgeographic.com/resources/ngo/education/ideas58/58regions.html
Teaching Generalizations about Native American Cultures Across the US
http://edsitement.neh.gov/view_lesson_plan.asp?id=347
"Why Do We Need Authority?" An upper elementary/middle school lesson on
the concept of authority
http://www.civiced.org/index.php?page=fod_ms_auth02_tg
"What Are the Possible Consequences of Privacy?" A middle school lesson
constructing a generalization about the advantages/disadvantages of privacy
http://www.civiced.org/index.php?page=fod_ms_priv06_tg

5

How Do Students Develop Citizenship in Democratic and Global Societies?

EXPLORATORY INTRODUCTION

In a "Point of View" article in the January/February, 2009 issue of *Social Education*, the premier journal of NCSS, you can read the following as a teacher's comment during an interview:

> ... we teach how a bill becomes a law, but that is not what democracy is all about. We haven't taught a problem in the community and then how to solve that problem. There is a great need to teach more civic engagement. "True Democracy" is not what teachers, administrators, and parents want taught. They want students to follow rules. [1]

The Civic Mission of Schools is a report issued in February 2003 by the Carnegie Corporation of New York and CIRCLE (Center for Information and Research on Civic Learning and Engagement). It provides a framework for creating more effective civic education in the schools and represented, for the first time, a consensus on the issues among the nation's leading scholars and practitioners. The report identifies six promising approaches to civic education from a review of the research: (1) Provide instruction in government, history, law, and democracy; (2) incorporate discussion of current local, national, and international issues and events into the classroom; (3) design and implement programs that provide students with the opportunity to apply what they learn through performing community service that is linked to the formal curriculum and classroom instruction; (4) offer extracurricular activities that provide opportunities for young people to get involved in their school and communities; (5) encourage student participation in school governance; (6) encourage students' participation in simulations of democratic processes and procedures.

---

[1]"Name withheld upon request, oral interview with Ann Ackerman, November 21, 2007."

What are your ideas about

1. When a social studies teacher feels it necessary to withhold her/his name when giving an opinion in an interview outside of the classroom, what does this say to you about the state of social studies education and the state of American society today?
2. Do teachers have the right to be critical of the school system for which they work?
3. Which of the six promising approaches to civic education identified in *The Civic Mission of Schools* do you remember experiencing in your K–12 education?
4. Which of the approaches do you think you would particularly like to use with your students when you teach?
5. On December 10, 1948, the General Assembly of the United Nations adopted and proclaimed the Universal Declaration of Human Rights [Resolution 217 A]. Article 19 of the Universal Declaration of Human Rights is:

   > Everyone has the right to freedom of opinion and expression; this right includes freedom to hold opinions without interference and to seek, receive and impart information and ideas through any media and regardless of frontiers.

   Which do you see as a better society, one in which people are orderly and obey its leaders or, one in which people are free to speak out on issues and express what they believe to be just and fair decisions or choices?

Chapter Overview

Since the end of the Cold War, many U.S. social studies educators have been asked by leaders and educators in nations who have not had democratic traditions for many years to help them plan new civic curricula and train teachers to teach for democracy. These requests and domestic problems have stimulated dialog concerning the practices of civics education in the United States. As a result of his experiences, John Patrick (2003) has concluded that the twenty-first-century civic mission of schools requires that at all levels of preadult education and in teacher education students should learn a minimal universal definition of democracy so that they will be able to compare and evaluate nations and regimes throughout the world according to a common basic understanding of democracy and democratic behaviors.

Being born in the United States or having an American parent makes a child a U.S. citizen. Citizenship, however, must be learned and practiced as the child grows and comes into contact with people and groups both in and out of the home. Patriotism, or love of country, is an attitude established early in life. Children and adolescents tend to be positive about national symbols, to like and trust their political leaders, and to be highly supportive of their political systems. Researchers have found such positive attitudes even when students have little understanding of their country or its government (Torney-Purta, 1990). But are love of country and positive attitudes toward symbols and leaders enough to live in a democracy in the twenty first century?

The school, especially a public school, is an important societal institution that greatly affects young people. It teaches, through formal and informal processes, attitudes and behaviors toward society. This chapter examines political knowledge, values, and law in light of concepts students need to learn to become responsible, participating citizens. It examines the ways in which children learn to become active citizens and the roles schools and teachers play in this process. As you read and reflect on the chapter, keep in mind that (1) the United States is more ethnically diverse than ever in our history, (2) citizens of a democracy must share common values, and (3) governmental actions must reflect those values while protecting the rights of minorities.

Chapter Objectives

1. Explain the importance of knowledge, values, and participation to citizenship.
2. Explain the importance of the individual in a democracy.
3. Explain the role of the hidden curriculum in forming students' ideas about power, authority, and governing.
4. Identify political science concepts and values that are essential to understanding democratic government.
5. Identify lesson characteristics that are helpful in accommodating learning in a multicultural democracy.
6. State a rationale for community participation or service learning.
7. Give examples of student participation activities that are appropriate for elementary and middle school students.
8. Explain how democracy can be modeled and practiced in the school and classroom.
9. Assess recommendations on ways in which elementary and middle school students can study law.
10. Explain the media's role in educating citizens.
11. Identify ways to help children make wise use of the media in school and their lives.
12. Reflect on the ethics teachers need to practice and model the learning of democratic ideals and practices in the school, community, nation, and world.

DEVELOPMENT

 ## Defining Citizenship in a Democratic Society

Because citizenship is a given to those born in a nation, how the population learns appropriate behaviors necessary to be a member of this group, called *citizens*, is determined by that group. Schools are one of the societal institutions that have an active role in helping children and youths learn to live and work in their nation. In the United States, the centrality of citizenship education in the social studies curriculum has enjoyed widespread acceptance. Political scientists, with their emphasis on rational thought and decision making, often criticize what is taught in the schools as being a naive, unrealistic, and romanticized image of political life. They say that the ideals of democracy are confused with the realities of politics (Jennes, 1990). The elementary curriculum is singled out for criticism because it tends to fail to recognize the presence of conflict and failure within a democracy. Ideals for the appropriate focus span a continuum from stressing patriotism and loyalty through examining and solving social problems to centering on social and governmental criticism.

During the 1970s, social studies educators involved with Project SPAN defined the role of the citizen as focusing on relationships between individuals and political entities and organized efforts to influence public policy (Superka & Hawke, 1982). Because such relationships are found at neighborhood, community, state, national, and international levels of government, citizenship activities fit into all levels (K–12) of the expanding horizons curriculum model that dominated the field for many years. Social studies is the subject that is primarily responsible for teaching the knowledge, skills, and values needed to understand and participate effectively in the political system and to deal responsibly with public issues.

Rapid changes in the 1980s and 1990s increased not only the amount of knowledge in the world, but the speed with which individuals encounter this knowledge and the need to process information critically and react appropriately. During this same time period, the old political balances and forces of the world changed greatly. As a result more nations tried, and are continuing to try, to implement democratic forms of government while at the same time becoming increasingly ethnically diverse and economically interdependent. New problems for people emerged or became more difficult to solve as the number and complexity of their variables increased. Unfortunately, given our time and resources, the ability of many adults and children to understand and intellectually grow as rapidly as the social world changes is limited.

During this same time, the National Council for the Social Studies (NCSS) developed standards for social studies programs that identified power, authority, and governance and civic ideals and practices as separate, equally important strands of the social studies K–12 curriculum. Also included were science, technology, and society and global connections, two often-neglected themes in past curricula.

In the 1990s, the International Association for the Evaluation of Education Achievement (IEA) began preparations for its second study of civic education. This study would assess not only knowledge about government and power, but also student attitudes and beliefs about government and the future in the United States and 23 other nations. Preparing instruments for such a large undertaking required careful planning and the establishment of common goals. Judith Torney-Purta, a distinguished educator and researcher on political socialization, who is currently chair of the International Steering Committee for the IEA Civic Education Study, summarized five views of citizenship education (March, 2000):

1. Knowledge of facts about government and constitutions, as "real citizenship"
2. Willingness to vote (and to look for information about candidates, their positions on issues, etc.)
3. A basic level of trust in institutions, sense of political efficacy, an ability to be thoughtfully critical about government policies, and other political attitudes (sometimes related to participation)
4. Respect for political opinions different from one's own and respect for the rights of ethnic, racial, or language groups
5. Participation in service learning or community projects (or politically relevant youth organizations)

Dr. Torney-Purta points out that her research and that of others clearly indicate that different people and different nations emphasize one or more of the five definitions.

 ## Developing Political Awareness

The model of civic education the IEA committee used to guide their planning and research for development of assessment instruments is given in Figure 5.1 on page 138. It is complex and illustrates the many contributing factors or forces in a person's political socialization (Torney-Purta, Schwille, & Amadeo, 1999). Its complexity suggests that even a carefully planned civic curriculum with explicit objectives might not be equally successful for each child or group of children to whom it is taught. The model applies to children in more than 20 nations.

In the center of the model is the individual child surrounded by socializing agents with various degrees of contact with the individual. In the United States, where various forms of media, including television, radio, movies, and the Internet, greatly affect the lives of children, perhaps media should be included in the circle surrounding the individual labeled *carriers of goals into actions*. The outer ring represents the more distant community of national and international institutions whose laws, policies, and theories impact nations and communities (Torney-Purta, Schwille, & Amadeo, 1999).

Political science is the discipline that studies governments. Political scientists focus their studies on three very different types of questions concerning governing:

Who has the right and power to govern?

How do governments organize themselves to make and enforce political decisions?

How do groups of people influence the political process?

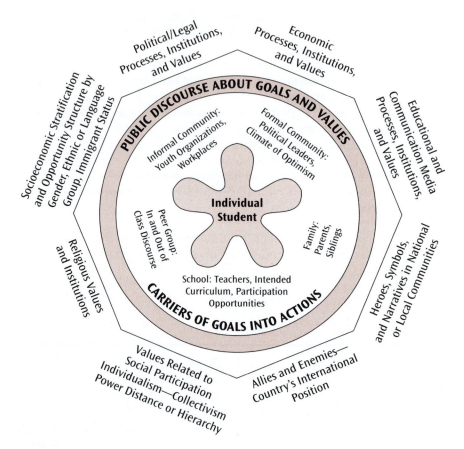

FIGURE 5.1

Model for IEA Civic Education

Source: Civic Education Across Countries: Twenty-four National Case Studies from the IEA Civic Education Project. (1999) Edited by Judith Torney-Purta, John Schwille, and JoAnn Amadeo. Amsterdam, Netherlands: IEA. Used by permission.

The first question examines historical and philosophical ideas; the second question deals more with the formation of governmental and public policies. The third question addresses politics as it is formally and informally practiced.

All citizens have the need for, and the right to, services from their governments. Citizens in a democracy have special powers and obligations:

- Bestowing both the power and right to rule on a government of their choice
- Selecting those who perform day-to-day governance
- Debating and compromising to instruct the government on the needs of the people and the types of policies desired
- Monitoring the actions of governments and keeping informed on issues related to the collective good
- Balancing their own self-interest with the collective good

Political scientists believe that the capacity to participate effectively in the politics of a free society requires knowledge of the political system and a real understanding of what one is trying to accomplish. Citizens must have the following qualities:

1. An interest in public affairs and a sense of "public regardedness"
2. Tolerance and respect for conflicts arising from divergent values and beliefs
3. The ability to examine consequences and to assess the likelihood of alternatives achieving desired goals
4. The ability to assess both long- and short-term consequences (Brody, 1989)

In summarizing the first phase of the IEA assessment in civics, the editors of the report identified a number of agreements in goals and some accomplishments, concluding that

> there is a universal or near-universal commitment to certain goals or themes. Civics education should be cross-disciplinary, participative, interactive, related to life, conducted in a nonauthoritarian environment, cognizant of the challenges of societal diversity, and coconstructed with parents and the community (and nongovernmental organizations) as well as the school. Despite extensive efforts, however, there has not been universal success in any country in formulating programs that optimize the possibility of achieving these goals for all students. (Torney-Purta, Schwille, & Amadeo, 1999, p. 30)

TIME FOR REFLECTION | **What Do You Think?**

1. As you examine the IEA model of civic education, at about what age do you think children are likely to begin functioning politically: that is, encountering and solving interpersonal problems with people whose viewpoints differ from their own? Explain your reasoning.

2. What are some possible ways in which teachers and educators can work with other community groups to help attain the goals of civic education?

 ## Citizenship and Standards

NCSS
Standard VI

In elaborating on the meaning of power, authority, and governance and civic ideals and practices, NCSS (1994b) identifies understanding the historical development of the structures of power, authority, and governance and their evolving functions in contemporary society as essential for civic competence along with examining the dynamics between individual rights and responsibilities. The study and practice of civic ideals with the goal of full participation in society through multiple interactions with individuals, groups, institutions, and organizations is the means to attaining a democratic government.

Goals 2000: Educate America Act of 1994 called for every U.S. adult to possess the knowledge and skills necessary to exercise the rights and responsibilities of citizenship. The Center for Civic Education directed the development of the *National Standards for Civics and Government* (1994). These K–12 standards focus on answering five questions:

1. What is government and what should it do?
2. What are the basic values and principles of U.S. democracy?
3. How does the government established by the Constitution embody the purposes, values, and principles of U.S. democracy?
4. What is the relationship of the United States to other nations and to world affairs?
5. What are the roles of the citizens in U.S. democracy?

These standards focus on both the content and students' actions that demonstrate that they understand and value the content. The skills are embedded in the standards through the use of verbs such as *identify, describe, explain, evaluate a position, take a position*, and *defend a position*. The development of participatory skills for democracy is present in recommended community and classroom activities. The goals of these activities are devoted both to monitoring politics and government and influencing politics and government. The standards provide specifics for two of the NCSS themes: VI (Power, Authority, and Governance) and X (Civic Ideals and Practice). As with other statements of standards, many state and local school systems used the *National Standards for Civics and Government* and incorporated its ideas into their own standards. So also did the National Assessment of Educational Progress and private testing organizations developing tests for states and school systems.

NCSS

Standards
VI, X

Key Concepts and Values

In some states, courses focusing only on civics have been designed for eighth grade. However, government and civics have also been assigned by the curriculum to all social studies classes. Emphasis in civics and government has been placed on preparing the individual to deal with the structure of U.S. government and its agencies and to be a future voter. The focus tends to be on the mechanics of government rather than on concepts and values underlying the procedures of governing and making and enforcing laws.

The task of identifying concepts to teach young students has been left largely to textbook authors. In K–4 textbooks, publishers have included political science concepts, but to a much lesser degree than geographic and economic concepts. The most frequently appearing concepts include *law, president, government, citizen, nation, rules, taxes*, and *Congress* (Haas, 1991). Table 5.1 suggests concepts that have been derived from the professional literature and through joint deliberation among civic educators worldwide. Despite the fact that political science concepts are often highly abstract, several of the organizing concepts listed in Table 5.1 have examples that are present in any situation where a

TABLE 5.1
Essential Concepts and Values in U.S. Democracy

amendment	decision making	international	pluralism
authority	democracy	justice/fairness	politician
Bill of Rights	diversity	law making	power
changing laws	due process	law/rule	privacy
citizenship	equality	leadership	representative democracy
civil servant	freedom	loyalty	respect for the individual
civil society	government	majority	rule of law
compromise	honesty	minority	security
conflict	human dignity	nation	self-discipline
conflict resolution	human rights	open-mindedness	social responsibility
consensus	influence	order	tolerance
Constitution	interdependence	participation	viewpoint

number of people interact, including at home and in the classroom. Creating a classroom community for learners is an important tasks for teachers at all grade levels. Creating a classroom community for learning is an important task for teachers and students at all grade levels.

School is often the first experience in which children interact with a variety of people who judge them on their actions. Schooling requires students to behave in new and different social situations. Lessons on political concepts such as rules, leadership, viewpoints, conflict resolution, and compromise, and the relationships among those concepts help students understand how to act in their school social situation in which they are one among equals. These lessons also provide rationales for desired classroom behaviors for the collective good of students and learning opportunities.

Socialization is the name given to processes whereby young people learn proper behaviors. Elementary and middle school teachers devote much time to socializing students. When elementary students attend school they are likely to learn to function in a larger, more diverse, and pluralistic group than they have previously encountered. Middle schools bring together students from several elementary schools and often create environments with a greater and more diverse pluralism than do elementary schools. Middle school students are engaged in another developmental task with political overtones: identifying appropriate roles in the larger community where, because of greater personal and cognitive powers, they are beginning to function more independently. Youthful maturing often brings countersocializing experiences. Students challenge the authority they previously assigned, without question, to certain people including parents, teachers, and government officials.

To function democratically, democracies have faith in their citizens to do what is right. Agreement on what is right comes from having common convictions and beliefs about what is important or of value. At a minimum, these include the provision for the basic needs of individuals and the respect for the human dignity of individuals. Such ideas are learned through socialization. However, socialization can become conformity for the wrong reasons and to the detriment of the human dignity of some or all of the population. For that reason, citizens are encouraged to question what is happening and decide whether the consequences of actions are those they consider important and of most worth or value. Democratic values and beliefs (civic ideals) associated with democracy and identified in formal position statements from the NCSS (1989, 1994b) are listed in Table 5.1.

Schools reflect the values of the society. Such values as self-discipline, consensus, equality, tolerance, fairness, loyalty, honesty, and freedom are of great concern in the functioning of all classrooms. Citizens must agree on the values and their importance if society is to function smoothly and have its laws observed. Elementary and middle school students need to examine the meanings of the values and predict what life would be like if people did not practice these values. In so doing, students decide on the type of society they want and need and come to understand the reasons for acting in ways that bring about such a society. Citizenship education in a democracy is going beyond conceptual understandings to include the development of *participatory skills*:

- *Interacting* through communication and cooperation in political and civic life
- *Monitoring* the work and actions of political leaders and institutions
- *Influencing* others and institutions to deal with issues consistent with democratic values and principles (Patrick, 1999)

The contribution of political science to social studies includes helping students find out how people use their own *personal power* to make a difference in their lives and others' lives. It also examines how individuals join together to make decisions *collectively* for their common good.

Research on democratic attitudes reports that the classroom climate and the hidden curriculum of the school directly affect students' attitudes. Even if they are not recognized formally in the social studies curriculum, concepts and values related to politics, law, and political science are presented indirectly throughout the K–8 curriculum and individual schools and classrooms. Students or groups of students may witness and experience discrimination, favoritism, and tyranny rather than tolerance, equality, and justice. This can result from classroom or school climates in which teachers accept stereotypes as facts about individuals or seek to keep particularly vocal or influential parents happy at the expense of equal opportunity for all individuals in the school to grow and learn.

Conflicting individual or small-group interests concerning school curriculum have resulted in various pressure groups seeking changes in school board policies or state and national laws. Formal instruction in democratic citizenship through the social studies curriculum is needed to help students overcome misconceptions and misunderstandings about democratic philosophy and U.S. government. A commitment to democratic principles, a willingness to engage in the democratic process, and the affirmation of core values are key elements of the bond that joins us as "We the People" (NCSS, 1997).

Michael Hartoonian, R. Van Scotter, and W. E. White (2007) point out that the American Revolution began the defining of the American citizen whose responsibility is to continue to work to "form a more perfect union." Debating current issues is a key element of American citizenship. They point out that all civic discourse creates tensions among four pairs of fundamental values:

- Law vs. Ethics
- Private Wealth vs. Common Wealth
- Freedom vs. Equality
- Unity vs. Diversity

Each of these pairs of values is in conflict. At any day or time period, the United States of America can be viewed as being in a continuum of tensions among the eight key values found in these four pairs. This is the struggle democratic minds must learn to embrace, reconcile, and balance in personal, local, and national situations. The continuity of America is maintained by deciding where along these four lines of tensions we need to function on each civic choice. American history is not without change. To move forward the America of our founders' dreams to a "more perfect union," these four pairs of values must be constantly examined and become an integral part of the beliefs and actions of citizens. Hartoonian and his colleagues suggest that when teaching social studies, teachers should be constantly looking for opportunities to examine one or more of the value tensions present. Teachers also must help students view problems within this struggle and reach personal decisions given their experiences and knowledge base.

The primary-grade Learning Cycle on page 144 defines *voting*, one of the most fundamental concepts related to decision making and the individual use of power. A clear understanding of the concept of voting and its consequences is essential if students are to be involved in the process of making some decisions concerning their activities in the classroom, school, clubs, or community.

NCSS

Standards

In the United States, citizens make their wishes known by voting for representatives, voting directly on issues in referendums, signing petitions, writing letters, displaying signs, taking part in support rallies, and giving speeches. The rights of freedom of speech, freedom of the press, peaceful assembly, and petitioning the government are guaranteed by the First Amendment of the U.S. Constitution. Participation in such activities is expected to reflect evidence of truthfulness and thoughtful consideration of the issues. Provisions are stipulated for legal redress of grievance for untruthful information and malicious intent. Information and the ability to use it gives a person the power to influence others, make better decisions, and exert control in his or her life. To make decisions on political issues, people must be informed. The information and skills learned in school contribute to the goals of informed citizens.

LEARNING CYCLE LESSON PLAN Voting Is a Way to Make Decisions

NCSS
Standards
VI, X

Grade Level: Primary

NCSS: Power, Authority, and Governance; Civic Ideals and Practice

Exploratory Introduction

Materials: A picture for each child to color that includes a boy wearing a shirt; crayons for each child

Objectives ⟶	Procedures ⟶	Assessments
1. Students recall decisions they have made in the coloring task given and during the day.	1. Provide each student with crayons and a picture to color. When pictures are completed, have a class discussion asking small groups to stand and show their pictures. Ask, "What are some of the decisions you made when you colored your picture?" Note that lots of individual decisions were made to color the pictures.	1. Students identify decisions made when coloring their pictures.
2. Students explain that people can make their own choices for many things.	2. Ask, "Besides the colors on the pictures, what are some other decisions you made today? Let's think about why we made these decisions today." Ask students to raise a hand if they colored the boy's shirt red. Ask, "How did you go about deciding to color the boy's shirt red? Who colored his shirt blue? Why did you pick blue instead of red?" Repeat with other colors. Ask, "Just because I like yellow (or another color) the best, does that mean everyone should wear yellow shirts? Why not?" Restate and affirm students' conclusion: When each person makes their own choice and does their own action, it is called *individual choice*. Practice saying the term *individual choice*.	2. Students give personal and logical reasons for their choices in the task, such as for their choices of color(s) to use.
		3. Students affirm and accept the right of others to make individual choices.
	3. Ask, "What is an example of an individual choice you made today? What might be an individual choice you will make later today when you are home?"	4. Students offer appropriate examples of individual choices.

continued

Lesson Development

Materials: Large poster for each group to color and crayons or markers

Objectives ⟶	Procedures ⟶	Assessments
1. Given a whole group problem, students discuss the problem and decide important ways in which individual decisions differ from group decisions. 2. Students decide that everyone should have a fair way to take part in the whole-group decision making and offer ways for this to happen. 3. Students list steps used in the voting process, placing them in logical order.	4. Tell students: "Suppose that the principal came to our room and gave us a great big picture like the one you colored earlier. Suppose she said that she wanted the class to color this picture to be displayed on the classroom door. Suppose she wanted the class to decide, as a group, how to color the picture so that everyone is happy with the way the picture looks. Ask, "How could we make the decisions on what colors to use for the various parts of the picture?" 5. Explain to students that a popular way groups of people in the United States make decisions is to vote on possible choices. Ask, "Has anyone heard of voting? Can anyone tell us about voting?" 6. Provide examples of possible voting choices if needed. Sometimes members of a family might vote on where to go for lunch or what to buy for someone's birthday present. 7. Ask, "Can anyone tell us what happens when a vote is taken?" List students' responses and continue discussion or fill in missing parts to get at least the following events. Number the statements in chronological order. Ask, "Of the things we have listed, which would be done first? Then what would happen?" 8. Be certain that the minimum steps include the following: a. A problem with two or more possible choices for answers is identified. b. Members of the group discuss the good and bad points of selecting each choice. c. Members think about what they have heard and decide what they believe to be the best choice. d. A vote is taken with everyone voting for only one choice. e. The winner is the choice with the largest number of votes.	1. Students identify at least two appropriate and important ways individual decisions differ from group decisions. 2. Taking a vote is suggested. 3. Students respond and give some information about voting taking place. 4. Students listen and offer suggestions for the steps in voting, placing events in logical order.

9. Practice the voting process, using the steps. Perhaps vote on the colors to use on a large poster of the picture colored earlier or some other poster. Follow the steps identified, referring to each as it is done.

4. Students decide that voting with the largest number as the winner is a fair way to make a choice.

10. Ask, "Are you pleased with the choice we made as a group?"

Have students take turns coloring the poster using the colors they voted to use. Then display the finished poster and discuss students' reactions to its appearance. Ask, "What steps did we follow in making our decisions?"

11. Ask, "Do you think you would like the poster as well if only one of the students in the class colored it and made all the choices? Would a poster completed by one person reflect what the class wanted?"

12. Ask, "What are some other times when we need to make choices in our class." List responses and post the list in classroom.

13. *Closure:* Ask, "How do you suggest that we make such choices? Will you remind me when we have choices to have a class vote?" Throughout the year, have students vote on these and add them to the list when appropriate.

5. Students suggest colors, give reasons, vote, and count votes in an orderly manner.

Students list steps and say the most votes wins.

6. Students offer logical times for voting decisions in the classroom.

Expansion

Objectives ➔	Procedures ➔	Assessments
1. Students explain that the winning choice is not everyone's first choice when voting is used. (Some people might not be as happy with the result of the vote as those who voted for the winning choice.)	1. Ask, "When we voted on the colors to make the large poster, did any of you get all of of your first choices? Raise your hand if that happened to you." (Some might not raise their hands.)	1. Students respond that not everyone got their first choice and that some people were not as happy as others with the choices made.

continued

2. Students state their acceptance of the principle of supporting the choice of the group to maintain harmony and fairness within the group.

3. Students state that citizens should accept the winner of a fair election and give appropriate reasons.

2. Ask, "Were you happy with the way the poster looked? Were you disappointed that your first choices were not all what the class selected?" Ask, "Think back, did anyone complain?" Ask a specific student why he/she did not complain. Ask others also. Discuss the responses.

3. Explain: When we vote on something, we are making an agreement with the others in the group. We are willing to go along with the group's choice.

4. Ask, "Why would someone be willing to do this? When have you done this before? Is there ever a time not to do what a group votes to do?" (Expect students to say when someone gets hurt, sick, etc.) Respond appropriately. Give hypothetical examples of group decisions and have students say whether they are acceptable decisions and explain their reasons. (1) We vote on what songs to sing for Grandparent's Day. (2) We vote that Betty should have a chocolate birthday cake.

5. Give examples of some adult group votes with which children might be familiar. For example: "Teachers in the school decided...."

6. Explain the election of the president is a vote by the citizens for someone who will represent the American people and work for all of the people. Ask, "Why do we need someone to make these decisions?" When a president is elected, those who voted for the winner celebrate.

7. When we elect a president, someone else doesn't get elected. Ask, "How do the people feel who voted for the person who did not win? How do they act? Why don't they move to another country?"

8. Explain that every four years, we have a presidential election and can select a new president. Citizens can replace a president with a new vote. Some people

2. Students respond that not everyone got their first choice and that some were not as happy as were others with the choices made.

3. Students identify times to accept and not to accept the group's decision. They indicate they want "fair votes" and appropriate group choice. Students say yes to 1 and no to 2. (Betty should select her own cake because it is her birthday.)

4. Students say that citizens should accept the winner of a fair election and give at least two appropriate reasons.

continued

will like the new president better than the old one. We also use the courts to be certain that the president makes fair decisions. The president also shares some of the law making with other elected people. The president can't just make any decision he or she wants to make. We will talk some more about how that is done on another day.

9. *Lesson Summary:* Ask: "What is the name of the way in which groups make decisions? Why is voting a good way to make decisions? Will people support the choice of a vote even if it is not their choice?"

5. Students respond with correct answers and logical related explanations.

Note: This lesson may be followed with

- Other lessons on decision making and alternative forms of decision making
- Practice voting on decisions made in class
- A lesson on the election of the president, especially in a presidential election year

TIME FOR REFLECTION | **What Do You Think?**

1. In what potential daily activities might teachers systematically help children learn to use their power for the good of the entire class?

2. List four typical classroom decisions you believe primary students could make during the school year to practice democratic procedures and values associated with voting.

3. For an exploratory introduction for primary-grade students, a teacher selected a coloring activity followed by reflecting on the decisions made in coloring the picture. How would you modify the beginning of the exploratory introduction for grade 4 or 5?

4. What additional values, concepts, and skills might you have to be ready to examine and teach as students begin to practice voting and accepting the results of a vote?

5. Older students may be familiar with formal voting carried out in elections. What concepts related to formal practices used in voting in the United States might you add to the learning cycle for older students?

If possible, discuss your responses with a peer.

Assessing Civic Education in U.S. Schools

The most recent assessment of what U.S. students have learned about government is the 2006 National Assessment of Educational Progress (NAEP) test in civics. Average scores of fourth graders on the civics 2006 NAEP test improved significantly over the 1998 testing, especially among the low performing students. Three of every four students or 73 percent of the fourth graders tested scored at or above the basic level, meaning that they demonstrated at least a partial mastery of civics knowledge and skill fundamental for proficient work for fourth grade. There were large differences between scores by race. In 2006 the gap between the races at all grades revealed a decrease in the gap between the white and Hispanic students at grade 4 and no changes between the white and black students. The 2006 scores for grades 8 and 12 did not yield an increase over those of 1998. When students were asked to identify related topics they studied, the results revealed similar responses as in 1998 including:

- Your community
- President and leaders of country
- Rights and responsibilities of citizens (a significant increase over 1998)
- Rules and laws
- How people solve disagreements
- How government works

Eighth-grade students indicated that of the topics that they studied there were a few changes:

- U.S. Constitution
- Congress
- Political parties and elections voting (a significant increase over 1998)
- How laws are made
- State and local government
- Court system (a significant increase over 1998)
- President and cabinet
- Other countries governments
- International organizations (a significantly lower response than in 1998)

Data Sources: http://nationsreportcard.gov/civics_2006/ (Retrieved June 28, 2009); http://www.nationsreportcard.gov/civics_2006/c0123.asp?tab_id=tab1&subtab_id=Tab_1#chart (Retrieved June 28, 2009) fourth grade; and http://www.nationsreportcard.gov/civics_2006/c0123.asp?tab_id=tab2&subtab_id=Tab_1#chart (Retrieved June 28,2009) eighth grade

Resources for Citizenship Education

Because many groups view citizenship education as one of their roles, the resources for citizenship education are literally countless and, all around us. Even before the Internet made materials readily available, many interest groups and businesses were working to promote their views about citizenship and their values by making free materials and guest speakers available to clubs and schools. These resources promote their perspectives on public or civic issues. Determining the quality of such materials for use in the classroom is important. Commercially prepared materials such as textbooks, video, film, and software often go through official state procedures to receive adoption approvals. But materials sponsored by interest groups and businesses generally do not go through such a screening process. Pressures to use sponsored materials may be great. Parents and teachers find it increasingly difficult to assume that the resource materials students can obtain are appropriate and within the abilities of students to understand and evaluate. To assist parents and teachers, various education agencies and organizations have joined forces to assess materials and to provide rating systems. The education department for the state of California provides a large database of resources matched to the state objectives.

The National Council for the Social Studies joins in coalitions with educators, business, government, and civic organizations to promote the teaching of powerful social studies. Professional education organizations make teachers aware of opportunities, issues, and resources through meetings and publications. They also investigate, debate, take positions, and speak out to promote their goals related to improving the teaching of their subject matter. Among the groups with which NCSS works are The American Promise and Children's Book Council.

Media Resources

Freedom to discuss and comment on the actions of government and its representatives is essential in a democracy. Freedom of the press is among the specific rights guaranteed by the first amendment to the U.S. Constitution. Throughout history, newspapers, magazines, and books have provided citizens timely information. The critical use of such resources is among the skills promoted in social studies education. Media plays a major role in forming public opinion because it controls the knowledge of citizens. Failure to be media literate is a major obstacle to successful adult civic participation (Nelson, 1990).

Special newspapers and magazines for students at various ages, such as *Scholastic Magazine* and *Time for Kids*, attempt to encourage them to develop skills and habits necessary to keep current with events and acquire civic knowledge. Local newspapers have allied to create a program called Newspapers in

Making a Literature Connection

Selecting a Trade Book That Stresses Social Studies

Teachers have an important role when using trade books for social studies instruction. Perhaps the most important is selecting a book to use as a read-aloud with all students. Such a book needs to focus on social studies content and objectives. Young learners need help in recognizing fact from fiction and identifying what is important for solving social problems from what is irrelevant, imaginative, or distracting. When taking class time to read a particular book, the teacher indicates to the students that this particular book is important. While reading a book to a class, the teacher has the opportunity to model critical reading behaviors with social studies content. This is not possible if the social studies content in not present or if the facts and issues addressed are not related to the learning objectives.

Two important advantages of using a good social studies book over other instructional resources are the ease of selecting to read only a part at one time period and reviewing portions by simply turning a few pages. Books that deal with the complexities of the American political system and its abstract ideals present a challenge to young learners. But do cartoon illustrations represent the topic in a way that is appropriate to the importance of the content or the office and its impact on people? Cartoons, as they are and have been used in newspapers, use symbols and exaggeration to comment on issues and send a message.

In learning social studies information, many topics are very serious, and a teacher must examine the illustrations that send lasting and powerful messages. The words that are used to explain pictures should guide the thinking of the reader to the important social studies information and attitudes. Gaining the attention of young learners is never more important than teaching accurate and important content and democratic, civic ideals and practices.

Teachers must be careful when they hear or read that a book has won an award because awards are given to books for different reasons. A book might excel in the criteria for the award and fall far short on other important aspects, especially the criteria of meeting the objectives for a lesson on the presidency. *Woodrow for President* (1999), *Woodrow, the White House Mouse* (1998), *Marshall, the Court House Mouse* (1998), and *House Mouse, Senate Mouse* (1996) by Peter W. Barnes are worth examining for the balance in treatment between interest for young readers and selection of important content. Although the mice are visually appealing for young learners, older students and adults can find many cleverly illustrated details and recognize many historical accuracies in American political life. The words, while rhyming, incorporate actual historical quotes and popular phrases. Future teachers who have used these books in field placements say that the students are quick to recognize some of the historical facts, such as the use of names of former presidents and office holders. They report that their younger students enjoy making detailed comparisons between the appearance of the real rooms in the government buildings and the illustrations in the books. Older students enjoy the challenge of using their textbooks or the Internet to search for references to historical events and quotations. Another idea would be to research the events of real presidential campaigns and compare them with what Woodrow G. Washingtail did to get elected. Woodrow G. Washingtail and his families and supporters also have values and character traits that can be identified and discussed.

A book about the legislative branch presented in an interesting way that appeals to elementary students is *My Senator and Me* by Senator Edward M. Kennedy. The process of passing a bill is related by Splash, the senator's Portuguese Water Dog, who accompanies the senator to his office and through Washington, D.C., as he works to pass an education bill.

The U.S. Constitution is one of the most important documents in American history. The poetic language of the Constitution and the fact that much of it was written in the eighteenth century makes it very difficult for twenty-first-century K–12 students to read and understand.

continued

continued

Cathy Travis provides a service to students and teachers with her book *Constitution: Translated for Kids*. The entire Constitution and its 27 amendments are printed on the left-hand column of the page with the corresponding translation in the right-hand column, creating an ideal opportunity for comparison of the language and vocabulary building. Additional features include a glossary of legal terms and explanations of all amendments and proposed amendments, with explanations of the positions for and against each. The book concludes with an extensive discussion of the fundamental concept in American democracy—*balance of powers*.

Phillip Hoose in *It's Our World Too! Stories of Young People Who Are Making a Difference* illustrates how students take stands to help others, to improve their local community and the environment, and to reduce crime and violence. Hoose provides a short chapter investigating courageous acts by youth. He also provides 14 examples of young peoples' projects and explains how to organize personal power to become active citizens in solving civic and global problems. A good trade book can be used to motivate students to study as well as provide information and raise important questions about how and why people behave in particular ways or make particular decisions.

Education whereby lessons on how to use the newspaper are provided to teachers, and the local paper is provided for every student in participating classes for a week. News magazines such as *Time* and *Newsweek* have created special educational programs in which students subscribe to the magazine at a reduced rate. Teachers receive weekly teaching guides and have the opportunity to select specially prepared packets on issues and enduring concerns prepared from the news agency archives. Most of these organizations also have websites that support teachers with lesson ideas and special sections for students that explain concepts related to stories receiving current media coverage.

Teachers often help students learn about events and the obligations and procedures for reporting news through activities such as producing a newspaper on events in their own classroom or in a time period under study. Often students or teachers ask questions about events in the local community or about international issues they encounter through studying current events. Such questions make excellent topics for units of study or local problem-solving activities. Students in grades 4 and 8 who took the 1998 NAEP in civics and who reported using newspapers, magazines, and books weekly or once or twice a month scored higher than students who said they rarely or seldom ever used them.

Elementary and middle school teachers who regularly use current events report doing so because they illustrate social studies content with current examples, helping students see the authenticity and need for studying the social studies curriculum. Current events is a vehicle through which students can learn about other nations. Students need important skills to become active citizens: gathering information, analyzing statements, identifying bias, defining problems, summarizing viewpoints, and drawing conclusions. These skills are taught and reviewed by studying current events. The outcomes of studying current events are values and attitudes such as developing empathy, reducing ethnocentric thought, building global awareness, recognizing interdependence, appreciating others and their views, encouraging tolerance, and realizing the need and importance of being an informed, active citizen. Teachers use a variety of resources when studying current events, with local newspaper and large urban papers being the most frequently mentioned, followed by television. News magazines including special youth editions and programs rank third in frequency of use (Haas & Laughlin, 2000).

Mary Hepburn, director of the Citizen Education Division at the Carl Vinson Institute of Government at the University of Georgia (1998), elaborates on the impact of electronic media as a socializing agent that needs serious reconsideration in the social studies curriculum. Hepburn relates that as early as 1979, Neil Postman predicted that television was fast becoming "the first curriculum," meaning that it would surpass the influence of schools as a civics education agent. Today, the vast majority of people in the United States receive their news through electronic media; nearly two-thirds of U.S. homes have more than one television; and more than half the children have their own televisions. The increase in individualized media use, especially by young children, means that both teachers and parents need to help students learn to use electronic media, including television, video, iPods, and computers, in meaningful and appropriate ways that help them gain knowledge and still have prosocial, democratic interactions with the great diversity of people who are their fellow citizens. More attention needs to be given to the power of the media to influence directly and indirectly people's knowledge and perceptions. Everyone needs to be aware of the media's potential to distort and mislead through repetition, bias, and stereotype.

Television relies on pictures to present its stories. Television journalists criticize their medium for having scripts so short that they distort the news. Time restrictions prohibit providing a perspective to frame stories and impede providing complete statements of the various viewpoints (Trotta, 1991). The Children's Television Act of 1990 limited the number of minutes of ads per hour in children's programs and required stations to air educational shows for children as a condition of license renewal.

Because all youth and especially those from lower socioeconomic backgrounds spend much time watching television, television is a socializing and educating force in their lives. Allen Smith (1985), a teacher in New York City, developed lessons critically examining popular television shows as a way of asking his students to examine the character traits of good citizens and ways in which people can influence the quality of programming.

A website devoted to creating critical viewers of the media is associated with the Yale University Family Television Research and Consultation Center. The site contains activities to help learn and teach about television viewing habits, careers in television, determining reality from illusion, avoiding the reinforcement of stereotypes, dealing with controversial issues, reasoning with ethics and morality, and researching the impact of acts of aggression and societal violence. Each of these topics reveals the great impact television has on U.S. culture. Another comprehensive site on media issues, containing teacher lesson plans for the elementary grades teachers, is the Media Awareness Network.

Computer usage is increasing in schools and holds great potential for social studies education and for bringing together people from all over the world to address shared issues and problems that are often global in scope and characteristic. C-Span provides teachers with daily lesson plans on breaking news that can be downloaded. It presents news broadcasts for use with students along with special newscasts that support school subjects. Computer use has created many new words, one of which is *teledemocracy*, which has three dimensions:

- Using the Internet for sources of public information
- Engaging people in electronic discussions
- Facilitating political participation, including signing petitions and communicating through letters and articles (Larson & Keiper, 1999)

Websites such as Speakout.com and UNICEF's Voices of Youth are examples of teledemocracy.

Computer usage places an increased demand on social studies educators to teach the full range of media literacy skills. This is particularly evident when computers are connected to the Internet with its wide use of video, pictures, and cartoons. With the glut of information, students more than ever need to be active in critically evaluating what they see, hear, and create. Teachers can accomplish these objectives through lessons in which students study and use each form of media and compare the various forms of media. Lesson ideas that accomplish these ends are included in the following list:

1. Examine the presentation of a story as it appears in a television news broadcast, a newspaper, and a news magazine. Compare how each medium covers the story. Use a chart with categories such as facts, background explanation, emotional words, opinions or viewpoints, and graphics or pictures.
2. Analyze news stories in the newspaper and television for their length and content. Discuss these findings and students' feelings about what they have found.
3. Compare different types of television programs and written articles. Have students identify what they like and dislike about various programs and articles and which are most appropriate in answering various types of questions.
4. Follow a big news story through its development over time. Make lists of the knowledge learned on each day. Ask new questions and form tentative conclusions as the study progresses. When the story is over, review the experience. Identify which of the tentative conclusions were accurate. Identify the most helpful questions asked. Make final conclusions and judgments on how objectively and completely the story was presented.
5. Examine the trade-offs involved in the quality of information and the speed of transmitting a story. Decide at what times speed or details are more important.
6. Ask students to generate questions that they still have after reading or hearing a news story. Research these questions.
7. Interview adults about some very significant event (past or present) and ask how they got their information.

8. Interview local journalists about their profession and the problems they encounter in their work.

9. Have students assume the role of a journalist. Have them write various types of articles and produce their own newspaper, video, or website. As they encounter the problems of the journalist, discuss these problems, having students describe their feelings about the problems and the solutions used by the class or by the editor.

Law-Related Education

The law-related education movement began because of the concern of lawyers and educators over the failure of the traditional textbook approach of civic education to provide a living content and vibrant activities for students (Starr, 1989). Advocates of law-related education (LRE) often criticize school civics curricula because students are taught the unrealistic perspective of a society that is in harmony and free from conflict. LRE provides many opportunities to examine the conflict between self-interest and the common good. Legal issues require careful examination of disagreements and conflicts. Mediation as a procedure for settling disagreements is usually taught as a way to avoid costly and negative actions that might lead to involving formal justice procedures. Examining the resolution of issues illustrates how society deals with conflicts for the common good and protects dissent through the concepts of individual, minority, and human rights.

LRE is supported and promoted by the American Bar Association, which can be contacted through its website. Often, local and state bar associations work with school systems by training teachers and by providing guest speakers. Judges, police officers, and lawyers are frequently asked to speak to classes. Field trips to courts to observe the daily meaning of the loss of personal freedom and to legislative bodies to observe the process of making laws supply students with information on LRE topics.

LRE lessons stress active student participation in learning concepts and performing value analysis. Role-playing, simulations, mock trials, structured discussion, and analysis of stories containing moral dilemmas or expressing viewpoints are frequently used. Lesson content centers on the need for laws, human and legal rights, individual and civic responsibilities, processes of the legal system, and the important legal principles and values found in the Constitution and the Bill of Rights. Special projects on criminal justice and the judiciary system have been developed for intermediate and middle school students.

LRE seeks to foster the growth and development in students of knowledge and behaviors needed by citizens living in a pluralistic and democratic society. It is appropriate to use with primary-grade students, and its topics are authentic problems children have as they relate to children, adults, and institutions (McBee, 1996). It is recommended that LRE programs be designed to promote growth in several of the LRE learning outcomes listed in Table 5.2 (Anderson, 1980). Table 5.2 suggests how

TABLE 5.2

Critical Learning Outcome Continuums in Law-Related Education

Outcomes Children Move Away From	Outcomes Children Move Toward
Perceiving law as restrictive, punitive, immutable, and beyond the control and understanding of people affected	Perceiving law as promotive, facilitative, comprehensive, and alterable
Perceiving people as powerless before the law and other sociocivic institutions	Perceiving people as having potential to control and contribute to the social order
Perceiving issues of right and wrong as incomprehensible to ordinary people	Perceiving right and wrong as issues all citizens can and should address
Perceiving social issues as unproblematic	Perceiving the dilemmas inherent in social issues
Being impulsive decision makers and problem solvers who make unreflective commitments	Being reflective decision makers and problem solvers who make grounded commitments
Being inarticulate about commitments made or positions taken	Being able to find reasoned explanations about commitments made and positions taken
Being unable to manage conflict in other than a coercive or destructive manner	Being socially responsible conflict managers
Being uncritically defiant of authority	Being critically responsive to legitimate authority
Being illiterate about legal issues in the legal system	Being knowledgeable about law, the legal system, and related issues
Being egocentric, self-centered, and indifferent to others	Being empathetic, socially responsible, and considerate of others
Being morally immature in responding to ethical problems	Being able to make mature judgments in dealing with ethical and moral problems

Source: "Promoting Responsible Citizenship through Elementary Law-Related Education," by C. C. Anderson, 1980, *Social Education 44*(5). © National Council for the Social Studies. Reprinted by permission.

teachers can evaluate their success in teaching about the law. The desired outcomes of LRE are listed in the right column. The left column lists behaviors and perceptions that not only are opposite, but also reflect a person who is uninformed and lacks both a sense and desire for community. Table 5.2 can be turned into an assessment record by adding a rating scale and comment space under each statement so teachers can track the classes' or individual student's responses over a period of time. By rewording the statements into sentences and adding a numbered rating scale between the statements, Table 5.2 can be changed into a self-rating attitudinal measure for older students.

At the basis of our nation is the importance of the U.S. Constitution and the principles of government set forth in the document and its amendments. The flag

text continues on page 160

LEARNING CYCLE LESSON PLAN Presidential Oath

NCSS

Standards
VI, X

Grade Levels: Middle and Intermediate

NCSS Standards: Power, Authority, and Governance; Civic Ideals and Practices

Exploratory Introduction

Materials: Several pictures of current and/or former U.S. presidents

Generalizations

The United States is a nation ruled by a body of laws, not by any one person. The U.S. Constitution is the guide for all laws and acts of our government.

Objectives ⟶	Procedures ⟶	Assessments
1. Students recall and identify different actions that the U.S. president can and cannot do.	1. Assign students to small groups. Show several pictures of the president or past presidents of the United States. Ask, "What are some of the things the president does?" Then ask, "What do you think the president can't do?" Assign small groups and ask students to create a list of responses for each question. Share lists, creating a class list on the board. 2. Discuss questions: "Would you want to be president? Why or why not?"	1. Record students' responses on a class list noting the accuracy of their responses.

Lesson Development

Materials: Picture of a U.S. president taking the oath of office; poster on which is written the presidential oath; Internet materials, or appropriate websites, through which students can explore process of becoming a president

Objectives ⟶	Procedures ⟶	Assessments
1. Students identify the steps a person follows to become president of the United States.	1. Ask, "What is the process by which a person gets to be president of the United States today?" Discuss and help students, in small groups, compile steps of the process using reference materials from Internet sites or the websites themselves. Share group ideas about the process and create a list. Add any of the following ideas students have not identified.	1. Students use materials and discussion to identify the steps a person follows to become president of the United States.

continued

a. Declare yourself a candidate.

b. Win pledges of votes in primary elections.

c. Be nominated by a political party as their presidential candidate.

d. Campaign for office.

e. Win the election.

f. Prepare to take over and appoint major helpers and advisors.

g. Be inaugurated (officially and formally sworn in by taking the presidential oath).

2. Students use the presidential oath in determining the relationships of the Constitution to the duties of the president

2. Display a picture of the president taking oath. Tell students that all U.S. presidents have taken the same oath. During the campaign, candidates for president promise they will do lots of things. Ask, "What are some of the things they promise? What do you want the president to swear to do?" List students' ideas. Ask, "Does anyone know what the actual oath is?" It is written in the Constitution, Article II, section 1:

I do solemnly swear (or affirm) that I will faithfully execute the office of president of the United States, and will to the best of my ability preserve, protect, and defend the Constitution of the United States.

3. This is the promise that tells us what a president must do, no matter what has been promised.

Discuss the meaning of the presidential oath Ask, "Are there any words in the oath that you don't understand?" (*Execute* means to carry out, not to kill.) "Does this oath include some or all of our ideals? Do you think it says all it should say? Why or why not? What appears to be the most important part of this oath?" How important is the Constitution to the United States? Is it more important than the president, Congress, the Supreme Court, and the military forces? Why? What does the Constitution do for us? What does having the president swear to preserve, protect, and defend the Constitution tell us about how our founders, and Americans in general, view the law? What does it say about the importance of particular people or particular offices or positions?"

2. Appropriate summary statements describe the relationship of the role of laws and the president.

continued

4. *Closure:* Ask students, in their small groups, to develop a summary statement describing how the United States is ruled. They should point out the role of laws as indicated in the lesson's key idea. Share statements. Develop a class statement.

Expansion

Objectives ⟶	Procedures ⟶	Assessments
1. Students predict which other occupations might take an oath to protect and defend the U.S. Constitution.	1. Review what was learned about the oath of the president. Present the following list of occupations and ask students to identify those for which the person swears an oath: lawyer, town council member, judge, teacher, doctor, soldier, governor, mayor, police officer, accountant, senator, member of Congress, citizen, member of the clergy. Ask, "For which of these occupations would a person be asked, as the president, to take an oath to preserve, protect, and defend the Constitution?" Mark the list according to the students' predictions.	1. Students create a logical list of predictions.
2. Students collect data to determine the accuracy of their predictions about who takes an oath to preserve, protect, and defend the U.S. Constitution.	2. Check the predictions. In pairs, have students write letters, do library or Internet research, or interview people in these occupations. Assign each pair one occupation. Ask about their oaths and how the oath influences what they do when working. Ask students to prepare a summary statement on the occupation for which they collected data. Conclude by discussing the summary statements and the importance of the Constitution to people in the United States.	2. Students prepare an accurate summary statement identifying who takes an oath to preserve, protect, and defend the U.S. Constitution.
	3. *Lesson Summary:* Ask students to review activities of the lesson. Then ask, "Who has responsibilities to preserve, protect, and defend the Constitution? Should all Americans, or just some, take an oath to the Constitution? How and when should they do this?"	

Note: Appropriate topics for learning cycles related to various aspects of the Constitution, political and legal occupations, and the process of naturalization might follow this lesson.

TIME FOR REFLECTION *What Do You Think?*

1. What types of things do you anticipate the students saying they want the president to do?

2. What answer would you accept from students to the question "What does the Constitution do for us?"

3. At the beginning of the Expansion, the plan says to review what was learned about the oath of the president. List several things that you would want the students to say.

4. Examine your answers to question 3. Which responses recall facts? Which require statements of conclusions?

5. Students might not finish their reports for the expansion in a short time during class, especially if they interview someone. How do you suggest handling this problem to complete the lesson including all responses?

and the president are the symbols of the United States with which most people, especially children, are most familiar. Knowledge about the Constitution, its content, and importance is an essential objective for social studies lessons. The Learning Cycle on page 157 addresses the importance of the Constitution.

 ## Participating in Democracy

Citizens are expected to participate in their communities. At the beginning of this chapter, you were asked to consider whether certain behaviors were those that would be performed by a good citizen.

In the nineteenth century, when fewer people were educated, most students were being prepared to become political, economic, or military leaders. Schools specifically taught students to be leaders and stressed the obligations of leadership as an important value. At the beginning of the twentieth century, when the rural nature of the United States was quickly giving way to the rise of industrial cities accompanied by a great influx of immigrants, Arthur Dunn of Indianapolis became one of the first public school educators to focus the social studies curriculum on identifying community problems and developing solutions. In 1915, Dunn became a member of the Social Studies Committee and convinced other members to incorporate service learning into two of their recommended course offerings: Community Civics for ninth grade and Problems of Democracy for twelfth grade (Wade & Saxe, 1996).

Even though service learning was promoted as an appropriate pedagogical model for citizenship education, it was largely replaced by other elements of the social studies curriculum, and only individual schools and teachers remained devoted to its use. Today, participation and service learning are being examined again because of changes in society. Some potential claims and benefits for community participation have been identified:

- Gaining a sense or a stake in the community
- Gaining a sense of self-worth and responsibility
- Practicing such important skills as cooperation, decision making, problem solving, and planning or organizing projects
- Gaining exposure to positive role models and career possibilities
- Increasing a sense of control over their environment
- Increasing personal interaction with a wider variety of people of other ages and cultural backgrounds (Procter & Haas, 1990)

Wade and Saxe (1996), in their review of empirical evidence for the impact of community service learning, reported that research was far from conclusive on the positive impact of service learning on social studies–related goals. Still, educators, politicians, business, and service communities consider service learning viable, and the number of people and schools taking part in it is increasing. A survey by the National Center for Education Statistics (Skinner & Chapman, 1999) found that 38 percent of middle schools in the United States had students participating in community service activities.

Traditionally, citizen participation has been categorized as one of four types of behavior:

1. Participation in aspects of the electoral process
2. Participation in grassroots citizen actions
3. Involvement in providing advice to form governmental policies and practices
4. Participation in obligatory activities

Recently, participation has been viewed with a broader sociopolitical definition: volunteer service through the donation of time and money and mutual self-help group projects addressing common problems (Langston, 1990). *Service learning* is a

TIME FOR REFLECTION **What Do You Think?**

Before reading further, record your answers to the following questions:

1. In what type of situation(s) might the average citizen assume a leadership role?

2. What are three ways in which citizens of differing interests and abilities might serve their community?

3. What variables can you think of that might help or hinder a citizen's ability to serve his or her community?

4. In what kinds of service activities can the elementary and middle schools involve their students?

5. What opportunities are present in the school for students to perform services?

particular form of community service that incorporates service in the community with curriculum objectives and classroom activities and discussions (Hepburn, 2000). In social studies, Rutter and Newmann (1989) advocate the connection be to issues such as social responsibility, improvement of the common good, and opportunities for meaningful political participation.

All people have personal power. Only a few people exert political power daily. The informal use of power most likely occurs within less formal social institutions, such as family, friends, neighbors, and community-based organizations or clubs. The organized and formal use of power and influence is associated with political institutions beginning at the community level. In today's world, many issues and concerns are not limited by geographical boundaries. The larger the distribution of the issue, the more likely it is that legal and political organizations play a role in the solutions. Whereas political activism receives the greatest amount of publicity, social activism has responded more quickly to the needs of people throughout history, improved the lives of vast numbers of people, and prompted many of the social organizations and much of the social legislation taken for granted today. Social action is of particular importance to a large and diverse democracy.

School-Based Community Service Projects

Today, citizens are greatly concerned with the apparent alienation of youth and various population groups. Many see volunteer and mutual self-help types of community service as having an important role in correcting societal problems. They seek to involve young people in community and service activities. Community participation programs include a "passionate commitment to promote reasonableness, tolerance, fairness, and respect" (Langston, 1990, p. 304). Eyler and Giles (1999), using the service-learning model, report that experience enhances understanding and this understanding leads to more effective participation and actions.

In 1996, NCSS and Farmers Insurance Group joined forces to start the American Promise Network to conduct educational outreach activities promoting the use of *The American Promise*, a video series and program that encourages service learning and community participation. This program encourages teachers and students to practice service learning and promote the values of preserving freedom, encouraging and acknowledging responsibility, fostering participation, making hard choices, using information, providing opportunity for all, using leverage for change, deliberating with others, and seeing common ground.

In addition to individual character-building attributes, community service is seen as having the potential to vitalize the curriculum through authentic life experiences that require students to use social and intellectual skills. Following an extensive survey of community service projects, Procter and Haas (1990) identified six specific types of school-based activities that are often labeled as community service:

1. Using the community as a laboratory in which to practice skills learned in the classroom as a part of the regular curriculum. For example, students might record an oral history of the community and prepare it for use in the school or local library.

2. Special events or co-curricular activities sponsored by the school or a club. An example would be students taking part in a disaster relief drive.
3. Service programs that require a minimum number of hours of service for graduation.
4. Specially designed courses with class work and participation components. An example is helping organize a recycling center.
5. Programs designed for specific groups of students, such as students at risk or those with disabilities. An example is having these students use their skills to tutor or read to younger students or to help with a Special Olympics contest.
6. Career-oriented programs with emphasis on specific work skills or a professional orientation in which the students work part of the school day.

Participation activities are undertaken by students after careful study and preparation. Students must know why they are involved and how to carry their projects to completion. Teachers and other adults assist students in preparing for such projects. According to Wade (2000), quality service-learning projects require willing and honest reflection throughout the project in a classroom climate based on caring, mutual respect, and openness to divergent ideas. Table 5.3 illustrates social participation. Three types of service found in schools today are school, community, and individual. Social participation is shown on a continuum of possible activities ranging from a one-time activity requiring only a small commitment of time to long-term projects requiring a regular commitment of time and using multiple intellectual and social skills. Sustained periods of service in the field are needed for gains in political knowledge, participatory skills, and a feeling of understanding politics (Hepburn, 2000).

School service projects are centered on activities in the school. Tutoring younger students, performing skits to teach safety or health information to other students, making tray decorations for hospital or nursing home patients, and collecting food or blankets for the needy are examples. Community projects involve

TABLE 5.3

Hierarchy of School-Based Community Service Projects and Learning Outcomes

Project Type	Skills	Values	Citizenship Concepts	Grade Levels	
School Service Project	Identifying needs, organizing, group dynamics	Cooperation, self-esteem, pride in accomplishment	Participation, activism	K–12	Basic
Community Service Project	Communication, critical thinking, decision making	Respect, brotherhood, empathy	Community and democratic values	3–12	
Individual Service Project	Time management, problem solving, adaptability, self-direction	Human dignity, justice, responsibility	Appreciation of cultural diversity, social justice	7–12	Complex

students in working with or through governmental and community organizations. Helping on a cleanup drive, planting trees in a park, and helping to build a children's playground are examples of community service projects. School and community projects are more predominant in grades K–8.

The individual service project is one in which the individual assumes the major responsibility in carrying out the service for an extended period of time. Tutoring in an adult literacy program, being a scout leader, and volunteering in a nursing home are examples of individual service projects. Table 5.3 also lists the skills, values, and citizenship concepts that are learned or practiced in each type of project. The projects are arranged in a hierarchical order to demonstrate that individual projects use the skills, values, and knowledge of the other two projects as well as those listed for individual projects. Individual service projects are more predominant in the upper grades (Procter & Haas, 1990).

Participation in Student Government

Student participation in the government of their own school through student councils has long been a tradition in middle and high schools. Such participation allows at least some students to practice democracy when the school administration gives students the freedom to initiate issues and solve problems. Today, many middle schools are attempting to encourage student government. In schools in which such programs are successful, the entire school and the principal have a strong commitment to the process. Student government is considered an important learning experience for all students.

Students elect representatives, who meet regularly, then return to share concerns and progress with classmates. Students identify the problems and needs of the school and are assisted in making the appropriate contacts in the school system and community to carry out their plans successfully. Students carefully research their ideas and develop workable plans. Students then present the plans to classmates, explaining the concerns of the adults and administrators and calling on fellow students to exhibit the behaviors needed to make the program a success.

Young children learn from observing and interacting in their surroundings including what they overhear adults saying. When entering kindergarten, students arrive with a variety of knowledge concerning being a member of a group. Teachers find that diversity in student group experiences needs to be molded into a common set of acceptable classroom behaviors. In twenty-first-century U.S. classrooms, many teachers face greater diversity in student backgrounds than in the K–12 schools they attended. Formally learning civic ideals and practices at the prekindergarten and kindergarten levels is now of greater necessity than ever. Building a classroom community whose members share skills, value cooperation, and value the common or community good is an essential foundation for all other forms of learning and for having safe schools. Practicing democracy in the organization and management within the classroom and the school is thought to be an important approach to teaching citizenship in a democratic society. States and educators frequently include official standards and curriculum objectives that call for learning essential civic values such as:

1. Demonstrating good citizenship by sharing, taking turns, assuming responsibility for daily chores and caring for personal belongings and for what belongs to others
2. Identifying the need for rules and the consequences for breaking rules
3. Resolving disagreements peacefully
4. Giving examples, and explaining why citizens voluntarily contribute their time and talents to the community
5. Explaining why rules are important and participating in developing rules
6. Giving examples of authority figures in the home, school, and community

The school curriculum is designed to assist youth in the development of their individual development and identity. Instructional procedures contribute much to the school and classroom environments that impact the personal development of individual students and also the faculty's development as professionals. Within individual classrooms teachers can make civic ideals and practices play a central role in all subjects. They do this by using and modeling the various civic procedures and values in personal statements, during their interactions with students, and in their expectations for the actions of their students. The *Democratic Classroom Interaction Model* is defined as systematic classroom use of five processes: communication, participation, interaction, application, and reflection, all of which are also required of citizens in democratic societies (Nielsen & Finkelstein, 1998; Nielsen, Finkelstein, Sehmidt, & Duncan, 2008). A key to students' learning of these skills is interacting over time in classroom and school environments as teachers gradually plan and relinquish complete control over the lessons. Another key is encouraging and enabling students to make decisions that plan and reflect on both the content and processes they use when learning.

In the first systematic large-scale study on youth and their knowledge of the democratic system in the United States, Hess and Torney (1967) reported that basic civic understanding and attachments to the political system were well developed by the eighth grade. But, they also found students failed to recognize the important roles of debate, disagreement, and conflict in the operation of a democratic political system. Could it be that students were limited to learning about the facts and concepts of the governmental system at the cost of making choices and encountering the difficulties of agreeing to common solutions? It may save time if teachers and staff make all the decisions, but what does that teach students about their needs and concerns, and their abilities to learn to control their own personal interactions and lives? Citizenship is granted at birth, but how *to be* a citizen is learned over time. Schools are expected to support the learning of citizenship, so governments fund them and control who is allowed to work in them. The twenty-first-century skills on which educators are focusing include being an active and participating citizen in the community and workplace. Social studies is the school subject expected to teach the governmental concepts, facts, and procedural skills needed to support development of the values supporting democracy. When teaching social studies, each teacher needs to use instructional procedures that involve students in making the types of choices citizens face daily at work, in their community, and as they make political choices.

Lessons and activities supporting learning about U.S. democracy include:

1. Examining leaders and followers, and their personal characteristics
2. Identifying problems in the schools, community, or world to examine
3. Applying age appropriate efforts toward solutions to the problems identified
4. Deciding on which actions to take, or projects to make
5. Evaluating the successes and failures of their own or historical efforts and projects
6. Cooperating with classmates in learning and playing
7. Contributing personal ideas and talents to finding solutions

The democratic classroom is another way of involving students in learning about democracy. The work in such classrooms in the upper elementary and middle school is designed to have students practice behaviors that reflect the democratic ideals of rights, responsibilities, and respect for self and others. Democratic classes make use of techniques such as cooperative learning, free expression and discussion of ideas, and the involvement of students in making decisions and setting goals (Holmes, 1991). Involving students in the assessment of projects is also an important aspect of the democratic school. The teacher models respect for all students and their ideas by inviting students to take part in making age-appropriate decisions. Through questions and involvement, students are guided to consider their needs and the common good. They are asked questions during the decision-making process and are involved in evaluating their choices and revising procedures or instituting new choices as needed. Teachers in democratic classrooms trust their students and allow them to make errors and face the consequences. However, they monitor the classroom activities carefully and encourage the realization and correction of errors before they become big problems.

Political Participation

Some elementary teachers work directly with their students to influence the formation of public policies at the local, state, and national levels. The political activities of third-grade students at Weber Elementary School in Fairbanks, Alaska, are a case in point. The students' activities included the selection of a current issue, in-depth study of facts and claims, and the use of communication skills and mathematics skills to gather data and inform citizens and politicians of their findings. Newspaper articles, guest editorials, and letters regularly flow from their classroom throughout Alaska and the continental United States as students study issues and share their knowledge and views. Not only do the students learn to gather and process information cooperatively, but they learn to respond appropriately and usefully in the democratic tradition. Their teacher, Grace Ann Heacock

Building on Diversity

The Challenges

In October 2006 the population clock at the U.S. Census Bureau (www.census.gov/population/www/popclockus.html) set the milestone of 300,000,000 people. Not only are there more citizens demanding goods and services, but also the ethnic diversity of the population is changing rapidly. According to the U.S. Census Bureau, as many as one-third of U.S. residents claim "minority" heritage. As of 2005, Hispanics were the largest single group in the United States. Our nation's minority population also is younger than the national average. Perspectives on population issues vary. Some people want the identity of Americans to remain as, they believe, it always has been. Others urge changes to fulfill the promised "American Dream" or advocate changes to meet the ever more global society. Educators find themselves in the midst of many challenges. Issues related to ethnicity and cultural differences are no longer found in a few locations within the United States and can come upon a school in a very short time. Changes in ethnicity impact not only classroom climate and learning, but also communications with parents, curriculum, and instructional resources.

The greatest amount of personal information elementary and middle school students possess comes from their personal experiences with their families. Young people also tend to be interested in details about the lives of youth across the world and throughout time. Many elementary and middle school educators approach the study of complex social studies concepts and issues through how issues impact families. Teachers discuss with their students both the impact of events and the potential for youth who can and are of service either within their families or the larger community. Examining the challenges families face through the use of trade books is one way teachers can seek to introduce students to other cultures and to the common characteristics of people regardless of ethnicity or age.

What's Happening To Grandpa? by Maria Shriver examines issues related to severe illness and old age that youth of all ethnic groups personally encounter or observe in today's world. This book not only provides information, but also illustrates how young people, out of love and respect for the elderly and other family members, can rise to challenges of bad news and use their talents in positive and helpful ways.

My Brother Martin: A Sister Remembers by Christine King Farris provides a different perspective on the life of an icon of African American history. She relates youthful memories of three children growing up in a city in the south, and Martin's first encounter with unjust behavior based on racial discrimination. She recalls how their parents, through words and actions, taught them to speak out against prejudice, hatred, and bigotry. In January, Martin Luther King, Jr. day is celebrated near the anniversary of his birthday. Adults listen to his famous "I Have a Dream" speech, but young people might better understand that dream by learning about the impact and response of a person who at their age dedicated his life to removing discrimination from the lives of all people because he remembered the pain he encountered from ethnic stereotyping as a young boy. In using this book, educators need to pay tribute to the King family, and the role families have in teaching character, civic ideals, and civic practices.

explains, "they are being empowered to keep a government of, for, and by the people" (Heacock, 1990, p. 11).

Over several years' time the efforts of the Extended Learning Program at Jackson Elementary School in the Salt Lake School District in Utah have resulted in the cleanup of a hazardous waste site, the passage of two laws, the planting of

Using Technology

Cybercitizenship

Cybercitizenship is one of the new terms introduced by the digital age of the twenty-first century in which we live. The definition, while still evolving, is based on combining the ideas of wise and good citizenship with the use of cyberspace in its multiple forms. New products have both positives and negatives, so the challenge to educators is to create a curriculum that takes advantage of the new positive resources while avoiding the negative potentials. Margaret Mead warned many years ago that, without guidance from adults, what happens to a society is that children bring up children and the end result is chaos. What is preferable is that the good ideas of the past remain, while changes brought to society are carefully weighed and only those ethically appropriate are chosen. This is not a new idea, as society changes and, we believe, evolves into one that is better than in the past.

We especially want society to continue to put into place the equal distribution of justice and the increased representative nature of governments. Learning to respect the rights of others and to respect yourself is not automatic. Learning to be an active participant in society also requires cognitive skills, especially questioning and gathering the best information available, and sharing this knowledge. Digital technology is impacting each of these skills. Thus far, two major emphases have been brought into the school curriculum. One is learning information literacy skills to access and evaluate information and share it in responsible and ethical ways. This is, perhaps, the easier challenge because it has previously been addressed for the print society. The second concern revolves around issues of safety and protection for rights and lives of individuals and groups. Much attention has been given to bullying of students by other students. While safety issues are not the sole concern of teachers, they are of concern because of the amount of time students are in the care of the professional staff of the schools, and because students bring personal and interpersonal issues to school that impact the learning atmosphere. Many schools have faced the safety issue by prohibiting the use of electronic tools and blocking access to particular computer services. Some educators worry that overcontrol ends up with less personal restraint and lack of critical consideration when using digital communication outside of school. There is a need for cooperation among responsible adults who have an interest in rearing youth who are responsible to themselves, communities, and the world. Middle school youth, in particular, have a number of oversimplified ideas concerning personal rights and responsibilities that need to be addressed with a positive approach, so they learn to accept democratic values and the role of being an active citizen. This increases the need for teaching democratic citizenship skills not only in social studies classes but within the entire school curriculum and in the school's extracurricular activities.

hundreds of trees, and $10,000 in neighborhood sidewalk improvements. Teacher Barbara Lewis writes: "Solving social problems will bring excitement and suspense into your life" (Lewis, 1991, p. 2). To assist other students, teachers, and interested adults, Lewis has written *The Kid's Guide to Social Action*. The following 10 tips are among her advice for taking action:

1. Choose a problem.
2. Do your research.
3. Brainstorm possible solutions.
4. Build coalitions of support.
5. Identify your opposition.

6. Advertise.
7. Raise money.
8. Carry out your solution.
9. Evaluate.
10. Don't give up.

Through actively taking part in examining political issues and trying to influence political decisions, students learn much about the functioning of the government. They also learn important principles concerning the use of power in society and test their reasoning skills and values. Such projects are filled with hard work and emotional ups and downs. Not every elementary or middle school teacher wants to use direct political participation with students. However, because many options for social action exist, all teachers can find a form of participation in which to engage their students.

Young people observe adults and model their behaviors on those of adults. Educators, especially social studies educators in a democracy, play a major role in helping youths to focus on civic choices and to encourage youths to evaluate possible choices, gather facts and opinions on issues, and make their decisions on the basis of the values that support democratic principles. Young people need to develop the full range of instructional goals that will lead to an ethical stance if they are to become good citizens who take civic action for the common good of their community, state, and nation. As part of examining the role of the social studies professional, members of the NCSS wrote and agreed to a code of ethics for the social studies profession. The code of ethics (see Figure 5.2 on page 170) identifies the six principles that describe how a social studies professional should approach teaching the knowledge, skills, and values associated with enlightened political engagement to young people. The entire statement that further explains each principle can be easily accessed through the NCSS Website.

TIME FOR REFLECTION | **What Do You Think?**

Read the six principles of the Code of Ethics for the Social Studies Profession in Figure 5.2 and answer the following questions:

1. What are the characteristics of classroom management that are most compatible with the free contest of ideas?

2. Who besides teachers are members of the social studies profession?

3. In teaching which of the NCSS Standards does the teacher have the opportunity to model good citizenship for students?

4. In teaching which of the NCSS Standards might the teacher have the opportunity to have students judge the civic virtues in the behaviors of a person or group?

5. When you think about your experiences with social studies professionals what specific principles of the code of ethics do you recall their exhibiting?

Principle One
It is the ethical responsibility of social studies professionals to set forth, maintain, model, and safeguard standards of instructional competence suited to the achievement of the broad goals of the social studies.

Principle Two
It is the ethical responsibility of social studies professionals to provide to every student the knowledge, skills, experiences, and attitudes necessary to function as an effective participant in a democratic system.

Principle Three
It is the ethical responsibility of social studies professionals to foster the understanding and exercise the rights guaranteed under the Constitution of the United States and of the responsibilities implicit in those rights in an increasingly interdependent world.

Principle Four
It is the ethical responsibility of social studies professionals to cultivate and maintain an instructional environment in which the free contest of ideas is prized.

Principle Five
It is the ethical responsibility of social studies professionals to adhere to the highest standards of scholarship in the development, production, distribution, or use of social studies materials.

Principle Six
It is the ethical responsibility of social studies professionals to concern themselves with the conditions of the school and community with which they are associated.

FIGURE 5.2
Revised Code of Ethics for the Social Studies Profession
Source: Retrieved on September, 16, 2003, from http://databank.ncss.org/article.php?story=20020402120622151.

An artist's sculpture interests this young man and illustrates national attitudes toward soldiers killed in action.

EXPANSION

Nobel Prize winner, Albert Einstein (1879–1955) said, "I never teach my pupils, I only attempt to provide the conditions in which they can learn" (Quotationspage. com, July 5, 2009).

Bertrand Russell (1872–1970), another Nobel Prize winner, said,

Passive acceptance of the teacher's wisdom is easy to most boys and girls. It involves no effort of independent thought, and seems rational because the teacher knows more than his pupils; it is moreover the way to win the favour of the teacher unless he is a very exceptional man. Yet the habit of passive acceptance is a disastrous one in later life. It causes man to seek and to accept a leader, and to accept as a leader whoever is established in that position. (Quotationspage.com, July 5, 2009)

1. Neither Einstein nor Russell is living today, nor did they work in close proximity to young learners day after day. What, in their quotations, are important ideas for someone who teaches youth in the twenty-first century?
2. Both of the men quoted above were associated with mathematics. Russell was British. Einstein emigrated from Germany as Hitler was rising to power and became a U.S. citizen. He refused to return to Germany for any reason during his lifetime. What positions do you think these men would take concerning the importance, or lack of importance, of including civic education in the schools?
3. Who do you think Einstein and Russell would say is responsible for the conditions of the world in which we live?

Summary

Citizens in a democracy must know the structure and procedures by which their government works and the ideals and values that support its beliefs and actions. They must also develop and practice civic skills and attitudes to carry out their responsibilities and duties as citizens. This includes examining the concerns of others and recognizing that differences and similarities exist within each society. Students need to learn to respect and appreciate the multicultural nature of U.S. society and view diversity as providing greater possibilities rather than as a threat.

Schools have long been viewed as a place where students learn to get along with others and acquire and practice the skills of active participation in society. Many are calling for youth to play a more active part in their communities. Schools are changing their curricula to increase the participation of their students in various aspects and efforts in their communities. Active participation by citizens is a requirement for democracy to flourish. Today, technology has increased the speed of communication between people and opened new sources of information to all. This dramatic change presents new opportunities and challenges for educating students to be civil individuals in their personal and civic lives.

Recommended Websites to Visit

Projects for students to participate in helping children in selected nations throughout the world have a better life.
www.freethechildren.org/

A middle school project and lessons on civics.
www.civiced.org/project_citizen.html

Ideas for how children can serve communities and people, especially other children.
www.50ways.org/main.php?nav=small_ways

Persuasive reading and writing graphic organizers (click on Persuasive writing tools on chart).
www.greece.k12.ny.us/instruction/ELA/6-12/Tools/Index.htm

Video about the National Archives and its importance
http://videocast.nih.gov/sla/NARA/dsh/index.html

Center for Information and Research on Civic Learning & Engagement
www.civicyouth.org/

An example of a service learning project that can save your school money is
http://www.nrdc.org/greensquad/intro/intro_4.asp

This project might also be applied to homes and other community locations.

6

What Is Social Studies' Contribution to Global Education?

EXPLORATORY INTRODUCTION

Read the following facts and then write your interpretation of those facts for teachers of social studies.

1. On June 18, 2009, the Cable News Network (CNN) showed a map of Iran that indicated all of the locations in Iran where people were uploading pictures and videos of the confrontations and protests associated with the 2009 Iranian election.
2. Soldiers serving in Iraq watched their children graduate from school, and at least one watched and coached his wife through the birth of their baby girl with the use of computers attached to webcams.
3. *Through the Lens*, a book of the best pictures from the National Geographic Society, was published in 20 different languages in 2003.
4. Much of the athletic equipment and clothing sold by major U.S.-owned producers and purchased by large numbers of American youths is made in the developing world by child labor in unhealthy working conditions.

Chapter Overview

NCSS Standard IX, Global Connections, is interdisciplinary. Often it is addressed in part during units focusing on economic and geographic problems. The impact of this standard on the lives of people can also be part of units focusing on history. Civic ideals and practices essential to American democracy, such as free enterprise, equality, freedom of expression and religion, and separation of church and state, are being adopted in nations around the world and challenged by some who believe that these ideals are not appropriate. We live in a world where no place seems safe from physical attack. Global Connections and the impacts of Science and Technology, another interdisciplinary theme, on people and groups (society) have both positive and negative consequences as a result of decisions made by people and leaders who represent various nations and interest groups.

Citizens need a sound foundation of knowledge, skills, and attitudes that support and examine democracy and the character and ideals of their nation's people. Citizens also need to critically examine the themes of Global Connections and Science and Technology and Society that were not a typical part of the curriculum in the past but were marginally present until recently. This is an important challenge for the curriculum in the United States because this country has such a large role in world affairs. In this chapter, issues related to global connections and their impact on the lives and decisions of people are examined.

NCSS

Standards
VIII, IX

Chapter Objectives

1. Explain how geography, economics, cultural institutions and practices, and human rights connect the people of the world.
2. Identify the characteristics of substantive cultural learning.
3. Explain how to confront misconceptions, stereotypes, and prejudice about people and groups through using instruction that focuses on substantive cultural learning.
4. Identify the multiple types of learning resources that provide accurate information and many perspectives on global and international issues.
5. Identify important issues that span national boundaries and potentially threaten the entire world.
6. Identify ways in which K–8 students can help take part in solving international and global problems.
7. Identify common characteristics of global education.

DEVELOPMENT

 ## Global Education: An Evolving Definition

Everyone's life is increasingly interdependent with the lives of people all over the world. American citizens directly and indirectly affect the lives of people throughout the world. Individual, group, state, and national decisions dealing with persistent global problems challenge our priorities and values. Governments, corporations, clubs, organizations, states, and individuals are all involved in transnational projects that contribute to global interdependence. Elements of global education can be found in all disciplines contributing to social studies content.

Why, you might ask, is there a special chapter devoted to this topic? Educators need to make decisions on what is appropriate to examine in the school's curriculum, when topics should be examined, and what instructional resources to use. Each of these decisions stimulates debate, requires research to gain answers, and results in decisions that must be carefully documented and evaluated. People have ideas and are implementing lessons and programs in global education. Yet little hard data is available on the success of such programs, and the definition of global education is still tentative in the minds of many people.

The media addresses globalism in ways that reflect the domestic economic, military, and governmental issues they cover every day. The concepts of sustainability, consumption, conflict, multinational, energy, and climate change are terms with which the public is familiar. When international issues are addressed, concepts such as terrorism, security, and national interests are used. Citizens need to understand these concepts and examine the generalizations that derive from the relationships among these ideas. The popular definition and perception of globalism or globalization, however, is not the same as global education or the NCSS theme of global connections. There are similarities, but there are important differences. The most notable are the differences in short-term and long-term meanings and responses. Differences come from the nature of the thinking and planning of various groups. Educators work with long-term goals and a very different product, one with very few similarities and lots of unpredictability. Educators also know that they alone do not have the power to reward or guarantee outcomes. So, educators rely on encouraging students to adopt particular habits in their thinking and acting and hope that what they attempt to teach lasts and grows throughout the years. Businesses and governments have more control over a product and more flexibility with their inputs and so have predictable outcomes, at least for the short term. There are bound to be some conflicts among those who advocate a global perspective because of such differences.

After more than 20 years of advocating, researching, and observing the teaching of global education, Merry Merryfield (2008) identifies three assumptions that underlie successful lessons with long-term learning potential.

First, *being open-minded* requires recognizing the tendency of people to respond quickly with answers. Quick responses are a result of our own closed-mindedness and parochialism because individuals have a tendency to accept their own responses based in their own experiences and cultures as correct and project it to all similar instances. Being open-minded means considering there are other possible perceptions and interpretations that provide new or different meanings and may be correct. Accepting the idea that you might not be correct is difficult. Solving complex problems, such as those associated with global issues, requires such thinkers. Most of the problems people face in daily life are not so complex; therefore, the quick response with a satisfactory outcome gets reinforced. Inquiry teaching strategies with their stress on testing your ideas and holding ideas as tentative in all areas of social studies helps students to master this essential skill needed in global education.

The second assumption is that *the knowledge base of global education is multidisciplinary*. Teachers need to work together. This means teachers must overcome personal barriers among themselves and problems associated with the traditional curricula often found with separate school subjects. Another problem is that the structure of the school day does not allow busy teachers to have the time to work together. Middle schools with successful teams of teachers may have an advantage in overcoming some of the institutional problems, so their students receive better presentations of global issues. Social studies teachers who see the need to integrate different perspectives from history and the social sciences and arts within their own subject have something to contribute to making integration of knowledge in global education more successful.

The third assumption for successful global education experiences is to *use relevant and authentic topics and procedures.* This applies to both instruction and assessment. To identify such topics and procedures, teachers continually learn and are open to assistance from community members in providing information to both teachers and students. Teachers who give up the idea of being the authority or dispenser of knowledge and model for their students by talking through their own learning are more likely to be successful in having relevant and authentic lessons. A classroom atmosphere respectful of students and supporting inquiry among individuals and groups who work together to examine problems is essential for using these strategies. Problem solving requires action to be taken on a problem. It can serve as assessment of knowledge and skills and dispositions. Problem solving also may require time that is outside of the regular school day and at locations very distant from the students' homes or schools.

Those advocating twenty-first-century learning support the goals for which these assumptions were identified by Merryfield. Much of the support for twenty-first-century education is coming from the electronics industry. It is true that the industry's successes have much to offer teachers as they attempt to gain information and contacts with those involved in today's authentic problems and their solutions. Many of the needs of today's students, however, are those associated with personal relations and development. Even though many educators have, for years, struggled to introduce inquiry skills and processes into the curriculum, they have not been as successful as the electronics industry. Giving up old perceptions of what makes a good teacher and good instructional strategies is difficult for teachers, students, and community members. Although not all of the states have adopted goals consistent with the needs of twenty-first-century learning, this effort is progressing and holds potential for creating change in education.

Robert Hanvey's book *An Attainable Global Perspective* (1976) is often identified as a most thoughtful statement concerning the knowledge and attitudinal bases for a global curriculum. Five dimensions of global education are identified:

1. **Perspective consciousness:** Understanding that others may view events and the world very differently from your own view.
2. **State of the planet awareness:** Knowing major trends in the world such as climate changes and population growth and the facts surrounding these trends.
3. **Cross-cultural awareness:** Knowing that there are differences in ideas and practices among nations and making an effort to view events from the vantage points of others.
4. **Knowledge of global dynamics:** Recognizing the interdependence of people and places because of dynamic world systems in the physical, cultural, and economic environments.

5. **Awareness of human choices:** Recognizing that events are shaped by the individual and collective decisions made by communities and nations. Decisions made in one area of the world may be prompted by decisions made by others or may affect the lives of people in far-off locations.

A set of guidelines for global and international education to assist teachers in establishing curricula was developed by H. Thomas Collins, Frederick R. Czarra, and Andrew F. Smith (1998). Their research led them to three broad K–12 themes for the curriculum:

1. Global challenges, issues, and problems
2. Global cultures and world areas
3. Global connections: the United States and the world

Their curriculum guidelines are built around these themes, including the knowledge, skills, and types of participation youths need to experience to gain a global or international perspective.

In designing a global curriculum, it is necessary to try to define what such a curriculum is. Parker, Ninomiya, and Cogan (2002) approached defining a global curriculum through research with people from nine nations. People from several nations were involved because Parker and colleagues assumed that defining the nature of a world citizen requires multiple perspectives from people from many nations concerning the world and its issues. Their participants arrived at a consensus about the content of the curriculum. They based the curriculum on six ethical questions that focus on problems affecting people across the world. In using such a curriculum, students focus their efforts on inquiry and deliberation concerning the six questions:

1. What should be done to promote equity and fairness within and among societies?
2. What should be the balance between the right to privacy and free and open access to information and information-based societies?
3. What should be the balance between protecting the environment and meeting human needs?
4. What should be done to cope with population growth, genetic engineering, and children in poverty?
5. What should be done to develop shared (universal, global) values while respecting local values?
6. What should be done to secure an ethically based distribution of power for deciding policy and action on the above issues?

Studying people and culture is essential in global education because people form global perspectives, and students must be aware of them and must also think about being aware of the state of our planet, of other cultures, of global dynamics, and of the choices we make. The questions and themes above incorporate these dimensions identified by Hanvey (1976).

Now, as a result of the many interdependent connections among people, businesses, and governments, as well as the increased use of technology to shorten both distances and the time for communications, the world has evolved into a global system. Columnist Thomas Friedman (2005) describes the world as now being flat. Technology has flattened, or broadened, opportunities putting people throughout the world on a more equal playing field. Global education is an important educational perspective especially in technologically developed nations. It encourages students to understand and discuss complex relationships about common social, ecological, political, and economic issues. Many issues citizens deal with today across the world involve inequality, justice, and conflict. Concepts important to understanding issues across the world include conflict resolution, social justice, values and perceptions, sustainable development, interdependence, human rights, and diversity.

Global Education Appropriate for Grades Kindergarten–8

In describing learning about people and places, Fran Martin (2007) points out that young students develop ideas about people without knowing where the people are located. She indicates that such perspectives and attitudes may be correct or may be a stereotypical view capable of leading to prejudice and bias. Because stereotypes occur, Martin's position is that global education is appropriate for students in the lower grades because correcting stereotypes, prejudices, and bias must be dealt at a young age. Failure to do so may result in reinforcing negatives and result in more difficulty confronting such ideas at a later age.

Many primary-grade teachers who teach students about people throughout the world are teaching global education. They are helping students become aware of the many commonalities we share. They are also helping students become aware of the differences that are found, especially those that are the result of human culture, such as religion, language, traditions, and the organization of communities. In addition, they are working to help young children better understand issues of which they are aware, including terrorism, environmental pollution, war, and health concerns.

As early as January 1991, the NCSS board of directors approved a report from the Task Force on Social Studies in the Middle School in which middle school students are noted as "developing a broad world view." Middle schools must engage their students "in examining the content and context of persisting global issues, the elements of human values and cultures, global systems, and global history." While global education has an important role in social studies, the need for a wide range of background knowledge to assure meaningful learning and understanding makes global education a particularly good theme for integrated units and joint efforts by teachers with various content specializations (Martin, 2007). In the social studies tradition, advocates of global education indicate that not only must accurate knowledge be examined in a critical way, but that actions based on using that knowledge need to be included among the learning activities.

Approaches to Global Education

Two major ways of approaching global education are the cultural approach and the problems approach. They share some perspectives, but they also have different emphases in their approach to global education.

The Cultural Approach to Global Education

Elementary students should experience in-depth learning about several countries that provides an accurate treatment of the content and avoids blatant stereotyping or dull and superficial learning. In-depth country units can positively influence students' attitudes toward learning about other cultures and areas of the world (Hoge & Allen, 1991). When elementary teachers provide such high-quality instruction about other nations, they are helping students to build the understanding, attitudes, and skills needed to sustain our nation as a leader in the world community (Hoge & Allen, 1991).

Teaching about cultures around the world is a way of examining important social issues related to the lives of people everywhere (Merryfield, 2004). The examination of cultures needs to be substantive and in-depth. Table 6.1) illustrates

TABLE 6.1
Substantive Culture Learning

Content and Pedagogy	Some Practices of Nonglobal Educators	Some Practices of Global Educators
1. Developing skills in perspective consciousness	Teach one mainstream point of view. Teach that other viewpoints are wrong. Imply that other people are inferior, so there is no need to understand why they think the way they do. Assume that Americans know why people in Africa, Asia, or the Middle East behave the way they do (so there is no reason to ask them).	Teach students to recognize and understand underlying assumptions and values in their own perspectives and how they change over time. Teach students to analyze the perspectives of others as part of understanding how different people view events and issues. Have students develop the habit of examining the experiences, knowledge, beliefs, and values that shape people's worldviews.
2. Using skills in recognizing stereotypes, exotica, and cultural universals	Ignore stereotypes their students may have. May teach that all people in a culture or region are the same. May use exotica to motivate students.	Identify stereotypes students bring to class. Address stereotypes directly. Teach students to recognize how exotica may interfere with cultural understanding.

continued

TABLE 6.1 (Continued)
Substantive Culture Learning

Content and Pedagogy	Some Practices of Nonglobal Educators	Some Practices of Global Educators
	May ignore or play down commonalities.	Aim for a balance between cultural differences and commonalities.
	Do not teach cultural universals.	Teach students to examine cultural universals.
3. Using primary sources from the cultures or regions under study	Use only American sources to teach about other cultures.	Use primary sources such as literature, documents, newspapers, and websites from the culture under study.
		Have students interact with people from the culture.
4. Understanding of the intersections of prejudice and power	Do not teach about intersections of prejudice and power.	Teach about prejudice and discrimination within and across diverse world regions.
		Teach about people's ongoing efforts to resist oppression or discrimination.
		Help students understand how minority cultures perceive the actions of those in power over them.
5. Understanding of dynamic change and increasing global interconnectedness	Do not teach how cultures change.	Teach the dynamic nature of cultural change and diffusion.
	Allow students to think a culture is static.	Help students understand how cultural norms change over time in real people's lives.
	May use images or content about a culture that are out of date.	Help students understand how cultural changes affect minorities and indigenous peoples.
	Do not teach global interconnectedness.	Teach economic, political, cultural, environmental, and other connections between their students and people in other cultures.
	Allow students to assume that the United States is not dependent on other nations or people in other countries.	Provide learning experiences to connect students with people in other countries.

Source: Merryfield, M. (2004). Engaging elementary children in substantive culture learning. *Social Education 68*(4) 270–274.

substantive knowledge and skills that should be applied to the study of cultures (Merryfield, 2004). The table contrasts the substantive global approach, which is a cultural approach, with the traditional approach that was often used in the past, which viewed other cultures through a narrow and nonglobal perspective.

The Problems Approach to Global Education

Global education is often conceived of as the study of economic, political, ecological, and technological systems and problems that extend across national boundaries. Four persistent problems encompass the entire globe and serve as the focus of global education:

1. Peace and security
2. National and international development
3. Environmental problems
4. Human rights

Building on Diversity

Finding the Views of People in Other Nations

Since September 11, people are more aware of their need to know of events in other countries and their potential impacts on their own community. Gaining a multicultural perspective includes learning about and considering the perspectives of subgroups within your community and nation and the great variety of cultural groups through out the world. The Internet provides many up-to-date resources on the views of various groups around the world. Major world news resources have websites that teachers and students can visit. The British Broadcasting System (the BBC) covers the world in written, video, and audio articles at www.bbc.co.uk/. Click an area of the world in the index on the left side of this webpage. The World News Network at www.wnnetwork.com/ provides similar information. Professional organizations such as The Asia Society provide links to articles about Asian nations and people (see www.asiasource.org/news/at_mp_01.cfm). Information and photo essays about nations that border Russia can be found at www.eurasianet.org. For an index of English-language newspapers go to www.chipublib.org/008subject/005genref/gisengfl.html. The same page has a link to ethnic newspapers in the United States, although not all are in English.

By visiting the websites of English-language newspapers, students can locate multiple perspectives on current events to compare with stories that they read or hear from major U.S. news organizations. Using computer software, students can produce their own news reports in formats such as newspaper, video, or PowerPoint presentations that incorporate multiple viewpoints. Students can be challenged to create an editorial or cartoon that expresses their own perspective on an issue or topic. Another important assignment that helps students to evaluate news sources is to ask students to examine selected articles on a topic and try to determine which articles are for government-controlled newspapers and which articles contain quotes from people who freely speak their mind on a topic versus those who carefully weigh their comments for various reasons.

All these problems impact people and societies throughout the world. All are greatly impacted by changes in scientific knowledge and technology.

One way to study these four problems is to organize our instruction around five major concepts: interdependence, change, culture, scarcity, and conflict (Kniep, 1989). These major concepts can serve as five themes we study throughout the year. Through these themes, we can examine each of the four persistent problems found across the world. As an example, let's consider the problem of human rights and the major concept of interdependence. Because we are interdependent in our own society, we need each other's services, and this can lead us to deny the rights of some people to make sure that we get the services we need and want. So we might enact laws that make it hard to change jobs. Nations also might do this to other nations. Trade agreements might be set up to make sure that we get a resource we need from another country, such as oil or coffee. Because we need the resource, we might overlook human rights problems and the low wages, long hours, and unsafe conditions workers in those countries must endure for us to get the resource.

TIME FOR REFLECTION | ## What Do You Think?

Select one of the other three persistent problems identified by Kniep—(1) peace and security, (2) national and international development, or (3) environmental problems—and describe how the major concept of interdependence can be studied with this problem.

Interdisciplinary Connections

Many interdisciplinary topics that are frequently studied in middle school have global connections, especially those connected with preservation of species and changes in climate and atmosphere (Cruz, 1998). Political science, law, and civics are subjects that address global issues because many actions that are needed to solve global problems require the cooperation of nations, international organizations, and people living in several nations.

Closely related to global education is the peace education movement. The connection is evident when we consider peace and security as one of the persistent problems in the world. Peace is also important when we consider the problems of national and international development of the environment and of human rights. Originally prompted by concerns about nuclear war, peace educators soon recognized that removal of nuclear weapons is not enough to stop war. Peace educators seek to preserve the world and to preserve the safety and security of our bodies and our consciences for all people.

These youths, born in America, visited their grandparents and family in northern Nigeria. Such students and their parents are potential resources for teaching about other nations and cultures.

 ## Teaching Global Education

Many interest groups' concerns fall under the umbrella of global education. Some of these groups sponsor special days or weeks throughout the year. These groups often supply free education materials and suggest activities that students might enjoy. Yet, if such activities are done in isolation, they do not contribute to meaningful learning. Instead, students might develop only a vague awareness of the issues. Some students might experience despair because they see only huge problems with no solutions or they might be encouraged to embrace simplistic solutions. Sufficient time needs to be devoted if students are to gain the in-depth knowledge needed to understand global issues.

Teaching units that define the problems and investigate subtopics and alternative solutions are a more appropriate instructional approach than is the celebration of single-day events. Students need to investigate the consequences of actions designed to solve global problems along with the values that support the proposed solutions. As students examine global problems and their causes and consequences, they need to decide whether the solutions promote practices that are consistent with democratic civic ideals and whether the solutions will appear positive or negative to people in other nations. Some unit topics that can address global issues in these ways include the following:

- How can the needs of all people be fulfilled?
- How are changes in communication technology helping and hurting people?
- What makes a person a hero or heroine?
- Why have people or groups been nominated for or won the Nobel Peace Prize?
- How do we help people in places where a natural disaster has occurred?
- How are the lives of women and children changing in today's world?

Elementary and middle school students should examine global issues to help them deal positively with such issues. At school, students can examine many difficult issues with less emotion using a more rational thought process than will happen when they are involved in incidents that affect and challenge the lives of family members or a friend. The school curriculum can also address problems that have occurred in the past and examine and evaluate the various ways in which people and nations have tried to solve their problems. Although many possibilities exist, teachers must make careful decisions about which global issues to study and how to investigate those issues. Dorothy Skeel (1996) points out that one of the questions that each teacher must answer when selecting a topic for study is "Are the students sufficiently mature and experienced to thoroughly understand the study?"

Hoge and Allen (1991) believe that young students can and should learn about people in other nations. They recommend that teachers approach studies of other nations and people as a resource provider and co-learner with their students. In this role, teachers model effective ways of seeking answers for thoughtful questions. Such teachers help students to form conclusions and generalizations and test and revise their ideas as they encounter new facts and viewpoints. However, not all topics are appropriate for all students. Angell and Avery (1992) report that if a topic or problem is not clearly related to local situations, students tend not to see the issue as having local applications and cannot see ways to personally take action on such a problem.

Focusing on helping young students identify multiple perspectives on issues and problems is a major learning outcome related to global issues. So also is discussing what are good and positive actions, moral positions, and appropriate behaviors. For example, one of the most negative issues in the social studies curriculum is genocide. Examining such a difficult topic only superficially can result in students deciding to conform to what those in power want because they are afraid of them. By carefully examining the Holocaust, many educators hope to assist students in dealing with negative behavior and provide support for human needs and the value of justice. Some advocate teaching about the Holocaust in the primary grades by focusing on self-concept, caring for others, prejudice, and human rights in stories about people in various ethnic groups (Sepinwall, 1999). Samuel Totten (1999), an educator who has devoted years to the study of genocide and the Holocaust, recognizes the great complexity of the content of this topic and makes it clear that he does not view the Holocaust as an appropriate topic at the K–4 levels. However, he does identify a number of social skills and values that he believes should be taught in K–4 so that students will be more able to carefully consider the Holocaust in later grades. He recommends examining and teaching these values and attitudes with content that does not include the violence and extreme negative behaviors that are a part of the Holocaust and genocides. Global topics involving the environment and social conditions such as child labor also have many negative attributes and solutions that are very complex. Very young students should be helped to develop such skills as critical thinking and problem solving and values such as respect for justice and human dignity within the more traditional curriculum topics. Middle school students have greater cognitive skills and might address the more complex topics with accurate information. Middle school teachers must be sensitive to the needs of the students who are involved in developing their personal identities and need adult support in facing individual moral decisions and pressures from peers and a world that sends them confusing messages.

The Learning Cycle on page 186, "Teaching about War to Help Create a More Humane World," is presented as a large unit that takes place over at least 10 days of teaching. The early part of this unit serves as the exploratory introduction to the unit, with the middle section serving as the development portion and the last part of the unit applying and expanding the key generalization taught forming the expansion. This unit uses a number of instructional strategies suggested for use in addressing global issues. The unit requires several days to complete

text continues on page 194

Students' artwork reveals what they learned about the need to manage the world's renewable resources.

LEARNING CYCLE UNIT PLAN   *Teaching about War to Help Create a More Humane World*

NCSS

Standards I, II, III, VIII, IX, X

Grade Levels: Intermediate and Middle School

NCSS Standards: Global Connections; Science Technology and Society; Culture; Time, Continuity and Change; Civic Ideals and Practices; and People, Places, and Environments

Generalization:

Because wars and civil wars kill some soldiers and civilians and severely change the lives of the surviving civilians and soldiers, warfare is an event that people and governments should work hard to prevent happening in the future.

Exploratory Introduction

Materials: Pictures from the U.S. Civil War from American history textbooks or the collection of the Library of Congress website (www.loc.gov)

Objectives →	Procedures →	Assessments
1. Given a set of pictures from the U.S. Civil War, students describe what they believe to be the characteristics of a war.	1. Arrange students in small groups and give each a set of pictures. Ask, "What do these pictures tell you about the characteristics of the Civil War?" Discuss this and be prepared to report your ideas to the class. Have groups share their ideas. 2. Ask the class, "Judging from your pictures, what did your group identify as characteristics of the people in the Civil War? From what you see in the pictures, who or what kinds of people were involved in the Civil War?" Have students point out or describe their sources of information in the pictures. Ask, "What messages did these pictures tell you about what things happened to the people in the pictures?" 3. Record students' answers on a chart titled "People and Events of War."	1. Students work together and share ideas.
2. Students indicate that only a few people's perspectives are present in the picture set.	4. Call attention to what is on the chart and ask, "Whose involvement in the war was not commemorated in the pictures? Why? Why do you think the photographers did not take pictures of old people, women, and children or why might the Library of Congress not have preserved such pictures? Do you think these other people had the same views toward the war as did the soldiers and politicians whose pictures we have seen? How can we find out what happened to	2. Students state that few views are present in the picture set.

continued

slaves, wives, families, farmers, and factory workers during the war?"

5. Announce that the class will keep the chart and see whether it needs to be changed as the class continues to study. (Keep the chart and add, cross out, or put question marks beside ideas after reading and discussing each story. Use a different color marker for each day.)

Lesson Development

Materials: A copy of each of the following trade books: Polacco, Patricia. (1994). *Pink and Say*. New York: Philomel Books; Breckler, Rosemary. (1996). *Sweet Dried Apples*. Boston: Houghton Mifflin; Cha, Dia. (1996). *Dia's Story Cloth*. New York: Lee and Low; chart paper and various colored marking pens; paper for drawing pictures for each student; world map

Objectives	→	Procedures	→	Assessments
1. Given the reading of *Pink and Say* and discussion of its content, students examine the impact of the U.S. Civil War on two young men and their families, providing evidence from the book to support their ideas.		1. Tell students you are going to read them a book written about the U.S. Civil War. Showing its cover, ask, "What do you think the young men or boys pictured on the cover are doing? What does this picture lead you to believe about the young men?" Accept and record students' predictions. On a map of the United States, locate Michigan, which was Say's home, and Georgia, where the events in the book took place. 2. Read the book, showing the pictures. Ask students to comment on the pictures, especially moods illustrated and facial expressions. After reading, say: "Think back on the pictures in this book and identify one that stands out in your memory. Tell me what is in the picture and what message the picture gives to you." After several students share, say, "Think about the picture you personally remember the most from the story or the picture that first comes to your mind and raise your hand if the picture could be described as happy." Count and record responses. Ask, "How many of you thought the first picture could be described as sad?" Count and record.		1. Students attend to comments and questions of teacher and classmates.

continued

3. Say, "Raise your hand if you think the story was sad. Next, raise your hand if you thought it was happy." Record the number of responses.

4. Begin a class discussion by noting that the book provides a few hints of what the lives of Pink, Mo Mo Bay, and Say were like before the war. Ask students to consider these questions and to support their responses with evidence from the story.

   a. What do you think the lives of Pink and Mo Mo Bay were like before the war?
   b. What do you think the life of Say was like before the war?
   c. What happened to Pink, Say, and Mo Mo Bay during the war?
   d. Describe how you think Mo Mo Bay felt about Pink and Say.
   e. Pink and Say have feelings about the war. What do their feelings have in common? How are they different?
   f. Why was touching Mr. Lincoln's hand "something important"?
   g. What was the last request Pink made of Say? What do you think was the significance of this request and the actions of the two boys?
   h. Why do you think Pinkus Aylee was killed within hours of entering Andersonville Prison and Say was not?
   i. Who do you think was the hero of the story? What did Mo Mo Bay do that was heroic? What did Pink do that was heroic? What did Say do that was heroic?

5. Make a list of the words that describe Pinkus Aylee (Pink).
   Make a list of the words that describe Sheldon Curtis (Say).
   Make a list of words that describe the marauders.

6. *Closure:* We have looked at a picture set and read a story of one soldier that was passed on through oral history in the family. Display the chart that was begun earlier. Ask, "Are there any statements on our

2. All students answer with a show of hands.

3. Students offer logical predictions and interpretations.

4. Students offer logical predictions and interpretations, supporting them with evidence from the book.

2. Students make changes on the chart that reflect their increased information

5. Students evaluate their ideas and offer additions and suggestions for removal

from the evidence they identified in *Pink and Say*.

3. Given the reading of the story *Sweet Dried Apples*, students identify the impact of the Vietnam War on the lives of Vietnamese people.

list that you think we should remove from the list at this time?" If so, cross them out. If a question remains, put a question mark beside the statement. Ask, "Are there any new statements you think we should add to our list that tell us important things about the people and events of the war?"

7. Display a world map, locating Vietnam, where the story takes place. Tell students that many people came to the United States from Vietnam after the war and most settled in California.

8. Read the story and follow similar procedures with this book as with the previous book. Show pictures and ask students to predict what the face would look like on those pictures where the illustrator shows the backs of the people. Review the events of the story through a discussion based on the following questions, asking students to give supporting evidence from the book with their responses.

   a. What was daily life like for the children before the war?
   b. Little is said of what life was like for the adults, but judging from the pictures and the few words, how would you describe the lives of the adults prior to the war?
   c. What were the first observable signs of the war that the children in the story encountered?
   d. What things did the grandfather, Ong Noi, do for the children and the family?
   e. How would you describe the relationship between the children and Ong Noi?
   f. Why do you think Ong Noi did not smile when he told the children, "You must never wander from home!"
   g. While the grandfather was gone, what did the children do as a surprise for him? Why do you think the children thought this would be a good idea? How was their village attacked during the war?
   h. In the morning after the attack, what was the grandfather's concern and what did he do?
   i. What happened to the grandfather?

using evidence from *Pink and Say*.

6. Students make logical inferences about the impact of the Vietnam War on the lives of Vietnamese, using evidence from the story.

7. Students answer questions with correct replies.

j. What happened to the members of the village?

k. The book does not tell us what happened to Ba. What do you think most likely happened to him? Why do you think this is the case? Have the class vote with a show of hands on the predictions of the different responders and record their votes on the board.

l. What do you think happened to the people who reached the large boat?

m. Why do you think the girl promised herself that she would return and do several things for Ong Noi?

n. Who in this story do you think is a hero and why do you think that is the case?

8. All students vote, and logical reasons are offered.

4. Students identify war as one of the causes of immigration.

9. Tell students that many people have come to the United States as immigrants because of war. Ask the students whether they have heard the terms *migration* and *immigrant*. Define these terms, if needed. Ask, "Can you name the nation from which one or more of your ancestors migrated when they came to the United States?" Record responses. Ask, "Do you know of anyone in the community who came to the United States from Vietnam?"

9. Students identify war as one cause of immigration and provide logically acceptable answers to questions.

5. Students make changes on the chart that reflect their increased information from the evidence they identified in *Sweet Dried Apples.*

10. When people migrate, what do they leave behind? Why do you think more people would be willing to migrate during a war or just after a war?"

11. *Closure:* Use same procedures as used for *Pink and Say.*

10. Students evaluate their ideas and offer additions and suggestions for removal, using evidence from *Sweet Dried Apples.*

6. Given the reading of the book *Dia's Story Cloth*, students trace the migration of the Hmong people and describe the lives of the Hmong during their migration.

12. Tell students that the people in the third book you are reading lived in Laos, a nation neighboring Vietnam, at the same time as the characters in *Sweet Dried Apples.* Locate both Vietnam and Laos on the world map. Note their shared border and the course of the Mekong River.

13. Ask, "If I asked you to record the events of a trip, how would you do it? What media would you use to record the events?" The Hmong people of Laos have long recorded events that are important to them by sewing on a piece of cloth. Show the picture of the entire cloth in the center of the book.

continued

14. Ask, "What is your first impression of this cloth?" Share ideas. Have the students look at the picture and try to identify what happened in one or two events recorded on the cloth.

15. Tell the students that the author of the book immigrated and now lives in the United States. The cloth shows the history of her ancestors' migration over many years. Read the names of the nations on the cloth. Use the map to locate these various nations where the Hmong people lived: China, Laos, Burma, and Thailand. Note the locations in relationship to the Mekong River.

16. Say, "As we read this book, identify things that are similar and different from yesterday's story." Read the book and examine the pictures in ways similar to the other books. Then ask and discuss the following questions. Ask students to support their responses with evidence from the book.

    a. Why have the Hmong people lived in so many different places?
    b. What was the life of the Hmong people like before the war in Laos?
    c. How were the lives of the Hmong people changed by the war?
    d. Could the Hmong men have avoided fighting in the war?
    e. How are the actions of a guerrilla soldier different from those of a regular soldier?
    f. What happened to Dia's father? (The family does not know.)
    g. What were the members of Dia's family forced to do to keep from being killed?
    h. Hmong means "free people." In what ways do you think the Hmong people were "free" before the war?
    i. Do you think the word *free* described the Hmong when they got to Thailand?
    j. What did Dia's family get in the refugee camp in Thailand that helped them to eventually migrate to the United States?

11. Students offer logical ideas based on scenes on cloth.

12. Students answer correctly and predict logically.

k. What were some of the problems Dia and the Hmong people had to overcome in the United States?

l. Is there anyone in this book you think is a hero?

7. Students conclude that the cloth tells the history of the Hmong just as the picture set recorded U.S. history.

17. All of the events described in the narrative are shown on the cloth. Examine the cloth again, locating the different events. Ask, "What weapons are shown on the cloth? Which weapons do you think were most destructive to the Hmong? Why? What is the importance of the story cloth to Dia and her family? To other Americans who are Hmong?"

18. Make a list of words that describe the cloth. Ask, "How has the explanation of the cloth and our detailed observation of it changed our thoughts about the cloth? What does the cloth tell us about the impact of war on people? In what ways are the presentation of the war on Dia's cloth different from what we saw in the picture set of the American Civil War? What does the cloth tell you happened to the people?"

13. Students agree that the cloth is a historical document that is important to all Hmong people and serves a function similar to that of photographs.

8. Students draw a picture that illustrates a way that war affects the lives of people.

19. *Closure:* Display the chart and read the statements. Ask, "Are there any statements on our list that you think we should remove at this time? Are there any new things to add about people, events, and war?" Read the final list aloud. Post the list on a bulletin board. Have students draw pictures to frame the poster that illustrate what they have concluded about war and its impact on people. Leave space at the top for a title to be added later.

14. Students offer appropriate changes to list.

15. *Formal assessment:* Students' pictures show the impact of war on people, including civilians.

Expansion Phase

Materials: Computers for research, a paper strip on which to write the title for the bulletin board, the list of past winners of the Nobel Peace Prize at http://almaz.com/nobel/peace/peace.html

Objectives →	*Procedures* →	*Assessments*
1. Given the request to reflect on their recent study, students describe what they have learned about how war affects the lives of people.	1. Call attention to the chart and pictures on the bulletin board. Refer to several pictures and ask, "Which statement on the chart do you think this picture illustrates? How are our pictures different from those we looked at from the Library of Congress?" Affirm the presence of civilian population and their losses as well as military.	1. Students indicate that more than soldiers are injured in war and mention immigration and refugees.

continued

2. Students use the Internet to gather information about people and organizations who help civilians and refugees affected by wars, identifying their roles and the types of help provided.

2. Tell students we need a title for our bulletin board that tells what we learned. Ask for suggestions, recording on the board, until there is a title on which students agree. Write the title on a strip of paper and attach it to the bulletin board.

3. Tell the students that World War I was called "the war to end all wars," but there have been hundreds of wars since then. Many people have jobs in which they help the civilian people and those who become refugees. Display a list of winners of the Nobel Peace Prize. Note that some are people and others are groups or organizations. Ask, "What do you think they have done to bring about peace or prevent wars? How can we find out more about the winners and others who help to prevent wars or help people during wars?"

4. Assign students to small groups to research the organizations that help people who are affected by wars today. They should find information on who works for the groups, how they get their money to work, where they are currently working, and what types of help they provide. (You may give a short oral presentation explaining a poster you make that illustrates the main findings.) Display a list of organizations for reports; students may add others if they know of them. Possible groups include the U.N. Commission for Refugees, Doctors without Borders, the International Red Cross/Red Crescent, Vietnam Veterans of America Foundation, winners of the Nobel Peace Prize, church-affiliated charities,[*] and nongovernmental organizations,[*] such as World Vision and Children International. Students select organizations and research the answers.

2. Students identify role and types of help provided.

3. Reports are formal assessments. Grade on inclusion of information assigned.

3. Students develop an action plan for sharing ideas about helping organizations and building an effort to support and participate in

5. Students present a short report with an illustration or PowerPoint presentation concerning the group researched. These illustrations may be added to the bulletin board under a heading that students select as appropriate.

6. Students decide how they can inform others about what they have learned and why it is important. Then

4. Students offer plans and decide on an acceptable plan of action to share ideas about their research and how to help an organization's work

[*]Teachers can search the Internet for names of such groups with local connections.

continued

the work of those organizations.

they develop an action plan in small groups and arrive at a whole-class consensus on a plan.

7. Alternative or additional options: Include a class visit from a person who works for such an organization or an interview with a person from the community who is a refugee.

8. *Lesson Summary:* Students briefly review the activities with which they have been involved and identify the generalization constructed as a result of those activities: Because wars and civil wars kill some soldiers and civilians and severely change the lives of the surviving civilians and soldiers, warfare is an event that people and governments should work hard to prevent happening in the future.

by supporting and participating in it.

5. Plan is assessed on its ability to be workable through student participation.

because it focuses on identifying multiple perspectives, using reflective discussion, and evaluating consequences of decisions. True stories from three trade books present the reality of war and its consequences in the lives of common people in different nations and at different times. The expansion phase of the lesson looks at responses caring people and organizations have made to the negative impacts of warfare both between nations and within nations.

 ## Resources for Teaching Global Education

Computers and the Internet

Many sources of information and multiple perspectives about people and events throughout the world are available today. Whereas in the past there were few opportunities for students to test or challenge perspectives or conclusions about how people live or feel in another area of the world, today students can communicate with students in classrooms throughout the world, read local reports in newspapers of many nations, and join in chats and discussions with individuals throughout the world. Technology also has changed the reporting of events, enabling reporters to provide live coverage as events are taking place that can include pictures and streaming video. All of these new sources of data provide more information but, in return, demand that students learn skills of critical thinking. Such skills are needed to evaluate information and decide which parts of the information are valid or biased, what conclusions can be made from the information, and how accurate those conclusions might be. In the past, students were likely to accept what was written in a book or presented in a single news presentation as true; today, that is less likely. When encountering the words of many people with varying wants and messages, students want to know the truth. Teachers need to help students by encouraging them to ask questions and by helping them to analyze and evaluate the many comments available. Many websites provide information in multiple languages. Large news media throughout the world can be visited for news and perspectives not present in US media sources.

Because young people are interested in the lives of youth in other nations and because so much of the athletic equipment and clothing worn by U.S. youths is made in foreign nations, U.S. students have become aware of the fact that the money they spend goes to workers and businesses around the world. The International Labor Organization website examines the plight of workers and the issue of child labor in today's world, and the U.N. website for teachers contains the texts and treaties on human rights that can help students examine working conditions.

The impact of war includes the many people who are severely wounded every day by land mines, and more mines are being deployed each day. Through the project materials section of the United Nations website, students can learn about the serious problem of land mines and how to help families and children living in dangerous areas to have safer lives. Mark Hyman explains how students at Tenafly Middle School in New Jersey became interested in helping to eliminate land mines and raised $30,000 to finance the removal of mines in the small city of Podzvizd in Bosnia-Herzegovina (Hyman, 2001).

TIME FOR REFLECTION | **What Do You Think?**

1. What do you anticipate the students' response will be to the focus question for the exploratory introduction of this lesson?

2. When did you last read or hear in the media about refugees from war or famine?

3. How can the NCSS Standard VIII (Science, Technology, and Society) be worked into this lesson?

4. Write a values statement that you think sums up this lesson.

Book Series

Books with a variety of formats provide the information needed to study global issues. There are a number of book series for young learners about families throughout the world. Especially helpful are those illustrated by photographs.

Series of books such as those by Lerner Publications of Minneapolis address topics such as visual geography, the world in conflict, and globe trotters. Such book series provide similar information on nations and cultures that allow students to identify commonalities and differences among nations and people.

Resources for Current Events

Many teachers at all grade levels use current events to illustrate the importance of history and social sciences to the lives of people today. Current events are also used to internationalize the curriculum. Most teachers use current events for a few minutes each day or as a weekly or biweekly focus during a class period. Some teachers develop units based on a current event (Haas & Laughlin, 2000). There are numerous sources of information about current events, and today's technology makes it possible to gain access to international news broadcasts and articles. Local problems can be linked to similar problems in other areas of the world. Almost all of the news programs and publications have websites, and many provide lesson plans for teachers. Programs are available for purchase for all grade levels from *Scholastic, Time*, and *Newsweek*. C-Span in the Classroom broadcasts programs early in the morning so that teachers can tape them for use in their classes. C-Span also provides lesson plans for many of these programs.

EXPANSION

Global education is a worldwide curriculum movement. Throughout the world resources for teaching global education are being produced by some nongovernmental organizations (NGOs), others by publishers or various interest groups. Using the resources of the Internet students far from each other can interact and learn about global issues. As you read earlier in this chapter, the meaning of global education is still evolving and educators are searching for common guidelines for teaching and producing educational resources. In 2008, the Global Education Week Network of the Council of Europe issued a set of guidelines to provide a common tool to help educators understand and implement global education. The types of activities recommended by this European group include:

- Use of project learning
- World-link methods
- International school partnerships
- Debate competitions on global issues
- Participative arts
- Community learning
- Learning to live together

You have probably heard of each of these approaches to learning and perhaps you have even taken part in them. Which approaches might be done in a classroom or community that does not have modern technological facilities? Which of the approaches would be best assisted through the use of modern technology? Do you believe that in the twenty-first century, global education will be more likely to be widely adopted as part of the school curriculum than it was in the twentieth century? Why or why not?

Summary

Social studies educators view examining real-world problems currently challenging people and nations as part of the socialization duty of civic education that creates active rather than passive citizens. Social studies professionals view the global perspective as one important perspective for citizens of all nations to develop. Having both a national and a global perspective helps to counter the extreme nationalism that led to world wars and the abuse of basic human rights, freedom, and justice among many people promoted by nations in the twentieth century. A curriculum that includes powerful and meaningful instruction in all 10 of the NCSS standards promotes the development of citizens who are well aware of the importance of the long struggle of people to obtain democratic rights. Such citizens are also aware that solving international problems may involve some compromises but see the need to understand multiple perspectives in viewpoints among people and nations. Through examining global connections and their causes and consequences, students come to understand that the consequences and costs of proposed solutions must be examined and evaluated before action is taken and must be reevaluated as time passes. Students become aware of the importance of individual decisions and of the collective decisions of groups and nations.

Recommended Websites to Visit

Global warming interactive sites and quizzes
http://environment.nationalgeographic.com/environment/global-warming/
Information on regions of the world
http://www.cotf.edu/earthinfo/main.html
Links to information about all the countries in the world
http://www.loc.gov/rr/international/portals.html
Population and the world
http://www.miniature-earth.com/me_english.htm
Animated maps of the world
http://www.sasi.group.shef.ac.uk/worldmapper/index.html

Play this game to learn of and try to solve problems faced by Peace Corps volunteers
http://www.peacecorps.gov/wws/educators/enrichment/wanzuzu/#servicelearning

Refugee movies
http://www.youtube.com/profile?user=UNFugeeMovies

Electro City, a computer game managing your own virtual towns and cities in New Zealand to learn about sustainability and energy use
http://electrocity.co.nz/

Translations of news articles appearing in the press in other nations
www.worldpress.org

Latest news from the United Nations on its efforts in all departments
www.un.org/News/

The International Education and Resource Network provides for joint studies between schools.
www.iearn.org/

Visit with children in other countries and learn about how they spend their days.
www.oxfam.org.uk/coolplanet/kidsweb/wakeup/index.htm

Unite for Children Against AIDS
www.unicef.org/uniteforchildren/index.html

Document-based questions and rubrics
www.kn.pacbell.com/wired/fil/pages/listdocumentpa.html#cat2

The American Forum for Global Education—Free lesson plans to download and opportunities for teachers
www.globaled.org/myself/intro.html

UNICEF Voices of Youth—Information about youth and issues related to their lives, opportunities for students to communicate with peers throughout the world, ideas for service and taking actions, teacher page
www.unicef.org/voy/

World Movement for Democracy—Learn about efforts to promote democratic education throughout the world. Links to many groups working on this task.
www.wmd.org

World News Network
www.wnnetwork.com/

Information on nations bordering Russia
www.eurasianet.org

Videos of the work of the Heifer Foundation helping families
www.heifer.org/site/c.edJRKQNiFiG/b.476481/

7

How Do Teachers Use and Manage Social Studies Instructional Strategies Effectively?

EXPLORATORY INTRODUCTION

Compare the following two instructional strategies and respond to the questions:

Strategy 1: A 30-minute teacher lecture supplemented by a PowerPoint presentation describing how a law is developed, argued, and passed by the state legislature.

Strategy 2: Two students in the class were hit while riding in cars by another car whose driver was talking on a cell phone. They know other states have laws against driving while talking on a cell phone. Their classmates agree that such driving and accidents are a serious problem. The class decides to find out how they might get a law passed in their state to forbid driving while talking on a cell phone. They search the Internet, identify and e-mail their local state congress representative, find statistics on auto accidents in which talking on a cell phone was a factor, and then invite their state representative to class to discuss how they might get their proposed law introduced and passed in the legislature.

1. What differences in student control are found in each method?
2. What differences would you expect in student learning from the two strategies for a third-grade student? For a sixth-grade student?

Chapter Overview

Meaningful and powerful social studies knowledge, supportively taught using effective instructional resources, requires thoughtful planning and ongoing assessment of short- and long-term objectives. It also requires teachers with

199

Standards

social studies pedagogical content knowledge (PCK) who understand and use strategies that facilitate students' construction of social studies knowledge. What students learn is influenced by how they are taught, the quality of individual and social processes occurring in the classroom, and the perceptions and understanding of social studies as a subject to be taught and learned (NCSS, 1994b). The social studies program is supported by a mixture of appropriate and adequate technology, classroom facilities, and resources.

Social studies teachers are like orchestra conductors as they select and combine teaching strategies and instructional resources to help students learn. They emphasize different strategies at various times during the lesson. Because every strategy has strengths and weaknesses, effective teachers select strategies matching the objectives toward which their students work. They also select activities their students enjoy or need to perform and learn.

Throughout this book, the classroom scenarios and learning cycles illustrate how individual teachers use their PCK to combine instructional resources and strategies to provide meaningful learning of powerful social studies skills, content, attitudes, and values. You will want to examine these carefully and to try them with students. They provide examples that we hope can inspire you to expand your own talents in lesson development.

Chapter Objectives

1. Describe instructional strategies that help students construct meaningful social studies learning of content, skills, values, and participation as an active citizen in a democratic nation.
2. Describe and evaluate cooperative group learning in a social studies lesson.
3. Describe and evaluate the teacher's role in social studies lessons focusing on fact acquisition, concept development, understanding generalizations, and developing cognitive and affective skills for active citizenship in a democratic society.
4. Describe the potential effects on social studies learning outcomes of varying the amount of student control in lesson activities.
5. Describe and evaluate appropriate instructional methods for each phase of the social studies learning cycle.
6. Describe important concerns to be addressed in an effective classroom management plan for teaching social studies lessons.

DEVELOPMENT

Social Studies Pedagogical Content Knowledge (PCK)

Teachers with effective social studies pedagogical content knowledge (PCK) set powerful social studies curriculum and instructional goals. Then, they plan the use of instructional strategies and assessment that enable students to accomplish

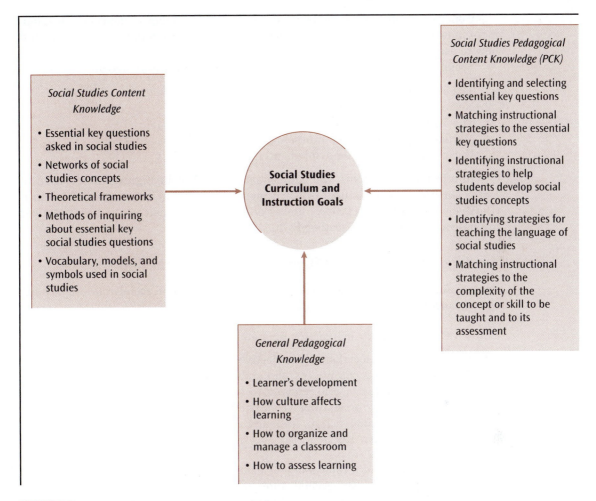

Social Studies Content Knowledge

- Essential key questions asked in social studies
- Networks of social studies concepts
- Theoretical frameworks
- Methods of inquiring about essential key social studies questions
- Vocabulary, models, and symbols used in social studies

Social Studies Curriculum and Instruction Goals

Social Studies Pedagogical Content Knowledge (PCK)

- Identifying and selecting essential key questions
- Matching instructional strategies to the essential key questions
- Identifying instructional strategies to help students develop social studies concepts
- Identifying strategies for teaching the language of social studies
- Matching instructional strategies to the complexity of the concept or skill to be taught and to its assessment

General Pedagogical Knowledge

- Learner's development
- How culture affects learning
- How to organize and manage a classroom
- How to assess learning

FIGURE 7.1

Social Studies Goals, Pedagogical Content Knowledge, and General Pedagogical Knowledge

those goals. Figure 7.1 describes how social studies curriculum and instruction goals are accomplished through social studies PCK, general pedagogical knowledge, and social studies content knowledge.

Social studies PCK involves five planning activities:

1. Identifying and selecting essential key questions for your students
2. Matching instructional strategies to the essential key questions
3. Identifying instructional strategies to help students develop social studies concepts
4. Identifying strategies for teaching the language of social studies
5. Matching instructional strategies to the complexity of the concept or skill to be taught and to its assessment

General pedagogical knowledge is teachers' knowledge of learner's development, how culture affects learning, how to organize and manage a classroom, and how to assess learning.

Social studies content knowledge involves teachers' knowledge of:

1. The essential key questions asked in social studies
2. Networks of social studies concepts
3. Theoretical frameworks
4. Methods of inquiring about essential key social studies questions
5. Vocabulary, models, and symbols used in social studies

In effective classrooms, the components described in Figure 7.1 are used to foster learning so that students learn most of what they are supposed to learn (Berliner, 1987; NCSS, 2008). A number of teaching dimensions and best practices are associated with social studies PCK.

Teaching Dimensions that Support Meaningful Learning

Several dimensions of effective teaching support meaningful social studies learning: *clarity, variety, task orientation*, and *student engagement*.

Clarity.   *Clarity*, or clear instruction, includes:

- Knowledge of the social studies objectives for the activities
- Directions students can understand and follow
- Experiences related to, and relevant to, students' lives
- Multiple modes for presenting social studies content
- Opportunities for interaction, feedback, and self-evaluation throughout lessons (Jacobowitz, 1997)

Variety.   Reading about a topic alone or using only a materials-rich activity is not sufficient. Combining instructional approaches such as materials-rich activities, student discussion, reading, and teacher questioning brings together the whole so that meaningful learning occurs.

Task Orientation.   Classrooms vary greatly in the amount of time and emphasis devoted to specific educational goals (Perie, 1997). Powerful social studies learning for *all* students requires student involvement in social studies for a significant amount of time at every grade level. Effective teachers manage and reduce interruptions, plan for transitions between topics, organize materials distribution and return, and are aware of efficient techniques for managing student traffic flow. Social studies lessons are cycles of active learning and feedback. Lessons build on one another, leading to accomplishing unit objectives.

Student Engagement.   Effective classrooms have a nonthreatening and supportive learning environment in which students focus on lesson activities with few interruptions or disruptions. If 40 minutes has been allocated for social studies but the students are engaged in learning only half that time, a powerful social studies program cannot result. The more consistently and completely students are engaged in lesson activities, the higher student achievement will be.

Best Practices: Teaching Strategies that Support Meaningful Learning

Some teaching strategies are frequently used to support meaningful learning. Two such strategies are *questioning* and *cooperative learning*. These strategies are used often throughout the Learning Cycles in this book.

Questioning. All learning begins by asking questions. The types of questions teachers use guide students' engagement in the lesson (Harvey & Goudvis, 2000). The amount of time a teacher waits between asking questions and calling on students for responses, or responding to answers, affects student responses (Rowe, 1996). Classroom research has found that teachers, on average, wait less than a second before calling on a student or responding to a student's comment. Waiting 3 or more seconds before calling on a student or acknowledging a response can increase the length of student responses, the number of appropriate responses, and the cognitive level of the responses.

Questions are planned in advance, relate to the lesson activities, and are written into lesson plans. Learning cycle lessons begin with questions that all students have a chance to answer, such as "What do you have to do to be elected president?" and "Why didn't many people settle in Florida until the middle of the twentieth century?" These are *open*, or *broad, questions*, which have many answers. Teachers accept all answers even though some answers may explain more than others. Such questions engage all students in the class. A central *key question* is planned for the exploratory phase of every learning cycle. In a lesson focusing on the concept of presidential elections, for example, the teacher may ask the key question "What do you have to do to be elected president?" It is an open question that involves each student in thinking about the main idea of the lesson.

During the lesson development phase, questions focus student inquiry on the main concepts, skills, and attitudes of the lesson. After watching an Internet video about the election campaigns of two recent candidates for president, the teacher might ask "From whom did each candidate get the money to fund the campaign?" This is a *closed, or narrow, question*. The focus is narrow because it has one or a few appropriate or correct answers. Many questions during the lesson development are narrow or closed.

During the expansion phase of the lesson, questions are used to help students apply the concept in a new context. The emphasis on open questions is greater although some closed questions may be used. For example, in the case of the presidential election campaign lesson just discussed, the teacher starts the expansion with an open question, such as "If you are going to design a winning presidential election campaign, what would it include?" Later, the teacher might ask the closed question "What is missing from our design for a winning presidential election campaign?"

NCSS
Standards VI

As we consider skills much needed by citizens in the twenty-first century, questioning that stimulates higher-level thinking is prominent. In social studies, we ask fundamental open questions such as:

- "Why and how do people establish, influence, and interact with systems of governance?"

To help students consider such complex questions, teachers use open questions that focus attention on more specific important ideas; for example, middle school students might consider:

- "How can world governments cooperate to make ethical decisions related to our global environment?"

Even more specific open questions that still allow for a variety of responses can be used, such as:

- "Why are third parties unsuccessful in U.S. politics?"

Beyond such a specific open question, the teacher might involve students in considering closed or narrow questions such as:

- "What regulations are followed in our state to decide whether a person is eligible to vote in the next election?" or
- "What are the three main reasons the people we interviewed gave for voting for _____ as our governor?"

To better understand the big ideas in social studies, teachers use closed questions but make sure to use open questions and build toward the powerful fundamental open questions around which social studies is built (Ratway, 2008, p. 394).

Cooperative Learning.   Cooperation is needed in all classroom learning as students share the time and talents of a teacher and learning resources. *Cooperative learning* is an approach and a set of strategies specifically designed to encourage student cooperation while learning. In a review of research on the use of cooperative learning, Slavin (1989) reported that students learn as well or better when using cooperative learning as when using competitive and individual learning strategies. Johnson and Johnson (1986) pointed out that students develop a positive self-image and an improved attitude toward, and acceptance of, classmates.

Because social studies is committed to fostering human and civil behaviors and active, responsible participation in the communities in which people live and work, cooperative learning should be integrated into the learning and participation of social studies lessons (Stahl, 1994). Cooperative learning is uniquely suited for social studies because the social skills it teaches are essential to democratic attitudes and beliefs (Johnson & Johnson, 1991). When diverse students are brought together for repeated face-to-face interactions in which they must use cooperative learning procedures, they become more supportive of each other (Johnson & Johnson, 1991). Students in cooperative groups show higher academic achievement and increased motivation.

Traditional group strategies create barriers in learning (Johnson, Johnson, & Holubec, 1990a). Two major barriers include leadership dominated by one person and work performed by a few in the group. Students do not develop group process skills unless they are taught them directly and required to practice them. Only through reflection on their cooperative efforts do students become committed to the value of cooperative learning. To be successful, group interpersonal skills are carefully planned for, taught, and reinforced by the teacher. Table 7.1 compares behaviors of students and teachers in cooperative groups with their behaviors in traditional classrooms.

Cooperative learning fosters four important goals (Johnson & Johnson, 1986). *First*, positive interdependence among students is created through the division of workload, responsibility, and joint rewards. Groups establish positive interdependence when they learn to work together to earn recognition, grades, rewards, and other indicators of group success (Slavin, 1989). They learn to work together for the common good. Discussions, explanations, questioning, and other verbal exchanges are important in sharing, exploring, discovering, applying, reviewing, and rehearsing the content.

Second, positive student interaction and accountability holds students individually accountable for their own learning and for the learning of others in the group. Assignments are frequently divided, with each student mastering a part and then instructing the other students in the area of mastery. Each student knows the others are depending on him or her. If one student chooses to do poor work or make trouble within the group, the other members of the group are sure to be affected and use peer pressure to change the student's behavior. Grades are often partially assigned by combining individual scores and group mean scores. Teachers and students evaluate and grade the working process of the group as well as the final product or presentation. They discuss the group process and how well the group accomplished its goals, and evaluate the individual roles of group members. Additional discussion topics include the sequence of tasks, procedures used in carrying out the tasks, and student responsibility for the tasks.

TABLE 7.1
Behaviors of Students and Teachers in Classrooms

Traditional Classroom	Cooperative Classroom
Do your own work	Work with others to learn
Eyes to front and be quiet	Eye to eye, knee to knee
Listen only to the teacher	Listen to group members
Learn only from teacher/materials	Learn from one's peers within a group
Work alone	Work within a small group as a group
"Silence is golden"	Productive talk is desired
Teacher only makes decisions	Students make decisions
Learners are passive	Learners are active

Source: "Cultivating Cooperative Group Process Skills within the Social Studies Classroom," by P. Roy, 1994, in R. J. Stahl (Ed.), *Cooperative Learning in Social Studies: A Handbook for Teachers*, Menlo Park, CA: Addison-Wesley. Used with permission.

Third, students work to develop adequate interpersonal and small-group skills. Students are taught effective communication, willingness to accept and support each other, skills to resolve conflicts, and appreciation for learning about each other. Students evaluate their group skills and performance in planning and working together. Instruction in cooperative learning begins with short lessons or with carefully structured activities presented by the teacher. As students become more familiar with the group processes, activities may be longer and involve the students in selecting topics and assigning membership responsibilities.

Fourth, students develop awareness of the need for group processing. In face-to-face encounters students discuss the group process, determine how well the group accomplished its goals, and evaluate individual roles in the group. Some discussion topics include sequence of tasks, procedures to carry out the tasks, and student responsibility for the tasks. Group functioning is monitored by students and the teacher. The teacher instructs students in effective group processes, creates and facilitates a nonthreatening work environment, and intervenes when members encounter difficulty with group processes. Group processes include group-formation skills, group-achievement skills, and group-interaction skills.

The method used in grouping students is important to the success of cooperative groups. Teachers plan heterogeneous, small cooperative groups. A typical group includes four students: one high achiever, two average achievers, and one low achiever. Leadership responsibilities for both the content of the lesson and the success of the group belong to all group members. One student might be the group *recorder*, writing down what decisions are made and keeping notes. Another student might be *materials manager*, collecting the materials needed and organizing them. Another student might be the group *spokesperson* in charge of communicating learning outcomes to others. One more student might be the group *organizer*, making sure that everyone has a chance to contribute to discussion and that each person has a clear task to do. Roles usually alternate over time among members of the group.

When large amounts of material are obtained for a topic, tasks are divided into about equal parts. For example, on the topic of the Great Depression in the United States in the 1930s, each group member focuses on one possible question:

- What were the major causes of the Depression?
- What were the effects of the Depression in our community?
- What major solutions were experimented with to try to ease the Depression?
- What was the role of the president, Franklin D. Roosevelt?

Each member may work with students in other groups who have the same question to answer. This division into specialist groups is called a *jigsaw*. An alternative sharing method requires each group member to develop a response individually, then to share it with his or her cooperative group.

Using Technology

Creating a Collaborative Classroom

Examples of powerful social studies lessons that engage students in collaborative learning with technology are available. A middle school example is "Why Did They Do It: What Were the Purposes of Lewis and Clark's Corps of Discovery Expedition?" (Sunal, Sunal, & Staubs, 2007). Students consider the key question posed and examine some scenes from along the Lewis and Clark Expedition's trail, which they can use to form hypotheses responding to the question. Next, small groups of students undertake tasks that investigate information on relevant Internet websites. Each group assigns a different task and set of websites to each member, who serves as the expert on this aspect of the expedition. The experts get together and share ideas in a jigsaw cooperative learning group format achieving a new level of expertise. The experts return to their home group where they present their expertise and enable the group to decide whether their hypotheses are supported by the evidence they have gathered. As an expansion of their work, the groups then examine other expeditions such as Richard E. Byrd's Antarctic expedition and Samuel Chaplain's northeastern North American expeditions. They consider whether their hypothesis continues to be supported by these other diverse expeditions. Without collaboration, a single student or the whole class could not have the opportunity to investigate the purposes of expeditions of discovery in the past in such great depth, nor to develop personal expertise that contributes to addressing an interesting problem. An example of a collaborative group project for fourth grade is "Westward Ho!" by Lori Mathys (2007) in which students become part of pioneer families. In another example, fifth and sixth graders work with partners and in small groups to examine and make inferences from statistics that address "Standard of Living Around the World: From Analysis to Action" (Libresco & Phua, 2007).

In social studies activities using cooperative learning, teachers tend to have less difficulty with classroom management. Students assume greater responsibility for materials and help each other by answering questions and assisting in the completion of assignments. Because students realize they have valid contributions to make, they become even more willing to participate in small-group work. Students use their creativity to solve more difficult and complex problems than they would be willing to try individually. Social studies teachers are helping students learn to live in their social world: cooperative grouping facilitates this effort.

A Continuum of Knowledge and Instruction

Teachers have different conceptions of the way social studies teaching and learning take place. One conception focuses on *fact acquisition*. The content to be learned is a list of facts and definitions of terms. Students receive and remember the information presented. Repetition is the key learning process. Students are evaluated by repeating facts and definitions provided by the teacher and textbook. The teacher sets most of the conditions for learning: exposing students to facts, providing drill and recitation sessions, and encouraging motivation in students through a variety of media and external rewards. This conception focuses on low student and high teacher control of learning.

A second conception of social studies teaching and learning focuses on *concept* or *idea attainment*. Students figure out the attributes of a concept by comparing and contrasting examples and nonexamples of the concept. In this view, students are learning concepts created by others. The teacher presents and explains concepts in a coherent and interesting way by involving students in using examples, anecdotes, and activities to illustrate the concepts. In this conception, students have greater control over their learning than in fact acquisition.

NCSS

Standards

A third conception of social studies teaching and learning actively engages students in developing important social studies ideas on their own, identifying and using them in the real world. The emphasis in *idea formation* is on activities involving students with interpreting and constructing representations of what they read, observe, and try out. Students decide what to investigate and the methods to use. Students are encouraged, in a safe setting, to challenge their previously learned ideas. Students integrate this information with their prior knowledge, making changes or replacing old ideas as needed and appropriate. Teachers guide student learning and monitor student behaviors, ideas, and interpretations. New alternative ideas are attempted by applying them and by providing new evidence and situations, allowing the student to choose the appropriate new idea (NCSS, 1994b). Effective social studies teaching through idea formation changes traditional student and teacher roles, giving students greater control over learning. No longer is the teacher just an information giver, motivating students to memorize concepts as understood by the teacher or text. Students actively participate in the learning process using exploration, testing their prior knowledge, and applying ideas in a variety of situations. Teachers help students learn, reducing their role as the knowledge authority.

The activities of learning and the processes for helping others learn fall along a *continuum of instruction*. One end is the giving and acceptance of information to be learned with low student and high teacher control; the other end is the search for learning and the puzzle of putting together data to create new meaning with high student and low teacher control of learning.

In the remainder of this chapter, you will learn about some teaching strategies that can be used in social studies to help students attain specific objectives. Each is grouped and presented according to the amount of teacher and student control over the lesson and is linked to the phases of the learning cycle in which it is most appropriately used. Figure 7.2 illustrates the relationships between types of activities and the behaviors of teachers and students.

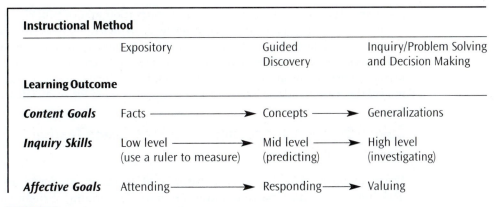

Instructional Method			
	Expository	Guided Discovery	Inquiry/Problem Solving and Decision Making
Learning Outcome			
Content Goals	Facts ⟶	Concepts ⟶	Generalizations
Inquiry Skills	Low level ⟶ (use a ruler to measure)	Mid level ⟶ (predicting)	High level (investigating)
Affective Goals	Attending ⟶	Responding ⟶	Valuing

FIGURE 7.2
Matching Learning Outcomes to Instructional Methods

Matching Instructional Strategies to Student Needs

NCSS
Standards

One aim of education is to help students be self-directing (NCSS, 1994a, pp. 11–12). A key factor is the amount of student control during the learning process. In order from least to greatest student control, the categories are *expository, guided discovery*, and *inquiry and problem solving/decision making*. These categories are described in detail in the next sections to demonstrate the range of social studies instructional methods. Teachers choose an appropriate instructional strategy that matches the student's level of social studies content, skill, attitudinal objectives, and developmental needs. Each instructional method is effective and appropriate in helping students attain a particular level of learning objective.

Expository, or Direct, Instructional Methods: Lower Student Control

Expository instructional methods, or direct instruction, provide students with little control over the direction or extent of the learning process. Lesson activities using expository methods include the following characteristics:

- The teacher controls the situation, providing adequate directions and motivation.
- The teacher provides ample opportunities to practice the skill in a wide variety of situations.
- The teacher supplies immediate and continuous feedback focusing on correct answers.
- The teacher uses lecture and closed, narrow questions to control the learning situation but must provide extensive and adequate directions for the student.

Expository methods require external motivation and careful classroom management. These methods produce only lower levels of learning: recall and memorization. Expository methods facilitate development of the affective areas of attending and willingness to receive information. These methods are occasionally useful in the lesson development phase of the learning cycle in which the teacher explains the key idea of the lesson and the lesson focus involves the need for recall (Rosenshine, 1986).

Guided Discovery Instructional Methods: Mixed Teacher and Student Control

When using guided discovery instructional methods, students are involved in activities related to a concept and form an understanding of them before they are offered or explained by the teacher. The teacher creates a problem to investigate and determines procedures and materials needed, but students collect and analyze data and evaluate the results as they relate to the problem. Guided discovery has four characteristics.

1. Students are provided with the time and opportunity to study relationships in data and form a new idea.
2. Students use several activities focusing on one concept, generalization, value, or skill.
3. Students' main role is to investigate and discover answers to the questions posed, discussing and displaying data to do so.
4. The teacher provides directions and asks questions that help students begin activities with the learning resources selected.

NCSS

Standards VI

An example of guided discovery methods is helping students develop the concept of law by examining two different city laws: no spitting on the sidewalk and no playing checkers in public, as they appear in the city code in 1902, 1932, and 1962. The students look for patterns, then discuss what they find. For example, students may find that the law forbids spitting in 1902, is revised to allow spitting "on downtown concrete sidewalks" in 1932, and disappears from the city code by 1962. A number of discovery activities involving the concept occur: interviews with city officials, a health department official, and members of the historical society and research using city records to determine where sidewalks were found during each year that was studied. Students can learn inquiry skills such as inferring, predicting, organizing, interpreting, and drawing conclusions from data.

Inquiry and Problem-Solving/Decision-Making Instructional Methods: Greater Student Control

The third social studies instructional method, inquiry, involves significant student control over the direction the lesson takes. Students create a problem to investigate, determine procedures and materials needed, collect and analyze data, and evaluate results. These lessons have five characteristics:

1. Students are competent in basic social studies inquiry skills.
2. Students select problem areas to investigate.
3. Students work in groups, orally reporting the results of investigations.
4. The teacher guides students in defining the problem to investigate and in helping to identify resources.
5. A safe and supportive classroom environment is maintained.

Inquiry method activities are intrinsically motivating because students direct their own learning. Even a first-grader is likely to use higher thought processes during an inquiry. A young student's social studies project, for example, could involve making a drawing showing where items in her personal materials basket (scissors, glue stick, crayons, etc.) should be placed. The drawing is made after the student lists three or more problems with the basket, such as the glue stick always falling over. The student asks questions, communicates information, makes inferences, and builds predictions. In writing stories about the experience, facts may form the basic content of the narrative, but students also often make inferences and construct generalizations.

Students involved in inquiry and problem-solving/decision-making method activities practice the full range of inquiry skills. Careful selection of key social studies ideas and skills is needed because inquiry methods reduce the amount of material covered to a greater extent than other instructional methods. Meaningful learning of generalizations and higher-order inquiry skills, as well as improved long-term memory and transfer of learning, occur. Inquiry focuses on problem solving and decision making. It is important to bring students into contact with other people's various views and conflicting values. Therefore, inquiry problems are most often those found in the school and local community. Students plan how they can participate and work together (Dunfee & Sagl, 1967; Meyerson & Secules, 2001).

Matching Types of Instructional Activities to Each Phase of the Lesson

Teachers of powerful social studies instruction select teaching strategies that match the desired learning outcome and the needs of each phase of the lesson. The learning cycle provides a framework for lessons using multiple teaching strategies. As you read the classroom scene below, identify each phase of the learning cycle and note the various teaching strategies employed.

A CLASSROOM SCENE: One Teacher's Planning Decisions

Mrs. Cooper noticed that *scarcity*, the most fundamental economic concept, is identified for first-graders in the social studies standards of her school district. Because scarcity is a situation that affects everyone, Mrs. Cooper wanted her lesson to help the students understand the concept and find solutions to a situation of scarcity.

NCSS

Standards VII

Mrs. Cooper's first-graders do not have strong reading skills, but she wanted to incorporate the learning of problem-solving skills, so she selected the guided discovery model. In a structured exploration activity, she engaged students in making a thank-you card for school cafeteria workers who had been helping these young children with their lunch trays. She suggested that a thank-you card should look happy. The students had previously said that yellow was a "happy color." She reminded them of their idea that yellow is a happy color, suggesting that every group might use some yellow on their card. However, Mrs. Cooper only had one piece of bright yellow paper. She introduced the concept of scarcity by asking, "How can each group have some yellow paper to decorate the card?" Students made a number of suggestions during a discussion in which they agreed on an idea that best solved their problem. After making their choice, the children started making their cards with their yellow paper and with a set of materials that included lots of other colored paper but not enough scissors and bottles of glue for all groups to use.

When the cards were completed, each group displayed their card, and the class noted how they had used the words *thank you* and the yellow paper. Then Mrs. Cooper asked whether any problems were encountered in completing the task, particularly with the materials. During the discussion, students identified the lack of enough scissors and bottles of glue. Mrs. Cooper asked students to tell her how they solved this scarcity problem, recording their solutions on a chart. Then she asked whether students noticed other times in the classroom or at home when there was not enough of something.

The children gave many examples, and Mrs. Cooper noted that everyone faces the problems of scarcity from time to time. She said, "When not enough of an item is available for you to use at a particular time and place, then there is a scarcity of the item." The children repeated the word *scarcity* and reviewed what was scarce when they made their cards. Mrs. Cooper read aloud the suggestions for solving problems of scarcity on the chart and asked, "What title should we give the chart?" and "Where should we post the chart so everyone can see it?" She encouraged the children to use the word *scarcity* in the title. The chart was posted so it could be used again when another situation of scarcity was encountered.

Later, when the students were using manipulatives in math, they discovered another situation of scarcity. They recalled, with Mrs. Cooper, how they had previously solved such a problem. Mrs. Cooper read the list and asked the students whether they could use one of these ideas to solve their problem or whether some new ideas could be added to the list. The students selected and used one of the ideas to solve the problem. The reuse of the chart during the mathematics lesson and throughout the week served as an expansion activity. As the week went on, the children became better at identifying situations of scarcity. They suggested additional ways to solve problems of scarcity, adding them to the chart. Mrs. Cooper found that her need to intervene in social problems involving scarcity decreased and that, if she reminded the students that a situation was one of scarcity, the children wanted to solve the problem for themselves rather than have her give them a solution. ■

TIME FOR REFLECTION | *What Do You Think?*

1. From the evidence offered in the description of Mrs. Cooper's teaching of scarcity, why would you say that she was or was not successful in teaching the concept to her students in a meaningful way?

2. In addition to learning the concept of scarcity, what other cognitive and affective objectives did Mrs. Cooper have for the lesson?

3. In what ways did Mrs. Cooper control the lesson?

4. In what ways did the students control what happened during the lesson?

5. What are some possible negative actions from students that might have controlled the lesson development?

6. How do you think Mrs. Cooper would have responded to the possible negative student actions?

Useful Instructional Activities for the Exploratory Introduction Phase

A sample of successful teaching methods for the exploratory introduction phase of a lesson is described next. The methods are sequenced from low to high student control.

Review.   During review, students recall related concepts and generalizations studied previously and relate them to the new idea that is developed in the current lesson.

Structured Exploration.   Structured exploration of a concept, attitude, or generalization to be developed can occur at the beginning of the lesson. An open key question introduces the lesson and helps organize students' experiences. In the classroom scene, Mrs. Cooper might have asked, "What might happen when not enough materials are available for each person in a group to do a project?" She may then have had students predict what they thought would happen and try it. Next, students could predict what would happen when a third person was added and try that. Students should describe what is happening in each activity.

Cooperative Group Challenge.   In a cooperative group challenge, a teacher describes what he is going to do and asks students to predict what happens next. For example, two students act out the beginning of a historical event but stop before it is finished. The class considers what happens next. Students are divided into cooperative groups based on their answers and each group provides evidence for its answer. Then each group gets information about the event and tests their predictions.

Confrontational Challenges or Discrepant Events.   Confrontational challenges, or discrepant events, confront students' conceptions of the way the world works. Students encounter a familiar experience for which they have an expectation of what happens next. But, surprisingly, they find a different result.

- Silently present an event in which two people interact without speaking.
- Have an event operate as students enter the room (e.g., students enter to find two close friends arguing).
- Present an unexpected situation through video or pictures. For example, students are shown pictures of a man and a woman. They hear a description of one person's accomplishments, including that the person is a boxer and volunteer firefighter. Most likely, they select the large man's picture, after which they learn that the boxer and volunteer firefighter is the woman.

Students then engage in discussion or manipulation of materials related to the inconsistent experience in an attempt to clarify their ideas. Students inquire into all the discrepancies, even those they had not expected. The teacher provides information only when requested, and only information that cannot be obtained through the students' own inquiry process.

Problem Exploration.   In a problem exploration, a teacher presents students with an open-ended problem and has them attempt to find a solution. Students might receive a map of a zoo showing drawings of animals, trees, restrooms, benches, picnic tables, waste cans, and snack machines. They are told that the city has received a gift of land next to the park that doubles its size. There is money to add pairs of moose, kangaroo, elephants, seals, and penguins. The number of tables in the picnic area will double. The zoo needs a new map, and the students have been asked to draw that map. But the city wants the size of the map to remain the same 8 ½ by 11 inches as the present map. Groups of students work to make a new map for the zoo.

NCSS

Standards
VII, X

Open Exploration.   Students explore an unstructured environment in response to an open key question. On a field trip to a tall building, for example, students observe the movement of people and goods in the community below them, then describe what they see and why this happens.

Useful Instructional Activities for the Lesson Development Phase

The second phase in the learning cycle, lesson development, explains a new idea or skill and leads students in practicing new skills and in using new content.

Instructional strategies ranging across a continuum from expository through inquiry-based problem solving and decision making are appropriate depending on the objectives for the learning cycle.

Field Trips.   Field trips of short or long duration should be a common event. These activities include everything from a trip to the school playground to make observations of how people safely use playground equipment to a trip to a historic farm. Field trips require more advance planning than do classroom activities. Teachers visit the site to determine the potential for learning and possible problem situations. Field trips have objectives similar to classroom-based activities. Depending on lesson objectives, the degree of student control of activities at the site varies.

Guest Speakers.   A guest speaker usually is welcomed with great interest. Whatever the speaker's focus, the teacher carefully prepares both speaker and students for the visit. Students often spend time studying the speaker's topic prior to the visit.

The objectives of the speaker's visit, how the students are prepared for the visit, what occurs during the visit, how the visit is expanded upon, and how it is evaluated must be identified in the lesson plan. Without a lesson plan, the visit is likely to be interesting, but it might not relate well to the specific social studies content.

Demonstration.   A demonstration involves the use of real objects, physical analogies, or models to illustrate a concept, generalization, skill, attitude, or behavior. Students look for a particular event or one student performs the activity for others. A teacher may use a demonstration to teach students how to find directions with a compass or how to introduce oneself to a person about to be interviewed. A short video clip may be appropriate for demonstrating skills. Some demonstrations provide students with information they use in a follow-up activity.

Lecture or Teacher Presentation.   Some lecture or teacher presentation is possible in the elementary and middle school. First-grade students should be exposed to a presentation of no more than 10 minutes if it is relevant to something they are studying and generates enthusiasm. Middle school students can attend to longer presentations. PowerPoint presentations often are illustrated lectures or presentations that may hold students' attention for a short time, as will video presentations.

Games.   Games are used during the lesson development phase or the expansion phase of a lesson. They provide an opportunity for students to practice both academic and social skills. Small-group games offer opportunities for players to interact directly, focusing on the educational content. Teachers in upper elementary and middle school classes may prefer to use whole-class games and model them on television game shows. Students help to prepare the game by writing questions and performing leadership tasks in such games.

Participation in answering questions can be increased by forming teams and requiring all team members to agree to an answer, or by having each team member

A field trip offers this student a unique opportunity to operate bellows once used by a nineteenth-century blacksmith.

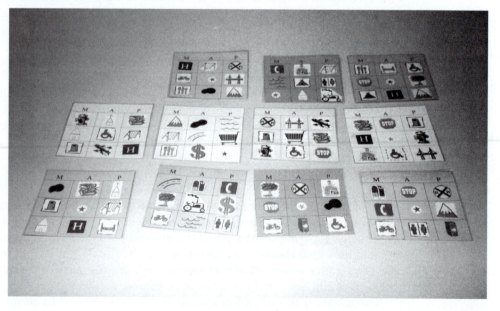

Teacher-made games help nonreaders recognize symbols, a skill used in map reading.

write the answer on a piece of paper. One or two response sheets are randomly drawn, and a point is awarded for each correct answer.

Games must have a winner so that they come to an end. Teachers can reduce the amount of emphasis placed on winning, and should keep in mind that a student's cultural background and experiences may focus not on individual wins but on contributing to the group's success.

Role-Playing and Simulations. Role-playing and simulations provide opportunities to learn content, use critical thinking, make decisions, and practice social and communication skills. They give students opportunities to hypothesize, test, revise, and retest their ideas. Done individually, role-plays tend more to examine value and social issues, whereas simulations tend to stress content and cognitive skills. Simulations also can incorporate role-playing, adding to their interest and complexity.

Role-Playing. Role-playing examines interpersonal relationships and social behavior. Students become conscious of their values when they have to express and criticize the views and behavior of the characters in the role-play. Young students role-play situations with which they are familiar, such as selecting team members. Older students may confront familiar problems or explore real problems faced by historical figures to learn how the problem can be solved. Role-playing is carefully taught. The teacher maintains a supportive class environment and is sensitive to the various personalities of the students. All students, including listeners, are actively involved in role-playing. Role-playing carries the risk of displaying emotions that might cause embarrassment or lead to criticism or ridicule. If the teacher takes time to develop a class atmosphere in which students respect individual differences and feelings, such problems are avoided.

A well-designed role-playing lesson typically has eight parts. A *warm-up* makes students aware of the general type of problem and introduces the specific role play to be considered. Student understanding is checked with specific questions about the various characters and their views. Predictions of possible actions help to identify alternatives.

Selection of participants considers students' personalities, their cultural experiences, and the content goal of the role-play. Different groups may replay the scene or subsequent scenes. More mature students should not be first to act out a scene because their choices might eliminate the consideration of alternatives and their consequences.

Setting of the stage occurs when the players come to a general agreement on the content to be portrayed in a scene but not its outcome—for example, "The scene is a conversation between a student and parent just after the parent has been called by the principal. The principal has said that the student cheated on a test."

The *listeners* in the audience are prepared for their role, receiving suggestions about what to listen for. The goal is to keep them intellectually involved in the role-play, preparing them to take part in the discussion that follows. Different listeners may be assigned specific tasks, for example, observing a character's responses.

NCSS

Standards IV

The actual *role-play is introduced* by establishing who are the participants and when and where the action takes place. An introduction may state: "Mary is the mother who has just heard from the principal about her son cheating on a test. Tom is the son who enters the house through a door over there and sees his mother."

Following the enactment, the teacher leads a *discussion* investigating the realism portrayed by the roles. The characters' words and actions are evaluated. A discussion of alternative responses that could have been made by the characters and the consequences of those responses dominates this section.

A *reenactment* of the role-play follows. Students portray different interpretations by the characters, so a new set of alternatives and consequences are examined. Additional scenes in the drama may also need to be portrayed. Different groups of students may act out these scenes to increase participation.

To bring *closure*, the teacher and students examine how representative is the problem they enacted. They may draw some generalizations about the ways people respond when facing a problem. During this time students may share similar problems with which they are familiar. A teacher never prods students into revealing personal problems that might cause embarrassment. Therefore, teachers ask appropriate questions:

Have you ever heard of someone having a similar problem?
Was the outcome realistic?
What were important comments or actions that led to this outcome?
What might have been said or done to change the outcome?
Can you imagine a situation in which a similar problem might take place?

Simulations.   Simulations are activities similar to a real-world situation or problem, simplified for use in a short time period. Students perform tasks or assume roles and act out a problem situation. Participants are provided with descriptions of their tasks, roles, and the problem situation. Very young students might take part in working in a class post office, sorting and delivering letters. Older students might take part in a simulated Nigerian marketplace, court of law, or stock market investment.

Teachers can construct simulations, locate them in resources, or purchase them. An example of a sixth-grade simulation found on the Internet is *Emperor of Rome* at http://www.pbsorg/empires/romans/special/emperorgame.html. Ideas for two simulations that can be used in middle schools to consider the question "What is the Best Way to Govern a Nation?" have been described by Jason Endacott (2007). One simulation considers democracy "Let's Plan a Party" while the other considers autocracy "Pizza My Way." Students apply their knowledge and skills as they solve the simulation problem. Teachers prepare the materials, introduce the simulation, and conduct the final debriefing discussion.

When they begin the simulation, students have all materials and clearly understand the problem and issues. Roles are assigned with care. Ideally, roles are equal in the amount of time and work needed for preparation. Simulation materials provide each student with a detailed written description of his or her role, including talents, concerns, and viewpoints about the topic.

When the teacher is certain that the problem and roles are clearly understood, the simulation begins. When the problem is solved, the simulation is completed. Debriefing of the simulation requires students not only to recall events, but also to reflect on their consequences and importance to the solution. The following are appropriate debriefing questions:

How realistic was the simulation?

Did the participants perform their roles realistically?

Are the participants happy with the outcome? What could have been done differently to increase their satisfaction?

What additional knowledge might help them better perform the simulation?

What are other possible outcomes for the simulation had different views prevailed?

What did we learn that might help us understand other similar problems?

The objective of a simulation is that the students learn through the process, including the debriefing, not that they get the "right" or "best" solution to the simulation problem. If grades are given in connection with a simulation, they should be assessed after the completion of the simulation and the debriefing discussion.

Teachers might choose to repeat the same simulation after students have studied the topic with the expectation that students create a more sophisticated and complex solution in the expansion phase. However, a short simulation experience cannot provide students with an adequate understanding or emphatic experiences for complex historical events such as the Holocaust or the slave trade (Totten, 2000). If a simulation is used for a complex cognitive and affective event, it may be best to reserve it for the exploration phase. Research and study on the issues and values of the real event can be undertaken during the lesson development phase. Students will have some ideas to research after experiencing the simulation.

Discussion Strategies. Discussion entails verbally sharing ideas with the goal of improving one's thinking on a topic (Parker, 2001a). Powerful discussions involve higher-order thinking. Students who take part in successful discussions come to the situation with a set of skills they have learned and are willing to use, and some knowledge about the topic to be discussed. The knowledge may come from real-life experiences or be acquired indirectly through media. The teacher has four roles in discussions (Eggen & Kauchak, 2001; Parker, 2001b). First, teachers create a focal point for the discussion that attracts students' thinking by framing a question or problem of interest to students.

Second, teachers orient students by giving clear directions for the specific tasks facing them. For example, a teacher might inform students that a homeless student living in a nearby shelter will become part of the class tomorrow and ask them, in pairs, to identify ways in which they can help the student maintain his school materials and be a successful partner in projects while respecting the difficulties of his situation. Next, the teacher uses small-group discussions in which each group focuses on a specific strategy that can be used to help the new student become a partner in the classroom. Finally, the whole group meets to share specific strategies discussed in small groups and plan how these will be implemented over the next week. The teacher might provide students with a discussion guide that presents a topic and asks them to perform certain tasks in keeping with the skills required for discussion of the topic (see Figure 7.3).

Third, teachers facilitate interaction during the discussion by the kinds of tasks they provide (e.g., starting with discussion among pairs, moving to small groups, and then to a whole group). Teachers also facilitate interaction through using open-ended questions such as Why? How? and In what ways? Teachers foster willingness to participate by personally modeling skills and by recognizing students' efforts in the discussion. To do this, teachers clarify students' comments: "We don't have the facts to make a conclusion or know whether this idea is accurate or realistic" or "Carol is right; you must make an inference to make this conclusion." Arranging seats so that students have eye contact with one another and easily hear each other promotes the interchange of ideas.

Teachers teach skills for discussion and have students practice them, including the following:

- Listening to others
- Asking questions to draw out or clarify the ideas of others
- Paraphrasing the views of others
- Identifying areas of agreement or disagreement

Fourth, teachers keep the discussion focused and on track. They use focusing questions such as "How does that relate to our question?" Teachers also summarize and review at critical points.

Before you examine the artifact, recall the rules for group discussions and decide on procedures you can use to help the group reach a conclusion.

- Listen to others and ask questions so you know what every other person in your group thinks.
- Give everyone a fair chance to express their ideas.
- Discuss what the group can do if you don't have the same idea at first.
- Discuss what the group should do if you can't all agree on an idea after talking about everybody's ideas for a while.

Each member of your group should examine your group's artifact carefully. When everyone has had a chance to examine the artifact, discuss and complete the following instructions.

1. Give the artifact a name.
2. Describe what you think the artifact is used for.
3. Describe what you think the artifact is made of.
4. Describe how you would make the artifact.

FIGURE 7.3
Discussion Guide: What Is This Artifact?

The biggest problem with discussions arises when a teacher does not allow students to develop ownership of them (Eggen & Kauchak, 2001). To give students ownership, teachers must sit back, take a less active role, and let student leadership develop. Teachers cannot, however, let discussion flounder but must provide sensitive direction that maintains students' central, active role. When some students dominate the discussion, teachers steer it by calling on a wide sample of students with comments such as "Let's hear another point of view from _____" and "We haven't heard from _____ yet. What do you think?"

Another alternative is to use small-group discussion in which everyone participates followed by a whole-class discussion. When the whole class is involved in a discussion, they usually are working toward the construction of a concept, generalization, value, or other portion of social studies content. This occurs during the lesson development phase. Discussions in the expansion phase often have students take the knowledge or skill constructed and consider its application in a new situation.

A discussion needs closure so that students feel their efforts have produced some results. Teachers can ask students to create a summary of major points made in the discussion or to indicate their agreement with a conclusion by a show of hands. Because discussions do not always lead to common conclusions, teachers address this point at the end of the discussion noting that "Different people have different ideas about our question. That's okay. What is important is to know what you think and why." The teacher emphasizes that the purpose of discussion is not necessarily agreement but the honest exchange of ideas and opinions.

Writing in Social Studies.　Writing can be utilized in many ways to create powerful social studies learning. Writing helps to process information, to examine point of view, and to determine what the information explains about an event, idea, or value. The steps of the writing process often are incorporated: prewriting, drafting, revising, editing, and sharing/publishing to organize facts and express conclusions and beliefs.

An "I used to be…, but now" poem or paragraph is one example of using writing to create meaningful social studies (Sunal, Powell, McClelland, et al., 2000). Students take a look backward at their own lives and the way they used to be. Initially, as a prewriting activity, the teacher asks students to bring in and share photographs of themselves at different ages and also favorite toys from different ages. The teacher follows up with questions: How have you changed since you were little? and How have you stayed the same?

Another prewriting activity has each student complete a then/now chart on any number of topics. For example, the following chart considers the topic of emotions:

	Then	Now
Emotions	looked up to older brother afraid of the dark—needed a light in the hallway	my older brother is a pain don't need a light any more

Next, students begin drafting a poem or paragraph using their then/now chart. The teacher may read the beginning of a piece she has partially drafted from her own then/now chart. Students put aside their drafts for a couple of days, then revise them focusing on their ideas rather than on mechanics. When satisfied with their ideas, they move to the editing stage in which they consider issues of form and correct grammar, spelling, and punctuation. Finally, students share their writing in a read-aloud from the classroom author's chair.

Students are helped to structure their writing in social studies using five sections: aim or purpose of the investigation, method or how it was carried out, results, conclusions, and action plan. Students can be told what type of information to write in each section and how it can be written. Table 7.2 shows how all these parts are related. The writing process can be used in creating the report of an investigation. Other social studies activities include creating a comparison and contrast chart, composing a photo essay, and developing a survey.

Difficulties in Reading Textbooks.   Today's teachers tend to use national and state standards and multiple resources, including appropriate sections of textbooks. Some teachers allow the textbook to define the social studies curriculum and the units they teach. Many social studies textbooks contain lots of pictures, illustrations, maps, and graphs. Teacher guides suggest activities to help introduce and expand on the text's presentation. Many students have difficulty reading social studies textbooks. Their difficulties often stem from a lack of experiential background.

TABLE 7.2
Guide for Writing Up a Social Studies Investigation

Heading	What to Write	How to Write It
State Problem, Aim, or Purpose	What do you think you were trying to find out in this investigation?	Write a short, single-sentence statement that begins "To find out…."
Method	Describe, in your own words, exactly what we did.	1. Write numbered statements. 2. Use the word *we* instead of *I*. 3. Use past tense: *was* and *were*, and so on.
Findings	What did you discover?	Write a few sentences about what you discovered. Illustrate with two or three examples of supporting evidence. Include a table, chart, or timeline showing the results.
Conclusions	What did you discover in this investigation?	Write a few sentences explaining what you found out.
Action Plan	What can or should people do to tell others about the situation and start to improve it?	Write one or two sentences about how people can use this information.

Social studies textbooks tend to have a heavy load of technical concepts and generalizations. Technical concepts are specialized ideas in social studies, such as interdependence and political party. Technical concepts are related to each other to form generalizations, for example, the economies of countries in today's world are interdependent on each other. Most students have an incomplete and inaccurate understanding of these concepts. Many social studies textbooks pile too many concepts and generalizations into a few paragraphs without enough supporting examples and with little discussion.

Textbooks are made more complex because they include hard-to-pronounce names of cities, faraway countries, and foreign words. References to long periods of time and huge distances are frequent. What does a 10-year-old student think when a textbook says, "Our country was founded over two hundred years ago" or "long, long ago"? What do expressions such as "far to the north" or "over a thousand miles to the east" mean to students who are not sure which direction is which and have never traveled farther than across the state (Hoge, 1986, p. 1)?

Doing a Content Analysis of a Textbook.

Teachers carry out a content analysis of their school curriculum guide and think about what they intend to teach. When they have identified a unit they plan to teach, they examine a copy of the textbook to see whether it contains relevant material. Next, teachers analyze the unit in a student edition of the text before reading the teacher's guide. Many teachers use textbooks as resources for students. When textbooks are used as a resource, they support a unit but do not directly determine its content.

The content analysis procedure in the next Time for Reflection activity also is useful in carrying out a content analysis of a curriculum guide, a unit, or other supplementary teaching resource. A content analysis helps teachers identify the most important skills, facts, concepts, generalizations, attitudes, and values in the resource. If these match what the teacher intends to teach, the resource provides good support.

Developing a Teaching Plan Using a Textbook.

Once the content of a textbook unit has been analyzed and the most important inquiry skills, facts, concepts, generalizations, attitudes, and values identified, the teacher develops a teaching plan. The teaching plan sets up one or more learning cycles for the important material identified. If students can learn important material, the teacher relegates other material to the more cursory treatment of reading about it in the textbook. It is critical to identify what is most important and implement learning cycles to teach it. The textbook, or a portion of it, can be used in the learning cycle but is best used during the lesson development phase.

A new teacher may have difficulty accomplishing effective teaching because of the demands of many subject areas. New teachers usually cannot develop more than one or two complete, well-elaborated units in each subject area during the first year of teaching. Therefore, a new teacher identifies the one or two most important social studies units in the textbook and develops a teaching plan using

TIME FOR REFLECTION **What Do You Think?**

Do a textbook unit content analysis by examining one unit in a student copy of a social studies textbook. Answer the following questions.

1. What should be learned from reading this unit?
2. What is most important here?
3. What are the most important facts presented?
4. What are the most important concepts presented?
5. For which of these concepts can students currently give an example?
6. Which concepts are likely to be completely new to students?
7. What inquiry skills are presented or required?
8. What attitudes are evident?
9. What values are incorporated?
10. Which words will students have difficulty pronouncing and understanding?
11. Do the objectives match those in the state or local curriculum guide?
12. Which national social studies standards are addressed?

learning cycles for those units. During the following year, the teacher can add one or two more units to his or her repertoire.

Most teacher's guides have activities to support the textbook, but they often do not match the social studies content well. Activities may try to integrate other content areas often including literature and math. This takes attention away from the social studies topic and might result in a neglect of the social studies skills students must learn (Alleman & Brophy, 1998).

When reading the textbook, students use a variety of strategies to help them with text material. Study guides help students identify important facts, concepts, and generalizations. In cooperative groups, students can each read passages and share their study-guide responses. Struggling readers can be grouped with more proficient readers so difficulties that arise in a particular passage, such as pronouncing a word or understanding a sentence, can be quickly overcome by seeking help from another group member. Passages can be audio-recorded by the teacher, an adult volunteer, or an older student for students having difficulty reading them.

Social Studies Kits. Social studies teaching materials can be purchased as individual items or as kits designed for a specific topic of study, such as ancient civilizations or mapping. Kits contain materials used to conduct activities that fit the yearlong social studies plan. Most kits are supplemented with a teacher's guide and multimedia support materials. Some kits contain several other materials, such as large pictures, posters, models, artifacts, or both informational and fiction books.

Making a Literature Connection

Reading Literature

Only high-quality trade books that are appropriate for social studies should be selected for use in a unit. To maximize their use, trade books are carefully selected for small-group, whole-group, and teacher read-alouds. Trade books are used to support or introduce attitudes and values. It is important for teachers to read the books they select and to consider both the accuracy of the content and the attitudes and values that can be affected by reading the book. The selection of trade books must accurately represent differing perspectives. A trade book does not replace other resources used in social studies, but is a support. Student self-selection of books to read from those identified by the teacher is a way to expand an individual's learning.

Reading provides the student with information and viewpoints on issues, people, and events.

Carefully guiding students in reading textbooks and factual books is important, because the styles of writing are different from a fictional story. Students need to identify the facts that illustrate ideas and recognize the conclusions made by the author. Help needs to be given to students in reading the words on maps and charts because writing on such items does not follow the same sentence construction as in the books they are familiar with reading. Indeed, some of the writing may be headings, which are not constructed in complete sentences. When reading documents, students also may encounter these same unusual ways of stating information.

Professional educational publishing houses, museums, government agencies, industries, and special interest groups all produce materials for classroom use. Often, they hire education specialists to work with them to produce professional-looking learning materials. Such materials may be free or inexpensive, but are always considered "sponsored" (Haas, 1985). Many sponsored materials are appropriate for classroom use, but they may express the viewpoint of the producer or sponsor. When teachers decide to use materials that have not been screened for overall appropriateness by official adoption committees, they have the additional responsibilities of examining the methods used to present the sponsor's message and of evaluating the potential impact that message may have on students.

Teachers must judge whether commercially prepared kits and units match the curriculum and abilities of the students. Additional criteria for judging social studies kits and units are important:

- How accurate is the information presented?
- Is the material in the kit illustrative of the diverse nature of the society?
- Do the materials present multiple viewpoints in an unbiased manner?

Visual Information and Literacy. Television, computer screens, cell phones, signs, symbols, books, magazines, movies, photographs, and even body language provide visual messages. Few people are visually literate enough to get full value from social studies pictures and illustrations (Benjamin, 2001). We do not always teach students to successfully read both a complex diagram and a photograph, although each of these requires different skills. Social studies visuals include realistic drawings, photographs,

Building on Diversity

Reading Activities

Prereading activities can involve students in making their own responses to literature that bring their cultural experiences into the social studies classroom.

Going Home by Eve Bunting, illustrated by David Diaz, is a picture book about a farm-worker family who takes a car trip to visit relatives in La Perla, Mexico. This book can be used with many unit topics, for example, a study of continuity and change. A teacher may have students create a contrast chart before reading the book. After reading, students revisit their charts, commenting on what they now think to add.

Contrast Chart for *Going Home*

Good Things About Moving	Bad Things About Moving

An anticipation guide is another form of prereading activity useful in social studies for getting students to explore their attitudes, opinions, and beliefs. After reading *Going Home*, students tell why they responded as they did during the initial discussion. Does their response come from direct experience, what they have read or seen, or what they have heard others say?

To develop an anticipation guide, determine the main ideas that you want students to learn in the reading and create true/false or agree/disagree statements for those ideas. For middle schoolers, you can put the statements on a transparency, have students write them in their notebooks, and then have them respond with a true/false or agree/disagree. This can be followed by polling your students for their answers. Older students, in particular, will ask you for the correct answers, but you can say "That is something we are going to investigate," so it serves as a motivator as well. The students complete a reading and then revisit the anticipation guide's questions and affirm or change their original responses (Yell, 2006, personal communication). A partial anticipation guide for *Going Home* follows (Sunal, Powell, Wiesendanger, 1985 McClelland etal., 2000, p. 255):

Anticipation Guide for *Going Home*

Agree	Disagree	
_____	_____	Most people who leave Mexico to live in the United States do this to make more money.
_____	_____	Farm workers have a hard life.

abstract diagrams, graphs, charts, tables, flowcharts, maps, line drawings, pictures, and symbols. In textbooks, there are three typical problems with illustrations. First, the written text conflicts with the illustration. Second, the illustrations are too simple, so they do not adequately support the level of the text. Third, the illustrations are too complex, so students do not take the time needed to examine and learn from them.

Before using any visual, teachers need to ask, "What is its purpose?" The purpose could be to gain attention, maintain interest, stimulate recall, or assist

Journaling is used to find out what students think about a book. The double-entry journal encourages students to select meaningful quotes (Barone, 1990). The quote is written in a column on the left side of the page. The reader writes on the right side, across from the quote, his or her reaction to what the author wrote. An example of a double-entry journal for *Going Home* follows (Sunal et al., 2000, p. 255):

Double-Entry Journal for *Going Home*

Quote	Response
"Mama looks so young and beautiful and Papa... so handsome. She has forgotten about her sore shoulders," I say. "And he's forgotten about his *bad knees*," Dolores adds.	Mama and Papa seem like they were young. Like when they met before they were married. It's like they are going back in time.

Venn diagrams and book charts help students compare two different texts. Students might read and compare *Going Home* with Allen Say's book *Grandfather's Journey* about the Japanese American narrator's grandfather and his move to the United States from Japan. An example of a book chart follows (Sunal et al., 2000, p. 256):

Book Chart

Title	Author	Narrator	Lessons Learned
Going Home	Eve Bunting	Carlos	Moving can be both good and bad. People miss where they were born.
Grandfather's Journey	Allen Say	Grandson	War creates big changes. Moving can be both good and bad.

Many nonfiction reading materials, as well as informational books, can be used to create powerful social studies. These include student magazines, such as *Cobblestone*, and magazines written for a general audience, such as *National Geographic*. As with the examples provided for fiction, many prereading, reading, and postreading strategies can be used. Some of the strategies that work well with nonfiction follow (Sunal et al., 2000, p. 257):

Prereading	Reading	Postreading
Anticipation guide	Double-entry journal	Venn diagram
Contrast chart	Directed reading/thinking activity	Book chart
K-W-L	Note taking	Summarizing
Questionnaire	Webbing of information	Response journal

in comprehension by clarifying the text. *Maps* as visual images are discussed in Chapter 12.

Charts, graphs, and *tables* are used frequently in social studies. An example in history is data describing the amounts of something (bridges, voters, soldiers, warships, deaths from smallpox) at a specific time in the past. Usually, these amounts are being compared (e.g., the number of soldiers compared to the number of warships needed for troop transport). Or changes are traced in the amounts over time (for example, the number of warships in 1840, 1940, and 2004).

In Figure 7.4 reading across the chart allows you to trace changes in the number of soldiers in a region following changes in 100-year intervals. You can note the change by region and also the rate of change. For example, there was slow change in North America until the 100 years following 1850. Reading down the chart, you can examine the number of soldiers in each region during the same time period. In North and Latin America in 1650, there were few soldiers compared to the numbers in 1950.

More complex comparisons can be made by reading down and combining the information with that gained by reading across (Benjamin, 2001). Thus, you will find that the number of soldiers in Africa did not vary greatly over the time periods, while those in North America showed great change. Information in a table can be presented differently to highlight various aspects of the data. For example, the data in Figure 7.4 could be presented as percentages of the total world's soldiers in each region, which would make it easier to compare regions.

Another way of representing data is by using graphs. Bar and line graphs make differences more obvious and comparisons easier but are less precise and require more space to convey the same information as a table (Benjamin, 2001).

Drawings, artwork, video, and *photographs* can be more difficult sources for gathering information than they may at first seem to be. You need to do more than look at them (Benjamin, 2001). First, you need to recognize the actual information they present, such as what Columbus's ships looked like or how Hiroshima appeared after the atomic bomb explosion. Then you need to interpret them by trying to understand what the artist or photographer is saying in the work. Artists do not just record a visual image, they make choices about which part of an event they focus on and how much emphasis they give that portion. Artists are sending a message to anyone who looks at their work. Interpreting visual material requires knowledge about the subject matter, the artist, the style, and the context in which it appeared. Like written descriptions, art does not simply speak for itself. There

Number of Soldiers by Region				
Region	**Year**			
	1650	**1750**	**1850**	**1950**
Europe	10,000	14,000	25,000	30,000
North America	20	500	2,500	57,000
Latin America	1,200	1,400	2,800	25,000
Africa	10,000	8,000	12,000	15,000
Asia	33,000	48,000	35,000	35,000

FIGURE 7.4
Chart of Soldiers by World Region

are different and controversial interpretations of some images, such as those of a public demonstration against the Vietnam War in 1970. But not all images are controversial. A photograph of the main street in your great-grandparents' small home town decades ago might tell you that the sidewalks were filled with people, while today few people are seen on the sidewalks because they now shop at a mall on the outskirts of town. There is a wealth of information about life at the time in such a town that requires interpretation and is not controversial.

Learning Centers. Learning centers provide students practice in making choices. Students choose which activities they do at the center and evaluate their own progress. Giving students the opportunity to choose their own activities allows them to select how they most want to learn. This selection process contributes to students discovering their best way to learn while building their self-esteem.

The availability of space plays an important role in the physical appearance of a learning center. In a cramped area, the learning center might be confined to a single box while students return to their desks to work on each activity. In other settings, learning centers might be large bulletin boards or sections of the room divided into cubicles for different types of activities.

The objectives of social studies learning centers vary widely. They may involve either gaining knowledge, developing skills, or examining attitudes and values, or incorporate two or more objectives. Learning center objectives have common characteristics:

- Clearly established learning objectives
- Self-checking and self-evaluating procedures for individual activities
- Progress charts or records for each student
- Multiple activities to accommodate various learning styles
- Student choice among the methods of accomplishing specific objectives
- Enrichment materials for both remedial and advanced study needs

Inquiry Invitation. An inquiry invitation helps focus students' attention on higher-level inquiry skills such as selecting variables, data interpretation, and data analysis. Students are presented with data for a given problem or situation; the students do not gather or collect the data because it is a time-consuming process. An inquiry invitation is a good task for cooperative learning groups. This strategy provides students with experience in later stages of the inquiry process where they tend to be weakest. Three examples of inquiry invitations follow:

- Bringing in a copy of a newspaper article about a particular event—a major earthquake in the United States
- Providing a table of data—the number of rainy days per month in a specific location
- Showing a picture or diagram of an event—the movement of troops in the Battle of Lexington during the American Revolutionary War

This learning center could address knowledge, skill, or attitudinal objectives.

Weekly inquiry invitations providing details from current event news reports, pictures, or video clips motivate students' interest in the news and in places and people throughout the world. Open questions accompany the data: "What does this mean to you?" or "What happened here?" Students do not have to provide, or even attempt, a "correct" answer, but they are expected to apply logical and critical thinking as they work. Periodic use of the inquiry invitation not only helps students practice their skills, but also provides teachers with an authentic assessment exercise they can use to document student progress in developing higher-order skills.

Using a WebQuest.   The WebQuest Page (http://webquest.sdsu.edu/) by Bernie Dodge is the best source of information about WebQuests (Haas, Channell, Linder, Vandevander, & Van Sickle, 2006). WebQuests are problem-solving activities that require inquiry and critical thinking from students and should not be mistaken for treasure hunts that only seek information (Sunal & Haas, 2002). A WebQuest presents students with a task or a problem. It provides scaffolding assistance as students complete a project addressing the task. The WebQuest provides some website addresses to assist students in researching the problem given them by the task. A quality WebQuest frames the essential question, has overall visual appeal, connects tasks to national social studies standards, uses an engaging scenario and tasks, has relevant resources, involves students in interesting roles, uses clear evaluation criteria, and demonstrates creativity. Two sources of examples of relevant and high-quality WebQuests appear in *Social Studies Research and Practice*: Haas, Channell, Linder, Vandevander, and Van Sickle (2006) in Volume I, Issue 1, and Courtney and Haas (2006) in Volume I, Issue 2.

Useful Instructional Activities for the Expansion Phase

In the expansion phase, students apply the new concept, generalization, attitude, and/or skill to additional examples. Without many widely varied applications, the meaning of the idea remains restricted to the examples used during its development in the lesson.

Teachers should select two or more different instructional strategies with substantial student control for the expansion of each learning cycle, such as:

- Find examples through or the use of technology.
- Present an inquiry invitation involving an application of what was learned.
- Identify examples of what has been learned on a field trip.
- Use or create games, role-playing, or dramatization to illustrate what has been learned in the lesson.
- Apply ideas learned through art, music, science, and/or mathematics.
- Revisit a confrontation challenge attempted early in the lesson for a different or improved solution.
- Investigate a new problem that applies ideas learned in the development phase.

Classroom Management Strategies for Powerful Social Studies

In teaching for meaningful social studies, students use materials and are involved in student-to-student interactions. Students have more movement about the room, more questions, and more control of their learning environment. General classroom management guidelines designed for a social studies program facilitate students constructing meaningful knowledge. These guidelines include advanced planning, giving directions, distributing materials, creating an organized beginning, grouping students, using classroom rules, creating lesson smoothness, and being a facilitator (see Figure 7.5).

Advanced Planning

Lesson planning is critical to effective classroom management and high student achievement. An effective teacher personally tries activities that students must perform in the classroom *before* they are used. Problem points are evaluated, and modifications are made if difficulties occur. Preparation eliminates delays that cause frustration.

- Locate materials where they are to be used.
- Prepare the lesson plan and materials ahead of time.
- Provide an overview to students before beginning.
- Give directions first before having students get materials.
- Plan materials distribution.
- Assign students to work in small groups.
- Direct students' energy toward the lesson objectives.
- Conduct smooth lessons.
- Post schedules.
- Reduce confusion.
- Serve as a guide.
- Ask broad, open questions.

FIGURE 7.5
Classroom Management Techniques for Powerful Social Studies Teaching

Giving Directions

Before students receive materials, they are given directions on how the materials are to be used. The directions do not have to be specific or step by step. They can include a statement such as "You will be receiving a box of materials. When you get your box, make observations of each object in the box and group them. Write your observations on the sheet provided." This approach introduces a focus for the activity. Providing instructions while students are already involved in activities with materials usually is not effective because they are too busy to listen.

Distributing Materials

Distribution of materials to students can be the single most difficult part of a materials-rich social studies lesson. It is important to set up stations and place materials in easily accessible locations. Appointing social studies helpers to distribute social studies resources is an effective technique. One role for cooperative groups is the resource manager, who collects, organizes, and returns instructional resources.

Distribution methods based on restaurant and home distribution of food at mealtime are a good analogy for planning materials distribution in classrooms. Social studies materials can be distributed *family style*. Designate a table or row of students as a group. A student distributes a set of materials to each group. Students in the group redistribute the materials among themselves. *Waiter/waitress style* involves identifying a student from each group to come up and collect a set of materials to be used by the whole group. The student delivers items to each individual member of the group or the whole tray to the group as a single set. In a *cafeteria-style* approach, one student from each team proceeds through a line in which items to be used by the team are picked up. *Food-court style* involves students going to different locations in the room to pick up needed materials. *Home style when dinner guests are late* involves distributing materials to student group locations before the lesson begins.

When making a decision about materials distribution, consider the following factors: time, amount of student involvement, amount of teacher time, and efficiency/smoothness. Reducing the amount of time is the most important factor. A distribution method that increases student involvement is preferable because it provides additional time for students to become aware of the materials and to understand how to use them, increasing their learning. The method that most reduces the involvement of the teacher provides more time to work with individual groups or monitor the classroom. The distribution method that gets the materials to the students quickly reduces class disruption. The importance of an individual factor depends greatly on classroom context. Factors to take into account include students' ages, number of materials to be distributed, type of materials, and amount of potential mess that could be caused during the distribution process.

Organizing the Beginning

When all materials are ready to be distributed and students are ready for the social studies lesson to begin, it is important to provide an introduction or overview to the lesson. This introduction provides students with an expectation of what is to come next and a focus for relating the events of the activity. Most introductions do not tell students the expected outcomes of the activities or the specific lesson objectives if doing so takes the excitement out of learning.

Grouping Students

Before beginning the lesson activities, students are grouped for cooperative learning. Not only do cooperative learning groups provide effective learning, but they also are useful in organizing the classroom for the distribution and return of materials. Groups should be given names or numbers and assigned work spaces.

Using Classroom Rules

Effective classroom management in powerful social studies requires that all classroom rules are taught and modeled. Posting daily and weekly classroom schedules and a student helper list is important. During the beginning of the lesson, teachers monitor and redirect the behavior of students who are not on task. Getting students involved in the learning task quickly enables teachers to identify topics that motivate students to remain engaged. Nonverbal communication is best when possible. If necessary, ask misdirected students to describe their task and to demonstrate responsibility. Refer to written directions if needed. When further redirection is required, discuss quietly the effects of the present behavior if continued, as well as the positive effects on fellow classmates of the requested behavior if observed.

Creating Lesson Smoothness

Students stay on task when teachers provide smooth, evenly paced, relevant lessons. Teachers are aware of the various ways the flow of learning can be disrupted or enhanced. Lesson confusion is handled by appropriate lesson planning. Knowing the sequence of activities, having all materials ready, and anticipating management problems creates a smoother lesson. Specific classroom management practices used during the teacher-guided part of the lesson can increase the smoothness and pacing of a social studies lesson:

- Completing instruction on the original idea before switching to a new idea
- Staying with an instructional activity
- Announcing only ideas or information relevant to the activity
- Avoiding disruption by overattention to minor student misbehavior (Kounin, 1970, Wolfgang, 2001)

Being a Facilitator

Teachers help students having difficulty and monitor the progress of individuals and groups during student activities. The teacher moves from group to group around the class, asking mostly open-ended questions to help focus or redirect student learning: What evidence do you have for making that statement? Why did you say that? Why have you been doing that? In small groups, students usually feel freer to ask questions or provide explanations that may not be well thought out. It is important to create an atmosphere in which students are willing to try out new ideas and explanations without fear of embarrassment. The teacher's role during the student activity part of the lesson is one of facilitator and helper.

Assessment Considerations

The learning outcomes of instruction with each of the strategies described in this chapter can be assessed. The assessment must be matched to the outcomes expected as a result of the instruction. If the focus is on using an instructional strategy with high student control of learning, then the assessment must enable students to respond in ways that allow for the differences among them. So, conducting a performance task, developing a role-play, or responding to an application scenario written on a card provide an assessment related to the instructional strategy used and to the learning outcomes expected. If high teacher control was evident in the instructional strategy, such as a short lecture, and if the learning outcome expected was recall of the requirements for election to a government position, for example, then the assessment will be narrowly focused. The social studies assessment must be matched to the expected learning outcomes, to the instructional strategy used, to the amount of student and teacher control over learning during instruction, and to the needs of the learners. The ability to make such matches is a characteristic of social studies PCK.

EXPANSION

 ## Making Decisions about Which Instructional Strategies to Use

Many instructional strategies are available to address the social studies ideas and skills we teach. Teachers carefully make decisions matching strategies to their students' developmental level and interests and to the topic under study. Teachers also take advantage of their own personal abilities and experiences. There is no set formula to follow when deciding on instructional strategies to use in a lesson or unit. In a unit (see Chapter 8) teachers may use different instructional strategies at the beginning of the unit, as they explore the topic, other strategies to develop the unit's ideas and skills, and still others as the ideas and skills of the lesson are expanded upon. Or, a strategy may be carried across all parts of the unit. Teachers are decision-makers weighing many factors.

Teachers recognize that it takes time to develop expertise in using any strategy whether it is cooperative group investigations or effective use of social studies kits. When a strategy is used, teachers often identify ways in which they will apply it a little differently next time, so their expertise grows. It is important to continue to work at developing best practices in using an instructional strategy.

It is important to keep in mind that any particular instructional strategy can be overused. When a strategy is overused, students can become bored so their motivation lessens and attention wanders. If, for example, the phrase "What do you know about...?" is overused, the responses may be negative such as "Nothing, and I don't want to know anything about it" or students may just be unresponsive. A teacher might, instead, begin with a short video asking "What do you think you know from viewing this section of the video?" The responses are likely to reveal both prior knowledge and stimulate interest.

TIME FOR REFLECTION: What Do You Think?

A CLASSROOM SCENARIO: Studying State and Local Historical Sites

Ms. Tafoya was teaching a social studies unit on major historical sites in her state. The unit was part of her fourth-graders' yearlong study of their state. She created a digital story on her computer to show the students. The study used some personal photos of historic sites taken during trips around the state (e.g., the first factory, first state capitol building, a trading post, a part of an ancient trail, a wall with very old cave paintings, the entrance to the first state park, an old bridge across a large river, a country railroad depot, the site where a treaty was signed between a Native American tribe and the U.S.

government, the street that was the first paved road in the state, and others). Other photos were selected from the Internet. She placed all of the photos together, added background music, and audio-taped the narrative that she had written to accompany the photos. After Ms. Tafoya showed the digital story, students discussed their observations of the historic sites and constructed lists of the characteristics of each one. Students used their lists to construct categories of historic places such as those associated with the first peoples, with government, and with industry. They discussed how it might be decided that a site is "historic." Students then looked for photos on the Internet of other historic sites they had read about or heard of from family members. Then Ms. Tafoya's students constructed a large classification chart, printed off copies of sites from the digital story and placed them on the chart in the category to which they best belonged. They also placed on the chart the additional photos they had collected from the Internet and some photos from their family trips. Ms. Tafoya engaged students in other related activities, and then she took them on a field trip to some local sites including a school from 1900, the building that housed the first local newspaper, and a visit to a nearby farm whose barns dated from the 1880s. Groups of students took digital cameras on the field trip taking photos of the places they visited. During the next few days, each group classified its photos, then created and presented their own digital story using their photos.

1. Identify the instructional strategy or strategies Ms. Tafoya used at the beginning of the unit on historical places.

2. Were some strategies continued from the beginning of the unit, were new ones added, or was a mix of strategies used to develop the unit's ideas and skills? Identify and discuss the strategies used.

3. How were students involved in practicing and applying the ideas and skills of the unit at the end of the unit?

Summary

Powerful instructional procedures promoting meaningful social studies learning not usually found in traditional classrooms include the following:

- Knowing general procedures for effective teaching and learning
- Using a repertoire of social studies best practices
- Grouping students heterogeneously and encouraging peer interactions
- Having adequate social studies content knowledge organized in a meaningful way
- Calling attention to discrepancies or creating confrontational challenges where students consider multiple perspectives or interpretations of the same event or idea
- Asking students to explain or justify their conclusions and predictions, rather than accepting a simple answer

- Proposing discrepant observations, unsatisfactory hypotheses, or incorrect conclusions and challenging students to evaluate them
- Introducing new terms during the lesson development phase by using concrete examples, a demonstration, or an activity
- Knowing where and how social studies information can be obtained when it is needed
- Matching the assessment to the instructional strategy used

Although state and national organizations provide guidelines, the teacher has the responsibility of creating the social studies program in the classroom. Having a basic set of criteria facilitates decision making. Teachers need to consider the amount of control given to students in various instructional strategies and where in the lesson a strategy can be used.

Recommended Websites to Visit

21st Century Visual Literacy Lessons
http://www.kn.pacbell.com/wired/21stcent/sitemap.html#visual
NOVA Online Teachers Site
http://www.pbs.org/wgbh/nova/teachers/
Virtual Jamestown
http://www.virtualjamestown.org/page2.html
Geography Action!
http://www.nationalgeographic.com/geography-action/index.html
Questioning Strategies to Improve Student Thinking and Comprehension
http://www.sedl.org/secac/rsn/quest.pdf
Strategies to Teach social Studies: SSCED Tool Kit
http://ritter.tea.state.tx.us/ssc/downloads/toolkits/Shared%20Sections/Resources/Strategies/
Strategies.pdf.

8

How Are Powerful and Meaningful Social Studies Units Constructed?

EXPLORATORY INTRODUCTION

You are giving feedback to a teacher at a fourth-grade-level teacher meeting. The group is reviewing a web planning a fourth-grade unit on Native Americans of the Great Plains in the early 1800s. You notice that one-fourth of the unit will be devoted to hunting practices. You ask your colleague why so much time will be spent on this topic. She tells you that she has a collection of locally found arrowheads that she can show the students. She thinks students will find the collection interesting and be motivated to study the topic. That is why she is going to spend this time on hunting practices. Because this is a lot of time to spend in the unit on this topic, you ask whether she had considered other ways to use the arrowheads in the unit. She tells the group she could not think of what other topics within the unit might be addressed by having students explore and talk about the arrowheads. She asks for ideas from the group because she agrees that devoting 25 percent of the unit to hunting practices probably is too much. What other ways to incorporate the arrowhead collection into the unit can you suggest?

1. Before making your suggestions, identify major characteristics of the cultures found among Native Americans of the Great Plains in the early 1800s that might be studied using the collection.
2. Describe three suggestions you will make that will both broaden and deepen the unit's content.

Chapter Overview

We receive many bits and pieces of information every day in isolation, ignore most of them, and choose to store just a few in our minds. Lessons are organized to encourage students to link ideas and experiences. These linkages result in meaningful learning that deepens understanding. Effective teaching is organized best in units built around significant questions that help students construct key concepts, generalizations, values, and inquiry skills. The *unit* is a set of interconnected, related lesson plans that introduce and explore, fully develop, and expand understanding of a topic. The construction of a unit requires the teacher to make many decisions using questions such as: What steps are needed in planning a social studies unit that helps students develop meaningful learning about the social world? What significant questions will be addressed? and What evaluation criteria can I use to determine how well students were able to accomplish the goals of the social studies unit?

Chapter Objectives

1. Explain the importance of significance, relevance, and coherence as evaluation criteria for developing social studies units.
2. Differentiate between various types of units built on social studies topics.
3. Describe unique problems in planning and teaching an integrated, interdisciplinary unit that are not found with units focusing only on social studies topics.
4. Identify systematic procedures for determining appropriate topics for social studies units.
5. Describe general steps in planning all types of social studies units.
6. Construct unit focus questions and link them to appropriate school subjects and content standards.
7. Analyze sample unit web diagrams.
8. Construct a web diagram illustrating relationships between focus questions, school subjects, and the information to be learned in a unit on a social studies topic.

DEVELOPMENT

 ## Planning the Appropriate Focus for Social Studies Units

Planning units can involve a single teacher, a teacher pair, a group of teachers, various subject area teachers, a whole school, or several schools through use of e-mail, discussion boards, and the Internet. When more than one person plans a unit, all participants respect the diversity of the planners, compromising and cooperating. This applies to both content issues and the use of a teacher's time for planning and instruction. Planning social studies units involves focusing on significant questions, key ideas, student needs, appropriate instructional strategies, and relevant assessments. To create powerful social studies learning, many teachers do yearlong planning.

Significance, coherence, and relevance are three evaluation criteria used when constructing social studies units. *Significance* means that the content taught is important to the discipline and to the student's need for powerful social studies. Less is more in the unit. Only the most critical concepts related to a topic are selected for the unit, and they are taught in depth (NCSS, 1994b).

Coherence means that the questioning and investigative nature of social studies cuts across all parts of the unit and across the curriculum. Students have direct experience with the inquiry skills and actions typical of work in the disciplines contributing to social studies. Units stress considering significant questions, acquiring and practicing inquiry skills, conceptual understanding, applications, and transfer of social studies knowledge to the student's own world. Coherent units recognize that the student's social world includes attitudes as well as agreements and conflicts on values.

Relevance means that the content, activities, and breadth of experiences in the social studies unit reflect the student's current life, future goals, and aspirations. The questions asked in the unit are significant to the student. Social studies content and skills have an impact on the decisions a student makes and on his or her quality of life.

Selecting a focus for a unit begins with determining the *goals* that will guide the unit. Teachers consider the social studies content and inquiry skills, students' developmental level, the amount of integration with other subjects, and the amount of time available for the study.

Some units focus on describing an event or idea from history or from the social sciences, such as community development, transportation, the voting process, or immigration. Other units focus on learning a skill used in organizing or processing social studies information, such as using a grid system to locate places on a map. Still other units focus on attitudes or values people in our nation believe to be important or in need of reconsideration, such as treating everyone equally and justly or recycling trash to conserve resources. Longer units that study themes, such as interdependence, or an issue, such as how to reduce drug use among young people, place more emphasis on learning content, attitudes, values, and skills. Each focus has its strengths and weaknesses. Each focus can be used in a thematic, integrated, and interdisciplinary unit or in a unit whose content is drawn only from the social studies.

Descriptive-Focused Units

The traditional organization of social studies curriculum and that found in most textbooks has a *descriptive focus* emphasizing students' acquisition of knowledge. The content topics frequently are introduced in the early grades and repeated at various points in higher grade levels. Each time they are repeated, more abstract and complex new information is introduced. When these topics are well taught, students gradually build an in-depth understanding of the topic. With a content emphasis, descriptive units may provide a clear view of a topic such as colonization but do not make clear connections with other topics. Learning is isolated with little application of the content possible. Descriptive units should be taught sparingly during the year and supplemented with greater emphasis on thinking skills. They can be used for current events or commemoration of an event, for example, the anniversary of the nation or of the constitutional amendment giving U.S. women the right to vote.

An example of a descriptive unit addressing an event follows.

Ms. Brown teaches her students about the census as ordered by the U.S. Constitution and taken by the government every 10 years. Her students encourage their parents to fill out the form that comes in the mail on Census Day, April 1. She shows them a sample form and they take a census of their classroom using the form.

Units based on descriptive textbook materials need to be greatly modified by focusing on the key social studies concepts and thinking skills identified for the topic in local, state, and national standards.

Thinking Skills–Focused Units

In a unit with a *thinking-skills focus*, the specific content learned is less important than the skills to be developed. A thinking, or inquiry, skill such as classification can be taught with almost any content. Students can classify agricultural products, types of government, or the climates of world regions. Students focus on a significant skill, developing and practicing it within a set of content. An example of a thinking skills–focused unit follows.

Mr. Goldman wants students to learn to develop and ask useful questions when interviewing. He builds a unit around the personal benefits of saving money in the bank and how banks play a role in the local community by investing customers' savings to help local businesses. To develop an understanding of how banks operate within the community, students design and try out possible questions for interviews they will conduct with two local businessmen invited to their classroom. They redesign their questions after trying them out, develop a final set of interview questions, use those questions with their invited guests, and then assess their guests' responses to determine how well the questions got at the information they were seeking.

A strength of a thinking skills–focused unit is that it allows the teacher to provide help for students who have difficulty and to focus students more on *how* they are learning. The weakness of this unit focus is that social studies ideas may not be covered systematically, jumping instead from concept to concept without full development of any one concept. Thinking skills–focused units are best when interspersed with other types of social studies units throughout the year and from grade to grade. They should be used to ensure that students develop a thinking skill needed in upcoming units.

Conceptual and Thinking Skills–Focused Units

Units can combine social studies concepts and thinking skills with equal emphasis. A *conceptual and thinking skills–focused unit* works best with inquiry and investigative instructional strategies. Students work with a coherent set of content. At the same time, they develop skills necessary systematically to study and construct an understanding of the concepts and their relationships. They also examine the values related to processing the information and the attitudes of people toward the content.

An example of a conceptual and thinking skills–focused unit follows.

> Ms. Herrera took a trip to western U.S. states, visiting a lot of historical sites. She uses her travels to help her students understand concepts related to the Westward Movement in U.S. history. Students plot the Oregon and Santa Fe trails on a map and the paths of the transcontinental railroads, using and further developing their mapping skills. They locate today's major cities along the two trails. Pictures of places Ms. Herrera visited are examined and then put into a digital presentation showing their location on maps of the trails. Students examine the appearance of the natural and cultural landscapes shown in the photos and describe these places in words. They read passages from diaries of people who traveled west during its settlement by people from the eastern United States. They look at pictures artists drew and photographers took of western landscapes and of the Native Americans who lived in the West in the 1800s. Students try to infer the places in which Native Americans were encountered, using evidence in the drawings and photographs in which they appear. Students use websites to view pictures of the cities and national parks in the West today, pointing out major changes in the natural and cultural landscape of the West since the mid-1800s. Finally, they debate whether the natural and cultural landscape of the West has changed positively or negatively, explaining their reasoning for their decision.

A criterion for selecting appropriate topics for this type of unit is that key ideas must lend themselves to investigation by students. This type of teaching requires significantly more time than does a traditional approach. So, it is important to select key ideas that are fundamental to powerful social studies.

 # Units that Integrate School Subjects

Two types of units can be used that integrate school subjects: theme units and issue and problem-solving units. *Theme units* cut across social studies topics and may include topics associated with other subject areas. An *issues and problem-solving unit* attempts to solve a problem that is relevant to somebody—an individual, a group of individuals, or society as a whole.

Theme Units

Powerful ideas often are used by people of all occupations. These ideas provide tools for thinking about the world and solving problems (NCSS, 1994b; National Research Council, 1996). Some examples include systems, classification, culture,

NCSS

Standards

interaction, production and distribution, models, time, decision making, interdependence, and scale. Other less broad but useful themes are concepts such as energy, neighbors, the dynamic earth, colonization, or space exploration (Mayer, 1995; NCSS, 1994b). The planning web in Figure 8.1 shows a plan for an interdisciplinary primary-grade unit.

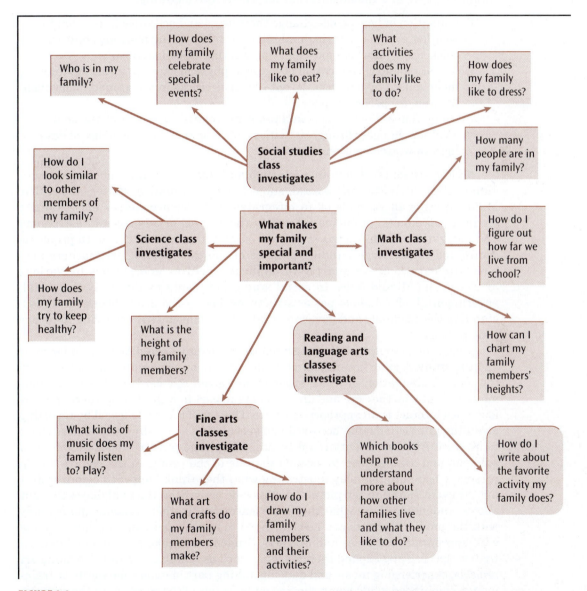

FIGURE 8.1

Planning Web for an Interdisciplinary Primary Grades Unit on What Makes My Family Special and Important?

Planning and development of *theme units* begin when meaningful integration of the selected subjects around an important theme can occur. After comparing the plan for the yearly topics of each of the major subjects, a theme that fits the curriculum and appropriate topics in each of the subject areas is identified. For example, patterns of continuity and change could be investigated during the early childhood years in a theme unit that integrates the following:

Examination of how people change their dress and activities in relation to weather events—carrying umbrellas on rainy spring mornings or wearing thick coats, hats, and gloves in cold weather (social studies)

Observation and classification of common physical changes in the environment caused by a weather event—such as cracks in the ground following a hot and dry period (science)

Investigation of number sets and problems related to daily and seasonal weather changes through activities—such as counting the hours of daylight in winter (mathematics)

Middle school teachers often jointly plan integrated units that include individual class activities in several subject areas around a chosen topic. The Middle Ages is an example of an integrated unit. Science classes may examine medical procedures, problems related to the plague, or advances in astronomy and navigation. Math lessons may focus on architecture and the math problems confronted in the large building projects of the time period. Art teachers may have students compare and try to duplicate pictures and statues by various artists of the Middle Ages. In social studies, students might study the social, governmental, or religious power structures, laying the groundwork for understanding the economic and governmental reform movements occurring in future time periods.

Classwide activities with integrated thematic units could be used to begin or end the study. A joint first-day project can provide an exploratory introduction to the topic. A simulation in which students are given role cards with a little information about who they are and directed to take part in a short task where the various roles interact is an appropriate choice. The simulation is followed by reporting about the interactions that occurred and speculating as to why various roles chose to interact. Another activity could be assigning large pictures to small groups of students and asking them to assume the role of the people in the picture and to present a 1-minute role-play illustrating what they think happened before or during the event shown in the picture. A classwide activity on the final day of the unit allows students to share what they have learned with other students and possibly with the public. Students can be challenged to appear as living museum exhibits with appropriate costumes and artifacts. Students can take part in simulated activities that use and expand their learning, such as building a model or making art projects, experiencing music and dancing, taking part in games for youth, or training for knighthood while being cheered on by ladies of the court. With the cooperation of the cafeteria staff, lunchtime can present typical foods accompanied with period music played or presented live.

For their integrated unit, "I Love the Knightlife: A Week in the Middle Ages," costumed teachers and administrators at Hudson Middle School in Hudson, Wisconsin, assisted in a classwide activity to begin their study.

The administrative, janitorial, and cafeteria staff often are needed to help with classwide events because of needed schedule changes. Parents, local clubs, museums, and universities may provide assistance as reenactors or as advisors or supervisors. Interactive, culminating events are enthusiastically remembered by students but require much planning and many physical resources, so a team approach spreads the work among two or more teachers.

Some themes do not lend themselves to integration of all subjects. When planning a unit, teachers consider whether strong examples that students can understand exist in the subjects included.

Issue and Problem-Solving Units

Many issues are complex and not easily resolved or not resolved at all. However, students can explore such issues, identify possible solutions, examine the arguments for and against each solution, predict which solution(s) might be best implemented, and try out a possible solution. Such a unit is likely to have a conceptual and thinking skills focus. The issue involves one or more significant concepts and requires students to apply and further develop thinking skills to work with it.

Selecting developmentally appropriate issues or problems for investigation is essential. The strength of a unit focused on a carefully chosen issue or problem is that it is motivating to students because they find it relevant. First-graders, for example, are likely to be interested in addressing the issue of taking responsibility for the care of classroom animals. They can consider the problems that would result from acquiring a new classroom animal such as a gerbil, lizard, or fish. They can investigate the kind of food it will need, the environment needed to sustain it, how it takes in water, the time of the day or night in which it is active, and so on. Then, the students can develop procedures for the animal's proper care. This unit investigates the general question "What are the responsibilities and problems of owning or caring for a pet?" At the middle school level, students often investigate current issues within their community. They might, for example, consider drainage problems that recently have led to flooded streets and homes in heavy rainstorms. In order to develop possible solutions, they first investigate causes of this new problem in the community such as cutting of trees on a hillside that allows water to cascade down it, or the filling in of streambeds. Now, they are ready to talk to civil engineers, geologists, and public officials about solutions. Working in cooperative groups, the students can lay out a solution, try to identify its possible cost, and develop a technology-assisted presentation to present to their city council and mayor. This unit investigates the general question "How can the flooding problems our town has been experiencing in the last five years be solved in a reasonable time and at a reasonable cost?"

In units addressing an issue or problem, all students are involved in the investigation at some level. These units require examining the issue from several viewpoints and might examine social, political, economic, scientific, historical, and technological aspects. There are many opportunities for students to follow different lines of thought, and find that life contains differences and controversies that can be resolved when we work democratically together.

Choosing a yearly curriculum based on issues requires planning and reflection by teachers. Perhaps this type of unit is best when interspersed with other units in a well-sequenced curriculum based on local, state, and/or national standards. One effective way of using an issue-focused unit is as a follow-up to a previous unit. Students investigate in some depth an issue that was discovered in a previous unit. Such a unit might ask the question "How does the historian or anthropologist know that they are telling us accurate information about people who lived long ago when no written messages or books were left for us to read?"

An issue-focused unit is complex to manage and assess. Students often are pursuing different aspects of an investigation at the same time. Teachers must make sure that projects have an underlying organization, that all information is sequenced and communicated to all participants, and that information is analyzed and shared in relevant and clearly understood formats. Graphs, maps, charts, computer databases, and other means of organizing and communicating information are used. Teachers often hold class meetings in which students discuss common problems and suggest possible solutions to one another. Teachers meet with small groups of students about their individual progress to help coordinate and support student learning. Carefully planned rubrics for assignments are used to help students evaluate their own progress.

TIME FOR REFLECTION | *What Do You Think?*

A question can serve as the focus for a unit based on an issue, for example, "Why do pet owners need to teach their pets to be good members of the community?" This general question brings students into contact with (1) the needs of other people in the community, (2) personal responsibilities citizens have to others, and (3) laws and jobs related to caring for pets.

1. Write two additional focus questions appropriate for lessons related to this issue.

2. Write a focus question that requires students to use either science or mathematical knowledge to answer it.

3. What are three social studies standards that are addressed in the focus questions you wrote in items 1 and 2 above?

4. What sources of information will students most likely use to get help to answer these questions?

5. How can the teacher help students understand the meaning and relationships among the pieces of information provided to them?

6. What skills do students need to learn or practice to answer these focus questions?

7. What value(s) do you anticipate students embracing to explain why a pet needs to learn to be a good member of the community?

How to Choose Appropriate Topics for Integrated Units

Perhaps the best way to start to think about the types of decisions required and the problems to be addressed in planning integrated social studies units is to consider an example of a theme-focused unit that is often taught in elementary schools: a unit designed around turkeys and the Thanksgiving Day holiday. In such a unit, students may make name tags in the shape of a turkey, read stories about turkeys, make turkey drawings from hand tracings, write stories about turkeys, make observations of a turkey egg and turkey feather, and visit a turkey farm. A major criterion for choosing these activities is how well they fit this particular theme.

It is difficult to identify an important concept or skill being taught in this unit. In selecting a topic, the teacher reflects on four questions:

1. What are the important *key concepts* central to each of the subject areas integrated?
2. What *essential*, or *focus, questions* lead students into thinking?
3. What *activities* engage the students in reflective thinking?
4. What are the natural and significant *connections* between key concepts?

An appropriate topic engages teachers and students in making choices that enhance the quality of student learning outcomes and the teacher's own feeling of the worthiness of the unit (Sunal et al., 2000). Although most topics interconnect subjects, *many* do not provide meaningful learning for the students, such as zoo animals or written communication. Integrated units are best used when they are appropriate for teaching important content and skills.

Planning Integrated Units

Two major planning techniques can be used for integrated teaching. The first is choosing a single key idea for a unit that interconnects the disciplines. The second major planning technique for integrated teaching is planning the yearly curriculum in several subjects. Teachers look at curriculum goals throughout the year, matching the goals for social studies to those for language arts, science, mathematics, art, music, physical education, and so on across several units.

Interconnections occur when students study Benjamin Franklin as a participant in the Constitutional Convention while considering other aspects of his life. Students could investigate his experiments with static electricity, for example. Within the next few decades following Franklin's experiments, liquid batteries were invented by Volta in 1800; electromagnetism was discovered by Oerstead in 1819; and laws of electrical interactions were devised by Ampere in 1822. Other inventions, such as electroplating, and the concept of basic circuits could be connected with events in history during and following this period. At the same time, a measurement unit in mathematics could be taught because the invention of the metric system occurred in this time period.

Using a Wheel Design.   Some teachers have used a wheel design to identify topics. Edith Merritt and Martha Lockard, teachers from Tuscaloosa, Alabama, report their use of a wheel design (Sunal et al., 2000). They draw a circle, then draw another circle inside of it, and another circle inside of that circle, creating rings in the circle. They add in as many rings as there are subjects under consideration for topics.

For example, one year they started with six major social studies topics on the outermost ring, so the circle was divided into six sections by topic. Each of the six topics was written in a section of the outermost ring. Next, they examined the science curriculum and listed, where possible, a topic related to each social studies topic. One science topic, for example, was classification of organisms. This topic was written, along with the other science topics, in the second ring, next to the corresponding social studies topics written in the outermost ring. They continued this process, filling in a third ring with language arts/reading topics.

Using a Column Design.   Another format for identifying possible themes for integrated units is a chart. The subject areas under consideration serve as the headings. Chart headings could be social studies, science, mathematics, physical education, art, or any other subjects. The teacher selects one subject with which to begin, such as social studies. Then all the topics to be taught in social studies that year are listed under the heading *social studies*. The second column may be reserved for science. Looking at the science topics, the teacher decides which ones correspond to the social studies topics and writes them in the column next, in the same row of the social studies topics they match. The process is repeated with mathematics and so on. An example of such a design follows (Sunal et al., 2000):

Social Studies	Science	Mathematics	Language Arts
Human communities	Animal communities	Numbers	Stories about communities
Graphing	Graphing	Graphing	Interpreting graphs

As the teacher fills in the chart, themes are built where many matches occur. When deciding whether to integrate instruction, the teacher reflects on five key questions:

1. What important *key concepts* are central to each of the school subjects and can be successfully learned or practiced in the unit?
2. What *questions* can focus and direct students' thinking?
3. What *activities* can engage students in reflective thinking about the unit?
4. What natural and significant *connections* can be made to the students' world beyond the school?
5. How can students *connect the key concepts and generalizations* to be learned from studying the unit?

 # Developing Integrated Units

Effective unit development requires thoughtful consideration of basic planning steps, purposeful organization, and reflective evaluation. Using any of the unit planning approaches and types of unit focuses already described requires a similar sequence of planning steps. The essential planning steps are summarized in Figure 8.2. The model set of procedures presented next has worked well for many elementary and middle school teachers. The procedures are based on classroom use as well as on related research results. Although the procedures provide a useful set of steps with which to work, teachers generally adapt them and develop their own set of procedures as they gain experience in planning and teaching units.

Step 1: Generating Ideas for the Topic of a Unit

Once a topic has been chosen, ideas about the content, skills, attitudes, and values related to the topic are generated. These ideas are a beginning point and are revised during the unit development process. Examples of initial ideas for an integrated unit on government at the fifth-grade level include laws, voting, structure of government, taxes, making inferences, school government, local and state government, comparing roles of government officials, problem solving, campaign literature and television advertisements, making changes in government, mapping electoral districts in our community and in our state, and decision making.

1. Generate ideas for the topic.
2. Research the topic.
3. Develop focus or guiding questions.
4. Identify and accommodate special needs of students.
5. Develop intended learning outcomes.
6. Categorize intended learning outcomes as knowledge, skills, and attitudes.
7. Create a web.
8. Develop a rationale and goals.
9. Begin the KWL chart.
10. Develop learning objectives.
11. Develop an assessment plan.
12. Develop lesson plans.
13. Develop accommodations for technology.
14. Implement the unit.
15. Evaluate student learning.
16. Reflect on the unit.

FIGURE 8.2
Summary of Suggested Steps in Planning a Unit

Questions to stimulate ideas include "How do people decide for whom to vote?" and "What role does government play in our daily lives?"

Step 2: Researching the Topic

Researching the topic enables teachers to assess their prior knowledge, to add to this knowledge base, to identify alternative concepts and perspectives that students may hold, and to update their knowledge.

Step 3: Developing Essential or Focus Questions

Teachers identify the main points or questions for a unit. This is especially important when the ideas have been planned for them, as in a textbook chapter. Textbook chapters and learning kits typically contain more information than students can meaningfully understand. Without essential, or focus, questions, it is difficult to help students see the main point. Focus questions help students to link with their prior knowledge as well as to establish a rationale for studying the unit. For a single unit, several questions are appropriate. An essential question guides the development of a single lesson or of several lessons. For example, a middle school unit on local and state government could start with several questions:

How are local and state government similar and different?
Who makes the rules by which local and state governments operate?
Who might provide these services if local and state government did not do so?

Once an initial list of essential, or focus, questions is developed, teachers ask themselves: "Which of the questions really get at the heart of the unit? What kinds of questions are being asked? Are they mostly where or when questions? Are there any how or why questions? Do the questions represent a variety of thinking skills from recall and comprehension to application, analysis, and evaluation? To what extent do the questions relate to the students' interests and needs?" If needed, the questions are modified to include a variety of social studies thinking skills and student interests and needs. For example, after evaluating the list of essential questions generated for a unit on local and state government, the teacher might decide to modify the following question: "How are local and state government similar and different?" The teacher might decide to change this question to read: "How can we create a Venn diagram showing similarities and differences of local and state governments?"

To focus the unit further, it is named as a significant question that students investigate and strive to answer during the course of the unit:

How does government take care of our needs?
Why is it important for citizens to be active in voting?
How can we work with our legislators to be sure our government serves everybody?

Step 4: Identifying Special Needs among Students and Making Accommodations

Students with special needs might require adaptation of lesson plans. A list of specific adaptions may be compiled on the basis of students' needs identified through the special education program and others noted by the teacher. Some of these needs might include (1) students who are having difficulties academically, (2) students whose native language is not English and who are not yet fluent in English, (3) students who have physical and emotional difficulties, and (4) students who are experiencing severe family stress, such as divorce, death, or relocation.

Step 5: Developing Intended Learning Outcomes

The teacher's reflection on the focus questions help to create intended learning outcomes, which usually are written as learning objectives. Intended *learning outcomes* are statements of what the teacher wants the students to learn. These statements can address inquiry skills, concepts, attitudes, or values. Learning outcomes are not activities the students do during the unit. Instead, they describe what students construct in their minds. The following list contains initial ideas for a middle school unit on government. Ideas marked with an X best represent potential intended learning outcomes. Those marked with an O are activities, not intended learning outcomes.

_O_ 1. Write a letter or use the Internet to obtain information about local and state government.

_X_ 2. Explain how local government carries out essential services such as trash collection and street maintenance.

_X_ 3. Conclude that government planning for roads makes an impact on our everyday lives.

_O_ 4. Look at an Internet video on views of the state capitol building.

_X_ 5. Explain the relationship of voting for an elected school board to the choices made for school calendars and events.

Step 6: Categorizing Intended Learning Outcomes

The next step is grouping the intended learning outcomes into categories. Each idea is defined as an inquiry skill, content knowledge, attitude, or value. Teachers ensure that outcomes are expected for each category. Inquiry skills, such as recalling, explaining, predicting, analyzing, creating, and evaluating, can be grouped into several levels. Content knowledge can be grouped into factual statements, concepts, or generalizations. Attitudes can be identified or explained in detail with possible consequences noted.

Step 7: Creating an Idea Web

The technique of webbing can be used to evaluate, complete, and relate the important ideas, skills, attitudes, and values in the unit. Webs are especially helpful when teachers jointly prepare units. As the web is constructed, additional ideas, skills, attitudes, and values may be identified to support the topic and create bridges among the components of the unit. Links represented by labeled arrows can be drawn to connect ideas and inquiry skills, showing relationships between facts, simple concepts, more abstract concepts, and generalizations. These links, or ladders, help students to understand relationships and integrate skills, concepts, and generalizations.

Two types of webs are generally used: a hierarchical web and a schematic components web (Novak, 1995). The teacher chooses one that best fits the topic. To construct a hierarchical web (Figure 8.3), the teacher performs the following tasks:

1. Selects the key idea(s), skill(s), attitudes, and values
2. Lists ideas, skills, attitudes, or values related to key ones
3. Ranks the ideas and/or skills from the most general to the most specific
4. Groups the ideas, skills, attitudes, and values into clusters, adding more if necessary
5. Arranges the ideas, skills, attitudes, and values in a two-dimensional array
6. Links the ideas, skills, attitudes, and values, and labels each link

Figure 8.3 shows part of a hierarchical web for a unit on "How Does Our Government Take Care of Our Needs?"

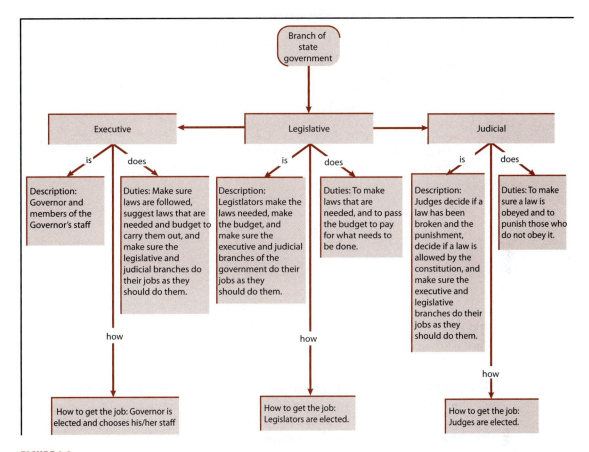

FIGURE 8.3
A Partial Hierarchical Web for a Unit on State Government

Many of the same procedures just listed for constructing hierarchical webs are followed in creating a schematic components web. In a schematic components web for the same unit in Figure 8.4, the unit topic is located at the web's center. Both web types connect main ideas, skills, attitudes, and values with interlinking inquiry terms, such as *how, is,* and *does*. Using a webbing technique is a way to analyze the nature of the unit at this stage. Does the web show meaningful ideas, skills, attitudes, and values? Are there too many abstract ideas? What concrete ideas, bridges, and ladders can be added to help students understand other concepts or more abstract ideas?

If a textbook serves as the source for a unit, the teacher lists important ideas, skills, attitudes, and values from it. This list is used to create a web. Using national, state, and local standards, the teacher modifies the web by changing or adding ideas, inquiry skills, attitudes, or values. Typically, social studies textbooks contain a large amount of content. The teacher de-emphasizes and eliminates textbook

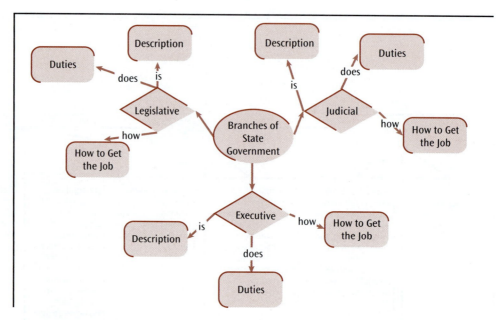

FIGURE 8.4
A Partial Schematic Components Web for a Unit on State Government

ideas and facts that are not compatible with the standards used to implement a unit based on appropriate key ideas for powerful social studies.

Modifications and deviations from the course of study in a fifth-grade textbook chapter on government, for example, may be made:

A field trip may be added to visit a session of the local city council.

A listing and discussion of all elected offices found in most states may be dropped and replaced with cooperative groups, each investigating one key elected office in the state such as the state highway commissioner or the state superintendent of schools.

Step 8: Developing a Rationale and Goals

It is important to think about the reasons for teaching the unit and how the *unit rationale* is communicated to students. A rationale statement is determined by the values influencing the teacher's perception of students, students' relationship to society, and students' interaction with social studies as a subject. A unit rationale statement answers the questions:

How is the unit *relevant*, affecting the future of the students as well as their current individual needs and interests?

How does the unit examine *societal* issues and help students deal responsibly with them?

How is the unit *developmentally appropriate* for the students?

How is the unit a *self-learning enterprise*?

A rationale for a unit on government might, for example, contain a goal statement such as "This unit is designed to give fifth-grade students insight into, and an appreciation of, the role of government in our daily lives as it serves the needs of citizens." A complete rationale contains a goal statement and briefly describes how instruction is intended to proceed.

> The unit begins with students' exploration of visual examples of government at work in their community such as trash collection, road paving, and construction of water lines. It continues with Internet searches and interviews with government officials and a range of citizens to collect more information on the role of government as it serves citizens' needs. Students identify general patterns of government roles relating to their schooling, their homes, family members' work, recreation, transportation, and health. The unit concludes by identifying limitations of government's service to citizens such as badly timed traffic signals, lack of a school nurse, limited hours at the public library, or the need for greater oversight of contamination in local streams. The role of society is addressed to provide students with the appreciation that active citizens can have an effect on the decisions government makes and the services it delivers.

Step 9: Beginning the KWL Chart

The *KWL* chart is used over time in planning and evaluating the unit. It provides the teacher with some indication of students' knowledge prior to instruction, what knowledge needs to be obtained before instruction begins or as instruction progresses, and what knowledge the students learn through the unit. At the beginning of a new unit, a teacher asks students, "What do you *know* about _____?" Then the teacher asks students, "What *would* you like to learn about this topic?" After the unit has been taught, the teacher asks students, "What did you *learn* about this topic?" Students' comments are recorded on a chart under three columns headed *K* (*k*now), *W* (*w*ould like to learn), and *L* (what was *l*earned), respectively. Teachers may develop a personal KWL for a unit.

The KWL is extended by interviews with a sample of students. Questions can be used to ascertain the K and W parts of the chart, or teachers can use photographs, maps, artifacts, or other items related to the topic to probe students' prior knowledge and interests. A teacher planning a fifth-grade unit on government, for example, might use a set of photographs including examples of government services, citizen protests, and/or citizens voting to probe students' prior knowledge during an interview. The KWL chart and interviews are used throughout the unit to help plan, modify, and assess to evaluate the extent to which the learning outcomes are being attained.

Because social studies lessons often deal with information about which students may have heard strongly voiced opinions, attitudes, or stereotypes, they may not want to share their ideas in the KWL for fear of being ridiculed or of offending others. Such as classroom is not providing the safe environment needed for using critical and creative thinking when constructing a KWL. When the social studies topic is one about which the teacher expects students will have usable prior knowledge, a KWL can be an appropriate strategy for planning a unit or a lesson. Because a KWL relies on students' verbal abilities, it may fail to be an observable premeasure for all students in the class. Many students, including those whose primary language is not English, may perform well with social studies content long before they can verbalize ideas in the English language (see Chapter 10 for a discussion of language development in social studies among English language learners). When bringing closure to the development phase of a unit or a lesson, students need to be engaged in reflection on what they have learned thus far and may want to learn in the future. There is a strong case for asking, "What would you still like to learn?" At the completion of a unit or lesson teachers need to ask students such questions as: "What have you learned from this unit (or lesson)?" "What surprising things did you learn?" "What did you learn about yourself by taking part in this unit (lesson)?" As students engage in an end of unit (or lesson), they should present their ideas instead of listening to the teacher tell them what they should have learned. By asking students questions and listening carefully to their replies, a teacher can identify differences among students and their learning, which is an important contribution to the teacher's planning and teaching abilities, or pedagogical content knowledge (PCK).

Step 10: Developing Learning Objectives

Initial learning outcomes are revised, written as objectives, and classified into practical categories for teaching. Several formats can be used to write learning objectives. All *objectives*, whatever their specific format, focus on what the student will learn and how success can be achieved. Examples of objectives indicating *knowledge* of a concept or generalization that students construct follow:

Students compare the duties of each branch of state government: executive, legislative, and judicial.
Students give reasons why citizens should vote.
Students state the meaning of "city council."

Examples of objectives indicating *inquiry skills* that students develop and use follow:

Students gather data by interviewing.
Students organize data into bar charts comparing two variables.
Students write and present a play portraying the roles of each branch of state government: executive, legislative, and judicial.

Examples of objectives indicating attitudes or values that students learn to appreciate and accept follow:

Students demonstrate respect for the voting process.

Students express a desire to seek out opportunities to learn more about the governor's official activities.

Students use e-mail to communicate their views to their local council member.

Step 11: Developing an Assessment Plan

Two purposes of assessment are important at this stage in planning a unit: (1) feedback about student learning of a key idea and (2) data about the effectiveness of the lesson plans on student learning outcomes. Assessment also is used to provide feedback to students about their learning and to teachers about the effectiveness of the unit.

TIME FOR REFLECTION | *What Do You Think?*

During a lesson, students participate in a series of activities that result in one or more of the following: acquiring content knowledge, enhancing skills, analyzing values, taking a position, and making decisions on how to participate in society in ways that support democracy and its citizens. The teacher's role is very different from that of students: facilitating student learning and development and assessing student progress toward learning. To perform this role, the teacher must constantly be aware of what the students are to be doing and must observe and assess whether students' behaviors are those that indicate they are likely to be mastering the objectives of the lessons. Knowing what you expect of the student is important to successful teaching. In evaluating a social studies teacher, the evaluation question is "Did the teacher help students to learn valuable and important things that will help them become good citizens in a democratic nation in an increasingly interdependent world?"

Once the topic of a lesson has been selected, the teacher decides just what about the topic the students should learn. The emphasis of every objective must be on the accomplishment of the student. Some educators say that the objective should clearly state what students will be able to do after instruction that he or she could not do before being involved in the instructional process. This view of an objective sees the student's mind as an "empty vessel" that is "filled up" during instruction. Clearly, during social studies instruction, students do acquire new content knowledge. Meaningful learning however, often requires learners to use skills they already have to reorganize their knowledge. This means that there are times when what the learners are doing during the instructional process is more important than new knowledge and the focus of the objective is on the use, or mastery, of a skill. At other times, students focus on what is important to do when making conclusions or decisions, placing the focus of the objective on attitudes/dispositions or values.

Perhaps you have learned to write behavioral objectives that include three parts:

1. Under what conditions (specific sources of information)

2. The action of the student (action verb)

3. The degree of acceptable accomplishment (minimum performance level) (Mager, 1962)

Some examples of such an objective are as follows:

- Given a map of the world and the latitude and longitude coordinates of 10 national capitals, the student will correctly *locate* the capitals with 90 percent accuracy.
- Given a list of the presidents and vice presidents of the United States, students will correctly *match* the vice presidents with their presidents with 90 percent accuracy.

The above form of an objective is helpful when the student is practicing a skill that has several rules to apply in performing the skill. Many social studies lessons, however, include tasks that do not follow a systematic series of steps. Social studies specialists tend to view behavioral objectives as statements of what students will learn or do during the instructional process. The key to writing such objectives is to use a verb that describes what is done by the learner during the lesson. Among the verbs that accomplish this are *name, list, identify, explain, compare, locate, graph, analyze, tell why, choose, defend*, and *evaluate*.

In the discussion of step 10 are examples of three types of educational objectives. Note how the descriptive verb hints at what will be done during the lesson and how the teacher might approach the evaluation of each objective.

1. What subtopics of the unit on "How Does Our Government Take Care of Our Needs?" do the knowledge objectives in step 10 indicate will be studied?

2. What are the three activities that students will be doing in the lessons guided by the skill objectives?

3. How might you motivate students to accomplish each of the attitudinal or value objectives shown in step 10?

4. Assume you plan to teach fourth-grade students about Washington, D.C., in three to five days.

   A. What significant question might the unit address?

   B. Write three knowledge objectives, three skill objectives, and three attitudinal or value objectives for the unit. Label each objective by its type.

   C. Which objectives will you address in the early, or exploratory, part of the unit? the middle, or developmental, part of the unit? and the last, or expansion, part of the unit?

   D. How many learning cycles will you use to help students in responding to your significant question?

Types of assessment used include a quiz or test, student writing projects, graphs and charts, cooperative group work, artwork, interviews, or group/individual projects. Informal and semiformal methods, as well as having students develop portfolios of their work, can be incorporated into an effective assessment plan. The assessment is designed to evaluate each type of learning outcome included in the unit: ideas, thinking skills, and affects. This requires several types of assessment methods. As part of a complete assessment plan, students are asked for feedback on their reaction to the unit (see Figure 8.5).

What Did You Think about Our Unit?

1. What were your favorite activities in this unit? Why?
2. What could you, your classmates, or your teacher have done to increase your satisfaction?
3. What were your least favorite activities? Why?
4. Circle the description that best describes your feelings about this unit.

   Very satisfied   Satisfied   Unsatisfied   Very unsatisfied   Not sure

FIGURE 8.5
Sample Student Feedback Form

Step 12: Developing Lesson Plans

Potential activities emerge from the list of learning outcomes. One way to view the activities is to consider the resources available and related activities possible using these resources. Next, the appropriateness of the resources and activities for the special and developmental needs of the students is considered. Examples of resources are textbooks, field trips, games, guest speakers, the Internet, commercial videos, homemade videotapes, digital cameras, case studies, debates, and simulations.

Consider a fifth-grade unit on government in which one objective is "Students will give reasons why citizens should vote." Possible resources and activities for accomplishing this objective could be:

- Observing citizens voting in the school gym in a local election and interviewing a sample of these voters asking questions about why they chose to vote.
- Using the Internet to obtain statistics on voting patterns for different age groups in the state.
- Following a teacher-approved blog on voting for five days to identify reasons given for not voting as well as for voting.

Each of these resources and resource activities can be used to achieve one or more different outcomes. The lesson plans drafted are based on the rationale and learning objectives that have been designed using the list of resources and activities.

Step 13: Developing Accommodations for Technology

Teachers ask themselves several questions:

How can technology enhance learning in this particular setting?
If concrete materials are not available for the concepts and skills involved, can technology provide the bridge to help students learn the concepts meaningfully?

Making a Literature Connection

Incorporating Social Studies Trade Books into Units

Social studies trade books are available for all themes found in the national standards.

Once a unit theme and the major national standard(s) on which the unit will focus have been identified, teachers can consider which trade books might best accompany the unit. Trade books should be read by the teacher and then chosen to fit students' interests and developmental level, challenging students' thinking and moving it to a higher level of complexity and reflection. Each teacher also will consider whether bias or stereotyping appear in the book and whether the book can be used along with other books and materials to present multiple perspectives on an idea.

Trade books often address more than one national social studies standard and might be used more than once throughout the year for different purposes. Younger students often enjoy hearing a book read to them more than once. Some examples of recently published trade books are presented below to indicate the range of social studies trade books available for use by teachers in units. These books are organized according to the national standard they address.

Culture

Amish Horses (2001) by Richard Ammon and illustrated by Pamela Patrick is a picture book describing the many tasks people and horses accomplish on an Amish farm (for primary grades).

Time, Continuity, and Change

When Esther Morris Headed West: Women, Wyoming and the Right to Vote (2001) by Connie Nordhielm Wooldridge and illustrated by Jacqueline Rogers is the story of Esther Morris, who not only voted but also ran for office and won before women were given suffrage throughout the United States (for primary grades).

People, Places, and Environments

Katie and the Sunflowers (2001) by James Mayhew depicts Katie's adventures in a museum and introduces us to the works of van Gogh, Gauguin, and Cezanne (for grades 3–5).

Individual Development and Identity

Just the Two of Us (2001) by Will Smith and illustrated by Kadir Nelson celebrates the dignity, maturity, and honor of being a father (for grades 3 and up).

Individuals, Groups, and Institutions

O'Sullivan Stew (1999) by Hudson Talbott retells an Irish folktale in which Kate decides to recapture a horse the king has taken in order to save her village from destruction by a witch (for grades K–5).

Power, Authority, and Governance

Red, White, Blue, and Uncle Who? The Stories Behind Some of America's Patriotic Symbols (2001) by Teresa Bateman and illustrated by John O'Brien is an easily read introduction to seventeen traditional American icons (for grades K–5).

Bound for the North Star: True Stories of Fugitive Slaves (2000) by Dennis Brindell Fradin uses primary source illustrations to tell the stories of fugitive slaves who took great risks to find freedom (for middle school).

Production, Distribution, and Consumption

Those Building Men (2001) by Angela Johnson and illustrated by Barry Moser is a picture book of the diverse men who build and the monuments they build including the Erie Canal, skyscrapers, and bridges (for grades K–5).

Made in Mexico (2000) by Peter Laufer and illustrated by Susan L. Roth describes a way of life in a remote Mexican village that touches music around the world (for grades 3–5).

Science, Technology, and Society

The Great Unknown (2001) by Taylor Morrison presents the efforts of artist and paleontologist Charles Wilson Peale to excavate and display the bones of the mastodon (grades 3–5).

Fire in Their Eyes: Wildfires and the People Who Fight Them (1999) by Karen Magnuson Bell uses vivid photographs and text to show the training, equipment, and courage needed by wildfire fighters (for grades 3–8).

Global Connections

Who Really Discovered America? Unraveling the Mystery & Solving the Puzzle (2001) by Avery Hart and illustrated by Michael Kline outlines the tools of inquiry, rules of evidence, and some historical methodologies and activities for students to help answer the question "Who really discovered America?" (for middle school).

Civic Ideals and Practice

Food Watch (2001) by Martyn Bramwell presents issues affecting the planet's food supply and introduces professionals in the field, using the phrase "A day in the life of…," then guides readers through experiments and actions they can take (for grades 5 and up).

Can technology provide additional practice or transfer experiences that are not possible in the real-life situation?

Is the use of technology economical in terms of the time it requires?

Is additional supervision necessary?

Step 14: Implementing the Unit

After planning, the unit is taught. Adjustments and fine tuning are made to meet the needs of the students and the context of the learning experience while it is being taught.

Step 15: Evaluating Student Learning

Students provide their ideas concerning the unit activities and what they learned through the unit either as part of a lesson or in a separate class or group discussion (see Figure 8.5). Teachers add their observations to information obtained from examining assessments. Students' ideas are recorded on the KWL chart. Teachers may conduct some postunit student interviews. Teachers compare the learning outcomes with the information they have and decide to what degree the students have accomplished them.

Step 16: Reflecting on the Unit

Unit development and instructional planning are part of a large cycle. One of the most important parts of the cycle is devoted to gathering feedback on the unit and reflecting on its effectiveness. Some questions to consider are as follows:

What evidence of motivation to learn about the topic was found?

What evidence of learning about the topic did you see?

To what extent did students accomplish the learning objectives?

Using Technology

Databases and Spreadsheets

Databases are files or sets of information students create about a topic made up of records, one for each event, each place, each monthly temperature, or each piece of data in any number of information categories. Databases and spreadsheets are useful in studying many unit topics. Each record in a database or spreadsheet has fields: subcategories containing information such as the name of a capital city and its height above sea level. Fields can be arranged or sorted in many ways. In using a database on U.S. cities, for example, students can ask for listings of those cities with a certain characteristic, such as population more than 100,000 or fewer than 500,000. Once a database has been set up, it is always available to answer questions related to the information it contains.

Ready-made databases are available on the Internet. Perhaps the largest is that of the U.S. Census Bureau. This database is helpful in learning about the people of the United States and each state and territory. Students can make their own databases quite easily. Most computers have programs installed that create databases.

Each student does research and then enters the products of the research efforts into the database. For example, students could set up a database focused on early settlers in their community. After deciding what sort of information to collect about each person (e.g.,

name, birthdate, date of death, whether married or single, occupation), each student searches and finds as much of the needed information as possible for a given settler and enters the information into the database. Once the database is complete, students ask questions and sort the data to help answer their questions. Figure 8.6 depicts screens from a fourth-grade class database.

When data are sorted to answer one question, the answer brings new questions to mind. As new questions arise, students carry out further research and add new information to the database. Sometimes the information is just not available. This clearly illustrates to students that not every question is readily answerable. Making databases as a class effort demonstrates the power of information and of cooperative efforts.

Spreadsheets can be used to extend data into the future. Data in a database can be put into a spreadsheet. Students can use the spreadsheet to add, subtract, multiply, and perform many other mathematical operations with numerical data. For example, a student might note that each year a state collects a certain amount of money from a gasoline tax. The average gasoline tax paid by a citizen can be obtained by dividing the total tax by the number of people in the state. Then it can be multiplied by an inflation error.

Did the ideas in the lessons flow together well?

What did the students remember and not remember from day to day?

Which lesson was the best? Why? Did you predict this?

Would you use this unit again in its present form? If not, what specific modifications would you make?

Written responses provide a starting point for a teacher when considering whether the unit should be kept and revised for inclusion in the curriculum for the future.

Teachers make many choices when planning a year-long curriculum. Because the year-long plan provides guidelines and encourages reflection on the purpose and success of the social studies program, some changes in the plan should be expected as the year progresses. Students may find one topic particularly interesting and

(Screen One: list of information items given about each president)

OUR PRESIDENTS

Main Menu
President's Name
President's Term of Office
President's Political Party
State President Was Born In
President's Occupation
President's Age at Inauguration
President's Age at Death

(Screen Two: specific information about a president, Harry S. Truman)

Truman, Harry S.
1945–1953
Democratic
Missouri
Businessman
60
88

(Screen Three: answer to the question "Which presidents were not lawyers?")

Washington, George
Harrison, William H.
Taylor, Zachary
Fillmore, Millard
Johnson, Andrew
Grant, Ulysses S.
Roosevelt, Theodore
Wilson, Thomas W.
Harding, Warren G.
Coolidge, John Calvin
Hoover, Herbert C.
Truman, Harry S.
Eisenhower, Dwight D.
Kennedy, John F.
Johnson, Lyndon B.
Carter, James E.
Reagan, Ronald W.
Bush, George H. W.
Clinton, William Jefferson
Bush, George W.
Obama, Barack H.

FIGURE 8.6
Three Sample Screens of a Database Developed by Fourth-Grade Students

Russian students gather with their teachers after a day at an outdoor camp to sing songs and discuss the unit they are just finishing on social issues and the environment.

want to pursue it further, or topics and ideas planned might not challenge students because they are too complex and abstract for their level of maturity or too simple to curry their favor. Unexpected issues of importance to the students and community may arise and stimulate students to investigate them.

EXPANSION

 ## Conceptualizing an Integrated Unit

Courses of study are found in many local school systems and also often at the state level. When examining a course of study for each of the subjects taught at a grade level, teachers find several consistent topics across the subjects. Some topics are inquiry skills such as classifying or problem solving that are used in each subject area. Other topics may be studied with a somewhat different focus depending on the subject but still belong under the same topic such as change and continuity or the environment. In these cases teachers may decide to plan and implement an integrated unit that helps students transfer skills and ideas across the subject areas with appropriate depth of study in each of the subjects.

TIME FOR REFLECTION | *What Do You Think?*

You are examining the courses of study for social studies, science, mathematics, and reading/language arts for your grade level. You find the following topics.

Social Studies: communication, communities, transportation, mapping, making rules and laws, inferring, predicting, and sequencing.

Science: simple machines, electricity, energy sources, classifying, sequencing, writing science journals, and plants.

Mathematics: counting to the millions place, communicating mathematical ideas, simple fractions, measuring, writing in a daily mathematics log, and the metric system.

Reading/Language Arts: the writing process, sequencing story events, identifying main characters, syllabication, summarizing, author study, and using story clues.

Identify one integrated unit that could be developed and implemented this year utilizing a component from each of the four courses of study.

1. Describe the components to be used from the courses of study.

2. Give a rationale for selecting these components to be part of the unit. In your rationale, describe how these relate to each other.

3. Identify three essential, or focus, questions the unit's lessons will help students answer.

Summary

The unit-planning process is a critical professional skill because key ideas are interrelated with each other and with students' prior experiences to make them useful. Units can be developed with emphasis on key social studies ideas or on integrated ideas from several disciplines. Three evaluation criteria are useful during the construction of units: significance, coherence, and relevance. Selecting an appropriate focus for a unit involves determining the rationale and goals of the unit. Emphasis can vary in content, inquiry skills, attitudes, values, and the amount of integration with other subjects. Different foci for unit planning include a descriptive focus on content, a thinking skill focus, a conceptual and thinking skill focus, and an issues and problem-solving focus. Within a year's time, a teacher can probably teach some integrated units and some units devoted to a single subject or skill.

In planning an integrated unit, an appropriate topic involves teachers and students making choices that increase the quality of student learning outcomes and the teacher's own feeling about the worth of the unit. When the goals for social studies can be matched to those for science, mathematics, physical education, fine arts, or language arts across several units, individual teachers and teams of teachers often find that students learn the topic better through the connections made during integrated units. Effective social studies unit planning with an appropriate focus requires thoughtful consideration of basic planning steps, purposeful organization, and reflective evaluation.

Recommended Websites to Visit

NESEA's curricular units are interdisciplinary on themes such as transportation, energy, and the environment.
www.nesea.org/education/
Social Studies School Service provides many resources in support of social studies units.
www.socialstudies.com
Yale-New Haven Teachers' Curriculum Institute: Index of Units (181 volumes of units)
http://www.yale.edu/ynhti/curriculum/indexes/
Free Global Education curriculum materials
www.globaled.org

9

How Do Social Studies Teachers Facilitate Students' Development as Individuals and Community Members?

Make a list of student characteristics that teachers should focus on in order to foster their development as active, responsible individuals. Make a second list of student characteristics to be fostered in order to help students be active, responsible participants in the classroom community. Construct a Venn diagram with one circle for individual development and one circle for classroom community participation. Place those characteristics found in both lists in the center overlap of the circles.

1. Analyze your diagram giving special attention to how much overlap there is between the two lists. Describe the results of your analysis.
2. Among the challenges confronting teachers in the classroom and making it difficult to foster student individual and community participation characteristics are instances of bullying, prejudicial responses, or shy withdrawal from an activity. Select one of these challenges, identify a grade level, and describe how you might respond to the challenge at that grade level if you were the teacher in the classroom.

Chapter Overview

Within social studies, *psychology* focuses on understanding and accepting our individuality, whereas *sociology* helps us understand our social nature and the groups formed within our communities, nation, and world. Developing a positive self-image and self-confidence, better accepting and understanding ourselves, and learning to accept and relate to others enable us to live with others as social beings (Pagano, 1978). Developing the attitudes and values integral to each person's personality supports goals for individual and social development. The National Council for the Social Studies Standard IV, *Individual Development and Identity*, Standard V, *Individuals, Groups, and Institutions*, and Standard X, *Civic Ideals and Practice*, emphasize the importance of developing each person individually and socially as members of groups that contribute to communities, nations, and the world (1994b).

NCSS

Standards
IV, V, X

Social studies programs work to develop civic-minded citizens who take on issues of concern to them. In doing so, both teachers and the curriculum confront individual selfish behavior, lack of experiences, and misinformation that contributes wrongly to classifying and stereotyping others. Developing attitudes and values that support responsible citizenship entails education that promotes the development of both character and ethical behavior. Character education refers to helping students build a set of values and attitudes enabling them to be responsible, active citizens. Ethical behavior refers to helping students make decisions to behave in ways reflecting a system of ethics focused on what is best for all people.

Various aspects of psychology, sociology, and values education are controversial. The disagreements revolve around what to teach and how to teach it. Controversy can be expected in a democratic society because such a society encourages a variety of opinions. This chapter describes methods for teaching individuals to develop into strong citizens who take on issues that concern them. Where controversy exists, a variety of viewpoints are presented.

Chapter Objectives

1. Explain how the classroom environment, curriculum, and instructional activities indicate the level of respect teachers and students have for each other.
2. Analyze classroom events in terms of the presence or development of values.
3. Describe social factors that affect the development of self-concept and teachers' ability to work positively with students from diverse social environments.
4. Identify three aspects of morality.
5. Describe theories of moral development.
6. Identify two means by which teachers can facilitate students' moral behavior.
7. Compare the goals and procedures of values clarification, value analysis, and teaching a specific value.
8. Explain the purpose of character education and its relationship to the social studies curriculum.
9. Explain how values are present and assessed in the school and its curriculum.

DEVELOPMENT

Respect for Diverse Students and for Oneself as a Teacher

When exploring students' conceptions and understandings of the idea of hero, Steven White and Joseph O'Brien (1999) found that students identify with people who demonstrate moral excellence, not with those who achieve prominence through displays of glitz and glamour that appeal, however superficially and temporarily, to society. As students mature, they move from exercising moral excellence in single events to actions sustained over a period of time. Teachers who create an environment of respect and encouragement promote such moral behaviors.

The Classroom Environment

Students sense, with their first step into a classroom, how much a teacher respects them. Room arrangements and instructional procedures suggest whether the teacher will encourage informal, frequent communication among students and between students and the teacher. The expectation for student discussion and cooperation is created by arranging the classroom into areas where small groups work together. Such an arrangement encourages students to exercise control over both their behavior and learning. Teachers view themselves as learners enthusiastically exploring new ideas and information along with students.

When reading through the learning cycle on sharing and negotiation, note teacher behaviors that encourage students to grow in confidence and respect for each other. The teacher uses an activity related to a holiday as a vehicle for setting up a dilemma students have to work through. Note how discussion is used to encourage reflection and draw out implications for how to better work together while appreciating individual differences and wants.

NCSS

Standards

The Curriculum Respects Diversity

Acceptance of, and respect for, students is communicated through the curriculum and the strategies used to teach it:

- Students have some responsibility for actively contributing.
- Discussions demonstrate a respect for students and diverse opinions.
- Students have responsibility for making decisions relating to the lessons.
- Family members are regularly involved in the curriculum and in lessons providing information or artifacts, in discussing ideas as part of homework assignments, and in visiting the classroom to examine students' presentations or to make guest presentations.
- Community members and public employees are requested to provide information and to help make connections between classroom studies and community experiences.

text continues on page 274

LEARNING CYCLE LESSON PLAN Sharing and Negotiation

NCSS

Standards
IV, VII

Grade Level: Primary

NCSS Standards: Individual Development and Identity; Production, Distribution, and Consumption

Exploratory Introduction

Materials: For each pair of students, provide two shoe boxes; one pair of scissors; one glue bottle and glue stick; 10 sheets each of red, pink, and white construction paper; one large, red, lacy paper heart; a set of marking pens; five small valentine stickers; one vial of glitter—all per each pair of students; one response sheet per student; one checklist per student; one observation sheet per observer

Objectives	Procedures		Assessments
1. Students construct a Valentine's Day mailbox using only materials supplied by the teacher.	1. Divide students into pairs and tell them they will be making a project. One pair of students acts as observers/reporters while the others work. Ask for volunteers for this job. Provide pairs of students with only the materials listed for use and have all other supplies put away. Tell students they are to make mailboxes to be used on Valentine's Day for collecting valentines. They must use only the supplies they are given to decorate their box.		1. Students complete mailbox using only materials given them.
	2. Point out that there are not enough supplies for each student to use at one time. Ask the *key question*: "What are some ways you can share some of your materials?" Hear suggestions from several students and ask students to begin working on their boxes. Show the observers how to use the checklist sheets.		

Lesson Development

Objectives	Procedures		Assessments
1. Students identify problems they encountered in making the mailboxes.	1. When all have completed their mailboxes, ask "Were you able to complete the mailbox in the way you wanted? Is anyone unhappy with the way their mailbox looks?"		1. Students share their feelings and problems.

continued

2. Students list ways to solve a problem of scarcity.

3. Students identify behaviors needed in sharing.

4. Students define sharing as dividing things equally or, if not exactly the same, dividing them in a way those sharing think is equal.

5. Students describe examples of negotiation.

---

2. Ask the observers: "Did you observe anyone who looked unhappy while making the box? Describe what you observed."

3. Ask the class: "Did you and your partner have any additional problems in completing your mailboxes with the materials you were given? What does sharing mean to you? Were you able to get equal amounts per person of all the supplies? Why? How? What are some behaviors, or ways you need to act, when you are sharing?"

4. Talk with students about scarcity, focusing on when there is not enough of something that is needed. Ask, "What were some examples of scarcity when you made your Valentine mailboxes? In what other school events or home events have you experienced scarcity?" Ask, "How do people solve problems of scarcity? Raise your hand if you thought sharing in the mailbox project was easy." Discuss their responses, asking: "Why? Why not?"

5. Ask, "What are some suggestions for behaviors to use when sharing?" Record student responses on board or chart.

6. Ask, "From the ideas we put on our list, how can we define sharing so that we can write a definition of it? Does everything have to be equally divided? What happens if two people have three things to divide? Is it sharing if one person takes two of the items and the other gets only one? How can that be fair?"

7. Explain how sometimes people decide that one person might get more of something and the other person gets more of something else that they want. I have heard students say: "I'll give you the purple marker if you will let me have the orange and yellow markers." They agree to do this. Ask, "Who has heard something like I described? Do you know what this is called?" It is called negotiation, or making a deal. The decision is made and agreed to before the people get what they want. Negotiating is a different way to solve the problem of scarcity, but it doesn't

---

2. Observers share their observations and others give evidences of listening to those observations.

3. Students identify behaviors indicative of sharing and identify behaviors that are nonexamples.

4. Students identify appropriate behaviors.

5. Students decide that "fair" is not always an equal division of everything in sharing.

6. Students share appropriate examples of negotiation.

continued

6. Students describe how negotiation and sharing can solve a problem of scarcity of materials and satisfy everyone.

work unless people agree to the way things will be distributed. Ask, "Why are sharing and negotiating worth taking the time to do?" Record answers in a list.

8. Closure: Ask, "What title should we give this list of reasons?" Title it appropriately.

7. Students include in their description the characteristics of jointly talking over what their problem is and deciding that each person has equal access to materials or they decide beforehand what is a fair way to share.

Expansion

Materials: Materials to decorate covers of work folders, with some scarcity present in certain colors of paper; glue and scissors, for each pair of students

Objective ⟶	Procedures ⟶	Assessment
1. Students apply sharing and negotiation in solving a new problem involving scarcity	1. Give pairs of students materials to decorate the covers of folders for their work, making sure that some materials are scarce. Explain that some of the supplies are scarce and suggest that they recall the discussion of sharing and negotiation. Encourage them to use the strategies previously discussed in the new task. 2. When the assignment is completed, ask, "Who used sharing in the task? Who used negotiation for supplies? Are you satisfied with the way your folders look? Where in the room can we post our ideas of sharing and negotiation behaviors so that we will remember to use them in the future?" Post a chart where students suggest and call attention to it at other times throughout the year. 3. *Lesson Summary:* Ask the students to briefly review the lesson activities and to identify the two important ideas with which they worked.	1. Students offer appropriate explanations of how they solved problems of scarcity in the assignment.

continued

Summative Evaluation Have students draw a picture of two people sharing or negotiating and have them write a sentence or two describing the situation and solution they are describing.

Determine if each student has presented an accurate description and drawing demonstrating an example of sharing and negotiating.

Checklist

Pair number: _____   Observer: _____

Observe the pair of workers once every 5 minutes, and record in a sentence or two the way they are behaving and working.

Observation 1   Time: _____

_____

_____

Observation 2   Time: _____

_____

_____

Observation 3   Time: _____

_____

_____

Observation 4   Time: _____

_____

_____

Observation 5   Time: _____

_____

_____

continued

Response Sheet

Name: _____

What was the main problem you had in using the materials you were given? _____

_____

_____

What was one way you used to solve this problem? _____

_____

_____

What does sharing mean? _____

_____

_____

How can sharing and negotiation help to solve the problem you had with the mailbox materials?

_____

_____

- Family members and volunteers, including older students, tutor or provide help for special activities, for field days or trips, and to photograph or record class activities (Alleman & Brophy, 1998).

Consider how the following examples of involving a family member in class strengthens students' understanding of, and respect for, each other.

Courtney's mother came to class with digital photos of her childhood home in Tennessee. She showed a photo of a panel in the kitchen that could be opened to reveal log walls of what was originally a cabin. Later, these walls had been covered with wood planks, and the cabin was expanded into a large farmhouse. She also told them some traditional Appalachian Mountain ghost stories.

A few weeks later, Rosa's father came to class and provided students with tamales traditionally made in El Salvador that are wrapped in corn leaves and cooked. He showed digital photos of his family's house in El Salvador, corn growing in a field, the elementary school he had attended, the square in the center of his home town, and pictures of Rosa and of some of her cousins in El Salvador. He talked about how important corn is as a crop and of how the volcanic soils provide rich farm land. Finally, he taught them the fight song for a Salvadoran soccer team.

As students interact with people representing a variety of cultures, they are likely to overcome their prejudices, becoming citizens who work for the common good of all.

TIME FOR REFLECTION | **What Do You Think?**

1. How could student independence be fostered during the lesson development phase in the learning cycle on sharing and negotiation?
2. What teacher actions in the learning cycle indicate that the teacher respects students?
3. What is a sample statement third-graders might make to define sharing?
4. What important characteristic do students need to add to their definition of negotiation to differentiate it from sharing?
5. How would you change the lesson plan if, during the making of the mailboxes, several students began arguing or became upset over the behaviors of others and complained to you or quit making their mailboxes?

 ## Development of Self-Concept in Diverse Students

An individual's self-concept is the complex product of all life's experiences (Christensen & Dahle, 1998). During the elementary and middle school years, students develop a sense of independence; they learn to cope with feelings of jealousy, fear, and aggression; and they form friendships and develop empathy (Kostelnik, Whiren, Soderman, Stein, & Gregory, 2002). Each of these social areas seems to be universal across cultures, although they may be expressed differently (Ekman & Davidson, 1994).

Independence and Responsibility

As elementary and middle school students develop cognitively and socially, they become better able to plan solutions to problems and to understand the social environment. They are more and more able to act independently. Teachers reward positive attempts to be independent, but when time is short, many teachers do not value student independence enough to provide the extra time needed for independent planning and decision making. Sometimes students' attempts result in unsafe or disruptive behavior. When students' independent attempts do not work, teachers assist them and guide them in learning from their mistakes (Macoby &

Masters, 1970). When help is given too quickly, it reinforces dependency, frustration, and sometimes aggression or withdrawal.

Students become independent when they are expected to be responsible (Quilty, 1975). For example, putting away materials when one is finished using them and keeping things in one's own locker both demonstrate responsibility. Expectations of responsibility are best met when accompanied with reasons. A teacher might demonstrate the benefit of being responsible by saying, "The scissors and stapler you need are on that shelf. The last person who used them returned them to where they belong; now everyone can easily find them when they need them." Students may work responsibly on a task, but they often start, then stop and attend to something else, then return to what they were working on, and so on. Teachers should recognize and reward efforts at responsibility.

Independence and responsibility depend on one another. Students from various cultural backgrounds can be expected to display independence and responsibility differently. For example, students from Asian backgrounds often assume responsibility for tasks and carry them out well but might not be as likely to organize others to do a task unless the teacher indicates permission to do so (Scarcella, 1980). These students are demonstrating respect for the teacher in a manner they have learned through their personal cultural experiences. Teachers help students develop independence and responsibility by (1) planning carefully, (2) anticipating difficulties, (3) giving clear directions, and (4) providing outlines of suggested procedures. Expecting and encouraging responsibility and independent behavior show respect for students as individuals who are in the process of growing up.

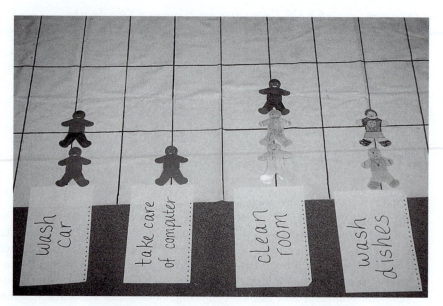

By graphing individually performed tasks, students see that they share some experiences with their classmates but not others.

Jealousy

Jealousy is a natural feeling that results partly from egocentrism, especially in younger students, who sometimes find it hard to accept another student being the center of attention even for a short while (Seifert & Hofnung, 2000). Reflecting on the learning cycle on sharing and negotiation, how much potential for jealousy is there in using this lesson's development with first-graders? With fourth-graders? Even though jealousy in students is normal, it threatens their self-respect because it often means that a person is uncertain of the affection of another person in the presence of a third party.

Students express jealousy in several ways, including aggression, immature behavior, and boasting. When a student displays any of these behaviors much more frequently than is common among his or her peers, teachers may have cause for concern. Teachers who use peer behavior as their basis for comparing students' behavior recognize that some behaviors are more common among certain groups of people than among others. Teaching that encourages students to discuss concerns and analyze their behavior, as suggested in the sample learning cycle, assists students in learning to cope with feelings of jealousy.

Contests resulting in winners and losers foster jealousy and reduce self-respect. Instead, an emphasis should be placed on each student performing as well as possible. Cooperative group efforts at completing a project are effective replacements for contests. Each student contributes personal strengths, gains in self-respect, and is less likely to be jealous of others. A closely related problem occurs when a teacher identifies one student as a model and tells others they should emulate this model. Students should examine historical situations, current events, and fictional situations whose development may have been influenced by jealousy and evaluate how people respond to jealousy. Teachers ask questions to help students do so, as in these examples:

- How much do you think jealousy influenced racist attitudes toward the baseball player Jackie Robinson?
- Students who work hard on their assignments and do well are being insulted by others. Why is this happening? Could some students who are making insulting comments be jealous of the success these students are having in their classes?
- Were Cinderella's sisters jealous of her beauty? Do you think this was why they were mean to her?

Literature can serve as a starting point for discussing jealousy. *Sophie and the New Baby* (Anholt, 1995) explores Sophie's initial excitement about having a baby brother followed by her jealous feelings about the attention he gets, ending with Sophie's realization that she does not have to be jealous. In *Herbert Binns and the Flying Tricycle* (Castle & Weevers, 1986) a mouse inventor makes a flying tricycle that causes jealousy in three other animals who try to sabotage his invention but fail. A cat becomes jealous in *Almira's Violets* (Fregosi, 1976) and eats the blossoms of plants in her owner's flower shop. Matthew Gollub's *The Moon Was at a Fiesta*

(1994) tells how the moon over Oaxaca, Mexico, was jealous of the sun and planned a fiesta so she could have fun like the sun, but discovered she caused an imbalance in nature.

Fears

Fear is part of life. Fear can produce wariness, anxiety, suspicion, dread, dismay, anguish, and panic (Kostelnik et al., 2002). Students often have fears that are not reasonable. Very young children develop fears frequently between ages 2 and 5. As they mature, their ability to interpret observations and events develops; fears weaken and students become more realistic. Teachers should remember that because students' thinking processes are immature and their personal experiences are limited, students think their fears are reasonable. Students usually grow out of their fears as they mature. Adults who use threats to enforce discipline, such as telling a child to eat her food or the police officer will make her eat it, may cause children to develop fears.

Fear often is expressed so strongly that the adult cannot help but be aware of it. The best approach is to listen to the student, discuss the fear, and show sympathy for the student's feelings (Kostelnik et al., 2002). Although the fear cannot be talked away, the student will know that the fear has been recognized as real and upsetting. Activities in which students describe situations in which they feel fear and how they try to cope with it can be helpful. Focus on inventing strategies with the students that are successful in helping them recognize and cope with their fears.

Middle school students often develop fears related to their social situations. They worry when placed in a situation they feel has the potential for ridicule, such as making an oral presentation. Young teens may be nervous, or freeze entirely, unable to remember a word of what they want to say. The growing pressure young teens feel in social situations and the fear of ridicule cause inhibitions and anxiety.

Teachers need to help students develop confidence. Because young teens often compare themselves with the polished presentations actors create for videos and commercials, it is important to discuss the bloopers that professional actors make and to encourage students to watch a program that features such bloopers. Once they realize that professional presentations are the result of many retakes and much editing, as well as years of professional training, they may be able to set more realistic expectations for themselves and their peers. Allowing students to video their presentations beforehand or to use PowerPoint to revise and perfect them before presenting them helps overcome fears. This can serve as an opportunity for experimenting with digital moviemaking (Hofer & Swan, 2006).

Teachers have limited ability to help reduce fears generated by personal situations and must recognize that some fears are legitimate, especially in cases of abuse or violence in the streets. It is important to work to reduce fears when possible but to be aware of whom to contact for assistance when a student is involved in a situation in which the teacher can provide only limited assistance or none at all.

Fears that may be shared by several students should be examined. Reflect on how fearful students were during a recent weather event—a tornado warning, a severe rainstorm with lots of thunder and lightning, a blizzard. Are students afraid of getting caught in the middle of older adolescents shooting at each other because of an insult? How frightened are they of getting AIDS?

Students should have opportunities to discuss stories and historical events in which an individual deals with fear. For example, *Island of the Blue Dolphins* (O'Dell, 1960) offers opportunities to discuss the fears of a young Native American girl surviving on her own for years on a Pacific island. For very young students, a book such as *Will I Have a Friend* (Cohen, 1967) engages them in considering how others cope with fears. Reading biographies, trade books, and historical fiction provides students with safe opportunities to encounter and critically discuss the diverse fears and feelings of people throughout history.

Aggressive Feelings, Bullying, and Conflict Resolution

Do you view yourself as more or less than, or about as aggressive as the average person? What situation(s) cause you to feel aggressive? Terms such as *desk rage* and *road rage* have surfaced in the news in recent years. Complaints about increased aggression in sports, even among young athletes and spectators, are of increasing concern. Other nations think that U.S. culture is so aggressive and violent that no one is safe on our streets.

Some students are consistently more or less aggressive than the average student. Their aggression is part of their personality because they are temperamentally noisy, active, and distractable with more difficulty in adjusting to changes in routine (Berk, 2000). Situations, however, also create many aggressive feelings. Some students are poor social observers, finding it hard to accurately interpret others' facial expressions and words. So they do not understand that no hostility was intended and develop a history of not getting along with peers. Some students become aggressive when frustrated. Often, positive reactions to frustration, such as sharing, cooperating, talking, and other prosocial behavior, have not been strongly reinforced in these students. Such students often associate with other aggressive students (Seifert & Hoffnung, 2000). Families who use erratic physical punishment often have aggressive children. These students believe the only reason not to be aggressive is to avoid getting caught and punished. Punishment often pushes them into further aggression. Aggressive models in real life and in the media teach aggressive behaviors. Some students come from cultural backgrounds that encourage higher or lower levels of aggression than are typical among most students. Most students also learn to feel guilt when they act aggressively in situations for which their society does not sanction aggression. As a result, they are more likely to avoid aggression as they get older (Seifert & Hoffnung, 2000).

Reducing Aggression.   One way to reduce aggression is to eliminate conditions that promote it. These include frustrating situations and aggressive media programs.

Another way to reduce aggression is to teach students that aggression does not reward them, for example, by using time-out procedures. Teaching students how to resolve conflicts and interact positively with others helps. Using cooperative learning exemplifies the type of learning students need to practice if aggression is to be reduced. Finally, helping students monitor and control their own behavior is important. These strategies help students realize that less aggressive behavior results in more positive attention, affection, and approval (Seifert & Hoffnung, 2000).

Children's literature also can be used to explore aggression. *The Runner* (Voight, 1985) offers an opportunity to talk about aggression and conflict in a family. *A December Tale* (Sachs, 1976) focuses on child abuse. *Cider Days* (Stolz, 1978) describes conflict and aggression in school caused by racial bias.

Students should examine the aggression that occurs in current events. One country fights with another: Who is the aggressor? A traveler is attacked on a subway train: Who is the aggressor? Historical events can be examined in light of aggression. How did the Choctaw first react to the aggression that settlers exhibited as they appropriated the native lands and began to farm them? One major source of aggression is being unable to identify alternative solutions to conflict situations.

When children can think of just a few ways to get their point across, they tend to use some kind of attack as the fastest, surest choice. Children who come up with several choices less often use violence. So, teachers have group discussions about possible solutions, teach assertiveness and negotiation skills, and teach conflict resolution.

Conflict Resolution.   Conflict resolution abilities are important for managing students' personal and interpersonal aggressive feelings. Conflict resolution refers to programs encouraging students to resolve disputes peacefully outside traditional school disciplinary procedures (Conflict Resolution Education Network, 2000, p. 27). Schools with conflict resolution programs teach, model, and incorporate the processes and problem-solving skills of mediation, negotiation, and collaboration. Fundamental to such programs is the idea that the disputing parties solve the problem themselves. Peer mediation is the most common type of conflict resolution process, having students act as neutral third parties to resolve disputes. This is most effective in middle school and to some extent in upper elementary grades. Components of conflict resolution can be used effectively with younger children.

Conflict resolution requires specific skills: knowing how to listen, empathizing, reasoning analytically, thinking creatively, and understanding another person's viewpoint. Generally, six steps are followed:

1. Agree to meet and set ground rules.
2. Gather information about the conflict.
3. Identify what the dispute is really about.
4. Suggest possible options for resolution of the dispute.
5. Select one or more workable options.
6. Reach agreement (Conflict Resolution Education Network, 2000, p. 27).

Conflict resolution programs support school polices to prevent violence by teaching skills and processes for solving problems before they escalate into violence. Such programs help students develop personal behavior management skills, act responsibly in the school community, and accept the consequences of their own behavior. Students develop fundamental competencies, such as self-control, self-respect, empathy, and teamwork, that are necessary throughout life. Students learn to respect others as individuals and as members of a group. Finally, students learn how to build and maintain responsible and productive intergroup relations (Conflict Resolution Education Network, 2000).

Bullying.   Bullies are unhappy children who likely make poor social and academic progress. Proactive strategies must be used with bullies and their victims. Students are bullied because of (Bullying UK, www.bullying.co.uk/):

Weight	Looks
Hair color	Their family
Their schoolwork	If they are not popular
If they work hard	If they have a disability
If they are a different religion, color, or culture	If they wear glasses or a hearing aid
If they have dyslexia or dyspraxia	If they've been off school due to illness

When dealing with a student who is being bullied, it is important to remember that the student will be very upset, although it might not show on the outside. If the student has found the courage to talk to you, then he or she needs to know you will take the problem seriously. How you react and respond to that student may make the difference between resolving the issue or allowing misery to continue that could affect the rest of the student's school life.

Students must be taught guidelines for protecting themselves from bullying:

- Tell a trusted adult about the bullying, and be persistent until the adult takes action.
- Tell a staff member at your school if the harassment is school related. Schools have bullying policies in place.
- Save threatening e-mail or written or text messages in case action must be taken later.
- Never agree to meet alone with the bully.
- If possible, block the bully from your chat or instant messaging accounts.
- If you are threatened with violence, inform the local police (I-Safe America, Inc. February 21, 2009, www.isafe.org/).

Teachers try to get students who might be bullies to recognize that any of the following behaviors indicates they are a bully:

- There's a boy or girl (or maybe more than one) whom you've repeatedly shoved, punched, or physically pushed around in a mean way just because you felt like it.
- You had someone else hurt someone you don't like.

- You've spread a nasty rumor about someone in conversation, in a note, or through e-mail or instant messaging.
- You and your friends consistently have kept one or more kids from hanging out or playing with you.
- You've teased people in a mean way, calling them names or making fun of their appearance or the way they talk or dress or act.
- You've been part of a group that did any of these things, even if you only wanted to be part of the crowd (Stop Bullying Now! http://stopbullyingnow.hrsa.gov/index.asp?area=main).

Bullies must be told that their behavior will not be tolerated and must be taught ways to control angry impulses (e.g., talking oneself out of a quick reaction, deciphering behavioral cues that tell how someone else is feeling, and experiencing logical consequences from bullying).

How to Intervene When You See Bullying.   When you see bullying occurring, immediately step in and stop it. Identify the bullying behavior and say that it is against school rules (e.g., "Name calling is bullying and is against school rules"). Then, support the bullied child so he or she can regain self-control. Help the child save face, if needed. Include bystanders in the conversation and give them guidance about how they could intervene or get help in the future. Do not require students to apologize or make amends in the heat of the moment. As appropriate, impose immediate consequences on the bully (e.g., take away lunch in the cafeteria). Let students know you are watching them and their friends. Notify your colleagues. Do not require the students to meet together to work things out. Give bullied students some time to process the event and vent (Stop Bullying Now! http://stopbullyingnow.hrsa.gov/index.asp?area=main). Assist victims by supporting verbal assertiveness so that they establish their desires and protect their rights. Assertiveness training reduces bullying. It helps to teach children how to appear more confident and how to interpret social cues. Also, helping children form friendships reduces their victimization.

Friendship

Throughout childhood, students add to the number of acquaintances they have and develop close friendships. At different ages, students have different expectations for friends, so the character of friendship changes over the years. Students usually are closest to others who are similar in age, race, sex, interests, degree of sociability, and values. Through the early elementary school years, students prefer a friend who is easily accessible, has nice toys, plays easily, and quickly rewards attempts at friendliness (Seifert & Hoffnung, 2000). During the middle of the elementary school years, shared values become important. Beginning in middle school, students really start to care about what happens to a friend. They stress mutual understanding and closeness but still expect friends to be useful to them.

Using Technology

Internet Safety and Cyber-Bullying

The Internet offers those who prey on children many opportunities. Teachers seeking information and help in protecting children from online predators will find assistance on the Internet. The National Center for Missing and Exploited Children (NCMEC) has many resources available at www.missingkids.com, including information on laws and legislation; tips and pointers for teachers, parents, and children; and lists of preventative resources on various aspects of exploitation. Teachers must report suspected illegal activity involving children and predators to school authorities and also should report online activity to the CyberTipline at 1-800-843-5678, which is cosponsored by the NCMEC and the U.S. Postal Service. Predators make the most contacts with children and youth in chat rooms, but they also use instant messaging and e-mail.

Middle schoolers are among the most vulnerable to predators. Young adolescents are moving away from parental control and are looking for new relationships outside the family. Under the guise of anonymity, they are more likely to take risks online without fully understanding the possible implications. Young people who are most vulnerable to online predators tend to be new to online activity and unfamiliar with netiquette, aggressive computer users, the type to try new and edgy activities, actively seeking attention or affection, rebellious, isolated or lonely, curious, confused regarding sexual identity, easily tricked by adults, and attracted by subcultures different from their parents' world. Children and youth think they are aware of the dangers of predators, but actually are quite naïve about online relationships.

Tell students not to respond to instant messages or e-mail from strangers. A good resource is the website, Online Predators, presented by Microsoft at www.microsoft.com/athome/security/children/kidpred.mspx.

i-SAFE at http://isafe.org/ is a valuable site for teachers and parents. A part of the site called i-LEARN provides virtual training modules for teachers and parents. Students grades 5 and up can become i-MENTORS helping others safely use the Internet. Many resources are available at i-SAFE that allow teachers to build a curriculum that enables students to respond to cyber-bullies and predators while becoming responsible Internet users. NetsmartzKids is another website that has Internet safety activities for children in elementary and middle school, for educators, and for teachers at http://www.netsmartz.org/.

Cyber-bullying is sending or posting harmful or cruel text or images using the Internet or other digital communication devices (see cyber-bully.org). Cyber-threats often are a part of cyber-bullying. A cyber-threat happens when online material threatens or raises concerns about violence. A direct cyber-threat is an actual threat to hurt someone or to commit suicide. Distressing material is not a direct threat but indicates someone is emotionally upset and might be considering hurting someone, himself, or committing suicide. Examples for educators are found at http://cyberbully.org/cyberbully/docs/cbcteducator.pdf. A cartoon posted on YouTube illustrates the effects of cyber-bullying on children and teens (see http://www.youtube.com/watch?v=xGKmlTtZnSk).

WiredSafety at http://wiredsafety.org is an extensive site dealing with cyber-bullying, cyber-abuse, and cyber-stalking. It contains resources in English and Spanish useful for teachers and parents. The site has many subsections dealing with a range of problems. It addresses emerging problems that the public may be just becoming aware of, providing ideas on how to respond. A game children find interesting teaches about cyber-bullying at http://www.mcgruff.org/Games/cyberbully.php. GetNetWise at getnetwise.org provides tutorials for teachers and parents on how to secure a computer and how to find out which sites a student has visited.

Students who make and keep friends are skillful at initiating interactions with their peers, maintaining ongoing interactions, and resolving interpersonal conflicts. These skills are developed through four primary strategies that teachers can help students develop:

1. Greeting another student directly ("Hi! What's your name?")
2. Asking appropriate questions ("What's your favorite videogame?")
3. Giving information ("I like to play checkers.")
4. Trying to include the new friend in their activities ("Do you want to play tag at recess?")

Students need to know that it is important to keep trying even when rejected. Teachers should recognize that the willingness to keep trying depends on self-confidence.

Through daily classroom activities, teachers coach students in social skills that help them begin and continue satisfying friendships. Coaching involves telling or showing students how to use a specific social skill. This includes giving students opportunities to practice the skill and giving feedback with suggestions for improving the use of the skill. Among the skills that are effectively taught are asking questions, learning to give positive reinforcement to others (such as smiles), making good eye contact, and taking turns (Kostelnik et al., 2002). Once a friendship has begun, many skills can contribute to its continuation:

- Rewarding a friend by smiling at him or her
- Imitating the friend's actions
- Paying attention to the friend
- Approving of what the friend does
- Complying with the friend's wishes
- Sharing things with the friend
- Communicating well
- Being a good listener
- Giving information needed by the listener
- Judging whether your own actions have shown or not shown respect for others' rights and welfare (Hartup, Glazer, & Charlesworth, 1987)

Friendships can be examined by discussing current events and historical situations. Consider the following questions as ideas for content that can be discussed within social studies units:

At one time the United States has been both a friend and an enemy of Germany. What might be the characteristics of friendships between the leaders of these nations?

What is meant by a media report that someone got a city building contract because he was the friend of the mayor?

Does a real friendship mean you do illegal things for your friends?

Henry Ford and Thomas Edison were close friends. What was the basis for their friendship?

Literature can be used to help students consider friendship. Two books by Leo Lionni are examples. In *Little Blue and Little Yellow* (1995), two characters explore their friendship while mixing their colors; in *It's Mine!* (1996), three frogs learn that sharing is important. In the series, *Franklin Collection: 10 Books* (Bourgeois & Clark, 1999), a turtle learns about friendship and finds that no one likes a friend who is bossy. *It's My Turn* (Bedford & Field, 2001) describes two friends who learn to share, take turns, and cooperate so they can enjoy the seesaw, a favorite ride at the playground. An industrious hen and her loafer friends are featured in *The Little Red Hen* (also in Spanish, *La Gallinita Roja*) by Lucinda McQueen (1985). In *My Friends* (Gomi, 2006), a very young girl describes all she has learned from her friends. Using photographs, a diverse group of students demonstrate the meaning of friendship in their activities in *Friends at School* (Bunnett & Brown, 2006). *Jennifer, Hecate, Macbeth, William McKinley, and Me* by E. L. Konigsburg (1976) describes how a shy child makes friends.

Empathy and Helpful Prosocial Behaviors

Empathy is the ability to vicariously experience the emotions of another person. It is thought to play an important part in developing friendships (Seifert & Hoffnung, 2000). Empathy relates to prosocial behaviors. These are positive social actions that benefit others such as sharing, helping, and cooperating. This chapter's learning cycle lesson plan on sharing and negotiation is an example of a lesson focusing on helping students develop prosocial behaviors.

As early as kindergarten, children demonstrate empathy by responding helpfully to another person's distress: comforting, giving things to another child, warning a child of further danger, and inquiring of a child in trouble. Teachers foster empathy and prosocial behaviors by encouraging high-quality peer contacts, such as those that often occur in cooperative group or pairs activities. Teachers foster empathy by (1) giving verbal approval to students' prosocial behaviors, (2) modeling empathy and prosocial behaviors, (3) using instructional practices that involve cooperative activities, (4) analyzing the words and acts of characters in stories and books for prosocial behaviors, and (5) using activities in which students' have greater control of their learning.

Self-Esteem

Self-esteem and self-concept are closely connected. If a person is pleased with his self-concept, he will have high self-esteem. Most students have formed a stable sense of self-esteem by the middle school years. Self-esteem appears to be related to social behavior. Students with high self-esteem participate frequently in discussions and other activities rather than simply listen passively. Expressing opinions, approaching new tasks with self-confidence, resisting peer pressure, and making friends easily are thought to be the result of high self-esteem based on positive self-concept. Teachers need to work to foster a positive self-concept in each student and to indicate respect and appreciation for each student's abilities and cultural background. Because self-esteem affects motivation and the desire to study and learn, teachers use instructional strategies and management procedures to support its formation.

Values and Moral Education in a Diverse Society

Our values are an important part of our self-concept. Values are decisions about the worth of something based on a standard we set. When an individual decides something has value, he or she decides that it is worthwhile and compares that worth to the importance and worth of other things. Something that is judged "right" is valued. Not all things of value are "moral" because their value may not be measured against the standard of "right" behavior.

Building on Diversity

Learning from the Voices of Our Family and Community

Teachers must offer family and community members opportunities to speak about their life experiences and give this knowledge an important place in the classroom (McCaleb, 1994). One way to accomplish these goals is to build student and community books on themes such as Our Family History, Teachings from My Childhood Community, the Wise Person I Remember, My Family's Dictionary: Words That Are Special to People in My Family, My Mother (or Father, Grandma, Big Sister, etc.) Is Special, Words of Advice from My Family, Friendship across Generations, the Most Frightening Time in My Life, or a Book for Peace (McCaleb, 1994).

To begin, a teacher might share a literature selection on the topic or have a brainstorming session. Next, a decision should be made about whether family or community members will be interviewed to obtain information. If interviews are to be used, questions are identified for the interview. Information from interviews can be discussed and put on thematic maps and charts. Many books should be joint student and family/community projects. Students will find that they have to weave together several stories and sometimes multiple perspectives. They might need assistance from their teacher and/or family members. A first draft can be edited with help from the teacher or other students. Some books, however, may be a coproduction of the student and family and may be brought to school as a completed project.

Even the youngest students can create a book. Their books may be mostly artwork of people or events. A description of the artwork may be short and written by the student or can be dictated to an adult who writes it down for the student. A special book day should celebrate the completion of books on a topic. Students from other classes can come in to listen to books as they are read, or the book can be shared with family members on a family night.

Three Aspects of Morality

Morality has three aspects: (1) moral reasoning, (2) self-evaluation, and (3) conscious resistance to unacceptable thinking and behavior. Growth in moral reasoning is aided by finding that others have different moral perspectives, which may conflict with one's own perspectives (Seifert & Hoffnung, 2000). Moral judgments depend on synthesizing several varieties of social information to arrive at conceptions of appropriate and inappropriate behavior (Bandura, 1977).

Self-evaluation views guilt as empathic distress accompanied by the belief that you are responsible for someone else's distress. When children are tempted to do something they are not supposed to do, the likelihood of succumbing to temptation depends on child rearing and school experiences, understanding of the misconduct, and situational factors. When children have families and teachers who firmly and consistently insist that they learn and practice habits of self-regulation, who justify their disciplinary action with inductive reasoning, who are warm and communicative, who avoid the use of unnecessarily harsh discipline, and who are models of self-controlled behavior, they are most likely to display desirable conduct away from adults. Parents' and teachers' use of explanations and inductive reasoning helps children learn to accept responsibility for their misbehavior. In inductive reasoning, an individual becomes familiar with examples and nonexamples of something and then uses them to develop a concept or generalization. Bandura (1977) suggests that children develop personal standards of appropriate conduct and that they learn to guide their behavior by rewarding and punishing themselves for attaining or falling short of goals they have set for themselves.

Children who are internally motivated to behave morally, pride themselves on good behavior, anticipate blaming themselves for misbehaving and know how to talk themselves out of misbehaving, and know how to avoid thinking about forbidden activities are better able to resist temptations than are children lacking these qualities. At a time when nobody else is nearby, a student might, for example, notice, on the desk of another student, a brightly colored, fancy new pencil that is considered the latest thing in pencils. This student is tempted because her mother won't buy her something just because it is a fad; she buys her only the customary yellow pencils. This student could take the pencil, hide it, and use it out of class so that nobody would know she took it. However, this student knows she would feel guilt and would not want to look the owner in the face. She understands that the guilt she would feel from this misconduct isn't worth it, so she quickly moves away from the area and puts the temptation well away from her.

Situational factors that can influence the likelihood for resisting temptation include specific aspects of the situation as well as of the individual. A specific situation often affects a person's reaction to each aspect of morality. For example, a student might feel guilt in one setting but not in another. In addition, depending on an individual's mood, concerns, or even health, the feeling of guilt might be present in one instance but not in another even when circumstances remain the same. These individual aspects also influence how a person faces temptations.

Moral Development Theories

Lawrence Kohlberg described moral development. Some disagreement exists about how accurately his theories predict moral development, but some implications should be considered in social studies education.

1. **The *Egocentric* Stage.** Children (about 4 to 7 years old) do not knowingly follow rules; they decide what is right and wrong on the basis of what adults permit or forbid them to do.
2. **The *Incipient Cooperation* Stage.** Children (about 7 to 10 or 11 years old) are more social and cooperative as they demonstrate an understanding that rules are made to help solve interpersonal conflicts.
3. **The *Real Cooperation* Stage.** Children (about 11 or 12 years old) begin to develop appropriate rules and understand why rules are needed.

Kohlberg (1969) tested individuals from a variety of cultures and economic levels, finding similarities in development. He outlined his ideas as follows:

1. As cognitive development occurs, understanding of morally appropriate behavior and the reasons for that behavior also occur.
2. Cognitive and social development occur in stages and each qualitatively different from the one that preceeded it.
3. Maturational factors and the continuing restructuring of behavior through experience and maturation result in the requirement that no new stage may be achieved unless all preceding ones have been achieved.

Kohlberg's theory has implications for teaching. Students cannot be expected to understand adult explanations of right and wrong because they do not have the cognitive ability to do so. Students are likely to be motivated by the reward or punishment an action brings rather than by whether it is right or wrong. Students can mature and begin to understand why if explanations are given. Eventually, they develop their own set of moral standards and values. They need to know and judge others' values and actions. Students need experience requiring reflection and logical reasoning to make moral decisions.

Judgment has been found to become increasingly abstract up to about age 16, indicating that Kohlberg's insistence that cognition cannot be separated from moral development is well founded. Because moral development requires practice in making and examining moral questions, teachers should concern themselves with providing students with lesson experiences in which they actively confront moral issues.

Carol Gilligan (1982) challenged Kohlberg's view that equal justice for all is the highest moral criterion. She stated that females have a concern for care and responsibility as the highest moral criterion that is missing from Kohlberg's work. The justice orientation results in ideals of equality, reciprocity, and fairness between individuals. The care orientation results in ideals of attachment to others, loving and being loved, listening and being listened to, and responding and being responded to. Brown, Tappan, and Gilligan (1995) indicate that children experience both perspectives and learn lessons about justice and care in early childhood relationships that generate expectations that are confirmed or modified in later childhood and adolescence. These lessons result in two moral injunctions—not to treat others unfairly and not to turn away from others in need—defining two lines of moral development; providing different standards for assessing moral thoughts, feelings, and actions; and pointing to changes in the understanding of what fairness means and what constitutes care.

Three ways are suggested for developing care (Brown et al., 1995). First, students should be helped to consider the peculiarities of a situation and to understand others in order to develop care. Activities fostering the development of care include: writing; reading fictional and historical accounts of human lives, societies, and cultures; demonstrating through art how meaning depends on context; frequent classroom discussion; constructing and discussing meaning as we interact with text. Second, students need opportunities to tell their own stories about their real-life moral experiences. Interviews with the teacher or other students enable students to tell their stories to an interested listener. Journals and essay assignments focus students on the moral decisions they have made in their own lives. Teachers must be sensitive and sympathetic, providing students with the kind of response to their stories that indicates they have heard and understood them. Third, students dramatize their own moral stories through skits, plays, or video productions. This requires sharing a story with a peer audience, which can be uncomfortable for some but provides an opportunity for students to learn important lessons from their peers' stories (Brown et al., 1995).

Teaching Approaches in Values Education

Three approaches have played important and often controversial roles in values education: values clarification, values analysis, and character education. Each requires preparation and thought to be used appropriately and effectively.

Values Clarification.   Values clarification is a teaching approach focusing on moral reasoning. It helps you make choices as you work toward enhancing your own moral development. This approach emphasizes the process of thinking about what is valued more than the specific values themselves. The values-clarification approach is used to help students decide what value they personally attach to something. Teachers help students explore a value such as being trustworthy by asking thought-provoking questions: Would they keep a friend's secret when another friend is curious? Would they keep silent when the teacher is threatening to punish someone else for altering a PowerPoint presentation made by a small group when they know their friend damaged it but have promised not to tell?

The teacher tries to remain neutral and to serve as a facilitator of students' own exploration of their feelings. In so doing, teachers help students recognize that they live in a complex society in which many different values are present and often conflict. The teacher tries to help students decide what they think is worth valuing and how great a value they place on it (Raths, Harmin, & Simon, 1978).

When values clarification questioning strategies are employed in a learning cycle lesson, the exploratory introduction presents a decision-making situation or scenario in which the students make a decision. In the lesson development phase, the first six steps of the seven-step process for values clarification developed by Raths et al. (1978) are followed. Figure 9.1 presents the seven steps with sample teacher questions appropriate for each step. During the expansion phase, the teacher engages students in step 7 by considering situations in which the same value as that examined in the original problem is appropriately applied or not applied. Values-clarification questioning is used as a whole-class, small-group, or single-student strategy.

Values-clarification exercises using paper-and-pencil responses include rank ordering alternatives, forced-choice sets of statements, and checklists. To rank order, students are given a list of statements, or items, to rank from most to least important, useful, desirable, or any of a variety of other categories. Figure 9.2 is a sample exercise for ranking the qualities students think are important in a good friend. Following the individual decisions, the students discuss their rankings and reasons for the rank ordering.

1. ***Choosing freely***
   "Where do you suppose you first got that idea?" or "Are you the only one among your friends who feels this way?"

2. ***Choosing from alternatives***
   "What reasons do you have for your choice?" or "How long did you think about this problem before you decided?"

3. ***Choosing after thoughtful consideration***
   "What would happen if this choice were implemented? If another choice was implemented?" or "What is good about this choice? What could be good about the other choices?"

4. ***Prizing and being happy with the choice***
   "Are you happy about feeling this way?" or "Why is this important to you?"

5. ***Prizing and willing to affirm the choice publicly***
   "Would you be willing to tell the class how you feel?" or "Should someone who feels like you stand up in public and tell people how he or she feels?"

6. ***Acting on the choice***
   "What will you do about your choice? What will you do next?" or "Are you interested in joining this group of people who think the same as you do about this?"

7. ***Acting repeatedly in some pattern of life***
   "Have you done anything about it? Will you do it again?" or "Should you try to get other people interested in this?"

FIGURE 9.1

The Values-Clarification Process   *Source:* Adapted from *Values and Teaching* (2nd ed.), by L. Raths, M. Harmin, and S. Shore, 1978, pp. 63–65, Columbus, OH: Merrill.

What Is Important in a Friend?

In class, everyone listed those qualities they thought were important in a friend:

_____ Has ideas for games   _____ Likes things I like

_____ Is happy   _____ Listens to me

_____ Does the same things as me   _____ Agrees with me

_____ Shares   _____ Does what I say

_____ Dresses like me   _____ Tells me what he or she finds out

Which of these qualities do you think are the most important in a friend? Number the qualities from 1 to 10 from the most important to the least important quality.

Most Important Quality in a Friend: _____

Least Important Quality in a Friend: _____

FIGURE 9.2
Sample Rank-Ordering Form

People have ideas about what makes a good friend. Some people's ideas about which qualities a good friend has are given below. Read each idea. If you agree with the idea, circle *Agree*. If you disagree with the idea, circle *Disagree*.

What Makes a Good Friend?

Agree	**Disagree**	1. A good friend smiles at you a lot.
Agree	**Disagree**	2. A good friend likes the same clothes you like.
Agree	**Disagree**	3. A good friend has ideas for things to do together.
Agree	**Disagree**	4. A good friend likes to do the same things you do.
Agree	**Disagree**	5. A good friend shares things with you.
Agree	**Disagree**	6. A good friend likes the things you like.
Agree	**Disagree**	7. A good friend listens to you.
Agree	**Disagree**	8. A good friend does what you say.
Agree	**Disagree**	9. A good friend agrees with you.
Agree	**Disagree**	10. A good friend takes the blame when something goes wrong.

FIGURE 9.3
Example of a Forced-Choice Questionnaire

Forced-choice activities have students choose between two or more choices in responding to a statement. Figure 9.3 illustrates a forced-choice exercise. Nonreaders may be asked to choose between drawings of situations, or they can raise their hands to register their choice as the teacher reads the items aloud. As student choices are discussed, the teacher uses clarifying questions, such as those in Figure 9.1 to help the students probe the reasoning for their responses.

What Is a Friend?

A class surveyed all the students in their school. Their survey was about what a friend is. After they put together all their information, they decided on the following description:

> A friend is someone who is just like you. A friend dresses like you, likes the same jokes, talks like you, and likes to play the same games. A friend never disagrees with you. A friend always lets you have first choice and shares everything. A friend never gossips about you and stands up for you to everybody else. A friend will lie about something if the truth will get you in trouble. A friend never gets mad at you.

What do you think about this description? Put a checkmark beside each word that tells what you think about this description.

_____ Helpful		_____ Silly		_____ Thoughtful
_____ Bad		_____ Impossible		_____ Important
_____ Wise		_____ Unimportant		_____ Good
_____ Strong		_____ Useful		_____ Weak
_____ Honest		_____ Tough		_____ Fair
_____ Mean		_____ Unfair		_____ Accurate

FIGURE 9.4
Sample Checklist

Figure 9.4 demonstrates a checklist approach. Students are first presented with a statement, situation, or story that involves valuing. Then they check off those adjectives from a list of positive and negative adjectives that describe how they feel about the statement, situation, or story. Student responses on the checklist are used as the focus of a discussion that follows.

The values-clarification approach has been criticized for three reasons: (1) its focus, (2) broad interpretation of what a value is, and (3) lack of attention to what cognitive structures are needed for this type of questioning to help students successfully clarify their values (Fraenkel, 1977). The values-clarification approach today is recommended as one component of a moral education program but not as the only part.

Value Analysis.   Value-analysis strategies help students think in an organized, logical manner about the following issues:

- Their values
- Their reasons for making specific choices
- The consequences of having a particular value
- The conflicts between their values and other people's values (Banks & Clegg, 1979)

Because value analysis involves asking questions, it is appropriate to use in all three phases of the learning cycle. Sometimes an incident from a person's life or a story might lead to using value analysis. In *Goldilocks and the Three Bears*, Goldilocks goes into someone else's house, eats their food, breaks their furniture, and sleeps in their beds. What values was Goldilocks displaying? Why did she do what she did? What were the results? Did her values conflict with the bear family's values? Students' skills in value analysis can be built using a sequence suggested by Banks and Clegg (1979). See Figure 9.5 for an example.

The values-analysis approach has been criticized as too logical to attempt to analyze what is affective. Certain values, particularly religious values, must be

1. **What is the value problem?**
   Is it right for Goldilocks to be in the bears' house?

2. **What is occurring that might involve values?**
   Goldilocks is eating others' food and sleeping in their beds without their permission and breaking their furniture.

3. **What does Goldilocks's behavior tell us about what she values? What does the bears' behavior tell us about what they value?**
   Students might decide Goldilocks values her own needs above all else and/or the bears value their right to privacy more than Goldilocks' right to satisfy her needs.

4. **How do these values differ or conflict?**
   Students may decide that Goldilocks's and the bears' values conflict. The bears cannot have their privacy if Goldilocks feels the only way she can satisfy her needs is not to wait until they get home.

5. **What are the sources of the values expressed?**
   Students may decide Goldilocks learned at home that she doesn't have to wait to satisfy her needs. The bears may live in a community that regards the right to privacy as important.

6. **What other values could be expressed? What alternatives are there?**
   Students might decide Goldilocks should respect the bears' right to privacy and wait until the bears get home to ask them to share their food and for a place to sleep. Or they might decide that the bears would expect Goldilocks to come into their home and would be upset if she didn't make herself comfortable in their home.

7. **What are the consequences if various choices are made?**
   Students might decide that the consequences of Goldilocks's present choice is that the bears find their food eaten and their furniture broken. Making another choice, Goldilocks might have waited until the bears came home and asked them for help. Or maybe Goldilocks would have looked like a tasty morsel to the bears and they might have eaten her!

8. **What choice do you make?**
   Students might decide that Goldilocks should wait until the bears get home and ask for their help.

9. **Why did you make this choice and what will its consequences be?**
   Students might decide that Goldilocks should wait until the bears get home and ask for their help because she wasn't dying of hunger and should have had some respect for the bears' privacy.

FIGURE 9.5

Value Analysis Sequence Using the Story of *Goldilocks and the Three Bears*

taken on faith and cannot be logically analyzed. Situations in which value analysis is helpful occur in pop culture (Joseph, 2000), legal cases (Naylor & Diem, 1987), classroom incidents, personal incidents, current events, and historical events. Value analysis may not always be appropriate, but it gives students a means by which they can analyze social issues and problems.

Character Education.   Character education is a movement that has become prominent in recent years. This approach is focused on teaching and modeling specific character traits, for example, honesty, courage, perseverance, loyalty, caring, civic virtue, justice, respect and responsibility, and trustworthiness. Both values clarification and moral reasoning focus on the processes of reasoning and selecting values. Character education focuses on demonstrating moral and ethical qualities in our emotional responses, thinking, reasoning, and behavior (Berkowitz & Bier, 2004).

Two types of values are associated with character education. *Personal values* are the behaviors people demonstrate that uphold their ideals such as honesty, courage, perseverance, self-discipline, responsibility, and integrity. *Social values* are demonstrated in our behaviors and attitudes toward others, especially those in our personal social environment such as our friends, teachers, and family members. These values include caring, respect, empathy, trustworthiness, fairness, and acceptance and tolerance of diversity. *Civic virtues* also are associated with character education. These are expressed by our behavior and attitudes toward the community, society, and government and include active citizenship, patriotism, and justice (U.S. Department of Education, 2007).

Character education sometimes is taught through standalone lessons. A standalone lesson focuses on a character trait, such as an elementary lesson about integrity using the book *The Empty Pot* (Demi, 1990), which is found at http://www.bu.edu/sed/caec/files/elemlesson.htm or a middle school lesson teaching an understanding of responsibility using *The Chronicles of Narnia* (Lewis & Baynes, 1949), which is found at http://www.bu.edu/sed/caec/files/mslesson2.htm. Standalone lessons are useful but limited. When using a book, for example, to focus on a character trait, teachers keep in mind how concepts are constructed. Active investigation of the concept and linking it to personal experiences should come before the book is used. This will allow students to apply their new knowledge of the character trait to the book with which they are working. Such standalone lessons are used best as Expansion activities in a unit focusing on the character trait.

The Task Force on Character Education in the Social Studies, formed by the National Council for the Social Studies (1996), recognized the role of character education in citizenship stating that citizens must be committed to core, or fundamental, values such as life, liberty, equality, truth, pursuit of happiness, and promotion of the common good. To accomplish such a commitment, social studies teachers foster students' meaningful understanding of core values. Teachers involve students in discussions and projects tied to issues about which the students have concerns.

A number of curricula address various aspects of character education, including different perspectives, content, and instructional approaches. Teachers and school systems critically examine these to decide which are appropriate for their students' needs and can best foster meaningful learning and understanding of behavior consistent with core values that underlie human societies.

Representative character education lessons and curricula are found at:

The Ethics Curriculum Project, http://www6.miami.edu/ethics/ecp/index.htm

The Center for Social and Character Development at Rutgers, http://www.rucharacter.org/LessonPlans/

The Center for the Advancement of Ethics and Character at Boston University, http://www.bu.edu/sed/caec/files/teacherresources.htm

The Institute for Character Education, http://charactered.ocde.us/ICE/lessons/index.asp

American Promise, http://www.farmers.com/FarmComm/AmericanPromise/guide_main.html

In character education lessons, the exploratory introduction typically involves preparing a situation in which the trait value is demonstrated. For example,

These students are working on projects using different resources they chose. Such projects foster perseverance, self-discipline, and responsibility, which are important values in character education.
Photographer: Lynn A. Kelley

students can role-play a situation, such as returning money they have found to its owner. During the lesson development, the trait or value is modeled, described, and discussed. Students read and analyze stories in which honesty is demonstrated. Honesty is then demonstrated by students during the expansion. The students devise their own role-plays to demonstrate honesty as a way of expanding the trait into new contexts. Concerns raised by this approach include the selection of traits and values for the content of character education and who selects them.

Advocates believe that it is impossible to have a value-neutral education but that it is possible to agree on a common set of core traits or values to be taught. Concerns exist about whether teachers are expected to indoctrinate students with a set of values selected by an elite group. Concerns also exist about whether young children can meaningfully understand character traits. The research literature on moral development indicates that cognitive development is important in understanding the abstract ideas represented by character traits and in knowing when and how to behave consistently with the values incorporated in those traits. Some traits, such as respect for others and taking responsibility for oneself, appear to have consensus. However, it is important to consider whether some traits represent the perspectives of one or more cultural groups but are not core values for peoples the world over.

We have discussed multiple approaches illustrating the range of purposes for values education. Values are basic to social studies curriculum and to all education. Yet this area has no clear specifications. Researchers and curriculum developers have put great effort into developing and testing the approaches described. Each has something to offer, but each must be considered with attention to how it is carried out and why it is being used.

Attitudes and Dispositions Promoting Powerful Social Studies

Attitudes and dispositions are affective responses that reflect out feelings and personal likes and dislikes. The development of attitudes promoting powerful learning is a fundamental goal of the social studies curriculum. We can plan for, model, and encourage these attitudes in a social studies lesson: curiosity, respect for evidence, flexibility, responsibility to others and the environment, and appreciation of the social and natural worlds. These attitudes are important for learning social studies, and essential to being an active and responsible citizen.

Curiosity

Curious students want to know about, to experience, to explore, and to investigate the things around them. This is an attitude that promotes all kinds of learning. Curiosity often is shown through questioning. Teachers foster curiosity by welcoming students' questions about people, objects, and events. Inviting students to pose questions is one way of valuing curiosity. Questioning brings satisfaction if it helps students share their pleasure and excitement with others. Curiosity is *wanting to know*, rather than a mere flow of questions. Wanting to know stimulates efforts to find out. A teacher encourages curiosity by asking students to explain a puzzling event related to a key idea. One goal of the exploratory introduction phase of a lesson is to create curiosity.

Respect for Evidence

Students gather evidence about their social world and use it to develop and test ideas. An explanation or theory is not useful to a student unless it fits the evidence or makes sense of what the student already knows.

Open-Mindedness.   Students show they know that an unsupported statement is not necessarily true when they ask, "How do you know that's true?" or say, "Prove it." If a teacher appears to accept statements from students without evidence or offers no evidence for a statement he or she makes to students, the attitude transmitted is that evidence is *not* necessary. Asking for evidence conveys the true nature of social studies as a process focused on solving specific types of problems.

Perseverance.   Obtaining convincing evidence takes perseverance; waiting for new evidence to be reported, being willing to try again, learning from earlier difficulties, and changing one's ideas as a result of what is learned. Teachers model perseverance and provide students with some assignments that require seeking out information rather than just accepting the most easily available evidence.

Consideration of Conflicting Evidence.   It is not easy to accept evidence that conflicts with what you think you already know. Students are more likely to consider conflicting evidence if their teacher models this behavior, accepts mistakes, and rewards their efforts.

Reserving Judgment

Respect for evidence requires reserving judgment. Information is willingly considered and used in making a decision. Students find this a difficult process that does not result in immediate satisfaction. Instead, a period of uncertainty and mental challenge exists before a judgment occurs.

Flexibility

Unless flexibility exists, each experience that conflicts with existing ideas causes resistance. It becomes a rival idea instead of a part of the process of modifying and developing an existing one. The ability to be flexible and the recognition that conclusions are tentative are important qualities. Elementary and middle school students might not fully understand the tentativeness of ideas, but teachers need to promote attitudes that enable them eventually to develop this understanding. One way of doing this is to preface conclusions with a statement such as "As far as we can tell...." It helps occasionally to talk with students about how their ideas have changed and how they used to think. Asking students to write and read about what they have learned in a small group helps them develop flexibility. Having students construct portfolios of their social studies experiences and receive feedback also promotes flexibility.

Responsibility to Others and to the Environment

NCSS

Standards
VIII, X

Growth of inquiry skills should be accompanied by the development of sensitivity and responsibility. This is expressed as an attitude of respect for, and willingness to care about, others and the environment.

A sense of responsibility toward someone or something is more likely to occur when a student has had experience with that person and thing or knows something about them. For example, students who have picked up litter in their classroom or from the school grounds understand the effort that goes into this task. These students are more likely to take care of their school or community than is someone who has not been so involved. Knowledge and experience help, although they are not enough to create an attitude of responsibility. Many of the concepts relating to responsibility for, and sensitivity to, people and the environment are complex. The interdependence of plants and animals in an ecosystem, for example, is not routinely considered when citizens make decisions in local communities. Concepts are often controversial, such as in the production of energy using nuclear fission.

Rules that teachers and students form together help students begin to act responsibly. These rules can expect students to pick up pencils or crayons off the floor rather than step on and mash them, to water classroom plants on a regular basis, to wash their hands after covering a sneeze to reduce the spread of bacteria, and to provide enough space when sitting in a circle on the rug so that their neighbors have enough room to sit comfortably. The way to accomplish this is gradually to transfer responsibility to students for making decisions about how they should behave in their social and physical world.

Values, Morals, and Aesthetics

It is an emotional aspect or implication that often prompts people to examine a problem and take action. The skills used to make value and moral choices are the same as those used to examine cognitive issues. The difference is the content of the problem under consideration. Affective questions focus on making choices about preference, importance, correctness, and truth.

Values are decisions about the worth or importance of something based on a standard we have set. When we value something, we believe it is important or that it has worth. Value decisions are *morals* when the judgments involve rightness or wrongness.

Aesthetics is the recognition of beauty and the assignment of value to it. People value that which they consider beautiful. Through painting, sculpture, ceramics, and weaving, artists express the beauty they see in nature and in social events. Musicians and writers also express the beauty they find in nature and in social events. Activities providing students with opportunities to search for beauty and examine values that people over the ages have assigned to the many designs and relationships found in nature and in the social world are incorporated into social studies.

NCSS
Standards III, VII

Each generation must be educated to recognize and preserve relationships between people, places, and environment as production, distribution, and consumption take place among a larger and larger population. We need to examine and institute ways that allow nature and people to coexist. Developing an appreciation for natural beauty is a starting point for students to learn to value the natural environment in which they live. By incorporating cognitive, affective, and aesthetic perspectives in lessons, students have opportunities to examine important aspects of a problem before making a decision. In so doing, students use many skills and apply them to information from both the cognitive and affective domains.

Making a Literature Connection

Demonstrating Powerful Attitudes and Dispositions

Attitudes and dispositions strongly affect our education. When teachers model curiosity, respect for evidence, flexibility, and other powerful attitudes and dispositions, students typically respond positively. Modeling involves demonstrating the trait in action and encouraging students to display it.

Literature selections that demonstrate attitudes and dispositions promoting powerful social studies are available. *Curious George* by H. A. Rey is beloved by very young children, who watch the monkey's curiosity get him into all sorts of trouble and find that he always has challenging experiences but comes out fine.

In *Straight to the Hoop* by John Coy, James, an inner-city 10-year-old, perseveres to prove himself on the basketball court. Responsibility toward others and perseverance are described in *Freedom School, Yes!* by Amy Littlesugar, as Jolie, her family, and friends, despite threats, persevere in aiding a young woman who has come to teach in a Mississippi Freedom School in the 1960s. *The Chimpanzees I Love: Saving Their World and Ours* by Jane Goodall clearly presents Dr. Goodall's respect for our environment as she enthusiastically works very hard to learn about and protect an endangered species.

Assessing How Diverse Students Relate to Individuals and Communities

Assessing students' individual and social development requires teachers to use authentic measures that focus on the performance of social behaviors and expressions of values and attitudes. Such measures are demonstrated in this chapter's learning cycle and the examples of a rank-ordering form, a forced-choice questionnaire, and a checklist. Students' journals, brief essays, drawings, and role-playing are products that teachers can use for assessment. It is important to have students make their views public while at the same time ensuring the classroom is a safe place in which to do so.

Teachers must know the community served by the school well because they are making interpretations of what students say and demonstrate. Students' prosocial behaviors, values, and attitudes are influenced by their family experiences and culture. It is within this context that students are developing as individuals and members of many communities—that of their family, their church, the people with whom they are involved in clubs and sports, among others. At the same time, students and their families deserve and expect privacy. Therefore, teachers must maintain confidentiality and carefully identify instructional activities that are appropriate and relevant to students' backgrounds and to the communities in which they live. Finally, assessment of attitudes and values and of individual and social development is not done in order to give a grade. These are components of individual and social development that are assessed in order to determine how best to scaffold students' continuing development. Grading such development implies judging students as individuals and is not a part of our role as social studies teachers.

EXPANSION

Confronting Challenges to Students' Active, Responsible Development as Citizens

Teachers play an important role in students' development as individuals, as members of the classroom community, and as members of the community beyond the classroom. Dilemmas with no easy solution often confront teachers. The focus of teaching must be on working through challenges in ways that students' develop as active, responsible individuals and community members.

TIME FOR REFLECTION | What Do You Think?

Reflect on the following questions, and develop a response that keeps in mind the key goal of students' development as active, responsible individuals and community members.

1. Violence in schools has been widely described in the media in recent years and schools have responded with increased security measures. What positive roles can technology play in such a context? What additional problems does technology present to educators who wish to support students' active and responsible community membership by allowing them greater control over activities in the classroom and school?

2. Why is it necessary for teachers at early childhood, elementary, and middle school levels to attend to students who observe acts of bullying and help them learn to voice their feelings and abilities to respond to such situations?

3. When, in the K–8 curriculum you experienced, do you recall teachers including an examination of what people think was proper behavior? Was "proper behavior" defined in such a way that it considered whether a decision was a just decision? Where in the K–8 social studies curriculum might a teacher have opportunities to ask students to consider and discuss what they believe to be just and proper behaviors and to give their reasons why such behaviors are or are not the correct choices for a responsible and active citizen?

4. Being a leader and an active follower are two roles that all citizens perform in a democracy. What are three actions leaders need to exhibit in leading a club, organization, community, state, or nation? What are three actions followers need to practice when deciding to support or reject a person as a leader worthy of following?

5. How can formative assessment during a lesson be used to promote students' development of a positive and realistic self-concept?

Summary

Personal and social development occur through maturation and experience. Teachers provide experiences encouraging students' development, help them cope with difficulties they encounter, develop morals and values, and develop prosocial attitudes conducive to citizenship. The teacher is a powerful person in a student's life and works to ensure a positive influence for the student as an individual and as a participating citizen in a democracy.

Each student has different needs, and each of these needs has a strong impact on the student. Because of the needs each student has, and because of the differences between students, controversy erupts over how psychology and values education should be taught. Moral reasoning and values clarification are two areas that have generated a lot of controversy. Much of the controversy is due, first, to the recognition that psychology and values education are both important and sensitive issues, and, second, to conflicting ideas on how to teach them well. The controversy often involves people's basic beliefs about morality and students' relationships with each other. Because this is an area in which issues have not been resolved, we most likely will continue to see debate.

Recommended Websites to Visit

The Conflict Resolution Education Network
http://www.creducation.org/
Character Education Resource for Teachers: An Online Guide, U.S. Department of Education
http://www.cetac.org/teacherresource/
U.S. Department of Education's Safe and Drug-Free Schools Program
http://www.ed.gov/about/offices/list/osdfs/index.html
Helping the Socially Isolated Child Make Friends
http://www.ldonline.org/article/19272
Northwest Regional Educational Laboratory: Developing Self-Directed Learners
http://www.nwrel.org/planning/reports/self-direct/index.php

10

How Can I Involve All Students in Meaningful Social Studies?

EXPLORATORY INTRODUCTION

Each of us experiences life differently and brings to the classroom a unique view of the topics social studies addresses. Teachers who engage each of us in active participation in social studies create a classroom in which we truly benefit from the opportunity of learning from each other. Consider and respond to the following questions.

1. Assume you are a teacher in either the second or seventh grade. In one class of 20 students at a school with which you are familiar, what estimates would you give of the percentage of students who are: male? Hispanic American? identified as having special needs? low income (qualifying for free lunch)?
2. How have your personal experiences influenced your estimates?
3. Describe the teacher in this class in terms of gender, ethnicity, abilities, and socioeconomic status. How does the teacher you described compare in these personal characteristics to the students?
4. What do the similarities and differences you identified between teacher and students imply for the kind of goals the teacher must set in order to involve all students in meaningful social studies during the school year?

Chapter Overview

Powerful social studies means that every student has an equal opportunity to learn social studies, regardless of culture, gender, or disability. We must step away from the traditional whole-class approach to teaching social studies and encourage students to use, interact with, and respect not only their own heritage but also those of their peers. *Curriculum Standards for Social Studies* (NCSS, 1994b) endorses the belief that students should be helped to construct a pluralist perspective based on diversity. This perspective respects differences of opinion and preference, race, religion, gender, class, ethnicity, and culture in general. Students need to learn that cultural and philosophical differences are not "problems" to be solved, but healthy and desirable qualities of democratic community life. Likewise, disabilities may limit individuals in some respects but enrich the group as students respond to and include each other in their work toward the common good of all.

This chapter describes the process for planning, developing, and carrying out lessons involving diverse students in a powerful social studies program. The types of accommodations that can be made to involve all students in a lesson are not unmanageable or difficult when included in a meaningful approach to social studies.

Chapter Objectives

1. Describe the purpose and rationale of social studies for all students.
2. Distinguish traditional social studies teaching from teaching that involves all students.
3. Describe general instructional strategies for social studies teaching in inclusive classrooms.
4. Describe the factors to be considered when adapting social studies instruction for students with special needs.
5. Identify and describe accommodations to be made in adapting a social studies concept for several specific special needs.
6. Define multicultural social studies teaching.
7. Describe modifications that are helpful in attaining meaningful social studies that accounts for differences in gender and cultural heritage.
8. Describe strategies for assessing social studies learning in diverse student populations.

DEVELOPMENT

 ## Meaningful Social Studies for All Students

Americans from all cultures need social studies to solve everyday problems. Multicultural education can be defined in many ways. A comprehensive definition describes multicultural education as at least three things: an idea or concept, an educational reform movement, and a process. Social studies is a critical component of multicultural education. Citizens need to observe events perceptively, reflect on them thoughtfully, and understand explanations offered to them (NCSS, 1994b).

All students should be as competent in civic matters as possible (Mastropieri & Scruggs, 2000). They should have knowledge, skills, and attitudes that enable them to "assume 'the office of citizen' (as Thomas Jefferson called it) in our democratic republic" (NCSS, 1994b, p. 3). Four other reasons for teaching social studies to *all* students are:

1. Social studies activities broaden and enrich personal experiences.
2. Special needs learners benefit from guided or selected activities that are based on reality and have predictable outcomes.
3. Social studies activities involve learning about cause-and-effect relationships.
4. Social studies develops and refines thinking and problem-solving skills.

"Best Practices": Giving All Students Greater Control of Their Social Studies Learning

The sections that follow describe guidelines and activities for working with diverse groups of students in the elementary and middle school social studies program. Teachers with social studies PCK recognize that no single instructional strategy fits all students. Such teachers also recognize that each student must perceive social studies as relevant, important, and interesting, and that this happens when the student experiences a positive sense of control over his or her learning. When teachers adapt social studies instruction and curriculum for learners with different needs and from different cultural backgrounds, they give students greater control over their learning. The best practices for social studies instruction are those that are adapted to learner's needs, experiences, and heritage and give greater control of learning to students. Such best practices move along the continuum of learning from teacher control toward student control.

Social Studies Education for Students with Disabilities

The U.S. Department of Education has interpreted the Individuals with Disabilities Education Act (IDEA) to mean that the regular classroom in the neighborhood school should be the first placement option considered for students with disabilities (Riley, 2000). IDEA requires that, to the maximum extent appropriate, children with disabilities "are educated with children who are not disabled, and that special classes, separate schooling, or other removal of children with disabilities from the regular environment occurs only when the nature and severity of the disability is such that education in regular classes with the use of supplementary aids and services cannot be attained satisfactorily" (IDEA, Sec. 612(5)(B)).

Students with disabilities who are placed in the regular classroom must have appropriate supports and services to succeed, including instructional strategies adapted to their needs. Some supplementary aids and services that educators have successfully used include modifications to the regular curriculum, the assistance of a teacher with special education training, special education training for the regular teacher, the use of computer-assisted devices, the provision of note takers, and the use of a resource room. In these classrooms, students are viewed as individuals who also share characteristics.

Teaching resources play a crucial role in social studies. As a resource is considered for use by students, teachers examine the resource's vocabulary level; its content in terms of how conceptually complex it is (concrete vs. formal ideas); the writing style; how it is organized; and features such as graphics, illustrations, and accompanying software.

A primary reason for including students with special needs in the regular classroom is to increase their contact with a broader range of students. Excellent opportunities exist during social studies activities to promote such contact. Most social studies curricula hold the potential for a wealth of activity-centered small-group experiences appropriate for a wide range of students. When students work together to achieve a social studies objective, the potential for positive interactions within the group increases. Group experience can reinforce the interaction skills of all students and develop an appreciation of differences among peers. Other positive results of having students with a varying range of attributes work together cooperatively include tolerance, better appreciation for what a person can do, and opportunities to perform services that help others.

Meeting the personal needs of students requires thoughtful consideration of many factors. The identification of conditions needing accommodation may require modification of the learning experience to most fully benefit the student. Student abilities and characteristics, combined with the specifications of the Individualized Education Plan (IEP), determine the degree of modification of instructional strategies, curriculum, and evaluation procedures necessary to best serve the student.

General Instructional Strategies for Inclusive Classrooms

Adapting social studies materials for students with disabilities is accomplished through six general steps:

1. Identifying the learning needs and characteristics of the students
2. Identifying the goals for instruction
3. Comparing the learning needs and goals to the teaching materials to determine whether the content, instructional techniques, or setting require modification
4. Determining specific modifications of the teaching materials
5. Modifying the materials
6. Conducting ongoing evaluation as the materials are used

As you plan a specific lesson or unit, you need to ask and answer four specific questions:

- What does the task/assignment/activity require?
- What physical, sensory, and cognitive skills are needed?
- What components of the task require accommodation?
- What accommodation options exist?

The following activities have proven useful in working with many special needs students. However, the teacher must have a clear understanding of the student's special needs and appropriate instructional strategies. When peers work with the special needs student, the teacher must monitor the situation. Appropriate preparation includes selection of peers for working with the student and giving thorough guidelines for the activity.

Multisensory Activities. Multisensory activities throughout a lesson provide positive experiences for all students because motivation is enhanced through working with materials. Activities incorporating more than one sense or a different sense from that commonly used increase access to learning for all. For example, asking students to create a picture of an event by building it with clay on a piece of paper lets a visually impaired student "feel" the reported event. Other students are engaged in considering their activity from a new perspective: Rather than writing a report of an event, they must communicate it through the clay model. Such a challenge can result in some students utilizing or adapting little-used skills. All students may better understand that those who lack the physical ability to perform some skills are able to use other skills to accomplish a task. When more modes of presentation are used, everyone is likely to benefit both cognitively and affectively. Open-ended, multisensory, exploratory learning

Using Technology

Adapting Instruction and Curriculum in the Inclusive Classroom

Technology both supports students with special needs and presents them with problems. While a SmartBoard can be used to project and display key questions and points to assist hearing impaired students, an alternative is needed by visually impaired students, such as digital voice recordings of the key questions and points. All students can benefit when teachers consider ways of using technology to support students with special needs. When a SmartBoard is used, for example, the ability to project large sizes of type assists those with less severe visual impairments and also helps other students who may sit in locations where it is more difficult for them to read typical writing on a whiteboard.

Technology includes specific adaptations for special needs such as Braille and large print keyboards, keyguards, wrist rests, trackballs, voice output, and computers with character readers. Common features of technology available in many classrooms offer further opportunities for adaptations. Teachers can increase type size, highlight important questions and vocabulary, provide concept maps showing connections between ideas, input short classroom videos onto a computer screen or SmartBoard, and use touch screen technology for students who have motor control problems or who benefit from manipulating objects on a screen. Teacher web pages are common in many schools and enable students and family members to follow up on school activities at home. Teachers also use sites such as TeacherTube (www.teachertube.com) to share ideas about adaptations for various student needs and to show how adaptations are implemented in real classrooms.

approaches are effective with students who have learning disabilities and related mild disabilities and for many students with visual, auditory, and physical
disabilities.

Cooperative Group Activities.   Cooperative group activities provide needed help
for students and assist in social integration. Each student within the group has
a role with a specific assignment. For example, a student might record responses, encourage contributions, or manage materials. Research on cooperative
learning involving special needs and regular students indicates that cooperative learning experiences, compared to competitive and individualistic ones,
promote more positive attitudes toward peers who have disabilities (Johnson &
Johnson, 1978).

Classwide Peer Tutoring.   Classwide peer tutoring involves assigning social studies
tutoring activities to all students in a classroom. Students can work with an idea,
a demonstration, or a procedure. Then they teach it to other students, perhaps
through a group activity such as a jigsaw. When they have mastered the idea,
demonstration, or procedure, they return to their home cooperative group and
teach it to the members of that group. Having opportunities to teach peers can reinforce students' own learning and motivation (Steedly, Dragoo, Arefeh, & Luke,
2009). Special needs students may have abilities that enable them to be effective
at carrying out a demonstration, creating a map, putting information to music, or
some other activity. Such abilities are used in classwide peer-tutoring sessions.
When the idea is taught by other students through various modes of presentation,
each student has multiple access to the idea, because each way of tutoring uses
different senses or different perspectives.

Peer Buddy System.   In the peer buddy system, students serve as friends, guides, or
counselors to fellow students who are experiencing problems. For example, a
student with an arm in a cast works with a peer buddy to complete a project such
as a map that sometimes requires both arms and hands to be used in making it.
A variation is to pair a student with special needs, such as one with a severe visual
impairment, occasionally with another student whose vision is normal. Another
variation is occasionally to pair two students who are experiencing similar problems so that they can give each other moral support. The opportunity to talk with
others about how they have approached problem situations can lead to sharing advice, greater motivation, and better learning.

Reciprocal Teaching.   Reciprocal teaching engages students in learning strategies
aimed at improving their comprehension of social studies textual material by
questioning, summarizing, clarifying, and predicting what is in a document, table,
book, children's magazines, Internet sites, and in instructions for carrying out an
activity. Students take turns leading discussions in a cooperative group that
focuses on each of the strategies.

- Questions the text raises
- Ways of best summarizing the ideas in the text
- Ways of explaining or clarifying the ideas in the text
- Predictions based on the ideas in the text

Reading Alone.   Reading alone can present difficulties, yet it is an integral part of most social studies activities and curricula. Although materials can be chosen to reflect the reading levels of most students, variations in individual reading levels within the classroom are still likely to be wide. Reading should be done *following* students' experiences with the events discussed in the reading materials. Reading is most effective when it is part of the lesson development phase of a learning cycle. It should occur after students have explored the lesson idea and formed the idea in their minds through active experiences. Students should be taught how, and encouraged to examine, the pictures and graphics in a book or on an Internet site before they read explanations. This helps them comprehend what they read.

Lecture-Based Presentation.   A lecture-based presentation is used primarily to give instructions, describe procedures, and provide short explanations. Lectures need to be supplemented to be successful in classes that include learners with special needs (Bulgren, Deshler, & Schumaker, 1993). Lectures can create problems when students in the class have very short attention spans. They can result both in inappropriate behavior and in students simply "tuning out." When lectures are used, they must be brief. Important concepts and vocabulary are learned best through a variety of activities involving a range of modalities. If repetition is necessary, short lectures may be audio-recorded so the student can hear them again.

The concept mastery routine has been described by Bulgren and colleagues (1993) as a way to assist students who have difficulty processing new information when trying to construct concepts. Teachers create a concept diagram including:

- The concept name
- The concept class or category
- Important information associated with the concept
- Examples and nonexamples of the concept
- A blank space for additions to the diagram
- A definition of the concept

Media Presentations.   Media presentations and the use of all types of *technology* can be a positive aspect of the curriculum for all students. Students with low reading abilities benefit from a multisensory approach. Media content may require reinforcement before and after its presentation. Repeated opportunities to work with the media presentation may be of value to any student in the class.

Strategies for Using Social Studies Textbooks.   Students need to be familiarized with the organization of the textbook over a period of days. Teachers first point out the overall parts of the textbook: table of contents, glossary, index, references, and appendices. Then the organizational system of the textbook is introduced: units, chapters within units, and sections within chapters. Next, specific features within chapters or units are examined: chapter objectives; chapter openers, such as motivating stories; chapter outlines; types and levels of headings and subheadings; use of boldface type, underlining, or colors; vocabulary; illustrations, maps, charts, diagrams, and graphs; chapter, section, or lesson summaries; follow-up activities or extensions; end-of-section, chapter, and unit questions; checks for understanding; different question-and-answer formats; skill builders; application activities; and critical or creative thinking extensions. Textbooks are complex!

Finally, teachers help students examine features associated with supplemental materials, such as workbooks, activity sheets, student directions, textbook-related websites, textbook-related CD-ROMs, the amount and types of practice activities, and the formats of materials (Mastropieri & Scruggs, 2000).

Social studies textbooks and materials differ in structure from other types of text materials used in classrooms (Cook & Mayer, 1988). Text structures include the following examples:

Time, order. Information is provided in a chronological sequence; clue words include *next, later*, and *after this*.

Cause–effect. Events or actions are related as causes with consequences; clue words include *because, caused*, and *resulted in*.

Compare–contrast. Similarities or differences are highlighted among concepts, events, or other phenomena; clue words include *in contrast, similar, differ*, and *difference between*.

Enumeration. Items are listed by number; clue words include *one, another, the next*, and *finally*.

Sequence. Items are placed in a specific order; clue words include *first, second*, and *third*.

Classification. Types of items are placed into groups; clue words include *type of, labeled, classified, member of*, and *group*.

Main idea. An overriding thought or concept is presented (often in the first sentence) followed by supporting or elaborating statements (Cook & Mayer, 1988; Mastropieri & Scruggs, 2000).

Teachers help students identify the essential information by verbally describing why they are selecting certain sections, and not others, to highlight. For example, a teacher might say, "This looks like a new social studies concept, so I will highlight it. This next section just provides more information on the new concept, so I won't highlight it." Teachers can provide students with a self-monitoring sheet for highlighting that contains questions such as the following.

Did I examine my book for boldfaced print, types of subheadings, and charts, maps, or figures that seem important?

Did I find what information in my book is important to highlight, by asking and answering the following questions:

Is it new information?

Does it describe an important event in history?

Does it list or order causes of events?
Does it tell a main idea?
Does it compare and contrast events?
Did my teacher emphasize it?
Did I select information to be highlighted?
Did I test myself on the highlighted information by asking and answering
questions about the highlighted information? (Mastropieri & Scruggs,
2000, p. 521)

Study Guides.   Teachers often make study guides to reinforce their lesson objectives. Students use information in the textbook or other materials to complete short-answer questions on the study guide form to reinforce major ideas and practice skills. Study guides are best used after students have had some exploration activity with an idea.

Semantic Feature Analysis.   A semantic feature analysis is an activity to help students learn concepts from a social studies unit and/or textbook chapter (Bos & Anders, 1990). In using semantic analysis, the teacher analyzes the content within a chapter and develops a web. The web contains ideas introduced in a hierarchy of main ideas to lesser ideas. Students discuss the web with the teacher and fill in sections the teacher has left blank, or add examples for the ideas on the web.

This young student shows his ability to sequence by size by matching and aligning these traditional Russian figures.

Another strategy for using social studies textbooks with special needs learners is POSSE (Englert & Mariage, 1991; Englert, Tarrant, Mariage, & Oxer, 1994). POSSE is an acronym:

Predicting ideas from prior knowledge
Organizing predictions based on the forthcoming text structure
Searching/**S**ummarizing for main ideas within the text structure
Evaluating comprehension

During instruction, POSSE begins with prediction activities. Students predict the content to be covered, activating their prior knowledge. As they discuss in small groups, or in the whole group, they record their predictions on sheets structured in the following way.

Students *predict* what ideas are in the textbook section: The Underground Railroad

Ideas	Questions
It's about a railroad.	Was there really a train?
Slaves try to run away.	Where could they go?
It is a long trip.	How did they get food to eat?

Standards

During the *organizing* component, students organize their ideas into semantically related groups. Figure 10.1 is an example of organizing ideas in a web format. After recording and organizing their ideas, students are asked to *search* for the structure in the ideas presented in the textbook (see Figure 10.2). Then they are asked to *summarize* the idea in their own words. Students use Figures 10.1 and 10.2 to help them make their summary explaining what they now see as the idea. Finally, students *evaluate* their work by comparing their summaries, using their search for the structure webs, clarifying their ideas, and perhaps predicting about a next related reading on the topic.

General Suggestions for Adapting Textbook Materials for a Diverse Classroom. Adapting textbook materials for a diverse classroom involves four components. First, the teacher might need to provide alternative text formats. Audiorecordings of texts or those developed by the teacher and a volunteer reader can be used. Computerized text with audio components can be helpful. Enlarged-type versions of materials or Braille versions of text materials can be acquired. Finally, peers can read the text to the student.

Second, the teacher develops or plans for the use of alternative curriculum materials. Study guides, outlines, or other types of guided notes can be prepared. Text materials can be supplemented with pictures, software, material from Internet sites, and activities.

Third, the teacher frequently talks with special needs students to find out what they are thinking and what meaning the material being investigated has for

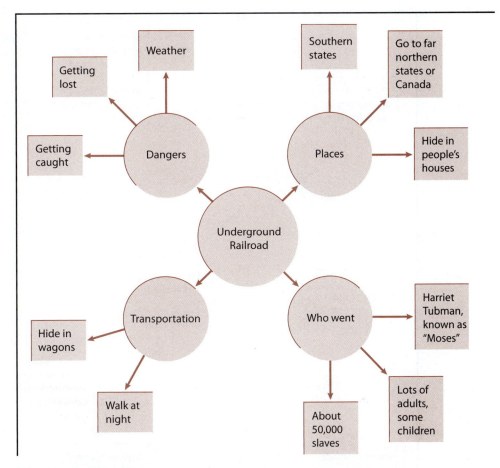

FIGURE 10.1
**Students Organize Their Thoughts in a Concept Web as Part of the POSSE Procedure
for Reading Text**

them. Students maintain journals that describe the meaning they are giving to
new concepts.

Fourth, teachers use peers and parent volunteers as assistants (Mastropieri &
Scruggs, 2000).

Factors to Be Considered in Adapting Social Studies Curricula and Instruction

Time is the variable that, more than any other, has to be considered in teaching
special needs students. Students with physical disabilities may need various sensory experiences to supplement learning. Students with visual impairments need
tactile and auditory materials to explore while visual materials are being set out

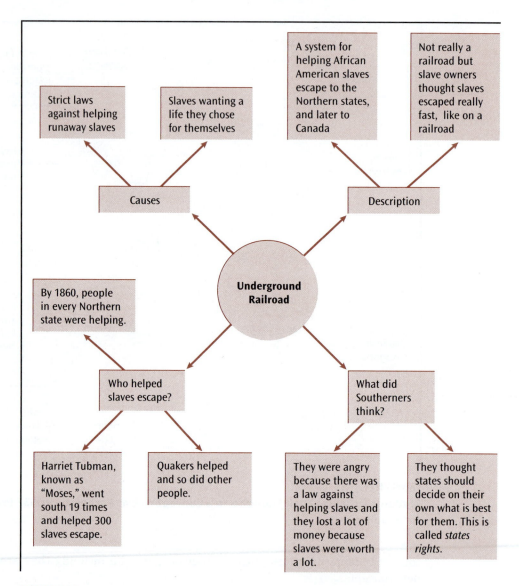

FIGURE 10.2
Students Create a New Web as They Search for Structure in the Text

for other students to pick up. Students with hearing impairments usually get less experience at abstracting information because they may have fewer opportunities to discuss their experiences with others. Their response time might be longer than that of other students in a specific situation because they have less experience and need more time to work through ideas.

Students with nonphysical disabilities might need more time and different learning strategies to supplement learning. Emotionally conflicted students often cannot suppress competing responses or ignore one stimulus to pay attention to another. As a result, they spend less time anticipating the course of some event and don't adjust accordingly. Students with mental retardation often cannot integrate events, assign meaning to them, or pick out an appropriate response. For all these students, making predictions over a short interval of time may be difficult, but the reasons for this difficulty differ and depend on the type of disability. Teachers need to provide appropriate opportunities to increase the amount of time these students are engaged in data-processing activities.

Different modalities take in information at distinctive rates. An individual's eyes, for example, can display a whole spatial array at one time. The eyes keep track of information as a whole set. By contrast, information that comes in over auditory tracts is strung out in time and must be sequenced and patterned by the listener before it becomes intelligible. The wide range and depth of distance over which the eyes pick up information permits people to "see ahead in time." Before an event reaches its conclusion, or even before it takes place, people who can see may anticipate and adjust their responses accordingly. Because vision permits interaction at a distance, it provides a little lead time in which to adjust a response before an event happens.

When experiencing events, students with visual impairments usually must arrive in the midst of them. They may use sound and other perceptive cues, but because these are received over a much shorter distance and range than vision, the lead time is shorter. The visual cues telling an inquirer what to look for and when to collect data must be supplanted with other devices for visually impaired students. Because students with visual impairments have so little information before arriving on the scene compared to sighted children, they require more time to collect comparable cues.

Students with hearing impairments often don't get sufficient early clues. The task of abstracting information from the social world and then processing it into language to be logically manipulated depends on the availability of language models or appropriate communication substitutes for sound. Schools frequently spend a huge amount of time teaching language in a standalone format rather than in the context of some concrete event. As a result, students with hearing impairments often are denied the chance normal students get of trying to map experience with language in social studies activities.

Students with hearing impairments need to engage in social studies activities in which they can observe the history of events or systems. Students with visual impairments usually come to use verbal information very efficiently. They usually can hold longer chains of directions and verbal information in their memory than can sighted students.

Involving Students with Visual or Hearing Impairments in Social Studies.   Much of what is done in powerful social studies programs can be adapted for use by students with visual and hearing impairments for whom early social studies instruction is even more important than for other students. Teachers have successfully used the following steps to adapt materials for students with visual and hearing impairments (Sunal & Sunal, 1983):

1. Identify the factors in an event.
2. Identify the kinds of evidence associated with the factors.
3. Identify all the modalities or combinations of modalities that could be used to supply evidence that is equivalent to what would be collected by students without visual or hearing impairments.
4. Adapt the materials where necessary.
5. Devise a technique for recording data that the student with hearing or visual impairments can use.

Doing Social Studies with Mentally Retarded or Emotionally Conflicted Students.
Emotionally conflicted students and students with mental retardation often share the problem of a short attention span. Almost without exception, however, teachers who involve these students in social studies activities find that attention to activities is much longer than attention to passive tasks. These students often repeat or practice the same interactions many times.

Social Studies Education in a Culturally Diverse Society

The United States is more culturally diverse than are most societies. This diversity has led to an important question: "How can all students participate in and meaningfully learn social studies?" (Hursh, 1997). Some students are recent arrivals from other countries and are learning English as a second or third language. Many children are raised in urban settings that differ greatly from the national mainstream experience. Some students have moved from an urban area to a small town. In all such instances, these students increase the diversity of a classroom.

TIME FOR REFLECTION ● What Do You Think?

Evaluate a classroom lesson you have taught or recently observed that included one or more special needs students. On a separate sheet of paper, answer the following questions:

1. Describe the social studies lesson taught in the classroom. What types and number of interactions occurred between the students and the teacher and between the students? What role in the learning process did the teacher play? What role did the students play?

2. What strategies involved all students in the lesson?

3. What learning outcomes do you infer for all students from the lesson? What difficulties did the students have in accomplishing the lesson objective(s)? Provide evidence supporting your evaluation.

4. During which tasks in the lesson did students with special needs have difficulties? During which tasks did they perform well? Why do you think this might be the case?

Important systems of beliefs are transmitted from one generation to the next. Children learn belief systems through direct teaching and through the behavior of those around them (Kostelnik et al., 2002). As a result, children learn different character traits. For example, in some societies, children learn to value cooperation more highly than in others; in some societies, children learn that competition is good. In some societies, time is treated as a commodity not to be wasted; in others, time is fluid and not so pressing. One cultural group might interpret a child's loud behavior as healthy exuberance, while another group might interpret it as disrespectful. Belief systems broadly define how people believe children should be treated, what they should be taught, and what behaviors and attitudes are socially acceptable (Shaffer, 2000).

People in most societies support social responsibility, behaving in ways that contribute to the common good. However, cultures place different emphases on prosocial behaviors such as sharing, helping, or cooperating. The emphasis that is placed on prosocial behaviors is expressed in laws, economic policies, the media, and the institutions people create. The ways in which people think about children, how children spend their time, what they see and hear, how they are treated at home and in the community, and the expectations people have for their behavior

Building on Diversity

Variations in Belief Systems

Children learn their culture's rules for how emotions are shown and for which emotions are acceptable in certain situations and which are not. Students carry these cultural rules with them into the classroom. For example, when most European American children are reprimanded, they are expected to maintain eye contact to show respect and to adopt a solemn expression to communicate remorse. Many Mexican American and Nigerian children are taught to cast their eyes downward to indicate respect. Chinese children might learn to smile as an expression of apology when being scolded. Navajo children often learn to lower their voices to express anger, whereas European American children learn to raise theirs in order to get the message across. In Japanese and Korean cultures, children typically learn to keep their emotional expressions in check and to avoid crying. In the United States, many people approve of young children expressing their emotions, but older children are expected to hide certain emotions out of consideration

for the feelings of others; for example, they should smile when they receive a gift even if they are disappointed because it is not what they hoped for. In all cultures, children who learn the rules of conduct are perceived as more likeable and socially competent by peers and adults (Kostelnik et al., 2002).

Information on cultural views among various Native American groups can be found at Students and Teachers Against Racism, http://www.racismagainstindians. org/AcademicPapers/NativeChildGuidance.htm. Other sites that may be helpful on various groups are: WWW Hmong Homepage, http://www.hmongnet.org/; Understanding the Latino/Hispanic Culture (for educators), http://www.coedu.usf.edu/zalaquett/hoy/culture.html; Asian American Culture Links, http://janet.org/~ebihara/aacyber_culture.html; African Culture: Africa South of the Sahara, http://www-sul.stanford.edu/depts/ssrg/africa/culture.html; and Middle East Cultures, http://www.mnsu.edu/emuseum/cultural/oldworld/middle_east.html.

are all culturally based. Across all cultures, adults at home and in school most strongly affect whether children become more or less prosocial. Teachers must understand the variations between cultures and even within a single culture because not all subgroups teach their children exactly the same rules or promote the same behaviors. Activities such as making the student–family–community books presented in Chapter 9 on themes such as "Words of Advice from My Family," "What Kind of Work Did My Grandfather Do?" or "Teachings from My Childhood Community" enable a teacher to gain some insight into the cultural rules a student has been taught at home.

In the United States, three significant minority student groups—African Americans, Hispanics from numerous Latin American countries, and Native Americans—often are underachievers in social studies. The National Assessment of Educational Progress (NAEP) documents very low performance for Native Americans on its tests. Asian American immigrants generally have limited English proficiency, yet many groups of Asian Americans are more successful in the United States than are members of some other minority groups who are native English speakers (Tobin & McRobbie, 1996). However, each group exhibits a wide range of performance. Subgroups within each group also vary widely. Yet, the members of each group tend to share cultural similarities. Teachers must consider these similarities because the needs of various groups within our culture differ.

Teachers need to think and learn about what makes a multicultural social studies program. In what ways is it different from a traditional program? The classroom has both a content and a context. To be responsive, teachers must present meaningful social studies that incorporates strands of specific content that are relevant to the experience of the students. Just providing a social studies program with a variety of experiences and an environment in which students are free to explore is not adequate. The social studies program must consistently invite all students to participate in experiences fostering different forms of communication: spoken, written, graphic, and mathematical.

All students—regardless of their gender and social class, their ethnic or cultural characteristics, and their special needs, if any—should have an equal opportunity to learn in school. Three basic premises of multicultural social studies education are as follows:

1. All students can learn social studies.
2. Every student can participate effectively in the social studies program.
3. Cultural diversity is appreciated in the social studies program because it enhances rather than detracts from the richness and effectiveness of learning.

Four goals have been identified for meeting the needs of culturally diverse students through a multicultural approach to social studies education:

1. Acquire the knowledge and skills needed to study children's heritage.
2. Present appropriate lessons for particular students, including powerful teaching strategies such as role-playing and cooperation to increase instructional effectiveness with diverse students.

3. Eliminate school and teacher stereotypes and expectations that narrow student opportunities for learning and displaying competence.
4. Create and sustain a communal setting that is respectful of individual differences and group membership where learning is valued, engagement is nurtured, and interests are encouraged (Holmes Group, 1986).

Each of these goals is achieved slowly over a long period of time. Celebrating Black History Month in February and Women's History Month in March, watching a video of Chinese New Year celebrations, breaking a piñata at Cinco de Mayo in May, or celebrating a Multicultural Day can be useful activities but are not enough to allow students to overcome stereotypes, understand cultural heritage, and appreciate the contributions of diverse people to our society.

Culturally Responsive Teaching

Using multiple instructional strategies adds variety and interest to lessons and helps provide learning opportunities for students with various learning styles. Some may conclude this is all a teacher has to do to be a culturally responsive teacher. This is not quite true. As Au (2009) notes, teachers also must be familiar with the ways in which students in a cultural group are taught to behave that are consistent with their particular culture. In many classrooms students may be asked to behave in ways that are counter to those of their ethnic community, and they may hear and observe students being rewarded for what they have been taught is disrespectful or improper behavior. Teachers need to take the time to learn about how values such as respect and cooperation are viewed and practiced in the cultures of their students. Research reveals that cooperatively working with others for the well-being and interdependence of the group, measuring success in spiritual ways, and living in harmony with the environment are cultural differences many ethnic groups promote. Various ethnic groups, however, may emphasize one of these ideas over another or exhibit these values in different ways. This means that the teacher must take the initiative to learn about the students and their cultures as well as about the individual differences among the personalities of the students in the classroom.

Sample Strategies for Multicultural Social Studies

In classrooms where all students learn powerful social studies, three major strategies have been successfully used. The first strategy is to use *history* and the lives of *historical figures* as illustrations of the concepts being taught. The second strategy is to provide examples from *present-day social issues*. The third strategy involves using examples and applications of social studies concepts that fit a student's *culture* and *ethnic background*.

Historical Approach.   Well-chosen examples of history incorporate a range of time periods, cultures, and genders to demonstrate a variety of perspectives. Long ago, Socrates taught through the use of questions and discussions in small groups; Sarah Winnamucca encouraged Native Americans to build schools for their children in the late 1800s; and Friedrich Froebel established the first kindergartens in Germany in the early 1800s. Examples from history can be used to illustrate how various people's perspectives on a concept have changed education and are a part of important, larger cultural changes. In so doing, students can learn that the average citizen's role is not universal, inevitable, or unchangeable. This kind of understanding is needed to encourage critical thinking about social studies concepts.

Current Social Issues. Providing examples and references from current social issues can have a bearing on students' lives and arouse their interest in social studies. Also effective is discussing the people involved with these issues and how they are affected by addressing them. Some examples of issues are water quality, health care for all, urban sprawl, discrepancy in wages between men and women, how to provide adequate housing for all, and gun control. Such national issues have local import, and specific examples often affect the lives of students.

Using Student Culture. Experiences that students have at home, in school, and in the community are rich opportunities for the development of relevant social studies concepts. It is important that the activities, problems, investigations, and variables in social studies lesson plans use student culture and relate to students' daily lives. They must encourage acceptance and appreciation of different views and behaviors by valuing all cultural and ethnic backgrounds.

Role Models and Relevancy

Limited experiences of students, especially those from some minority groups, mean that they do not always have models who understand the role of social studies in their lives and occupations. Therefore, they might not see how social studies is relevant to their lives. The factors that have produced this problem are complex.

Role Models. Professionals from all cultures make outstanding contributions in their fields. African Americans, for example, follow occupations that heavily rely on social studies knowledge, such as being government employees or managers of local businesses. Many African American youths, however, do not realize the need for a strong early education in social studies or understand how to prepare for a professional career.

The investigation of the lives of people pursuing a wide range of occupations, both historical and contemporary, is important if all students are to have opportunities to succeed economically. Such an investigation must move beyond the individuals

The curriculum is enriched when students are encouraged to bring in objects associated with their ethnic heritage.

who are typically studied, such as George Washington Carver (a botanist and agricultural researcher) and Benjamin Banneker (a self-taught mathematician and astronomer). By restricting study to "great men and women" from a cultural group, recognition is removed from the important roles and services of average citizens. It is with average citizens that young people can interact and through whom they identify the important role of their own cultural group within the community. Most important of all is the chance to talk with local community members. These people are real and meaningful to students. When they come from the local area, they demonstrate to students what can reasonably be achieved with some effort and guidance.

Internet resources may be helpful for learning about potential role models in historical periods or from cultural groups at a distance from your community. These include the Biographical Dictionary with thousands of biographies of people over a wide range of time periods in a searchable database, http://www.s9.com/; African-American History: Biographies A–Z, http://afroamhistory.about.com/library/blbiographies.htm; National Women's History Project: Honored Latinas, http://www.nwhp.org/resourcecenter/honoredlatinas.php; Women in World History Biographies, http://www.womeninworldhistory.com/heroine.html; and Academy of Achievement: People in the 20th Century Who Have Shaped History, http://www.achievement.org/.

Making a Literature Connection

Role Models

Role models from the community and local cultural group are an important component of social studies. These can be extended through biographies and autobiographies to include diverse role models from different locations and times. Examples include the following:

Bad Boy: A Memoir (2001) by Walter Dean Myers tells about growing up in Harlem in the 1950s and becoming aware of racism and his own identity as a black man (for middle school).

Hokusai: The Man Who Painted a Mountain (2001) by Deborah Kogan Ray and illustrated by the author is a picture book biography of Hokusai, one of Japan's most famous artists, and gives an intimate look at the life of peasants in late eighteenth-century Japan (for grades 3–5).

John Blair and the Great Hinckley Fire (2000) by Josephine Nobisson introduces readers to a not-well-known firestorm that devastated Hinckley, Minnesota, in 1894, burning a huge area and killing many. John Blair, an African American railroad porter, led 300 passengers out of burning rail cars to safety at a nearby lake (for grades 3–5).

America's Champion Swimmer: Gertrude Ederle (2000) by David A. Adler discusses the first woman to swim the English Channel and her never-give-up attitude (for primary grades).

Pick-and-Shovel Poet: The Journeys of Pascal d'Angelo (2000) by Jim Murphy focuses on an Italian immigrant's determination to write poetry as he teaches himself to read and write in English while earning his living with a pick and shovel (for middle school).

Tallchief: America's Prima Ballerina (1980) by Maria Tallchief uses extensive pictures to tell Tallchief's story through her own words (for grades 3–5).

The Journal of Sean Sullivan: A Transcontinental Railroad Worker (1999) by William Durbin and illustrated with photographs and prints tells about a boy working on the transcontinental railroad and how he witnesses the legacy of the Civil War; the growth of the West; the courage, and also the racism, of some workers; and the appalling conditions that were part of working on the Union Pacific Railroad (for middle school).

Boss of the Plains: The Hat That Won the West (1998) by Laurie Carlson tells how John Batterson Stetson created the most popular hat west of the Mississippi (for K–5).

Seven Brave Women (1997) by Betsy Hearne highlights the brave exploits of seven of Hearne's female ancestors, celebrating the determination of "ordinary" women who have found many ways to be brave (for grades K–6).

Relevant Social Studies.   One way of addressing the needs of all students is to use everyday objects and experiences for social studies activities to make concepts more relevant. Although few students may become historians or politicians, they "will all become citizens with civic responsibilities and rights" (Rea, 1999, p. 4). Historical ideas in social studies can be made more relevant by tying them into students' prior knowledge, encouraging students to consider alternatives and reactions. Teachers could ask, "Has anything ever gotten you fighting mad?" and then help students tie their experiences to those of the American colonists who were "fighting mad" about the British Tea Acts (Rea, 1999, p. 4). Likewise, slaves and laborers reacted violently on some occasions. They also rebelled by slowing down tasks or only minimally performing them.

Not everything can be experienced firsthand, yet teachers can strive to make vicarious social studies experiences relevant. Teachers may use audiobooks, the Internet, trade books, guest speakers, storytellers, biographies, and video as ways of bringing experiences alive and increasing their relevance. An audiobook, with accompanying trade book, that would enable students to have vicarious experiences of a very different ecosystem is *Whalesong* (Siegal, 1998). This audiobook has strong emotional impact, enabling students to explore the Pacific Ocean world into which humpback whales are born and mature and the dangers they face from pollution as well as calls for renewed commercial whaling, both caused by humans.

Using such an example helps students contextualize social studies concepts (Sunal, Pritchard, & Sunal, 2000). The example makes use of an experience that many students have not had but ties it to experiences with which they are familiar. Teaching that works at making social studies relevant and that provides role models for students is good teaching for everyone. Other chapters discuss and give examples of teaching appropriate for diverse students.

Culture and Gender Differences in Student–Teacher Interactions

Many teachers interact differently with different students. Male students often are given extended teacher help when answering questions. Females who give wrong answers usually are not asked to elaborate on their answers. Females often are rewarded for the neatness, but not the correctness, of their work. African American males might be ignored until they misbehave. Few African American females are praised for their learning. Native Americans often are introduced to social studies concepts in a manner that is not meaningful to them. The research indicates that teachers need to focus their attention on how they interact with students. They need to reflect on their observations of themselves to decide whether their interactions are based more on their expectations of students and preconceived ideas than on what each student needs and how each student participates in class.

Although it can be a time-consuming and complex process, teachers must read about the cultures represented by their students and interact closely with students and their families to learn about their cultural experiences. Gradually, teachers will develop an understanding of the cultural backgrounds of the students with whom they work. Teachers can address gender concerns by paying attention to how they interact with boys and girls, how they respond to both passive and active behaviors from boys and girls, whether and how their expectations for the behaviors of boys and girls differ, and how they include both males and females as role models in the curriculum.

Specific teaching strategies are needed to provide a powerful social studies program for students of both genders and of all cultural heritages. Many strategies have been shown to be effective in the research literature: (Zainuddin, Yahya, Morales-Jones, & Ariza, 2002)

1. Having high expectations for all students
2. Varying social studies learning activities
3. Addressing the affective dimension, considering feelings and motivations
4. Overcoming language barriers
5. Respecting different cultural mores and traditions by learning about them
6. Discussing gender and cultural inequities
7. Analyzing classroom management for equity
8. Providing role models of both genders, who represent a range of cultural heritages
9. Acknowledging and using the culture and home environment as a vehicle for learning

Helping English Language Learners Participate in Social Studies

English language learners (ELL) bring diversity to the classroom that can be enlightening and educational. Encouraging ELL students to contribute to the classroom is a key to fostering their desire to learn a new language and to be academically proficient in the classroom (Cruz et al., 2003). Teachers are not likely to have a basic knowledge of several languages but can be expected to use strategies that help ELL students no matter what their primary language. The nature of social studies requires more language use, both verbal and written, than many other school subjects, such as mathematics (Cruz et al., 2003). Learning some basic words in your students' primary languages will help you to provide a comfortable, safe, and secure classroom environment.

Recognizing and Scaffolding Language Learning

There are two types of language use: basic interpersonal communications skills (BICS) and cognitive academic language proficiency (CALP) (Cummins, 1984). Language that is used to interact with others for social purposes, BICS, is developed through social interaction when students talk with others about a new pair of shoes or a school day off last week because of a severe storm. Specialized language used for academic purposes, CALP, is acquired at school and used for academic purposes. For example, classifying city, county, state, and nation in a hierarchy in which one includes another as a subcategory requires a high degree of CALP. Some English language learners developed CALP in their native country if they had adequate schooling; others did not develop it because of inadequate or no schooling. Those with CALP in their primary language develop it more easily in English when some support is provided. Those without CALP need greater support for a longer time. Social language proficiency, BICS, takes about two years to develop to an age-appropriate level, whereas CALP will take five to seven years. Teachers may assume that because social language is well developed, academic language is equally developed, but this should not be expected.

Four proficiency stages in communication are found with ELL students (Cruz et al., 2003; Zainuddin et al., 2002). At the *preproduction stage*, students point to items and can follow commands but mostly listen. Teachers use gestures and act out directions, use repetition, use pictures and props, and ask simple yes or no questions. In the next stage, *early production*, students give one or two word responses, label and match items, and list items. Teachers model tasks and language, use simple role-plays, ask either/or questions, and ask who and where questions. In the third stage, *speech emergence*, students use phrases and simple sentences, compare and contrast items, and describe items. Teachers focus content on key concepts, use frequent comprehension checks, use expanded vocabulary, and ask how and why questions. In the fourth stage, *immediate fluency*, students demonstrate beginning CALP, participate in dialog and discourse, demonstrate reading and writing abilities, and comprehend academic text. Teachers provide alternative assessments, check for language bias and cultural bias, and provide contextual support. Teachers identify their ELL students' stages and focus on using the instructional strategies that are appropriate for each student.

Effective communication with ELL students includes modified input and modified interaction (Cruz et al., 2003). Modified input occurs every time the teacher directs something specifically at an ELL student, such as providing pictures, speaking slowly and clearly, and focusing on the here and now (Cruz et al., 2003). Also important is the interaction between teacher and student and the ELL student and native speakers in cooperative groups. Interactions are modified to scaffold the ELL student's comprehension and production of the language and content. The teacher uses more comprehension checks and supports negotiation of meaning by teaching ELL students to use phrases such as, "Please repeat that," "What does ___ mean?" and "How do you say ___?" (Cruz et al., 2003, p. 21). Peer students in cooperative groups are taught how to rephrase, expand, and check for indications of miscommunications. As ELL students advance through the communication stages, teachers match their development with appropriate instructional strategies.

Instructional Strategies for Helping ELL Students Understand Social Studies Content

Authentic and active involvement of ELL students is vital to meaningful social studies learning. Social studies has an academic language of its own, as do all subjects. Two types of learning have been found to be particularly effective for engaging ELL students in social studies learning: inquiry-based learning and project learning (Moje, Collazo, Carrillo, & Marx, 2001; Stoddart, Pinal, Latzke, & Canaday, 2002). Project work and investigations involve ELL students in everyday and academic discussions that help them acquire relevant language and concepts. When students have responsibility over a project of their own or as part of a group project, limitations in English language skills are reduced. Often, many parts of a project can be accomplished with limited language skills. While involved in the project, the ELL student learns English vocabulary to identify items and events being experienced and through talking about the project with others.

Some of the strategies and techniques that help to provide a comfortable, safe, and secure classroom environment in which academic competency in social studies is the goal include the following (Cruz et al., 2003):

- Learn to correctly pronounce the names of your ELL students.
- Use a community resource person to help you send a letter home to family members in their native language on class expectations and policies, major topics, projects, and the like.
- Provide a visual for class routines with a picture to depict each routine.
- Invite ELL students to make a presentation about their culture to the class. If their English proficiency is low, or if they decline, assign more proficient students to investigate the cultures of your beginning ELL students and to present the information to the class.
- Provide clear directions verbally, following up with written directions on the board and modeling of directions.
- Label items in the classrooms in the languages of your ELL students and in English.
- Set high expectations for all students with an understanding that it is often a language barrier, not an academic one, that impedes instruction.
- Check continuously for comprehension by asking for simple one-word responses, asking yes-or-no questions, and making true-or-false statements.
- Assign ELL students to an English-speaking classmate.
- Monitor your classroom, placing ELL students in the middle or at the front of the room, where they have your attention and you have many opportunities for frequent eye contact and interaction.
- Send home updates, weekly assignments, or class news in the ELL students' languages, if possible, through help from a community resource person.

 ## Assessment of Social Studies Learning for All Students

Tests fail to consider interpersonal skills, language abilities, and talents that students need in the real world. Culturally relevant alternative assessment is needed to improve educational options for students from diverse backgrounds. Alternative formats for assessments are discussed below.

Group Assessment through Cooperative Learning.   Through discussion, students construct and negotiate a shared meaning of their social studies experiences, beginning to understand and appreciate cultural and other differences. Research indicates that cooperative learning experiences, more than competitive and individualistic ones, promote positive attitudes toward members of a different ethnic group or gender (Johnson & Johnson, 1978).

Graphic Organizers.   Culturally diverse students share ideas, discuss, and agree on meanings through the use of graphic organizers.

Oral Interviews.   Students are given an opportunity to share experiences through personal narratives. This enables them to demonstrate their individual questions, perspectives, and understandings (Kelley, 2009).

Projects.   Projects allow students to display their learning, how they applied data they collected, and how they can complete tasks on their own. Teachers can assess understanding even when students have difficulties expressing themselves.

Portfolios.   Use of the portfolio provides multiple sources for profiling student growth and helps ensure equitable treatment of culturally diverse students.

Maintaining an Equitable Approach

Social studies must be taught equitably to all students. Each student must be treated as an individual with a heritage, needs, and abilities that are recognized and addressed by the teacher. It is not enough to treat each student equally because all students differ, so, the aim is equitable teaching of social studies. This is complex and takes time to achieve. We begin by finding out as much as possible about a student's heritage and by working to establish ties with families. We use grade-appropriate content standards, recognize the difference between social language and academic language for ELLs, adapt instructional materials to varying students' needs, use cooperative learning groups, maintain ELLs native language through bilingual materials support, engage students with role models, and use authentic assessment.

TIME FOR REFLECTION | What Do You Think?

Evaluate one of your previously written social studies lesson plans or one that you find on the Internet or in a collection of lesson plans. Consider how appropriately the planned lesson involves culturally diverse students in the classroom. Answer the following questions:

1. What strategies would involve all students in the social studies lesson?

2. What additional strategy could be added to increase the effectiveness of the lesson for students from all cultural backgrounds?

Journal Writing.   This activity encourages students to connect social studies to their personal experiences. It is more culturally relevant when it becomes a personal process in which grammar and punctuation are unimportant. These continuous entries throughout the unit provide evidence of learning in the context of the student's life experiences. When students share their journal comments in pairs or in their cooperative group, they communicate with each other about their learning. A continuous sharing back and forth of ideas helps students accept each other's ideas and the evaluation of their own ideas by others.

Assessment Using Technology

The availability of interactive technology today supports authentic social studies assessment of *all* students. Technology can be used with the kinds of authentic assessment discussed above. It also can be used for:

- Paired presentations recorded via digital video in which a student explains a concept to a partner, then they reverse roles and the partner explains his understanding of the concept. The video of the paired presentation can be assessed by the pair and the teacher considering (1) the quality of their questions, (2) their ability to summarize what the explainer said, (3) their helpfulness in making the ideas clear, and (4) the appropriateness of their interruptions (San Antonio Home Education, 2009).
- Progress interviews that are short digital video recordings in which students describe their progress on a project or in accomplishing a goal at specific points in a grading period allowing the teacher to follow the student's progress and adjust the assignment as needed.
- Constructing products such as classroom maps, appropriate period costumes, laying out a Native American village, commercials advertising a classroom business, "Me bags" that provide a personal introduction of a student, and scrapbooks of important events related to a concept being studied. Such products can be assessed with rubrics and through discussion with the student.

Specific technology tools to support authentic assessment from rubric developers to programs that store all data related to electronic portfolios are available commercially.

EXPANSION

 ## Applying Ideas for Helping All Students Learn Meaningful Social Studies

Participating in a community is essential in civic life, so it is an important focus in a meaningful social studies program for all students. One way of participating in community life is through working in a small group that tries to solve a problem or provide a service or product that improves the community and the lives of people. Within a classroom teachers involve students in such participation, helping them learn skills that make it possible to reach out to the community and act for the common good. Small-group activity provides a means by which each student can work with others, bringing individual strengths while accommodating individual differences and needs.

Students participate in many communities ranging from their own classroom, to the after-school groups that play in football or soccer leagues, to groups such as the American Cancer Society or the American Red Cross for whom they might collect money through being part of a Walk-a-Thon, to the world as the largest community when they work to conserve how much paper they use. Whether the community is the classroom or the world, getting along with people who are similar and different is part of showing respect for oneself and for others. It requires communication skills, a willingness to share ideas, honestly evaluating your own and others' ideas, and building dispositions to come to common solutions for the betterment of the community. While each of these is a skill that individual students develop to different levels, teachers work to help each student develop these skills to his or her best level.

In the classroom, teachers help students address specific participation problems such as being prompt in performing tasks, so that others do not have to wait to complete their work because another group member is late. Teachers also focus on helping students develop overall skills in working with others. Students are encouraged to identify problems, sharing and considering each other's ideas about clarifying the problem. When all have agreed on what the problem is, students work to seek solutions, decide on the most workable solution, then follow through by trying out that solution. Participants are encouraged to reflect on their efforts and to reach a decision about whether the problem is solved. Fully participating in the communities to which we belong is a lifelong effort and one that must be part of social studies at all grade levels.

TIME FOR REFLECTION | *What Do You Think?*

Your 25 middle school students have decided to volunteer to help out at a local hospital as a community service project. The hospital has identified a big need for volunteers to deliver donated magazines and personal hygiene products (e.g., toothpaste, small bottles of moisturizing soap, etc.) to patients. It has asked that these volunteers stop to chat with the patient, try to fill requests regarding items a patient would appreciate receiving, and report requests for items not currently available to patients. One student in your class has developmental disabilities and cannot read, another is wheelchair bound, and three others are recent immigrants who speak just a little English. All of the students want to be involved in the project. How can you structure the project so that each student will be involved in it? Describe the following.

1. What advantages and disadvantages might result from assigning students to work in pairs?

2. How will students keep records of their visits and patients' requests?

3. How will students be involved in discussing their experiences, describing successes and problems, and finding solutions to problems encountered?

4. How will students be involved in evaluating the effects of their participation as a contribution to the common good of the local community?

Summary

A powerful social studies program is a planned and deliberate effort to help students, regardless of special needs, cultural heritage, or gender. It is an effort to maximize their potential for success in social studies and as active citizens. Teachers focus on making social studies relevant and meaningful to each student. They expect that all students can learn social studies and that doing so is a worthwhile endeavor.

Recommended Websites to Visit

Authentic Assessment Toolbox
http://jonathan.mueller.faculty.noctrl.edu/toolbox/index.htm
TeacherVision: Adaptations and Modifications for Students with Special Needs
http://www.teachervision.fen.com/special-education/resource/5347.html
World-class Instructional Design and Assessment Consortium (WIDA). *English language proficiency standards for English language learners*
http://www.wida.us/standards/6-12%20Standards%20web.pdf
Ethno-Pedagogy: Cross cultural teaching techniques
http://www.literacynet.org/lp/hperspectives/deepcult.html
Selected Links for ESL & EFL Students: Easy to navigate
http://iteslj.org/ESL.html

11

How Do I Engage Students in Examining History?

Ms. Wasserman overheard several of her first-graders saying they felt sorry for their grandparents because they didn't have fun toys when they were children so their lives must have been boring. She wanted to correct her students' misconception and thought a study of the history of toys would help. She decided to use an old family picture from the early 1900s showing two children and their toys for the exploratory introduction for the lesson.

1. Why do you think she made this choice?
2. How do you anticipate the children will respond to the appearance of the children in the picture?
3. How would you respond if the children laughed at the picture?
4. What do you think these first-graders will conclude about the children in the picture and the toys they had?
5. Whom might you contact in your local community to help you to teach your students about the toys available 50 to 100, or more, years ago?

Chapter Overview

People need to know about their pasts and their places in world history. This chapter is concerned with how we learn about our past and how that past can be made meaningful to us as individuals and as citizens of an increasingly interdependent nation and world. The study of history is personal and exciting but is often viewed by students as remote and uninteresting. Students have difficulty giving reasons for studying history because it does not seem to serve a utilitarian need. Perhaps this is more a factor of what and whose history has been taught than of the nature of history and its importance to people.

Elementary teachers play an important role as they provide students with formal learning experiences in history. Recent investigations into how elementary and middle school students understand history have described the naïve concepts or imaginative and inaccurate assumptions students hold. These investigations challenge the validity of past ways of introducing the study of history to young people. Therefore, the curriculum and instructional strategies that adults often experienced in their elementary and middle school years are being seriously questioned and reevaluated. This chapter investigates several reasons for studying history, the skills required to study history, the role of interpretation and evidence in the study of history, and research on how young students begin to examine and interpret history to identify the contributions it makes to their lives.

Chapter Objectives

1. Differentiate between the definition of history given by scholars and that used in schools.
2. Identify four goals or purposes for the study of history.
3. State a rationale for the study of history in all grades, K–8.
4. Distinguish between the roles of primary and secondary resources in studying history.
5. Explain why the teaching of history must include the examination of conflicts.
6. Explain why studying particular historical topics is suggested for elementary and middle school students.

7. Describe how timelines are used to assist in developing an understanding of time.
8. Reflect on how the learning cycle approach to lessons is appropriate to the needs of students studying history.
9. Identify various resources that can be used to teach history to students.
10. Explain why the role of narrative in teaching and learning history needs additional study.
11. Suggest multiple roles for the Internet in the teaching of history and evaluate the practicality of each.

DEVELOPMENT

 ## Definition of History

History means different things to different individuals. Even historians do not agree on a single definition of history or on what constitutes an appropriate historical problem for investigation. Historians actually refer to themselves by different names: social historian, military historian, oral historian, archivist, public historian, interpreter, reenactor, genealogist, and archaeologist. However, historians generally agree on three important aspects: History is a chronological study that interprets and gives meaning to events and applies systematic methods to discover the truth.

Unlike social scientists, historians cannot rely on direct observations and experiments to gain facts. The historian has only what has been left behind and preserved to provide hints as to what may have taken place. Some people leave much; others leave practically nothing. Like the detective, the historian conducts exhaustive research to find many clues. Discoveries are mostly just clues, not complete records. They reflect the perspectives and memories of their preservers. Therefore, the historian *interprets the evidence,* deciding on the degree of its importance and accuracy. This is done by applying logic and "best guesses" to knowledge about the people and their times.

Often a discovery leads to more questions than it can answer. The ability to place times and events in chronological order is important in establishing cause-and-effect relationships. Historians not only examine the motives and actions of people, but also often apply principles from science and scientific discoveries to help them interpret the evidence. Working in history requires logic and persistence. The task is not complete when the answer is found; the results must be communicated to others, or the knowledge could be lost forever.

Actually, this explanation is not quite what a professional historian might indicate. Elliott West, a specialist in the social and environmental history of the American West, explains that history has no beginning and no end. There is always more to learn. Of necessity, historians bound their studies with a beginning point and an end point. But in reality, events took place that predate the topic of your study, and more history transpires afterward. Knowing about these events can contribute to a deeper and greater understanding and a more meaningful interpretation of what you have learned. West describes history as an infinite study "that celebrates a diversity of viewpoints and emphasizes our continuity with, and responsibility to, the past and future" (West, 2000, p. 1). West goes on to say that in this infinite quality, the study of history has much in common with the nature of education for teachers.

Students have various experiences before coming to school and return to different situations each afternoon. Teachers try to bound their teaching by knowing developmental characteristics of students at particular ages, but this is only a small help. Teachers who know the details of the lives of individual students have a better understanding of the students' interests, fears, and behaviors. Like the historian, the more teachers know about their students, the better they understand them.

When studying history, the more students know, the better they can learn. Young students with limited knowledge and experiences can learn history but not with the same understanding that the teacher, parent, or scholar has. Just what students know and are capable of doing at different times throughout their school careers is largely unknown. Only in recent years has research tried to discover how students learn history.

Additionally, if constructivists are correct, the problems of teaching history today differ from those perceived as problems of teaching history in the past. What you knew and could understand as a child might not be, because of changes in society and the world, what today's child can understand. Recent research points out that students understand time and lots of other concepts needed to learn history in more sophisticated ways than educators realized in the past. Other research, particularly large sample test results, illustrates that students might not know things that we think they know or what we think we knew when we were their age. Teachers must decide how to use the research findings to improve the teaching of history while resisting the temptation to do what has always been done or what others who have little experience with teaching tell you to do.

Brophy and Van Sledright (1997), in reviewing the new research concerning elementary students' understanding and learning of history, recommend that teachers ask themselves the following questions to reflect seriously on their approach to teaching history:

What are the big ideas I need to teach?
How can the study of history pique students' interests?
How can I encourage students to ask important questions about what happened in the past?
What inaccurate conceptions do my students hold that keep them from completely understanding the objectives?
How can I help students understand the past and get inside others' experiences?
How can I help students understand that history is an interpretive construction based on evidence?

They also remind us that some students introduce imagination into their interpretation of events. They recommend that teachers create assignments and opportunities to recognize the improper use of imagination and replace it with analysis of facts to help students make more accurate and logical interpretations.

History in Schools

Historians have played a major role in all the national commissions and committees since 1892 that have addressed both history and social studies (Hertzberger, 1989). History is one of the specifically identified subjects in goal 3 of the U.S. Department of Education (1990), which states that history helps to prepare students for "responsible citizenship, further learning, and productive employment in our modern economy." The statement goes on to say that "all students will be knowledgeable about the diverse cultural heritage of this nation and about the world community" (U.S. Department of Education, 1990, pp. 5–6).

Two important dimensions of citizenship education in a democracy are identified by Engle and Ochoa (1988). One dimension is *socialization,* the process whereby a child comes to accept and support his or her culture. This provides for the continuity of the society. Engle and Ochoa suggest that for a democracy to continue to reflect the will of its people, its citizens must also experience a second dimension, the *forces of countersocialization.* Such forces require people to examine their personal and social beliefs and analyze the problems of their nation and world. Countersocialization activities require views to be supported with *reason* and *evidence.* Such behaviors are needed if citizens in a democracy are to be able to decide which ideas, institutions, programs, and behaviors should continue, change, or be abolished.

The study of history provides the opportunity for both socialization and countersocialization experiences. Engle and Ochoa suggest that very young children receive instruction that is largely socialization but that some countersocialization instruction is appropriate in the later elementary grades. The learning cycle on page 336 on learning from the paintings and drawings of artists is an example of how to get data from pictures and how artists show events.

The role of the study of history in the schools has been mostly to socialize students in the U.S. democratic tradition and to prepare them to be citizens. Much study has been devoted to learning about the origins of the nation and its struggles to grow physically, politically, and economically. Famous people and events have tended to dominate the study of history. Perhaps your definition of history greatly reflects this traditional approach to history. In recent years, social and ethnic groups have argued for the inclusion of important events and groups of people not previously studied in an attempt to present a more accurate interpretation of the nation and world. When asked to reflect on changes in social studies during their careers, more veteran social studies educators identified the inclusion of multicultural/global/gender-related education within the scope of social studies programs as the most important single change in the field of social studies. Catherine Cornbleth described this broadening of social studies to include more people as an important force because it "enables greater numbers of people to believe that they are a part of the U.S. and have a stake in it" (Haas & Laughlin, 1999b, p. 10).

LEARNING CYCLE LESSON PLAN

Learning from the Paintings and Drawings of Artists

Grades Levels: Intermediate and Middle Grades.

Primary teachers might use portions of the lesson with success.

NCSS Standards: Time, Continuity, and Change; Culture; People, Places, and Environments; Individuals, Groups, and Institutions

Teacher Background Information: In 1940 and 1941, large numbers of poor African Americans moved from the South, where there were few jobs and segregation, to the cities of the North, where industrial production related to World Wars I and II was increasing. In his paintings, Jacob Lawrence recorded events of the migration from the perspective of the African American migrants he observed and knew. This event is usually missing from general history textbooks, in which the events of World War II dominate.

Generalizations: (1) Artists, like writers, create works illustrating events they consider to be important. (2) Painters interpret events through the use of color, lines, textures, and shapes. For higher grades only: (3) Information about some people is only available from paintings "paintings" and drawings. (4) When combined with written works, paintings and drawings can add depth to our understanding of an event.

Skills practiced include: Making observations and generating inferences, hypotheses, and conclusions. Communicating through discussion, writing, and drawing.

Exploratory Introduction

Materials: An action painting such as *The Stampede* by Frederick S. Remington (available at www .allposters.com/-sp/Stampede-Posters_i309914_.htm). Packets for each group containing three or four paintings or drawings illustrating different events with two pictures in common. Obtain paintings through Internet searches at the National Gallery of Art, the Metropolitan Museum of Art, and by searching for such artists as Grandma Moses, Bernice Sims, Homer Winslow, Frederick Remington, or Norman Rockwell. Select events that are personal, family related, or local. With older students, include one or two paintings of major historical events.

Objectives $\longrightarrow$	Procedures $\longrightarrow$	Assessments
1 Students examine pictures and identify the events that are depicted.	1. Show students a copy of the painting *The Stampede* by Frederick S. Remington. Ask, "What do you think is being shown in this picture?" "Have you ever witnessed an event similar to this one?" Listen to and accept all student comments. 2. Ask, "What words would you use to describe the event?" "Raise your hand if you would like to be the man on the horse." "What do you think he might be thinking or feeling?"	

continued

"How does the painter convey these feelings about the rider to us?" Help students to recognize that the lines of the body parts of the horse, rider, and cow indicate forward movement. Help them to see that the use of light and dark colors adds to the excitement of the picture and the blurring of background details helps the viewer focus on the action at the front of the picture.

3. Ask, "Can you see the expression on the face of the rider?" "What do they think his face would look like?" Ask students to try to duplicate their idea of the expression with their own faces.

4. Say, "Raise your hand if you think the painter was a good artist." Call on several students to tell why or why not. Inform students that Remington was a famous artist whose works depict the American West he observed.

5. Place students into small groups and tell them that each group will receive a packet with new paintings or drawings and that some are unique to their group. Each group is to examine the pictures and decide the events being depicted. Ask students to explain how the artist calls attention to parts of the picture using the tools of color, line, texture, and shape. Each group should select words that describe the event(s) illustrated in the pictures. Group members should decide which of the pictures they like best and explain why it is their favorite.

6. Groups share their descriptive words about the common pictures and show the class their unique painting(s), describing each. Using a show of hands, students indicate the painting that is their personal favorite. Review the ways the artists help make events come alive for an observer.

1–6. Use a checklist to record:
   a. students sharing materials
   b. opinions to research conclusions
   c. selecting a favorite picture

Lesson Development

Materials: Downloaded paintings by Jacob Lawrence from 1940–1941 Migration of the Negro series (available at www.moma.org, and at www.phillipscollection.org/american_art/artwork/Lawrence-Migration_Series1.htm). Search for Jacob Lawrence. Prepare sets of 5 to 8 pictures for small groups each

continued

containing three common pictures. The book *The Great Migration* (1993) New York: HarperCollins Children's Books is helpful.

Objectives ⟶	Procedures ⟶	Assessments
1. Students recall artists' tools for paintings and drawings.	1. Review the ideas student have about how artists inform them of events and the tools the artists use to add details and feelings to their paintings. 2. Tell students that they will examine a series of paintings that a famous African American artist, Jacob Lawrence, painted in the early 1940s called the Migration of the Negro. Set the paintings in the context of the time period (consult teacher background). Tell the students to think for a moment what they might see in the paintings. Have a few students share some ideas and explain their reasoning. Say: "Let's see how Lawrence viewed the story of the migration." If possible, use the games for Kids at http://www.Phillipscollection.org/migration_series/flash/games_landing.cfm.	1. Students list color, lines, texture, and shape as important tools of the artist.
2. Given a sample of pictures from the series the Migration of the Negro 1940–1941 by Jacob Lawrence, students describe the pictures and hypothesize about the story being told in the series of pictures.	3. Ask students to return to the groups. Distribute envelopes containing a sample of the pictures. Ask students to examine the pictures in ways similar to what they did with the paintings from the previous day and use details from the paintings to agree on the story that is illustrated. Groups write this story in several sentences and pick a member to read the story. Tell the students to be certain to include the feelings and beliefs of the people in the pictures. 4. Ask the selected students to read their group's story. List the common characteristics of the stories and the differences in columns on a chart. Ask groups to explain their differences and to show those paintings that led them to their conclusions, pointing out what they consider to be important evidence.	2. Students cooperatively examine the pictures and make appropriate conclusions based on evidence from the pictures.
3. Students compare their stories for common and different conclusions.	5. Display the common pictures. Did all groups find the same message in these pictures? Ask members of the group to come forward and hold up the	

continued

paintings that were unique to their group. Students can also be asked to show with their facial expressions and posture how Lawrence illustrated the people in the unique pictures. As each group presents their pictures, ask, "What new messages or ideas do you get from these pictures?"

6. Say, "Raise your hand if you think Lawrence described the event of the 1940–1941 migration of African Americans well." Ask for reasons and accept student opinions.

7. Ask, "How would you describe the colors and texture of Lawrence's paintings compared to what you saw in the Remington picture?" "Do you think Jacob Lawrence should be classified as a good artist?" "Why or why not?"

8. Ask, "What questions would you like to ask Jacob Lawrence about his series of paintings on the African American migration of 1940–1941?" "Do you have any other questions about him as an artist or his other paintings?" List students' questions on a chart. Ask, "How do you think we might find the answers to these questions?" Use the book *Story Painter: The Life of Jacob Lawrence* by John Duggleby. It shows additional paintings and provides some details of his life and career. Get additional pictures from the Internet. Ask, "From the additional pictures we have seen and the words we have found about Lawrence, what would we like others to know about Jacob Lawrence the artist?" List students' ideas.

9. Have students individually write a short statement that informs others about how they might identify a painting as being done by Jacob Lawrence. Tell them to describe how he uses the artist's tools and identify the most likely subjects or events for his painting. Tell students to include something about Lawrence's life that can help people understand his paintings.

10. *Closure:* Ask students to relate what they have learned about Jacob Lawrence as an artist and invite students to volunteer to read their statements.

4. Students express their view on the status of Jacob Lawrence as an artist, defending their viewpoints.

5. Students seek out additional information about Jacob Lawrence to better understand his career.

6. Students reflect and write what they believe others should know about Jacob Lawrence and his paintings.

3. Students state conclusions and seek evidence to support differences or revise original conclusions.

4. Students recognize that artists use their tools differently and have different styles of painting.

5. Statements are formal assessment; use rubric at end of plan.

6. Students express their views and seek to understand the reasoning of those with different ideas.

continued

Expansion

Materials: Paper of various types, colors, roughness, or quality; crayons, tempera paints, various sized brushes, markers, and colored pencils. For older students, materials and screens to add texture. Computer and projector or copies of pictures from sites provided.

Objectives	Procedures	Assessments
1. Students conclude that different materials and personal preferences contribute to the variety in the appearances of paintings.	1. Display several pictures by various artists to the students. Review that all artists have the same tools of color, texture, line, and shape to use in their drawings and paintings. Ask, "What do you think accounts for the fact that not all of the pictures by a single artist look exactly alike and that different artist's paintings may look very different from those of other artists?"	1. Students identify different surfaces and the qualities of the paints used. Some artists prefer to show objects as being very realistic, with sharp lines, whereas others use fuzzy lines and shapes.
2. Given a selection of prehistoric drawings, students identify herding and hunting as activities. 3. Students describe paintings as a way to learn about people who left no written languages that we can read. 4. Students view drawings of trades in Ancient Egypt and indicate the types of work done by the people.	2. Show new paintings one at a time and ask the class to agree on the event shown by the artist: http://astronomy.nmsu.edu/tharriso/ast110/cavepaint.jpg www.fjexpeditions.com/tassili/aboteka/ab1.jpg www.fjexpeditions.com/tassili/sefar/sf6.jpg www.fjexpeditions.com/tassili/jabbaren/ja3.jpg Ask, "What event is shown?" "Whom do you think did this painting?" "What evidence do you see that leads you to this conclusion?" "Do you think this is an important painting?" "Why or why not?" www.ancientegypt.co.uk/trade/home.html Ask, "What do you think is being done in this picture?" "Do you think this picture was drawn at the same time, before, or after the other pictures?" "Do you have any idea who painted this picture?" 3. Click "Explore" in the index on the left and view the pictures of the jeweler's workshop and the carpenter's workshop. Click on the pictures to enlarge portions for better viewing.	2. Students identify hunting and herding activities drawn on rocks. 3. Students indicate that the people could not write, so we only have these drawings to tell us about their lives.

4. Visit www.ancientegypt.co.uk/life/explore/main.html. Click on the pictures to enlarge and learn about them. Ask, "What can we conclude from these pictures about Ancient Egypt?" "Do you think these paintings were done by professional artists?" "Why or why not?"

5. Given a choice of art supplies, students illustrate their personal event using lines, shapes, and color.

5. Ask the students to think of an event that they have witnessed and to draw a picture of that event, showing how they remember it and including their beliefs and feelings about the event. Allow students to select their own choice of paper and colors. Suggest that if students want, they could try to copy the style of one of the artists' paintings they have seen in the lessons.

6. Display students' paintings/drawings and ask students to tell about their paintings and how they used the materials, lines, shapes, and colors to tell about their event. Painting and explanations are formal evaluations. Rubric follows lesson plan.

7. *Lesson summary:* Ask students to recall the various works of art that they encountered in the lessons and to suggest some of the things they learned about drawings and paintings. Have students share their ideas about the following question with a partner: "How would you respond to a person who said that everyone is an artist?" After a minute or two, ask several students to share their thoughts with the class. Ask for a show of hands of students who agree with the various statements as they are made. If someone has a different answer, ask student(s) to share it with the class. Ask, "If you are reading a textbook or a trade book and there is a drawing or painting on the page, how will you respond to it?"

4. Formal assessment; use rubric at end of plan. Students create drawings that express a feeling of the event and explain their pictures.

continued

Summative Evaluation Rubric

Rubric criteria for paragraph	Beginning (1)	Mastery (2)	Exceptional (3)
Comments on artists' tools	Describes use of one tool	Describes use of two tools	Describes use of more than two tools or explains how his materials impact the style of his paintings
Identifies subject/event	Are of African Americans	African American people in day-to-day activities	Painted African American experiences he saw and famous African Americans
Comments on artists' life	Identifies one fact about life	Identifies two or more life experiences	Relates his life experiences to his art work

Summative Evaluation Rubric

Criteria for Painting and Explanation	Beginning (1)	Mastery (2)	Exceptional (3)
Painting's appearance	Completed, neat, use of one tool evident	Completed, neat, use of two tools clearly evident	Completed, use of three tools clearly evident
Event	Shows an event that is visually understandable	Shows an event with actions or emotions present	Shows an event with actions and emotions present on picture's major actors and minor actors
Oral explanation	Describes the event in a voice loud enough to be heard	Describes event in an expressive voice, loud enough to be heard. Tells how the artists' tools are used in pictures	Describes event in an expressive voice, loud enough to be heard. Explains event's importance or atmosphere. Tells how artists' tools were used in picture to convey ideas.

TIME FOR REFLECTION | ## What Do You Think?

When using social studies textbooks, many students fail to give attention to the pictures and graphics; at the other extreme, some students think they can just look at the pictures and know what happened.

1. What similarities are there between a painting of an event and several written paragraphs about the event?

2. How is it possible for an artist or a writer to create something that is accurate if he or she did not witness an event?

3. Do you think that an observer gets more meaning from the work of an artist or of a photographer? Explain.

4. What attitudes and process skills necessary to understand history or social studies does a lesson such as this one reinforce for an elementary or middle school student?

5. Many different artists and pictures could be used for this lesson. Why do you think the developer selected Jacob Lawrence for the Lesson Development phase and ancient artwork for the Expansion phase?

6. Why do you think the developer did not include grammar as criteria for the rubrics?

Standards for History

Standard II

NCSS Standard II, "Time, Continuity, and Change," names three key concepts for the study of history: "Social studies programs should include experiences that provide for the study of the ways human beings view themselves in and over time" (NCSS, 1994b, p. 22). In seeking to understand their historical roots and locate themselves in the expanse of time, students are linked to people and ideas that remain the same over generations. They also come to see the struggle to institute change as a way of exerting control over their lives. Developing a historical perspective helps individuals and groups answer the following questions:

> Who am I?
> What happened in the past?
> How am I connected to those in the past?
> How has the world changed and how might it change in the future?
> How do our personal stories reflect varying points of view and inform contemporary ideas and actions? (NCSS, 1994b, p. 22)

Young children are studying history when they sequence and order events in their daily lives, hear stories about today and long ago, recognize that other individuals hold different views, and understand links between their actions and decisions and their consequences. The curriculum, beginning in kindergarten, has plenty of opportunity to examine these basic historical concepts. Students enjoy solving puzzling questions about an unusual site they see on a walk through their community or about their school in years gone by, as pictured in old photographs brought in by a visitor. They might also learn about the people for whom local buildings and streets have been named. Through the study of people and events in world and U.S. history, middle school students experience expanded historical inquiry. They have in-depth instructional opportunities to learn about people's lives in various time periods by comparing, contrasting, and judging the lives, actions, decisions, values, and cultural traditions of individuals and groups.

After dialog and a major revision, the National Standards for History were published in 1996. The standards address U.S. history, world history, and historical thinking skills. Figure 11.1 explains the five common historical thinking standards (skills) for grades K–12: (1) chronological thinking, (2) historical comprehension, (3) historical analysis and interpretation, (4) historical research capabilities, and (5) historical issues analysis and decision making. As you read descriptions of behaviors needed to perform historical thinking, you might wonder whether you were asked to do these tasks when you studied history. Note that some skills the historian uses are not common to the thinking skills elaborated for the various social sciences. This is a result of the differences in the available data and ways data are obtained.

In Figure 11.1, skills in italics are for introduction and mastery in grades 5–12 when students are more likely to be formal operational thinkers. Although these skills are similar to those for K–4, they differ qualitatively in the complexity and number of tasks the student must perform before making a final conclusion. Note the emphasis in Standard 5 on multiple perspectives and alternative viewpoints that encourage the historian to view history as an infinite story. Historians recommend that all five standards be approached in grades K–4 at a beginning, but not superficial, level that goes beyond retelling a story and beyond accepting only one possible outcome. They want teachers to emphasize the need for evidence to support ideas.

Because of differences in the cognitive and affective development of students and in the curricula found in various states, two sets of standards for historical knowledge are presented: one with a K–4 or primary grades focus and one for grades 5–12. The recommended content standards are identified by eras of time. Each standard may be addressed in multiple ways. Teachers, states, and school systems make many decisions concerning the specifics to be addressed. However, addressing history with elementary students through topics and events with which they are likely to have some personal knowledge or experiences clearly must be emphasized.

The National Center for History in the Schools describes activities keyed to the National History Standards for grades 5–12 in two sourcebooks, titled *Bring History Alive*. One sourcebook is devoted to U.S. history, and one focuses on world history. These illustrate the Center's recommendations for using multiple resources to teach history. Students use both primary and secondary resources and a range of intellectual skills to interpret the data and assess the interpretations that others have made of historical events and trends. The entire set of K–12 National History Standards are on the Internet and also listed as a recommended website at the end of this chapter.

Note: Skills listed in italics are additions from the grades 5–12 standards for historical thinking.

Standard 1: Chronological Thinking

a. Distinguish between past, present, and future time.
b. Identify the temporal structure of a historical narrative or story.
c. Establish temporal order in constructing students' own historical narratives.
d. Measure and calculate calendar time.
e. Interpret data presented in timelines.
f. Create timelines.
g. Explain change and continuity over time.
h. *Reconstruct patterns of historical succession and duration.*
i. *Compare alternative models for periodization.*

Standard 2: Historical Comprehension

a. Identify the author or sources of the historical document or narrative.
b. Reconstruct the literal meaning of a historical passage.
c. Identify the central questions(s) the historical narrative addresses.
d. Read historical narratives imaginatively.
e. Appreciate historical perspectives.
f. Draw on data in historical maps.
g. Draw on visual and mathematical data presented in graphs.
h. Draw on the visual data presented in photographs, paintings, cartoons, and architectural drawings.
i. *Evidence historical perspectives.*
j. *Utilize visual and mathematical data presented in charts, tables, pie and bar graphs, flow charts, Venn diagrams, and other graphic organizers.*
k. Draw on visual, literary, and musical sources.

Standard 3: Historical Analysis and Interpretation

a. Formulate questions to focus their inquiry or analysis.
b. Compare and contrast differing sets of ideas, values, personalities, behaviors, and institutions.
c. Analyze historical fiction.
d. Distinguish between fact and fiction.
e. Compare different stories about a historical figure, era, or event.
f. Analyze illustrations in historical stories.
g. Consider multiple perspectives.
h. Explain causes in analyzing historical actions.
i. Challenge arguments of historical inevitability.
j. Hypothesize influences of the past.
k. *Identify the author or sources of the historical document or narrative.*
l. *Differentiate between historical facts and historical interpretations.*
m. *Analyze cause-and-effect relationships and multiple causation, including the importance of the individual, the influence of ideas, and the role of chance.*
n. *Compare competing historical narratives.*

FIGURE 11.1

Standards in Historical Thinking   *Source: National Standards for History Basic Edition*, by the National Center for History in the Schools, 1996, Los Angeles: National Center for History in the Schools.

o. *Hold interpretations of history as tentative.*
p. *Evaluate major debates among historians.*

Standard 4: Historical Research Capabilities

a. Formulate historical questions.
b. Obtain historical data.
c. Interrogate historical data.
d. Marshal needed knowledge of the time and place, and construct a story, explanation, or historical narrative.
e. *Identify the gaps in the available records, marshal contextual knowledge and perspectives of the time and place, and construct a sound historical interpretation.*

Standard 5: Historical Issues Analysis and Decision Making

a. Identify problems and dilemmas in the past.
b. Analyze the interests and values of the various people involved.
c. Identify causes of the problem or dilemma.
d. Propose alternative choices for addressing the problem.
e. Formulate a position or course of action on an issue.
f. Identify the solution chosen.
g. Evaluate the consequences of a decision.
h. *Marshal evidence of antecedent circumstances and contemporary factors contributing to problems and alternative courses of action.*
i. *Identify relevant historical antecedents.*
j. *Evaluate alternative courses of action.*

FIGURE 11.1 *Continued*

 # Benefits of Studying History

In response to concerns over what they saw as an inadequate quantity and quality of history teaching in U.S. elementary and secondary schools, historians formed the Bradley Commission on History in the Schools in 1987. The Bradley Commission says that the study of history is "vital for all citizens in a democracy, because it provides the only avenue we have to reach an understanding of ourselves and of our society, in relation to the human condition over time, and how some things change and others continue" (Bradley Commission, 1989, p. 5). The benefits can be grouped into three categories:

1. Personal benefits derive from helping individuals attain their identity by finding their own place in the history of the world.
2. The study of history helps individuals better understand and study other subjects in the humanities.
3. Studying history helps unify citizens into communities by creating a national identity.

The intellectual skills used and promoted by the systematic study of history help people develop cognitively. The Bradley Commission refers to these intellectual skills

TABLE 11.1
Habits of the Mind Associated with History

Perspectives	Modes of Thoughtful Judgment
Understanding the past is significant to individuals and society	Distinguish between significant and inconsequential
Comprehend the diversity of cultures and shared humanity	Develop historical empathy
Comprehend the interplay of change and continuity	Identify causal factors
Accept uncertainties of life	Determine consequences
Consider conclusions and generalizations as tentative	Idenfity multiple causation Evaluate ethics and character
Read widely and critically	Explain role of geography and time
	Identify assertions, inferences, facts, and evidence

Source: Historical Literacy: The Case for History in American Education, by the Bradley Commission on History in the Schools, 1989, New York: Macmillan Publishing Company.

as the "habits of the mind" (1989, p. 25). The Commission goes on to say that the principal aim of the study of history is the development of perspectives and modes of thoughtful judgment (social studies skills) associated with its study. Table 11.1 lists the perspectives and particular modes of thought historians use in making their critical judgments and interpretations of people, institutions, and events. The modes of thoughtful judgment are similar to the tasks of critical thinking required in making decisions whereas the perspectives are more similar to conclusions about the world from the study of history. Thus, historians view the benefits of studying history primarily from a personal perspective whereas the creators of the school curriculum tend to see the benefits of studying history deriving from its contribution to a sense of community and national unity.

Peter N. Stearns (1998), writing for the American Historical Association, summed up the responses to the question "Why study history?" when he wrote "because we virtually must, to gain access to the laboratory of human experience."

 ## Students and the Learning of History

Although students might not be able to understand history as completely as do historians, they are able to address some aspects. In recent years, researchers have shifted their focus from understanding time to broader concerns about how children learn history. As a result, they are more able to make research-based recommendations for activities that help children construct a more meaningful understanding of history. Students know more about some historical topics than others. Children often know a great deal about the content and interpersonal relations of social history but very little about the nature and purpose of government, politics, and economics (Barton, 1997b). This has great implications for the type of history to select, the topics to be addressed, and the need to provide motivation and links to the reality and importance of specific events and people when teaching history at various grade levels and various locations.

The National Standards for History are used by most states in establishing state social studies standards and they have incorporated many research findings into their recommendations. In the remainder of this chapter you will encounter specific references to research related to instructional strategies and resources for teaching history to elementary and middle school students. You also are provided a learning cycle lesson and ideas that model the proper use of research findings. Much of the research has been done in single classrooms using in-depth interviews and analysis of students' discussion and activities. These intense studies provide a type of data that has not previously been gathered systematically or in large amounts. Most of the studies indicate that students in a class do not view historical events or individuals in the same way, although their explanations and responses might show some possible trends.

Also available are the analyses of extensive tests such as the National Assessment of Educational Progress (NAEP). The NAEP has redirected the focus of their testing to attempt to gain information on both the learning of historical content and historical skills. In 2006, the scores for fourth- and eighth-grade students in U.S. history on the NAEP were slightly higher than in 2001 and several of the subcategories of questions were significantly higher than in 1994. Fourth- and eighth-grade teachers reported teaching about events during all of the four time periods tested: before 1815, 1815–1865 through the Civil War, 1865–1945, and 1945 to the present. According to the teachers, more time was spent teaching U.S. history through the Civil War at both grade levels. Disturbing, however, was the finding that 48 percent of the fourth-grade teachers and 56 percent of the eighth-grade teachers did not spend any time teaching about the time period 1945 to the present. This is of concern because grandparents and other citizens in the community might be interviewed by students or come as guest speakers to the school, and this time period has greatly impacted the lives of the students' immediate families. At present, the NAEP is the best single test educators have to measure both present successes and failures and any large-scale impact of reforms in the teaching of history.

Using Timelines to Develop Chronology

The concept of time is very abstract. Timelines are concrete devices used to assist students in understanding time-related concepts. Physically making a timeline is only part of the process. Questions and exercises using the timeline are essential if students are to discover the meaning and relationships embedded within the timeline.

Whereas the primary emphasis on the calendar in kindergarten might appear to be the recognition of numbers and counting, the calendar also helps to mark the passage of time and important changes that occur over time. Recording changes in the weather and seasons and recognizing holidays and birthdays are beginning points for the study of time in history. By acknowledging these events, the teacher helps students to recognize important ideas related to history. As time passes, certain things change and others remain the same, illustrating continuity. Students need to recognize these and mark regularities in the passage of time. Appropriate questions related to the calendar include the order in which things were done during the day and the recall of past activities. Marking the class calendar with a favorite event from their day is a way students record the history of their school year together.

The first timelines that students are assigned to make are concerned only with the correct ordering of events. Recording one event for each day of the week or one event for each year of their life is a helpful structure for young students to use when creating personal timelines (Hickey, 1999). Using a clothesline on which items are attached with clothespins is a good way to make a timeline in the classroom. In the classroom, timelines are placed where they are easily seen and easily reached to make additions.

Complete timelines not only identify dates or time periods for which the events occurred, but also order them over the uniform passage of time. Placing events along the timeline requires the ability to add and subtract. When long periods of time are considered, multiplication and division are needed. Neatly placing drawings or pictures on a timeline and labeling events with words are physically difficult tasks. Young students need large pieces of paper and small timespans with which to work. Equal timespans are marked along the timeline. This can be done with the help of colored paper or knots along a rope. As students progress through the grades, longer timespans are studied. A century is a very abstract concept. Large timespans are divided into more understandable divisions. A decade represents the entire lifetime of fourth- and fifth-graders. A generation, 20 years, is a time period that is understandable and helpful.

When considering events over a longer period of time, students can be asked questions linking the passage of time to generations to assist them in their understanding:

How many generations passed between the events (e.g., the Civil War and the Spanish-American War)?

Are there many people still alive who had firsthand experience with the Civil War and its aftermath or is their understanding based on secondary sources?

Have there been any important events that might change the probabilities of what events are likely to happen to people in a war or because of a war at the time we are working with?

Thinking about cause-and-effect relationships and hypothetical predictions can be stimulated by activities involving removing and/or moving events along the timeline. Question are also stimulating; for example, ask students what events might not have happened if the compass had been invented 200 years earlier. Teachers can also rearrange the events on the timeline, asking students whether the new arrangement is a possibility. Students can be asked to consider if a particular event were removed from or added to the timeline, what other events might also be removed or added (Sunal & Haas, 1993). Timelines are a part of most history chapters in textbooks, and they are often illustrated with words, colors, and pictures. Advanced timelines may be created as a series of bars that include events related to other topics associated with the major topic being studied such as social reforms, inventions, literature, Asia, or Europe that are placed under the timeline. Such timelines help to put events into the context of the world's history. Today's digital timelines such as *(Ben) Franklin's Interactive Lifetime* http://www.benfranklin300.org/timeline/ have imbedded pictures and links to primary documents and videoclips. Special software programs such as Tom Snyder Productions, *Timeliner,* help teachers and students produce digital timelines of their own and include pictures and links to primary documents and videoclips. Teachers need to encourage students to read and interpret the timelines in the texts as well as the words and pictures of a book.

 # Resources for Teaching History

When teaching children about history, educators use a variety of resources in addition to, or instead of, textbooks. Additional resources provide opportunities to learn history by using a greater variety of learning skills. Part of learning history is learning how the historian gets and processes information. See Figure 11.1 for the list of skills (modes of thoughtful judgments) used in historical thinking. Historians use many resources. Each learning resource is evaluated for its usefulness, accuracy, and limitations. Some resources are readily available; others can be obtained through inquiries and using the Internet. Access to most of the great libraries and museum collections in the United States and in much of the world is possible through the Internet. These resources greatly extend the resource base available to all teachers and students and hold the potential of changing the way history is taught to K–8 students.

Locating and Using Historical Resources

Resources for teaching history can be obtained by asking for help. People are very willing to help when they are asked politely for specific things. Students' family members often have much to offer. Students should write a letter of thanks, including some of the things they learned as ways of reviewing and illustrating their attention and learning. Students are prepared in advance for any special behavior needed in encountering or handling resources. Make students aware of their learning objectives in advance before the experience and excitement of encountering the resources distract their attention. Prepare data collection sheets that match the learning objectives for use during the resource experience. A word of warning: many online archives are very difficult to navigate so it may be wise to use some of the prepared collections such as American Memory at the Library of Congress with younger students.

People as Resources

History is a part of everyone's life. Through examining similarities and differences in lifestyles and using resources from various racial, ethnic, and social groups in the community, a multicultural dimension is added to the study of history (Hickey, 1999; Singer, 1992). Whereas some people can relate experiences firsthand, others can tell about them because they remember what others have told them. Begin by talking to students' family members or neighbors. Have students write letters to local history buffs, leaders of business and civic organizations, or the local newspaper asking for specific information or for answers to questions. Some teachers have had great success in dealing with senior citizen's groups or nursing home residents whereas others have worked well with collectors or craft makers. Not all people might want to visit a class, but many are happy to receive one or two students. Students in small groups or as a whole group prepare a written list of meaningful questions to ask. Tape or video recording presentations helps to get information correct, but permission must be obtained before recording. For longer units of study, it is often useful to have one or two individuals who work well with the age group visit several times as the study progresses.

Artifacts and Museums

Museums are an important source of artifacts, but so are attics and antique stores. Larger museums often make reproductions available at reasonable prices. One or two carefully selected artifacts can provide many opportunities for students to use their observation and thinking skills. Interesting questions and discussions that lead to forming hypotheses and investigations can be initiated by examining artifacts. Artifacts are successfully used as instructional resources in each phase of the learning cycle. Examining the materials, craftsmanship, and workings of artifacts reveals much about the values and lifestyle of both the maker and user. Artifacts provide the opportunity to examine concepts such as change, continuity, and creativity and offer clues to the local habitat and level of scientific knowledge and its application during the time period when they were used.

A trip to a museum or restoration is often reported as a positive memory in the study of history. Many small local museums have some very different or unusual things students have never seen. Sometimes observers are surprised to find items displayed that they see every day but never think to be of value or related to history. Because museums display collections, they are often appreciated by middle grade students who delight in collecting and learning all about their own collections. Many museums and restorations provide active programs especially for students: allowing them to handle things, to take part in live demonstrations, or to remain several days to live and work in another time period.

Students learn best if the opportunity for instruction both before and after the visit is provided. Teachers should contact the facility well in advance of the visit. Many museums have planned activities or reading lists to assist the teacher in preparing for the visit. They also provide special guides or programs for student groups. One of the largest collections of artifacts in the world is that of the Smithsonian Institution, sometimes referred to as "America's attic," in Washington, D.C. Through the educational services of the National Portrait Gallery of the Smithsonian Institution website for example, students can visit the 1999 special exhibit of the portraits of George and Martha Washington.

The Community as a Resource

State and local history is often included in the elementary and middle school curriculum. These provide the opportunity to gather data firsthand as a historian might and to process it into meaningful conclusions and displays. Third-grade teacher Caroline Donnan (1988) explains that she was able to meet all the social studies skill objectives through a third-grade study of the local community.

Cemeteries are often the locations of commemorative monuments to events or people. A trip to the cemetery can help teach students about the life cycle and about how and why people are remembered. Older students can look more closely at tombstones and discover changes in lifespans and the reduction of infant and child mortality. Rubbings can be made or epitaphs copied to provide information about a person and the times in which he or she lived. Often, ethnic, religious, or racial groups are buried in separate cemeteries or sections. Examining this phenomenon can raise a number of interesting questions:

> Why did a family bury their son with other soldiers rather than in the family plot?
> Why are people of one religion all buried together?
> How many generations of a family are buried in one plot? What might this tell you about the people?

The architecture of your community illustrates the origins of ethnic groups, changes in preferences, and the wealth of each owner. It indicates the technology and materials available to the builder. The names of streets reflect their functions and the people and places admired by the citizens. Some buildings have been used for a variety of purposes, and some are no longer in use. Speculation and investigation of their future usage are worthy activities. Many communities have special memorials, statues, and buildings. These acknowledge important people, businesses, and events of local concern. They often link the community to national and world events students read about in textbooks. In small communities, walking field trips provide students with opportunities to gather data and

Visiting a restoration involves learners in the lives of people who lived in other times.

Interesting artifacts can be found in homes as well as museums and restorations.

identify questions for future study. Sketching, photographing, and interviewing are helpful on a walking field trip and serve as discussion and project inspirations when students return to the classroom. Dot Schuler (2002) took her class on such a walking tour, which eventually led to their writing and illustrating a book that is sold as a guide to their community for tourists.

Documents as Resources

Every U.S. citizen should be aware of the content of important documents such as the Declaration of Independence, the Constitution, and the Emancipation Proclamation. Many textbooks include reproductions of such major documents. Here, documents are defined as the official or public record of events in the lives of individuals, businesses, communities, and institutions. Historians examine many documents.

Locally, documents often can be obtained through government offices, individual businesses and organizations, and local museums. Families may have deeds, wills, and certificates to share. The National Archives and Records Administration has prepared teaching resources and regularly publishes lessons based on a historical document from their collection in *Social Education*. Original documents are often handwritten and difficult to read. Most educational packets of documents include more easily read printed copies. As part of the federal government's emphasis on putting information online for use by citizens and in education, it is possible to gain access to many collections of documents through the National Archives (visit 100 milestone documents http://www.ourdocuments.gov/content.php?page-milestone) and historical data from the U.S. Census manuscripts are at their website after the information is 50 years old.

Questions to be answered when examining documents include those that help in gathering information, interpreting it, and establishing its meaning. Data-gathering questions follow:

> What does the document say?
> What values are expressed in the document?
> Does the document include any words indicating bias or prejudice?
> Does the document order action? By whom? To whom?
> Is the document sworn to or legally binding?

Questions that assist in establishing meaning and interpretation follow:

> What things happened as a result of issuing the document?
> Does the information in the document agree with other resources?
> Is this document likely to be more accurate than data in another source?
> Why might this document have been preserved?
> At what specific truth or what conclusion does this document help me arrive?

Diaries, Letters, and Pictures as Resources

Diaries, letters, and pictures are also primary sources of data. Some books contain these resources pertaining to specific events and time periods. Local families and museums may have such items that can be copied to share. Estate and garage sales are good sources of old pictures. The learning cycle on page 336 develops skill in gathering information and comparing pictures. Because those who produce primary sources are likely to state their opinions or interpretations, questions concerning the author's or photographer's credentials and views must be asked:

> Who wrote the material or took the picture, and for what reasons?
> How likely was the author to know the facts and to make accurate conclusions?
> Does the author or photographer have a reason to support one view or another?
> Are any facts present or does the writer present only conclusions?
> What other sources agree with the facts or views presented?
> What word(s) might indicate a bias or lack of objectivity?
> What does this document help me understand?

Teachers can make documents into learning resources. Teachers Leah Moulton and Corrine Tevis (1991) found the local museum a great source of historical pictures of their community. On the back of each picture, they copied and then covered the museum's description. As their second-graders examined the pictures, they identified the first thing they noticed, and two things they might not see at the location today. Finally, they gave each picture a title. Following class discussion, the descriptive paragraphs were uncovered and read aloud. This allowed students to check the accuracy of their predictions and to learn more about what was in each picture.

Visual Literacy and History

Before photography was available, artists preserved the likenesses of people and landscapes in paintings, on the walls of caves and on pottery, in stone, or on canvas. Artwork decorates buildings, homes, and tombs. Artists and, more recently, photographers made a living preserving images of the rich and powerful or what governments or news agencies paid them to photograph.

Study of ancient civilizations often calls on the evidence recovered by archaeologists. Because the languages of many people are not written or cannot be translated, works of art provide us with our best sources of information about many people and how they lived. For nonreaders in the primary grades or for students whose first language is not English, works of art provide important sources of information and are instructional resources for learning social studies. Children often like to handle pictures, examining them closely. Smaller pictures cut from magazines, or travel folders and postcards, which can be laminated or placed in page protectors, make good instructional resources for small groups. Or they can be placed in learning centers with questions to prompt exploration and data-gathering tasks. Another technique is to project a large image in which people are shown. Students discuss what they see, focusing on the people and how they might feel in this situation and what they are doing. Finally, small groups of students role play the scene several times and discuss their various interpretations and the likelihood of the role-play being an accurate depiction.

Pictures do not always tell the truth. Painters and photographers include and exclude things from pictures. A painting, drawing, or photograph is an interpretation of what was. Cartoon drawings are especially known for carrying messages, but messages in other visual images are often overlooked. Visual literacy requires skills in interpretation, the exercise of judgment, and the desire to question what is seen. It also requires taking time to look carefully at the whole and at its parts. Questions that promote visual literacy follow:

Does the object contain a signature or clues about the creator?
What is being shown?
What does the artist want you to see first and foremost?
Does the work contain secondary messages?
Do regular patterns or shapes present a message or feeling?
What use do you think the owner intends to make of this object?

Films and children's film-length cartoons are resources with which students are very familiar. When films and videos are used, students need to analyze differences between fact, fiction, artistic license, and the need to create a story that sustains the viewers' interest. Many children's versions of films use a grain of truth, lots of special effects, and creative imagination. Ethnic groups particularly charge that stereotyping is used and untrue facts are presented in many popular children's films. The use of dialog, music, emotion, and visual stimuli make film and video powerful presenters of information that may not be accurate or fair. As with all learning resources in the classroom, teachers carefully evaluate these. When using them, teachers address the errors and try to assist students to differentiate between fact, fiction, and entertainment. When teachers have students present their learning in video or PowerPoint presentations, students' special effects need to support accurate facts and interpretations of events.

 ## Reenactments and Drama

Visits to historic sites and weekend festivals often bring people into contact with reenactors who assume the role of people who lived and worked during the period being reenacted. History is taught by reenactors through presentations and answering questions as if the spectator had stepped into the historic scene. These historians are quite knowledgeable about the individuals they portray and how the individuals performed their work and lived their daily lives. It is possible to arrange for these historians to come to schools for special presentations or for special days of celebration. A day in a one-room school, at a medieval or Renaissance festival, visiting a colonial village, or at a frontier fort are activities used by many

TIME FOR REFLECTION | ## What Do You Think?

1. An assistant superintendent attended a presentation of the Boston Tea Party by a fifth-grade class. Native Americans tossed the tea overboard and then set fire to the ships. If you had been the assistant superintendent who was called on to comment after the students' program, what would you have said?

2. How might the teacher have facilitated the students' recognition of the differences between fact, fiction, and dramatic presentations so that the Boston Tea Party presentation reflected these understandings?

3. Children's literature is often beautifully illustrated. As students learn the importance of reading and the written word, they often entirely neglect the illustrations in a book. What questions can teachers ask to encourage students to identify the facts, emotions, and interpretations present in the pictures of books?

4. Identify at least three appropriate categories of tasks for a rubric for a history project that requires the students to illustrate what they have learned in drawings or through other artistic endeavors.

teachers. These are usually done during the lesson development or expansion phases of the learning cycle. Older students, after researching a topic or skill, might take part in a schoolwide presentation. They become instructors, presenters, or members of living displays to inform and teach classmates, younger students, community visitors, and family members about a particular era. These types of presentations may be part of a learning assessment.

Some teachers use the acting out of history as a regular instructional strategy. Students use their background knowledge to role-play people and events while teacher questions focus their thoughts and help them to reflect on and evaluate the likelihood of their interpretations. Teachers carefully plan these scenarios so that students focus on acquiring and using facts and interpersonal understandings to attain meaningful learning of social studies objectives. Students are confronted with making decisions as they believe people of the era would have made them. Then they reflect on, and perhaps revise, their dramas. This strategy gives students control over the direction of the lesson and their learning assessment. In the process of using drama and acting to learn history, students develop affective skills related to empathy and skills to interpret acts and events, giving them greater meaning. Students often say that they learn and remember more having engaged in the acting out of history (Morris & Welch, 2000). Teachers help students successfully act out history in several ways:

1. Researching the historical topic or event thoroughly
2. Mentally summarizing all the research in a series of events and relationships
3. Making a large chart to post in the classroom of the objectives, in the form of questions, to consider about the event:

   What actually begins the situation?
   Who are the leaders of the action?
   How do the poor people in the community view the importance of this situation?

4. Focusing students' attention on learning and answering the questions in an accurate or realistic manner
5. Providing for large amounts of verbal student expression
6. Allowing students freedom in their learning and interpretations, but helping them examine their reasoning and interactions through discussion, reflections, and writing
7. Keeping a record of students' daily participation using rubrics with which the students are familiar and on which students know they will be assessed

 ## Biographies and Historical Literature

Each May, *Social Education* publishes an annotated list of notable children's books in conjunction with the NCSS Book Review Committee and the Children's Book Council. All the books are related to social studies content and classified by grade-level topic. These lists serve as excellent resources for teachers and resource learning center coordinators. The decision to use these books as part of the curriculum depends on their contribution to appropriate social studies objectives.

Many believe that trade books provide a better, or at least an important, source to use in learning history and social studies. Claims for their success include the illustrations and engaging language are an improvement over dull textbooks, and literature expresses feelings and emotions with which students can identify. Some students seem to prefer trade books because of these characteristics (Levstik, 1986). The storylike format is familiar and can help students to read and understand the material because the story links information with causal relationships. However, the author of the story provides an interpretation of the facts that may or may not be accurate. Students tend not to question these relationships if the story plot makes sense or if they personally identify with a character in the story.

Because historical events are open to multiple and conflicting interpretations, the study of history must deal with such conflicts. No one story can substitute for a study of an event or historical issue. Simply reading, discussing, or acting out a story is not a study of history. What is necessary is the examination of stories by different authors and documents that present new and conflicting information. Conflicting information prompts students to look for the truth of what really happened. Historical fiction books must be written in the context of the real historical events involving a particular place and time period.

A story may be used as part of an exploratory introduction to help raise interest in or questions about events. During the lesson development phase, narrative histories and biographies, both fictional and factual, can serve as the source of data to be

Building on Diversity

Pitfalls in Selecting Multicultural Books

One book does not adequately present the variety that is present within a cultural group, nor does one source of books for youth have books about the wide range of cultures and subgroups of a single culture.

Inaccurate information in the narrative and illustrations of a book often results when a well-meaning individual writes a book portraying another culture. The book's theme ends up being presented from the author's own understanding, which typically fails to represent the views or traditions of the cultural group presented. Closely related is the pitfall of presenting incorrect information because of a failure to perform the in-depth research necessary to gain the facts. The problems in multicultural books are hard to identify, because finding the errors requires more information than the vast majority of teachers have about a particular cultural group.

A number of organizations and individuals provide guidelines on how to include specific ethnic and religious groups in literature and give awards to accurate and positive efforts. NCSS provides both guidelines and awards. Assistant Professor Debbie Reese is a Native American who helps educators by critically reviewing children's literature and issues related to Native Americans. Visit her blog at http://americanindiansinchildrensliterature.blogspot.com/ to benefit from her scholarly explanations and the perspectives of Native Americans.

analyzed and evaluated. Teachers may read to students, stopping and discussing difficult passages with them. This helps students relate other information they know to the passage to clarify understanding. This approach models good historical thinking and reading skills. Alternatively, a teacher may have students select from a group of books on one topic and share their findings and questions with others. Using multiple books provides an opportunity to accommodate students with different abilities. Various authors are likely to present different facts, come to different conclusions, and express different viewpoints and interpretations. The use of multiple books requires students to examine different opinions, just as the historian does.

Successful experiences with the use of narratives and biographies in the study of history in grades 3 through 6 have been examined (Drake & Drake, 1990; Levstik, 1986; Zarnowski, 1990). In each case, multiple books were used, and the study lasted for a month or more. These studies reported that students tended to react strongly to the characters and their situations and that history knowledge was learned. Researchers have found that the meaningful examination and learning of history from trade books is not automatic.

Teachers should not be surprised to discover that students often read stories differently from adults because they have different interests and experiences. Zarnowski (1990) reported that an examination of the biographies students wrote while studying biographies showed that students tend to include more details and reactions concerning the early life of the person but only a rather matter-of-fact statement concerning the person's adult accomplishments. Perhaps this happens because students bring a better understanding of youthful experiences to their reading and do not have a great enough understanding of adult work and the challenges and interactions required in adult society. Each student provides her own meaning to every educational encounter.

Many have advocated the use of literature in the study of history and social studies. Some states, such as California, require its use as part of the curriculum guidelines. Middle schools often require literature study to help provide additional practice in reading to improve reading test scores. Middle school teams often use a novel or chapter book with their integrated units or as the inspiration for an integrated unit. Teachers in a team relate their instruction about the book to their school subject. The social studies teacher might help students to understand the story in relation to its historical context.

Difficult and potentially controversial or emotional topics such as slavery, the struggles for labor and women's rights, the immigration of Chinese to the United States in the mid-nineteenth century, and the Holocaust are present in textbooks. However, because of the nature of textbooks, the amount of coverage is limited. Teachers often use trade books to assist in bringing the life experiences of people to such topics and to help students recognize that laws and history are influenced by the combined impact of personal decisions. Depending on the focus of the content in a particular book, a trade book might be used in any of the phases of a learning cycle. The Making a Literature Connection feature in this chapter reviews several trade books and their potential uses to increase knowledge in lessons related to the Holocaust.

Biographies and historical fiction are two types of trade books that have long been popular among young readers. Biographical series abound and are written for all grade levels. Often authors stress the subject's childhood, emphasizing the values learned at a young age and used or practiced that led to an important accomplishment. Teachers might use such books to stress the importance of civic values. Another popular use of biographies is to expand the coverage of women and minorities to fill in the gaps of what they consider limited coverage in the textbooks.

Books of historical fiction are also available for all grade levels. For the youngest students, these books tend to present a storyline about a historical event and make extensive use of pictures or drawings. These make good read-aloud selections. Good historical fiction presents a plausible story in the context of a particular time period in which the sequences of events, buildings, dress, customs, and various attitudes and dialects are historically accurate for the time and setting. Real people referred to within the book should have lived and performed the actions ascribed to them by the author. The popular American Girl Series of books that describe a year in the life of a girl at various time periods in America is an example of historical fiction that attempts to promote positive images in young girls. Books of historical fictions are often selected by middle school teams for integrated units. The social studies teacher's contribution to the unit is to help students examine the events and the historical context and values. *Storm Warriors* (2001) by Elisa Carbone is the story of Nathan and his fictional family, who moved to a small cabin near the Pea Island Life Saving Station on the Outer Banks of North Carolina in the 1890s. The descriptions of the storms and rescue efforts of the African American station keeper and crew are true. As a postscript, the author includes a description of her research procedures and a dedication that lists the names of the keeper and crew who inspired the book.

Helping students understand that biographies are much more than a story is an important lesson in historical interpretation. As Barton (1997c) warns, only using studies of biographies may result in students' thinking that individuals have complete and independent control over the potential of their lives instead of realizing that lives are greatly impacted by historical conditions. To help students to learn that people are important agents within a historical context, Gary Fertig and Frederick Silverman (2009) note the frequent use of asking students to read and report on a biography, and suggest instead that a more powerful approach is to take additional time during which students add their personal expression of understanding as they examine persons in their historical context. This examination is accomplished through five activities. As each activity is completed, the whole class discusses what issues and events students are encountering in the life of the persons whom they are studying. This whole-class discussion time also allows teachers to stress why personal interpretations are a normal expectation in studying historical lives. Even though students sometimes work in pairs to share ideas and responses, each student creates a chart displaying the final versions of the five activities in a web presented to the class and serving as a formal evaluation. Through their active investigations, students seek to learn how individuals' values and opportunities are impacted by the institutions, inventions, and mass movements of their time. The activities are as follows.

1. Students read a biography and design a new book jacket illustrating the historical significance of the person. Students also write the jacket's flaps. The front flap describes the meaning of the cover, while the back flap has short first-person statements telling who and what the person did. The jacket is placed at the center of a web on a large piece of chart paper, and the other activities are placed in one of the four corners of the chart.
2. Students create timelines to identify significant events from the person's life and incorporate parallel important events in science, the arts, and society.
3. Students select the five events they consider the most important from the person's life and identify an artifact to represent each of the events.
4. Students display photographs that can be related to the individual's past and write their own captions for each photograph.
5. Students map the movement of the individual to important locations that impacted the person during the individual's lifetime.

There are several new trends in history trade books that attempt to present individual and social history to youth. One style is called the *catalog book* because it includes lots of pictures and illustrations with brief explanations grouped by topics such as entertainment, transportation, children's lives, and life inside a particular building. These books require that a reader observe the illustrations, many of which are quite small, for details and to make connections between items on the page. The narration tends to set the items in the context of the times and to comment on some details to illustrate and explain trends. Such books appeal to young learners who are great seekers of new, clever, or different ideas. They contain so many facts that the book can be examined many times and still bring out new findings and questions. These books are not appropriate for read-aloud strategies. Mary E. Haas (2000) illustrates how teachers can use small-group and whole-class discussions that prompt students to explore and ask questions about such books. A sample of individual and series of catalog books include *A Street through Time* (1998) written by Anne Millard and illustrated by Steve Noon, *A Farm through Time* written by Eric Thomas and illustrated by Angela Wilkes, *Pompeii: The Day a City Was Buried* (1998) by Melanie and Christopher Rice, *A Medieval Castle* (1990) by Fiona MacDonald and Mark Bergin, and *Welcome to Addy's World 1864* (1999) by Susan Sinnott.

Few research studies support claims of better content learning with the use of literature. Research is needed on the effects of a literature approach, especially its impact on skill development and values formation (Eddington, 1998; McGowan, Erickson, & Neufeld, 1996). Naturalistic studies have revealed that some student responses can actually have a negative impact on learning social studies or history thinking skills. Students might identify so strongly with the character of the story that they are inhibited from critically examining the issues that the character encounters (Levstik, 1986).

After considerable review of research and their own investigations, Van Sledright and Brophy (1992) concluded that students need to be taught how historical narratives are created if they are to develop meaningful understandings of the differences between evidence-based accounts and fanciful elaborations. Barton (1997c) says that educators need to be extremely cautious in their use of historical narratives. History must be based on evidence, and this necessity must be made clear to students. Books selected for students to read and learn history must have, as an essential criterion, descriptions of the sources of their information and acknowledgment of the conflicts among the sources (Levstik & Barton, 1997).

Making a Literature Connection

Using Trade Books to Add Depth to History Units

Many educators believe that history should be used to help youth examine the character traits needed for a civilized world. Youth see many examples of improper behaviors in the media and in society. Intermediate- and middle-grade students need help in identifying and explaining the positive character traits needed for citizens in democratic nations. The Holocaust is one topic that provides such opportunities, and several states have laws that require its teaching. In approaching the Holocaust, teachers might want to use one or more trade books.

Terrible Things: An Allegory of the Holocaust by Eve Bunting illustrates how stereotypes, prejudice, and isolation destroy a community and points out that being a bystander actually supports the aggressor and encourages more intolerance. The book's characters are meadow animals, and its general message makes it appropriate for the exploratory introduction phase of a learning cycle. In discussing the book, examples of students' observations, feelings of helplessness, prejudice, or fear will be brought out and students will have the opportunity to identify bullying and unfair treatment as being important to eliminate.

The lesson development phase is where students need to gain the facts and form conclusions. Youth identify with the lives of other people, especially young people. In an autobiography, Isaac Millman relates his story of surviving the Holocaust in *Hidden Child*. He tells of his feelings of sadness, confusion, and uncertainty and his experiences with kindness and harshness as he was shifted from place to place. He had to take on a new name and pose as a Christian child in order to survive the war and avoid the fate of the rest of his family members. This book is a good choice for teachers with little time. Because of the behaviors of many diverse characters, the book provides the opportunity to respond to questions with reasons and empathy.

Told from the perspective of a young boy who is confused when vandals try to intimidate his family and community, *The Christmas Menorahs: How a Town Fought Hate* by Janice Cohn relates the true story of how the people of Billings, Montana, joined together to make it clear that hatred against Jews and other minorities would not be tolerated in their community. This book is appropriate for the expansion phase. Students need knowledge of the Holocaust to understand the story. This book teaches students that bad things in history do not need to be repeated if good people are informed and stand up for human rights when they see a problem.

Using Technology

Using Interactive Activities and Games in Learning History

Using electronic interactive games for learning content and skills is an approach to engaging students in history. Many such games ask students to solve problems similar to those used by the historian and archeologist using primary data in the form of artifacts or documents. Others are drill-and-practice activities that may be found for the computer or constructed by teachers who may involve students in the process, for use in learning centers or as evaluation projects shared with other students and classes (Haas & Laughlin, 2007). Some label interactive timelines as games if they allow students the freedom to ask their own questions. Instructional games do not need to be elaborate, but must match the objectives of the lesson. Imbedding electronic games and simulations into station activities, WebQuests, small-group activities, and class discussions may provide motivation, previews/introductions, practice of skills, or review of information. Students need to be asked to help reflect upon and evaluate their successes during discussions using questions such as:

- What social studies knowledge or experiences did you use to help you work through this activity?
- What do you think you learned from completing this game or simulation?
- If you repeated this activity, how did you change your choices? Did you get a similar or different outcome?
- What was the most difficult choice you had to make?
- Were there any similarities between life today and the lives of people in the game or simulation?

Franklin's Interactive Lifetime is narrated with a range of options that allows investigation and discovery of the many activities of a colonial American citizen who greatly impacted American life.
http://www.benfranklin300.org/timeline/
You be the Historian allows students to examine artifacts from a family's house in the late 1700s.
http://www.americanhistory.si.edu/kids/springer/index.htm

The British Broadcasting Corporation (BBC) offers many history-related interactive sites for students on topics from Rome through World War II.
http://www.bbc.co.uk/history/forkids/
The site *What Came First?* encourages observing pictures for changes in daily activities through time.
http://www.bbc.co.uk/history/walk/whatfirst_index1.shtml
Ancient Egypt is associated with the mummy. Here students try to create a mummy and learn its relationship to religion and pyramids.
http://www.bbc.co.uk/history/ancient/egyptians/launch_gms_mummy_maker.shtml
Visit the website for *Colonial Williamsburg.* Use the pull-down menus under History and Education or Kids and the History to find lessons and interactive activities.
http://www.history.org/
Inca Investigation examines a site of the Inca to determine from archeological data how individual sites at a dig might have been used. This game from the American Museum of Natural History is an elementary inquiry exercise requiring higher-level thinking.
http://www.amnh.org/ology/index.php?channel=archaeology#features/inca?TB_iframe=true&height=540&width=750
Colonial House allows students to examine life in colonial New England.
http://www.pbs.org/wnet/colonialhouse/history/index.html
Teaching with Historical Places has good examples of state and local lessons and ideas. It provides teachers with background information and ideas.
http://www.nps.gov/history/nr/twhp/
American Memory at the Library of Congress has materials and lessons on many major topics in American history.
http://memory.loc.gov/ammem/index.htm

Expanding Your Skills in History

In-service programs for teachers are widely available to help expand their skills in teaching history. The Internet helps to meet teachers' needs to increase their knowledge when they need skills at a low cost. The website Dohistory is an excellent site to help teachers and older students develop the skills historians use. This site concentrates on the lives of ordinary people using as its primary resource a diary written by Martha Ballard more than 200 years ago. From the age of 50 until she died in 1812, Martha Ballard served her community as a midwife, delivering 816 babies. The site helps you examine the entries in Martha Ballard's diary as would a historian. Also included is a historian's tool kit.

Membership in professional organizations and attendance at state, regional, and national meetings is helpful. Professional journals and newsletters provide the opportunity to learn and think about issues and to become aware of workshop opportunities, and conferences providing scholarships for teachers. Individual membership brings all the benefits to your own address and the opportunity to become involved in leadership positions within the organization. NCSS membership information and publications information is available on the Internet, along with a list of the state and local affiliates and links to other social studies related organizations.

EXPANSION

Below is a worksheet for use in the Exploratory Introduction of a unit on Abraham Lincoln. As presented, the worksheet is for upper elementary and middle school students. If you wish to adapt this idea for use with primary grade students, the worksheet should be shortened so it ends with looking at the pictures of the new tails and asking students what they observe on the new tails.

Lincoln Penny Worksheet

Abraham Lincoln was the first American whose face was placed on a U.S. coin. This was done 100th years ago to mark the 100th anniversary of his birth, or the centennial, of his birth. The year 2009 is the 200th anniversary, or bicentennial, of Lincoln's birth. The bicentennial was celebrated in many locations that were important in Lincoln's life. The U.S. government is creating new pennies that honor Lincoln's life for the bicentennial.

You have seen many pennies in your lifetime. Below are two circles. Take a few minutes to sketch what you remember of the face and tail of the Lincoln penny. Include the words that are on the penny as well as the pictures, because they are all a part of the design of the penny.

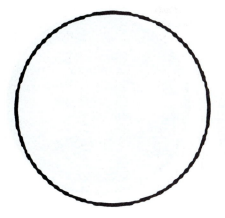 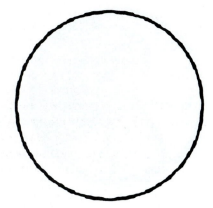

Compare your pictures with a partner. Then, work with your partner to do the tasks below.

1. Did both of you include the same pictures and words in your drawings?

2. What stands out the most in your drawings of the Lincoln penny?

3. If you did not put words on your drawings, what words do you think might be best?

4. On the next page are three circles that include the face and the two tails that have been used on the Lincoln pennies. Compare these to your drawings. The tail of the penny we see most often has the Lincoln Memorial because it is the newest design, made in 1959. The tail on the far right was the original design. The face has remained the same. Which tail do you think is more representative of Lincoln? Can you see the statue of Lincoln in the memorial (clue: look in the middle)? Can you see the heads of wheat in the older design?

In 2009 new pennies remembering Lincoln were issued. The face on the head remained the same, but the tails had four new designs. See these designs in the pictures on pages 367–368. Why do you think each of these designs was chosen?

Design 1:

Design 2:

Design 3:

Design 4:

What messages do the images in each design give you about Lincoln's life and values?

Design 1:

Design 2:

Design 3:

Design 4:

The same three phrases are included on each design but the locations on the tails are different. What are these three phrases?

1.

2.

3.

Why do you think these phrases are the same on all of the designs?

Why do you think scenes on the tails were from different locations in the United States of America?

Why do you think the scenes are of different sizes?

Which of the tails do you like the best? Why?

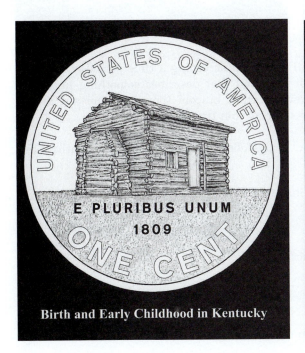

Birth and Early Childhood in Kentucky

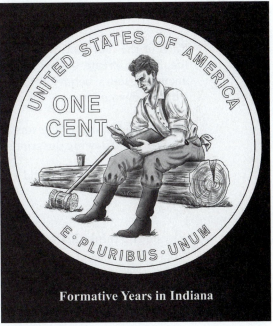

Formative Years in Indiana

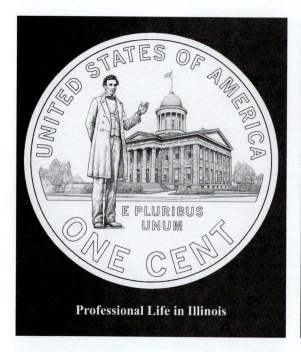

Professional Life in Illinois

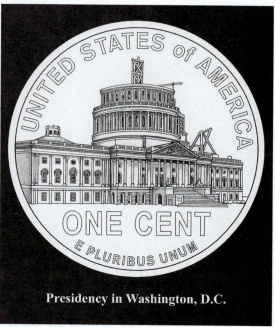

Presidency in Washington, D.C.

Each of the four pictures of a tail is labeled according a time period of Lincoln's life. Try to create a new title for each tail that describes something important about Lincoln's behaviors and reveals what Lincoln thought important and to what he devoted most of his efforts during that time period.

Be prepared to share your answers to the following questions with the entire class. Answer the following questions.

For which of the pictures did you have the most difficulty creating a good title?

Why do you think this was the most difficult?

Where could our class find help in understanding the symbols on the tails?

TIME FOR REFLECTION | ## What Do You Think?

The previous materials are for the Exploratory Introduction of an inquiry lesson about Abraham Lincoln who is remembered as the greatest president of the United States.

1. What type of resources might you use with students at the beginning of the development phase of an inquiry learning cycle lesson (or unit) that would provide accurate information concerning Lincoln's life and values for fifth-grade students? for students whose reading or language skills are below grade level or who are ESL/ELL students? In an inquiry lesson, why is a book or a video an appropriate choice near the end of the development and NOT the beginning of that phase?

2. In an inquiry learning cycle students' conclusions at the end of the Development might be considered hypotheses that could receive further testing. What might you ask students to do in the Expansion that would help them affirm the conclusions they made in the development phase? What type of learning resources would you use?

3. This learning cycle also might be used to focus on a study of the characteristics of those who have been president of the United States of America. The Exploratory Introduction is for an inquiry learning cycle on Abraham Lincoln. Your Task is to write the Lesson Development and the Expansion for the learning cycle. Select an upper elementary or middle school grade level and use several different types of learning resources. Remember that, in an inquiry lesson, students are to form their own ideas and not accept something that is told to them by an author, teacher, or producer. After making their own choices and decisions, however, students may check to see if others agree with their ideas; therefore, a video or book may be appropriate at the end of the Lesson Development.

Summary

History is an important subject for students to study in grades K–8. Many ways of stimulating and maintaining students' interest in the meaningful learning of history are available. Most researchers agree on the need for in-depth study of historical topics, the use of multiple resources, and the consideration of multiple perspectives. Rossi (2000) concludes that the clear implication for curriculum development of the research on the teaching of history is the need for in-depth study providing a conceptual framework that allows studnts to find meaning in the details.

Some controversy exists over what content and type of history to stress, but there is no shortage of potential content. Our families, the things around us, the issues influencing our lives, and our common heritage of values and beliefs all provide ample content. The data, too, are present if we look for and examine it carefully. The study of history can stimulate us to examine our present behaviors with an eye toward making appropriate changes while maintaining continuity with our worthy past.

Recommended Websites to Visit

Library of Congress with its lessons and American Memory Collection
www.loc.gov
The Smithsonian Institution, sometimes called "the nation's attic," with its museums and teacher pages
www.si.edu
The National Archives and Record Administration of the U.S. government with its educators' pages
www.archives.gov/
The National Standards for History 5–12
www.ssnet.ucla.edu/nchs/
Plimoth Plantation presents the site and life of early settlers
www.plimoth.org/
A portal for African American history and culture
http://blackquest.com/link.htm
A site to help teachers and older students develop the skills historians use
www.dohistory.org
The History Network, which provides links to the history of other nations and many ethnic groups
www2.h-net.msu.edu/lists/
A graphic organizer for cause and effect (click on cause and effect in chart)
www.greece.k12.ny.us/instruction/ELA/6-12/Tools/Index.htm
U.S. National Archives and Records Administration
www.archives.gov/index.html
Teaching with Documents and Worksheets for Analysis of Documents
www.archives.gov/education/lessons/
Evaluate documents on Internet sites: Reference and User Service Association of History Section of the American Library Association
www.lib.washington.edu/subject/History/RUSA/
Debbie Reese's blog: American Indians in Children's Literature
http://americanindiansinchildrensliterature.blogspot.com/

12

How Do I Engage Students in Interpreting the Earth and Its People Through Geography?

EXPLORATORY INTRODUCTION

Which of these are your students likely to be familiar with doing?

1. Watching the sky to see if dark clouds are heading your way
2. Eating strawberries, blueberries, or bananas in a salad or on cereal
3. Consuming a cup of shade-grown coffee
4. Searching *MapQuest* for directions
5. Viewing an image on the news that zooms in on a location using *Google Earth* or GPS

How is each of the actions above related to geographic knowledge?

Chapter Overview

Geography is an integral part of daily life. When was the last time that you were conscious of using geography? When was the last time that you sought out specific geographic information to help you make a personal or family decision? What issue in your community or in the nation are politicians discussing that is better understood and answered with the help of geographic information? In this chapter, geography is viewed as an integrated subject fundamental to people's lives and to the social studies curriculum. This chapter discusses the many ways we use geography in our lives and how children can meaningfully learn it.

Chapter Objectives

1. Evaluate your own experiences learning geography and compare them to the practices in today's elementary and middle school classrooms.
2. Analyze geography standards to develop a comprehensive definition of geography that is more than a tool for locating places.
3. Explain how geography is an integral part of all subjects and is used in many careers and daily work.
4. Identify and locate resources for teaching geography.
5. Identify activities that help students describe the three-dimensional characteristics of the world and translate them into a two-dimensional map.
6. Describe the advantages of using the globe with students.
7. Identify key concepts and skills geographers use to describe and interpret their world.
8. Analyze geographic lesson plans.
9. Identify variables that positively and negatively impact meaningful geography learning.
10. Hypothesize actions educators can take to increase geographic achievement for all.
11. Identify potential impacts of new technologies on processing geographical data and it impacts on using and learning geography.

DEVELOPMENT

 ## Defining Geography

Everybody wants to know what is happening around them. Joe Stoltzman (1990), a longtime geography educator, explains that geographically literate citizens are aware of (1) what is happening in the world, (2) why it is happening, and (3) how it affects other people throughout the world as well as themselves. Therefore, geography is good citizenship education.

Geographers are unique because they apply their efforts to understanding both the physical and cultural characteristics of the world. They have the perspective that location is an important characteristic of everything on earth. Through the study of locations and their relationships to each other, geographers help to explain the dynamics of what is happening in the world or in various places in the world. Geographers begin their study by asking where, but spend the vast majority of their time investigating the questions: Why is this where it is? If people do something in this location to change the physical or cultural conditions, what will be its impact on other locations? In what ways will the impact be positive and in what ways will it be negative? Because everything that has happened, is happening, or will happen must take place at a location, geography is a part of all 10 social studies standards.

The Five Themes of Geography

Before the standards movement, geography was defined by a joint committee from the American Association of Geographers and the National Council for Geographic Education, through using five themes: (1) location, (2) place, (3) relationships within places, (4) movement, and (5) regions as a working definition for K–12. Today, many teachers and geographers still use the five themes as they confront the daily pressures and tensions of the classroom.

Theme 1: Location, Position on the Earth's Surface.   The importance of location is the fundamental assumption of geography. Sometimes, we need to know an absolute or exact location, such as in which classroom we can find Mr. Lopez's fourth-grade class. At other times, we can be satisfied with a more general or relative location; for example, much of the world's oil is found near the Persian Gulf. Some learning activities including the location theme help students learn to locate places in the community, state, or nation; on the earth; or on a map or a globe.

Theme 2: Place, Natural and Cultural Characteristics.   This theme is descriptive of both the natural and human features of the landscape. Concepts describing features on the earth include mountains, capital cities, and the developing world. All are part of the place theme. Students gather data and answer questions such as the following to help them describe place:

> What does the land look like?
> How much water is present at this place?
> Does the water usually come from the atmosphere as rain or snow or from a
>   stream or body of water?
> Why don't wild animals live in the area?
> Do plants dominate the landscape or is the land largely barren or filled with
>   buildings?
> Why do so many (or so few) people live in this place?
> What have people done to change the appearance of the area?

Theme 3: Relationships within Places, Humans and Environments.   The natural environment tends to limit what people can do in a place. However, throughout history, people have been quite clever in dealing with these limitations. In dry areas where water was not sufficient to grow needed food, people found ways to import water. Today, people in dry places use advanced transportation to import food. The learning cycle lesson plan on page 374 addresses the theme of relationships within places.

Theme 4: Movement, Humans Interacting on the Earth.   People often do not remain in one place, nor do they use only resources from the place where they live. The movement of ideas and products affects not only places of origin and destination but also places along the way. Raw materials are extracted, new products are grown or

text continues on page 377

LEARNING CYCLE LESSON PLAN *People Change Their Environments*

NCSS
Standard III

Grade Levels: Primary and Intermediate

NCSS Standards: People, Places, and Environments

Exploratory Introduction

Materials: Tape of soft music, tape player, flower-scented room freshener, marking pens, response strips

Objectives ⟶	Procedures ⟶	Assessment
1. Students suggest what the word *environment* means to them.	1. While the students are out of the room, rearrange the desks, turn off the lights, start a tape of soft music, and spray the room with a flower-scented room freshener. If the students do not notice the changes when they return to the room, ask them how the room has changed. Ask, "What changes in the environment do you notice? Do you like them? What do you think when you hear the word *environment*?" Record each response on a strip of paper and place it on the bulletin board.	1. Students offer logical associations for the concept of *environment*.

Lesson Development

Materials: Three sets of 10 pictures illustrating natural and human changes, various natural and cultural scenes of rural and urban areas, and pictures showing scenes including some of pollution or natural disasters, homes, roads, schools, stores, and so on

Objectives ⟶	Procedures ⟶	Assessment
1. Students identify changes in the environments shown in pictures and suggest whether the changes were caused by nature or people.	1. Over two or three days, students use different sets of teacher-selected pictures and work in small groups. Teachers carefully select pictures for each group because the content of the pictures guides the classification possibilities. Each group uses a different set of pictures each day. Follow the identical procedure each day but address one of the content classification objectives each day.	1. Students work cooperatively.
2. Students classify elements of the environment into natural	2. Group activities: Students classify the pictures as: a. Examples of natural and human changes. b. Scenes similar to or different from their community scenes.	2. Groups classify pictures as assigned or create their own logical classifications.

and cultural (human made) landscapes.
3. Students identify pictures that appear similar to and different from their own community.
4. Students judge changes in the environments in the pictures as positive or negative and give reasons for their judgments.

c. Changes they consider good or bad. When doing this, students must give reasons for their choices.

3. Each day, students share their group's conclusions with the class. Groups decide on one picture to show the class to illustrate their classification and judgment. A different spokesperson makes the group report each day. Students ask clarification questions as needed.
4. *Daily closure:* After each day's class discussion, teacher asks, "Are there any pictures or words we should add to or take off our bulletin board because of what we have learned today?" Changes are made when class agrees. Ask, "How does our bulletin board summarize what we have been studying about the environment?"

3. Students offer logical reasons for classifying a change as good or bad.
4. Groups share work, listen to each other, and ask appropriate questions.
5. Checklist for group work:
   a. Students ask appropriate questions.
   b. Disagreements are clearly stated.
   c. Class makes appropriate and logical changes.
6. Students summarize accurately, giving important ideas.

Expansion

Materials: Chart paper and markers

Objectives $\longrightarrow$	*Procedures* $\longrightarrow$	*Assessment*
1. Students tell what they have learned about changes in the environment.	1. Tell students, "Think about what you have been learning and doing with the pictures of the environment this week. Will someone give me a brief statement of something you learned about the environment and how the earth is changed?" Call on several students. After each comment the teacher says, "If you have also learned what Johnny said, raise your hand."	1. Students state what they have learned clearly. 2. Students raise hands in agreement.
2. Students identify occupations that bring changes to the environment.	2. Display a list of occupations including doctor, clerk, contractor, janitor, tree trimmer, architect, fire fighter, farmer, and gardener. Ask, "Which of these people have jobs that cause them to change the environment as they work?"	3. Students offer answers and explanations.

continued

3. Students list ways they can change their classroom environment.
4. Students agree on a set of changes to make in their classroom.

3. Ask students: "How might students change the environment of their classroom?" List responses. If appropriate, have students also address how they could change the room to reflect a topic to be studied or coming season or holiday. (This procedure can be repeated during the school year.)
4. Through voting and discussion select several changes to make in the classroom. Have students make these changes then reflect on their quality in a short note to the teacher explaining how and why they believe the changes are good or bad.

4. Students offer logical answers in response.
5. Discuss and reach a conclusion by voting.
6. Students take part in carrying out the changes on the classroom and express their concerns and willingness to make additional appropriate changes. Formal evaluation is note to teacher. See rubric.

Note: This lesson may also be expanded by students taking part in a school or community cleanup campaign or students extending their knowledge by learning about laws concerning the environment.

Summative Evaluation Rubric

Criteria for Note	Beginning (1)	Mastery (2)	Exceptional (3)
Says change is good or bad.	Evaluates, but without a reason.	Evaluates as a personal preference or reason.	Evaluates identifying personal and community impact.
Identifies change.	Names a change.	Describes change before and after.	Describes change with a reason for the change.
Tells how change was done.	Says who made change.	Gives one specific act done to change the environment.	Gives several specific behaviors done to bring about the change.
Note is neat and uses acceptable grammar.	Uses only phrases or single words, more of a list than a note.	Writes two sentences.	Uses more than two complete sentences.

TIME FOR REFLECTION | *What Do You Think?*

1. Why do students quickly notice changes in the classroom set up for the exploratory introduction of the learning cycle on *People Change Their Environments*?

2. What initial terms do you anticipate students associating with the word *environment*? Why do you think these are the words?

3. What procedures would you use to prevent or solve the problem of students being curious about the pictures that other groups of students have?

4. Modifying the bulletin board helps students reconstruct their ideas about the environment and changes in it. What other activity might you use to help illustrate students' thoughts as they study?

---

produced in factories, and transportation centers are expanded or established. Ideas such as preservation, conservation, and democracy are being attempted in new places. People travel to other nations to visit and may spend part of their lives working or living in other nations. There are systematic movements among the natural forces on the earth. For example, currents carry warm and cold water to new locations; they also carry pollution created by people to new locations throughout the globe. Global problems are concerns of geographers as they study movements between places and regions.

Theme 5: Regions, How They Form and Change. It is difficult to conceive of the scale of the entire world, so geographers frequently divide it into regions. Within a region, geographers study all the places and activities defined by the other four themes. After studying many regions, geographers begin to get a picture of how the entire world works as they investigate the interactions between regions. Because the criteria for establishing a region are determined by the person doing the study, a region can be as small as an individual classroom, school, neighborhood, or community with which very young students are familiar. In this region, they can observe and investigate. As students develop their understanding of the five themes of geography, and develop their skills, they begin to study larger and more formal regions defined by physical and topographic features or political control. Those regions, such as the Middle East and Southeast Asia, defined by the interaction of many complex features, are appropriate for study by students who have well-developed concrete reasoning schemata or are formal thinkers.

The names given to each of the Five Themes of Geography are major organizing concept of geographic knowledge. Table 12.1 shows several geographic concepts related to each of these five concepts. Lessons that address a concept in one of the lists help to provide greater meaning to the theme under which it is listed.

TABLE 12.1
The Five Themes of Geography and Related Concepts

Location	Place	Relationships	Movement	Region
Absolute	Environment	Attitudes	Migration	Nation
Grid system	Landform	Adaptations	Diffusion	Physical
Map/globe	Climate	Inventions	Barriers	Cultural
Legend/key	Land use	Technology	Systems	Community
Relative	Vegetation	Pollution	Currents	States
Directions	Elevation	Changes	Winds	Middle East
Distance	Population	Industry	Transport	Europe
Scale	Rural/urban	Deforestation	Communicate	Historical
Equator	Buildings	Conservation	Causes	District

Geography and the National Social Studies Standards

NCSS

Standard III

Clearly, geography is strongly evident in the social studies standard for People, Places, and Environments. Geographers know that places do not exist in isolation; all parts of the world are interrelated and important. Global systems in the natural habitat, such as winds and currents, impact people's lives. There also are many connected cultural systems, such as communications, transportation, economic development, environmental quality, and human relations. Geography helps citizens understand our nation and interdependence with other people. This cross-national interdependence and the potential for regional and cultural conflicts is an important assumption underlying the problems encompassed in the social studies standard Global Connections.

NCSS

Standard IX

The social studies standard, Culture, is addressed in geography when people make decisions about the use of the earth's resources that are influenced by their culture. Some cultures exploit as many resources as possible, often bringing about major changes in the habitat. Other cultural groups view nondisruption of the habitat to be the correct decision. The final decision often is related to which group has the greater political or economic power or the legal authority to enforce decisions. Or it is related to who will devote time and effort to get their way or to force another group to compromise. Active citizens need to understand how geography is related to the social studies standard Power, Authority, and Governance and the standard Civic Ideals and Practices.

NCSS

Standard VI, X

Geography Education Standards: The Six Elements of Geography Education

Geography for Life is a statement of geographic education standards prepared by a committee of geographers and geographic educators. It details the basic concepts and generalizations of physical and human geography and illustrates how geography systematically approaches the study of the earth and its people. It explains how locations and interactions between people and natural habitats help students understand events and places today, in the past, and possibly in the future. These standards are helpful in selecting appropriate geographic content, concepts, and skills for lessons, curricula, and assessments.

The 18 standards are grouped into 6 major categories, or *elements*. Figure 12.1 identifies the 6 elements and the 18 standards. The standards subsume the five themes.

> **Element 1: The World in Spatial Terms.** Element 1 incorporates the theme of location, reminding instructors that finding places is not the only skill one uses when dealing with maps. It also identifies the variety of maps that students need to study and use.

Element 1: The World in Spatial Terms
1. How to use maps and other geographic representations, tools, and technologies to acquire, process, and report information from a spatial perspective.
2. How to use mental maps to organize information about people, places, and environments in a spatial context.
3. How to analyze the spatial organization of people, places, and environments on the earth's surface.

Element 2: Places and Regions
4. Know and understand the physical and human characteristics of places.
5. Know and understand that people create regions to interpret the earth's complexity.
6. Know and understand how culture and experience influence people's perceptions of places and regions.

Element 3: Physical Systems
7. Know and understand the physical processes that shape the patterns of the earth's surface.
8. Know and understand the characteristics and spatial distribution of ecosystems on the earth's surface.

Element 4: Human Systems
9. Know and understand the characteristics, distribution, and migration of human populations on the earth's surface.
10. Know and understand the characteristics, distribution, and complexity of the earth's cultural mosaics.
11. Know and understand the patterns and networks of economic interdependence on the earth's surface.
12. Know and understand the processes, patterns, and functions of human settlement.
13. Know and understand how the forces of cooperation and conflict among people influence the division and control of the earth's surface.

Element 5: Environment and Society
14. Know and understand how human actions modify the physical environment.
15. Know and understand how physical systems affect human systems.
16. Know and understand the changes that occur in the meaning, use, distribution, and importance of resources.

Element 6: The Uses of Geography
17. Know and understand how to apply geography to interpret the past.
18. Know and understand how to apply geography to interpret the present and plan for the future.

FIGURE 12.1
National Geography Standards   *Source: Geography for Life: National Geography Standards,* by the Geography Education Standards Project, 1994, Washington, D.C.: National Geographic Research and Exploration.

Element 2: Places and Regions. Element 2 combines two of the five themes, clarifying their meanings by pointing out that places are culturally defined by people, that they can be small or large, and that they may vary in importance over time.

Element 3: Physical Systems. Element 3 serves as a reminder that the earth has patterns that are related to its physical nature, that many changes are a result of the physical processes acting on the earth, and that natural forces change Earth by moving materials.

Element 4: Human Systems. Element 4 stresses ongoing changes in human patterns related to settlements, the movement of resources, and the struggles and conflicts regarding control of the earth's surface. The inclusion of these two systems reminds teachers to include detailed considerations of both.

Element 5: Environment and Society. Element 5 shows how people, at times, adapt their behaviors to fit the environment, whereas at other times, they try to change the environment to fit their own needs and desires. This element ensures that teachers consider environmental perspectives and ask students to think about how various people view the earth.

Element 6: The Uses of Geography. Element 6 encourages teachers to ask students to apply geographic knowledge to other school subjects and consider how people use geographic knowledge and skills in their jobs when making decisions.

 ## Resources for Teaching Geography

An inexpensive but important primary teaching resource is just outside your school. Field work is possible on every walk or trip outside. With a little planning and encouragement, students can study geography. Even the youngest students can talk about, draw, list, and photograph what they consider important observations. In doing so, they begin to learn the usefulness of major geographic tools, such as graphs, charts, maps, photographs, aerial photographs, and remotely obtained information from satellites circling the earth. Making accurate observations and recording observations require instruction and practice using instruments and skills. But the first geographers began with nothing more than paper and pencils, tools that are readily available to all students.

As students explore the local geographic outdoors laboratory, they come to appreciate and take pride in some of its aspects. Some might express negative feelings or concerns and want to seek ways to improve a place, such as cleaning an empty lot or making a playground for neighborhood children. Such efforts recognize that the study of geography involves values. Conflicts among the values of people and groups become obvious, as does the need to consider civic ideals and practices for the common good.

Geography is integral to abilities to locate, move, or control natural resources in ways that contribute to the quality of our lives. So governments and private businesses collect, organize, and publish much of the geographic information that citizens may need as they make both personal and group decisions. Maps are available from governments at various levels. The most detailed and up-to-date maps in the United States are produced by the U.S. Geological Service, the U.S. Census Bureau, and the U.S. Weather Service.

State offices responsible for natural resources, highways, and tourism frequently produce maps. The U.S. Department of Commerce and the U.S. Department of State organize and distribute information about various parts of the country and world. These are valuable resources for teaching, as are the employees of such offices. As guest speakers, these employees help to teach the proper use of maps and photographs as well as explain how they use geographic knowledge and skills in their work. Workers in the private sector, such as builders, architects, travel agents, and real estate agents, also encounter geographic problems and use geographic knowledge.

Using Technology

An Important Contributor to Learning Geography

Inexpensive cameras and the ease with which digital pictures and streaming video can be placed on class websites or sent through email enable teachers and students to share their homes, community, and field work with parents and students in other schools and nations. Students get to share what they consider important with other students and directly ask questions rather than receive a secondhand interpretation or outdated information from hard-to-obtain printed sources. Students can also conduct joint research studies with students in other locations and in other nations. GLOBE is a website that assists in locating current data, provides tools for processing the data, and has projects with options for sharing data between schools and with scientists. GLOBE works with agencies of the U.S. government to coordinate these projects.

The proliferation of websites makes information more readily available to youths and teachers. News agencies' websites provide coverage of events all over the world 24 hours a day. Agencies and departments of governments, especially the U.S. government, provide easy access to data in the form of graphs and maps about weather, landforms, agricultural products, population demographics, and population distributions. The Census Bureau, U.S. Geological Survey, and the National Parks Service are just a few of the many U.S. government agencies whose websites provide data to teachers and students and lessons that assist in the use of their data. Organizations such as the United Nations, CARE, Oxfam, the Red Cross/Red Crescent, the National Wildlife Federation, and the National Geographic Society provide data and often have teacher and student pages to teach about their work. There is no hard data that indicates how effective using technology is in increasing geographic knowledge and understanding among American students. However, NAEP data indicates that students who report having such experiences in their classes do score higher on the NAEP Geography Test.

Developing Geographic Concepts, Generalizations, and Skills

Geographic knowledge is found throughout the elementary curriculum in both social studies and science. When emphasis is placed on the people of a region, their culture is part of the study of geography. Geographic concepts, generalizations, and skills are all present in the classroom, on school grounds, and in larger regions such as local communities, states, nations, and throughout the entire world.

Even though geography is so much a part of our lives, it was often largely neglected in the school curriculum. Textbooks tended to reduce it to long lists of detailed facts and occasional map skills lessons. Geography often has been represented in textbooks by only the place and location themes. Textbooks have emphasized the place theme by discussing concepts such as mountain, river, plain, continent, equator, suburb, community, transportation, and lake. The location theme has been emphasized through map exercises in which students locate places and symbols and identify directions on maps of classrooms and familiar locations such as shopping centers. A major problem of emphasizing only the location and place themes is that studying geography becomes a chore of trying to commit isolated lists of information to memory. The most important reason for learning geography is its usefulness, which is made clear through the relationship and movement themes (Pigozzi, 1990). It is only through learning all the themes that students combine a sufficient number of appropriate concepts to form generalizations in geography. The generalizations that students make are tested by examining how concepts that are developed with information from one region can be applied to another region.

All five themes of geography, or all six elements of the standards, are stressed in every grade level. Very young children begin learning geography through personal interactions with their own local environments and regions. They observe their surroundings in the school and on short walks or field trips, and they record their information in simple stories, drawings, and maps. As they increase their information and skills through direct experiences, they begin to use more indirect sources of information to learn about places they cannot visit in person. Gradually, they use pictures, maps, films, charts, and written descriptions to begin to compare places. By identifying similarities and differences, they refine and elaborate their concept definitions. They form conclusions and make generalizations about various relationships among geographic phenomena. In so doing, they develop an elaborate mental map of their world. The mental map helps them to understand events and problems they encounter.

Two chief characteristics of a powerful geography curriculum are (1) the organization of geographic information and (2) the involvement of students in minds-on learning through inquiry and the use of inquiry skills. Information is presented in connected ways so that students are assisted in organizing this information. Authentic activities show the usefulness of geography by involving students in hands-on geographic investigations that are not limited to watching television programs, looking at Internet sites, or reading a book. When information is presented in a connected way, students are better able to construct meaning from it. Research by Brophy and Alleman (2000) reveals that whereas primary grades students can identify details in pictures and give reasons why different people might construct houses from different materials, they need help from teachers. Such help includes involvement in lessons with activities and prompting questions that enable them to construct geographic generalizations, such as that people build houses from the natural materials found in their physical environments.

NCSS

Standards

It is no coincidence that the NCSS standards use important superordinate concepts, such as People, Places, and Environment, as labels for their themes. Among the important superordinate concepts suggested by geographers in the five themes and six elements of geography are location, place, movement, physical systems, human systems, environment, and society. Questions using these superordinate concepts and relationships among them make excellent focus questions for units and curriculum for the entire year. Following is an example of a classroom scene showing how geography is meaningfully learned. As you read it, consider and examine the following:

- How students' prior knowledge is activated
- How concepts are developed
- How students use and expand on their new knowledge

This young man's interest in places is enhanced by studying the atlas and sharing information with family and friends.

A CLASSROOM SCENE

Mr. Boyd noticed that his state's third-grade social studies guidelines included teaching landforms and bodies of water and emphasized reading maps of the United States and the world. He knew that, although their community was located on the coast of one of the Great Lakes, most of his students had not seen a river. He planned and implemented a short unit using river as the superordinate concept to organize it.

He began by asking the students to think about Lake Michigan. Then he asked, "What can you tell me about the lake?" After students responded, Mr. Boyd refocused the discussion by asking, "Using the information we have been talking about, tell me how a river is similar to or different from Lake Michigan?" After some discussion, the children agreed that rivers are long and skinny and that you can see across them and build bridges to cross over them. Valesca said, "I saw pictures on television where a river had flooded over fields and into a town." Some students agreed with Shenana, who said, "Rivers are dirty and not pretty and blue like our lake." Mr. Boyd told the students, "In the next few days, we will be learning more about rivers and thinking about how the people who live along them might use rivers and what they think about rivers."

The next day, Mr. Boyd began the lesson development by putting students into small groups and giving them each a black-and-white outline map of the United States. He told the students, "Take a close look at the lakes and rivers on your maps. Then, make lists of differences and similarities." After a few minutes, he told them, "Look carefully at these colored maps and the pictures your group has. Add to your lists of similarities and differences."

The students' lists lengthened. They noted that cities were located along both the rivers and the lakes and that both rivers and lakes were shown in blue on the colored map. Some rivers seemed to be way down among rocks, whereas others were even with the land as the lakes were. All the groups decided that rivers that were even with the land did not look like they were moving.

Students grouped their pictures of rivers into those they thought might cause flood damage and those they did not think would be likely to cause flood damage. The students responded by placing those that were in rocky areas in the "not likely to flood" category. Mr. Boyd showed the students pictures of rivers that had flooded. The students concluded that their classifications were correct.

Mr. Boyd explained, "Rivers that flood have flood plains. This is an area that is expected to be covered with water in an average flood." He asked, "Where would you find the flood plain of a river?" Then Mr. Boyd told the students that one frequently flooded river in the United States today is the Mississippi River and that another great river that floods is the Nile River. After locating the Nile River on a world map, he showed the students pictures taken along the banks of the Nile River and asked them, "Where is the Nile River's flood plain?" The students quickly identified the flood plain. They explained why it was planted in crops, whereas the villages were on higher ground just beyond the flood plain.

Next, the students examined a map of the Nile River as the teacher called their attention to the various colors on the map along the course of the river. Students consulted the legend and discovered that elevation was shown by various colors. Part of the Nile River was at very high elevations shown in brown, whereas green indicated the lowest areas. The teacher then asked, "Where along the Nile do you think the pictures of the flood plain were taken?" The students decided that these pictures had been taken in green areas in Egypt.

The teacher then asked, "Where does the Nile River begin and where does it end?" The students found one end of the Nile but had trouble with the other end. So Mr. Boyd suggested starting at the end they found and tracing the Nile with a finger until they could not trace it any further. A controversy developed when they reached the city of Khartoum, Sudan, over whether this was the source of the Nile. The students said that each of the two rivers beyond the city, the Blue Nile and the White Nile, had *Nile* in its name and each came from high areas. Mr. Boyd took the opportunity to define the *junction* as a place where rivers flow together, forming a bigger river. He then asked the students to decide whether there would be a Nile River if there were no Blue Nile or White Nile. After some discussion, the students decided the source of the Nile River was the source of both the Blue Nile and the White Nile. At this point, Mr. Boyd provided the names for the regions in which rivers begin and end, telling the students that the region where rivers begin is called a *source* and where it ends (by flowing into the ocean or a lake) is called the *mouth*.

The students had noted that the Nile River divided at its mouth into branches with a triangular shape. Mr. Boyd told them the region in which a river divides is a low swampy area called a *delta*. He explained that *delta* is a letter in the Greek alphabet that looks like a triangle, and he drew this letter on the board.

Then Mr. Boyd refocused the students' attention on the junction of the Blue Nile and White Nile at the city of Khartoum. He wrote the word *tributary* on the board and said that the Blue Nile and White Nile were tributaries of the Nile. He asked, "Knowing they are called tributaries, what do you think the word *tributary* means?" After some discussion and looking at maps, the students developed a class definition: "A tributary of a river is a smaller river that comes in and helps to make the big river."

Next, Mr. Boyd challenged the groups to look at the map of the United States and trace the course of the Mississippi River. They had to identify the states where its source and mouth are located and count and record the names of its tributaries. They also decided whether the Mississippi and its tributaries had deltas. After about 10 minutes, the groups shared their findings. Mr. Boyd ended the session by asking for a volunteer to trace the course of the Mississippi River on a map of the United States he put on the overhead projector. He called on several students to name one of the parts of a river that they had learned about that day. Then they briefly summarized the lesson activities and the major concepts they had investigated related to the superordinate concept of river. These were similarities and differences between rivers and lakes, what rivers look like, which rivers might flood, flood plain, river junction, river source and mouth, delta, and tributary.

On the next day, the small groups traced the courses of the Ohio, Colorado, St. Lawrence, Columbia, Snake, Missouri, Arkansas, and Rio Grande rivers. They predicted, with evidence, which rivers might have large flood plains and where flooding might frequently present problems. Then they described inconveniences flooding might cause people living along the rivers. They made predictions on why cities located beside rivers. Then they were asked to decide whether the locations of these cities were in places where flooding might cause lots of problems. To conclude, Mr. Boyd said, "Both lakes and rivers are bodies of water." He asked the students to review the lists they had made previously of ways in which rivers and lakes are similar and different. Mr. Boyd asked one group of students to list on the board the concepts discussed. Another group added one concept that had been overlooked.

As an evaluation, Mr. Boyd asked students to write about the following in their journals:

Imagine that you and your family are moving to a new community. Which type of community would you want to live in: one located on a lake or one located along a river? Explain the reasons for your choice. ■

When planning, the teacher keeps in mind students' experiences, skills, interests, and developmental level, as well as the themes and standards of geography. Because a single theme or standard can be studied through the use of a variety of content, teachers decide what important content students should learn. A first-grade teacher in an area where flash flood watches are common might include a discussion of such watches and how to respond to them. A teacher in Iowa might teach about flooding resulting from snowmelt or rainstorms, whereas a teacher in Oklahoma would be more likely to examine tornadoes rather than floods.

As students develop their skills, they study more complex regions and issues. The complexity of the region makes it more difficult to understand—not its distance from the student as the expanding environments curriculum assumes. There is a difference between actual geographical distance and psychological distance. What is understood is directly related to common experience and empathy. Therefore, it is possible for young students to be interested in, and learn, accurate and legitimate information about areas of the world that are geographically at long distances from them. With young students, it is particularly important to carry out the following tasks:

- Provide enough accurate information
- Have students look for similarities
- Link similarities with familiar concepts
- Help students imagine how people in other places feel or respond to an issue

TIME FOR REFLECTION | *What Do You Think?*

1. How did Mr. Boyd help students construct the concepts of *delta* and *tributary*?
2. What inquiry skills did the students use to gather information?
3. Why do you think Mr. Boyd asked the students to make the decision about living by a lake or a river as the evaluation activity?
4. What criteria would you include on a rubric for this writing assignment? How many examples would you expect in the highest quality responses?

For example, young students who learn about children in northern Nigeria celebrating a holiday with special foods and dancing should be led to see that the children in other cultures get treats on special occasions just as they do.

Whether a teacher thinks of geography as elaborated in the NCSS standards, the five themes, or *Geography for Life*, geography education should stress content, concepts, skills, and generalizations across the range of the standards. Many people limit geography to map skills. Geographers use map skills far more frequently than the average citizen or people in other careers, but they also use many other skills commonly practiced by all social scientists. Table 12.2 identifies these

TABLE 12.2
Student Behaviors Illustrating the Five Geographic Skills

Ask Geographic Questions	Acquire Geographic Information	Organize Geographic Information	Analyze Geographic Information	Answer Geographic Questions
Ask questions: Where is it? Why is it there? What is important about its location?	Locate, gather, and process information from a variety of maps and primary and secondary sources.	Prepare maps to display data; construct graphs and tables displaying geographic information.	Use maps to observe and interpret geographic relationships.	Prepare oral and written reports that use maps and graphics.
How is one location related to other locations of people, places, and environments?	Make and record observations of physical and human characteristics of places.	Construct graphs, tables, and diagrams displaying geographic information.	Use tables and graphs to observe and interpret trends and relationships.	Acquire geographic information; draw conclusions; and make generalizations.
Distinguish between geographic and nongeographic questions.	Make and record direct field observations.	Summarize data integrating various types of materials.	Use text, photos, documents to observe and interpret trends and relationships.	Apply generalizations to solve problems and make decisions.
Plan ways to gather information.	Locate information in computer databases.	Make models of physical and cultural landscapes.	Make inferences and draw conclusions.	Assess validity of generalizations and revise if needed.
Formulate geographic hypotheses and plan their testing.			Interpret geographic information.	Apply theories from geography to help explain events and places.

Source: Adapted from *Geography for Life: National Geography Standards*, by the Geography Education Standards Project, 1994, Washington, D.C.: National Geographic Research and Exploration.

inquiry skill categories and illustrates them with specific examples of classroom activities. Because geographically literate citizens need to become familiar with these skills, they also must be an integral part of the curriculum.

TIME FOR REFLECTION | ## What Do You Think?

Thoughtful decision making by citizens is essential in a democracy and therefore is an important social studies goal.

1. Which of the five geographic skills helps to define a problem?

2. Which of the five geographic skills helps to process information to be able to understand and interpret relationships and evaluate their importance?

3. Which of the five geographic skills is used when students evaluate or revise their conclusions and generalizations?

Research Findings on Geographic Education

Reviews of research on geographic learning by the teams of Rice and Cobb (1978) and Buggey and Kracht (1985) concluded that elementary students have the ability to learn geographic skills. Carefully planned instruction in the elementary and middle grades is effective in increasing both geographic knowledge and skills. In 1985, the president of the National Geographic Society (NGS), Gilbert Grosvenor, noted that U.S. students taking part in an international test on geography had done poorly compared to students in other nations. With the support of geographers, the NGS launched Geographic Awareness Week in 1987 to promote the study of geography at all grade levels and raised money to fund the teaching of geography.

The results of the 2001 National Assessment of Educational Progress (NAEP) test in geography showed improvements in achievement over the 1994 NAEP tests (National Center for Education Statistics, 1995, 1996, 2002). Most likely, the higher levels of performance were related to efforts to increase the study of geography in the United States. Examining results of the 2001 NAEP assessment in geography provides information on what students knew and could do. This can help in making decisions for teaching geography to elementary and middle school students. Students scoring at the higher percentiles were more able to work with a range of geographic tools, create maps based on tabular or narrative data, grasp processes and relationships, bring outside knowledge to bear on answering questions, and analyze data.

The results from the NAEP geography test make it clear that some groups of students perform better than others. Some individuals in lower-performing groups do well on geographic tasks. But group differences indicate that schools in certain regions or serving specific demographic groups need extra efforts and assistance.

Making a Literature Connection

Books Provide Different Cultural Perspectives

Most people experience a geographer's curiosity when encountering spectacular sites prompting thoughts about origins and creations. Today, the appearance of the surface of the earth is explained as the result of erosions, depositions, and plate tectonics. Today's scientific culture makes explanations in relationships and theories from science. But people in other cultures have explanations concerning important events and places that have been passed on for hundreds and thousands of years. *Legends of Landforms: Native American Lore and the Geology of the Land* (1999) by Carole G. Vogel presents pictures and contrasting explanations about the creation of many striking landforms from across the United States. A teacher can use this book to stimulate discussions that encourage learning about and appreciation for the cultures and values of the people that formulated the explanations. Speculative questions prompt students to think and examine the nature of cultures, including their own. For example, why would Native Americans want to provide explanations for certain locations? How might nomadic or settled people use stories to help them teach their youths? Who are the actors in the stories and why do you think they were given their specific roles in the story? What do you think is the role stories play in the culture of the Native Americans? When reading various explanations, help students examine their personal reactions to the stories. Ask students, "Which explanations do you like the best? What did you learn from each explanation? Which explanation do you understand the best? Which do you think you will remember the longest? How has each explanation helped you to remember the characteristic of the site? Which explanation would you tell another person who looked at this site in wonder? What does the scientific explanation tell you about our society and its culture? Does the scientific explanation make sense to you or does it make you want to ask more questions? What do the Native American explanations tell you about their views of the world?"

In *Story of the Nile: A Journey Through Time Along the World's Longest River* by Anne Millard, the reader visits unique sites along the 4,350-mile course of the Nile River, from its sources to its mouth. Examining the details and relationships between the many individual drawings of daily life and the important events in the large pictures enables students to construct their understanding of the importance of the Nile River to the economic life of people and empires throughout time and in various environments.

All places are not alike. This generalization accounts for some of the differences in the way people act, the things they like or dislike, and potentially the things they can do or how they might differ when performing specific tasks. Young students are curious about the lives of others their age, but they tend to think that all young people live the same way they do. Reading *Recess at 20 Below* by Cindy Lou Aillaud can help young students restructure their thinking about the impact of location on human activities. Begin by asking students to share why they like to go outside for recess and what might be a good reason for canceling going outside. Examine the location of Alaska, the Arctic Circle, and the Alaska Highway. Ask students for predictions on how living in the far north of the United States might impact school activities and recess. The book uses words and photographs to describe the characteristics of the Arctic climate, illustrating special winter gear and clothing, the fun, and the dangers of going outside for recess when the temperature is 20 degrees below zero and daylight is short. Cold weather is not a reason for canceling recess, because the students adapt to the cold through actions of their own. However, some elements of their environment cannot be controlled, and sometimes schools must cancel the fun of recess outside. The book ends by implying that when the long hours of darkness, snow, and cold are gone, students look forward to long days and riding a bike in bright sunlight after 10 P.M. *Recess at 20 Below* can be used to not only address the single lesson of people in places, but it also is an opening for additional geography lessons about earth–sun relationships throughout the year and how they impact the lives of all people on the earth, including those living in the tropics, the middle latitudes, and the upper latitudes.

Many primary-grade teachers read trade books with settings in other nations to their classes. By linking these books to the study of the geography through a focus on the locations and a comparison of environments, students are encouraged to use skills in reading and listening comprehension while gaining greater understanding of the world in which they live. Such a procedure also models strategies for using books as learning resources for use in making small-group and individual reports.

Personal activities, such as doing geography projects, and home activities, such as discussing geography topics with a parent, also resulted in differences in performance on the test. Differences associated with demographic variables (as defined by the U.S. Bureau of the Census) include the following:

- White and Asian students had higher scores than African American, Native American, and Hispanic students.
- The higher the level of parents' education, the better the performance of students.
- Overall, male students performed better than female students.
- Students attending nonpublic schools performed at higher levels than did those in public schools.
- Students who were not eligible for free or reduced-price school lunch scored higher than students who were eligible for the program.

Differences in home and school behaviors include:

- Eighth-grade students who reported studying countries and cultures scored higher than those who said that they never or hardly ever studied countries or cultures.
- Those fourth- and eighth-graders using the Internet scored higher than those in classes whose teachers did not have students use the Internet.

TIME FOR REFLECTION   **What Do You Think?**

1. How do you think the results of national tests are best used to improve student learning?
2. Using the previous information, identify the out-of-school variables that seem to impact student learning of geography that hint at what parents or communities can do to provide geographic learning experiences to the students.

Research on Map and Globe Skills

Students in grades K–5 understand space differently from the geographer. Even older students may have difficulty understanding the world as it is spatially presented on maps. This means that the types of maps used in grades K–5 should differ from those used by older students. The types of information included on a young student's map or observed by a student on an adult's map will probably be interpreted differently by the student and the adult.

Spatial understanding begins developing in the first few months of life. Early development of spatial understanding is influenced greatly by the egocentric nature of the learner. At first, children view things from their own perspective. Later, they come to recognize multiple perspectives from various locations. Last, they are able to use an abstract reference system to locate items in relationship to one another. The three types of space children come to understand are topological, projective, and Euclidian. Teachers who recognize the characteristics of these types of space help children organize and gain information from maps in developmentally appropriate ways throughout the elementary and middle school years. These teachers also recognize opportunities to integrate the learning of geography and mathematics.

In helping students to develop spatial relationships, teachers integrate geography and mathematics. The three types of spatial knowledge include topographical space, projective space, and Euclidian space. Topographical space deals with shapes, separation, closure, continuity, and order. It is one of the first elements of a map and geometry that students learn. Projective space deals with the fact that items are seen differently depending on the direction from which they are viewed. Preschoolers have experiences with looking straight at objects or from a high point such as a hill. The above-vertical perspective, or "bird's-eye" view, is associated with reading maps and aerial photographs. Euclidian space, the most abstract type of spatial knowledge, focuses on where things are in relation to one another or to coordinates, such as the prime meridian, the equator, and the poles. Elementary and middle school students can best be taught about spatial relations with experiences using concrete materials and images that can be viewed and manipulated. Students make extensive use of spatial skills when reading or creating maps. *Google Earth* is a new tool that allows students and teachers to manipulate spatial perspectives and change data at locations from symbols to pictures at will.

 ## Helping Students Learn and Use Map and Globe Skills

Maps and globes are important tools for geographers because they provide a convenient way to organize information by location. By their very nature, maps and globes are quite different from the real world. They are not a picture of the world but an interpretation by the mapmaker, containing only information the mapmaker considers important to include for the purpose of the map. The title tells the reader the major idea shown on the map.

One of the best ways to learn the definition of a map is to make your own maps. When doing so, students encounter and solve the same kinds of problems professional mapmakers encounter. Mapping the classroom, schoolyard, or route taken on a neighborhood walk are excellent experiences for primary-grade students. Such mapping might begin with making three-dimensional models in a sandbox or on the floor with blocks or plastic models. Older students might map their individual routes to school or their rooms at home. Students of all ages should examine a variety of maps so that they can compare and judge their own ideas against those of professionals.

Globes and maps today are durable, less expensive than in the past, and made from a variety of materials. Schools can afford to have several globes so that small groups of students can explore and mark on a globe rather than gaze at it from afar. It is possible to buy inexpensive maps and atlases so that each student or pair of students has an atlas or placemat-like map. Such instructional materials provide students with opportunities for more active involvement in learning. Publishers of atlases and globes produce research-based materials that are appropriate for students at the various elementary grade levels. Many schools are painting maps on their parking lots and playgrounds, providing children with the opportunity to stand and walk across maps representing large areas such as the United States or the entire world.

If you put a globe where young children can get to it easily, they explore it and ask questions. This model of the earth is studied before maps are studied for several reasons. First, a globe is more concrete and realistic than a map. Second, students are familiar with models because of their toys. Third, although maps may include more specific information, all the information that is required in reading a map is available on a globe, and the globe presents the information more accurately. Shapes, locations, relative locations, distances, and sizes are all more accurately represented on a globe than on a map. Because of their two-dimensional nature, maps represent distances and shapes inaccurately. Such inaccurate information can lead to misconceptions.

Misconceptions not only limit a student's ability to answer geographical questions correctly, but often remain even after instruction tries to correct them. For instance, many U.S. children believe that Alaska and Hawaii are islands located just a little west of California and Mexico or in the Gulf of Mexico. It is

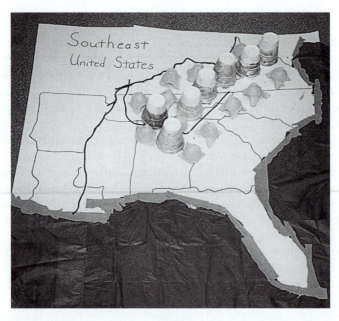

Making three-dimensional maps helps students see new ways to illustrate elevation.

the visual impact of the items on a map that helps to create and maintain such misconceptions. By using a globe first, children are more likely to learn geography correctly. After becoming familiar with a globe, students are likely to question the inaccuracies on maps. Through their own questions or those of adults, students can discover why the mapmaker must make choices about what to include on a map and how to show it as accurately as possible.

Reading a map or globe requires knowledge of the five superordinate concepts of (1) shape or pattern, (2) symbols, (3) directions, (4) distance, and (5) grid systems, as well as the conventions of their presentations on globes and maps. Like most concepts, each of these can be understood at a variety of levels. It is possible to use these concepts correctly on a map without thoroughly understanding them, just as it is possible to drive a car without understanding how its various systems work. However, understanding accounts for greater success in using globes and maps and for knowing when maps are most effectively used. Each of these concepts needs to be introduced, practiced, and refined by the student throughout the elementary and middle school grades.

The first maps students use should depict familiar locations with only few symbols. Map and globe publishers such as Nystrom, Cram, and Rand McNally produce instructional programs and sets of globes, atlases, and maps for children starting in kindergarten. By the sixth grade, most textbook series include various types of maps usually found in commercial atlases. Because students at this age are just beginning to develop their understanding of the abstract Euclidian space on which these maps are based and just starting to read locations, distances, and elevations with exact measurements, teachers need to encourage lots of discussion and involve students in a wide range of activities with these maps.

Geographers divide map and globe work into three sets of skills: mapmaking, map reading, and map interpretation. The interpretation of data on maps is related to the complexity of the question being asked and to the data students can read and understand from the map. Young students can make inferences and interpret data from a map based on their mastery of spatial concepts. Older students begin making inferences from data shown on two or more maps. Modern technology combining GPS and charted information such as census or production data can be combined to organize information more quickly. This allows teachers and students to answer questions that range from the local to the international.

Shapes and Patterns

Continents, nations, states, and distributions covering areas such as a state or nation or the jet stream have distinct shapes or form patterns with a shape. The ability to recognize these patterns and describe them is key to the study of geography. The first step is to be able to recognize the patterns, and the second step is to be able to identify the pattern when it is seen again. Because maps are made in different scales, patterns based on shape must be recognized when shown in various sizes. How people determine what they see as a shape of a portion of the earth is a matter of personal choice. Few patterns repeat, and few have simple shapes, such as a square. Teachers encourage students to describe places by the shape they have when a dark line is drawn around the edges. This is helpful in learning the locations of states and nations. Very young children are capable of doing this task. Many children enter kindergarten knowing various states because they played with a puzzle of the United States. Teachers encourage children to make associations to help them learn patterns. They allow children to make their own shape description rather than tell them what shape someone else has decided. Teachers might need to encourage children to do so with examples, by suggesting, for instance, that Indiana is shaped like a stocking or that Antarctica is shaped like a toy rubber duck.

Symbols

The idea that something represents another thing is learned in the preoperational stage, around ages 5 to 7. Globes and maps are symbols and they make extensive use of other symbols. Two types of geographic symbols are point symbols and area symbols. *Point symbols* identify those locations that cover small areas appearing as a point on a globe or small-scale map. The simplest point symbols to identify are called pictorial symbols because they appear similar to a picture of the real item. Maps for the beginner use a few pictorial or semipictorial symbols. As mapmakers include more information on a map, they simplify the symbols by making them more abstract. *Area symbols* show features that cover acres or square miles of land. Shading and colors are used for area symbols, and they are very abstract. Few universal symbols appear on maps and globes, partly because so many features might appear on a map. Even the meaning of a color may change from map to map.

Maps have legends or keys to specify the meaning of symbols used on them. Students must learn the habit of using the legend to be able to read maps. Symbol is one of the first superordinate concepts a student must come to understand to be able to read a map. Complex maps layer area and point symbols on top of one another.

Direction

Directions are learned first in relationship to oneself and then to other objects. Pointing to things and describing where they are in relation to yourself, to other people, and to objects is the beginning of directional activities. Students in the early primary grades can do this. Knowing left from right is important for learning map directions because east is 90 degrees right of north and west is 90 degrees left of north. Take students outside to locate north. As they face north, have them locate east and west by raising their arms. Tell students that south is to their backs when they are facing north. Then label the walls in the classroom with correct directions. Using the cardinal directions, have students locate items outside and inside in relation to people and objects. For example, a student might say, "Mary sits two desks north of Joan."

When maps and globes are introduced, they should be oriented toward the north. Because maps show what is on the earth's surface, they are best placed on a desk or on the floor parallel to the surface of the earth. Students are encouraged to trace directions with their fingers over the surface of the globe or map. In the early primary grades, many children quickly memorize directions on a map and give correct answers to questions, but this does not mean that they understand direction or can use directions, except on a map.

Distance

Correctly measuring distance on a map with the use of a scale is complex. It requires accurate use of mathematics knowledge, an understanding of proportionality, and the ability to divide quickly. Students must be able to conserve distance, recognizing paths of the same length. Distance is not only a straight-line measure; it is also important in determining the correct size and shape of an area. Therefore, exact measures of distances are best attempted in the intermediate grades. However, relative distances are used in the primary grades. Near, farther away, and farthest can be introduced to young children, as can measures such as small, big, and very big.

Because the globe provides a more accurate presentation of distances in all directions than does a world map, measurement of world distances and comparison of the sizes of regions is done first on the globe. Pieces of string are stretched over a globe between two points to get a relative measure of distances between places. The pieces of string are cut and compared to see whether they are the same length and, if not, which is longer. As the string is laid on the globe, the student observes the direction of the path one would travel to get between the points. When actual measurements in miles are needed, a string or thin strip of paper is placed between the two points and cut at the end point. The string or strip is moved to the scale where the distance is read by placing the paper or string next to the scale. Pieces of string or dental floss are used when measuring curved rivers or roads because their flexibility yields more accurate measures. Measuring with string the equator, meridians (longitude), and lines of latitude on a globe and comparing the lengths greatly assist students' meaningful learning of these concepts, along with the concepts of sphere and hemisphere. Without an accurate understanding of these concepts, students can't master the grid system of latitude and longitude.

Grid Systems

The grid system is the most complex of the concepts. It is a way of finding locations. A vertical line and a horizontal line intersect at only one place. To use a grid system, the student needs to understand this principle and practice locating intersections. Grid systems are taught first by using a system similar to that used in locating a seat in an auditorium with numbers for the rows and letters for the seats. When transferred to a map, letters are placed along the horizontal axis and numbers along the vertical axis. Road maps of individual states usually include this type of grid system as do city maps. Such a grid system gives an approximate location. The grid system can also be introduced with a dot-to-dot game.

For additional practice, letters can be placed in the boxes formed by a grid and secret messages can be decoded for practice. For example, Kathleen's mailbox address might be C5. Some teachers have labeled the tiles on the floor or ceiling of the classroom and encouraged students to practice locating people and things in the classroom. So the aquarium might be at E8. Exact locations are given by the system of latitude and longitude. Each line of latitude and longitude is identified by a number and a direction. Because every line of latitude or longitude is not on a map, locating places by latitude and longitude requires the ability to sequence numbers in relationship to the rectangular grid. It also requires the ability to estimate and understand directions on a map.

The trade book *Flat Stanley* is an inspiration for a widely used lesson to learn about states. In the lesson, students send a letter to someone in another community, asking the person to take Stanley to a place where they do something then send back a postcard or picture and letter telling about the activity and place. The letter indicates that the information will be put on the class bulletin board. A similar activity occurs when the teacher gives a person who is going to travel a stuffed animal with an attached card containing the school's address and two requests: (1) send a postcard from your destination and (2) pass the animal on to another person who will send the class a postcard, then passes the animal on to someone else until a specific date when the last person is asked to send the animal back to the school. Activities such as these help students become familiar with locations and places and can prompt additional learning when the teacher follows up as the cards are received. Quick follow-up activities include: measuring the distance the postcard traveled on the globe, visiting a website about the location or state named on the card, or reading a trade book about the location. The postcards might be used with older students to begin a more in-depth study of selected states or nations, and communicating information related to several more of the six elements in the geography standards.

Remote Sensing and Digital Maps in the Teaching of Geography

Most people use maps so that they can travel to a chosen location. In the United States, virtually all locations with a street or road address are included in one or more digital databases. Similarly, satellite images and historical data also are available. This has enormous potential for teachers and students who access these types of data via the Internet through a number of government websites and free commercial services such as Google. You can examine your own community or any place in the country by using Google Map.

Google Map can help students answer the most fundamental question: "What is a map?" Call up your city by entering its name into Google Map, click on the map, and then click on the satellite view. Ask students, "What differences do you notice?" This broadly worded question starts an inquiry lesson on important ideas about maps that can yield not only the definition of a map and aerial photographs, but that can also help students to construct conclusions and generalizations about the multiple uses of maps and data from remote-sensing sources. Click the hybrid button to combine the two images, creating an image that is even more helpful. Students and the public see such hybrid images on news broadcasts and in newspapers and magazines, especially when the reports are about weather or disasters.

Most students reveal great interest in exploring their own community, and more so when using these digital tools. Throughout the year, elementary teachers can use Google Map when preparing for walks or field trips. Students can help to plan the route and use the map to record or review their observations during or after a field trip. Students should be asked to verbalize the field trip's route by naming landmarks, intersections, and roads. Cardinal directions should be used to indicate turns and locations from one site to another. When debriefing field trips, teachers can use the map, aerial photograph, or hybrid to help review the trip. Students can explain the observations made at various locations on the trip, including short descriptions of what made a place special, along with information about what they learned at the final destination. Such verbalization helps in building and reinforcing social studies vocabulary. Students might also compare their routes with the directions for car drivers printed by a computer service.

View the whole world by downloading Google Earth, a globe that displays information about places around the world. Interested in adding your own information or information from other databases? For a small fee, you can use a version that allows you to add your own data files to the program and see them displayed. Geographers and businesses make extensive use of remote-sensing data, as do many agencies of the U.S. government, such as the National Ocean and Atmospheric Agency, the U.S. Department of Defense, the Census Bureau, the National Aeronautical and Space Administration, and the U.S. Geological Survey. Each of these agencies offers multiple maps on their websites.

Google Earth can help students understand current events because it displays data across large areas. Students can examine relationships between and among similar locations that are great distances from each other or explore patterns that transcend national boundaries, such as hurricanes and earthquakes.

With the use of GIS software, geographers and students are able to create displays or overlays of data on physical or political maps of the earth to answer geographic questions. All maps are made of layers of information. Learning to read and interpret maps and aerial photographs requires the ability to mentally isolate a layer of information, question the data's spatial relationships, and combine that layer of data with other data on another layer of the same map. Choosing sites to locate new places, targeting markets, planning a transportation network to distribute products and services, or respond to an emergency are problems that geographers answer in providing services to individuals, businesses, and governments. In doing so, geographers can help save multiple billions of dollars and time. Important information about people cannot be easily viewed by observing the landscape, but when it is digitized as, for example, the U.S. Census is, that information can be put onto maps and the spatial patterns examined. Atlases prepared for use in the upper elementary and middle schools include maps that illustrate distributions of such topics as population density and agricultural production for nations and continents, but such maps do not provide the most recent information and cannot show local differences or a general pattern. Digitized maps are therefore more likely to be both more detailed and up to date than maps in a printed atlas.

The third-, fourth-, and eighth-grade curricula of most states focus on communities and the state. Resources such as Google Map and Globe can be used to develop lessons and units to locate spatial relationships between economic resources and businesses or to examine the cultural and governmental services in their community and state. This assists students in understanding problems in their community and adds interest and realistic meaning to the study. Although such activities do not require Internet resources, the costs and scarcity of teacher time to locate, travel to, and obtain needed resources make it difficult for most teachers to do so.

Local and national media often display images gathered from satellites orbiting the earth. Digitized data on the Internet provide students and teachers with the opportunity for greater interactions, knowledge, and understanding of their world.

Numbers: The Amount or Quantity on Maps, in Atlases, and in Textbooks

Geographers cannot escape encountering and interpreting the meaning of large numbers. Population, gross national product (GNP), dollar value of crops, acres, miles, and elevations are just some of the geographic facts that are given as numbers. Comprehending the amount in a large number is quite difficult. Therefore, many people ignore the numbers and end up with great misconceptions about important characteristics of places. Geographers use charts and graphics, particularly histograms, pie graphs, bar graphs, and population pyramids. These graphics provide a visual image of numbers and sometimes compare parts to a whole or make symbols in graduated size to allow for more meaningful comparisons. Sometimes graphs are placed directly on a map to focus on location as well as amount. One of the most common graphs combines a line graph of the average monthly temperature and vertical bars indicating the average monthly precipitation at a location. These graphs are often shown on or with the maps that illustrate the types of climates and illustrate the variations in the temperature and precipitation during the year. Population pyramids are often printed with population distribution maps to indicate the age and sex distribution of the people. Other maps use area symbols to illustrate the amount of rainfall, length of growing season, and values of products produced in a state, nation, or continent. Typically, the colors on such maps use shades to indicate amounts, the lightest shades indicating small amounts and the darker shades the greater amounts.

Atlases prepared for grade 6 are filled with graphic representations of facts and concepts. Maps for primary grades may categorize cities by size, such as small city, medium size city, and big city. Atlases for primary grades also use aerial photographs of the region with the map to help students gain the vertical perspective from which the map is drawn and to illustrate how symbols represent real objects. Teachers use such maps to encourage students to make predictions and conclusions that can be tested. Students who examine the variety of maps in an atlas should be asked, "Why is the information important in explaining the characteristics of a place?"

Activities using maps and graphs to learn about places include the following:

1. Students explain why a map shows only some of the objects visible in the aerial photograph and tell why they think the mapmaker omitted several specific items. Students make their own map of a familiar location, explaining what they included and identifying several things they decided not to include.
2. Students explain why there are so many more young people or old people in some nations than in other nations. They predict the special needs that a region has because there are many old people or young people living there.
3. Using climate maps and graphs, students decide what clothing they would take if they were to travel today to a specified place. Then they decide what would be the best time for a tourist to visit that location.
4. Students pretend that they are starting a fudge factory that will need tons of various ingredients each month. Using the product maps, students decide from where in the United States they will purchase their products and where in the world they will find the chocolate and nuts needed for the fudge.
5. Using land use maps, students identify places that are home to cowboys and cowgirls, miners, and those who catch fish or raise fish.
6. Examine the climate and product maps and predict where people might have a harvest festival and the month in which they would be celebrating the harvest.
7. Students write reports on a nation explaining how the people earn their living and how they spend their recreational time using only resources available in an atlas. Students are challenged to provide at least six specific facts to support their ideas.

Reading and Maps

Reading words on a map is different from reading words in a story. Except for the title of the map, words on a map are labels for specific locations. Reading left to right is not always the standard convention on a map. Sometimes the words are written at odd angles and spread out to cover the areas being designated. Many words are spread out much wider than the normal reading eye span. This is particularly true on large wall maps and road maps. The style of print is also used as a symbol. More important features have fonts that make them more visible. The same font is used to designate all features or regions of the same type. The teacher needs to assist students in discovering the unique ways in which words appear on a map.

Creating a complex mental map of the world is a worthy goal for each student. Building this knowledge of locations is accomplished throughout the years.

The following instructional activities help students to construct map and globe concepts and practice using the skills needed to read and interpret information from maps and globes:

1. Students arrange a box of crayons, a pencil, a book, and a pair of scissors on their desktop and draw a map illustrating the arrangement. They remove the items and give them and their map to a partner. The partner uses the map to place the items on a desktop. The mapmaker checks to see whether the arrangement is correct.
2. Young students make Me Maps. A tracing is made around the body. Then the children use previously agreed-on symbols to draw their eyes, nose, heart, knees, ears, mouth, waist, and elbows in the correct locations.
3. Students follow a map to go on treasure hunts within the school or on the school grounds. The map may be drawn by the teacher or other students.
4. Students map their classroom or school grounds, selecting information to include and symbols to use. Then they place each symbol in the appropriate location. Actual measurement of distance is used if the students have such skills.
5. Each student makes a map illustrating the route taken to school. Older students also write directions to their homes, which classmates follow to mark a route on a city or county map.
6. When taking a field trip, students use a city or state map to plan the routes to and from their destinations. Older students measure the distance involved and try to locate the shortest route. They also write out a set of directions for the trip.
7. Students plan trips to visit famous cities and landmarks. They measure or compute the distance traveled.
8. Students use a world atlas and an outline map of the world to locate a natural resource or crop and draw its transportation route to the factory or marketplace where it is used or sold.
9. Students use a gazetteer to find the latitude and longitude of cities they hear about or read about in the news so they can locate them on the map.
10. Using the equator, prime meridian, and other selected meridians and parallels as a guide to location, students make freehand drawings of regions of the world, placing them in the correct locations relative to each other.

Meaningful learning of map and globe skills is linked to real-life experiences and to the use of maps. Too often, textbooks and teachers have taught map and globe skills as something unrelated to gathering and interpreting information. Using latitude and longitude is one of those skills often taught without consideration of its use beyond answering a question correctly on a standardized test. The learning cycle on page 402 teaches how to perform the skill of locating things exactly. It helps students consider the practical use of latitude and longitude.

LEARNING CYCLE LESSON PLAN   Latitude and Longitude

Grade Level: Middle school

NCSS
Standard III

NCSS Standards: People, Places, and Environments

National Geography Standards: The World in Spatial Terms

Exploratory Introduction

Materials: Two cards with information about specific cities or vacation sites for each small group of three students (each group should have different cities or sites on its cards); maps and atlases

Objectives	Procedures	Assessments
1. Given questions about places to eat lunch at a mall, students explain the difference between seeking a specific site or a general site.	1. Present the following puzzle to the students: "Imagine that you have been shopping at a large mall and that you are hungry and start to think about eating a hamburger. Your friend suggests going to the food court because she wants a slice of pizza. Will going to the food court meet your want for a hamburger? How would you respond to your friends' suggestion?" Ask, "Why do you think the owners of malls include food courts in their plans? Would a restaurant owner want to locate in a mall with a food court? Is there any time when you would definitely not want to go to the food court for lunch?" 2. Ask, "Can you think of other examples of times when specific locations rather than general locations are the place to go?"	1. Students respond with logical suggestions and explain that, when a person has specific wants, he or she must go to a place that can fill those specific wants.
2. Given a city or vacation site to visit, students try to describe its location to classmates so they can locate the mystery place.	3. Divide the class into groups of three and provide them with information about a particular city or vacation site. Without naming the place, students try to develop clues that enable their classmates to determine the site. 4. Have the class establish a number of tries the class has for each clue. Then have groups present their clues and have students try to determine the locations. 5. Ask, "Why was it hard to determine these locations?"	2. Students make an effort to describe city locations and try to guess the cities described. Students say that they need a way to find the exact location of a place. 3. Students try to locate the places in the clues. 4. Students discuss the difficulties of finding

the places from the clues concluding that it is difficult to locate places in other cities or nations. They decide that there should be a way to do this.

Lesson Development

Materials: A globe for each small group with locations marked with three differently colored stickers; a diagram for each small group showing the world divided into northern and southern halves by the equator and into eastern and western halves by the prime meridian; a grid for each student labeled with the equator and prime meridian and with other lines of latitude and longitude unlabeled; a world map for each group; a task sheet for each group with a set of 10 cities in the world whose location the group identifies; an atlas for each group; plain paper and one pair of scissors per group

Objectives $\longrightarrow$	Procedures $\longrightarrow$	Assessments
1. Given a globe on which are placed three colored stickers, students attempt to describe all three locations in words.	1. Tell students we have learned about using a grid system to find an approximate location on a city or state map. Ask, "Can someone explain how we found the location of the city, vacation site, or store on the map?" 2. Ask each group's materials manager to get a globe. Tell them you have put three stickers, each a different color, on the globe. Tell them, as a group, to try to figure out a way of describing the locations of each of the colored dots. Tell them they will have 5 minutes to try to figure out how to describe in words the locations of the three dots. (Note: A blue dot is located on the equator, a green dot is at the intersection of the prime meridian and a line of south latitude on the globe, and a red dot is between a line of north latitude and a line of longitude either east or west and near but not on a city that is labeled on the globe.) 3. After 5 minutes, ask, "How are you doing? Can you describe the locations of the dots? Which was the easiest to describe? Why?"	1. Students respond that, after finding the area, they searched the area for the specific symbol and name on the map. 2. Students use the lines and perhaps the names of the lines (numbers) to identify the locations.

continued

4. Tell students, "When we used the grid system, each square had an address or two names, what did we use to label the coordinates of the grid?"

5. Ask, "Did you find any labels on the line on the globe that we could use to name the lines?" Help the students find the numbers and the words *equator* and *prime meridian*. Students should already know that the equator divides the world into a northern and a southern half while the prime meridian divides the world into an eastern and western half. Review this and give each small group a diagram to reinforce the point. Ask review questions.

2. Given a latitude and longitude grid and several locations, students practice locating places with latitude and longitude, circling the correct locations on the grid.

6. Provide students with a grid with a labeled equator and prime meridian. Help students label the other lines of latitude, also called *parallels*, in intervals of 20 degrees. Label each line with the number and an appropriate direction. Repeat similarly for longitude lines (also called *meridians*). Stress that each line has an address. Make an analogy to each line having a first and last name just as each student does. (The first name is a number and the last, a direction— north, south, east, or west.)

7. Have students note that any combination of a vertical line and a horizontal line can cross, or intersect, at only one place.

8. Provide practice locating several intersections and circling them (0 and 20E, 30N and 40W, 50S and 0). After a few additional practice numbers, have the groups give you the locations of the green dot on the globe.
   Follow these steps to locate places by latitude and longitude:
   a. Begin at the equator and locate the correct latitude N or S.
   b. Mark that line.
   c. Begin at the prime meridian and locate the correct longitude E or W.
   d. Mark the line.
   e. Find the place where the two lines meet.

3. Students reply that letters and numbers were used.

4. Students look carefully at the globe finding the words *prime meridian* and *equator* and numbers.

5. Students follow directions, accurately labeling lines and circling locations on the grid.

9. Present the question: "Is the line for 15N on the grid? 28E? We must estimate the locations of these lines." Stress always starting by looking from the zero line (*equator* when locating the N or S parallel and the *prime meridian* when locating the E or W meridian).

10. Practice several of these as a class. Have the groups locate the red sticker on their globe. Ask, "Why aren't all the lines drawn on the globe?"

3. Students identify lines of latitude and longitude as a *parallel* and a *meridian*.

11. Review the terms *latitude* and *longitude* and *meridian* and *parallel*. Ask, "Which line is also called a parallel? What directions will be the last name for a line of latitude?"

6. Students identify meridians and parallels accurately.

12. Provide each group with a world map and have them locate the parallels and meridians. Ask, "Are the lines labeled the same on the map and the globe?"

13. Provide the groups with a set of 10 world cities to locate on a globe and a world map. Each pair locates all cities on both the globe and on a world map. Include the coordinates of your own city or that of a nearby city that can be found in the gazetteer in the back of an atlas (5N, 0W; 41N, 72W; 48N, 2E; 34S, 139E; 37N, 122W; 33S, 70W; 14N, 90W; 52N, 40E; 1S, 36E; 35N, 139E).

4. Working in groups, students correctly locate cities on the globe and on the world map.

7. Students work cooperatively in pairs correctly locating the cities on the globe and world map.

14. Ask, "Was it easier to locate places using latitude and longitude on the globe or on a world map? Why? Why do you think a map of a city uses a number and letter grid and not latitude and longitude grid?" (Answer: The city is too small an area for different numbers to be read and estimated.) "What are the latitude and longitude coordinates of our own city?"

15. Ask, "If you hear or read the name of a place and want to know its latitude and longitude so you can locate it on a map, where can you find the latitude and longitude?" Show students how to use the gazetteer in the atlas.

16. Provide for additional practice by using volcanoes, mountain peaks, or other cities. Have students use the gazetteer to find locations and write them on slips of paper to use in additional practice. (Such practice activities can be in a learning center also

continued

for those who need additional practice or are curious and want to do more.) Students can draw slips of paper at random from a box and locate the sites on a globe or map.

17. *Closure:* Ask students to describe and demonstrate how to identify the location of a city using its latitude and longitude.

8. Use a checklist to record if students find the locations correctly.

Expansion

Materials: Large world map, grids and list of hurricane plots downloaded from NOAA Internet site (given below) for each small group

Objectives →	Procedures →	Assessments
1. Students direct another student in how to locate a new place on a transparency or wall map of the world.	1. Ask review questions on vocabulary associated with latitude and longitude. Present a new place. Students give verbal directions for locating the place to another student, who tries to find it. Ask, "What is the first step John must do to locate the city? What next?" and so on.	1. Students give accurate answers and directions and check for correctness.
	2. Explain, "There are some occupations in which people use latitude and longitude because exact locations are very important to the success of their jobs." Ask, "Can you think of one such job?"	
2. Given an activity of plotting the course of a hurricane, students identify the need for weather services to track and predict hurricanes and other dangerous storms to help many people.	3. Explain the assignment: "You will need to plot a number of locations using latitude and longitude. Because the places to plot are close together, I am giving you a large map of a small region of the world."	
	4. Provide student groups with a new grid for tracking hurricanes (obtain from the NOAA). Using a world map, locate this area and show students that this map has symbols for individual degrees of latitude and longitude. When you estimate locations on the larger grid, you should notice that the lines are 1 degree apart. Ask, "New Orleans is located 30N and how many degrees west?" and "What is the latitude and longitude for Key West?"	
	5. Provide small groups of students with lists of places to plot. When they complete the plots they should connect the locations.	2. Students complete assignment correctly.

continued

6. Ask, "What do you think is plotted on the map? Who would want to know this information?" Consult Internet sites on weather for information on hurricane paths to plot for the lesson.

7. Ask, "When does the average citizen need to use latitude and longitude to help them locate places? People in which occupations might need to use latitude and longitude?" Ask students to describe the regions in the United States where hurricanes often strike.

3. Students conclude that shippers, tourists, farmers, and people living in potential hurricane paths would be interested.

8. *Lesson Summary:* Ask students to describe the activities in this learning cycle.

TIME FOR REFLECTION | What Do You Think?

Read the learning cycle on pages 402–407 and then reflect on it as you answer the following questions:

1. Think about when you were taught how to use latitude and longitude. How well did you accomplish the task? What did you find most difficult? Did you find anything relatively easy about latitude and longitude?

2. How would you describe your memory of the study of latitude and longitude?

3. Have you used latitude and longitude or seen references to them outside a school setting? If so, how were they used?

4. In a skill lesson, the teacher must provide practice in the use of the skill. Where in the learning cycle are practice opportunities suggested or provided?

5. What are some of the strategies the teacher uses to help students succeed in using latitude and longitude?

6. How does the teacher assess students' progress toward learning these skills?

7. Skill lessons are best taught as part of larger units that focus on geography content. What would be an appropriate content focus for a unit that incorporates the teaching of latitude and longitude?

8. During the remainder of the school year, when might a teacher provide some additional practice using latitude and longitude?

EXPANSION

"What is the name of the mystery nation?" is an activity with clear objectives that can be used in a number of different situations and requires critical thinking to solve the puzzle. It might, for example, be the Exploratory Introduction for a unit, a way to encourage learning current events, practice in developing a mental map of the world, or practice in learning to use an atlas and reading the various types of maps.

Five clues are prepared. Four are general and reflect the relative location and general physical and cultural characteristics. These four clues are given first. When the students have narrowed the possible choices to several nations, a fifth specific clue is provided that points the search to the exact nation. Teachers initially begin giving the clues, but after time, students or groups of students might write the clues. Try identifying these mystery nations:

Mystery Nation 1	Mystery Nation 2
1. The equator passes through this nation.	1. This nation is north of the equator and east of the prime meridian.
2. Many of this nation's mountains are volcanoes.	2. Through this nations flows one of the world's largest rivers.
3. This nation has thousands of islands including some of the world's largest.	3. This nation exports large amounts of petroleum.
4. This nation is an exporter of petroleum.	4. This nation is both multiethnic and multilingual.
5. This nation is one of the world's leading producers of tin and rubber.	5. This nation has the largest population of all of the nations in Africa.

Select a region of your state, nation, or of the world and six pictures. Three of the pictures should describe the physical characteristics of the region you selected. The other three pictures should describe the cultural characteristics of the region. Ask students to suggest one way in which the people in the region have used the physical environment to earn a living and one way in which they have been limited or challenged by the physical environment in performing normal daily activities. Ask the students to write several sentences telling how people change their environment for good or bad. Analyze the responses for the most and least common ideas identified. Are there common characteristics among the students who made any of the responses? Which pictures appear to have the greatest impact on the lesson's outcome? Did students fail to use the information in one or more of the pictures? How do you explain this lack of use? What changes in your selection of pictures can you make to help more students identify the characteristics of the region?

Summary

In recent years, more emphasis has been placed on teaching geography. Geographers recommend that map skills be taught beginning in the primary grades through the use of developmentally appropriate activities. They see drawing maps, reading maps, and making inferences and comparisons as techniques that help students develop thinking skills and knowledge of geography (Winston, 1984). The emphasis in the elementary grades on learning map skills has given the impression that location is geography. Approaches such as the introduction of a completely meaningful definition of geography, teacher training in geography, and preparation of standards and themes to be taught at all grade levels help students learn the importance of geography in everyday life. Students learn that through their own actions they decide how the physical and cultural resources of the earth can and should be used.

Recommended Websites to Visit

National Geographic My Wonderful World, educational website for teachers and students.
http://www.mywonderfulworld.org/
See GIS in Action allows students to answer questions using map overlays.
http://www.mywonderfulworld.org/toolsforadventure/games/gis.html
Learn all about Japan and the activities of Japanese children today at a website prepared for youth by the Ministry of Foreign Affairs of Japan available in many languages.
http://web-japan.org/kidsweb/explore/index.html
The National Geographic Society
www.nationalgeographic.com/
World Heritage sites are recognized internationally as places of great importance or beauty. A separate page is available for each of the 750-plus sites throughout the world
http://whc.unesco.org/nwhc/pages/sites/main.htm
A list of the world's 100 most endangered historic, artistic, and architectural heritage sites identified by the Word Monuments Fund, a private, nonprofit organization dedicated to preserving cultural heritage
http://wmf.org/a/watchlist.htm
The U.N. Environmental Programme World Conservation Monitoring Center monitors endangered species and environmental concerns and reports
www.unep-wcmc.org/
World gazetteer with statistics on nations and cities
www.gazetteer.de/
GLOBE is a worldwide hands-on, primary and secondary school-based education and science program with a free site for creating maps and graphs
www.globe.gov/globe_flash.html

The Environmental Protection Agency's portal to environmental issues and U.S. laws that affect the environment
www.epa.gov/highschool/
Hurricane Tracking Chart for the learning cycle
www.nhc.noaa.gov/gifs/track_chart.gif
Data on classic hurricanes for the learning cycle
http://weather.unisys.com/hurricane/index.html
National Atlas of the United States provides maps for downloading and information and a program to make your own maps
http://nationalatlas.gov/
U.S. Census Data
www.census.gov
Mapping Our World:
www.oxfam.org.uk/coolplanet/mappingourworld/mapping_our_world/l/home/index.htm
Connecting the Dots. 300 Million Reasons and Mysteries of the U.S. Pyramid: Three Lessons Using Geography:
www.populationeducation.org/staticpages/300million.jsp

13

How Do I Assist Students in Making Economic Decisions?

Madison, age five, asked her aunt, "How do you make money?"

Her aunt replied, "You get a job."

"No!" replied Madison, "How do you make money?"

Thinking she needed to provide an explanation with an example, her aunt replied, "When you have a job, you work for someone and that person pays you money for your work. That is how you make your money."

"No, how do you make *the* money?" asked Madison.

"Oh, you cannot make money, only the government can," replied her aunt.

"Well, how do they make the money?" asked Madison.

"It's a little bit complicated, but I know of a good video, and when we go home, I will take you to it on the Internet, and you can see how they make coins," said her aunt.

Madison reminded her aunt when they got home, and together they viewed *The Money Factory* with great interest, and Madison's 7-year-old brother also joined in the viewing.

1. If kindergarteners have interest in and seek knowledge about money, why do you think older students and adults lack the knowledge and ability to handle money well?
2. What, if anything, can elementary teachers do to help young students to understand money and its many uses and roles?

Chapter Overview

Economics is encountered every day by everyone. Chances are you cannot remember the first time you were told that you could not have everything you wanted; you were most likely too young to remember this incident. But you have probably heard it over and over again since then. This frequent statement is the basis of economics. The solutions people use to get around the reality that they cannot have everything they want is the study of economics. Economics is not limited to money, although this is the way most people view it. As a student you are likely to have a shortage of money, but you probably feel the shortage of other things as well, and perhaps even more. This chapter examines ways to help students understand the role of economics in their lives, their families' lives, their community, their nation, and the world. It also focuses on the process of making rational personal and group decisions about the use of the world's scarce resources. This chapter will give you ideas on how to approach teaching the NCSS standards Production, Distribution, and Consumption; Global Connections; and Science, Technology, and Society. All very much a part of citizenship needs in the 21st century.

NCSS

Standards VII, VIII, IX

Chapter Objectives

1. Clarify the differences between microeconomics and macroeconomics.
2. List the key concepts for the study of economics and of economic decision making.
3. Explain why scarcity and decision making (cost–benefit analysis) are considered the key to economic understanding.
4. Explain how to use the economic decision-making model with students.
5. Explain how economics influences the lives of all people, communities, and nations.
6. Explain how interdependence impacts all nations bringing them benefits from economic cooperation and how a lack of cooperation works against some nations and for others.
7. Identify ways in which economic education is integrated into the social studies curriculum through such topics as career education, geography, history, community studies, and consumer education.
8. Reflect on the ways in which economic education is authentically taught and assessed.
9. Locate potential resources for teaching economics to students.
10. Examine ways computers and technology can help teach economics.

DEVELOPMENT

 ## Economic Literacy

The National Assessment of Educational Progress (NAEP) does not have a test for economic literacy. However, in 1999 the National Association of Economic Educators (NAEE) tested adults and high school seniors on fundamental economic concepts. Half the adults and two-thirds of the high school students failed, showing a lack of understanding of fundamental concepts such as money, inflation, and scarcity. Of the high school students, 35 percent admitted that they did not know what effect an increase in interest rates would mean. Just over half (54 percent) of the adults and fewer than a quarter of the high school students knew that a budget deficit occurs when the federal government's expenditures exceed its revenues for the year.

Many people in the United States have high rates of personal bankruptcies, large credit card debts, and no savings or investments. At the same time, others are reaping financial rewards for investing. Such findings are spurring a national campaign for economic literacy and the promotion of more economically sound behaviors in which social studies education has a major role.

Defining Economics

Several different groups of professionals deal with the economy, and they do not always agree on the goals for economic education. One group is composed of academics, who look at economics as a rational study of concepts, their relationships, and the decision-making process. Another group is composed of members of the business and labor communities who see economics as related to the importance of work, jobs, and production. A third group is the consumer advocates, who seek to help individuals learn how to get accurate information to make personal decisions. A fourth group is the conservationists, who seek to save natural and human resources from exploitation by what they claim is ignorance at best and a conspiracy at worst. The emphasis found in the economics curriculum of a particular state or school district tends to reflect the views of the economic education leaders in the community or state. All the groups agree that teaching economics is important, but what to teach and emphasize and how to instruct students are sources of much controversy.

Economics is based on the realization that people want more than the resources available can provide. *Scarcity* is the term economists use to indicate the imbalance of wants and resources. For some, the goal and definition of economic education centers on the analysis of how goods and services get produced and distributed. Others stress examining ways to make the system of production and distribution work better through the formation of governmental and business policies. Perhaps the most inclusive definition is the one that defines economics as both a set of knowledge and a way of thinking (Banaszak, 1987).

Economics as a body of knowledge includes the concepts, generalizations, and theories developed by people to try to extend their scarce natural, human, and capital resources so that they can fulfill their basic needs and as many of their wants as possible. An important key to the accomplishment of this goal is a systematic way of thinking and making economic decisions. Economic educators today recommend an in-depth understanding of scarcity and the influence of incentives and strategic thinking about how scarcity applies to personal examples and to the more complex and morally difficult issues in the international realm. Scarce resources have at least two valuable uses, and people are willing to make a sacrifice to obtain them. Entirely giving up one use is the sacrifice because the other use is considered more important or satisfying.

The National Council on Economic Education (NCEE) promotes and evaluates economic education. In recent years, changes in curriculum and technology and the collapse of command economies such as that of the Soviet Union have resulted in new efforts by the NCEE. Five trends in economics education have been identified by Nelson (1997):

1. Economics and citizenship education
2. Economic education in Russia and Eastern Europe
3. Consideration of the importance of the global economy
4. Content standards
5. Use of computer technology in economic education

Economists have made a continuous and long-term commitment to increasing and improving the teaching of economics, producing guides, standards, and instructional materials. They also evaluate their successes and failures. The human resources of economists, businesses, and educators are organized through state councils and centers of economic education. These organizations raise funds for selected projects that produce many high-quality supplemental instructional materials for grades K–12, applying the results of research into how economics is learned. Today, NCEE and its state councils and economic education centers continue to work to fulfill new needs in economic education, providing training for both prospective and veteran teachers.

National Social Studies Standards Related to Economics

National social studies Standard VII: Production, Distribution, and Consumption focuses on the study of economics. All the remaining standards include consideration of aspects of economics. Standard IX: Global Connections and Standard VIII: Science, Technology, and Society are closely related to the current changes in the economy of the world. Throughout history, and across the world, people have had wants that exceeded their limited resources. People have tried, through decisions by rulers, inventors, and workers, to answer four fundamental questions:

1. What should be produced?
2. How should the production be organized?
3. How will goods and services be distributed?
4. What are the most effective allocations for their land, labor, capital, and management?

Science and technology often help to extend and make more productive some scarce resources, but these efforts come with opportunity costs. Siegfried Ramler

Standard VIII

(1991) describes the degree to which countries are interconnected. He says that connections occur in virtually every aspect of life: through world markets for the consumer goods we purchase and in such important elements of productive resources as labor, technology, and energy. The realities of global interdependence mean the impact of decisions go far beyond the local area in which they are made. In making economic decisions today, other cultures and nations must be considered. Social studies helps citizens to construct and build the knowledge needed to consider global influences on economic decisions. Taylor (1997) urges U.S. elementary schools to teach the impact of global issues on individuals and societies by giving attention to the interdependence of nations and the role of the United States in a global economy.

Voluntary National Standards in Economics

In examining the various published social studies standards, economists were concerned that some errors were present in the use of economic content. They also were concerned that students were being asked to do abstract thinking or perform tasks for which they were unprepared. They assembled a team of economists, teachers, and economic educators who wrote a set of standards stating 20 economic generalizations that can be addressed by K–12 students. Sample assessments were provided to guide teachers in determining whether they were being successful in teaching students about economics and economic decision making. Table 13.1 presents these standards in the left column and the assessment suggestion in the right column. By downloading the National Voluntary Standards (1997) from the NCEE website, you can receive a rationale and benchmarks for grades 4, 8, and 12, with suggestions for activities on how to measure students' progress in their understanding of each standard.

National Standards in Personal Finance

Although not a part of the movement that produced national standards, a rising concern over the lack of understanding personal finance prompted the development of *The National Standards in Personal Finance* prepared in 2002 by the Jump Start Coalition for Personal Financial Literacy. These standards identify four topics—Income, Money Management, Spending and Credit, and Savings and Investing—that all people need to understand to personally handle their finances. Table 13.2 further defines these topics. Both the NCSS and the NCEE endorse these standards. Others endorsing these standards include the national associations for elementary and secondary principals and the Council of Chief State School Officers.

TABLE 13.1
Voluntary National Standards for Economics and Assessments

Standard	Assessment
1. Productive resources are limited. Therefore, people cannot have all the goods and services they want. They must choose some things and give up others.	Students identify what they gain and what they give up when they make a choice.
2. Effective decision making requires comparing the additional costs of alternatives with the additional benefits. Most choices involve doing a little more or a little less of something: few choices are all-or-nothing decisions.	Students make effective decisions as consumers, producers, savers, investors, and citizens.
3. Different methods can be used to allocate goods and services. People acting individually or collectively through government choose which methods to use to allocate different goods and services.	Students evaluate different methods of allocating goods and services by comparing the benefits and costs of each method.
4. People respond predictably to positive and negative incentives.	Students identify incentives that affect people's behavior and explain how incentives affect their own behavior.
5. Voluntary exchange occurs only when all participating parties expect to gain. This is true for trade among individuals or organizations within a nation, and usually among individuals or organizations in different nations.	Students negotiate exchanges and identify the gains to themselves and others. They compare the benefits and cost of policies that alter trade barriers between nations such as tariffs and quotas.
6. When individuals, regions, and nations specialize in what they can produce at the lowest cost and then trade with others, both production and consumption increase.	Students explain how they can benefit themselves and others by developing special skills and strengths.
7. Markets exist when buyers and sellers interact. This interaction determines market prices and allocates scarce goods and services.	Students identify markets in which they have participated as a buyer and seller and describe how the interaction of all buyers and sellers influences prices. Also, they predict how prices change when a shortage or surplus of the product is available.
8. Prices send signals and provide incentives to buyers and sellers. When supply or demand changes, market prices adjust, affecting incentives.	Students predict how prices change when the number of buyers or sellers in a market changes, and explain how the incentives facing individual buyers and sellers are affected.
9. Competitions among sellers lowers costs and prices, and encourages producers to produce more of what consumers are willing and able to buy. Competition among buyers increases prices and allocates goods and services to those people who are willing and able to pay the most for them.	Students explain how changes in the level of competition in different markets can affect them.

TABLE 13.1 (Continued)
National Standards in Personal Finance

Standard	Assessment
10. Institutions evolve in market economies to help individuals and groups accomplish their goals. Banks, labor unions, corporations, legal systems, and not-for-profit organizations are examples of important institutions. A different kind of institution, clearly defined and enforced property rights, is essential to a market economy.	Students describe the roles of various economic institutions.
11. Money makes it easier to trade, borrow, save, invest, and compare the values of goods and services.	Students explain how their lives would be more difficult in a world with no money, or in a world where money sharply lost its value.
12. Interest rates, adjusted for inflation, rise and fall to balance the amount saved with the amount borrowed. This affects the allocation of scarce resources between present and future uses.	Students explain situations in which they pay or receive interest, and explain how they would react to changes in interest rates if they were making or receiving interest payments.
13. Income for most people is determined by the market value of the productive resources they sell. What workers earn depends, primarily, on the market values of what they produce and how productive they are.	Students predict future earnings based on their current plans for education, training, and career options.
14. Entrepreneurs are people who take the risks of organizing productive resources to make goods and services. Profit is an important incentive that leads entrepreneurs to accept the risks of business failure.	Students identify the risks, returns, and other characteristics of entrepreneurship that bear on its attractiveness as a career.
15. Investment in factories, machinery, new technology, and in health, education, and training of people, can raise future standards of living.	Students predict the consequences of investment decisions made by individuals, business, and governments.
16. There is an economic role for government in a market economy whenever the benefits of a government policy outweigh costs. Governments often provide for national defense, address environmental concerns, define and protect property rights, and attempt to make markets more competitive. Most government policies also redistribute income.	Students identify and evaluate the benefits and costs of alternative public policies, and assess who enjoys the benefits and who bears the costs.
17. Costs of government policies sometimes exceed benefits. This may occur because of incentives facing voters, government officials, and government employees; because of actions by special interest groups that can impose costs on the general public; or because social goals other than economic efficiency are pursued.	Students identify some public policies that may cost more than the benefits they generate and assess who enjoys the benefits and who bears the costs. They explain why the policies exist.

continued

TABLE 13.1 (Continued)

Voluntary National Standards for Economics and Assessments

Standard	Assessment
18. A nation's overall income levels, employment, and prices are determined by the interaction of spending and production decisions made by all households, firms, government agencies, and others in the economy.	Students interpret media reports about current economic conditions and explain how these conditions can influence decisions made by consumers, producers, and government policy makers.
19. Unemployment imposes costs on individuals and nations. Unexpected inflation imposes costs on many people and benefits others because it arbitrarily redistributes purchasing power. Inflation can reduce the rate of growth of national living standards because individuals and organizations use resources to protect themselves against uncertain future prices.	Students make informed decisions by anticipating the consequences of inflation and unemployment.
20. Federal government budgetary policy and the Federal Reserve System's monetary policy influence the overall levels of employment, output, and prices.	Students anticipate the impact of federal government and the Federal Reserve System's macroeconomic policy decisions on themselves and others.

Source: National Council for Economic Education (1997). *The Voluntary National Content Standards in Economics.* New York: National Council on Economic Education.

TABLE 13.2

National Standards in Personal Finance

A. Income

  1. Identify sources of income.

  2. Analyze how career choice, education, skills, and economic conditions affect income.

  3. Explain how taxes, government transfer payments, and employee benefits relate to disposable income.

B. Money Management

  1. Explain how limited personal financial resources affect the choices people make.

  2. Identify the opportunity cost of financial decisions.

  3. Discuss the importance of taking responsibility for personal financial decisions.

  4. Apply a decision-making process to personal financial choices.

  5. Explain how inflation affects spending and investing decisions.

  6. Describe how insurance and other risk-management strategies protect against financial loss.

  7. Design a plan for earning, spending, saving, and investing.

  8. Explain how to use money-management tools available from financial institutions.

TABLE 13.2 (Continued)
National Standards in Personal Finance

C. Spending and Credit

1. Compare the benefits and costs of spending decisions.
2. Evaluate information about products and services.
3. Compare the advantages and disadvantages of different payment methods.
4. Analyze the benefits and costs of consumer credit.
5. Compare sources of consumer credit.
6. Explain factors that affect creditworthiness and the purpose of credit records.
7. Identify ways to avoid or correct credit problems.
8. Describe the rights and responsibilities of buyers and sellers under consumer protection laws.

D. Savings and Investing

1. Explain the relationship between saving and investing.
2. Describe reasons for saving and reasons for investing.
3. Compare the risk, return, and liquidity of investment alternatives.
4. Describe how to buy and sell investments.
5. Explain how different factors affect the rate of return of investments.
6. Evaluate sources of investment information.
7. Explain how agencies that regulate financial markets protect investors.

 # Economic Concepts and Values

The National Council for Economic Education (NCEE) identified concepts providing the basis for both understanding economics and making reasoned economic decisions. Table 13.3 identifies these concepts and groups them to illustrate important relationships. The concepts within each of the major divisions vary in their degree of difficulty. The concepts shown in Table 13.3 are not comprehensive but are the broader organizing, superordinate concepts. A comprehensive list of concepts labeled Content Keywords is found on the Voluntary National Standards Contents: Index of Standards, at the NCEE link at the Companion Website. These are classified under each of the 20 standards for which they would most logically be taught.

The fundamental concepts are necessary to understand all the aspects and specializations within economics. As you are teaching units, you might want to include only a small part of economics or perhaps a portion of one of the longer standards. You will always include at least some of the fundamental concepts. You are probably familiar with their meanings even if you do not call them by the term

TIME FOR REFLECTION | What Do You Think?

1. Look at Table 13.1. Read the 20 standards in the left column. On the left side of your answer sheet, indicate the numbers of those you clearly recognize. On the right side, write the numbers of those you need help to understand.

2. Read through the assessments in Table 13.1. List the numbers of those that you think could be done by students who by the end of grade 4 have received appropriate content instruction. List those that you think could be done by students in grade 8 who have received appropriate content instruction.

3. Read the assessment tasks. List the numbers of the standards where the assessment focuses mainly on individual and family tasks. What are two curriculum implications of this focus?

TABLE 13.3
Basic Concepts and Social Goals

Fundamental Economic Concepts

1. Scarcity
2. Opportunity costs and tradeoffs
3. Productivity
4. Economic systems
5. Economic institutions and incentives
6. Exchange, money, and interdependence

Microeconomics Concepts

7. Markets and prices
8. Supply and demand
9. Competition and market structure
10. Income and distribution
11. Market failures
12. The role of government

Macroeconomics Concepts

13. Gross national products
14. Aggregate supply and aggregate demand
15. Unemployment
16. Inflation and deflation
17. Monetary policy
18. Fiscal policy

International Economic Concepts

19. Absolute and comparative advantages and barriers to trade
20. Exchange rates and the balance of payments
21. International aspects of growth and stability

Measurement Concepts and Methods

1. Tables, charts, and graphs
2. Rations and percentages
3. Percentage changes
4. Index numbers
5. Real vs. nominal values
6. Averages and distributions around the average

Broad Social Goals

1. Economic freedom
2. Economic efficiency
3. Economic equity
4. Economic security
5. Full employment
6. Price stability
7. Economic growth
8. Other goals

Source: A Framework for Teaching the Basic Concepts and Scope and Sequences K–12 by P. Saunders and J. V. Gillard, 1995, p. 10, New York: National Council on Economic Education.

economists use. The University of Omaha Center for Economic Education has a matrix of economic concepts recommending the grade levels (K–6) for appropriately teaching or reviewing each concept.

Microeconomic Concepts

Microeconomics is the study of individual households, companies, and markets and of how resources and prices combine to distribute wealth and products. The price of a new car at a given time helps to determine the demand for such cars. High prices may stimulate employers to work overtime to produce more cars. When lots of products are unsold, businesses hold sales to stimulate purchases. The government regulates those businesses that have a monopoly to protect consumers and ensure an adequate supply of the products produced by these businesses. Local, state, and national governments often own and operate some special facilities, such as power production, sanitation, roads, and transportation. Governments regulate taxes to help distribute fairly the burden of paying for public services in the society. Interest rates, the number of sales, and wages also distribute money throughout the economy because of the circular flow of wealth through various markets.

Macroeconomic Concepts

Macroeconomics is the study of the big picture, of the economy as a whole. Macroeconomics provides an overview of the conditions in an entire nation. The gross national product (GNP) is the value of all the goods and services produced in a nation for a year. This information enables us to compare production among nations. When the GNP is divided by the population of a nation, the outcome is the GNP per capita. This figure gives an idea of how much money is generated per person. If the GNP per capita is $50, the lives of the people are quite different from the lives of people living in a nation with a GNP per capita of $3,000.

At various times during the year, different levels of employment occur because of temporary changes in the business rate. For example, before the Christmas holiday, more people in the United States are working, and the unemployment rate is lower because consumers are doing extra purchasing. After Christmas, the unemployment rate is higher because fewer people are buying products and services.

Inflation occurs when the prices of all goods and services tend to go up in the nation during the same time period. Monetary policy is the regulation of the amount of money in the nation's economy. This is regulated in the United States by the actions of the Federal Reserve System in raising and lowering interest rates. Lower interest rates offer incentives to people to expand and borrow, whereas higher interest rates tend to encourage investment and savings. Fiscal policy is the combined actions of the national government in taxing, spending, and borrowing, which adds to, or subtracts from, the supply of money available to business and individuals. Fiscal and monetary policies are means by which the economy is managed. Some people and some economists do not think that the national

Making a Literature Connection

Trade Books Illustrating Economic Concepts

Using the story in a trade book to examine the impact of economics on the lives and actions of people, families, groups, and nations is a recognized procedure for examining economic ideas and theories (VanFossen, 2003). In examining economic principles within another cultural setting, students are helped to internalize concepts and to test the explanatory power of their economic generalizations. *The Ox-cart Man* (1979) written by Donald Hall and illustrated by Barbara Cooney describes a year in the life of a subsistent farmer family living in Appalachia during the 1800s. In contrast to today's family, each member of the farm family contributes to the production of what is needed by using his or her special abilities to produce something that the father takes to sell in the city at the end of his 10-day walk leading the ox and the cart he built to hold the products of their labors. The father sells all of the products, including the ox and cart. Then he purchases capital resources at the store and two pounds of wintergreen peppermint candy. He walks home, and the family continues their daily and evening activities. But what will the family purchase with the money that father brought home? And from whom will they purchase goods and services? Why do you think the farmer made such a long trip to the city rather that trading the family's products with people in the nearby villages? What would your students want their parent to bring back to them from a trip to a place very different from where they live?

Beatrice's Goat (2001), written by Page McBrier and illustrated by Lori Lahstoeter, is a true story of a subsistent farm family today. Beatrice, age 9, lives with her mother and five younger siblings in the small village of Kisinga in western Uganda. Beatrice helps her mother tend their crops and chickens, wash the clothes, and take care of her brothers and sisters. The book describes the changes that the gift of a goat from the Heifer Project International brings to Beatrice and her family. Beatrice did not understand how being the recipient of the goat would help her to attend school. In fact, she thought the family would never be able to save the necessary money for books and a uniform. At first, having a goat meant more work. Fetching water and elephant grass and selling their extra milk became additional daily tasks for Beatrice. The book provides details that allow students to answer such questions as these: What are some differences in the lives of children in the developing world from the lives of American children? Why did mama consider school for Beatrice more important than other needs of the family? How are schools in Uganda different from our school? Looking at the pictures, what other things do you think the family really needs? How can we find out how many boys and girls get to attend school in Uganda or other developing nations? How does the labor of the young people contribute to the common good of their families and community?

The illustrations in both of these books show landscapes that illustrate productive resources and the typical possessions of the subsistent farmers in the stories. Students should examine these illustrations to help gain a more accurate understanding of the quality of life for the subsistent farmers in different times and places.

To learn more about the work of the Heifer Project International and how your students might send another family in the developing world the gift of an animal and instructions in how to care for it, visit the project's website, which is listed at the end of this chapter.

A Basket of Bangles: How A Business Begins (2002) written by Ginger Howard and illustrated by Cheryl Kirk Noll relates how poor women in Bangladesh learn to work and support each other as they start businesses. Follow their progress as they learn how to get loans from a bank for their investment capital and the role of hard work, cooperation, and persistence in improving their daily lives and being able to pay back their loans with interest. This book prompts many questions about the lives of women throughout the world and the role of private enterprise, such as the following: Why would a bank want to loan money to women with no formal education? How do the women help each other throughout the year? Why doesn't the bank lend their money to men? Why, after paying off their loans, would the women want to get new loans that they will have to pay back with interest this year? Who, other than their own family members, benefits from the businesses the women start? Do you think the women will successfully expand their businesses and be able to pay off their new loans? How is starting a business in the United States similar to or different from the way these women started their businesses? Invite a local merchant to your class to explain how his or her business got started and how the business continues to use the services of a bank.

government always manages the economy correctly. These conflicts have the potential of making economics a controversial subject to teach in some communities.

International Economic Concepts

Nations have always been interrelated economically, but they are more so today than in the past and will probably become even more so in the future. Nations trade because they have something that other nations want and need and because they want products and resources from other nations. Some nations have an absolute advantage because they can provide something that other nations or regions cannot. Yet other nations provide a good or service better, faster, or in larger amounts and have what is called a comparative advantage. Because foreign-produced goods compete in the market with domestic products, some people want tariffs to stop the importing of certain products. However, when nations erect trade barriers, international trade slows. This slowdown can affect nations that have not raised their tariffs. Leaders in the U.S. government stress the need for free trade or trade without tariffs to promote the largest amount of sales between nations. Some economists warn that a complete free-trade policy may not always be in the best interest of a nation. The study of U.S. and world history is filled with discussions of international trade issues and their domestic and international consequences. Human rights advocates suggest that the international economy encourages lower salaries and poor working conditions in some nations and exploitation of poor people including children. When studying these ideas, students are also studying the NCSS Standards X (Civic Ideals and Values), II (Time, Continuity, and Change), and VI (Power, Authority, and Governance).

Nations do not want to buy much more from other nations than they sell. They seek a balance of payments between nations. If a nation does not sell about the same amount that it buys, it must find the wealth internally to pay for its international purchases. Such actions take away wealth for purchases and investments from the domestic economy. As a result, fewer domestic workers may be employed because money for workers' salaries and benefits must go to pay off the trade deficit. Nations can always print more money, but that money must be of constant worth or no other nation will want to take it in payment. The exchange rate is the price of one nation's money compared with another nation's. Most nations cooperate to keep the values of their currencies consistent.

The economic conditions within a nation can prompt the movement of both goods and people. Throughout U.S. history, many people have migrated to countries such as the United States for economic opportunity. Such movements are often the sources of domestic problems in the nations receiving the immigrants. Because the most educated are often those who migrate, nations whose populations migrate face different types of economic problems prompted by the loss of human resources. Therefore, international economics cannot be totally separated from the other economic concepts previously discussed. The learning cycle lesson plan on pages 424–427 illustrates how the fundamental concept of interdependence is present in microeconomics and international economics.

NCSS

Standard VII

NCSS

Standard X, II, VI

LEARNING CYCLE LESSON PLAN   *Economic Interdependence*

NCSS

Standards
VII, IX

Grade Level: Middle school

NCSS Standards: Production, Distribution, Consumption; Global Connections

National Economic Standards

When individuals, regions, and nations specialize in what they can produce at the lowest cost and then trade with others, both production and consumption increase.

Exploratory Introduction

Objectives	→ Procedures →	Assessments
1. Students give examples of situations where they are dependent on and independent from others.	1. Discuss the meaning of the concepts *dependent* and *independent* as the students understand them. Do this by asking: "What is an example of being dependent and being independent?" Encourage students to role-play. Then form students into small groups and have them assign roles: chairperson, recorder, reporter, and materials manager. Ask groups to try to describe a situation involving two people when both of them are dependent on each other.	1. Students offer appropriate examples of dependent and independent situations.

Lesson Development

Objectives	→ Procedures →	Assessments
1. Students define *interdependence* as "two people needing goods or services and providing them to each other so that both benefit and have some needs or wants fulfilled."	1. Tell the following two stories to the students: **Story 1** Mrs. Patrick was having a special dinner. She wanted to serve cheesecake with fresh strawberry topping. She went to her favorite fruit and vegetable stand and found bright red berries. "This is just what I need," she told the owner. "Don't ever go out of business!" "I won't," replied Mr. Fry, "as long as I have faithful customers like you."	

continued

Story 2

The Carmels' baby woke up early in the morning crying. On investigation, his mother discovered the baby had a temperature. She took the baby to the pediatrician, Dr. Walker, that morning and got medications. That evening, when Dr. Walker left the office, the battery in her car was dead. She called Carmels' Garage to get the car back in running order.

2. Ask the student groups to make a list of the things the two stories have in common. Then ask them to identify differences. As groups report, list commonalities and differences on the board. Ask, "In our stories, what did Mr. Fry do for Mrs. Patrick? Mrs. Patrick for Mr. Fry? The Carmel family for Dr. Walker?" and so on. Ask, "Are these examples of two or more people being dependent on each other?" Discuss.

3. Ask, "Does anyone know the word that describes two or more people being dependent on each other?" Introduce the term *interdependent*.

4. Review the meaning of words with the prefix *inter*, such as *intercom, intercept, interface, international, interchangeable*, and *Internet*. Reach a consensus on what the prefix *inter* means.

5. *Closure:* Develop a class definition of interdependent. Ask students to look at the list of what the two stories have in common. Ask, "What does it take to have an interdependent situation?" Write their definition on board.

1. Students respond with correct answers.

2. Students' definition contains the elements: two people, those people's needs for goods or services, those people's provision of goods or services, those people benefiting from the process, and those people having some wants and needs fulfilled.

Expansion

Materials: A card with a different occupation written on it for each student; one card with the occupation of child written on it; one safety pin for each student; and a ball of string

Objectives ⟶	*Procedures* ⟶	*Assessments*
1. Students give correct examples of how people in a community are interdependent.	1. Give each student a card with an occupation on it. Have students pin on their cards and get into a circle. Give the student with the term *child* a ball of string. As the child holds on to the end of the string, he or	1. Students identify correct interdependent relationships, focusing on the connection between people.

she passes or tosses the string ball to someone with whom a child would be interdependent and explains that choice. As students get the ball of string, they repeat the procedure until all students are holding on to the string. When everyone has had a chance, the teacher asks, "What does this illustrate about interdependence?"

2. Students predict that international independence is, or is not, a possibility and provide their reasons.

2. Ask, "Do you think we are only interdependent with people in our own community? Why? How could our families be interdependent with people in other areas of the world?" Students respond and explain as needed.

2. Students conclude that people are connected to each other through such economic concepts as jobs, goods and services, and needs and wants.

3. Give students the following homework assignment. At home, tonight, identify three examples each of clothing, food, and appliances that were made in another country. Record the item by name and the country where it was made.
Suggest how to find this information and that they might get help from family members. Provide a survey form on which to record information.

3. Students discuss in a respectful, orderly way their predictions, supporting them with reasons.

3. Students make conclusions about their interdependence with other nations based on data collected in homework surveys.

4. In small groups, have students combine their examples, report, and compare the results. All the nations are located on a world map with a line drawn attaching the nation of origin to your city. Different maps can be made for the different categories of information by small groups, and displayed. Decide on a title for the map and put it on the map. Display maps and note similarities and differences. Ask, "Do we trade with the same nations of the world for all types of products? Can we find alternative sources for each of these products in the United States?"

4. Students explain their answers based on the data on the maps and may add other data. Use a checklist to record participation.

4. Students predict economic consequences of accidents and behaviors.

5. Discuss what would happen if their families stopped buying clothing, food, and appliances from other nations. Ask, "What things and why? What would happen if a bad storm destroyed a crop or a big fire destroyed the port and its warehouses in Brazil or Korea?" and so on. "Do you know of any products from our community or state that are sold in other nations? How can we find out about this?" Students write letters asking local or state producers where products are sold in the United States and the world.

5. Students make logical responses, citing examples from past events and news items.

continued

5. Students help plan additional data-gathering experiences and carry them out.

6. Students conclude that people all over the world have more goods and services because they are interdependent.

7. Students state that their actions can affect people all over the world in both positive and negative ways.

6. Assign students, or have them volunteer singly or in pairs, to interview produce managers in grocery stores to find out where foods such as tomatoes, strawberries, and grapes come from at different times during the year. Assign other students, or have them volunteer, to talk to older people to learn about the types of foods and produce available when they were young. Ask students to write a three-paragraph report discussing the survey results. In paragraph 1, they discuss the home survey; in paragraph 2, they discuss the produce manager or older adult survey; and in paragraph 3, they draw conclusions regarding interdependence.

7. Read sample paragraphs and read letters from local companies as received. A class map can be made of the answers received, with lines from your community to other nations drawn according to responses received.

8. Conclude the lesson by discussing the pros and cons of being economically interdependent with people in other areas of the world. Make a chart of the students' points. Post it with the maps the groups made from their home surveys and the map of local exports still under construction.

9. Ask students to write three to four sentences telling:
   a. How their actions can affect people elsewhere in the world
   b. Whether the effects are positive, negative, or both
   c. The reason for their answer to part 2

6. Students develop and carry out usable plan for additional data gathering. Record participation on a checklist.

7. Students state the conclusion that people all over the world have more goods and services because they are interdependent.

8. *Formal assessment:* Students give appropriate reasoning for their view concerning whether their actions can impact people all over the world in both positive and negative ways.

Measurement Concepts and Methods

To help understand and interpret data concerning the economy, economists organize information into tables, charts, and graphs. Young elementary students can begin to use tables, charts, and graphs to help them organize economic information.

Middle school students can use percentages and averages. In the study of economics more than any of the other social sciences, students are called on to apply the knowledge and skills they have gained in mathematics to help them understand economic relationships. Integrated unit topics on economic issues and problems can involve the social studies teacher and the mathematics teachers. However, because many important economic concepts do not involve the use of mathematics, teachers of other subjects work on economic problems and issues as well.

Economic Decision-Making Skills

Because people encounter scarcity every day, they have to make choices (Standard 1 in Table 13.1). Rather than accepting the first solution that comes to mind, people are encouraged by economists to make rational decisions that consider the economic long- and short-term consequences. The decision maker must weigh alternatives and be aware of the opportunity cost of what is given up when one alternative is selected. The alternative that is selected must be considered to give more benefits than the opportunity cost. Helping students to identify alternatives, criteria, and consequences and to select what they see as the best alternative is the essence of teaching decision making. It is also the essence of cost–benefit analysis. James Laney (1993) identifies cost–benefit analysis as the concept that should receive primary emphasis during the elementary school years. He identifies this concept because it is a problem-solving or decision-making model that works with elementary and middle grade students. This is consistent with recognizing that in making a choice for the use of scarce resources, some other opportunity to use the resource is seen to be of less value and is lost or given up forever.

People of all ages make snap decisions and impulse purchases. The rationale for teaching decision making is that it reduces such decisions. When students face an important decision, these skills help them take time to identify and weigh alternatives carefully. Students should be helped to see when they need to seek additional information from printed sources or ask for professional advice to help them make decisions. They need to learn to ask for specific information and evaluate it. The abstractness in the decision-making process is made more concrete for students when they investigate real problems with which the students are familiar and use a decision-making chart on which alternatives and consequences are recorded and rated.

Table 13.4 shows the type of decision-making chart used in the successful elementary video series *Trade-Offs*. The chart title is the question to be answered by the decision. Alternatives are listed in the column on the left, and the criteria are listed across the top of the chart. Students are asked first to identify specific criteria for their problem and then to offer alternative choices. Sometimes, as alternatives are listed or rated, new criteria or alternatives are discovered and added to the chart. The discussion of the solution is guided by the information written on the chart.

TABLE 13.4
Decision-Making Chart

Question: Which three students should represent our class at the program planned for the entire school day on March 3?

	Alternatives			
	Completes Regular Classwork in Advance	**Has Good Speaking Voice**	**Clearly Understands Ideas to Be Presented**	**Will Represent Class Seriously**
Tom	+	+	?	–
Betty	+	+	+	+
Mohammed	–	+	+	+
Cassandra	+	–	?	+
Mei Lin	–	+	+	+
Jacques	+	+	+	+
Cynthia	+	+	+	+

The teacher directs the discussion by asking questions about the chart and how various parts of the chart compare. Each alternative and criterion is discussed and given a rating in the box created by the intersection of the appropriate row and column. Symbols such as smiley faces, frowning faces, question marks, pluses, zeroes, or minuses are drawn on the chart to conclude the discussion on each alternative and criterion. Rarely do all the ratings for an alternative contain positive symbols. The rating process does, however, narrow the list to the better alternatives. Next, the students reconsider each of these and decide which they believe is the best choice and second-best choice. The second-best choice is the opportunity cost. Students must decide whether their best choice is more to their liking than is the opportunity cost.

A second, more abstract, type of decision-making chart is shown in Table 13.5. In this chart, the students are asked to predict long- and short-term consequences, classifying them as having either positive or negative outcomes. After such information is recorded on the chart, students discuss the importance and chance of each consequence happening, and make their decision using information from the chart and its discussion. Making the final decision is important, just as letting students live with the consequences of their choices is a realistic learning goal for economics education and social studies—and for life.

Citizens make many personal decisions that affect the economy through the sales of goods and services and the use of productive resources. Their votes influence the ways in which governments spend and acquire money. Even rationally made decisions may not work out as predicted, because some criteria involve chance, or perhaps not all criteria are identified. Nevertheless, the consequences of

TABLE 13.5
Consequences Decision-Making Chart

Question: Should the tariff on foreign-made cars be increased?

Alternatives	Consequences	
	Short Term	**Long Term**
Yes	(+) Auto workers pleased, higher employment rate	(+) More U.S. cars produced
	(−) Auto agencies for foreign cars angry because sales decline	(−) Price of foreign cars up; nations raise tariffs on U.S. goods
No	(+) Price of foreign cars remains same; special sales on U.S.–produced cars	(+) United States produces better cars at lower prices through increased productivity and design improvements
	(−) United States produces fewer cars, more unemployed autoworkers	(−) Some U.S. auto plants close or reduce workers' hours

such decisions cannot be avoided. Teachers should not come to the rescue of a poor decision with an unrealistic save. Instead, they should help by asking problem questions designed to stimulate thinking from a particular view.

Sometimes, teachers may suggest possible alternatives or consequences if students fail to mention them. Students are encouraged to take the time to consider these new alternatives before making a final decision. Revisiting a decision after several days, if the choice does not appear to be working well, is acceptable. It can result in the generation of new criteria, alternatives, consequences, and even a new choice of action. Indeed, it is a very authentic approach to problem solving and decision making.

Teachers make many decisions each day, yet some of these can be made by students. Such practice helps students to recognize their personal control over their lives and the responsibilities they have for their personal and group behavior. Economic decisions involve the use of scarce resources. Time is a scarce commodity in the classroom, as are art supplies, library books, computers, and individual moments with the teacher or an adult helper. Teachers provide students with opportunities to make age-appropriate decisions and practice the decision-making process. Although it takes time to teach decision-making skills, students become equipped to perform the task in small groups or individually. The teacher can assess and evaluate students' thought processes with a quick glance at the chart.

Students who make decisions are more accepting of the decisions of others, provided they see the rationality of such decisions. Teachers who encourage students to make some class decisions might find their own decisions questioned from time to time and might be asked to support their choices or to change them. In this way, teachers serve as role models of rational decision makers and citizens.

Economic Goals and Values

The correct decision for an individual or group is based on their values and morals. A society or nation holds some agreed-on values, beliefs, and morals. However, not all of the values and beliefs are universally held or are given the same priority by all the people in the group. Economists do not always agree on the priority of economic values when making decisions and policies. Individuals may find the priorities of their values conflict when fulfilling their different roles. For example, for consumers, a lower price is important, but for union members, job security and the unity of action that give unions power are also important. Citizens might want to help protect local jobs, but they also want government services that require increased taxation of individuals and businesses. This can be a problem when citizens vote on raising property taxes to pay for school improvements.

The NCEE has identified eight important goals in the economy that reflect some of the values encountered in economic decision making and policy formation:

Economic freedom	Economic equity
Economic efficiency	Economic security
Full employment	Price stability
Economic growth	Other goals

Economic freedom is an important characteristic of the market economy. This is the opportunity to make your own choices concerning how to use resources and how to obtain additional resources.

Economic equity, or fairness to all, comes from the realization that some differences in the abilities of participants, such as physical disabilities, are beyond their control. Policymakers need to take these differences into account to make things equal for all. Various groups in society often point out that their needs go unrecognized by the policymakers and that they do not have economic equity.

Economic efficiency has two distinct definitions. One is *technical efficiency,* which is measured by getting the most output from the least input or resources. It is a reflection of high productivity. The second definition takes a broader view (macroeconomics), looking at the markets affected by the single decision and encouraging the choice that is best for all the markets. The total benefits must exceed the total costs. It is possible for a single person or company to benefit greatly while those choices have sum total effects that hurt many and cause an overall loss in productivity. Thus, the desire for economic efficiency creates situations in which the individual person or group is forced to place the larger group or society before his or her own good.

Economic security is a value highly prized by both individuals and society. We make economic decisions on the basis of the probability that we continue to be healthy, that we have employment, and that our savings and future are safe as long as we are willing to work. Individuals and citizens are often called on to make decisions that might affect economic security. In the United States, private and public policies have been made to try to give economic security to people. These include the Federal Deposit Insurance Corporation, worker's compensation, seniority rights, social security, and unemployment compensation. History is filled with examples of personal and group conflicts that relate to the values of economic security, and such conflicts will continue.

Full employment exists when everyone who wants a job has one. Although full employment seems desirable, it is probably never possible to attain this goal. There is always some unemployment as people enter the labor market for the first time, or decide to move or to seek new positions. When unemployment becomes larger than just these workers, it causes undesirable hardship because of the lack of economic security.

Price stability is another desirable value and goal that is probably never attainable. Prices do not all remain the same at all times. Controversy arises when increases and decreases in prices constitute inflation or deflation, which are damaging to the economy. Controversy also arises over managing the economy for price stability.

Economic growth is seen as necessary to continue to provide more products and jobs for a growing population, for investment, and for research incentives. Like many of the other goals and values, economic growth is interrelated with factors in a nation's economy and in the international economy. An economy can actually produce more, but the growth may not keep up with increases in the population as a whole or in the workforce. Controversy exists as to the best ways to promote economic growth.

Perhaps you do not see how elementary or middle school students are involved in or concerned about some of these goals and values. Many values, such as hard work, accuracy, high standards, honesty, reliability, promptness, cooperation, competition, and social responsibility, are facilitated by the schools and related to economics. Unfortunately, other negative values, such as extreme self-interest, immediate gratification, and cheating, are also present and sometimes reinforced by schools, society, and the media.

Young people receive mixed messages concerning which values are important. Economic educators claim that by learning economics, how to use cost–benefit analysis for decision making, and how to examine the rationale for economic values, students come to see the reasons why they should act in particular ways and adopt desirable values and behaviors. Knowledge alone, however, does not bring about prosocial behaviors. Teachers need to actively facilitate and support their use.

Children and the Learning of Economics

By the mid-1970s, economists and educators had reached a consensus on what aspects of economics to teach and how most effectively to accomplish the task. Their consensus includes the following four points:

1. An understanding of basic economic concepts is more important than a heavy dose of factual knowledge.
2. Instructional efforts should concentrate on aiding students to achieve a fundamental understanding of a limited set of economic concepts and their relationships.

3. Students should be given a conceptual framework to help them organize their understanding of economics, and they should be exposed to a manner of thinking that emphasizes systematic, objective analysis.
4. The real personal and social advantages of economic understanding become apparent as individuals achieve competence in applying their knowledge to a wide range of economic issues they themselves confront (Saunders et al., 1984, p. 2).

Economic education researchers have studied economic concepts presenting students with problems and asking them to explain what happened. Without formal instruction, economic reasoning begins to emerge between the ages of 5 and 7. Concepts with which students have the greatest personal experiences, usually the fundamental or microeconomic concepts such as *work, want,* and *scarcity,* appear to be the first that are understood (Armento & Flores, 1986). Two important conclusions come from these studies:

1. Children's economic ideas tend to follow a developmental sequence. Their thinking becomes more abstract and flexible with age.
2. Although economic thinking shows a gradual improvement with age, mature reasoning appears more quickly for some concepts than for others (Schug & Walstad, 1991).

With systematic instruction, even kindergarten students can learn economic concepts and economic decision making—weighing alternatives and what to give up against the benefits received (Kourilsky, 1977). Teacher behavior in teaching the concepts of specialization in grades 3–5 was examined by Armento (1986). Student achievement was greater when teachers did the following:

- Gave more concept definitions and more positive concept examples and reviewed the main ideas of the lesson
- Used accurate economic conceptual and factual knowledge relevant to the objectives of the lesson
- Included more of the relevant knowledge generalizations and more of the related concept labels
- Expressed more enthusiasm and interest in the content of the lesson (Armento & Flores, 1986, p. 98)

Research indicates elementary and middle school students can learn ideas about economics (Schug & Walstad, 1991). Even kindergarten students have been able to master concepts such as scarcity, decision making, production, specialization, distribution, consumption, saving, supply and demand, business organization, and money and barter (Kourilsky, 1977, p. 183).

Approaches to Teaching Economics

Students at all grades, at all ability levels, and from all socioeconomic levels can learn economics. "Although certain instructional approaches, techniques, and strategies have been shown to yield better results than others, comparative studies have concluded that elementary school students can learn economics at some level of understanding through a variety of approaches" (Kourilsky, 1977, p. 200). Economics plays an integral part in all societies, including the one that exists when students interact within the classroom. Involving students in analyzing and solving classroom problems is the overall goal of two programs developed by Marilyn L. Kourilsky: the Mini-Society and Kinder-Economy. Both programs are for elementary-age students, although the Kinder-Economy is especially designed for students in kindergarten. Each concept is presented in a sequence of three types of lessons. First, students experience the concept in their own classroom society and decide how to solve the situation. Second, the teacher helps the students debrief the situation to learn the names, definitions, and relationships between the economic concepts. Third, the teacher provides reinforcing activities such as role-plays, games, exercise sheets, stories, and art projects for the students to complete.

In beginning the study, the teacher performs two important tasks: arranging the initial scarcity situation in the classroom and leading the students toward reaching their own decision on how to solve their scarcity problem. Alternatives are generated, consequences are predicted, and the best choice is agreed to by the students. The students come to see that scarcity is frequently present in the classroom society and agree that the problem needs to be systematically reduced. Then students set about determining who in the classroom should get the scarce resources. Students usually decide that earning and free choice in spending are the best solutions. Once the decisions about the name of the society, the design of the money, the pay of officers, and pay procedures are established, the role of the teacher changes from leader to facilitator.

Instead of the teacher creating the experiences, the students, through their interactions, create the different problems to be solved. The teacher encourages them to examine the alternatives and consequences and to decide on the answer. If students make a poor decision, it becomes evident in new problems and can be corrected. The goal of these programs is to teach economic concepts and the relationships between concepts within society. The original opportunities to earn money must be activities that all students have an equal opportunity to engage in so that money gets into the classroom society. The key to the success of these classroom societies is the teacher's faith in the students' ability to discover problems and come to an acceptable decision supported by the class. For example, students might want to open businesses and sell items and services. Problems such as where to locate the business and when sales can take place must be solved. Can students sell services such as taking tests and doing homework for others?

The teacher, as a member of the class, has a role similar to that of the students in helping solve the problems. The teacher prods the students to use what they have learned about alternatives and consequences to help solve problems and, if necessary, suggests alternatives and consequences. Teachers have the additional responsibility of reinforcing learning through closure activities in the lessons and assignments. The teacher informs parents of the activities and their goals. Parents give written permission for students to bring items to school, specifying whether they are for use or may be sold or bartered.

The goals of classroom society programs go beyond the recognition of concepts requiring students to apply and analyze concepts and make decisions. The students must learn to live with both short-term and long-term consequences of their decisions. Because the Kinder-Economy and Mini-Society require a long-term, consistent time commitment during the week for students to accomplish their goals, the teacher needs to study the available books devoted to the program carefully. More information on mini-society is at http://www.mini-society.com/secure/. The Stock Market Game is a 10-week simulation sponsored by the Securities Industry Association. It runs three times each year for students in grades 4 through 12. Currently, there are two versions: a paper-and-pencil version and an Internet version. Student teams invest $100,000 and follow the progress of companies and markets as they interact with current events over 10 weeks. Students are allowed to buy and sell stocks and are guided and encouraged to learn the reasons for market changes. Teachers can enroll their classes through the NCEE website.

Mark Schug, author of *Economics for Kids: Ideas for Teaching in the Elementary Grades* (1997), suggests the following criteria for elementary economics lessons:

- Activities enhance citizenship understanding and skills.
- Activities provide opportunities for manipulating data and using concrete examples.
- Activities are formally planned, but informal opportunities are used to analyze and review concepts as they arise in the news and classroom.
- Activities link to children's own experiences.
- Activities link to the school district's curriculum.

A learning cycle lesson employing Schug's criteria in a lesson appropriate across grades K–8 is provided on pages 436–439.

 ## Resources for Teaching Economics

Special resources for teaching economics are widely available. In addition to those resources generally available for educators, teachers often employ local citizens who are knowledgeable about specific economic issues impacting local government and businesses. Field trips to local businesses that include entrance into areas from which the general public is normally excluded are very enlightening to young people who know little about the specifics of many jobs and careers. Teachers also use locally conducted surveys and send out written questionnaires to gather information. All governmental agencies and institutions face economic issues. Printed government materials and government speakers prepared for the general public may be of help to students.

LEARNING CYCLE LESSON PLAN — Advertisements and Making Good Choices

NCSS
Standard VII

Grade Level: Modifications suggested for K–8

NCSS Standards: Production, Distribution, and Consumption

National Economic Standard

Effective decision making requires comparing the additional costs of alternatives with the additional benefits. Most choices involve doing a little more or a little less of something: few choices are all-or-nothing decisions.

Materials: Three boxes of different sizes (one the size of a box that holds a birthday cake), each wrapped differently from plain to very fancy and colorful and containing one of the following: a stick of gum for each child, a box of cake mix, or a note providing an activity students would enjoy, such as a popcorn party at the end of the day, 15 minutes of free reading time, or choosing a book for a read-aloud; a video containing commercials students might see on prime-time television or in children's television shows; chart paper and markers for each small group; and a selection of advertisements from magazines, fliers, and newspapers.

Exploratory Introduction

Materials: Three boxes (described above)

Objectives ⟶	Procedures ⟶	Assessments
1. Students offer logical ideas on what might be in the three boxes the teacher presents.	1. Show the students the three boxes and ask, "Which box do you choose for your prize?" Tell the students you know that they will like each item but that they would especially like to have the cake. If they select the cake, you can call it an unbirthday party for all those whose birthdays are not on school days. Allow the students to discuss and decide which box to select. You might suggest thinking about the size of the cake or try to entice the students to take the most elaborately decorated box because it is wrapped like a birthday present.	1. Students make at least one suggestion that is appropriate for each box.
2. Students offer appropriate suggestions for arriving at a joint decision with which everyone will be satisfied.	2. After the discussion, ask, "How should we go about making the decision so that we know everyone will be satisfied?" Follow through with their choice and open the boxes. 3. Begin with the boxes not selected and ask, "Would you have enjoyed getting these surprises? Why or why not?" If the box containing the cake mix is selected, open it and wait for the students to respond. Ask, "Why did you respond this way? Isn't this a cake? What did I do or say that made you think there	2. Students make suggestions that consider everyone's viewpoints or decide that it is very difficult to satisfy everyone's wants.

continued

was a cake in here? What do we need to have before we have a cake to eat?" (With older students, the teacher might have them do things in class to earn the extra ingredients and frosting.) "Where do these extra items come from? How would you feel if we didn't have the eggs, oil, frosting, pans, and stove to complete the cake? What have we learned from this experience?" (If the box with the cake mix is not selected, provide the reward in their box and ask whether they enjoyed their present when finished. If the cake mix is selected, determine with the students a time when the cake is completed and served.)

Lesson Development

Materials: A video as described above, and chart paper and markers for each small group

Objectives →	Procedures →	Assessments
1. Students relate their past experiences with advertisements and the product advertised.	1. Ask, "Can someone tell me what we did with the three boxes? What did we say we learned from that experience? Were you satisfied with the present? Have you ever had another experience in which you thought, or were led to believe, that something was different from what it actually was? When?" After some discussion, explain that you are going to help them make better decisions by understanding advertisements and advertising.	1. Students identify instances of believing misleading advertisements.
2. Students characterize advertisements as attempts to try to get people to purchase something.	2. Form the students into small groups. Ask them to assign roles including recorder, chairperson, reporter, and materials manager. Show two advertisements from the videotape. Write questions on the board or overhead projector and ask each group to discuss the questions and record their answers on chart paper. "What do we call these two segments? Why are they on television? What do they have in common?" 3. After groups share their responses to the questions, ask each group to discuss the following question, then share with the class: "What can we say is a definition for an *advertisement*?"	2. Students state that, because television needs money to keep on air, time is sold for advertisements that get people to buy something.

continued

4. Show the two television ads from the videotape, one at a time. After each one, ask, "How did you feel when you watched this commercial? Why? Would you buy this item? Which of the two commercials did you like better? Why? What are some of your favorite commercials on television?" Get a quick list of four or five answers. Using a show of hands, ask, "Who remembers and likes each commercial listed?" (Keep the list for future use.)

3. Students identify examples of the use of advertising or propaganda techniques presented by the teachers, such as repetition, humor, endorsement, bandwagon, feeling good, glitz, or colorful language.

5. Depending on the time available and the age of the students, select several propaganda techniques and provide direct instruction on each as a separate concept. Use examples of each from the video and a short test for comprehension with a couple of commercials for which students are asked to identify the technique used and give their reasons. Affirm or explain answers.

6. On the next day, review and perhaps teach an additional technique or two using advertisements from magazines. Have students draw their own ad and tell which technique they used as an assessment of comprehension.

4. Students reword their definition to include using symbols and appeals that encourage buyers to make a choice that may not fit either their wants or their needs.

7. Discuss, with the students, their responses to the statement: Advertising is a bunch of lies. Ask the students whether they now want to add anything to their earlier definition of an advertisement.

8. *Closure:* Ask, "What would be your advice to a consumer when seeing or hearing a commercial?"

3. Students work cooperatively as a class or in small groups to identify types of ads.

4. Students correctly identify the various techniques in the commercials.

5. Students' definition includes use of symbols and appeals by advertisements, and the reaction of consumers who buy what they did not originally want or need.

Expansion

Materials: Advertisements taken from magazines, fliers, and newspapers; chart paper and markers for each group

Objectives	Procedures	Assessments
1. Students conclude that newspaper advertisements and local ads use fewer special techniques than	1. Ask, "What have we concluded about advertisements and your making a choice as a consumer?" 2. Give each small group several advertisements from magazines, fliers, and newspapers. Ask each group to identify, and record on chart paper, their response to the question, "What advertising technique is being	1. Students identify less color, no famous people, and other logical observations

continued

television and magazine ads.

2. Students conduct an interview or use e-mail to find out why business owners think advertisements are needed.

3. Students decide when they should consult ads for help and justify their answers.

used?" Have groups share findings. List techniques identified on the board. Ask the class to draw conclusions from their observations with the question, "What are the differences you observe in these new ads and those on TV or in magazines?" List on the board.

3. Ask, "Do you think you will remember the ads using fewer special techniques as long as the other ads? Why or why not? Why do these ads differ from the ones we looked at earlier? Can you think of any reason to advertise except to sell a specific item? Do you think there might be other reasons to advertise? How could we find out?" Revise to include interview data.

4. Interview local business owners, advertising people from the local newspaper, TV channel, or radio station, or people who sell or produce advertisements. Ask them why advertisements are needed. Alternatively, e-mail such individuals for their replies, which students analyze for similarities, differences, and new ideas. "Is our revised definition from yesterday still accurate?"

5. As final closure, relate the following problem to the students for class discussion. Imagine that you moved to a new community and you need to get the following: a haircut, your bike repaired, a quick lunch, and a nice present for someone's birthday. For which of these items would you consult advertisements and for what reasons? Have students share their responses orally or in writing.

6. *Lesson Summary:* Ask students to describe briefly the major activities in this learning cycle and the important ideas each helped them to understand concerning decision making and advertising.

from the ads, concluding that newspapers and local fliers use fewer special techniques than television and magazine ads because less money is available.

2. Students identify at least two reasons for the use of advertisements by business owners. Students consider changes in wording for their definition.

3. Students identify logical instances when they can use advertisements to help them make a decision to satisfy a need.

Note: Definitions of the various propaganda strategies can be found in books on propaganda and advertising and through the Internet.

1. How are the commercials for sporting events similar to and different from commercials focused on school-age students?

2. How would you change the expansion of this lesson to focus on the study of elections?

Using Technology

Investigating How to Use a WebQuest with Your Students

Although computers and other forms of technology may interest students in a lesson, using technology does not ensure that learning takes place. Presenting the content in ways through which the user can best learn is important in lessons that employ technology. Teachers find many Internet articles advocating for the use of specific resources. Yet, few researchers have investigated the impact of technology on actual learning. Carrying out an action research project to gain data on how all students in the class respond rather than just relying on observations is a better strategy for examining the impact of a technology on your students and determining if continuing, increasing, or ceasing its use is appropriate for a class.

A WebQuest is a sound approach for presenting a lesson, and it is simple for busy educators to use. By downloading and editing a template, educators can make their own WebQuests without learning the coding needed to create a webpage. The most important decision the teacher needs to make is selecting the websites for students to use in the WebQuest. Reflection on the qualities of good WebQuests and effective teaching for the variety of learners is also needed to develop WebQuests that are effective with learners.

The National Council for Economic Education link (EconEdLink, www.econedlink.org) has many WebQuests that are exemplary in their use of a variety of activities to help students learn and apply economic knowledge. Visit the website and search for elementary or middle school lessons. Next, examine three lessons with EconEdLink prefaces suggested for the grade level in which you have an interest or field placement. Select one lesson to use. Have a group of students of varying abilities work through the selected WebQuest. As you observe your students' successes and difficulties using this WebQuest, helping only when necessary, note the types of problems various learners encounter. As your students complete the WebQuest, ask each student predetermined questions about the lesson's content and how they felt about learning it through the WebQuest. Invariably, teachers report that K–8 students prefer the interactive exercises incorporated into the WebQuests and complain about long passages that require reading. Through this short action-research-like experience, you will become more aware of the characteristics to incorporate into your WebQuest to make it appropriate, yet challenging, for most of your students. You will identify multiple types of learning activities and ways of presenting information so that a wider range of students are able to successfully complete the WebQuest.

WebQuests developed by students who completed the EconEdLink activity, as described above, can be viewed in articles at http://socstrp.org, the website of the online journal *Social Studies Research and Practice*. See volume 1, issues 1 and 2 (Haas, Channel, Linder, Vandevander, & VanSickle, 2006; Courtney & Haas, 2006).

Federal institutions such as the Federal Reserve Banks, the U.S. Treasury, and the Internal Revenue Service have developed educational materials. Other economic institutions such as trade organizations, private corporations, insurance groups, and financial organizations have designed materials for use in schools. Many of these organizations are affiliated with NCEE and various state councils. One way to locate these materials is to contact your state's council on economic education. Your state department of education should be able to provide you with the appropriate address. Because economics is filled with controversy, some instructional resources have specific viewpoints.

EXPANSION

Parents and teachers alike say it is difficult to teach children about money and how to handle it. There is much more to learn than just saving money in a bank. Many careers specialize in finance and money including helping others with their money. Credit and debt are major problems for people, businesses, and governments. With all of the recent problems in the economy many teachers and schools believe they should increase teaching about economics and money. But, the problem is, where do you go for help? If you are like most teachers, you need more help than this chapter provides; you need ongoing help.

The most useful type of website for a teacher or school system seeking information about a topic is a portal devoted to that topic. Portals are one-stop locations trying to address all needs and wants. An example of such a portal for the topic of economic education is the website of the Council for Economic Education (NCEE)—http://www.councilforeconed.org/ea/program.php?pid=1. It offers many resources including instructional resources the NCEE created in cooperation with educators, business, and governmental agencies dealing with the distribution or regulation of money. On the left side of the home page is a long list of resources for educators. One of the most helpful for teachers is EconEdLink with over 630 lessons for grades K–12. Lessons are prepared by an educator, reviewed by educators and economists, and revised before posting. The digital model for these lessons is the WebQuest. Once students learn to navigate this model, it is easier to use additional lessons. Interactive learning and inquiry, the important characteristics presented in this textbook, are incorporated into the lessons at EconEdLink. Searches by grade level, economic concept, and author's name contribute to its friendly use. Teachers who wonder how students receive a lesson may find voluntary comments posted on the teacher's page. These comments often indicate the characteristics of their classes, strengths in the lesson, and adjustments they tried or would try. Across the top of the home page are additional helpful features such as weblinks, data links, cyberteach, standards, and current events. The current events section provides highlights of some of the latest economic-related news and provides references to EconEdLink lessons that deal with the content mentioned in the news stories. At the standards site, you are only one click away from the national economic and personal finance standards and individual states' standards. A 2007 survey reports that personal finance is a part of the curriculum in 40 states but tested in only a few. Personal financial problems and the banking crises are likely to bring about a greater emphasis in coming years.

1. In your K–12 schooling did you learn about personal economic issues?
2. What is something you would like to teach about economics to students you teach?
3. What are some of the concepts and/or skills that schools can teach to youth that will help their future employers to view them positively?
4. The websites at the end of this chapter contain active learning exercises and games. Take some time to examine one of these sites and share your ideas about it with a classmate.

Summary

Economics is integral to the lives of individuals and nations. Economists and economic educators place emphasis on research, teacher training, use of computers, and preparing instructional resources to improve economic knowledge. Although a variety of methods are successful in teaching economics, the best approaches emphasize economic concepts and rational economic decision making. Many economic concepts are present in elementary and middle school social studies curriculum. A study of economics for young teens is thought to be especially helpful because it has the potential to encourage students to make careful career choices and to develop good spending habits at a time in their lives when they begin to make their own decisions on many purchases and need to begin to select and prepare for working careers.

Recommended Websites to Visit

Council for Economic Education (NCEE) website.
http://www.councilforeconed.org/ea/program.php?pid=1
The most complete sources of information on WebQuests.
http://www.webquest.org/index.php
Games with a financial education focus.
http://www.fffl.councilforeconed.org/
Run a business.
http://disney.go.com/dxd/index.html?channel=108602#/disneygroup/hotshotbusiness/
Webkinz: Experience handling money by taking care of your Webkinz pet. Purchase of a stuffed pet required.
http://www.webkinz.com/us_en/
The Power of Green: An interactive activity for learning to save money in your home by conserving energy.
http://www.coned.com/thepowerofgreen/game/
Mini-society information and video.
http://www.mini-society.com/secure/video-reg.asp

Heifer International's education resources for teachers.
http://www.heifer.org/site/c.edJRKQNiFiG/b.3813431/

Minyanland: Learn about money through this free virtual world game.
http://www.Minyanland.com/

The Stock Market Game for middle school.
http://www.smgww.org/

The EconEdLink of the National Council for Economic Education provides lessons for all grade levels linked to the standards, most of which are WebQuests.
www.councilforeconed.org/ea/program.php?pid=1

The U.S. Mint has information on coins and includes games for young people and lesson plans on coins.
www.usmint.gov/

Information and games for children at the money factory
www.moneyfactory.com/

Definitions of the various propaganda strategies can be found in books on propaganda and advertising and through the Internet.
www.cyfc.umn.edu/Documents/C/C/CC1026.html

How Everyday Things Are Made helps students learn about production of goods.
http://manufacturing.stanford.edu/

The Federal Reserve Bank of Richmond has an education site and teacher programs.
www.rich.frb.org/econed/

Curriculum for personal economic fitness
www.fffl.ncee.net/

14

How Do I Teach Students to Learn Through Multiple Assessments and Evaluation?

EXPLORATORY INTRODUCTION

Think of a paper-and-pencil test you have taken. Now, examine Figures 14.1 and 14.2, which present questions from the 1994 National Assessment of Educational Progress (NAEP) tests in geography and history for fourth-graders and eighth-graders, respectively. Answer the questions about geography written for fourth-graders in Figure 14.1 and about history written for eighth-graders in Figure 14.2. Review your test-taking experience by answering the questions below.

1. In what ways are they different from the tests you took in fourth and eighth grades?
2. How can subjectivity be removed from grading these questions?
3. Explain whether you think the questions are fair to all children living in various conditions and regions of the United States.
4. Explain whether you think most students would be able to answer these questions.
5. On the 1994 NAEP test in geography, 44 percent of fourth-grade students were able to draw an island and correctly place the mountains, lake, houses, and forest. Only a very small percentage omitted answering the questions or produced a map that had no appropriately drawn elements. When the scores were analyzed by race/ethnic group, 51 percent of white, 17 percent of black, and 33 percent of Hispanic students answered the question completely. On the 1994 NAEP test in U.S. history, 32 percent of the eighth-grade students answered correctly. The breakdown by race and ethnic difference was 34 percent whites, 31 percent blacks, and 30 percent Hispanic students answered correctly. What might account for these differences?

Geography Questions

In the box below, draw a map of an island.
On the island, draw in the following details by hand:

    —Mountains along the west coast
    —A lake in the north
    —Houses along the east coast
    —Forests in the south

Be sure to use the symbols shown in the key.
Use your colored pencils to help you draw the map.

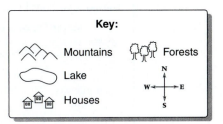

A **complete** response includes a continuous perimeter for the island and all four of the other features correctly located.
An **essential** response had three of the five specified elements correct.
A **partial** response had one or two correct.
An **inappropriate** response did not include any elements located correctly.

FIGURE 14.1
Sample NAEP Geography Questions   *Source: Learning about Our World and Our Past: Using the Tools and Resources of Geography and U.S. History—A Report of the 1994 NAEP Assessment,* by E. Hawkins, F. Stancavage, J. Mitchell, M. Goodman, and S. Lazer, 1998, Washington, DC: National Center for Educational Statistics.

Using a Chart to Consider Trade Between Countries
The two questions below refer to the following chart.

Major Exports of Three Countries

Country A	Country B	Country C
Oil	Cars	Computers
Natural Gas	Televisions	Airplanes
Coconuts	Cameras	Wheat

1. The situation shown in the chart will probably lead to
   a. trade among all three countries.
   b. trade only between countries A and B.
   c. trade only between countries B and C.
   d. a decision by each country to produce all nine goods listed.
2. Is the United States most likely country A, B, or C? Give one reason why.

_____

_____

A **complete** response correctly identifies country C and gives one appropriate reason why.
A **partial** response correctly identifies country C but gives either no reason why, or an inappropriate reason for the choice.

FIGURE 14.1 CONTINUED

History Questions
To answer the two questions refer to the newspaper report below.

> A city of desolation, of vacant houses, of widowed women, rotting wharves, of deserted warehouses…acres of pitiful and voiceless bareness—that is Charleston.

1. The news report was most likely written in
   a. 1835.
   b. 1845.
   c. 1855.
   d. 1865.[*]

2. The new report best supports which statement?
   a. Cities on the coast saw the worst of the fighting in the Civil War.
   b. During the Civil War urban areas in the South suffered.[*]
   c. The destruction of cities had little effect on the progress of the Civil War.
   d. The Civil War had little effect on city life in the North.

FIGURE 14.2
Portion of 1994 NAEP Test in U.S. History for Eighth-Graders   *Source: Learning about Our World and Our Past: Using the Tools and Resources of Geography and U.S. History: A Report of the 1994 NAEP Assessment,* by E. Hawkins, F. Stancavage, J. Mitchell, M. Goodman, and S. Lazer, 1998, Washington, DC: National Center for Educational Statistics.

Chapter Overview

How do you know whether the game has started as you approach the stadium? Does the crowd display certain behaviors that mark the beginning of a game? Suppose that, as you approach, a loud roar emanates from the opponents' side of the stadium. What would you suspect is happening? As you are considering such questions, you are assessing the situation. If teachers were asked what they do during the day, they might not mention assessment. However, teachers continually assess the behaviors of students to ensure that they are on task and accomplishing objectives. Administrators, state departments of education, politicians, and the public tend to pay attention to particular assessments they believe indicate students are learning. That selective coverage often calls forth negative feelings about a process that should be viewed for its positive role in education. This chapter examines the multiple ways in which teachers use assessment to determine the success of instruction and to adjust instructional procedures to improve individual learning and the curriculum. It also discusses ways to engage students in assessing their own progress toward learning.

Chapter Objectives

1. Explain the differences between assessment and evaluation.
2. Differentiate between informal and formal assessments and evaluations.
3. Describe how to modify assessments to determine more accurately the progress of students with various learning disabilities, culturally diverse students who lack English proficiency, and nonreaders.
4. Give examples of how students can be encouraged to assess their own progress and that of other students with whom they work.
5. Analyze and try writing rubrics appropriate for assessing projects and essays.
6. Examine test results and infer students' success and errors for the social studies curriculum.
7. Analyze how a middle school teacher uses assessment in teaching and planning.
8. Describe how reflection and action research can help guide your development as a professional.

DEVELOPMENT

 ## Assessing and Evaluating Social Studies Learning

Assessment has received increasing attention over the past 15 years. States, teachers, parents, and school systems have reexamined traditional assessment and evaluation. Educators have learned new skills and invented ways to more fairly and accurately assess students' social studies learning. Michael Yell, a seventh-grade teacher from Hudson, Wisconsin, and 1998 NCSS middle school National Social

Studies Teacher of the Year, describes his efforts to overhaul his assessment practices as follows:

> The journey toward using multiple types of assessment is compatible with the move toward constructivist and engaging teaching. I became dissatisfied with my methods of assessment. I realized that I was not teaching just for recall, and that assessing just for recall was defeating. As my journey continues, I want to expand my repertoire to include more student self-assessment, portfolios, and student-created rubrics. (Yell, 1999, pp. 328–329)

Aligning objectives and instructional procedures with assessment is the key to success in helping students attain standards and learning benchmarks. Learning is a journey. Unless you know where you are going (learning objectives), you don't know what roads and landmarks to look for (evidence), and you have no idea if and when you will get there (learning outcome). *Assessment* is collecting evidence of learning as you journey toward accomplishing your learning objectives. Unless you have accomplished your objectives, you won't know how well you like the results of your efforts. *Evaluation* comes after you complete the journey and ascertain how well that journey met your expectations. Evaluation in education comes when there is a collection of assessments that can be examined and compared with a set of expectations. Jane Pollock (1992), in reporting the outcomes of the Aurora, Colorado, schools' attempts to reform assessment, identified three results of the effort: (1) alignment with district goals, (2) improved instruction, and (3) greater student learning. Students are informed of the assessment criteria from the beginning, so they are more engaged in their learning tasks because they know what to accomplish during instruction.

When Evaluation and Assessment Are Needed

Evaluation is the process of using information to judge whether a program is meeting students' needs effectively. An evaluation should tell us (1) what students' needs are, (2) how well we have met those needs, and (3) what we might reform to better meet students' needs in both the affective and cognitive domains. Evaluation in social studies looks at students' understanding of their social world. The evaluation process is used to provide information with which the teacher can more effectively plan instruction for individuals and groups. It is also used to collect information so communication with parents and guardians is based on documentation of students' work and how they perform it.

Each evaluation serves one of two general purposes: formative or summative. *Formative evaluation* ascertains how well students engage in a lesson or unit and how well students are accomplishing the objectives toward which they are working. It begins with the exploratory introduction in which students' prior learning related to the lesson is diagnosed. Changes are made if it is evident students already know the content or skill to be taught or if reteaching of ideas and skills not mastered is needed. Throughout the unit, formative evaluation provides the teacher with information to determine whether and when students are ready to move on to new topics, objectives, or treatment of the information or whether additional time and effort are needed. Formative evaluation related to learning knowledge or inquiry skills often is completed quickly as the teacher assesses students' comments, questions, and answers during discussions, in writing assignments, or while performing learning tasks.

In *summative evaluation*, students' progress is examined at the end of an activity, unit, or part of the curriculum. Teachers usually have available copies of students' work to examine for evidence of learning the necessary standard. If and when percent or letter grades are given, they are given for work on summative assessment materials.

The evaluation process depends on assessment. Assessment is the process of observing, collecting, recording, and otherwise documenting the work students do and how they do it. Evaluation is the process of interpreting the evidence collected through assessment and making judgments and decisions based on the assessment (Trochim, 2006).

Guiding Principles for Assessment and Evaluation

Social studies requires assessments reflecting all the content areas supporting the social studies—aspects of cognitive and social skills, values, and the predispositions for action required for competent citizenship and participation in our democratic society and in a global world (NCSS, 1991). One of the major complaints social studies educators have about standardized tests is that they assess only a limited range of what needs to be assessed for outcomes in social studies. Assessment is a special challenge to social studies educators and one they need to spell out for the public, for politicians, and especially for students.

Students often complain that social studies is not relevant and wonder why they study it. Yet, the same students are very interested in their social world and in the lives of people. Social studies educators need to help students find connections between what they study and its importance to their lives and to the world in which they live. One way is to assess a wider range of what is expected to be learned and to recognize students' progress in an entire range of content, skills, attitudes, and dispositions. Students often have the misconception that only those ideas that are tested are worth learning. When testing and assessment focus on what is easy to test with a short reply, students are not given credit for their complete progress. They may react by focusing on the parts that are tested. Efforts to change the curriculum objectives and teachers' teaching methods must be accompanied by changing assessments and evaluations of the outcomes.

In 1991, NCSS adopted a position statement on testing and evaluation: "Only carefully designed evaluation strategies and tests will enable social studies educators to assess both the academic content and the thinking or performance skills stated in or implied by the objectives" (p. 4). To improve assessment and evaluation, the following guidelines were recommended:

1. Evaluation instruments should:
   - Focus on stated curriculum goals and objectives
   - Be used to improve curriculum and instruction
   - Measure both content and process
   - Be chosen for instructional, diagnostic, and prescriptive purposes
   - Reflect a high degree of fairness to all people and groups
2. Evaluations of students' achievement should:
   - Be used solely to improve teaching and learning
   - Involve a variety of instruments and approaches to measure students' knowledge, skills, and attitudes
   - Be congruent with both the objectives and the classroom experiences of the students examined
   - Be sequential and cumulative (NCSS, 1991, pp. 4–5)

When making decisions about grades, class placement, promotion, or retention, the same NCSS document states, "Social studies educators can and should use all the information available about their students' social studies achievement—data gathered from a variety of assessment instruments and techniques..." (1991, p. 5).

If assessment and evaluation are to bring about improved learning, they must be made public and understood by those most involved in student learning: teachers, students, parents, administrators, and the public and its representatives, who make laws and spend state and school board monies. Finding ways to involve students in the assessment and evaluation of their own learning, or using assessment as a teaching strategy, is not an entirely new idea, but one that is and will continue to be increasingly practiced.

Teachers plan assessments as a part of their lessons and the curriculum. The assessment questions in a textbook or standardized test should not be used unless the questions align with the objectives of the classroom. Groups of teachers cooperate to help each other improve their assessment skills and apply them to curriculum and classroom reform. When evaluating students' thinking, Buchovecky (1996) suggests that teachers

- Focus on the evidence present in their work
- Look openly and broadly and not be led by expectations
- Look for patterns and clues as to how and what the student is thinking

Teachers reflect on the curriculum and their teaching in light of evidence provided by the students' work. In the process, questions for action research may be identified. Following are helpful procedures and questions for curriculum changes and action research:

- Compare what you see and what you think about the students' work with what you do in the classroom.
- Note what you saw in the students' work that surprised you or that you found particularly interesting.

- Consider what inferences you can make about students' thinking from their work.
- Consider what questions about teaching and assessment the students' work raised.
- Consider how you might pursue these questions further.
- Ask whether there are things you would like to try in your classroom as a result of looking at the students' work. (Buchovecky, 1996)

As teachers have developed their skills in using multiple assessments that enable them to assess and evaluate the social studies accomplishments of diverse students, they have been pressured by a strong push toward standardized testing resulting from No Child Left Behind (NCLB) (2001) legislation and state initiatives. To ensure that standardized testing indicates that students are making the Adequate Yearly Progress (AYP) required under NCLB, teachers feel pressure to "teach to the test." Assessment in any form, including standardized tests, must align with the curriculum. However, a standardized test does not always align well. Many teachers feel they must teach the content on the test whether or not it is part of the curriculum or addresses their students' needs. Other high-stakes standardized testing, such as high school exit exams, puts pressure on teachers at all levels to teach what is on the exam so that their students will pass it when it is finally taken. Teachers may select not to teach content that is not on the test. Or, teachers may move nontested topics to late in the year, after the required testing has been completed, at which point there is not enough time to teach them for meaningful understanding.

Assessment, evaluation, curriculum, and instruction in social studies are intertwined. Teachers recognize that students must be assisted in doing as well as they can on high-stakes tests. But, teachers also know that it is their responsibility to provide a powerful social studies curriculum and use instructional methods that focus on students' needs and give students a sense of control over their learning. Such a focus has been shown to enable students to do well on tests because they have a foundation of both content and thinking skills. More importantly, research reports that these students also express the desire to be active and responsible participants in their communities.

National Testing of Social Studies

A visit to the website of the National Assessment of Educational Progress at http://nces.ed.gov allows you to read sample test questions and the summaries of the most recent testing of geography, history, and civics. These tests provide the largest assessment of students throughout the United States. U.S. history and geography were retested in 2006, and economics was tested for the first time. World history will be tested for the first time in 2012. Testing of this type reveals trends in the learning of the various social studies contents and skills. When combined with demographic data and responses to survey questions, the data can be broken down to reveal average scores by groups. The information from such NAEP tests provides a snapshot of the accomplishments of the students at the time of the administration of the test. It does not tell us what causes differences in the accomplishments. There are consistencies in the findings over the years that, when combined with other types of research, indicate that the following five ideas are probably helpful in improving the scores and by implication the learning of students in social studies as summarized from *The Civic Mission of Schools* (Carnegie Corporation, 2003):

- Provide instruction in social studies on a regular basis beginning in the earliest grades.
- Discuss current local, national, and international events and allow students to examine a number of perspectives and to hold different perspectives on the issues.
- Use active learning strategies, including simulations.
- Apply what is learned in the school and community by taking part in service learning activities.
- Allow students to take part in governance in school and extracurricular activities.

TIME FOR REFLECTION | **What Do You Think?**

1. What do you think might account for variations in the scores of students in different parts of the United States?

2. What might account for differences in the ethnic and gender scores?

3. What can teachers, administrators, and the public learn from the NAEP tests that cannot be learned from state testing or from classroom assessments?

4. How do the recommendations from *The Civic Mission of Schools* support the vision of teaching social studies stressed in this textbook?

Assessment and Evaluation Beyond Testing

Effective democratic citizenship requires gathering information, thinking, decision making, communications, social interaction, and civic participation. Assessment and evaluation limited only to testing fail to provide information about many of these requirements for citizenship. The essence of twenty-first century skills is an emphasis on what students can do with knowledge, rather than what units of knowledge they have. So, more authentic assessments of students' work and behavior through projects, performances, essays, and portfolios are needed (Silva, 2008). Such forms of assessment require students to make decisions based on value judgments and to support their selections with facts and explanations. Continual assessment and evaluation of progress along the path to student learning help to facilitate thinking and actions that make students productive learners.

Students must learn to assess and evaluate their own progress and that of their classmates in meaningful ways. When they do not like the way things are going, students need to recognize specifics that can be changed and approach these changes in ways that improve the quality of their efforts individually and collectively. When teachers facilitate students' development and integration of assessment and evaluation skills as part of the instructional process, they honor students' efforts by accepting and supporting their suggestions for changes. In this way, students assume some control in the assessment and evaluation process and are encouraged to use individual and group evaluation in ways that increase meaningful learning. When this is done, assessment and evaluation become instructional strategies. Such strategies are most often incorporated into the Development and Expansion phases of a learning cycle.

Learning takes time. Long-term assessment records are kept and charted so that teachers, parents, and students can see that adequate progress is being made and can identify areas of strength and weakness. One of the problems with relying only on teacher-made or standardized tests is that these tests are summative and do not provide the opportunity to refocus a student's efforts or to correct errors in a timely fashion. Summative-only assessment and evaluation reinforce poor habits and errors because students are unaware of the need to change. Teachers need to gather baseline data formally or informally through various forms of pretesting and then periodically evaluate progress. With the involvement of students and parents, a plan of action for each student is developed. An example of a progress report for incorporating the principles that guide assessment and evaluation appears in Figure 14.3. Such a report might be completed during teacher–student conferences or teacher–parent–student conferences.

Many school systems have moved away from traditional report cards containing a letter grade per subject. These have been replaced with reporting forms containing greatly increased amounts and types of information related to class work or with conferences. States are relying more and more on some form of test and/or standardized requirements for entering and graduating from high school. Many assessment instruments are being modified from traditional, quickly scored, multiple-choice tests to open-ended instruments that use questions like those found on NAEP tests.

In many classrooms, self-assessment habits begin in the earliest grades with collaborative goal setting. Students help to decide what is to be learned through a task and what makes a complete assignment. Teachers post learning goals, stated as questions, and encourage students to refer to them when needed and at specified reflective times. Students may write a more formal final reflection or the teacher may conduct a reflective discussion focused on how well the students believe they attained their goals and ask for evidence to support their claims of success or failure (Hart, 1999).

Group evaluation reports and rating of projects and working habits are used. Students also individually rate their group participation. These reports are combined with teacher observation and the final project to provide grades for cooperative group work. Young students begin rating only a few tasks, whereas older students have more

---

Progress Report Form: Social Studies

Name _____ Date _____

Task	Amount of Progress	Teacher Comments
	Low ◄──────► High	
1. Concept understanding as evidenced in		
a. Writing	◄──────►	
b. Speaking	◄──────►	
c. Graphic expression	◄──────►	
2. Problem-solving ability as evidenced in		
a. Participation in discussions	◄──────►	
b. Participation in activities	◄──────►	
c. Willingness to take risks	◄──────►	
d. Suggesting unique solutions	◄──────►	
e. Focused thinking	◄──────►	
f. Making appropriate responses	◄──────►	
3. Thinking-skill development as evidenced in		
a. Exhibiting creativity	◄──────►	
b. Exhibiting logical thought processes	◄──────►	
c. Grasping main idea	◄──────►	
d. Vocabulary		

FIGURE 14.3
Sample Progress Report

tasks because of their increased skill and cognitive levels. Questions that students might address when rating the progress of their group and their own efforts within the group are shown in Figure 14.4. The questions address skills and attitudes required for students to be successful in cooperating within the group. Questions ask students to identify specific tasks they do toward completing a project or assignment, for example, "What ideas did you contribute to how the project should look?"

Conferences with Diverse Parents and Families. Assessment and evaluation of individual students often is performed in collaboration with family members and the student. In student-led conferences, students present the information concerning their work and progress to the family members and teacher who ask questions. Then, all help to develop a focus plan for the student's efforts in the next grading period. Supporting activities can be agreed to, so that family members and the teacher work with the student to increase student knowledge and skills related to current events or to relate ideas learned through language and graphic means. Teachers offer students guidance in deciding what to present and how to approach the presentation as part of their classwork. With individual students, teachers may discuss particular selections and offer suggestions

---

Suggested Questions for Self-Evaluation of Group Work
_____

1. Did the group get to work promptly?
2. Did we understand our task?
3. Did everyone in the group have the opportunity to share their opinions and ideas?
4. Did everyone participate?
5. Did we wander off the topic to other things?
6. Did we offer facts and experiences to help in solving problems?
7. Were disagreements settled through compromise and with agreement of all?
8. Did we seek help from each other when needed?
9. Did we listen to each other?
10. Did we ask for help from the teacher only when we did not understand or could not solve the problem on our own?

Individual Self-Evaluation of Group Participation
_____

1. Did you have enough chance to talk about your ideas and information about the topic?
2. Were you happy during the group work?
3. What would have made you happier during the group work?
4. Did anyone seem to do most of the group's work?
5. Who in the group listens to you?
6. Who in the group doesn't listen to you?
7. Did anything bother you during the discussions? If so, what was it?
8. What should the group do to work together better?
9. Considering your abilities, the tasks you did, how much work you did, and how well you did your work, what grade do you think you should receive?
10. Suggest a grade for each member of your group. Consider the tasks each person did, how much work each one did, and how well done the work was.

FIGURE 14.4
Guiding Questions for Self-Evaluation during Group or Independent Study

and encouragement. Students decide what to present and practice presentations in small groups to refine their presentation skills.

Involving parents and students in assessment is an important learning experience for all, including the teacher (Read Write Think, 2008). In areas with large immigrant populations, teachers need to develop skills in relating to and talking with families who are not proficient in English and whose cultural views of parent and teacher roles may differ from those of the teacher. Teachers need training in assessment and evaluation and in sensitivity, communications, and multicultural behavior. In some instances, students may serve as translators in conferences with family members. When teachers have large enrollments of students whose families do not speak English or do not speak it well, the teacher attempts to learn to greet family members and thank them for coming using short phrases from their language, even if these phrases have to be written out phonetically and read from cards. Such actions show respect for the efforts family members make in coming to the conference as well as respect for their culture.

Performance Assessment.   Performance assessments are testing methods in which students demonstrate both knowledge and skills. Formats vary, but in all instances, students construct or perform rather than simply select a response. For example, a performance test occurs when a student is asked to identify cardinal directions in the gym. More elaborate performance tests assess presentations on research projects, including reporting on research findings, proposing solutions to problems, supporting findings with reason and evidence, working cooperatively with others, or planning a study. Lesson activities in the expansion phase of the learning cycle often provide opportunities for performance testing. Products of these activities are collected and graded or observed with the help of a checklist and rating scale.

Because many social studies activities cannot be completed without students applying learned skills and knowledge, the successful completion of social studies lessons and projects can serve as a form of evaluation. In addition to the project, students can write a description of the skills and steps used in completing the project or be interviewed about them. Performance assessment also may be a form of authentic assessment if the performance is the type of task that a citizen or an employee would be asked to perform as part of their work, and not just a contrived exercise for classroom use. In using performance assessments, students' performances can be positively influenced in several ways:

1. Selecting assessment tasks clearly aligned or connected to what has been taught
2. Sharing and scoring criteria for the assessment task with students prior to working on the task
3. Providing students with clear statements of standards and/or several models of acceptable performances before they attempt a task
4. Encouraging students to complete self-assessments of their performance
5. Interpreting students' performance by comparing them to developmentally appropriate standards, as well as to other students' performances (Elliot, 1995)

When performance assessment is used in standardized tests, it may be measured by open-ended questions. Many questions concerning history and the social sciences have more than one cause, effect, or result. Open-ended questions require students to apply concepts and make inferences at a level beyond that required by the multiple-choice questions. They allow students to bring divergent thinking, relevant information, and different outlooks to their answers.

Rubrics.   Assessing and evaluating authentic assignments and tasks requires obtaining information about the many parts of the task and the skills necessary to complete it. Terms such as *tasks*, *proficiency*, and *scoring criteria* are commonly used when discussing rubrics. Rubrics are used to identify both the content presented and the quality of the performance or presentation of information, skills, and values. Figure 14.5 on page 458 contains rubrics for projects intended to assess the variety of tasks a student needs to perform in preparing for and presenting a project. Students usually vary in their knowledge of, and ability to do, the various tasks required to complete a performance assessment. The use of rubrics identifies individual strengths and weaknesses so that students may set specific and individual goals for their learning efforts.

Students can be encouraged to participate in developing rubrics by asking several questions: What must be included in the answer for it to be complete? How important is it to make sure everyone has a chance to participate in their group's work? How will we know if the project is complete? Students can suggest a list of criteria that would be appropriate to include. The teacher adds to the list his or her expectations or asks a probing question, such as "We have learned how to write paragraphs, and our project includes writing, so do you think we should expect the answer to be written in complete paragraphs?" Alternatively, the teacher might suggest that because the class has learned that examples help to make ideas clear, the teacher expects students to include examples in their explanations. The teacher and students might discuss this idea and, together, agree on a minimum number of examples to include.

Students like to use rubrics because they help them see what is a complete and acceptable report or project. Setting standards against which to evaluate work as acceptable, of high quality, or in need of improvement presents an additional set of problems. To be fair in evaluation, students need to know the rubrics or criteria before they begin their work. As they work, they use the rubrics to help them assess their progress and evaluate the quality of their work. Students also help each other evaluate their work by applying the rubric and asking questions for clarification.

Teachers often are not familiar with all that the students have learned and do not know what criteria to set until they have had experience reviewing the work of many and varied students. Rubrics and their scoring criteria often are developed over several years. At first, rubrics may resemble lists of criteria or tasks students perform. Many teachers start with general guidelines for evaluation, such as noting that grammar is acceptable, especially good, or needs improvement. After several years, the scoring criteria may be spelled out in detail, including the specific number of examples or types of examples to be provided and the types of reasoning strategies used for work of varying quality. Recommended scoring techniques call for using a checklist approach, narrative/anecdotal recording, or rating-scale approach (Brualdi, 1998).

For rubrics to be successful once the scoring criteria are established and distributed to them, students must be able to trust that fulfilling them as stated results in the grade indicated. Should a teacher find that one or more papers go well beyond the stated scoring criteria, the teacher cannot change the grading standard and award to these papers the best grades, while lowering the grades of all who met the highest score (Nickell, 1999). Should this happen, Nickell recommends that students whose papers are exceptional receive the top grade plus written comments from the teacher. These additional comments note the outstanding characteristics of the assignment and compliment the student's efforts. Other students who have accomplished the criteria for the top grade also receive that grade. Should many exceptional products be produced, scoring criteria might be modified

FIGURE 14.5

Rubrics for Assessing Students' Projects and Related Tasks

Student Assessment Rubric

Student Name _____

Category	4—Exemplary	3—Accomplished	2—Developing	1—Beginning	Score
Content	A. All unit objectives are mastered B. Topics are covered in depth C. Many pertinent details included D. Went beyond assignment requirements	A. Most unit objectives are mastered B. Topics are covered C. Includes pertinent details	A. Some unit objectives are mastered B. Covers topics in superficial manner C. Few details are included	A. Few unit objectives are mastered B. Topic is not fully covered C. Few or no details	
Inquiry Skills	A. Evidence that all content has been carefully analyzed and evaluated B. Substantial evidence that students sought out and found other relevant sources that have been carefully synthesized C. Students can carefully explain or defend their reasons for choosing sources in their presentation	A. Evidence that content has been evaluated and analyzed, but not effectively synthesized B. Clear evidence that students sought out additional source materials and made a good attempt to integrate them into a coherent statement C. Some attempt to explain why materials were chosen	A. Some evidence that content has been either evaluated or analyzed, but no evidence it has been synthesized B. Some evidence that additional materials have been sought out C. Little evidence that student can explain why materials were chosen	A. Little evidence that the content has been evaluated, analyzed, or synthesized B. No evidence that additional materials were sought C. No evidence that student can explain why materials were chosen	
Technology	A. Used a variety of multimedia effects (images, sounds, video, etc.) B. Used a variety of appropriate sources beyond the *CongressLink* site and	A. Used more than one multimedia effect (images, sounds, video, etc.) B. Used more than one appropriate source beyond the *CongressLink* site	A. Used one or no multimedia effects (images, sounds, video, etc.) B. Used one or no appropriate sources external to *CongressLink* and limited their use of	A. Used one or no multimedia effects (images, sounds, video, etc.) B. Used no sources external to *CongressLink* and no other technology	

	...employed at least various technologies: scanner, other Web sources, digital recording, or digital camera to bring materials together	...and employed at least one of the following technologies: scanner, other Web sources, digital recording, digital camera	technology to the *CongressLink* website	
Presentation	A. Presentation is highly organized, thorough and cohesive B. Uses original approach effectively C. Terms and concepts are fully clarified for the audience D. Sources used greatly enhanced understanding of the topic E. Presentation of appropriate length. Used multiple appropriate sources external to *CongressLink*	A. Presentation is organized, thorough and cohesive B. Used original approach C. Terms and concepts are clarified for the audience D. Sources used enhanced understanding of the topic E. Presentation is of appropriate length. Used some appropriate sources external to *CongressLink*	A. Presentation needs work with its organization thoroughness and cohesiveness B. All terms and concepts are not clarified for the audience C. Some sources enhanced understanding of the topic D. Presentation is almost of appropriate length	A. Presentation is not organized, thorough, or cohesive B. Terms and concepts are not clarified for the audience C. Few sources enhanced understanding of the topic D. Presentation is of an inappropriate length
Teamwork	A. Consistently demonstrated vital leadership B. Consistently on-task throughout the unit C. Maintained positive attitude throughout the unit D. Played a critical role in organizing and facilitating group learning E. Met all due dates	A. Frequently demonstrated leadership B. Regularly on-task throughout the unit C. Maintained positive attitude throughout the unit D. Played a role in organizing and facilitating group learning E. Met all due dates	A. Regularly contributed to group effort B. Usually on-task throughout the unit C. Generally had a positive attitude D. Played a limited role in facilitating group learning E. Met most due dates	A. Sometimes contributed to the group effort B. Rarely on-task C. Not always a positive attitude D. Played a very limited role in facilitating group learning E. Frequently missed due dates

Source: From CongressLink (www.congresslink.org), a service of the Dirksen Congressional Center, Perkins, IL.

in the future for this assignment. Table 14.1 is an adaptation of one of the sample social studies performance tasks and rubrics that have been distributed to Wisconsin teachers as part of the Wisconsin Student Assessment System (WSAS) materials. It illustrates the alignment between the content standards, performance standards, task objective, and rubrics suggested as appropriate for use with students in grades 4 or 5.

The federal government is providing some leadership in the use of authentic assessments that incorporate rubrics for scoring. The most recent testing by

TABLE 14.1
Social Studies Performance Task and Rubric for Comparing Advertisements Grade Level 4/5

Related Content Standard	Students will learn about production, distribution, and consumption in making informed economic choices
Performance Standard	Students will give examples that show how scarcity and choice govern our economic decisions.
Objectives	1. Given three examples of newspaper or magazine advertisements with the prices removed, students will write two paragraphs or complete sentences that a. Identify similarities and differences between advertising claims b. Conclude whether these claims are describing meaningful differences c. Predict which products might be the most expensive, less expensive, least expensive, and give the reason for their decision
Rubrics	4. High Proficiency Highly organized, shows creative thinking Demonstrates a thorough understanding of basic content and concepts Sentences are complete without flaw, and mechanics are without error
	3. Proficiency Organization is logical—gets the point across Demonstrates an adequate understanding of basic content and concepts—minor errors do not detract from overall response Sentences are complete and mechanics are of quality
	2. Partially Proficient Presentation is ordered in an acceptable manner Demonstrates a marginal understanding of basic content and concepts—major errors of fact are present Sentences are of inconsistent quality; errors in mechanics are visible
	1. Minimal Response Poorly planned and disorganized Demonstrates little understanding of basic content and concepts Sentences are fragmented and mechanics are full of errors

the National Assessment of Educational Progress (NAEP) in history (1994), geography (1994), and civics (1998) included some short-answer questions scored with rubrics. Many of these questions are published at the NAEP website (http://nces.ed.gov/nationsreportcard). These publications report the success students have with each question given, provide the scoring rubrics, and illustrate each level with student sample responses. Figures 14.6 and 14.7 provide samples from the NAEP tests and illustrate a range of types of questions they ask. As you study these figures, take note of those questions for which a partial score is awarded and notice the rubrics suggested.

U.S. Department of Education statistics concerning how many students correctly complete each NAEP question and analysis of the test using group comparisons stimulate questions about social studies curricula. Whereas politicians might

After we anchored our ship in the ocean and went ashore to explore, we marched west. The forest was so thick we could only travel three miles in the first two days. Then we came to the mountains and climbed to the top. A rushing river flowed west out of the mountains. We continued to march two miles west and came down out of the mountains. Two miles further we came to the coast. It was obvious that the area we were exploring was an isthmus.

In the box below, draw a map of the region described above. Be sure to include all of the geographical elements mentioned in the description. Include a scale to indicate distance.

An **essential** response includes a map in which three elements are correctly placed. The response may be a peninsula or an island.

A **partial** response includes a map in which at least two elements are correctly placed.

FIGURE 14.6
Portion of 1994 NAEP Test in Geography for Eighth-Graders   *Source: Learning About Our World and Our Past: Using the Tools and Resources of Geography and U.S. History: A Report of the 1994 NAEP Assessment, by E. Hawkins, F. Stancavage, J. Mitchell, M. Goodman & S. Lazer, 1998, Washington, DC: National Center for Educational Statistics.*

> Scott wants to be a police officer when he grows up. He says the police get to wear uniforms with badges, use handcuffs, and drive cars as fast as they want.
> What is wrong with Scott's ideas about why he wants to be a police officer?
> <u>He thinks he gets to be big and powerful because he gets to brake [sic] the rules of others.</u>
> Think about the things police officers do in their work. What are two good reasons to be a police officer?
>
> 1. <u>You discipline people so they can learn from their mistakes.</u>
> 2. <u>Make peace between people that are fighting and fix the problem.</u>

These constructed-response questions are designed to measure fourth-grade students' ability to make distinctions between power and authority. The response received a score of 3, or acceptable, on a 4-point scale in which a score of 4 was considered complete and a score of 1 was considered unacceptable. The first part of the responses did not receive credit because its meaning was unclear. However, both reasons for being a police officer were credited. Overall, 67 percent of fourth-graders wrote an acceptable answer.

FIGURE 14.7
Completed Portion of 1998 NAEP Test in Civics for Fourth-Graders *Source*: The NAEP 1998 *Civics Report Card for the Nation* (NCES 2000–457), A. D. Lutkus, A. R. Weiss, J. D. Campbell, J. Mazzeo, & S. Lazer (1999, p. 25), Washington, DC: U.S. Department of Education, National Center of Educational Statistics.

focus on how well students in various groups (regional, racial, or ethnic) score, educators ask what results reveal concerning knowledge and skills being taught in the curriculum at various grade levels. When authentic tasks and thinking skills are included on tests, teachers provide practice with lessons and modify their own assessments to reflect the state or national test given. Because of time constraints, however, many state and national tests still include a greater portion of questions that ask students to recognize the best answer suggested by the test writer, rather than to construct their own answer.

In recent years, states have placed great emphasis on revising the learning standards and establishing benchmarks of learning for the more broadly stated standards. States are administering standardized tests to measure their success in meeting these benchmarks. The tests incorporate new types of questions to measure higher levels of learning and the multiple skills students must use to complete the questions at satisfactory and proficient levels.

Using documents such as letters, posters, and diary entries in teaching social studies is a standard procedure, but many students have not been formally tested on their abilities to use documents to form conclusions, make decisions, and solve problems. Document-based questions (DBQs) are appearing in larger numbers in social studies tests for elementary, middle, and high school students. Students are given several documents of various types (e.g., diary, cartoon, picture, legal papers, newspaper clippings, advertisements, or sections of government documents ranging from speeches to laws and the Declaration of Independence) that provide information on a social studies topic. The tests present a selected response question for each document and then present an essay question on the topic. Students write an essay of several paragraphs in which they examine the documents' positions, explain relationships between the documents, and explain the importance of the topic to the social studies topic. Students are expected to relate the content of these documents to other information they know about the topic and to state a conclusion or position.

The Bethpage school district in New York has an example at http://www.bethpagecommunity.com/Schools/socialst/k5/eriedbq.htm of document-based questions used by fourth-graders as they study transportation, specifically the Erie Canal. Fourth-graders look at a map of the Erie Canal, identify four cities along it, and then identify the waterway that connected the canal to New York City. Next, they look at a chart comparing travel by dirt road and by canal around 1845 and find it took 15 to 45 days by dirt road to ship goods that would only take 9 days to be delivered by canal boat. The chart also tells them that the shipping cost was $100 per ton by road but only $6 per ton by canal. Then, they identify and list advantages of using the canal over dirt roads. Other DBQ activities use a photo and other resources to continue the students' investigation of transportation via the Erie Canal.

Standardized testing can provide educators with information that helps to improve classroom instruction for the students. Teachers in the Greece, New York, Central School District provide a model for use of data from standardized tests. They examined the scores of their students on DBQs across the grade levels, noting common accomplishments and where students failed to receive credit on their essays. They made inferences about student behaviors and knowledge when using the documents and writing the test essays. Next, they interviewed students to learn whether their inferences were correct. The teachers noticed that the students did not write complete answers to the questions, writing well on one point and neglecting to provide the multiple examples and reasons asked for by the questions. Middle school students tended not to apply the rubrics given for the correct answers. Students told the teacher that they were confused about how to proceed with writing the essay because each year their teachers taught different approaches to writing essays. The teachers developed a common approach that focused on the claim, the evidence for the claim, and an interpretation of the meaning or importance of the claim. Teachers used this approach with a graphic organizer for writing essays using documents. They developed or located documents and used a DBQ essay writing assignment three times per year on topics selected by individual teachers in their own classrooms. They developed and used a generic rubric and had the students also apply the rubric by helping to evaluate their essays. As a result, student performance on the DBQ portion of the state tests improved.

NAEP tests a sample of students every four years in a particular content area. It also asks students and teachers to self-report selected behaviors that might help explain student scores. By law, NAEP is not allowed to ask questions that measure attitudes and predispositions for action. Therefore, neither the NAEP nor state tests can provide a complete measure of all social studies goals and objectives. Many questions remain for teachers and researchers to ask beyond those raised by

Building on Diversity

Promoting Individual Needs

The law requires that some students with special needs have individual learning plans. Often these recommend specific ways to change learning activities and identify modifications needed in testing conditions. For those with special needs, the teacher aligns assessment strategies with changes in learning goals and changes in the duration or physical conditions of lessons in which students are taught.

When multiple types of assessments are used and teachers and students work together to assess and evaluate learning progress, one result is that many more students receive help in establishing their own individual short- and long-term learning goals. Students with attention disorders may find alternative assessments provide them with a more accurate assessment of what they can do than do traditional tests for several reasons: (1) Alternative assessments do not necessarily require students to sit quietly for extended periods of time. (2) Alternative assessments actively involve students in learning activities. (3) Alternative assessments tolerate constructive noise.

Teachers can make specific arrangements to address individual needs:

1. Provide additional time to complete assessments to address problems of anxiety, attention span, language, vision, and reading difficulties.
2. Provide recorded directions or readings of test questions students can listen to using headphones.
3. Use Web Quests that set a task and guide a student or pair of students through using resources at their own pace to complete the task. For further discussion of Web Quests, see: http:socstrp.org/ISSUES/PDF/1.1.8.pdf.

4. Provide the opportunity for students to dictate their answers into recorders.
5. Use pictures and graphics to illustrate directions and questions for those with reading difficulties or second-language learners; encourage students to express answers with combinations of graphic representation and words.
6. Post written directions and schedules for assignments so that students can refer to them for additional assistance as they work.
7. When students are asked to present materials orally for authentic assessments, allow them to make presentations using digital audio or video so that they can stop, start, and redo.
8. Establish a quiet work area in the room away from sound and visual distractions.
9. Cooperate with special education teachers who work with inclusion students or with aides for those with special physical needs.

Gifted students have special needs. They may be gifted in one or more ways. Often, they are very creative in their thoughts and presentations of what they know and learn. Not being forced into thinking and performing like everyone else is important in supporting these students. During assessments and evaluation, it is important to look at and listen carefully to the entire message a gifted person presents in his or her works, giving recognition to novel perspectives and encouragement for future independent efforts. When teachers conference with family members, they should support the use of special mentors who have talent in the same areas as the gifted student. Conversations with such a mentor are a way of learning how to better encourage a gifted student and to help that student work cooperatively with all classmates.

standardized test results. Some argue that the best or most effective research is done by individual teachers in their own classrooms. Their rationale is that the individual teacher is most likely to use this information in a timely manner to bring about changes in classroom practices and curriculum for students.

Modes of Assessment

Assessment systems are evaluated to determine whether they provide teachers, students, and family members the kinds of information needed to foster meaningful social studies learning. Only then can results be used to make decisions about what is and is not working. Teachers work to ensure that both their informal and formal assessments consider each student at some point in a lesson. Procedures such as regular student–teacher conferences, teacher–parent conferences, student–teacher–parent conferences, and team meetings have been instituted in many schools to share information about students and plan for future learning. Such sharing is more productive when teachers increase their use of the following assessments.

Checklists.   Checklists identify desired student behaviors for lessons throughout the day. They provide a running record of the teacher's perceptions of students' participation and accomplishment. Table 14.2 illustrates such a checklist.

Individual Portfolios.   Individual portfolios are samples of student work illustrating what students are correctly able to do. Students select and organize best examples of work to illustrate clear progress over time. They present their portfolios to the teacher and family members. A portfolio contains a variety of products to

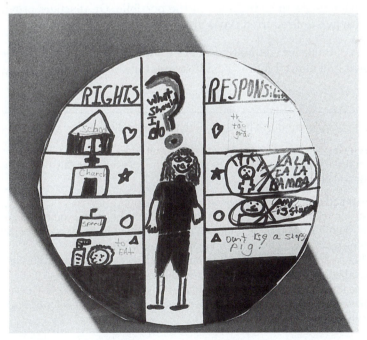

A student's drawing can be part of a portfolio.

TABLE 14.2
Sample Economics Education Checklist for the Student

Topic: Wants and Needs		Glenn	Sue
	Activity		
Needs	1. Identifies food as a need	X	X
	2. Identifies shelter as a need	X	X
Wants	1. Identifies a television as a want	X	
	2. Identifies a computer as a want	X	X
	3. Identifies roller blades as a want	X	
	4. Prioritizes wants	X	X
	5. Develops a timeline for obtaining the item prioritized as #1 on the want list		X

demonstrate the range of knowledge and skills the student is developing. Students periodically remove and replace materials in their portfolio or they begin a new section within it.

Teachers of younger students begin incorporating this form of assessment and evaluation by providing students with opportunities to select products from some of the assignments to be included in the portfolio. Or, teachers provide young students with a list of required types of assignments to be included.

Interviews.   Interviews enable teachers to talk with students in some depth about their ideas and plans. Figure 14.8 illustrates questions a teacher might ask students

---

The interviewer introduces the student to what will follow.

Interviewer: We have been exploring Hausa culture in West Africa. Because everybody has been following up different parts of Hausa culture, I wanted to talk to you about what you have found out.

1. What part of the culture did you decide to explore?
2. Can you tell me what you think is the most interesting thing you have found out?
3. Do you think this is really important for everyone to know, or is it something that is interesting but not something everyone should know? Why?
4. What are three things you have found out that you should share with everyone in this class because you think everyone should know them? Why?
5. If we think about these three important things, do you think we will decide that they are not very different from what we have here in our culture, or will we decide that they are really different? Why?

FIGURE 14.8
Interview Guide on Hausa Culture

in an interview to help them organize their thoughts while informing the teacher of their progress on an individual research topic on the Hausa people of West Africa. A key set of questions for each interview is preplanned. Additional questions probe students' ideas as the interview progresses. A record is kept of the types of responses students make and of any agreed-on goals identified as a result of the interview. All students in the class participate in interviews and are able to tell the teacher anything they want.

Classroom Websites.　Assessment should involve not only the teacher and student, but also the parents and guardians. Family members can be asked to share comments with their child on assignments and topics. By filling out short questionnaires or reports for the teacher on their child's learning and homework, parents help the teacher gain a better understanding of their child's interests, abilities, and needs. Parents should be encouraged to share such reports with their children and to offer encouragement and praise for studying and learning in school. Students can contribute to positive benefits from assessment by assisting in making class newspapers or websites designed to inform parents or to provide information on class activities. Even very young students can help select pictures that illustrate their school day and projects to put on a website and encourage their parents to visit a class website where the teacher may also post information and suggestions on ways parents might support student learning on current topics of study. In posting pictures from a field trip, for example, the teacher provides parents and students with a prompt for questions and discussion. Posting of student artwork and writings concerning class activities shows parents a range of the class activities and skills in the class. Class websites provide an e-mail address so that parents can easily communicate with the teacher. The computer provides an opportunity for busy parents and teachers to communicate more often and for the continuous assessment of a student's learning. Websites may include daily assignments to aid family members in discussing or supervising homework. They also provide opportunities to download assignments for students who must miss class. An example of a middle school teacher's home page for students and family members to use is that of Sue LeBeau at www.suelebeau.com.

Journals.　Journals are diaries or logs in which students reflect on their school experiences. They are especially helpful when students have individualized assignments. Journals encourage the use of writing as a learning process and as individual communication with the teacher.

Quality Circles.　Quality circles are class or small-group evaluation sessions. They may be teacher led or guided with a questionnaire or rubric, or students might write and share a report similar to a journal entry. Figure 14.4 suggests questions that might guide a group quality-circle discussion.

Self-Evaluation Reports.　Self-evaluation reports are filled out by each student concerning his role in a group. They give the student the opportunity to reflect on personal contributions to the group and how he could better benefit from group efforts. The lower section of Figure 14.4 suggests questions for a self-evaluation.

The Letter to ___.   Another form of self-assessment that works well in middle school is "a letter to __." Each student writes a letter to the teacher, a family member, an imaginary friend, etc. The teacher reminds the students of each of the goals of the unit, project, or lesson. The letter responds to each of the goals. Students can share their letters in class or on a discussion board and the teacher might record results, or the letters can be ready by only the teacher. An example of such a letter follows.

Goal 1:   The students will identify elements of the unit on political parties in which they demonstrated personal success and which should be useful to them in the future.

> *Favorite experiences:*
> My favorite experience was that I found that, if I divided up all the work into steps, I could get each part done and before I knew it, the whole thing was done.
> My favorite experience was that I was able to really get into political party websites and came up with a way to chart how much space was devoted to different ideas about a topic by each party. Then, I could really compare what they were saying about the topic.
>
> *Most important idea of the unit:*
> Everybody needs to know why we have political parties in this country (their history) and that they have succeeded mostly because they have represented the moderate view.
> We can get a really big job done if we all do our part and try to do it as best as we can, whether you are the political party or you are in a group working on this unit.
>
> *I will remember this about the unit:*
> A citizen needs to get beyond the 15 second sound bites and to use the Internet carefully to really find out what a political party is standing for in an election.
> It is very hard to get a new political party started and several people have tried in the last 25 years. People are more comfortable with the parties they have and don't contribute the money to really promote a new party.
> I am good at working on tasks with other people because I can work as part of a team or as a leader and can switch between these jobs.

The Self Study.   The self study is another form of self-evaluation report that lends itself well to use by middle schoolers. After a unit studying advertising and propaganda techniques, for example, students might develop their own commercials for a favorite product and digitally record them on video. They identify the techniques they tried to use to sell their product. Then, the whole class, a small group, or a partner analyzes the techniques in the commercial and gives written feedback to the commercial's producer. The producer follows up by writing a reflection on (1) why this product personally was important enough to choose for the commercial, (2) how well the group/partner analysis identified the technique(s) used and why there might be differences between what was intended and what was identified, and (3) how much influence the media and the propaganda techniques it uses seem to have on me. A self study can take many forms, but requires students to have some trust in the teacher.

Identifying Assessments Within a Lesson Plan

Formative assessment takes place throughout a lesson as the teacher engages students in activities and students make decisions that control their learning. It also occurs as the teacher asks questions and students share their ideas and products and develop consensus statements. As formative assessment occurs, the teacher determines whether students are constructing the ideas and skills that are the lesson's objectives. If a formative assessment indicates that students are not accomplishing the objective, the teacher does not move forward with the lesson plan. Instead, another instructional strategy is inserted to help students work through the problem and clarify ideas. It is important that a teacher incorporate formative assessment into the lesson to assist students at the most appropriate points in their learning. In the Learning Cycle, Making Good Rules, italicized comments indicate where and for what reasons the teacher is using formative assessment. Summative evaluation is used at the end of the lesson to determine how well each student constructed his or her understanding of the idea that good, useful rules have common characteristics.

Action Research and Reflection: Becoming an Effective Social Studies Teacher

Reflection on their practice is the primary way in which teachers enhance their professional development. Teachers use student data, observations of teaching, and interactions with their colleagues to reflect on and improve teaching practice.

Prospective and experienced teachers have beliefs about what good teaching is and what students should do and learn to understand social studies. These beliefs guide their teaching. Teachers use a variety of metaphors to describe their role in the social studies classroom: *expert*—tells students what they are to understand; *coach*—stands behind the students and tells them what to do in every step;

text continues on page 473

LEARNING CYCLE LESSON PLAN *Making Good Rules*

● **Grade Level:** Primary

NCSS Standards: Power, Authority, and Governance

NCSS

Standards VI

Concept: a good rule. The characteristics of a good rule are that (1) it is needed for a good reason, (2) it is clearly worded, (3) it applies fairly and equally to all, (4) it is easy to use or follow, and (5) it is agreed to by all.

Exploratory Introduction

Materials: Eraser

Objectives	→ Procedures	→	Assessments

1. Students discuss and identify reasons why rules are needed in a game.	1. Assign students to relay teams of 8 to 10 students for an eraser relay.
	2. Start the game, but do not give any rules. Stop students for not playing correctly and give one or two directions and then restart game only to stop it again. Repeat three to six times. Game rules include:
	  a. Pass the eraser down the row and then back up. The winning team is the first to complete this.
	  b. Players must hold the eraser with both hands.
	  c. The first player bends down and passes eraser to the next player by reaching through his or her legs.
	  d. The next player passes the eraser over his or her head, and so on.
	  e. Players turn around after passing eraser.
	  f. When the eraser gets back to the first player, everyone on the team sits down on the floor.
	3. After the game is played correctly, repeat it several times. Ask the key questions *each time* the game is played: "Is there a problem?" and "Is everyone playing fair?"
	4. Ask, "How can rules help us?" List students' responses on chart paper or the board (*formative assessment*). Ask, "How did you like playing this relay?" "How important was it that everyone knew all of the rules?" "Does everyone have to obey rules?" "What would happen if there were no rules?" (*Additional formative assessment of students' thinking and ideas that are related to the context in which the objective is set.*)
			1. Use a checklist to record those students who identify reasons explaining why rules are recorded in a game. (*Formative assessment; objective is assessed here.*)

continued

Lesson Development

Materials: Two statements on cards (see Procedures)

Objectives ⟶	*Procedures* ⟶	*Assessments*
1. Students analyze a good rule and a poor rule, applying a list of five identified characteristics of a good rule.	1. Assign pairs. Display two statements and read them to the students: "When the stoplight is red, stop and wait until it is green before going on." "When the stoplight is red, stop and wait until it is green before going on, except if you are wearing red shoes." Ask, "Could both of these statements be rules?" "How are they different?" "Is one a better rule than the other?" "Why?" (*Formative assessment of students' describing of criteria to identify good and poor rules.*)	1. Use a checklist to record which students applied the characteristics to a rule. (*Formative assessment; objective is assessed here.*)
	2. Have pairs develop a list of characteristics that make a rule a good rule.	
	3. Share ideas and list them on chart paper or the board. (*Formative assessment of students' offering of characteristics of a good rule. Documented by list developed.*) Together, develop a class consensus statement that lists the characteristics of a good rule and write it on the board. Focus students on including the following:	
	a. It is needed for a good reason.	
	b. It is clearly worded.	
	c. It applies fairly and equally to all.	
	d. It is easy to use or follow.	
	e. It is agreed to by all.	
	4. Ask, "Besides playing games, when do you have to obey rules?" Discuss and have students decide whether their characteristics of a good rule apply in situations other than playing games. (*Formative assessment of whether students offer suggestions for rule characteristics in other settings.*)	
	5. Ask, "Who makes rules?" Discuss. (*Formative assessment of students' ability to identify rules as being made by many people in various situations.*)	
	6. Ask, "What are some rules (laws) people have to obey?" Write these out and check them against the	

continued

list of characteristics of a good rule. (*Formative assessment of students' ability to apply characteristics in list to rules.*)

7. Have students select a rule from class or home and check it against the list of characteristics, writing down the letters of those that apply. Have students describe their work.

8. *Closure.* Review the list of characteristics together and decide whether it needs revision. Copy on to chart paper and post for all to see.

Expansion

Materials: Rules for fire drills or the bus

Objectives ⟶	Procedures ⟶	Assessments
1. Students write rules using characteristics of a good rule, then apply and evaluate them.	1. Have pairs examine the school's rule for fire drills or the bus using the list of characteristics for a good rule and their experiences with how it works in practice. Discuss students' findings. (*Formative assessment of students' attempt to use their experiences as well as the list of characteristics to determine whether a rule is good.*)	
	2. Ask pairs to develop a rule for a specific classroom activity, such as art class or free reading time, and to write it on the board. Share, deciding whether the rule meets the characteristics of a good rule. (*Formative assessment of whether the class is applying the list of characteristics.*)	
	3. Have the class select one of the rules to follow the next day or during the rest of the day. Afterwards, ask, "How well did the rule work?" "Do we need to revise the rule?" "Should we keep using it?" (Repeat process with other rules developed until all have been tested over a period of days.) (*Formative assessment of whether students attempt to develop, use, critique, and revise a good rule.*)	

continued

4. Ask each student to develop a rule the fits the list of characteristics or an activity at school or home that he or she thinks needs a rule. This activity should be one for which no pair has developed a rule.
5. *Lesson summary.* Have students tell you what they did in this lesson and what they think the lesson's "big idea" was.

Summative Evaluation: Apply the list of characteristics to the rule each student has developed, assigning one point for each included characteristic using the rubric.

Summative Evaluation Rubric

1. Each characteristic is included in the rule. Each characteristic is worth one point.

Characteristic	Point
a. It is needed for a good reason.	
b. It is clearly worded.	
c. It applies fairly and equally to all.	
d. It is easy to use or follow.	
e. It is agreed to by all.	
Points for characteristics:	

2. The rule is for an activity at school or home. Two points. Points: _____
3. The rule is for an activity for which no pair developed a rule. Three points. Points: _____

Total points out of 10 possible: _____

cheerleader—provides support for all student actions in their attempts to learn; *cook*—puts things in the pot and stirs while hoping for the best, providing many hands-on materials, and lots of time; and *facilitator*—assists students in carrying out their own plans.

Each of these descriptions or metaphors portrays aspects of teachers' tasks and behaviors that can be observed in classrooms. A relationship exists between what teachers believe and what they do in classrooms (Haney, Lumpe, &

TIME FOR REFLECTION | *What Do You Think?*

Read and reflect on the Learning Cycle Lesson Plan, Making Good Rules. Respond to the following. Share your responses with a peer, if possible.

1. Do the formative assessments in the lesson assist the teacher in tracking students' progress toward constructing the lesson's major concept?

2. Do the formative assessments in the expansion phase enable the teacher to identify whether students are applying the concept?

3. Does the summative evaluation enable the teacher to determine how well each student has constructed the major concept of the lesson?

4. Construct a checklist rubric for a social studies lesson plan. If possible, work with a partner. Choose an inquiry skill or social studies concept as an objective for the social studies lesson.

   a. What is the highest level of progress students are expected to reach with this skill or concept? State the skill or concept using an operational definition. Consider the question: "What do you want the students to be able to do, or make, at the completion of the lesson, if they have reached the highest level?" Label this statement as "level 3."

   b. Write down the lowest level of the skill or concept you expect to find among your students at the beginning of the lesson. Label this statement "level 1."

   c. Write down one additional level below the highest level you expect students to reach at the lesson's end. Label this statement "level 2."

   d. Write the three levels for a new list that is appropriate as an observational checklist rubric to be used for assessing students during the lesson.

Czerniak, 2002). Not only do teachers have beliefs about classroom teaching, these beliefs guide much of what teachers do in social studies. Better performance and continuous progression toward the goal of powerful and meaningful social studies teaching takes more than learning new strategies. The process requires changing beliefs and accommodating new situations.

Personal preferences, beliefs, and perceptions are only private and untested guesses or hypotheses about what is needed to facilitate students in learning social studies. How can we determine which of our preferences or beliefs about good teaching actually results in an individual student's development of a meaningful understanding of a significant social studies idea? If it works for one student, does it work with other students? Which of our beliefs work and which are "misconceptions," and for which students are these misconceptions? How does one change his or her beliefs?

Beliefs are personal convictions one holds about the way things work. Beliefs are persistent, resistant to change, and they guide our personal actions. Beliefs activate knowledge in classroom settings. If a person has knowledge, it generally will not be used unless the person's beliefs provide an action agenda. For example, even though cooperative learning groups have many positive effects on student achievement in social studies, a teacher may be reluctant to use the strategy because of an untested belief that groups foster student dependence on others to do the work.

Reflection as a process for personal change is seen in the early writings of such reformers as John Dewey (1929). Dewey described inquiry and the processes of reflection as being an intentional act on the part of teachers. Reflective inquiry distinguishes poor teachers from effective teachers. Becoming an expert teacher requires teachers to actively participate in research (Dewey, 1929). Today, more than ever, teachers are required to prove they are effective teachers. More importantly, you need to know that you are an effective teacher and that the ways in which you conduct your social studies lessons are successful in bringing meaningful social studies to the students you teach.

Teachers carry out practical research in their classrooms all the time. Action research is purposeful and personal. Action research is planned, systematic, and collaborative. It begins with finding or becoming aware of a generalized problem that is developed into a focus question. It involves methods and skills teachers use to solve classroom problems, but it is more systematic and collaborative. The teacher's efforts provide information about the new classroom practice that allows for decisions to be made concerning classroom changes.

Consider an event where students cannot understand the concept of interdependence due to the extended time needed to collect and organize lots of information from a variety of experiences. What is the problem? Will use of technology help? The focus question for the teacher's action research becomes: "Can using a simulation help students meaningfully understand interdependence?" To address this question, the teacher considers, "Where will I find information and help?" See Figure 14.9 for critical questions guiding action research. Other questions arise: "How will I investigate this question to find an answer in my classroom?" "What information is needed to answer the question?" "How can I gather data on students to answer this question?" "What classroom observations must be made?" If the results of the investigation of the problem are analyzed and evaluated as significant, the teacher develops an action plan to implement those results. The implementation is evaluated along with student responses to check whether the results provide a solution to the original question. Questions such as "How big a group should work on the simulation?" and "When students participate in the simulation do they understand the concept better than when reading the textbook or examining a flow map?" are best answered by action research in the classroom. Action research is self-assessment by teachers who want to continue their development of the PCK needed to effectively teach social studies.

Action research creates a deeper understanding of the ideas questioned as well as more powerful and meaningful social studies learning in students. Teachers regularly ask questions about everyday social studies teaching. Teachers who purposely use action research generate more questions about their teaching. They develop more effective strategies for systematically observing classrooms, testing out their questions, and solving teaching/learning problems. Solutions to complex problems take time to identify and implement. Introducing

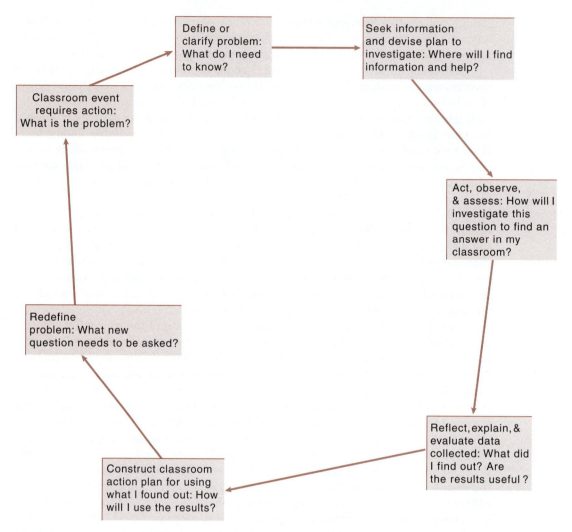

FIGURE 14.9
Critical Questions Guiding Classroom Action Research Activities

a new strategy, such as cooperative learning, inquiry learning, or simulations, requires time. Teachers using action research are more likely to value the results achieved and formulate effective plans of action based on what they have learned (Lumpe, Haney, & Czerniak, 2000).

Researchers have identified a number characteristic behaviors of expert teachers of social studies:

- They collaborate with colleagues to inquire into the needs and abilities of their students.

TIME FOR REFLECTION | ## What Do You Think?

Select a social studies textbook to examine for a particular topic. Obtain both the student and teacher's editions. Choose one chapter and review the suggested assessments in both. If possible, work with a partner on this activity. Record the following information:

- Textbook publisher and author
- Chapter title
- Chapter goal(s)

Create a table based on the example below and record your evaluation of the different assessments.

Page Number	Type of Assessment (e.g. True/False)	Evaluative Use of the Information (i.e. prior knowledge, monitoring, or summative)

Write a general description of the assessments suggested in the chapter. What areas are covered? What is missing? Evaluate the adequacy of the assessments suggested for a standards-based, hands-on, minds-on social studies program. What must be added to create effective assessment?

- They provide instruction for students from diverse backgrounds after reflection and feedback from their colleagues.
- They have their teaching performance evaluated by their colleagues (Lumpe, Haney, & Czerniak, 2000).

EXPANSION

 ## Practicing Skills in Pre-Assessment

Assessment and evaluation are major components in a social studies program. They provide information both to students and teachers that is used in short- and long-term planning. In the short term, a teacher uses formative assessment during a lesson to decide whether to move to the next phase of a lesson or whether further examples and explanations are needed by students. Short-term assessment also is used throughout a unit to determine whether students can work with the challenges of the next lesson and are able to build on what they know using the skills they have. Long-term planning occurs as a teacher lays out plans for a grading period and for the school year. Assessment and evaluation allow the teacher to restructure long-term plans so they best involve students in active participation in social studies and take advantage of newly developed content knowledge and skills.

TIME FOR REFLECTION   *What Do You Think?*

Assessing your students' prior knowledge is widely recognized as critical in effective teaching, but it is an instructional skill that takes time and practice to develop. Use the following method to help you plan a lesson.

1. Show individual elementary or middle school students several pictures of a historical event or era that you plan to teach. Ask students to tell you about the pictures listening carefully to their comments and taking notes. Ask a probing question only if needed to get a student to respond.

2. Write your reflection on the interviews. Identify the characteristics of each student and his/her responses, describing what they told you.

3. Describe any characteristics you expected students would mention, but found they did not.

4. Summarize your findings about their knowledge of the place and time period in the pictures, the sources of information they used, the accuracy of their knowledge, and their interest in the events and people represented in the pictures.

5. Describe the implications your findings have for the lesson you will plan.

6. Complete your lesson plan based on your new understanding of the students' prior knowledge of the topic.

Summary

Each student is special, and all students deserve complete assessments and fair evaluations. Each student must be treated first as a student, and evaluated in terms of similar needs to learn, grow, and develop into a productive citizen respectful of himself or herself and of others. Assessment and evaluation are positive processes involving the learner and helping teachers structure learning environments. Their goal is to meet the students' needs to reach the goals of the social studies program.

For proper evaluation, assessment begins with learning what the students know and do not know. It continues throughout the lesson as formative assessment guiding the instructional process until students attain their unique degree of success in understanding the social world in which they live and act. Teachers take the time to learn about the students they teach and work with others to improve student success. They realize that students' physical, emotional, and cultural needs must be addressed to help them get the most they can from school and to be measured fairly and recognized for their accomplishments. Most often, teachers who use a range of assessment and evaluation strategies, coupled with rubrics that spell out required levels of expectations, find that they are able to evaluate their students appropriately. Teachers own reflection and action research helps them assess and evaluate their teaching so it better addresses students' needs.

Recommended Websites to Visit

Website of the National Assessment of Educational Progress is the nation's report card
http://nces.ed.gov/nationsreportcard/

Exemplary rubrics for assessing research skills
www.fno.org/libskill.html

Help your students become good writers and publish on the Web
www.education-world.com/a_tech/tech042.shtml

Rubric Generator allows you to use prepared or customized rubrics
www.teach-nology.com/web_tools/rubrics/

Examine a sample document-based question for the primary grades
http://comsewogue.k12.ny.us/∼ssilverman/documents/example.htm

Sources of primary documents and document-based questions prepared by Paula Goldstein
www.kn.pacbell.com/wired/fil/pages/listdocumentpa.html#cat2

Looking at Student Work
http://www.lasw.org/

Sue LeBeau's home page for students, family members, and others
www.suelebeau.com

Action Research: A Strategy for Instructional; Improvement
http://www.newhorizons.org/strategies/action_research/front_action.htm

Action Research Resources
http://www.scu.edu.au/schools/gcm/ar/arhome.html

References

Alleman, J., & Brophy, J. (1994). Trade-offs embedded in the literary approach to early elementary social studies. *Social Studies and the Young Learner 6*(3), 6–8.

Alleman, J., & Brophy, J. (1998). Strategic learning opportunities during out-of-school hours. *Social Studies and the Young Learner 11*(4), 10–13.

Allen, R.(1996). The Engle-Ochoa decision making model for citizenship education. In R.Evans & D. Saxe, (Eds.), Handbook on teaching social issues, *NCSS Bulletin 93* (pp. 51–58). Washington, DC: National Council for the Social Studies.

American Association for the Advancement of Science. (1993a). *Benchmarks for science literacy* (pp. 3–4,322). New York: Oxford University Press.

American Association for the Advancement of Science. (1993b). *Science for All Americans.* New York: Oxford University Press.

Anderson, C. C. (1980). Promoting responsible citizenship through elementary law-related education. *Social Education 44,* 383–386.

Anderson, O. R. (1997). A neurocognitive perspective on current learning theory and science instructional strategies. *Science Education 81*(1), 67–89.

Anderson, O. R. & Krathwohl, D. (2001). *A taxonomy for teaching, learning, and, assessing.* New York, NY: Longman.

Angell, A. V., & Avery, P. G. (1992). Examining global issues in the elementary classroom. *The Social Studies 83*(3), 113–117.

Anholt, L. (1995). *Sophie and the New Baby.* Morton Grove, IL: Albert Whitman & Co.

Appleton, K., & Asoko, H. (1996). A case study of a teacher's progress using a constructivist view of learning to improve teaching in elementary science. *Science Education 80*(2),165–180.

Armento, B. J. (1986). Promoting economic literacy. In S. P. Wronski & D. H. Bragaw (Eds.), *Social studies and social science: A fifty-year perspective, Bulletin 78.* Washington, DC: National Council for the Social Studies.

Armento, B. J., & Flores, S. (1986). Learning about the economic world. In V. A. Atwood (Ed.), *Elementary school social studies: Research as a guide to practice, Bulletin 79* (pp.85–101). Washington, DC: National Council for the Social Studies.

Atherton, J. S. (2005). Learning and teaching: Constructivism in learning. Accessed December 1, 2008 from: http://www.learningandteaching.info/learning. constructivism.htm.

Ayers, W. (1993). *To teach: The journey of a teacher.* New York: Teachers College Press.

Baker, D. R., & Piburn, M.D. (1997). *Constructing science in middle and secondary school classrooms.* Boston: Allyn & Bacon.

Banaszak, R. A. (1987). *The nature of economic literacy.* Bloomington, IN: Clearinghouse for Social Studies/ Social Science Education. (ERIC Digest No. 41).

Bandura, A. (1977). *Social learning theory.* Englewood Cliffs, NJ: Prentice Hall.

Banks, J. A., & Clegg, A. (1979). *Teaching strategies for the social studies: Inquiry, valuing and decision making* (2nd ed). Reading, MA: Addison Wesley.

Baral, C. (2003). *Knowledge representation, reasoning and declarative problem solving.* New York, NY: Cambridge University Press.

Barone, D. (1990). The written responses of young children: Beyond comprehension to story understanding. *The New Advocate 3,* 49–56.

Barton, K. C. (1997a). "Bossed around by the queen": Elementary students' undestandingof individuals and institutions in history. *Journal of Curriculum and Supervision 12,* 290–314.

Barton, K. C.(1997b). History—It can be elementary: An overview of elementary students' understanding of history. *Social Education 67*(1), 13–16.

Barton, K. C. (1997c)."I just kinda know": Elementary students' ideas about historical evidence. *Theory and Research in Social Education 25*(4), 407–430.

Barton, K. C. & Levstik, L. S. (2004). *Teaching History for the Common Good.* Mahwah, NJ: Erlbaum.

Bedford, D. & Field, E. (illus.) (2001). *It's My Turn.* Tower.com: Bt. Bound.

Benjamin, J. R. 2001). *A student's guide to history* (8th ed.). Boston, MA: Bedford/St.Martin's.

Berk, L. (2000). *Child development* (5th ed.).Boston: Allyn and Bacon.

Berkowitz & Bier. (2004). Research-based character education. *The Annals of the American Academy of Political and Social Science, 59*(1), 72–85.

Berliner, D. (1987). Knowledge is power: A talk to teachers about a revolution in the teaching profession. In D. Berliner & B. Rosenshine (Eds.), *Talks to teachers.* New York: Random House.

Beyer, B. (1974). *Ethnicity in America.* Pittsburgh, PA: Carnegie Mellon University,Social Studies Curriculum Center.

Bianchini, J. A. (1998). What's the big idea? *Science and Children 36* (2), 40–43.

Blackwood, G. L. (2002). *The Year of the Hangman.* New York, NY: Dutton Children's Books.

Bos, C. S., & Anders, P. L. (1990). Interactive teaching and learning: Instructional practices for teaching content and strategic knowledge. In T. E. Scruggs & B. Y. L. Wong (Eds.), *Intervention research in learning disabilities* (pp.166–185). New York: Springer-Verlag.

Bourgeois, P. & Clark, B. (illus) (1999). *Franklin Collection: 10 Books.* London: Kids Can Press Ltd.

Boyle-Baise, M., Hsu, M-C., Johnson, S., Serriere, S. C., & Steward, D. (2008). Putting reading first: Teaching social studies in elementary classrooms. *Theory and Research in Social Education 36*(3), 23–255.

Bradley Commission on History in the Schools. (1989). Building a history curriculum: Guidelines for teaching history in schools. In P. Gagnon (Ed.), *Historical literacy* (pp. 16–50). New York: Macmillan.

Bunnett, R. & Brown, M. (illus). (2006). *Friends at School*. Long Island, NY: Star Bright Books.

Brody, R. A. (1989). Why study politics? In national commission on social studies in the school, *Charting a course: Social studies for the 21st century* (pp. 59–63). Washington, DC: National Council for the Social Studies.

Brophy, J. & Alleman, J. (2008). Early elementary social studies. In L. S. Levstik & C. A. Tyson (Eds.) *Handbook of Research In Social Studies Education*. New York, NY: Routledge.

Brophy, J., & Alleman, J. (2000). Primary grade students' knowledge and thinking about Native American and pioneer homes. *Theory and Research in Social Education 28*(1), 96–120.

Brophy, J., & Van Sledright,B.(1997). *Teaching and learning history in elementary schools*. New York: Teachers College Press.

Brown, L. M., Tappan, M. B., & Gilligan, C. (1995). Listening to different voices. In W. M. Kurtines & J. L. Gewirtz (eds.), *Moral development: An Introduction* (pp. 311–336). Needham Heights, MA: Allyn and Bacon.

Brualdi, A. (1998).Implementing performance assessment in the classroom. *ERIC/AE Digest.* (ERIC Document Reproduction Service No. ED 423 312.)

Bruner, J., Goodnow, J., & Austin, G. A. (1962). *A study of thinking*. New York: Science Editions.

Buchovecky, E. (1996). Learning from students' work. *Horace 30, 2.*

Buggey, J., & Kracht, J. (1985). Geographic learning. In V. A. Atwood (Ed.), *Elementary school social studies: Research as a guide to practice, Bulletin 79* (pp. 55–67). Washington, DC: National Council for the Social Studies.

Bulgren, J. A., Deshler, D. D., & Schumaker, J. B. (1993). *The content enhancement series: The concept mastery routine*. Lawrence, KS: Edge Enterprises.

Buysse, V., Goldman, B., & Skinner. M. (2003). Friendship formation in inclusive early childhood classrooms: What is the teacher's role? *Early Childhood Research Quarterly, 18*(4), 485–501.

California State Department of Education. (1988). *History–social science framework for California public schools: Kindergarten through grade 12*. Sacramento, CA: Author.

Carnegie Corporation. (2003). *The civic mission of schools: A report from the Carnegie Corporation of New York Ad Circle: The center for information and research on civic learning and engagement*. New York: Carnegie Corporation.

Castle, C. & Weevers, P. (1986). *Herbert Binns and the Flying Tricycle*. New York, NY: Dial.

Center for Civic Education. (1994). *National standards for civics and government*. Calabasas, CA: Author.

Center for Multicultural Education. (2000). *Essential principles for teaching and learning in a multicultural society*. Seattle: University of Washington Center for Multicultural Education.

Christensen, L. M., & Dahle, K. B. (1998). Is social studies different because I am included? The Docket: *Journal of the New Jersey Council for the Social Studies 8,* 19–23.

Chu, S., Chow, K., Tse, S., & Kulthau, C. (2008). Grade 4 students' development of research skills through inquiry-based learning projects. *School Libraries Worldwide. 14*(1), 10–37.

Clark, T. (1990). Participation in democratic citizenship education. *The Social Studies 81,* 206–209.

Collins, H., Czarra, F. & Smith, A. (1998). Guideline for global and international studies education: Challenges, culture, and connections. *Social Education 62*(5), 311–317.

Conflict Resolution Education Network. (2000). Conflict resolution in schools. *The ERIC Review 7*(1), 27.

Cook, L. K., & Mayer, R. E. (1988). Teaching readers about the structure of scientific text. *Journal of Educational Psychology 80,* 448–456.

Costa, A. (1991). The inquiry strategy. In A. Costa (Ed.), *Developing minds: A resource book for teaching* (Rev. ed., Vol. 1, pp. 302–303). Alexandria, VA: Association for Supervision and Curriculum Development.

Costa, A. (2002). Mediating the metacognitive. In A. Costa (Ed.), *Developing minds: A resource book for teaching* (3rd. ed., pp. 408–412). Alexandria, VA: Association for Supervision and Curriculum Development.

Council of Chief State School Officers. (1988). *Geography education and the state*. Washington, DC: Author.

Courtney, A., & Haas, M. E. (2006). How is today's consumer affected by advertising? *Social Studies Research and Practice 1*(2), http://socstrp.org.Retrieved July 28,2006.

Cruz, B. C. (1998). Global education in the middle school curriculum: An interdisciplinary perspective. *Middle School Journal 30*(2), 26–31.

Cruz, B. C., Nutta, J. W., O'Brien, J. O., Feyten, C. M., & Govoni, J. M. (2003). *Passport to learning: Teaching social studies to ESL students. Bulletin 101*. Silver Spring, MD: National Council for the Social Studies.

Cummins, J. (1984). *Bilingualism and special education: Issues in assessment and pedagogy*. San Diego: College-Hill.

Cummins, J. (1996). *Negotiating identities: Education for empowerment in a diverse society*. Los Angeles: California Association for Bilingual Education. Davis, B. G. Diversity and Complexity in the Classroom: Considerations of Race, Ethnicity, and Gender, accessed November 6, 2008 http://teaching.berkeley.edu/bgd/diversity.html

Demi (1990), *The Empty Pot*. New York, NY: Henry Holt and Company.

Dewey, J. (1929). *Democracy and education*. New York: Free Press.

DiSessa, A. A., Elby, A., & Hammer, D. (2002). J's epistemological stance and strategies. In G. Sinatra and P. Pintrich (Eds.), *Intentional conceptual change* (pp. 237–290). Mahwah, NJ: Lawrence Erlbaum Associates.

Donnan, C. S. (1988). Following our forebears' footsteps: From expedition to understanding. In V. Rogers, A. D. Roberts, & T. P. Weiland (Eds.), *Teaching social studies: Portraits from the classroom, Bulletin 82*. Washington, DC: National Council for the Social Studies.

Drake, J. J., & Drake, F. D. (1990). Using children's literature to teach about the American Revolution. *Social Studies and the Young Learner 3*(2), 6–8.

Dreyfus, A., Jungwirth, E., & Eliovitch R. (1990). Applying the cognitive conflict strategy for conceptual change—Some implications, difficulties, and problems. *Science Education 74*(5), 555–569.

Dunfee, M. (1977). *Social studies for the real world*. Columbus, OH: Merrill.

Dunfee, M., & Sagl, H. (1967). *Social studies through problem solving: A challenge to elementary school teachers*. New York: Holt, Rinehart, & Winston.

DuSessa, A, Elby, A. & Hamner, D. (2005). J's epistemelogical stance and strategies. In G. M. Sinatra & P. R. Pintrich (Eds.), *Intentional Conceptual Change*, (pp. 237–290). Mahwah, NJ: Erlbaum.

Eddington, W. D. (1998). The use of children's literature in middle school social studies: What research does and does not show. *The Clearing House 72*(2), 121–125.

Educational Broadcasting Corporation (2004). Concept to Classroom: Workshop: Inquiry Based Learning. Accessed December 14, 2008 http://www.thirteen.org/edonline/concept2class/inquiry/

Eggen, P., & Kauchak, D. (2001). *Strategies for teachers: Teaching content and thinking skills*. Englewood Cliffs, NJ: Prentice Hall.

Eggen, P., Kauchak, D., & Harder, R. (1979). *Strategies for teachers*. Englewood Cliffs, NJ: Prentice Hall.

Ekman, P., & Davidson, R. (Eds.). (1994). *Fundamental questions about emotions*. New York: Oxford University Press.

Elliot, S. N. (1995). Creating meaningful performance assessments. *ERIC Digest E531*. (ERIC Document Reproduction Service No. ED 381 985.)

Endacott, J. (2007). What is the Best Way to Govern a Nation? In L. Bennett & M. Berson, Eds. *Digital age: Technology-based K–12 lesson plans for social studies* NCSS Bulletin #105, (pp. 77–81). Washington, DC: National Council for the Social Studies.

Engle, S. H., & Ochoa, A. S. (1988). *Education for democratic citizenship: Decision making in the social studies*. New York: Teachers College Press.

Englert, C. S., & Mariage, T. V. (1991). Making students partners in the comprehension process: Organizing the reading "POSSE." *Learning Disabilities Quarterly 14*, 123–138.

Englert, C. S., Tarrant, K. L., Mariage, T. V., & Oxer, T. (1994). Lesson talk as the work of reading groups: The effectiveness of two interventions. *Journal of Learning Disabilities 27*, 165–185.

Ennis, R. (1991). Goals for a critical thinking curriculum. In A. Costa (Ed.), *Developing minds: A resource book for teaching* (Rev. ed., Vol. 1, pp. 68–71). Alexandria, VA: Association for Supervision and Curriculum Development.

Evans, R., Newmann, F., & Saxe, D. (1996). Defining issues-centered education. In R. Evans & D. Saxe (Eds.), *Handbook on teaching social issues, NCSS Bulletin 93* (pp. 1–5). Washington, DC: National Council for the Social Studies.

Eyler, J. & Giles, D. E. Jr. (1999). *Where is the "Learning in Service Learning?* Indianapolis: Jossey-Bass Publishers.

Farris, P. J., & Cooper, S. M. (1994). *Elementary social studies: A whole-language approach*. Madison, WI: William Brown & Benchmark.

Fertig, G. & Silverman, F. (2009). Creating biography webs to investigate individuals' historical contexts. *Social Education 73*(5): 244–248.

Flaitz, J. (Ed.). *Understanding your international students: A cultural, educational, and linguistic guide*. Ann Arbor, MI: University of Michigan Press.

Fraenkel, J. (1977). *How to teach about values: An analytic approach*. Englewood Cliffs, NJ: Prentice Hall.

Fregosi, C. (1976). *Almira's Violets*. New York, NY: Greenwillow.

Friedman, T. L. (2005). *The world is flat*. New York: Farrar, Strauss and Giroux.

Gagne, R. (1965). *The conditions of learning*. New York: Holt, Rinehart and Winston.

Gilligan, C. (1982). *In a different voice: Psychological theory and women's development*. Cambridge, MA: Harvard University Press.

Ginsburg, H., & Opper, S. (1988). *Piaget's theory of intellectual development* (3rd ed.). Englewood Cliffs, NJ: Prentice Hall.

Global Education Week Network. (2008). Global education guidelines: Concepts and methodologies of global education for educators and policy makers. Lisbon: North-South Centre of the Council of Europe. http://www.coe.int/t/dg4/nscentre/GEguideline_presentation_en.asp (Retrieved June 23, 2009)

Gollub, M. (1996). *The Moon Was at a Fiesta*. New York, NY: Tambourine Books.

Gomi, T. (2006). *My Friends*. San Francisco, CA.: Chronicle Books.

Graue, B. (2006). Introductory essay: Section six: Challenges in writing, voice, and dissemination of research. In Conrad, C. & Serlin, R. (Eds.) *The sage handbook for research in education: Engaging ideas and enriching inquiry*. (p. 506). New York, NY: Sage.

Haas, M. E. (1985). *Evaluating sponsored materials. How To Do It Series 4 Number 3*. Washington, DC: National Council for the Social Studies.

Haas, M. E. (1989). *Teaching geography in the elementary school*. Bloomington, IN: Clearinghouse for Social Studies Social Science Education. (ERIC Digest No. ED-SO-89–6.)

Haas, M. E. (2000). A street through time used with powerful instructional strategies. *Social Studies and the Young Learner 13*(2), 20–23.

Haas, M. E., & Laughlin, M. A. (1999a). *Meeting the standards: Social studies reading for K–6 educators*. Washington, DC: National Council for the Social Studies.

Haas, M. E., & Laughlin, M. A. (1999b). *Perspectives on social studies over a quarter of a century: Reflections from veteran social studies leaders*. (ERIC Document Reproduction Service No. ED 432 516.) Bloomington, IN: Social Studies Development Center and ERIC Clearinghouse for Social Studies/Social Science Education.

Haas, M. E., & Laughlin, M. A. (2000). *Teaching current events: Its status in social studies today*. (ERIC Document Reproduction Service No. ED 440 899.) Bloomington, IN: Social Studies Development Center and ERIC Clearinghouse for Social Studies/Social Science Education.

Haas, M. E., & Laughlin, M. A. (2001). A profile of elementary social studies teachers and their classrooms. *Social Education 65*(2), 122–126.

Haas, M. E., Channell, J., Linder, M. T., Vandevander, H., & Van Sickle, A. (2006). Developing social studies WebQuests with Teacher candidates. *Social Studies Research and Practice 1*(1), retrieved from http://socstrp.org. July 8, 2006.

Hampton, E., & Gallegos, C. (1994). Science for all students. *Science Scope 17*(6), 5–8.

Haney, J., Lumpe, A., & Czerniak, C. (2002). From beliefs to actions: The beliefs and actions of teachers implementing change, *Journal of Science Teacher Education 13*(3), 171–187.

Hanvey, R. G. (1976). *An attainable global perspective.* New York: Center for Global Perspectives.

Hart, D. (1999). Opening assessment to our students. *Social Education 63*(6), 343–345.

Hartoonian, M., Van Scotter. R., & White, W. E. (2007). An idea called America. *Social Education 71*(5), 243–247.

Hartup, W. W., Glazer, J., & Charlesworth, R. (1987). Peer reinforcement and sociometric status. *Child Development 38,* 1017–1024.

Harvey, S., & Goudvis, A. (2000). *Strategies that work: Teaching comprehension to enhance understanding.* New York, NY: Stenhouse.

Heacock, G. A. (1990). The we-search process: Using the whole language model of writing to learn social studies content and civic competence. *Social Studies and the Young Learner 2*(3), 9–11.

Hepburn, M. A. (1998). The power of the electronic media in the socialization of young Americans: Implications for social studies education. *The Social Studies 89*(2), 63–71.

Hepburn, M. A. (2000). Service learning and civic education in the schools: What does recent research tell us? In S. Mann & J. J. Patrick (Eds.). *Education for civic engagement: Service learning and other promising practices* (pp. 45–59). Bloomington, IN: ERIC Clearinghouse for Social Studies/Social Science Education.

Hertzberger, H. (1989). History and progressivism: A century of reform proposals. In P. Gagon (Ed.), *Historical literacy* (pp. 69–102). New York: Macmillan.

Hickey, M. G. (1999). *Bringing history home: Local and family history projects for grades K–6.* Boston: Allyn & Bacon.

Hofer, M. & Swan, K (2006). Standards, firewalls, and general classroom mayhem: Implementing student-centered technology projects in the elementary classroom. *Social Studies Research and Practice, 1*(1), 129–144.

Hoge, J. (1986). *Improving the use of elementary social studies textbooks.* (ERIC Digest No. 33.) Bloomington, IN: Clearinghouse for Social Studies/Social Science Education.

Hoge, J. D., & Allen, R. F. (1991). Teaching about our world community: Guidelines and resources. *Social Studies and the Young Learner 3*(4), 19, 28–32.

Holmes, E. E. (1991). Democracy in elementary school classes. *Social Education 55,* 176–178.

Holmes Group. (1986). *Tomorrow's teachers: A report of the Holmes groups.* East Lansing, MI: Author.

Hughes, P. (2003). Guerilla Season. New York, NY: Farrar, Strauss, and Giroux.

Hursh, D. (1997). *Multicultural social studies: Schools as places for examining and challenging inequality* (pp. 107–120). Albany, NY: State University of New York Press.

Hyman, M. (2001). One step at a time: A land mine removal initiative. *Middle Level Learning 14,* 10–15.

I-Safe America, Inc. (July 20, 2006). Bullying. Retrieved July 20, 2006, from www.isafe.org.

Jacobowitz, R. (1997). 30 tips for effective teaching. *Science Scope 21*(4), 22–25.

Jennes, D. (1990). Making sense of social studies. New York: Macmillan.

Johnson, D., Johnson, R., & Holubec, E. (1990a). *Circles of learning.* Edina, MN: Interaction Book Company.

Johnson, D., Johnson, R., & Holubec, E. (1990b). *Cooperation in the classroom.* Edina, MN: Interaction Book Company.

Johnson, D. W., & Johnson, R. T. (1978). Cooperative, competitive, and individualistic learning. *Journal of Research and Development in Education 12*(1), 3–15.

Johnson, D. W., & Johnson, R. T. (1991). Group assessment as an aid to science instruction. In G. Kulm & S. Malcolm (Eds.), *Science assessment in the service of reform* (pp. 281–289). Washington, DC: American Association for the Advancement of Science.

Johnson, R. T. & Johnson, D. W. (1986). Action research: Cooperative learning in the science classroom. *Science and Children 24*(2), 31–32.

Joseph, P. R. (2000). Law and pop culture: Teaching and learning about law using images from popular culture. *Social Education 64*(4), 206–211.

Joyce, B., & Weil, M. (1992). *Models of teaching* (pp. 159–179). Englewood Cliffs, NJ: Prentice Hall.

JumpStart Coalition for Personal Financial Literacy. (2002). *National Standards in Personal Finance: With benchmarks, applications and glossary for K–12 classrooms.* Washington D.C.: JumpStart for Personal Financial Literacy. www.jumpstartcoalition.org (retrieved July 3, 2009).

Keeler, C. & Langhorst, E. (2008). From PowerPoint to podcasts: Integrating technology into the social studies. *Social Studies Research and Practice, 3*(1), 164–176.

Kelley, L. A. (2006). Learning to que4stion in kindergarten. *Social Studies Research and Practice 1*(1), 45–54.

Kelly, L. A. (2009). *An examination of second graders' construction and interpretation of questions used during social studies interviews.* Unpublished doctoral dissertation. Tuscaloosa, AL: The University of Alabama.

Kniep, W. M. (1989). Social studies within a global education. *Social Education 53,* 399–403.

Kohlberg, L. (1969). Stage and sequence: The cognitive developmental approach to socialization. In D. Goslin (Ed.), *Handbook of socialization theory and research* (pp. 118–140). Chicago: Rand McNally.

Konigsburg, E. L. (1968). *Jennifer, Hecate, Macbeth, William McKinley, and Me, Elizabeth.* New York: Atheneum.

Kostelnik, M. J., Whiren, A. P., Soderman, A. K., Stein, L. C., & Gregory, K. (2002). *Guiding children's social development: Theory to practice.* Albany, NY: Thomson Delmar.

Kounin, J. (1970). *Discipline and group management in classrooms.* Huntington, NY: R. E. Kreiger.

Kourilsky, M. L. (1977). The kinder economy: A case study of kindergarten pupils' acquisition of economic concepts. *Elementary School Journal 77,* 182–191.

Kuhn, D., Black, J., A., & Kaplan, D. (2000). The development of cognitive skills to support inquiry learning. *Cognition and Instruction, 18(4),* 495–523.

Kuhn, D., Black, J., A., Keselman, D. & Kaplan, D. (2000). The development of cognitive skills to support inquiry learning. *Cognition and Instruction, 18(4),* 495–523.

Laney, J. D. (1993). Economics for elementary school students' research-supported principles of teaching and learning that guide classroom practice. *The Social Studies 84*(3), 99–103.

Langston, S. (1990). Citizen participation and citizenship education in the 21st century. In W. T. Callahan, Jr.,

& R. A. Banaszak (Eds.), *Citizenship for the 21st century* (pp. 297–310). Bloomington, IN: Social Studies Development Center.

Larson, B., & Keiper, T. A. (1999). Creating teledemocracy. In Joseph A. Braun, Jr., & C. Frederick Risinger (Eds.), *Surfing social studies: The Internet book, Bulletin 96*(pp. 49–52). Washington, DC: National Council for the Social Studies.

Leming, J. S., Ellington, L. & Porter-Magee, K. (2003). *Where did we go wrong?* Washington, D.C.: Thomas B. Fordham Institute.

Leming, J. S., Ellington, L. & Schug, M. (2006). *Social studies in our nation's elementary and middle schools: A national random survey of social studies teachers' professional opinions, values, and classroom practices.* Center for Survey Research and Analysis. University of Connecticut.

Levstik, L. (1986). The relationship between historical response and narrative in a sixth grade class. *Theory and Research in Social Education 15*(1), 1–17.

Levstik, L., & Barton, K. (1997). *Doing history: Investigating with children in elementary and middle schools.* Mahwah, NJ: Erlbaum.

Lewis, B. A. (1991). The kid's guide to social action. Minneapolis, MN: Free Spirit.

Lewis, C. S. & Baynes, P. (illus). (1949). *The Chronicles of Narnia.* London: C. S. Lewis Pte.

Libresco, A. & Phua, K. (2007) Standard of Living around the World: From Analysis to Action. In L. Bennett & M. Berson, Eds.*) Digital age: Technology-based K–12 lesson plans for social studies NCSS Bulletin #105,* (pp. 52–57). Washington, DC: National Council for the Social Studies.

Lionni, L. (1995). *Little blue and Little Yellow.* New York, NY: Harper Collins.

Lionni, L. (1996). *It's Mine!* Melbourne, Australia: Dragonfly Press.

Lopach, J., & Luckowski, J. (1989, March). The rediscovery of memory in teaching democratic values. *Social Education 53,* 183–187.

Lutkus, A. D., Weiss, A. R., Campbell, J. R., Mazzeo, J., & Lazer, S. (1999). *The NAEP 1998 civics report card for the nation,* NCES 2000–457, Washington, DC: U. S. Department of Education, Office of Educational Research and Improvement, National Center for Education Statistics.

Lynch, E. W. (1998). Developing cross-cultural competence. In E. W. Lynch & M. J. Hanson (Eds.), *Developing cross-cultural competence: A guide to working with children and their families* (pp. 47–86). Baltimore: Paul H. Brookes.

Macoby, E., & Masters, J. (1970). Attachment and dependency. In P. Mussen (Ed.), *Carmichael's manual of child psychology* (3rd ed., Book 2). New York: Wiley.

Mager, R. (1962). *Preparing instructional objectives.* Belmont, CA: Fearon.

Marshall, C., & Rossman, G. B. (1995). *Designing qualitative research* (2nd ed.). Thousand Oaks, CA: Sage.

Martin-Kniep, G., & Soodak, L. (1995). Curriculum integration: An expanded view of an abused idea. *Journal of Curriculum and Supervision 10*(3), 227–249.

Martin, F. (2007). The wider world in the primary school. In D. Hicks & C. Holden (Eds.) *Teaching the global Dimension: Key principles and effective practice.* (pp. 163–175). New York: Routledge.

Massachusetts Institute of Technology. (1990). *Education that works: An action plan for the education of minorities.* (Quality of Education for Minorities Report.) Cambridge: Massachusetts Institute of Technology.

Mastropieri, M. A., & Scruggs, T. E. (2000). *The inclusive classroom: Strategies for effective instruction.* Columbus, OH: Merrill.

Mathys, L. (2007). Westward Ho! In L. Bennett & M. Berson, Eds.*) Digital age: Technology-based K–12 lesson plans for social studies NCSS Bulletin #105,* pp. 24–28). Washington, DC: National Council for the Social Studies.

Mayer, V. (1995). Using Earth System for Integrating Science Curriculum. *Science Education 79*(4), 375–391.

McAninch, L., Swan, K. & Hofer, M. (2007). Podcasting: A beginner's guide to technology's latest trend. *Social Studies Research and Practice, 2*(3), 510–517.

McBee, R. H. (1996). Can controversial topics be taught in the early grades? The answer is yes! *Social Education 60*(1), 38–41.

McCain, T. (2005). *Teaching for tomorrow: Teaching content and problem solving skills.* Thousand Oaks, CA: Corwin Press.

McCaleb, S. P. (1994). *Building communities of learners: A collaboration among teachers, families, and community.* New York: St. Martin's Press.

McGowan, T. M., Erickson, L., & Neufeld, J. S. (1996). With reason and rhetoric: Building the case for the literature–social studies connection. *Social Education 60*(4), 51–60.

McQueen, L. (1985). *The Little Red Hen,* New York: Scholastic.

Merryfield, M. M. (2004). Elementary students in substantive culture learning. *Social Education 68*(4), 270–274.

Meyerson, P. & Secules, T. (2001). Inquiry cycles can make social studies meaningful-Learning about the controversy in Kosovo. *The Social Studies, 92*(5), 267–271.

Mitsakos, C. L. & Ackerman, A. T. (2009). Teaching social studies as a subversive activity. *Social Education 73*(1), 40–42.

Moje, E., Collazo, T., Carillo, R., & Mary, R. (2002). What is quality? Language, literacy, and discourse in project-based science. *Journal of Research in Science Teaching 38*(4), 469–498.

Morine-Dershimer, G., & Kent, T. (1999). The complex nature and sources of teachers' pedagogical knowledge. In Gess-Newson, J. & Lederman, G. (Eds). (pp. 21–50). *Examining pedagogical content knowledge.* Boston, MA: Kluwer.

Morris, R. V., & Welch, M. (2000). *How to perform acting out history in the classroom to enrich social studies education.* Dubuque, IA: Kendall/Hunt Publishing Company.

Moulton, L., & Trevis, C. (1991). Making history come alive: Using historical photos in the classroom. *Social Studies and the Young Learner 3*(4), 12–14.

National Archives and Records Administration. 100 Milestone Documents. http://www.ourdocuments. gov/content.php?flash=false&page=milestone Retrieved June 29, 2009.

National Center for Educational Statistics. (1995). NAEP 1994 geography: A first look: Findings from the National Assessment of Educational Progress. Washington, DC: Office of Educational Research and Improvement, U. S. Department of Education.

National Center for Educational Statistics. (1996). *NAEP 1994 geography report card: Findings from the National Assessment of Educational Progress.* Washington, DC: Office of Educational Research and Improvement, U. S. Department of Education.

National Center for Educational Statistics. (2002). *Geography highlights: The Nation's report card 2001.* Washington, DC: Office of Educational Research and Improvement NCES 2002–485, U. S. Department of Education.

National Center for Educational Statistics. (2006). Civics Report Card 2006. http://www.nationsreportcard. gov/civics_2006/ Retrieved Jun 28, 2009.

National Center for History in the Schools. (1994). National standards for United States history: Exploring the American experience; National standards for world history: Exploring paths to the present;and National standards for history: Expanding children's world in time and space. Los Angeles: University of California Press.

National Clearinghouse for English Language Acquisition. (2001). Survey of states' LEP students and available educational programs and services 1999–2000 summary report. www.ncbe.gwn.edu/ncbepubs/seareports/ 99-00/sea9900.pdf. Retrieved August 16, 2003.

National Council for Economics Education. (1997). *Voluntary national content standards in economics.* New York: Economics America.

National Council for Geographic Education. (1994). *Geography for life: National geography standards 1994.* Washington, DC: National Geographic Society.

National Council for the Social Studies. (1976). *Curriculum guidelines for multiethnic education.* Washington, DC: Author.

National Council for the Social Studies. (1989). In search of a scope and sequence for social studies report of the task force on scope and sequence. *Social Education 53,* 376–387.

National Council for the Social Studies. (1991). *Testing and evaluation of social studies students.* Washington, DC: National Council for the Social Studies. Retrieved on February 3, 2001, from www.sociastudies.org/ standard/positions/testingandeval/html.

National Council for the Social Studies. (1994a). *Charting the course: Social studies for the 21st century* (pp. 59–63). Washington, DC: Author.

National Council for the Social Studies. (1994b). *Expectations of excellence: Curriculum standards for social studies.* Washington, DC: Author.

National Council for the Social Studies. (1996). *Fostering civic virtue: Character education in the social studies.* Washington, DC: Author.

National Council for the Social Studies. (1997). *Position statement: Fostering civic virtue: Character education in the schools.* Washington, DC: Author.

National Council for the Social Studies. (2008). *A Vision of Powerful Teaching and Learning In the Social Studies: Building Social Understanding and Civic Efficacy. A Position Statement.* Washington, DC: Author.

National Council of Teachers of Mathematics. (1989). *Curriculum and evaluation standards for school mathematics.* Reston, VA: Author.

National Research Council. (1996). *National science education standards.* Washington, DC: National Academy Press.

Naylor, D., & Diem, R. (1987). *Elementary and middle school social studies.* New York: Random House.

Nelson, L. R. (1997). Recent trends in economic education. *ERIC Digest.* (ERIC Document Reproduction Service No. ED 412 171.)

Nelson, M. (1990). A future for civic education. In W. T. Callahan, Jr., & Banaszak, R. A. (Eds.), *Citizenship for the 21st century* (pp. 42–57). Bloomington, IN: Social Studies Development Center.

Nickell, P. (1999). The issue of subjectivity in authentic social studies assessment. *Social Education 63*(6), 353–355.

Nielsen, L. E. & Finkelstein, J. M. (1998). Citizenship education: Looking at government. *Social Studies and the Young Learner 1(1),* 10–13.

Nielsen, L. E., Finkelstein, J. M., Schmidt, A. & Duncan, A. (2008). Citizenship education: Engaging children in building community. *Social Studies and the Young Learner 21(1),* 20–23.

Novak, J. D. (1995). *Concept maps help teachers learn.* New York: Cornell University.

Nugent, G., Kunz, G., Levy, R., Harwood, D., & Carlson, D. (2008). The impact of a field-based, Inquiry-focused model of Instruction on preservice teachers' science learning and attitudes. *Electronic Journal of Science Education, 12*(2), Accessed December 14, 2008 from http://ejse.southwestern.edu

Ovando, C., Combs, C. C. & Collier, V. P. (2006). *Bilingual and ESL classroom: Teaching in multicultural contexts,* 4th ed. Boston: McGraw-Hill.

Padrón, Y., Waxman, H. C. & Rivera, H. H. (August, 2002). *Educating Hispanics students: Effective instructional practices.* Center for Research on Education, Diversity & Excellence, Practitioner Brief #5.

Pagano, A. (1978). Children learning and using social studies content. In A. Pagano (Ed.), *Social studies in early childhood: An interactionist point of view* (pp. 82–94). Washington, DC: National Council for the Social Studies.

Paige, R. (2002a). Press Release, May 9. Retrieved from www.ed.gov/print/news/speeches/2002/05/5092002.html.

Paige, R. (2002b). Press Release, June 21. Retrieved from www.ed.gov/print/news/speeches/2002/06/062102a.html.

Pajaras, M. F. (1992). Teacher's beliefs and educational research. Cleaning up a messy construct. *Review of Educational Research 62,* 307–332.

Parker, W. (2001a). Classroom discussion: Models for learning seminars and deliberations. *Social Education 65*(2), 111–115.

Parker, W. (2001b). Toward enlightened political engagement. In W. B. Stanley (Ed.), *Critical issues in social studies research for the 21st century* (pp. 97–118). Greenwich, CT: Information Age.

Parker, W., Ninomiya, A., & Cogan, J. J. (2002). Educating world citizens toward multinational curriculum development. In W. Parker (Ed.), *Education for democracy: Context, curricula, assessments* (vol. 2, pp. 151–182). Greenwich, CT: Information Age.

Partnership for 21st Century Skills, Information, media, and technology skills. Accessed December 15, 2008 http://www.1stcenturyskills.org/index.php?option=com_content&task=view&id=61&Itemid=120

Patrick, J. P. (2003, May 7). Teaching democracy globally, internationally, and comparatively: The 21st century civic mission of schools. Paper presented at the third annual R. Freeman Butts Institute on Civic Learning in Teacher Education in Indianapolis, Indiana.

Patrick, J. J. (1999). *The concept of citizenship in education for democracy.* (ERIC Digest No. EDO-SO-1999-6.)

Patrick, J. J., & Hoge, J. D. (1991). Teaching government, civics and law. In J. P. Shaver (Ed.), *Handbook of research on social studies teaching and learning* (pp. 427–436). New York: Macmillan.

Perie, M. (1997). *Time spent teaching core academic subjects in elementary schools. Comparisons across community, school, teacher, and student characteristics. Statistical analysis report.* Washington, DC: American Institutes for Research in the Behavioral Sciences.

Perkins, D. (2009). Making learning whole: How seven principles of teaching can transform education. San Francisco, CA: Jossey Bass.

Perkins, D., & Blythe, T. (1994). Putting understanding up front. *Educational Leadership 51*(5), 4–7.

Peterson, P. E. & Hess, F. S. (2008). Few states set world-class standards. *Education Next*, summer 70–73. http://media.hoover.org/documents/ednext_20083_70.pdf Accessed June 13, 2009.

Phillips Collection. (2009). Washington, D.C.: Author http://wwwphillipscollection.org/migration_series/flash/games_landing.cfm Accessed June 19, 2009.

Pigozzi, B. (1990). *A view of geography and elementary education* (Elementary Subjects Center Series No. 18). East Lansing: Michigan State University, Institute for Research on Teaching, Center for the Learning and Teaching of Elementary Subjects.

Pollock, J. E. (1992). Blueprints for social studies. *Educational Leadership 49*(8), 52–53.

Potari, D., & Spiliotopoulou, V. (1996). Children's approaches to the concept of volume. *Social Studies Education 80*(3), 341–360.

Procter, D. R., & Haas, M. E. (1990). *A handbook of school-based community projects for student participation.* (ERIC Document Reproduction Service No. ED 326 467.) Bloomington, IN: Social Studies Development Center and Eric Clearinghouse for Social Studies/Social Science Education.

Pugh, S. L., & Garcia, J. (1996). Issues-centered education in multicultural education. In R. W. Evans & D. W. Saxe (Eds.), *Handbook of teaching on social issues, National Council for the Social Studies Bulletin 93* (pp. 121–129). Washington, DC: National Council for the Social Studies.

Quilty, R. (1975). Imitation as a dyadic interchange pattern. *Scandinavian Journal of Psychology 16,* 223–239.

Ramler, S. (1991). Global education for the 21st century. *Educational Leadership 48*(7), 44–46.

Raths, L., Harmin, M., & Simon, S. (1978). *Values and teaching* (2nd ed.). Columbus, OH: Merrill.

Ratway, B. (2008). Asking the right questions: Developing thinking skills through Wisconsin's grade level foundations. *Social Education, 72*(7), 302–305.

Ravitch, D. (1999). Higher, but hollow, academic standards. *The New York Times,* February 6, 1999. http://www. edexcellence.net/detail/news.cfm?news_id=219& id= Accessed June 13, 2009.

Ravitch, D. & Schlesinger, Jr. A. The new, improved history standards. *Wall Street Journal* 4/3/96. http://www.edexcellence.net/detail/news.cfm?news_id=75&id= Accessed June 13, 2009.

Rea, D. (1999). Serious fun in social studies. *Middle Level Learning 6,* 2–5.

Read. Write. Think (2008). Involving students and families in ongoing reflection and assessment. Accessed December 6, 2008 http://www.readwritethink.org/lessons/lesson_view.asp?id=973

Rice, M., & Cobb, R. (1978). *What can children learn in geography?: A review of the research.* Boulder, CO: Social Science Education Consortium. (ERIC Document Reproduction Service, ED 166 088).

Richards, J. C. & Lockhart, C. (2000). *Reflective teaching in second language classrooms.* Cambridge: Cambridge University Press.

Riley, R. (2000, May). *U. S. Secretary of Education Richard Riley announced the grantees for 2000 under the Partnerships in Character Education Pilot Projects Program.* Washington, DC: U. S. Department of Education.

Rosenshine, B. V. (1986). Synthesis of Research on Explicit Teaching. *Educational Leadership, 43*(1), 60–69.

Rossi, J. A. (2000). At play with curriculum development in history. In S. W. Bednarz and R. S. Bednarz (Eds.), *Social science on the frontier: New horizons in history and geography.* (pp. 52–66). Boulder, CO: Social Science Education Consortium.

Rowe, M. B. (1987). Wait-time: Slowing down may be a way of speeding up. *American Educator 11*(1), 38–47.

Rowe, M. B. (1996). Science, silence, and sanctions. *Science and Children 34*(1), 35–37.

Roy, P. (1994). Cultivating cooperative group process skills within the social studies classroom. In R. J. Stahl (Ed.), *Cooperative learning in social studies: A handbook for teachers* (pp. 18–50). Menlo Park, CA: Addison-Wesley.

Rutter, R. A., & Newmann, F. M. (1989). The potential of community service to enhance civic responsibility. *Social Education 53,* 371–374.

San Antonio Home Education. (2009). Alternative Assessment and Technology. Accessed February 3, 2009 from http://www.homeesa.com.

Sanger, M. J., & Greenbowe, T. J. (1997). Common misconceptions in electrochemistry: Galvanic, electrolytic, and concentration cells. *Journal of Research in Science Teaching 34*(4), 377–398.

Saunders, P., Bach, G. L., Calderwood, J. D., & Hansen, W. L. (1984). *Master curriculum guide in economics: A framework for teaching the basic concepts* (2nd ed) New York: Joint Council for Economic Education.

Saunders, P., & Gilliard, J. V. (Eds.). (1995). *A framework for teaching the basic concepts and scope and sequences K–12.* New York: National Council on Economic Education.

Saunders, W. (1992). The constructivist perspective: Implications for teaching strategies for social studies. *School Science and Mathematics 92*(3), 16–27.

Scarcella, R. (1980). Teaching language minority students in the multicultural classroom. Englewood Cliffs, NJ: Prentice Hall.

Schug, M. C. (1997). Economics for kids: Ideas for teaching in the elementary grades. In M. E. Haas & M. A. Laughlin (Eds.), *Meeting the standards: Social studies readings for K–6 educators* (pp. 166–168). Washington, DC: National Council for the Social Studies.

Schug, M. C., & Beery, R. (1987). *Teaching social studies in the elementary school: Issues and practices.* Glenview, IL: Scott Foresman.

Schug, M. C., Todd, R., & Beery, R. (1984). Why kids don't like social studies. *Social Education 48,* 382–387.

Schug, M. C., & Walstad, W. B. (1991). Teaching and learning economics. In J. P. Shaver (Ed.), *Handbook for research on social studies teaching and learning* (pp. 411–419). New York: Macmillan.

Schuler, D. (2002). Studying the Community. *Social Education 66*(5), 320–324.

Schwab, J. (1974). The concept of the structure of a discipline. In E. Eisner & E. Vallance (Eds.), *Conflicting conceptions of curriculum* (pp. 162–175). Berkeley, CA: McCutchan.

Sears, R. (1963). Dependency motivation. In M. R. Jones (Ed.), *Nebraska symposium on motivation, 2* (pp. 25–64). Lincoln, NE: University of Nebraska Press.

Seifert, K. L., & Hofnung, R. J. (2000). *Child and adolescent development* (5th ed.). Boston: Houghton Mifflin.

Sepinwall, H. L. (1999). Incorporating Holocaust education into K–4 curriculum and teaching in the United States. *Social Studies and the Young Learner 11*(3), 5–8.

Setti, A. & Caramelli, N. (2005). Different domains in abstract concepts. Accessed December 16, 2008 http://www.cogsci.rpi.edu/csjarchive/Proceedings/2005/docs/p1997.pdf

Shaffer, D. R. (2000). *Social and personality development.* Pacific Grove, CA: Brooks/Cole.

Shulman, L. S. (1986). Those who understand: Knowledge growth in teaching. *Educational Researcher 15*(2), 4–14.

Siegal, R. (1998). *Whalesong.* (Cassette Recording YA 965) Read by Don West. New York: Listening Library.

Silva, De. (November, 2008). Measuring Skills for the 21st Century. Education Sector Reports. Accessed June 8, 2009 www.educationsector.org

Singer, A. (1992). Multiculturalism and democracy: The promise of multicultural education. *Social Education 56,* 83–85.

Skeel, D. J. (1996). An issue-centered element curriculum. In R. Evans & D. Saxe (Eds.), *Handbook on teaching social issues* (pp. 230–235). Washington, DC: National Council for the Social Studies.

Skinner, R., & Chapman, C. (1999). *Service learning and community service in K–12 public schools.* (NCES 1999–0443). Washington, DC: U. S. Department of Education, National Center for Education Statistics.

Slavin, R. E. (1989). Research on cooperative learning: Consensus and controversy. *Educational Leadership 47*(4), 52–54.

Smith, A. (1985). Channeling in on good citizenship. *The Social Studies 76*(91), 28–31.

SSCED (2008). SSCED tool kit, curriculum, instruction, and assessment. Accessed December 17, 2008 http://www.tea.state.tx.us/ssc/downloads/toolkits/Shared%20Sections/Resources/Strategies/Strategies.pdf

Stahl, R. J. (1994). Cooperative learning: A social studies context and an overview. In R. J. Stahl (Ed.), *Cooperative learning in social studies: A handbook for teachers* (pp. 1–17). Menlo Park, CA: Addison Wesley.

Starr, I. (1989). The law studies movement: A brief commentary on its history and rationale. *ATSS/UFT Journal 44*(10), 5–7.

Stearns, P.N., (1998). Why study history? American Historical Association http://www.historians.org/pubs/free/WhyStudyHistory.htm Accessed June 17, 2009

Steedly, K., Dragoo, K., Arefeh, S., & Luke, S., Effective Mathematics Instruction, Accessed February 4, 2009 http://www.nichcy.org/Research/EvidenceForEducation/Pages/MathEffectiveInstruction.aspx#top

Stoddart, T., Pinal, A., Latzke, M., & Canaday, D. (2002). Integrating inquiry science and language development for English language learners. *Journal of Research in Science Teaching 39*(8), 664–687.

Stoltzman, J. (1990). *Geography education for citizenship.* (ERIC Document Reproduction Service No. ED 322 081). Bloomington, IN: ERIC Clearinghouse for Social Studies/Social Science Education.

Sunal, C. S. (2008). What is a Citizen? Changing Definitions. In Vanfossen, P. J. & Berson, M. J. (Eds.), *The Electronic Republic? The Impact of Technology on Education for Citizenship.* Purdue, IN: Purdue University Press.

Sunal, C. S., & Haas, M. E. (1993). *Social studies and the elementary/middle school student.* Fort Worth, TX: Harcourt, Brace, Jovanovich.

Sunal, C. S., & Haas, M. E. (2002). *Social Studies for the Elementary and Middle Grades: A Constructivist Approach.* Boston, MA: Allyn & Bacon.

Sunal, C., McCormick, T., Sunal, D., & Shwery, C. (Spring/Summer, 2005). The demonstration of teaching values in elementary pre-service teachers' e-portfolios. *International Journal of Social Education, 20*(1), 64-80.

Sunal, C., Powell, D., McClelland, S., Rule, A., Rovegno, I., Smith, C., & Sunal, D. (2000). *Integrating academic units in the elementary school curriculum.* Fort Worth, TX: Harcourt Brace.

Sunal, C., Pritchard, G., & Sunal, D. (2000, June–May). Whales in depth: An interdisciplinary study. *Middle Level Learning 8,* 11–15.

Sunal, C., & Sunal, D. (1983). *Adapting science for the hearing impaired, Resources in Education.* (ERIC Document Reproduction Service No. ED 273 177).

Sunal, C. S., & Sunal, D. W. (1999, April). Reasoning and argumentation. Paper presented at the annual meeting of the American Educational Research Association, Montreal, Canada.

Sunal, C. S., Sunal, D. W. & Staubs, M. O. (2007). Why did they do it? What were the purposes of Lewis and Clark's corps of discovery expedition? In L. Bennett & M. Berson, (Eds), *Digital age: Technology-based K–12 lesson plans for social studies* NCSS Bulletin #105, pp. 60–65). Washington, DC: National Council for the Social Studies.

Superka, D., & Hawke, S. (1982, May). Social roles: A focus for the social studies in the 1980s. *Social Education 44,* 362–369.

Taba, H. (1967). *Teacher's handbook for elementary social studies.* Palo Alto, CA: Addison Wesley.

Taylor, H. E. (Ed.). (1997). *Getting started in global education.* Alexandria, VA: National Association of Elementary School Principals.

Tennyson, R., & Cocchiarella, M. (1986). An empirically based instructional design theory for teaching concepts. *Review of Educational Research 56,* 40–71.

Thagard, P. (1992). Analogy, explanation, and education. *Journal of Research in Science Teaching 29*(6), 537–544.

Thagard, P. (2008). Conceptual change. Accessed December 17, 2008 http://cogsci.uwaterloo.ca/Articles/conc.change.pdf

The Benjamin Franklin Tercentenary. Franklins Interactive lifetime. http://www.benfranklin300.org/timeline/ Retrieved June 29, 2009.

The Quotations Page. http://www.quotationspage.com/quote/29311.html Retrieved July 5, 2009 Bertrand Russell quotation.

The Quotations Page. http://www.quotationspage.com/quote/40486.html Retrieved July 5, 2009 Albert Einstein quotation.

Tobin, K., & McRobbie, C. (1996). The significance of cultural fit to the performance of Asian Americans. Paper presented at the annual meeting of the American Educational Research Association, New York.

Tom Snyder Production. (2008). *Timeliner XE.* Watertown, MA: Tom Snyder Productions, Inc.

Torney-Purta, J. (1990). Political socialization. In W. T. Callahan, Jr., & R. A. Banaszak (Eds.), *Citizenship for the 21st century* (pp. 171–198). Bloomington, IN: Social Studies Development Center.

Torney-Purta, J. (2000). Comments in E-mail discussion. American Political Science Association. Posted March 28. Retrieved from APSA CIVED@H-Net.msu.edu March 18, 2008.

Torney-Purta, J., Schwille, J., & Amadeo, J. A. (Eds.). (1999). Civic education across countries: Twenty-four national case studies for the IEA civics education project. Delft, Netherlands: Eburon Publishers.

Totten, S. (1999). Should there be Holocaust education for K–4 students? The answer is NO. *Social Studies and the Young Learner 12,* 36–39.

Totten, S. (2000). Diminishing the complexity and horror of the Holocaust: Using simulations in an attempt to convey historical experiences. *Social Education 64*(3), 165–171.

Trocham, W. M. (2006). Introduction to Evaluation. Web Center for Social Research Methods. Accessed December 6, 2008 http://www.socialresearchmethods.net/kb/intreval.htm.

Trotta, L. (1991). *Fighting for air: In the trenches with television news.* New York: Simon & Schuster.

U. S. Department of Education. (2007). Mobilizing for Evidence-based Character Education. Available online at: http://www.ed.gov/programs/charactered/mobilizing.pdf.

U. S. Department of Education. (2001). No Child Left Behind Act of 2001. Public Law No. 107–100. [On-line]. Available: www.loc.gov/.

U. S. Department of Education (2007). *Character Education: Our Shared Responsibility.* Retrieved October 20, 2010 from http://www.ed.gov/admins/lead/character/brochure.html/

Van Fossen, P. J. (1998). World wide web resources for teaching and learning economics. *ERIC digest.* (ERIC Document Reproduction Service No. ED 424 289).

Van Sledright, B. A., & Brophy, J. (1992). Storytelling, imagination and fanciful elaboration in children's historical reconstructions. *American Educational Research Journal 29,* 837–859.

Wade, R. C. (Ed.). (2000). *Building bridges: Connecting classroom and community through service-learning in social studies, Bulletin 97.* Washington, DC: National Council for the Social Studies.

Wade, R. C., & Saxe, D. W. (1996). Community service-learning in the social studies: Historical roots, empirical evidence, critical issues. *Theory and Research in Social Education 24*(4), 331–359.

West, E. (2000). At play with education and history. In S. W. Bednarz & R. S. Bednarz (Eds.), *Social science on the frontier: New horizons in history and geography* (pp. 1–17). Boulder, CO: Social Science Education Consortium.

White, S. H., & O'Brien, J. E. (1999). What is a hero? An exploratory study of students' conceptions of heroes. *Journal of Moral Education 28*(1), 81–95.

Willingham, D. (2007). Critical thinking: Why is it so hard to teach? *American Educator, 31*(2), 8–19.

Winston, B. (1984). *Map and globe skills: K–8 teaching guide.* Indiana, PA: National Council for Geographic Education.

Wolfgang, C. (2001). *Solving Discipline and Classroom Management Problems: Methods and Models for Today's Teachers.* New York, NY: Wiley.

Yell, M. (2006). Personal communication with Mary E. Haas, June 27, 2006.

Yell, M. M. (1999). Multiple choice to multiple rubrics: One teacher's journey in assessment. Social Education 63(6), 326–329.

Zainuddin, H., Yahya, N., Morales-Jones, C. & Ariza, E. (2002). *Fundamentals of teaching English to speakers of other languages in K–p12 mainstream classrooms.* Dubuque: Kendall/Hunt

Zarnowski, M. (1990). *Learning about biographies.* Washington, DC: National Council for the Social Studies. Children's and Youth Literature

Index

A

Adler, David A., 322
Advertisements
  expansion, 438–439
  exploratory introduction, 436–437
  lesson development, 437–438
  rubrics for comparing, 460
Aesthetics, with morals and values, 298–299
African Americans, 320–321, 323, 336, 339, 360
  voting and, 100
Aggression
  conflict resolution, bullying and, 279–282
  constructing concepts of, 95–97
  reducing, 279–280
AIDS, 279
Aillaud, Cindy Lou, 389
Alleman, 383
Allen, 184
Almira's Violets (Fregosi), 278
American Association of Geographers, 373
American Bar Association, 155
American Cancer Society, 329
American Historical Association, 347
American Memory, 364
American Red Cross, 329
The American Promise, 150, 162
America's Champion Swimmer: Gertrude Ederle (Adler), 322
Amish Horses (Ammon), 260
Ammon, Richard, 260
Ampere, André-Marie, 248
Ancient Egypt, 364
Ancona, George, 120
Angell, 184
Anholt, Laurence, 278
Application, 108
Approval, 100
Area symbols, 394
Artifacts, 220
  in homes, 353
  museum, 351–352
Artwork, 228
The Asia Society, 181

Assessment modes
  checklists, 465
  classroom websites, 467
  identifying assessment within lesson plans, 469
  individual portfolios, 465–466
  interview guide on Hausa culture, 466
  interviews, 466–467
  journals, 467
  letter to…, 468
  quality circles, 467
  sample economics education checklist for students, 466
  self-evaluation reports, 467–468
  self study, 468–469
  student drawing, 465
Assessments
  cooperative learning and group, 326–327
  developing plans for, 257–259
  formative, 49
  formative evaluation and, 128
  graphic organizers, 327
  guiding principles for evaluations and, 449–451
  journal writing, 328
  maintaining equitable approaches with, 327–328
  management strategies and considerations for, 234
  modes of, 465–469
  national testing of social studies and, 451–452
  necessary evaluations and, 448–449
  oral interviews, 327
  portfolios, 327
  projects, 327
  of social studies learning for students, 326–328
  students learning through evaluation and multiple, 444–479
  beyond testing with evaluations and, 452–464
  using technology, 328
Assessments, beyond testing with

completed portion of 1998 NAEP test in civics for fourth-graders, 462
conference with diverse parents and families, 454–455
guiding questions for self-evaluation during group or independent study, 455
performance assessments and, 456
portion of 1994 NAEP test in geography for eighth-graders, 462
promoting individual needs with, 464
rubrics, 456–457
sample progress reports, 454
Atlases, 399–400
An Attainable Global Perspective (Hanvey), 176
Attitudes
  curiosity, 296–297
  demonstrating powerful dispositions and, 299
  flexibility and, 297–298
  reserving judgment and, 297
  respect for evidence and, 297
  responsibility to others, environment with, 298
  student development, dispositions and, 296–299
  values, morals, aesthetics and, 298–299
Attributes, 94, 95
Au, 319
Austin, 105
Authority, 15
Avery, 184
Awareness, 108
Aylee, Pinkus, 188

B

Bad Boy: A Memoir (Myers), 322
Ballard, Martha, 363
Banks, 293
Banneker, Benjamin, 321
Barnes, Peter W., 151
Barton, 362

Basic interpersonal communications skills (BICS), 324–325
Basic skills
  classifying, 61
  communicating, 61
  estimating, 62
  inferring, 61
  measuring, 62
  observing, 61
  predicting, 61
A Basket of Bangles: How A Business Begins (Howard), 422
Bateman, Tess, 260
BBC. *see* British Broadcasting System
Beatrice's Goat (McBrier), 422
Bedford, David, 285
Behavioral learning theory, 31–32
Behaviors
  classrooms and student/teacher, 205
  geographic concepts and student, 387
  inquiry skills and associated, 61
  integrative thinking skills and sample student, 74
  learning theory and, 31–32
  prosocial, 285
Belief systems, 317, 474
Bergin, Mark, 361
Bethpage school district, 464
BICS. *see* basic interpersonal communications skills
Bilingual and ESL Classroom: Teaching in Multicultural Contexts (Ovando, Combs, Collier), 110
Bill of Rights, 92
Biographies
  historical literature and, 357–362
  pitfalls selecting multicultural books and, 358
  using trade books to add depth to history and, 362

Blackwood, Gary, 77
Books
  adapting materials for
    diverse classrooms and
    text, 312–313
  adding depth to history
    with trade, 362
  content analysis of
    text, 223
  cultural perspectives
    and, 389
  developing teaching plans
    using text, 223–224
  difficulties in reading
    text, 222–223
  global education series,
    195–196
  illustrating economic
    concepts, 422
  incorporating social
    studies trade, 260–261
  pitfalls selecting multi-
    cultural, 358
  strategies for using social
    studies text, 309–311
  trade, 23, 151–152
*Boss of the Plains: The Hat
  That Won the West*
  (Carlson), 322
*Bound for the North Star:
  True Stories of
  Fugitive Slaves*
  (Brindell Fradin), 260
Braille, 307
Bramwell, Martyn, 261
Breckler, Rosemary, 187,
  189, 190
Brindell Fradin, Dennis, 260
Bring History Alice, 343
British Broadcasting
  System (BBC), 181
Brophy, 334, 362, 383
Brown, 289
Brown, Matt, 285
Bruner, 105
Buggey, 388
Bulletin No. 89 (NCSS), 14
Bullying
  aggression, conflict reso-
    lution and, 279–282
  how to intervene
    with, 282
  Internet and cyber-, 283
Bunnett, Rochelle, 285
Bunting, Eve, 226–227, 362
Byrd, Richard E., 207

C
Cabot, John, 28
CALP. *see* cognitive academic
  language proficiency
Carbone, Elisa, 360
CARE, 381

Carlson, Laurie, 322
Carl Vinson Institute of
  Government, 153
Carnegie Corporation of
  New York, 133, 452
Cartier, Jacques, 28
Carver, George
  Washington, 321
Castle, Caroline, 278
Cause-effect, 310
CD-ROMs, 13
Center for Civic Education,
  15
Center for Information
  and Research on
  Civic Learning
  and Engagement
  (CIRCLE), 133
Cezanne, Paul, 260
Cha, Dia, 187, 191–192
Chaconas, Dori, 120
Challenges
  instructional activities
    and confrontational, 214
  instructional activities
    and cooperative
    group, 214
Change, 14, 15
Channell, 231
Chaplain, Samuel, 207
Chapman Catt, Carrie, 100
Checklists, 465
Children. *see also* Students
  learning economics,
    432–433
Children's Book Council,
  150, 357
Children's Television Act of
  1990, 153
*The Chimpanzees I Love:
  Saving Their World
  and Ours* (Goodall), 299
*The Christmas Menorahs:
  How a Town Fought
  Hate* (Cohn), 362
The Chronicles of Narnia
  (Lewis), 294
Chronology, history time-
  lines and, 348–350
CIRCLE, 452. *see* Center
  for Information and
  Research on Civic
  Learning and
  Engagement
Cities and rivers lesson
  plans
  expansion, 127
  exploratory introduction,
    125
  lesson development,
    125–126
  summative evaluation,
    127

Citizenship
  chapter objectives, 135
  chapter overview,
    134–135
  civic education in U.S.
    schools and, 149
  cyber, 168
  democratic societies and
    defining, 135–137
  developing political
    awareness with,
    137–139
  education for active,
    12–14
  education resources for,
    150
  exploratory introduction,
    133–134
  key concepts and values,
    140–148
  law-related education
    and, 155–160
  media resources and,
    150–155
  participating in democ-
    racy and, 160–171
  standards and,
    139–140
  students,
    democratic/global
    societies and develop-
    ing, 133–172
  summary, 172
  websites, 172
Civic education
  assessing U.S. schools
    and, 149
  model for IEA, 138
Civic ideals, 16, 99
Civic practices, 16
*The Civic Mission of
  Schools* (Carnegie
  Corporation of New
  York and CIRCLE),
  133, 134, 452
Civic virtues, 294
Civil War, 348
Clarity, 202
Clark, William, 13, 207
Classifications, 61, 310
Classrooms
  adapting instruction and
    curriculum in inclu-
    sive, 307
  creating collaborative,
    207
  environments, 269
  first-grade scene, 3–5
  fourth-grade scenes,
    93–94
  general instructional
    strategies for inclusive,
    306–313

geography concepts in,
    384–386
  management strategies,
    231–234
  rules, 233
  sixth-grade scene, 5–6
  social studies taught in
    today's, 30
  student/teacher behavior
    in, 205
  studying state/local his-
    torical sites in,
    235–236
  teacher planning
    decisions in, 212–213
  websites, 467
Classroom scenarios, 1–2
  constructing concepts of
    aggression, 95–97
Clegg, 293
Closure, 20, 35, 218
CNN, 173
  Interactive, 13
Cobb, 388
Cody Kimmel, Elizabeth,
  120
Cogan, 177
cognitive academic
  language proficiency
  (CALP), 324–325
Cohen, Miriam, 279
Coherence, 240
Cohn, Janice, 362
Cold War, 134
Collier, V., 110
Collins, H. Thomas, 177
Colonial House, 364
Colonial Williamsburg, 364
Columbus, Christopher,
  28, 228
Column designs, 248–249
Combs, C., 110
Common wealth *v.* private
  wealth, 143
Communication, 61, 66
Communities, 286, 352–353
Community service projects
  democracy and school-
    based, 162–164
  learning outcomes and
    hierarchy of, 163
Compare-contrast, 310
Computers, 194–195
Concept, names, 98–99
Concept analysis, 103
Concept learning cycle, 107
  expansion, 109–110
  exploratory introduction,
    108
  lesson development, 108
Concepts, 94–95
  boundary, 106–107
  concrete, 105–106

conjunctive, disjunctive and relational, 105
coordinate, 103
cultural factors and, 110
differences in complexity/abstractness of, 103–106
economic measurement, 427–428
formal, 105–106
forming, 97–98
identifying attributes of, 97
interrelationships among, 101–103
key citizenship concepts and values, 140–148
productive resources and, 111–113
school as concrete, 106
sensory, 105–106
sub, 103, 104
superordinate, 103
teaching, 107–113
teaching complex and abstract, 110
types of, 98–101
values and economic, 419–428
Conclusions, 62
Concrete concepts, 105–106
Conferences, family/parent, 454–455
Conflict resolution, bullying, aggression and, 279–282
Conjunctive concepts, 105
Constitution: Translated for Kids (Travis), 152
the Constitution, 92
Constructivist theory, 30–31
Consumption, 15
Content knowledge, 10, 11
Continuity, 14, 15
Cooney, Barbara, 422
Cooperative group activities, 308
Cooperative learning, 204–205
Coordinate concepts, 103
Cornbleth, Catherine, 335
Countersocialization, forces of, 335
Coy, John, 299
Creative thinking, 75–76
Critical thinking, 73, 74
Cross-cultural awareness, 176
Cruz, B., 110
C-Span, 154, 196
Cuban Kids (Ancona), 120

Cultural diversity. *see also specific ethnicities*
Asians, 277
culturally responsive teaching and, 319
current social issues and, 320
historical approach and, 319–320
role models, relevancy and, 320–323
social studies education and, 316–323
strategies for multicultural social studies and, 319–320
student culture and, 320
variations in belief systems and, 317
Culture, 14, 15, 99
cultural diversity and student, 320
interview guide on Hausa, 466
Korean and Japanese, 317
student-teacher interactions and difference in gender and, 323–324
Curiosity, 296–297
Curious George (Rey), 299
Current events, 196
Curriculum
applying knowledge about learning to social studies, 30–32
diversity and respect for, 269–275
ethnic heritage and, 321
social studies, 14–17
Curriculum Standards for the Social Standards (NCSS), 53
Curtis, Sheldon, 188
Cyber-bullying, 283
Cybercitizenship, 168
Czarra, Frederick R., 177

D
Dancing with Katya (Chaconas), 120
Databases, 262
Data gathering skills, 64
Data-organizing skills, 64
Data-processing skills, 64
A December Tale (Sachs), 280
Decision making, 62, 73
chart, 429
chart for consequences, 430
economic skills with, 428–430

Declaration of Independence, 78
Delta, 385
Demi, 294
Democracy
concepts and values in U.S., 141
expansion, 170–171
hierarchy of school-based community service projects, learning outcomes and, 163
participating in, 160–171
participation in student government and, 164–166
political participation and, 166–170
school-based community service projects and, 162–164
tele, 154
Democratic Classroom Interaction Model, 165
Democratic societies, students developing citizenship in global and, 133–172
Demonstrations, 215
Dennenberg, Dennis, 120
Dependent, 424
Descriptive-focused units, 240–241
Descriptive study, 72
Dewey, John, 475
Diaries, 354–355
Dia's Story Cloth (Cha), 187, 191–192
Digital timelines, 350
Directions
giving, 232
maps, globes and, 394–395
Direct teaching, 31
Discussions
guides, 220
strategies, 219–221
Disjunctive concepts, 105
Distance, 395–396
Distribution, 15
Diversity
cultural factors and concepts with, 110
early inquiry skills and building on, 59
learning values/morals from family and community with, 286
multiple perspectives and building on, 48
pitfalls selecting multicultural books and, 358

political participation challenges an, 167
promoting individual needs and, 464
reading activities and, 226–227
social studies and building on, 9
social studies education and cultural, 316–323
unity *v.*, 143
Documents, 353–354
Dohistory, 363
Donnan, Caroline, 352
Drama, history reenactments and, 356–357
Drawing conclusions, 62
Drawings, 228
learning from artists' paintings and, 336–342
student assessment, 465
Duggleby, John, 339
Dunn, Arthur, 160
Durbin, William, 322
Durrant, Lynda, 23

E
the Earth
geography and students interpreting people and, 371–410
location and position of surface, 373
movement and humans interacting on, 373, 377
in spatial terms, 379
Economic concepts
economic interdependence and, 424–427
international, 423
macroeconomic and, 421, 423
measurement concepts and methods with, 427–428
microeconomic and, 421
social goals and basic, 420
trade books illustrating, 422
values and, 419–428
Economic decisions
approaches to teaching economics and, 434–435
chapter objectives, 412
chapter overview, 411–412
children, learning of economics and, 432–433
defining economics and, 413–414

Economic decisions
    (*Continued*)
  economic concepts and
    values with, 419–428
  economic decision-making
    skills and, 428–430
  economic goals, values
    and, 431–432
  economic literacy and,
    412–413
  expansion, 441–442
  exploratory introduction,
    411
  national social studies
    standards related to,
    414–415
  national standards in
    personal finance and,
    415–419
  resources for teaching eco-
    nomics and, 435–441
  students making, 411–443
  summary, 442
  voluntary national stan-
    dards in economics
    and, 415
  websites, 442–443
Economic education check-
    lists, 466
Economic freedom, 431
Economic goals
  economic efficiency, 431
  economic equity, 431
  economic freedom, 431
  economic growth, 431, 432
  economic security,
    431–432
  economic stability, 431
  full employment, 431, 432
  other, 431
  price stability, 431, 432
  values and, 431–432
Economic growth, 431, 432
Economic interdependence
    lesson plans
  expansion, 425–427
  exploratory introduction,
    424
  lesson development,
    424–425
Economic literacy, 412–413
Economics
  defining, 413–414
  national social studies
    standards related to,
    414–415
  scarcity and, 212–213, 413
Economic security, 431–432
*Economics for Kids: Ideas
    for Teaching in the
    Elementary Grades*
    (Schug), 435
Edison, Thomas, 284

*Educating Hispanic
    Students: Effective
    Instructional Practices*
    (Padrón, Waxman,
    Rivera), 110
Education
  for active citizenship,
    12–14
  assessing U.S. schools
    and civic, 149
  character, 294–296
  law-related, 155–160
  model for IEA civic, 138
  research findings on
    geographic, 388, 390
  resources for citizenship,
    150
  six elements of geogra-
    phy, 378–380
  social studies influencing
    global, 173–198
  standards for geography,
    378–380
  students with disabilities
    and social studies,
    305–316
  values in diverse society
    with moral, 286–296
Egocentric stage, 288
Einstein, Albert, 170, 171
Elementary lesson activity
    choices, 46–47
Elementary schools, 13
  first-grade classroom
    scenes in, 3–5
  fourth-grade classroom
    scenes in, 93–94
  global education
    appropriate for K-8
    and, 178
  hypotheses constructed
    by students in, 71–72
  lesson activity choices
    and, 46–47
  sixth-grade classroom
    scenes in, 5–6
  social studies in middle
    and, 3–6
ELL. *see* English language
    learners
Emotions, 221. *see also
    specific emotions*
  students with conflicted,
    316
Empathy, 285
The Empty Pot (Demi), 294
Engle, 335
English language learners
    (ELL), 324, 326
Enumeration, 310
Environments, 14, 15,
    99, 298
  people changing, 374–376

relationships within
    places, humans
    and, 373
  society and, 379, 380
Equality *v.* freedom, 143
Equator, 404
Essential attributes, 95
Estimating, 62
Ethics *v.* law, 143
Evaluations
  assessment and forma-
    tive, 128
  guiding principles for
    assessment and,
    449–451
  necessary assessments
    and, 448–449
  students learning
    through multiple as-
    sessment and, 444–479
  summative, 49
  beyond testing with as-
    sessments and,
    452–464
Evidence
  consideration of
    conflicting, 297
  respect for, 297
Examples, 95
Expansion phase, 33,
    37, 38, 39, 43–44,
    109–110
  history, 363–369
  interactive activities,
    games in learning
    history and, 364
  Lincoln penny worksheet
    and, 363, 365–368
*Expectations of Excellence:
    Curriculum Standards
    for Social Studies*
    (NCSS), 12, 14, 15
Exploratory introduction
    phase, 33, 37, 38,
    39–40, 108–109
  confrontational chal-
    lenge, discrepant
    events and, 214
  cooperative group chal-
    lenge and, 214
  open exploration and, 214
  problem exploration
    and, 214
  review, 213
  structured exploration
    and, 213
  useful instructional
    activities for, 213–214
Eyler, 162

F
Facilitators, 234
Facts

acquisition, 207
  generalizations, concepts
    and, 117–118
  social studies concepts
    and, 94–97
Family, 286
  conferences, 454–455
A Farm through Time
    (Thomas), 361
Fears, 278–279
Federal Reserve Banks,
    441
Feedback form for stu-
    dents, 259
Fertig, Gary, 360
Feyten, C., 110
Field, Elaine, 285
Field trips, 155, 215
  student, 216
*50 American Heroes Every
    Kid Should Meet*
    (Dennenberg and
    Roscoe), 120
*Fire in Their Eyes:
    Wildfires and the
    People Who Fight
    Them* (Magnuson
    Bell), 261
Flaitz, J., 110
Flat Stanley, 396
Flexibility, 297–298
Food Watch (Bramwell), 261
Ford, Henry, 284
Formal concepts, 105–106
Formal definitions, 98–99
Formative assessment, 49
Franklin, Benjamin, 248
*Franklin Collection: 10
    Books*, 285
*Franklin's Interactive
    Lifetime*, 364
Freedom School, Yes!
    (Littlesugar), 299
Freedom *v.* equality, 143
Fregosi, Claudia, 278
Friedman, Thomas, 178
Friends at School (Bunnett
    and Brown), 285
Friendship, 97, 282, 284–285
From Wood to Paper, 18
Full employment, 431, 432

G
Gagne, Robert, 105
Games
  instructional activities
    and, 215–217
  learning history and
    using interactive
    activities and, 364
  student fieldtrips
    and, 216
  teacher-made, 216

Gauguin, Paul, 260
Gender, 323–324
Generalizations
    defining, 116–117
    developing geographic
        concepts, skills and,
        382–391
    facts, concepts and
        distinguishing, 117–118
    forming, 115–116
    learning cycles, 122–123
    literature connections
        with messages as, 120
    making, 119
    predictions made using,
        118–119
    relationship between
        concepts and, 115–122
    social studies concepts
        and, 91–132
    teaching powerful,
        121–122, 123
    types of, 120–121
General pedagogical
    knowledge, 11
Geographic concepts
    classroom scene,
        384–386
    developing generaliza-
        tions, skills and,
        382–391
    literature connections to,
        389
    place, 383
    research findings on
        geographic education
        and, 388, 390
    research on map and
        globe skills and,
        390–391
    student behaviors illus-
        trating five geographic
        skills, 387
Geography
    chapter objectives, 372
    chapter overview, 371
    defining, 372–380
    developing geographic
        concepts, generaliza-
        tions, and skills in,
        382–391
    education standards,
        378–380
    expansion, 408
    exploratory introduction,
        371
    five themes of, 373,
        377–378
    people changing environ-
        ments with, 374–376
    questions, 445
    resources for teaching,
        380–381

sample NAEP questions
    for, 445–446
students interpreting
    earth and people
    through, 371–410
students learning/using
    map and globe skills
    with, 391–407
summary, 409
uses of, 379, 380
websites, 409–410
*Geography for Life:
    National Geography
    Standards 1994*
    (National Council for
    Geographic
    Education), 14–15,
    378, 387
Geography standards
    environment and society,
        379, 380
    geography uses, 379, 380
    human systems, 379, 380
    national, 379
    physical systems, 379,
        380
    places and regions, 379,
        380
    world in spatial terms,
        379
Geography themes
    five, 373, 377–378
    related concepts, 378
    theme 1: location,
        position on the earth's
        surface, 373
    theme 2: place, natural
        and cultural character-
        istics, 373
    theme 3: relationships
        within places, humans
        and environments, 373
    theme 4: movement,
        humans interacting
        on earth, 373, 377
    theme 5: how regions
        form and change, 377
Giles, 162
Gilligan, Carol, 288, 289
Global connections, 14,
    16, 99
Global dynamics, 176
Global education
    approaches to, 179–182
    appropriate for K-8, 178
    awareness of human
        choices and, 177
    book series, 195–196
    chapter objectives, 174
    chapter overview,
        173–174
    cross-cultural awareness
        and, 176

cultural approaches to,
    179
evolving definition of,
    174–178
expansion, 196–197
exploratory introduction,
    173
interdisciplinary
    connections, 182–183
Internet, computers and,
    194–195
knowledge of global
    dynamics and, 176
people's views from other
    nations and, 181
perspective consciousness
    and, 176
problems approach to,
    181–182
resources for current
    events and, 196
resources for teaching,
    194–196
social studies influencing,
    173–198
state of planet awareness
    and, 176
student artwork and,
    185
substantive cultural
    learning and, 179–180
summary, 197
teaching, 183–194
war, humane world and,
    186–194
websites, 198
Global societies, 133–172
GLOBE, 381
Globes
    direction and, 394–395
    distance and, 395–396
    grid systems and,
        396–397
    helping students learn
        maps skills and,
        391–407
    latitude, longitude and,
        402–407
    numbers, amount/
        quantity on maps, in
        atlases, textbooks
        and, 399–400
    reading maps and,
        400–401
    remote sensing, teaching
        geography, digital
        maps and, 397
    research on map skills
        and, 390–391
    shapes and patterns, 393
    symbols and, 394
    three-dimensional maps
        and, 392

GNP. *see* Gross national
    product
Goals
    economic concepts and
        social, 420
    general pedagogical
        knowledge and social
        studies, 201
    integrated units, devel-
        oping rationale and,
        254–255
    objectives and, 79
    values, economic deci-
        sions and, 431–432
*Goals 2000: Educate
    America Act of 1994*,
    140
Going Home (Bunting),
    226–227
*Goldilocks and the Three
    Bears*, 293
Gollub, Matthew, 278
Gomi, Taro, 285
Goodall, Jane, 299
Goodnow, 105
Google Earth, 391, 398
Google Map, 397, 398
Governance, 15
Government, 101, 110
    integrated units and
        partial hierarchical
        web for state,
        251–252
    partial schematic compo-
        nents web for state, 254
    student, 164–166,
        202–203
Governors, 99
Govoni, J., 110
Grandma Moses, 336
Graphic organizers, 327
The Great Migration, 338
The Great Unknown
    (Morrison), 260
Grid systems, 104, 396–397
Gross national product
    (GNP), 399, 422
Grouping, 79
Groups, 15
Guerilla Season (Hughes),
    77
Guest speakers, 215
Guiding hypotheses, 70, 72
Gundisch, Karin, 120

H
Haas, 162, 231
Haas, Mary E., 361
Hall, Donald, 422
Hanvey, Robert, 176, 177
Hart, Avery, 261
Hartoonian, Michael, 143
Hausa culture, 466

Have You Seen Trees?
(Scholastic), 23
Heacock, Grace Ann, 166
Hearing impairments,
315–316
Hearne, Betsy, 322
Hepburn, Mary, 153
*Herbert Binns and the
Flying Tricycle*
(Castle), 278
Hess, 165
Hidden Child (Millman),
362
Hiroshima, 228
Hispanics, 167
Historical approach,
319–320
Historical sites, 235–236
History
benefits of studying,
346–347
biographies, historical
literature and,
357–362
chapter objectives,
332–333
chapter overview,
331–332
definition, 333–334
expanding skills in, 363
expansion and, 363–369
exploratory introduction,
331
habits of mind associated
with, 347
reenactments, drama
and, 356–357
resources for teaching,
350–355
in schools, 335–343
standards for, 343–346
students and learning of,
347–348
students engaged in
examining, 331–370
summary, 370
timelines to develop
chronology with,
348–350
visual literacy and,
355–356
websites, 370
History resources
artifacts in homes as, 353
community as, 352–353
diaries, letters, pictures
as, 354–355
documents as, 353–354
locating and using,
350–351
people as, 351
visiting restoration
communities as, 353

Hitler, Adolf, 171
Hoge, 184
*Hokusai: The Man Who
Painted a Mountain*
(Kogan Ray), 322
the Holocaust, 56, 184, 362
Hoose, Phillip, 152
*House Mouse, Senate
Mouse* (Barnes), 151
Howard, Ginger, 422
How I Became an American
(Gundisch), 120
Hughes, Pat, 77
Humans
choices, 177
resources, 114
systems, 379, 380
Hyman, Mark, 196
Hyperactivity, 99
Hypotheses, 71–72
developing and using
guiding, 70
evaluating, 70
formulating, 62
helping students
develop, 69–70
observations, inferences
and, 68–70

I

ICT. *see* Information and
Communication
Technology
IDEA. *see* Individuals with
Disabilities Education
Act
Ideas
inquiry skills and social
studies, 58–59
integrated units and
generating topical,
249–250
main, 310
student involvement and
applying, 328–330
Idea webs, 252–254
Identity, 15
IEA. *see* International
Association for the
Evaluation of
Education
Achievement
IEP. *see* Individualized
Education Plan
"I Have a Dream" speech
(King), 77, 167
Immigrants, 190
Inca Investigation, 364
Incipient cooperation
stage, 288
Independence, 275–276, 424
Individualized Education
Plan (IEP), 306

Individuals, 99
choice, 144
development, 15
portfolios, 465–466
Individuals with
Disabilities Education
Act (IDEA), 305
Inferences, 61, 68–70
Information and
Communication
Technology (ICT), 66
Information literacy
skills, 66
Inquiry invitations, 229–230
Inquiry skills, 4
abilities needed for, 57
assessing use of, 83–85
early, 59–60
fostering, 76–77
functions of social
studies, 65
hierarchy of, 85–89
planning activities to
teach, 79
social studies, 60–67
social studies and
learning, 173–198
students developing
social studies ideas
using, 58–59
Inquiry skills assessment
record of student skill
development and, 84
sample development as-
sessment for curiosity
and, 84–85
task performance record
of student social
studies activities
and, 83
Inquiry skills hierarchy, 89
backyard mystery class-
room scenario and,
87–88
developmental use of
thinking skills in
social studies lessons
and, 85–86
learning cycles and
teaching, 86
Institutions, 15
Instruction
continuum of knowledge
and, 207–209
factors in adapting social
studies curricula and,
313–316
Instructional activities
expansion phase and
useful, 231
exploratory introduction
phase and useful,
213–214

instructional strategies,
lesson phases and
matching types of,
210–211
lesson development
phase and useful,
214–231
selecting, 41
teacher planning deci-
sions and, 212–213
Instructional strategies
adapting instruction
and curriculum in
inclusive classrooms
and, 307
chapter objectives, 200
chapter overview,
199–200
classroom management
strategies and,
231–234
classwide peer tutoring
and, 308
continuum of knowledge,
instruction and,
207–209
cooperative group activi-
ties and, 308
exploratory introduction,
199
general suggestions for
adapting textbook
materials for diverse
classrooms and,
312–313
greater control of
students and, 210–211
guided discovery and
mixed teacher/student
control and, 210
inclusive classrooms and
general, 306–313
lecture-based presenta-
tions and, 309
lower student control
and, 209–210
making decisions about
using certain, 235–236
matching types of in-
structional activities to
lesson phases with,
211–231
media presentations
and, 309
multisensory activities
and, 307–308
peer buddy system
and, 308
reading alone and, 309
reciprocal teaching and,
308–309
semantic feature analy-
sis and, 311–312

social studies PCK and, 200–207
social studies teachers managing, 199–237
social studies textbooks and, 309–311
student needs and matching, 209–211
students organizing thoughts in concept web as part of POSSE procedure for reading text, 313
study guides and, 311
summary, 237
websites, 237
Integrated units
choosing appropriate topics for, 247–248
column designs used with, 248–249
conceptualizing, 264
developing, 249–264
partial hierarchical web for state government, 251–252
partial schematic components web for state government, 254
planning, 248–249
step 1: generating topical ideas for, 249–250
step 2: researching topics for, 250
step 3: developing essential/focus questions for, 250–251
step 4: identifying special needs among students and making accommodations for, 251
step 5: developing intended learning outcomes with, 251–252
step 6: categorizing intended learning outcomes with, 252
step 7: creating an idea web for, 252–254
step 8: developing rationale and goals for, 254–255
step 9: beginning KWL chart for, 255–256
step 10: developing learning objectives for, 256–257
step 11: developing assessment plans for, 257–259

step 12: developing lesson plans for, 259
step 13: developing accommodations for technology, 260–261
step 14: implementing, 261
step 15: evaluating student learning for, 261
step 16: reflecting on, 261–264
summary of suggested planning steps for, 250
wheel designs used with, 248
Integrative skills
formulating hypotheses, 62
isolating and using variables, 62
organizing, interpreting, drawing conclusions from data, 62
solving problems, making decisions, investigating, 62
thinking critically and creatively, 62
Integrative thinking skills
creating thinking and, 75–76
critical thinking and, 73
fostering, 76–77
investigating, 73, 75
problem solving, decision making and, 73
sample student behaviors when using, 74
students using, 72–77
Interactive activities, 364
Interdependence, 104, 424
International Association for the Evaluation of Education Achievement (IEA), 136
civic education model and, 138
Internet, 2, 4, 116, 154, 194–195, 196, 321, 350
safety and cyber-bullying, 283
Interviews
assessment modes and, 466–467
guide with Hausa culture, 466
oral, 327
Investigating, 62, 73–74, 75
Island of the Blue Dolphins (O'Dell), 279
It's Mine! (Leonni), 285

It's My Turn (Bedford and Field), 285
It's Our World Too! Stories of Young People Who Are Making a Difference (Hoose), 152

J
Jamestown colony, 77
Japanese culture, 317
Jealousy, 91, 277–279
Jennifer, Hecate, Macbeth, William McKinley, and Me (Konigsburg), 285
Jews, 56, 362. *see also* the Holocaust
John Blair and the Great Hinckley Fire (Nobisson), 322
Johnny Appleseed, 23
Johnson, 204
Johnson, 204
Johnson, Angela, 260
Journals
assessment modes and, 467
writing in, 328
The Journal of Sean Sullivan: A Transcontinental Railroad Worker (Durbin), 322
Judgment, 297
Jump Start Coalition for Personal Financial Literacy, 415
Junctions, 385
Just the Two of Us (Smith, W.), 260

K
Katie and the Sunflowers (Mayhew), 260
Kelley, Lynn, 45
Kennedy, Edward M., 151
Key terms/concepts, 42, 140–148
The Kid's Guide to Social Action, 168
King, Martin Luther, 77, 167
King Farris, Christine, 167
Kirk, Cheryl, 422
Kline, Michael, 261
Knowledge, 30. *see also* Pedagogical Content Knowledge
content, 10, 11
continuum of instruction and, 207–209
global dynamics and, 176
prior, 31, 32, 33, 55
social studies and teacher, 11

social studies goals and general pedagogical, 201
social studies pedagogical content, 200–207
Kogan Ray, Deborah, 322
Kohlberg, Lawrence, 288
Konigsburg, E. L., 285
Korean culture, 317
Kourilsky, Marilyn L., 434
Kracht, 388
KWL chart, 255–256

L
Ladies First: Forty Daring Women Who were Second to None (Cody Kimmel), 120
Lahstoeter, Lori, 422
Laney, James, 428
Langhorst, Eric, 77
Language learning, 324–325
Latitude
expansion, 406–407
exploratory introduction, 402–403
lesson development, 403–406
longitude and, 402–407
Law-related education (LRE), 155, 160
critical learning outcome continuums in, 156
presidential oath lesson plan and, 157–159
Lawrence, Jacob, 337, 338–339, 343
Law v. ethics, 143
Learning
assessing and evaluating social studies, 447–464
assessment of concept, 113–115
categorizing intended outcomes for, 252
children, economics and, 432–433
cooperative, 204–205
developing intended outcomes for, 251–252
giving students greater control of social studies, 305
global education and cultural, 179–180
group assessment through cooperative, 326–327
history, using interactive activities and games, 364
"minds-on," 17

Learning (*Continued*)
 from paintings and
  drawings of artists,
  336–342
 recognizing and scaffolding language, 324–325
 teaching dimensions
  supporting meaning-
  ful, 202–203
 teaching strategies sup-
  porting meaningful,
  203–205
Learning centers, 229, 230
Learning cycle lesson
 phases
 choosing activities for,
  45–49
 consistent and inconsis-
  tent actions during
  development of, 41
 consistent and inconsis-
  tent actions during
  expansion phase of, 43
 consistent and inconsis-
  tent exploratory
  introduction, 40
 development, 40–42
 elementary lesson activity
  choices and, 46–47
 expansion, 43–44
 exploratory introduction,
  39–40
 learning cycle format
  and, 37
 lesson summary, 44–45
 middle childhood lesson
  activity choices and,
  47–49
 opportunities to include
  multiple perspectives
  and, 48
 questions for, 38
 scale lesson plan, 34–36
Learning cycle lesson plans
 advertisements and
  making good choices,
  436–439
 classifying Native
  American food plants,
  81–82
 economic interdepend-
  ence, 424–427
 latitude and longitude,
  402–407
 learning from paintings
  and drawings of
  artists, 336–342
 making good rules,
  470–473
 people change environ-
  ments, 374–376
 presidential oaths,
  157–159

productive resources,
 111–113
scale, 34–36
sharing and negotiation,
 270–274
teaching about war for
 humane world, 186–194
from tree to paper,
 18–21, 22
voting as a way to make
 decisions, 144–148
why cities exist where
 rivers come together,
 125–127
Lecture-based presenta-
 tions, 309
*Legends of Landforms:
 Native American Lore
 and the Geology of the
 Land* (Vogel), 389
Lesson development phase,
 33, 37, 38, 39, 40–42,
 108–109
 artifacts discussion guide
  and, 220
 chart of soldier by world
  region and, 228
 demonstration, 215
 difficulties in reading
  textbooks and, 222–223
 discussion strategies,
  219–221
 emotions and, 221
 field trips, 215
 games, 215–217
 guest speakers, 215
 inquiry invitation and,
  229–230
 instructional activities
  for, 214–231
 learning centers and,
  229, 230
 lecture or teacher
  presentation, 215
 reading activities and,
  226–227
 reading literature and,
  225
 role-playing and, 217–218
 role-playing and simula-
  tions with, 217
 simulations, 218–219
 social studies kits and,
  224–225
 teaching plan develop-
  ment with textbooks
  for, 223–224
 textbook content
  analysis and, 223
 using WebQuests and,
  230–231
 visual information
  literacy and, 225–229

writing guide for social
 studies investigation
 and, 222
writing in social studies
 and, 221–222
Lesson plans. *see also*
 Learning cycle lesson
 plans
 developing, 259
 identifying assessment
  within, 469
Lesson summary
 learning cycle lesson
  phases and, 43–44
 scale lesson plan and, 36
 tree to paper lesson plan
  and, 21
*Letter from President
 Thomas Jefferson*, 5
Letters, 354–355, 468
Lewis, Barbara, 168
Lewis, C. S., 294
Lewis, Meriwether, 13, 207
Lincoln, Abraham, 7, 188.
 see also Lincoln penny
 worksheet
Lincoln penny worksheet,
 363, 365–368
Linder, 231
Lionni, Leo, 285
Literacy
 economic, 412–413
 ITC, 66
 visual information and,
  225–229
Literature connections
 books illustrating eco-
  nomic concepts, 422
 books providing cultural
  perspectives, 389
 demonstrating powerful
  attitudes and disposi-
  tions, 299
 incorporating social
  studies trade books,
  260–261
 reading literature and,
  225
 role models, 322
 trade books, social
  studies and, 151–152
 using trade books in
  social studies, 23
 using trade books to add
  depth to history, 362
*Little Blue and Little
 Yellow* (Lionni), 285
Littlesugar, Amy, 299
The Little Red Hen
 (McQueen), 285
Location, 93
Lockard, Martha, 248
Lockhart, C., 110

A Log's Life (Pfeffer), 23
Longitude
 expansion, 406–407
 exploratory introduction,
  402–403
 latitude and, 402–407
 lesson development,
  403–406
LRE. *see* Law-related
 education
Lynch, 110

M
MacDonald, Fiona, 361
Macroeconomic concepts,
 421
Magellan, Ferdinand, 28
Magnuson Bell, Karen, 261
Main idea, 310
Making good rules lesson
 plan
 expansion, 472–473
 exploratory introduction,
  470
 lesson development,
  471–472
 summative evaluation
  rubric, 473
Management strategies
 advanced planning and,
  231–232
 assessment considera-
  tions and, 234
 creating lesson smooth-
  ness and, 234
 distributing materials
  with, 232–233
 facilitators and, 234
 giving directions and, 232
 grouping students
  and, 233
 organizing beginnings
  and, 233
 for powerful social
  studies, 231–234
 techniques and, 232
 using classroom rules
  and, 233
Maps, 104, 227
 direction and, 394–395
 distance and, 395–396
 grid systems and,
  396–397
 helping students learn
  globe skills and,
  391–407
 latitude, longitude and,
  402–407
 numbers, amount/quan-
  tity in atlases, globes,
  textbooks and,
  399–400
 reading and, 400–401

remote sensing, teaching geography and digital, 397

research on globe skills and, 390–391

shapes and patterns, 393

symbols and, 394

three-dimensional, 392

Marrin, Albert, 120

Marshall, the Court House Mouse (Barnes), 151

Martin, Fran, 178

Materials
distributing, 232
manager, 207

Math, 13

Mathys, Lori, 207

Mayhew, James, 260

McBrier, Page, 422

McCain, Ted, 24

McQueen, Lucinda, 285

Mead, Margaret, 168

Measuring, 62

Media
literacy skills, 66
presentations, 309
resources, 150–155

Media Awareness Network, 153

A Medieval Castle (MacDonald), 361

Memorization, 31

Merritt, Edith, 248

Merryfield, Merry, 175, 176

Metacognition, 33

Mexican Americans, 317

Microeconomic concepts, 421

Middle childhood lesson activity choices, 47–49

Middle schools, 13
global education appropriate for K-8 and, 178
hypotheses constructed by students in, 71–72
lesson activity choices and, 47–49
social studies in elementary and, 3–6
Task Force on Social Studies in, 178
U.S. history for eighth-graders and portion of 1994 NAEP test in, 446

Migration, 190

Millard, Anne, 361, 389

Millman, Isaac, 362

"Minds-on" learning, 17

Modeling, 78

Monarchy, 31

The Money Factory, 411

The Moon Was at a Fiesta (Gollub), 278

Moral development theories
egocentric stage, 288
incipient cooperation stage, 288
moral education and, 288–289
real cooperation stage, 288

Moral education
learning from family and community, 286
moral development theories and, 288–289
three aspects of morality and, 287
values in diverse society with, 286–296

Morrison, Taylor, 260

Moser, Barry, 260

Moulton, Leah, 354

Movement, humans on earth and, 373, 377

Multiple assessments
becoming effective social studies teachers with, 469–477
chapter objectives, 447
chapter overview, 447
evaluating social studies learning through, 447–464
exploratory introduction, 444
modes, 465–469
practicing skills in pre-assessment with, 477–478
students learning through evaluation and, 444–479
summary, 478
websites, 479

Multisensory activities, 307–308

Murphy, Jim, 322

Museums, 351–352

My Brother Martin: A Sister Remembers (King Farris), 167

Myers, Walter Dean, 322

My Friends (Gomi), 285

My Senator and Me (Kennedy), 151

N

National Assessment of Educational Progress (NAEP), 13, 149, 388, 444
complete portion of civics test for fourth-graders, 462
portion of 1994 geography test for eighth-grader, 462
sample geography question, 445–446
U.S. history for eighth-graders and portion of 1994's test, 446

National Council for Geographic Education, 15, 373, 420

National Council for the Social Studies (NCSS), 12, 53, 56, 136, 200, 208, 243, 304, 382
position statement, 8–9
standard I, 6, 75, 81, 186
standard II, 75, 78, 125, 186, 336, 343, 423
standard III, 3, 34, 96, 125, 186, 299, 336, 374, 378, 402
standard IV, 268, 270
standard IX, 81, 173, 174, 186, 378, 412, 414, 424
standard V, 268, 336
standard VI, 76, 139, 140, 144, 157, 203, 210, 378, 423, 470
standard VII, 18, 111, 214, 270, 299, 412, 414, 423, 424, 436
standard VIII, 18, 174, 186, 196, 298, 412, 414, 415
standard X, 140, 144, 157, 186, 214, 268, 298, 378, 423

National Council on Economic Education (NCEE), 414–415

National Geographic Society, 173, 381

National Standards for Civics and Government (Center for Civic Education), 15, 140

National Standards for History: Expanding Children's World in Time and Space (Grades K–4), 14

National Standards for United States History: Exploring the American Experience (Grades 5–12), 14

National Standards for World History: Exploring Paths to the Present (Grades 5–12), 14

The National Standards in Personal Finance (Jump Start Coalition for Personal Financial Literacy), 415

National Voluntary Standards, 415

National Wildlife Federation, 381

Native American food
plants lesson plans expansion, 82
exploratory introduction, 81
lesson development, 81–82
summative evaluation, 82

Native Americans, 11, 238, 317, 320, 358, 389

Nazis, 56

NCEE. *see* National Council on Economic Education

NCSS. *see* National Council for the Social Studies

Neighbors, 94

Nelson, Kadir, 260

Newmann, 162

Newsweek, 152, 196

New York Times, 76

Nigerians, 317

9/11. *see* September 11, 2001

Ninomiya, 177

Nobisson, Josephine, 322

No Child Left Behind Act of 2001, 13, 32, 451

Nonexamples, 95

Noon, Steve, 361

Nordhielm Wooldridge, Connie, 260

Not One Damsel in Distress: World Folktales for Strong Girls (Yolen), 120

Numbers, with maps and globes, 399–400

Nutta, J., 110

O

Objectives
developing learning, 256–257
goals and, 79

O'Brien, John, 260

O'Brien, Joseph, 110, 269

Observations, 68–70

Observing, 61

Ochoa, 335

O'Dell, Scott, 279

Oersted, Hans Christian, 248

Oh, Rats! The Story of Rats and People (Marrin), 120
On the Same Day in March: A Tour of the World's Weather (Singer), 120
Open-mindedness, 297
Operational descriptions, 98–99
Oral interviews, 327
Order, 310
Organizing, 62
O'Sullivan Stew (Talbott), 260
Ovando, C., 110
Oxfam, 381
The Ox-cart Man (Hall), 422

P
Padrón, Y., 110
paintings/drawings of artists lesson plan
  expansion, 340–342
  exploratory introduction, 336–337
  lesson development, 337–339
Parallels, 404
Parent conferences, 454–455
Parker, 177
Participatory skills, 142
Passport to Learning: Teaching Social Studies to ESL Students (Cruz, Nutta, O'Brien, Joseph, Feyten, Govoni), 110
Patrick, John, 134
Patrick, Pamela, 260
PCK. *see* Pedagogical Content Knowledge
Peale, Charles Wilson, 260
Pedagogical Content Knowledge (PCK), 10, 11, 12, 17, 26, 305, 475
  creating collaborative classrooms with, 207
  social studies, 200–207
  social studies goals, general pedagogical knowledge and, 201
  teaching dimensions supporting learning and, 202–203
  teaching strategies supporting learning and, 203–205
Peer buddy system, 308
Peer tutoring, 308

People, 14, 15
  geography and students interpreting earth and, 371–410
  as historical resources, 351
People change environments lesson plan
  expansion, 375–376
  exploratory introduction, 374
  geography and, 374–376
  lesson development, 374–375
  summative evaluation rubric, 376
Performance assessments, 456
Perseverance, 297
Personal finance
  national standards in, 415–419
  voluntary national standards for economics and assessments with, 416–418
Personal power, 142
Personal values, 294
Perspective consciousness, 176
Pfeffer, W., 23
Photographs, 228
Physical systems, 379, 380
Pick-and-Shovel Poet: The Journeys of Pascal d'Angelo (Murphy), 322
Pictures, 354–355
Pink and Say (Polacco), 187, 189, 190
Places, 14, 15
  developing geographic concepts with, 383
  natural and cultural characteristics of, 373
  regions and, 379, 380
  relationships with humans, environments and, 373
Planet awareness, 176
Point symbols, 394
Polacco, Patricia, 187, 189, 190
Political awareness, 137–139
Political participation
  challenges with, 167
  cybercitizenship and, 168
  democracy and, 166–170
Pollock, Jane, 448
Pompeii: The Day a City was Buried (Rice and Rice), 361

Portfolios, 327, 465–466
POSSE, students with disabilities and, 312, 313
Power, 15
Predicting, 61
Predictive study, 72
Presentations
  lecture-based, 309
  media, 309
Presidential oaths lesson plan
  expansion, 159
  exploratory introduction, 157
  lesson development, 157–159
Price stability, 431, 432
Prime meridian, 404
Prior knowledge, 31, 32, 33, 55
Private wealth *v.* common wealth, 143
Problem solving, 62, 73, 74
Procter, 162
Production, 15, 99
Productive resources lesson plan
  development, 111
  expansion, 112
  exploratory introduction, 111
  natural and capital resources rubric, 113
  productive resources rubric, 113
  summary, 112
  summative evaluation, 112
Progress reports, 454
Projects, 327
Project SPAN, 136
Prosocial behaviors, 285
Psychology, 267

Q
Quality circles, 467
Questioning, 203–204
Questions
  classroom action research activities and, 476
  developing essential/focus, 250–251
  geography, 445
  sample NAEP geography, 445–446
  self-evaluation with group/independent study and guiding, 455

R
Rankin, Jeanette, 100
Ratification, 100

Reading
  alone, 309
  maps, 400–401
Real cooperation stage, 288
Reason, 335
Recall, 31
Recess at 20 Below (Aillaud), 389
Reciprocal teaching, 308–309
Reconstruction, 108
Recycle Every Day (Wallace), 23
Red, White, Blue, and Uncle Who? The Stories Behind Some of America's Patriotic Symbols (Bateman), 260
Red Cross/Red Crescent, 381
Reenactments, history and, 356–357
Reese, Debbie, 358
Reflecting skills, 62, 66–67
Reflection, 93–94
Reflective Teaching in Second Language Classrooms (Richards and Lockhart), 110
Regions
  formation and change of, 377
  places and, 379, 380
Relational, 105
Relevancy, 240
  curriculum, ethnic heritage and, 321
  role models, literature connections and, 322
  role models and, 320–323
  social studies and, 322–323
Remington, Frederick S., 336, 339
Remote sensing, 397–399
Resources
  citizenship, 150–155
  education, 150
  global education, 194–196
  history, 350–355
  media, 150–155
  productive, 111–113
  productive lesson plan, 111–113
  for teaching economics, 435–441
  for teaching geography, 380–381
Responsibility, 275–276, 298
Restoration communities, 353

Rey, H. A., 299
Rice, 388
Rice, Christopher, 361
Rice, Melanie, 361
Richards, J., 110
Rivera, H., 110
Robinson, Jackie, 278
Rockwell, Norman, 336
Rogers, Jacqueline, 260
Role models
    curriculum, ethnic
        heritage and, 321
    literature connections
        and, 322
    relevancy and, 320–323
    relevant social studies
        and, 322–323
Role-playing, 218
    closure, 218
    introduction, 218
    listeners and, 217
    reenactment and, 218
    selection of participants
        and, 217
    simulations and, 217
    stage setting and, 217
Roscoe, Lorraine, 120
Rossi, 370
Rubrics
    advertisements/social
        studies performance
        task and, 460
    for assessing students'
        projects and related
        tasks, 458–459
    assessments/evaluation
        beyond testing and,
        456–457
    natural and capital
        resources, 113
    productive resources, 113
    summative evaluation,
        21, 376, 473
Rules, using classroom, 233
The Runner (Voigt), 280
Russell, Bertrand, 170, 171
Rutter, 162

S
Sachs, Marilyn, 280
Saxe, 161
Scale, 104
Scale lesson plan
    closure, 35
    expansion, 35–36
    exploratory introduction,
        34
    lesson development,
        34–35
    lesson summary, 36
    summative evaluation, 36
Scarcity, 212–213, 413
Scholastic Magazine, 150

Scholastic Time, 196
Schools. see also
    Elementary schools;
        Middle schools
    as concrete concept, 106
    democracy, community
        service projects and,
        162–164
    first-grade classroom
        scene in, 3–5
    fourth-grade classroom
        scenes in, 93–94
    history in, 335–343
    sixth-grade classroom
        scene in, 5–6
    social studies in elemen-
        tary and middle, 3–6
    violence in, 300–301
Schug, Mark, 435
Schuler, Dot, 353
Science, 14, 15
Scotter, R. Van, 143
Self-concepts
    aggressive feelings,
        bullying, conflict reso-
        lution and, 279–282
    diverse students and de-
        velopment of, 275–286
    empathy, helpful proso-
        cial behaviors and, 285
    fears, 278–279
    friendship, 282, 284–285
    graphing individually
        performed tasks and,
        276
    independence and
        responsibility, 275–276
    Internet safety, cyber-
        bullying and, 283
    jealousy, 277–278
    self-esteem and, 285–286
Self-esteem, 285–286
Self study, 468–469
Semantic feature analysis,
    311–312
Sensory concepts, 105–106
September 11, 2001, 181
Sequence, 310
Seven Brave Women
    (Hearne), 322
Sharing/negotiation lesson
    plan
    checklist, 273
    expansion, 272–273
    exploratory introduction,
        270
    lesson development,
        270–272
    response sheet, 274
Shelterwood (Shetterly), 23
Shetterly, S. H., 23
Shriver, Maria, 167
Significance, 239–240

Silverman, Frederick, 360
Sims, Bernice, 336
Simulations, 217, 218–219
Singer, Marilyn, 120
Sinnott, Susan, 361
Skeel, Dorothy, 184
Skills
    basic, 61–62
    communicating, 66
    data gathering, 64
    data-organizing, 64
    data-processing, 64
    developing geographic
        concepts, generaliza-
        tions and, 382–391
    expanding history, 363
    information literacy, 66
    integrative, 62
    map and globe, 391–407
    media literacy, 66
    participatory, 142
    pre-assessment and
        practicing, 477–478
    reflecting, 66–67
    research on map and
        globe, 390–391
    social studies and learn-
        ing inquiry, 173–198
    students using integra-
        tive thinking, 72–77
SmartBoard, 307
Smith, Allen, 153
Smith, Andrew F., 177
Smith, Will, 260
Social Education, 133,
    353, 357
Social goals, 420
Social issues, 320
Socialization, 141, 335
Social studies
    assessments and national
        testing of, 451–452
    chapter objectives, 3
    chapter overview, 2
    concepts and generaliza-
        tions developed for,
        91–132
    constructing powerful and
        meaningful, 238–266
    curriculum, 14–17
    defining, 12
    education for active
        citizenship and, 12–14
    elementary and middle
        school, 3–6
    essential, 23–24
    exploratory introduction,
        1–2
    global education influ-
        enced by, 173–198
    kits, 224–225
    learning inquiry skills
        for, 56–90

multicultural, 319–320
    planning powerful
        lessons in, 17–23
    powerful and meaning-
        ful, 1–27
    purposeful and powerful,
        6–11
    relevancy and, 322–323
    students developing
        citizenship in
        democratic/global soci-
        eties with, 133–172
    students engaged in
        examining history
        with, 331–370
    students engaged in
        powerful, meaningful,
        28–55
    students interpreting
        earth and people
        through geography
        and, 371–410
    students involved in
        meaningful, 303–330
    students learning
        through multiple
        assessment and evalu-
        ation with, 444–479
    students making eco-
        nomic decisions with,
        411–443
    summary, 26–27
    teachers facilitating
        students' development
        as individuals and
        community members,
        267–302
    teachers managing in-
        structional strategies
        for, 199–237
    twenty-first century
        teaching and impact
        of standards with,
        24–26
    websites, 27
    writing in, 221–222
Social studies, engaging
    students
    applying knowledge
        about meaningful
        learning to, 30–32
    chapter objectives, 29–30
    chapter overview, 29
    choosing activities for
        learning cycle phases
        with, 45–49
    exploratory introduction,
        28–29
    learning cycle lesson
        phases with, 33–45
    optimal length of time
        for learning cycles and,
        50–51

Social studies (*Continued*)
principles of teaching and learning to support curriculum standards for, 53–54
strategies promoting conceptual change with, 32–33
student assessment in learning cycle phase with, 49
summary, 54–55
teaching in classrooms today, 30
websites, 55
working with learning cycles and, 51–53
writing learning cycles and, 50
Social studies concepts/generalizations
applying, 129–130
assessment, 113–115
chapter objectives, 92–93
chapter overview, 92
complexity differences and abstractness of, 103–106
concept teaching and, 93–94, 107–113
expansion phase of learning cycle and, 124–128
exploratory introduction, 91–92
exploratory introduction phase of learning cycles and, 122–123
facts as content with, 94–97
formative evaluation and assessment with, 128
forming, 97–98
inquiry teaching and national standards in, 128–129
interrelationships among, 101–103
lesson development phase of learning cycles and, 124
relationships between, 115–122
summary, 131
types of, 98–101
websites, 132
Social studies curriculum, 17
applying knowledge about learning to, 30–32
behavioral learning theory in, 31–32
constructivism theory in, 30–31

ten themes of standards for, 14, 15–16
Social studies inquiry skills
applying learning cycle to teach, 80–83
assessing use of, 83–85
chapter objectives, 58
chapter overview, 57–58
communicating skills and, 66
creating conditions to promote student thinking with, 77–79
data gathering skills and, 64
data-organizing skills and, 64
data-processing skills and, 64
developing students' ideas with, 58–59
developing/using guiding hypotheses with, 70–72
early, 59–60
exploratory introduction, 56–57
functions, 65
hierarchy of, 85–89
information and ICT literacy with, 66
K–8, 61–62
observations, inferences, hypotheses and, 68–70
reflecting skills and, 66–67
summary, 89–90
teaching lessons, students using integrative thinking skills and, 72–77
websites, 90
Social studies lessons
planning powerful, 17–23
from tree to paper, 18–21
using trade books, 23
Social Studies Research and Practice, 231
Social studies units, construction of
chapter objectives, 239
chapter overview, 238–239
choosing appropriate topics for integrated, 247–248
conceptual and thinking skills-focused, 241–242
descriptive-focused, 240–241
developing integrated, 249–264

exploratory introduction, 238
integrated, 245
integrating school subjects with, 242–249
issue and problem-solving, 245–246
planning appropriate focus for, 239–242
planning integrated, 248–249
planning web for inter-disciplinary primary grades, 243
powerful and meaningful, 238–266
summary, 266
theme, 242–245
thinking skills-focused, 241
websites, 266
Social values, 294
Societies, 14, 15
environments and, 379, 380
social studies education in culturally diverse, 316–323
students developing citizenship in democratic and global, 133–172
Sociology, 267
Soldiers, 228
Sophie and the New Baby (Anholt), 278
Speakers, guest, 215
Special needs, accommodations for and identifying, 251
Spreadsheets, 262
The Stampede, 336
Standards. *see also* National Council for the Social Studies
citizenship and, 139–140
common concerns about social studies, 25–26
economics, assessments and voluntary national, 416–418
economics and national social studies, 414–415
economics and voluntary national, 415
geography education, 378–380
in historical thinking, 345–436
history, 343–346
personal finance and national, 415–419
ten themes of social studies, 14, 15–16

Stanton Blatch, Harriet, 100
Stearns, Peter N., 347
Storm Warriors (Carbone), 360
Story of the Nile: A Journey Through Time Along the World's Longest River (Millard), 389
Story Painter: The Life of Jacob Lawrence (Duggleby), 339
Straight to the Hoop (Coy), 299
Strategies
classroom management, 231–234
discussion, 219–221
ELL students and instructional, 325–326
inclusive classrooms and general instructional, 306–313
multicultural social studies, 319–320
social studies teachers managing instructional, 199–237
teaching, 203–205
for using social studies textbooks, 309–311
A Street through Time (Millard), 361
Structuring, 78
Student development
as active/responsible citizens and confronting challenges, 300–301
attitudes and dispositions promoting powerful social studies with, 296–299
chapter objectives, 268
chapter overview, 267–268
exploratory introduction, 267
relating to individuals, communities and assessing diverse, 300
respect for teachers and diverse, 269–274
self-concept in diverse, 275–286
social studies teachers facilitating, 267–302
summary, 301–302
values and moral education in diverse society with, 286–296
websites, 302
Student government
democracy and participation in, 164–166
engagement, 202–203

Student involvement
applying ideas for help-
ing students learn
meaningful social
studies with, 328–330
assessment of social
studies learning for
students and, 326–328
chapter objectives, 304
chapter overview, 303–304
culture and gender
difference in student-
teacher interactions
and, 323–324
exploratory introduction,
303
helping English-language
learners participate in
social studies with,
324–326
in meaningful social
studies, 303–330
meaningful social studies
and, 304–305
social studies education
for students with dis-
abilities and, 305–316
social studies education
in culturally diverse
societies and, 316–323
social studies learning
and giving greater
control to, 305
summary, 330
websites, 330
Students
artwork, 185
assessment drawings
and, 465
assessment of social
studies learning for,
326–328
behaviors illustrating five
geographic skills, 387
being developed as
individuals and
community members
by social studies
teachers, 267–302
building concepts, 114
classroom behavior of
teachers and, 205
creating new webs while
searching for structure
in text, 314
cultural diversity and
using cultures of, 320
developing citizenship
in democratic/global
societies with social
studies, 133–172
developing hypotheses,
69–70

economic education
checklists for, 466
emotionally conflicted,
316
engaged in examining
history with social
studies, 331–370
engaged in powerful,
meaningful social
studies, 28–55
fieldtrips, 215
grouping, 233
guided discovery instruc-
tional strategies and
mixed control of
teachers and, 210
instructional methods
and greater control of,
210–211
instructional strategies
and greater control of,
210–211
instructional strategies
and lower control of,
209–210
instructional strategies
for ELL, 325–326
integrative thinking
skills and behaviors
of 74
interpreting earth and
people through geogra-
phy and social studies,
371–410
involved in meaningful
social studies, 303–330
learning of history and,
347–348
learning through multi-
ple assessment and
evaluation with social
studies, 444–479
making accommodations
for and identifying
special needs in, 251
making economic deci-
sions with social
studies, 411–443
matching instructional
strategies to needs of,
209–211
organizing thoughts in
concept web as part of
POSSE procedure for
reading text, 313
projects in character ed-
ucation, 295
rubrics for assessing
projects/tasks by,
458–459
Russian, 264
sample feedback form,
259

sample screens of
databases developed
by fourth-grade, 263
technology and using
WebQuest with, 440
using integrative
thinking, 72–77
Students with disabilities
adapting instruction and
curriculum in inclusive
classrooms with, 307
classwide peer tutoring
and, 308
cooperative group
activities and, 308
creating new webs,
searching for structure
in text and, 314
doing social studies with
mentally retarded and
emotionally conflicted,
316
factors in adapting social
studies curricula and
instruction for,
313–316
general instructional
strategies for inclusive
classrooms and,
306–313
general suggestions for
adapting textbook
materials for diverse
classrooms and,
312–313
lecture-based presenta-
tion and, 309
media presentations
and, 309
multisensory activities
for, 307–308
organizing thoughts in
concept web as part of
POSSE procedure for
reading text with, 313
peer buddy system
and, 308
reading alone and, 309
reciprocal teaching and,
308–309
semantic feature analy-
sis and, 311–312
social studies education
for, 305–316
strategies for using social
studies textbooks with,
309–311
study guides and, 311
visual/hearing impair-
ments and involving,
315–316
Study
descriptive, 72

guides, 71–72
predictive, 72
Study guides, 311
Subconcepts, 103, 104
Suffrage, 100, 121
Summarizing, 95
Summative evaluations, 49
*The Sun, the Rain, and the
Apple Seed* (Durrant),
23
Superordinate concepts, 103
Sweet Dried Apples
(Breckler), 187, 189,
190
Symbols, 104, 394

T
Talbott, Hudson, 260
*Tallchief: America's Prima
Ballerina* (Tallchief),
322
Tallchief, Maria, 322
Tappan, 289
Task completion, 83
Task Force on Social
Studies in the Middle
School, 178
Task orientation, 202
Task performance, 83
Taylor, 415
Teachers
becoming an effective
social studies,
469–477
classroom behavior of
students and, 205
classroom planning deci-
sions and, 212–213
facilitating students' development as individu-
als and community
members, 267–302
games made by, 216
guided discovery instruc-
tional strategies
and mixed control of
students and, 210
knowledge needed for
social studies, 11
lectures or presentations,
215
managing instructional
strategies for,
199–237
TeacherTube, 307
Teaching
approaches in values
education, 289–296
approaches to economics
and, 434–435
clarity and, 202
concept, 107–113
culturally responsive, 319

Teaching (*Continued*)
  dimensions supporting
    meaningful learning,
    202–203
  direct, 31
  generalizations and pow-
    erful, 121–122, 123
  materials, 79
  national standards in
    social studies and
    inquiry, 128–129
  reciprocal, 308–309
  resources for geography,
    380–381
  resources for history,
    350–355
  strategies supporting
    meaningful learning,
    203–205
  student engagement and,
    202–203
  task orientation and, 202
  traditional, 31
  variety and, 202
Teaching strategies
  cooperative learning,
    204–205
  questioning, 203–204
  student/teacher behavior
    in classrooms, 205
*Teaching with Historical
  Places*, 364
Technology, 14, 15
  adapting instruction
    and curriculum in
    inclusive classrooms
    with, 307
  assessment using, 328
  creating collaborative
    classrooms with, 207
  cybercitizenship,
    political participation
    and, 168
  databases and spread-
    sheets, 262
  deciding whether and
    when, 13
  developing accommoda-
    tions for, 260–261
  helping students build
    concepts with, 114
  as important contributor
    to learning geography,
    381
  information and ICT
    literacy with, 66
  interactive activities,
    games in learning
    history and, 364
  Internet safety, cyber-
    bullying and, 283
  investigating problems
    using, 124–128

investigating using
  WebQuest with
  students, 440
Teledemocracy, 154
*Terrible Things: An Allegory
  of the Holocaust*
  (Bunting), 362
Tevis, Corrine, 354
Textbooks, 343. *see also*
  books
  adapting materials for
    diverse classroom,
    312–313
  developing teaching
    plans using, 223–224
  difficulties in reading,
    222–223
  doing content analysis
    of, 223
  maps, globes, atlases
    and, 399–400
  strategies for using so-
    cial studies, 309–311
Themes
  geography's five, 373,
    377–378
  social studies curriculum
    and standard's ten, 14,
    15–16
  social studies units and
    construction of, 242–245
Theories
  behavioral learning,
    31–32
  constructivist, 30–31
  moral development,
    288–289
Thinking
  behaviors and integra-
    tive skills with, 74
  conceptual, 241–242
  creating conditions to
    promote student, 77–79
  creative, 75–76
  critical, 73, 74
  critically and creatively,
    62
  integrative skills and,
    72–77
  lesson characteristics to
    promote, 78–79
  planning activities to
    teach inquiry skills
    and, 79
  promoting student, 77–79
  skills and developmental
    use, 85–86
  standards in historical,
    345–346
Thomas, Eric, 361
Those Building Men
  (Johnson), 260
Thought patterns, 38

Through the Lens
  (National Geographic
  Society), 173
Time, 14, 15, 49, 50–51,
  99, 310
Time, 152, 196
Time for Kids, 150
Timeliner, 350
Timelines, 7
  chronology and history,
    348–350
  digital, 350
Topics
  generating ideas for
    social studies, 249–250
  researching social
    studies, 250
Torney-Purta, Judith, 136,
  137, 165
Totten, Samuel, 184
Trade books, 23, 151–152,
  187, 260–261
  adding depth to history
    with, 362
  Flat Stanley, 396
Trade-Offs, 428
Travis, Cathy, 152
Trees and Forests, 23
Tree to paper lesson plan, 22
  closure, 20
  expansion, 20–21
  exploratory introduction,
    18–19
  lesson development, 19–20
  lesson summary, 21
  summative evaluation
    rubric, 21
Tributary, 385

U
*Understanding Your
  International Students:
  A Cultural, Educa-
  tional, and Linguistic
  Guide* (Flaitz), 110
Unit rationale, 254
Unity v. diversity, 143

V
Values
  analysis, 292–294
  character education and,
    294–296
  clarification, 289–292
  economic concepts and,
    419–428
  education and teaching
    approaches, 289–296
  learning from family and
    community, 286
  moral education in
    diverse society with,
    286–296

morals, aesthetics and,
  298–299
personal, 294
social, 294
Values education
  analysis and, 292–294
  character education and,
    294–296
  forced-choice question-
    naire and, 291
  *Goldilocks and the Three
    Bears* and, 293
  rank-ordering form
    and, 291
  sample checklist, 292
  student projects and, 295
  values-clarification
    process and, 290
Van Aspert, Elly, 56, 57
Vandevander, 231
van Gogh, Vincent, 260
Van Sickle, 231
Van Sledright, 334, 362
Variables, 62
Variety, 202
Videos, 228
Vietnam War, 78, 189,
  229
Violence, 300–301
Visual impairments,
  315–316
Visual information, literacy
  and, 225–229
Visual literacy, 355–356
Vogel, Carole G., 389
Voigt, Cynthia, 280
Volta, Alessandro, 248
*Voluntary National
  Content Standards in
  Economics* (National
  Council on Economic
  Education), 415,
  416–418
Voting, 114, 143
  African Americans
    and, 100
  suffrage and, 100, 121
Voting lesson plan
  expansion, 146–148
  exploratory introduction,
    144
  lesson development,
    145–146

W
Wade, 161, 163
Wallace, Nancy
  Elizabeth, 23
War and humane world
  lesson plan
  expansion phase, 192–194
  exploratory introduction,
    186–187

lesson development, 187–192
Washing, George, 352
Washing, Martha, 352
Washington Post, 76
Waxman, H., 110
WebQuests, 41, 230–231, 440
    using, 230–231
Websites, 5, 6, 13, 27, 76, 154, 282, 440
    Bethpage, 464
    biographical, 321
    classroom, 467
    Dohistory, 363
    GLOBE, 381
    interactive activities/games, 364
    Internet safety, 283
    NCEE, 415
    news, 181

Welcome to Addy's World (Sinnott), 361
West, Elliott, 333–334
"Westward Ho" (Mathys), 207
Whalesong, 323
What Came First?, 364
What's Happening to Grandpa?, 167
Wheel designs, 248
When Esther Morris Headed West: Women, Wyoming and the Right to Vote (Nordhielm Wooldridge), 260
White, Steven, 269
White, W. E., 143
Who Really Discovered America? Unraveling the

Mystery & Solving the Puzzle (Hart), 261
Wilkes, Angela, 361
Will I Have a Friend (Cohen), 279
Winnamucca, Sarah, 320
Winslow, Homer, 336
Wisconsin Student Assessment System (WSAS), 460
Women, suffrage and, 100, 121
Woodrow, the White House Mouse (Barnes), 151
Woodrow for President (Barnes), 151
World News Network, 181
Writing journal, 328

in social studies, 221–222
social studies investigation and guide for, 222
WSAS. *see* Wisconsin Student Assessment System

Y
Yale University Family Television Research and Consultation Center, 153
The Year of the Hangman (Blackwood), 77
Yell, Michael, 447
Yolen, Jane, 120
You be the Historian, 364

Z
Zarnowski, 359